The Radical Republicans

and Reconstruction, 1861–1870

THE AMERICAN HERITAGE SERIES

THE

American Heritage

Series

UNDER THE GENERAL EDITORSHIP OF

LEONARD W. LEVY AND ALFRED YOUNG

The Radical Republicans

and Reconstruction

1861–1870

EDITED BY

HAROLD M. HYMAN

University of Illinois

THE BOBBS-MERRILL COMPANY, INC.

INDIANAPOLIS • NEW YORK

To Miss Bessie Gladding,
teacher

Foreword

History, goes the saying, is written by the victors. Yet it has taken a century for the North to forge ahead on the "dark and bloody" battleground of Reconstruction historiography, and a Union victory in fiction, the movies, secondary school texts, or in any other indicator of popular understanding is nowhere in sight. Even at the highest level of scholarship the history of Reconstruction is only now being written, or rather rewritten. Harold M. Hyman's book is simultaneously a critical review of the scholarly literature—by itself "worth the price of admission"—and a pioneering guide to the rediscovery of Reconstruction. Professor Hyman gives Reconstruction a new temporal dimension by considering it as a phenomenon that began the day after Sumter, not the day after Appomattox. Indeed, he sees Reconstruction as a reform movement whose roots were well planted before Sumter. Moreover, from the perspective of the Union as a whole, rather than any section of it, he views 1865 as the beginning, not of a tragic era, but of a much better time than the ante-bellum days! Most historians have been blind to that great fact for nearly a century. Professor Hyman explains this blindness and, in doing so, outlines the way in which changing times conditioned the image historians have had of the Negro, the Civil War, Reconstruction, and the Republicans. He gives historiography its due as a form of intellectual and cultural history.

The very generous array of original documents included here ranges widely over political, economic, constitutional, religious, and military sources, only a few of which are the old familiar ones. The freshness and importance of the documents and the incisive headnotes which indicate their significance prove, once again, that tireless mining of the archives, when combined with intellect, can extend the frontiers of our knowledge. Readers will note with profit the documentation on the nature of pre-Sumter Radicalism, on the fading of Radicalism long before Reconstruction ended, on the relation of Republicans to such little-studied constituencies as the ministers and the army, and on the Freedmen's Bureau. Nothing in print can vie with the section on that agency in showing how its administration and policies reflected the innate dilemmas of Radicalism arising from the crosscurrents of the time. The materials also enlarge vistas for our understanding of the effects upon Radicalism of the impeachment of Johnson, the elections of 1868 and 1872, and the new amendments to the Constitution. Rarely has a book of documents reflected such a blending of provocative editorial commentary and new sources of indispensable value.

This book is part of a series whose aim is to provide the essential primary sources of the American experience, especially of American thought, from the colonial period to the present. The series when completed will constitute a documentary library of our history. These volumes will fill a need of libraries, scholars, students, and even general readers for authoritative collections of original material. These materials will illuminate the thought of significant individuals, such as James Madison and Louis Brandeis; groups, such as Puritan political theorists and American Catholic leaders on social policy; and movements, such as those of the Antifederalists or the Populists. There are a surprising number of subjects traditionally studied in American history for which there are no documentary anthologies. This series will be by far the most comprehensive and authoritative of its kind. It will also have the distinction of presenting representative pieces of substantial length that have not been butchered into snippets.

Leonard W. Levy
Alfred Young

Preface

Recently, Professor David M. Potter offered as "fairly illustrative of well-known types of historical information" the following statement of his own devise: "The Radical Republicans defeated Lincoln's mild [Reconstruction] program and inaugurated the era of drastic reconstruction." Next Potter showed how complex and unsatisfactory this statement is.

This relatively simple sentence, though apparently devoid of theory, contains at least three very broad generalizations, each one treacherous in the extreme. First is a generalization which ascribes to an unstated number of individuals a common identity strong enough to justify classifying them as a group—namely, the Radical Republicans—and ascribes to this group a crucial role in defeating one policy and implementing another. Yet, in terms of analysis historians have had great difficulty either in defining what constituted a Radical or in proving that any given aggregate of individuals formed a truly cohesive Radical bloc. Second is a chronological generalization—that a certain time span was pre-eminently significant for the process of what is called "Reconstruction"—setting up new regimes in the Southern states and restoring them to the Union—rather than for other developments, such as industrialization. Yet that process lasted for very diverse intervals of time in various states, and the long-range problem of the relationship of Negroes and Whites continued to be important long after the so-called Reconstruction was "ended." Third is a generalization about the degree of severity of Reconstruction, which involves not only a verdict on the over-all effect of a whole series of acts of Congress but also an opinion on what kind of settlement can be considered as drastic in the case of a defeated belligerent. Many of the measures adopted during Reconstruction are now regarded as salutary—for instance, the establishment of public education in some [Southern] states—and other measures, such as the Amnesty

Acts, do not conform to the generalization that Reconstruction was drastic.[1]

What follows is an attempt to re-evaluate the relationships of the Radical Republicans to Reconstruction policy, while avoiding, hopefully, semantic pitfalls and other dangers that face travelers on the dim and gory terrain of Reconstruction historiography. The historian's favorite recourse, a return to sources, offers one means of retraveling this route from which flows so much more recent history.

Of persons and institutions who have aided me in this effort, I thank particularly the University of Illinois. Its resources brought forth as assistants Messrs. Charles H. Clark, Ralph Flynn, and Donald Shepardson, who with good will helped me to solve many of the problems involved in assembling this book. Indefatigable staffers of the University of Illinois Library moved me ahead at good speed, and their opposite numbers at the Widener Library of Harvard University provided equivalent aids. Manuscript collections that I employed are cited in appropriate footnoting. I want, however, to thank sincerely, if not adequately, all the archival custodians who made available the treasures of their holdings.

Fawn Brodie, James McPherson, Grady McWhiney, August Meier, and Hans Trefousse, among colleagues, offered suggestions, data, and criticisms. Co-editor of the series in which this volume appears, Leonard W. Levy, a rediscovered friend, provided the inestimable encouragement of patient overseeing. Ferne knows that she is first, always.

HAROLD M. HYMAN

Champaign, Illinois
September 1966

---

[1] Potter, "Explicit Data and Implicit Assumptions in Historical Study," in *Generalizations in the Writing of History: A Report of the Committee on Historical Analysis of the Social Science Research Council*, ed. Louis Gottschalk (Chicago: University of Chicago Press, 1963), pp. 184–185.

Contents

PART ONE

The Year Before Sumter:
Radicals on the Defensive

PART TWO

War: The Concentration of Extraordinary
Power for Beneficent Purposes—1862

PART THREE

Radicalism Takes the Offensive

PART FOUR

Reconstruction Policy
and Republican Crisis

PART FIVE

Peace Will Soon Break Out

PART SIX

The Freedmen's Bureau:
Self-Help Versus *Paternalism*

PART SEVEN

The Critical Year—1865

PART EIGHT

Fruits into Ashes

PART NINE

Year of Decision—1866

PART TEN

Congress Acts on Reconstruction—1867

PART ELEVEN

Reconstruction and Impeachment

PART TWELVE

The Issues of '68

PART THIRTEEN

Thirty-Five Years of Antislavery Agitation
Fittingly Rounded Out

PART FOURTEEN

1870 and Following

PART FIFTEEN

Conclusion

page 521

Introduction

"Who Won the Civil War, Anyway?" demanded Fawn M. Brodie, the able biographer of Radical Republican congressman Thaddeus Stevens, in a centennial survey of outstanding literature on that unceasing struggle. She charged that for far too long a time, the South has swept the field. In estimates of the war and especially of the Reconstruction that the large majority of Americans commonly accept, Mrs. Brodie found that the Stars and Bars wave on as though Appomattox had never been. The evidence she amassed of a Southern victory in the war of words was so convincing that she was moved to remark how "by some quixotic reversal the Lost Cause is no longer lost."[1]

This Southern victory is evident most spectacularly in mass entertainment media. Ever since *Birth of a Nation* fifty years ago, a succession of motion pictures have provided reinforcements for the ghostly hosts of Secessia and for the robed ranks of the Ku Klux Klan. By such cinema depictions, Confederate military commanders were abler and nobler than their opposite numbers northward, and Southern white civilians were made of purer stuff than their Yankee counterparts. Until very recently, Negroes almost always appeared on screen and stage in the roles of menials, grading downward to the slow-witted character portrayed for so long by Stepin Fetchit.[2]

---

[1] *New York Times Book Review,* August 5, 1962, pp. 1 ff.

[2] Richard Bardolph, *The Negro Vanguard* (New York: Vintage Books, 1961), p. 240; and see John D. Roche, *The Quest for the Dream: The Development of Civil Rights and Human Relations in Modern America* (New York: The Macmillan Company, 1963), pp. 79–87.

Aping Hollywood's jaded themes, television has immeasurably broadened the spread of moonlight-and-magnolia stereotypes. As example, a television spectacular in 1961 carried into millions of homes the unprovable and improbable allegation that Lincoln's murder was a product of Northern conspirators, chiefly Radical Republicans centering on Secretary of War Edwin M. Stanton, rather than of pro-Confederate Northern extremists who took their cues from John Wilkes Booth.[3]

Though little studied, the proposition appears to be reasonable that the attitude of members of a society toward its history offers more insight into present felt needs than into the actualities of the past. Granting the worth of this assumption, it is easy also to allow that the Orwellian "twistory" on the Civil War and Reconstruction may have ample justification as drama.[4] Have such depictions, amounting to a demonology in which the Republican Radicals do the Devil's work, also worth as history?

Perhaps so, if the assumptions of winner-take-all democracy apply to matters of historical interpretation. Grotesqueries similar to those against which Mrs. Brodie inveighed exist in history textbooks widely employed across the nation, and in levels of instruction ranging from elementary to college. It is reasonable to assume that the message of the South's victory issues daily in classrooms almost everywhere, as well as through channels of more popular entertainment. When the numbers of students in schools are added to those who attend, through novels or drama, to the delights of fictionalized history—even with due allowance for duplications—the size of

---

[3] Harold M. Hyman, "Second Look at Stanton," *Columbia University Forum*, VI (Spring 1963), 43–45.

[4] For the word "twistory" I am indebted to Jerome Frank, *Fate and Freedom: A Philosophy for Free Americans* (New York: Simon and Schuster, 1945), ch. 2. Will Herberg, in "The Civil War in New Perspective," *Modern Quarterly*, VI (Summer 1932), 54–61, looked into the significance of the attitudes of Americans of the 1920's and 1930's toward the Civil War.

the built-in audience that the South has enjoyed for its modes of thought on certain matters of great significance in mid-twentieth-century America is staggering.

A catalogue of subjects commonly distorted because of this pro-Southern gleam is simple to assemble. It includes the causes of the war, the conditions of slavery and the likelihood of permanence for slavery had there been no war or Union victory, and the alleged unreadiness of the slaves for immediate freedom and political participation. Other persisting distortions center on the quality of the peace that was won, the nature of the Reconstruction, and the personalities and purposes of the architects of the Reconstruction, the Radical Republicans.

Great numbers of Americans have learned, and still receive, unbalanced views on these matters as part of everyday exposure to mass entertainment and mass education, because substantial consensus exists that the white South has the right of history.[5] This Southern bent has been all but complete not only among scriptwriters, playwrights, and novelists, but also in the academic world, especially among historians, from whose works the more popular artists largely draw their materials.

Magnifying further the effects of these vast numbers and this harmony among chroniclers is the impact of continuity. The South has enjoyed a half century of hegemony, as mass

---

[5] The factor of equity of subject treatment in textbooks recently has received a large amount of attention, especially in the "sensitive" subject area of race relations during the Civil War and Reconstruction. See Mark M. Krug, "On Rewriting of the Story of Reconstruction in the U.S. History Textbooks," *Journal of Negro History,* XLVI (July 1961), 133–153; and Patrick J. Groff, "The Abolitionist Movement in High School Texts," *Journal of Negro Education,* XXXII (Winter 1963), 43–51. Related and useful are Carl N. Degler, "The South in Southern History Textbooks," *Journal of Southern History,* XXX (February 1964), 48–57; and Frederick S. Allis, Jr., "The Handling of Controversial Material in High School Textbooks in American History," Massachusetts Historical Society *Proceedings,* LXXII, 323–329.

education has reached its flowering. For fifty years mono-graphic scholarship on the men and measures of 1860–1877 has presented Dixie's story with great sympathy, though adorning it with the apparatus of objective scholarship. Little wonder that textbooks and teachers, taking their cues from research frontrunners among historians, have repeated themes set forth in prestigious monographic literature, leading to Mrs. Brodie's indignant question, "Who Won the Civil War, Anyway?"

To be sure, the evolution, transmission, and reception of ideas, ideals, and attitudes are not parts of a numbers game. Nevertheless, whatever a great many people believe is always very important in a political democracy. As example, intran-sigence on the part of Southern whites in the 1960's with re-spect to demands by Negroes for a proper share in the promise of American life appears to be intimately linked to tightly cherished misconceptions concerning the roles that Negroes supposedly played during Reconstruction. On the coin's other face, with the Civil War's centennial just past, and with the South the long-time victor in defining the meanings of the war and of the Reconstruction, the rising aspirations of Negroes in the 1960's are mocked by demeaning depictions of black men of the 1860's and 1870's.[6]

The Reconstruction "period," far more than that of the war, has suffered in scholarly literature as well as in more popular forms. To advert first to the latter, consider how en-thusiastically Americans embraced the centennial celebrations that took place between 1961 and 1965. The scope and pop-ularity of the observances indicate that in addition to enjoying good shows, Americans North and South sense the significance of the war to their historical situations, present conditions, and aspirations for the future.

But with 1965, recreations of Civil War battles ceased.

---

[6] John Hope Franklin, "A Century of Civil War Observance," *Journal of Negro History*, XLVII (April 1962), 97–107.

Members of patriotic societies have given up the blue and gray uniforms in which they re-enacted the Antietam surge and the Vicksburg siege. Mass pilgrimages that since 1961 brought many Americans before monuments honoring the heroes of the war years have lessened in number. Centers of special interest to tourists, such as the Lincoln Memorial and the Gettysburg battlefield, are quieter places than they were during the years of the centennial—perhaps because the Illinois Pavilion at the New York World's Fair, with its "talking Lincoln," usurped at least temporarily their favored places on tourists' itineraries.[7]

In 1965 the quasi-official commemorative organizations commissioned since 1961 in three dozen states to mark the significance of their respective states' contributions to the Union victory or to the Confederate experiment closed up shop. And to cap the sense that Lee's surrender marks the last event of a past century that Americans today should mark with pride and commemorate with ceremony, the United States Civil War Centennial Commission has rung down the curtain on its work.[8]

Now that it has, the odds are very heavy that no one in Washington, in the fifty state capitals, in patriotic societies, or even at the Round Tables, will recommend the creation of a Centennial Commission to mark and to honor achievements and heroes of Reconstruction years. Indeed, the popular and scholarly consensus has been, and in large part remains, that Reconstruction produced no heroes and few accomplishments worthy of celebration, that Reconstruction is the North's de-

[7] An Associated Press dispatch, July 23, 1964, judged that "the individual star of the World's Fair is none other than Abraham Lincoln . . . the creation of the Walt Disney organization." Champaign-Urbana (Ill.) *Courier*, July 23, 1964.

[8] Among the associations of Civil War enthusiasts, only the dedicated brotherhoods of the Civil War Round Tables will predictably retain an undiminished level of interest and activity in the men and measures of Lincoln's time.

feat, as Appomattox is the South's.[9] As example of this consensus, the late Fred A. Shannon, former Professor of History at the University of Illinois and Pulitzer Prize-winning
author of *The Organization and Administration of the Union
Army,* wrote in 1947 that "hardly anybody today has anything
to say in favor of Congressional Reconstruction in the South
in the decade following the Civil War."[10]

Indeed, "hardly anybody" has said much that was favorable
about Reconstruction or about the Radical Republicans since
shortly before the turn of the century. Until that time, however, many writers who had participated in the antislavery
crusade, fought in the Union's armies, or been prominent Republican politicians (and in some instances all three) rang the
changes on the theme of Southern war guilt. They believed in
the existence of a prewar conspiracy between Southern slavo-
crats and Northern doughfaces and doughsouls—conscience-
less men of malleable features—to control the United States
government or to smash it. In these analyses, slavery threatened Christian morality as well as white Americans' liberties,
and Reconstruction was a necessary and proper continuation
of the war.

These accounts were partisan, polemical, and pungent, and
their Republican one-sidedness and excessive analytical sim-
plicity required balance and correction.[11] The decade of the
1890's appears logically to have been the proper time for the
introduction of restraint, moderation, and humility in newer
judgments. Mortality had silenced many of the penmen of the

---

[9] Thomas J. Pressly, *Americans Interpret Their Civil War* (New York:
Collier Books, 1962), p. 163.

[10] In a review of E. Merton Coulter, *The South During Reconstruction,
1865–1877,* in *A History of the South,* ed. Wendell Holmes Stephenson and E. Merton Coulter, VIII (Baton Rouge: Louisiana State University Press, 1947). The review appeared in the New York *Socialist Call,*
Dec. 19, 1947.

[11] Pressly, pp. 53–77.

first phalanx of Republican writers, and sectional passions had ebbed in North and South. Aging veterans of Grant's and Lee's campaigns enjoyed joint conventions—to which, to be sure, the tens of thousands of Negro veterans of the Union Army were not invited. Before the new century bowed in, North and South joined in a common and most satisfying war against Spain. The road to reunion appeared to be straight and narrow.

Adding to the prospects in the 1890's and after for more rational, better balanced, and more dependable considerations of the war and Reconstruction was the arrival on the literary and academic scene of the professionally trained historian. Armed usually with a Ph.D. degree from a German university, or at least from a prominent American one, these men brought the approaches of the "social scientist" to research in the American past, combining writing with teaching, especially of graduate students who in turn went forth to teach teacher-writers. Thus the impact of the new breed of historian swiftly spread far beyond their campuses, persisting on into the present.

The consensus of these scholars and of their disciples was not the expectable one of moderation, however. Instead, their writings diverged sharply from earlier accounts. The new scholarship, whether of the so-called Dunning school of thought or of the more recent "revisionist" cast that persists today and that is the major source of the Southern victory with respect to popular and scholarly attitudes, centered attention on the causes and results of the war and of the Reconstruction.[12]

Any attempt briefly to summarize fifty years of historiography is best put aside in favor of reference to the several major

---

[12] Harvey Wish, *The American Historian: A Social-Intellectual History of the Writing of the American Past* (New York: Oxford University Press, 1960), pp. 209–235. On general aspects of the softening of sectional exacerbation, see Paul H. Buck, *The Road to Reunion, 1865–1900* (Boston: Little, Brown, 1947). For a definition and further discussion of "revisionism" see footnote 31 below.

works on the subject that deserve close attention.[13] Instead, I wish to consider why so many writers, whose careers spanned such a long period of time and who disagreed on many major questions concerning the war's causation and conduct, agreed that the Reconstruction was unnecessary, unconstitutional, and excessive, and that the Radical Republicans were Lincoln's enemies before Appomattox and Andrew Johnson's foes after. To most of these commentators, the Radicals were vengeful fanatics bent on ruining the prostrate South, regardless of the repentance felt by ex-Confederates, through the unwise military enforcement of Negro suffrage—a sinful gift of the ballot's power to blacks who, because of natural limitations, could not wield it with the white's responsible independence. At worst, according to the new consensus, the Radicals were low hypocrites who exploited war-born passions and Northern humanitarian concern for the freedman in order to perpetuate Republican party successes at the polls. A later refinement of this trend of analysis, still tenaciously persisting, was that the Radicals were willing and corrupted lackeys of Northern entrepreneurs who were forcing the massive alterations in America's production and transportation technologies and who wanted the South's traditional opposition to such advances subdued.[14]

This sudden alteration, during the 1890's and after, in the pattern of historical interpretation of the Reconstruction

[13] In addition to the volumes by Pressly and Wish, see Howard K. Beale, "What Historians Have Said About the Causes of the Civil War," *Social Science Research Council Bulletin,* 54 (1946); David Donald, "American Historians and the Causes of the Civil War," *South Atlantic Quarterly,* LIX (Summer 1960), 351–355; and Roy F. Nichols, "The Problem of Civil War Historiography: A Discussion of the Points of View of Professors [D.W.] Brogan, [J.B.] Duroselle, and [Pieter] Geyl," *American Philosophical Society Proceedings,* CVI (February 1962), 36–40. Nichols' reference is to articles by the specified men, appearing in the same issue of the *Proceedings* as his, pp. 1–35.

[14] A recent, able, and restrained restatement is in C. Vann Woodward, "The Political Legacy of Reconstruction," *Journal of Negro Education,* XXVI (Summer 1957), 231–240.

closely paralleled off-campus developments in politics and in race relations, although in theory the footnote-laden products of the new seminars eschewed anything but "objective" facts. In 1877 the Republican party, no longer Radical, made its famous deal with the Democracy. The price of inaugurating Rutherford B. Hayes as President that year was Republican abandonment of the last fragments of their Reconstruction effort in the South. White Republicans, with few objectors, were willing to give up the South's Negroes to the white South's mercies.[15] Save for infrequent and ineffective relapses into concern over the Negro's plight, the national government left off efforts to oversee the quality of citizenship in the former Confederate states, as measured by color, until almost the present time.

Matters of skin pigmentation again assumed a worrisome political significance just twenty years after Hayes's entry into the White House—precisely when the historians' reversal of judgment on the merits of the Reconstruction and the Radical Republicans took place. During the 1890's the Populist upsurge in politics caused Southern state legislators and constitution drafters to work out the varied, now-familiar roster of Jim Crow laws. These disfranchisement and segregation policies effectively "nullified" the Fourteenth and Fifteenth "Reconstruction" Amendments to the federal Constitution.[16] The rise, chiefly in the South and Southwest, of sharecropping and similar economic relationships in some ways undercut the effect of the Thirteenth Amendment as well.[17]

---

[15] Stanley P. Hirshsohn, *Farewell to the Bloody Shirt: Northern Republicans and the Southern Negro, 1877–1893* (Bloomington: Indiana University Press, 1962), admirably complements Vincent P. De Santis, *Republicans Face the Southern Question—The New Departure Years, 1877–1897* (Baltimore: Johns Hopkins Press, 1959).

[16] C. Vann Woodward, *The Strange Career of Jim Crow* (New York: Oxford University Press, 1955).

[17] Theodore Saloutos, "Southern Agriculture and the Problems of Readjustment: 1865–1877," *Agricultural History*, XXX (April 1956), 58–76.

Whatever the motivations of Northern Republicans in abandoning the Negro in the mid-1870's and of Southern Democrats in disfranchising and segregating Negroes in the 1890's, the question intrudes why most Northern whites, including leading Republican politicians, acquiesced in these retrograde motions, and why professional historians approved them in their writings. After all, spectacular sensitivity to the existence of oppression and want had marked prewar and wartime America, at least in the North. By the 1850's the attention of morally sensitive Northerners had come to center on the Southern Negro. Moving during the war into politics, antislavery reformers had succeeded finally in energizing the weakened spring of the national government and transforming it for the purposes of war into a reform agency. For many of these reformers, Reconstruction was a continuation of their decades of humanitarian effort to employ the nation's augmented force and institutions on behalf of black men.

Then something happened. Northern whites lost their penchant for being their brothers' keepers. Moral stewardship gave way to other interests, which often centered on economic, instead of civil, liberty. Other reforms—women's rights, good government, prohibition—took precedence over the Negro's welfare. A new view of science made this sharp decline in the white man's concern for the Negro respectable and acceptable and altered the climate of opinion concerning the nature of man, especially colored man. Commanding almost complete popular and scholarly acceptance by the mid-1880's, this new scientific attitude permitted Northern acquiescence, without much sense of guilt, in the abandonment and then in the disfranchisement of Negroes. It also underlay the shift, among historians of the 1890's and after, to the opinion that the Reconstruction effort had been a tragic error.

By 1860 science was on its way to becoming the playboy of the Western world. The conclusions of Louis Agassiz and

Darwinian concepts especially (the latter's *Origin of Species*
appeared in 1859 and *The Descent of Man* in 1871) corroded
deeply into the Gilded Age (they still retain currency in the
twentieth century). Extrapolating from these assumptions
about the origins and ascent of man, commentators miscon-
strued the merits of the races of men.[18] The "scientific" conclusion was that the Negro could not measure up, on the evolutionary scale, to the demands of American citizenship.

In a sense, therefore, Radical Reconstruction was the
triumph of older, traditional views stemming from the eight-
eenth-century idea that all men were equal, and the early-
nineteenth-century ideal that all men were divine. The abandonment by 1877 of the Reconstruction effort represented the
triumph of the new scientific substantiation for racial differences and inequality, translated into no-politics. Naturally,
many men did not need to have the racial prejudices they
cherished buttressed. For others, evolutionary data merely reinforced romantic prejudgments—long antedating the Victorian era—regarding the superiority of white people over
colored.

But the scientific confirmation of such myths lifted them
out of the category of bigotry onto levels acceptable to re-

---

[18] Patrick W. Riddleberger, "The Radicals' Abandonment of the Negro
During Reconstruction," *Journal of Negro History*, XLV (April 1960),
88–102; and for the pre-Civil War growth of a "scientific" affirmation
of alleged Negro inferiority, see William Stanton, *The Leopard's Spots:
Scientific Attitudes Toward Race in America, 1815–59* (Chicago: University of Chicago Press, 1960). On the impulsion toward good works,
see Clifford Griffin, *Their Brother's Keeper: Moral Stewardship in the
United States, 1800–1865* (New Brunswick: Rutgers University Press,
1960). The vigilant abolitionists did not fall prey to this lure, at least
not until abolition was won. See James M. McPherson, "A Brief for
Equality: The Abolitionist Reply to the Racist Myth, 1860–1865," in
Martin Duberman, ed., *The Antislavery Vanguard: New Essays on the
Abolitionists* (Princeton: Princeton University Press, 1965), pp. 156–177.
But after 1865 many abolitionists accepted some idea of white superior-
ity, with James Pike serving as a prominent example.

spectable men and women. Radical Republican reformers, who during the war and Reconstruction brought the government into action to make real the Jeffersonian credo, came to seem, in genteel estimates, quaintly antique and faintly fanatical. How else explain, in those pre-economic-determinism years, the Radicals' efforts on behalf of Negroes, when science had proved biracial coexistence undesirable in terms of political and social equality?

The point is that whatever motivated individual Republicans who worked out the 1877 deal by which Southern Negroes lost the last remnants of national protection, science justified the arrangement for most Northern whites. By 1877 few people any longer cared enough to raise a contradictory voice adequately loud to be heard in politics, in the face of such weighty evidence that Negroes were not worth further effort or risk. Bigots who employed Darwin in order to wed prejudice with politics, and who named the offspring "principle," had almost an unopposed road in enlarging areas of statutory and customary discriminations against Negroes, especially in Southern states, but in the North as well. "Proofs" of the Negro's ineradicable inferiority quieted the consciences of men of good will. American society lost its penchant for reform—or reduced its awareness of distress—less out of a hardening of the nation's heart than from rigidity in the nation's brains. Because white men would no longer look at the Negro's declining condition, Negroes by the 1890's were on their way to becoming America's invisible men. The neglect was in striking contrast to the century-long concern over their plight that had culminated in the Reconstruction effort.

Thirty years after Appomattox, Northern historians and chroniclers who had been participants in the events they described were passing from the scene. By then, Darwinian extrapolators had assumed clear leadership in theology, law, social sciences, and history.[19] Tenets sacred to the Darwinian devout were heard in 1896, when the United States Supreme Court sanctioned "separate but equal" educational provisions for Negroes, in an opinion that rested for its support far less on law than on pseudoscientific folklore about race.[20] Historians of the new look—John W. Burgess, William A. Dunning, James Ford Rhodes, James Schouler, and Woodrow Wilson, among others—during the 1890's and later took on the task of interpreting Reconstruction in this comfortingly scientific context. However these writers differed on other matters, they agreed that the Reconstruction process and the Radical Republican leaders deserved adverse descriptions and judgments. Here, as an extreme example, is a 1902 estimate of Congress' attempts, under Republican prodding, to enfranchise Negroes in the Southern states during Reconstruction; it appeared in Burgess' influential *Reconstruction and the Constitution, 1866–1876.*

> But there is no question now that Congress did a monstrous thing and committed a great political error, if not a sin, in the creation of this new electorate. It was a great wrong to civilization to put the white race of the South under the domination of the Negro

---

[19] Donald Fleming, "Social Darwinism," in *Paths of American Thought,* ed. Arthur M. Schlesinger, Jr., and Morton White (Boston: Houghton Mifflin Company, 1963), pp. 123–146; Richard Hofstadter, *Social Darwinism in American Thought,* rev. ed. (Boston: Beacon Press, 1955), pp. 3–104, 170–184: referred to hereafter as Hofstadter, *Social Darwinism.* The most succinct statements are in Paul F. Boller, Jr., "New Men and New Ideas: Science and the American Mind," in *The Gilded Age: A Reappraisal,* ed. H. Wayne Morgan (Syracuse: Syracuse University Press, 1963), pp. 221–243; and Henry Steele Commager, *The American Mind: An Interpretation of American Thought and Character Since the 1880's* (New Haven: Yale University Press, 1950), pp. 277–292.

[20] Barton J. Bernstein, "Case Law in Plessy v. Ferguson," *Journal of Negro History,* XLVII (July 1962), 192–198.

race. The claim that there is nothing in the color of the skin from the point of view of political ethics is a great sophism.[21]

So complete was the reversal from earlier views, which had praised the Republicans for their Reconstruction venture, that Dunning, in a rare mood of jest, wrote in 1901 to his friend Frederic Bancroft: "Lord, how the reconstructors have been reconstructed! I'm going to . . . take the ground that the whole [Reconstruction] business was ethically, socially, and politically right; that's the only way in which a man can attract any attention now."[22]

But in his publications Dunning steered clear of such heresy. Instead, he and his numerous, influential, and long-lived disciples helped to cement Jim Crow concepts into the new, "objective" historical scholarship. Consider this estimate of Negro behavior and capacities, offered in Dunning's 1907 book, *Reconstruction, Political and Economic:*

> The negro had no pride of race and no aspiration save to be like the whites. With civil rights and political power, not won, but almost forced upon him, he came gradually to understand and crave those more elusive privileges that constitute social equality. A more intimate association with the other race than that which business and politics involved was the end toward which the ambition of the blacks tended consciously or unconsciously to direct itself. The manifestations of this ambition were infinite in their diversity. It played a part in the demand for mixed schools, in the legislative prohibition of discrimination between the races in hotels and theaters, and even in the hideous crime against

---

[21] Burgess continued: "A black skin means membership in a race of men which has never of itself succeeded in subjecting passion to reason, has never, therefore, created any civilization of any kind." (New York: Charles Scribner's Sons, 1902), p. 133.

[22] April 5, 1901, Bancroft Papers, Special Collections, Columbia University Library.

white womanhood which . . . assumed new meaning in the annals of outrage.[23]

A few weak voices were raised in unavailing protest against the triumph of the "Dunning school" of interpretation. As example, Francis N. Thorpe in 1905 presented a warning that deserves repetition today, just as it rated, but failed to receive, attention sixty years ago. He wrote that "Reconstruction is a word whose full meaning . . . cannot be known for many years—perhaps for centuries. The ebb and flow of civil affairs in the South during Reconstruction are yet too imperfectly understood to warrant any anticipation of the final decision on the exercise of the suffrage by the negro in America."[24]

Notwithstanding this wise injunction and disregarding later protests—voiced in scattered publications, in the main by Negroes, and culminating in the mid-1930's in W. E. B. Du Bois' *Black Reconstruction*—the Dunning version marched on far into the twentieth century.[25] Dunning and his coadjutors ap-

---

[23] (New York: Harper and Brothers, 1907), pp. 213–214; and see Alan D. Harper, "William A. Dunning: The Historian as Nemesis," *Civil War History*, X (March 1964), 54–66; Kenneth M. Stampp, "The Tragic Legend of Reconstruction," *Commentary*, XXXIX (January 1965), 44–50; and David Donald's introduction to the recent Torchbook reprint of Dunning's *Essays on the Civil War and Reconstruction* (New York: Harper and Row, 1965).

[24] Thorpe's introduction to Peter Joseph Hamilton, *The Reconstruction Period* (Philadelphia: United States Edition, 1905), pp. ix-x.

[25] Du Bois, *Black Reconstruction: An Essay Toward a History of the Part Which Black Folk Played in the Attempt to Reconstruct Democracy in America, 1860–1880* (New York: Harcourt, Brace and Company, 1935). See too the significant recollection by a Negro Mississippian who was a state legislator there during the Reconstruction; in John R. Lynch, *The Facts of Reconstruction* (New York: Neale, 1913). Pressly, pp. 249–262, surveys the near monopoly on the part of Marxists on protests against the Dunning tide. Note too that in the late 1930's Hitler analyzed the American Civil War and its impact as follows: "Since the Civil War, in which the Southern States were conquered against all historical logic and sound sense, the Americans have been in a condition of political and popular [i.e., racial] decay. In that war, it was not the Southern

pealed strongly to many Americans who, looking at their land during the first quarter of this century, were not too pleased at what they saw and not too critical of what they read. The Dunning warning was that the real danger to democracy was not in the loss of Negro rights but in the lessening of states' rights and in the sinister secret links of big business to corrupt and demogogic public officials. Science proved fruitless any attempt, especially any by the national government, to raise the Negro's condition too quickly or at all.

This distorted and prejudiced view of the past was given an immensely popular expression in 1929 in Claude G. Bowers' *The Tragic Era: The Revolution After Lincoln,*[26] which one trenchant commentator, Bernard Weisberger, has called a "zestful work of the imagination." That "familiar story," Weisberger wrote,

> told how 'Vindictives' and 'Radicals' in Congress shouldered aside Johnson and the Supreme Court and imposed 'Carpetbag' and 'Scalawag' and 'Negro' governments on the South by bayonet. These new governments debauched and plundered a proud but helpless people until finally, desperately harried whites responded with their own campaigns of violence and persuasion. These respectable folk at home at last took advantage of mount-

---

States, but the American people themselves who were conquered. . . . The beginnings of a great new social order based on the principle of slavery and inequality were destroyed in that war, and with them also the embryo of a future truly great America that would not have been ruled by a corrupt caste of tradesmen, but by a real *Herren*-class that would have swept away all the falsities of liberty and inequality." Quoted in Gerhard L. Weinberg, "Hitler's Image of the United States," *American Historical Review,* LXIX (July 1964), 1011. I do not suggest that Hitler read Dunning or Bowers, or that they were philosophers for Nazism, but only that the assumptions of the historians named were more widespread in the world than they or their successors could have imagined.

[26] (Cambridge: Houghton Mifflin Company, 1929).

ing Northern disgust with 'carpetbag crimes' to restore 'home rule' unopposed.[27]

Were the impact, diffusion, and tenacity of the views presented in *The Tragic Era* less great, the book could easily be dismissed as pseudo scholarship. But as Francis Butler Simkins, an eminent historian and a Southerner, has shown, the Dunning-Bowers depiction of Reconstruction has become more real than the truth to Southerners less critical than Simkins himself is. "In mid [twentieth] century," Simkins wrote in 1939, "the masses of white Southerners [still] accepted these judgments as axiomatic. . . . The wickedness of this [Reconstruction] régime and the righteousness of the manner in which it was destroyed were fundamentals of his [the white Southerner's] civil code."[28]

Events of the 1950's and 1960's offer continuing affirmation of the keenness of Simkins' insight. The passionate distortion concerning the Radical Republican and Reconstruction continues to have a vast impact on popular attitudes and present problems. Consider that in July 1964 the Imperial Wizard of an Alabama-centered group called the Knights of the Ku Klux Klan, Robert Shelton, told a reporter that "the Klan symbolizes the Reconstruction. We try to keep the Klan today on the same pedestal of history, of the Reconstruction past, when there were no laws to defend the [white] Southerner under the heel of Federal oppression."[29]

As Simkins noted in 1939, the historian's duty is not to sustain or to condemn "the everlasting South" but to "foster more

---

[27] Weisberger, "The Dark and Bloody Ground of Reconstruction Historiography," *Journal of Southern History*, XXV (November 1957), 428.

[28] Simkins, "New Viewpoints of Southern Reconstruction," *Journal of Southern History*, V (February 1939), 50–51.

[29] Quoted in Margaret Long, "The Imperial Wizard Explains the Klan," *New York Times Magazine*, July 5, 1964, p. 25.

moderate, saner, perhaps newer views."[30] This is still the historian's duty. To be sure, the new wave of "revisionist" scholarship helped partially to correct some of the more egregious distortions of the Dunning and Bowers genre. But the correctives departed less from Dunning's pathways than some revisers have realized or admitted; they have kept alive the most important of his conclusions, if not all of his presuppositions; they have rested also on subjective and emotional foundations and been less "objective" and "scientific" than at first appeared.

If dating is meaningful in such an evanescent question as shifts in intellectual attitude, then the years of World War I deserve description as a turning point. The reactions of American historians of the Civil War to their experiences in, and attitudes toward, World War I provided the springboard for the re-evaluations of the Civil War and Reconstruction.[31] This transposition of values led the new scholars into the continuation of old errors.

Most intellectuals had ushered in the twentieth century in the optimistic mood engendered by Darwinian modes of

---

30 "New Viewpoints of Southern Reconstruction," p. 67.

31 The word "revisionism" suffers from variant interpretations and much imprecision, and I have avoided employing it except as it meshed with the argument of this essay. Professor Fehrenbacher has provided the following useful frame for this employment: " 'Revisionism' as a general outlook can be found throughout Civil War historiography, from a book by James Buchanan in 1866 to a centennial series of newspaper articles by Bruce Catton in 1961. But as a recognizable school of interpretation it emerged during the years between [the Treaty of] Versailles and [the Japanese attack on] Pearl Harbor, a time when the American people, significantly, were experiencing a great revulsion against their participation in the First World War." Don E. Fehrenbacher, "Disunion and Reunion," in *The Reconstruction of American History*, ed. John Higham (New York: Harper & Brothers, 1962), pp. 111–112 and *passim*. Pressly, pp. 291–328, offers more detail. Affection for the South as a region also figures as a source of revisionists' inspiration. Many historians of the post-World-War-I period were Southern born. But the impact of this factor is simply less provable, however real and large its significance.

thought. They envisaged history as a happy catechism, not as a prelude to cataclysm. Priests and professors continued to teach that man was climbing a high wave of progress, with greater ascents soon to come. Modern man was on the way to curing all ills through the application of science to society. Europe's great powers surely were too civilized to study war any more. After all, the last mass conflict had ended way back in 1815. In sharp contrast to the Napoleonic holocaust, intervening wars, with the sole exception of the American Civil War, had been brief, localized, and restrained in conduct. The most recent clashes—the transoceanic fray between the United States and Spain, and the Asian duel between Japan and Russia—fitted neatly with this inspiring trend toward rational limitation of the horrors of war, a trend solemnized further in the Hague agreements.

Americans shared in this comfortable consensus. They were busy at home, in conformable spirit, attempting the reformation of political institutions through the broadening of political democracy and the application to government of the exciting new insights provided by the social scientists. So-called Progressives were assuming leadership of both major political parties. Through their efforts, federal, state, and local agencies began watchdogging over corporate practices, overseeing the conservation of certain natural resources, and offering some protection to consumers. By 1912, when Progressives were Presidential candidates in all parties, the triumph in politics of the new-style reformer appeared to be complete; the old-fashioned "boss" was surely obsolete. The expectation was widespread that the shocking liaisons between machine politicians and greedy corporations, which had so tarnished the Gilded Age, were henceforth impossible. A cleaner, more efficient, and more democratic American society soon would be the outcome of this wedding of the science of politics with the morality of reformers, a union epitomized by Wilson's election and the subsequent ratification of the Sixteenth and Seventeenth Amendments to the national Constitution.[32]

To be sure, few of these optimistic reformers of the early twentieth century were much interested in matters that had consumed the energies of Lincoln's generation. Jim Crow practices, including racial segregation in the federal civil service, were products of Wilson's first administration, and they came in virtually unopposed in Congress or elsewhere in the nation.[33] The reform literature of the Progressive years ignores the fact that millions of Americans—immigrants generally, members or would-be members of labor unions, Negroes and other pigmented minorities—were restricted in the things that they might say or write, the places in which they could live, learn, or play, and the ways in which they should make their livings. Except for the puny cadre that the NAACP represented, the Negro remained an invisible man. The symbol for the time was not the heated activism of John Brown but the illuminating insights of Charles Beard, Frederick Jackson Turner, and Thorstein Veblen, whose ideas centered on economic factors as the compelling forces underlying the actions of men and nations.[34]

Then, just fifty years ago, came World War I, and three

---

[32] See the provocative interpretation in Charles Forcey, *The Crossroads of Liberalism: Croly, Weyl, Lippmann, and the Progressive Era, 1900–1925* (New York: Oxford University Press, 1961). It is an admirable supplement for Commager, *The American Mind*, ch. 20; George F. Mowry, *The Era of Theodore Roosevelt: 1900–1912* (New York: Harper, 1958); and Richard Hofstadter, *The Age of Reform: from Bryan to F.D.R.* (New York: Alfred A. Knopf, 1955).

[33] Kathleen L. Wolgemuth, "Wilson and Federal Segregation," *Journal of Negro History*, XLIV (April 1959), 158–173.

[34] Roche, *The Quest for the Dream*, pp. 1–25. An extraordinarily useful insight into the numerous intellectual pathways that men opened in the pre-World-War-I decade is available in Howard K. Beale, ed., *Charles A. Beard: An Appraisal* (Lexington: University of Kentucky Press, 1954).

years later the American involvement took place. The vile conditions in which men fought the war, the brutal treatment that prisoners and noncombatants suffered, the monstrous new weapons that armies employed, upset the cherished beliefs regarding the rising rationality of mankind in international relations. Brutal, total, and ruinous in its effects on European monetary, ethical, and political systems, the war took on, in historical and popular accounts that appeared soon after the armistice, the lineaments of retrogression into the Dark Ages, rather than appearing as the successful containment of the aggressively expansive, militaristic German Empire.[35]

Perhaps the worst of it was that the sacrifices and horrors of 1914–1918 appeared after 1919 to have been worthless. Clearly the world after 1918 was not safe for democracy. Instead, the Bolshevik growth held on in eastern Europe, and the fascist creation soon rooted in Italy. Instability and inflation plagued the governments and currencies of the succession states of central Europe. Unrest troubled Ireland, Palestine, most of Asia, North Africa, and Latin America. And the League of Nations, the focus of so many hopes, was failing to perform as its well-wishers had anticipated.

Accentuating further the disillusionment and cynicism for intellectuals, revelations grew in number of unsavory secret treaties between the wartime Allies regarding the disposition of the enemy's colonies. Common allegations had it that all atrocities attributed to the German enemy before 1918 were fictional or were exaggerated by Allied propaganda agencies; and though these allegations were untrue, the uncritical consensus insisted that they were fact. Investigations in this country and others brought to light supposed links between muni-

---

[35] *War and Intellectuals: Essays by Randolph S. Bourne, 1915–1919,* ed. Carl Resek (New York: Harper Torchbooks, 1964), pp. 3–47; Henry F. May, *The End of American Innocence: A Study of the First Years of Our Own Time, 1912–1917* (New York: Alfred A. Knopf, 1959).

tions producers and other corporate "merchants of death," who had fattened on cost-plus profits and, by implication, had deliberately prolonged the meat-grinding on the Western Front in order to garner even greater wealth. How could a monopoly of guilt adhere to Germany, historians asked, when the evidence was impressive that all nations in 1914 followed selfish, amoral, economic imperatives?

But the real shocker in this avalanching logic was that the war might be judged to have been unnecessary as well as worthless and dreadful. Once the assumptions took root that the war was an irrational and fruitless irrelevance, the next steps followed ineluctably. If the guilt for causing the war or the blame for the awful conditions of combat and the excesses committed on civilians was not particularly Germany's, how justify the Versailles attempt to restructure German society into more democratic and less militaristic lines?[36]

By and large, American intellectuals came quickly to accept the judgment of relativism as to German war guilt. Freudian and neo-Marxian concepts reinforced that judgment, and a pattern of unsavory domestic developments garnished the assumption of scientific relativism with an overlay of apparent cynicism and disillusionment.

During the period of American involvement in the war, the home front had become a happy hunting ground for superpatriots, who were often closely linked to war-emergency agencies on all levels of the federal system. The armistice was adequate to stop war abroad, but at home Red raids, deportations, race riots, and vigilantism continued on into the 1920's, attended by the illiberal and anti-intellectual excesses that

---

[36] Louis Morton, "From Fort Sumter to Poland: The Question of War Guilt," *World Politics*, XIV (January 1962), 386–392, deals succinctly with this matter, in reviewing A.J.P. Taylor's *The Origins of the Second World War* (New York: Atheneum, 1962). See too, Arthur Link, "What Happened to the Progressive Movement in the 1920's?" *American Historical Review*, LXIV (July 1959), 833–851.

marked that decade.[37] Repelled by the unanticipated irration-
ality of their countrymen, Americans of sound conscience were
disgusted also to learn that the hard-won prewar improvements in democracy's machinery had not after all insulated
politics from corrupt politicians or from corrupting special
interests. Another Gilded Age was upon the land, more tawdry
and vulgar than the worst of Grant's era. Men of taste and
integrity looked backward from the 1920's and from the De-
pression- and war-ridden 1930's and 1940's to the decades
immediately preceding American entrance into the First
World War and saw a lost Eden, from whose happy paths
the nation had gone astray when it linked its fortunes to
Europe's problems and thereby lost its virtue.

Some distinguished men of letters were so repelled by the
unsavory characteristics of Harding's "normalcy" that they
temporarily became expatriates in their search for a more
sympathetic milieu. Not so historians. Almost to a man they
preferred faculty benches to the Left Bank. From campus fast-
nesses they hit out at what they found distasteful in modern
America by redrawing, through their scholarship, the major
lineaments of Civil War and Reconstruction America.

These historians deserved and deserve respectful attention.
Their work is marked by far more rigorous standards of com-
pleteness in research than had obtained previously in the
earlier corps of writers such as Rhodes and Dunning, and
more latterly in Parrington. As Professor T. Harry Williams
noted in 1946, "these new viewpoints have provided a desirable balance and proportion to the historical treatment of
Reconstruction." Unquestionably, the post-World-War-I writ-

---

[37] Harold M. Hyman, *To Try Men's Souls: Loyalty Tests in American
History* (Berkeley and Los Angeles: University of California Press,
1959), pp. 267–324; Harry N. Scheiber, *The Wilson Administration and
Civil Liberties, 1917–1921* (Ithaca: Cornell University Press, 1960);
Robert K. Murray, *Red Scare: A Study in National Hysteria, 1919–1920*
(Minneapolis: University of Minnesota Press, 1955).

ers improved the over-simple drama of good against evil that had marked and marred earlier analyses of the Civil War and Reconstruction. These historians, Williams wrote,

> have forced several modifications in the Reconstruction story. They have demonstrated, among other things, that the corruption of the Reconstruction state governments has been exaggerated and that in any case corruption was a national, not a purely southern, phenomenon, with an expanding capitalism as the chief corrupting agent; that the Democrats were quite as willing as Republicans to be bought by business; that the supposed astronomically high appropriations of the Reconstruction governments seem so only in comparison with the niggardly budgets of the planter-controlled governments of the ante-bellum period; that although the Reconstruction governments were corrupt and dishonest, they must be credited with definite progress in the fields of popular education and internal improvements; and that the national reconstruction program was radical only in a superficial sense in that it gave political power to the Negro but failed to provide economic power through the promised confiscation and ownership of land, and thus that because the position of the Negro had no lasting basis his rule was easily overthrown.[38]

The new scholarship swiftly assumed front-running leadership among historians. It was not only quickly successful but almost overwhelmingly so. A survey of reviewing media reveals how few critics took issue with the revised estimates of the Civil War and Reconstruction. The major carpers were Marxians or Negroes—Du Bois, Allen—and this added weight to the altered analysis of the past.

This scholarly blitzkrieg was successful undoubtedly because its practitioners were, and are, able. Consider only a few outstanding members of the first wave: Howard K. Beale, William B. Hesseltine, Avery O. Craven, Allan Nevins, Roy F. Nichols, and James G. Randall, among the academics. They represent extraordinary talent.

---

[38] Williams, "An Analysis of Some Reconstruction Attitudes," *Journal of Southern History,* XII (November 1946), 469–470.

Diligence is another characteristic that helps to account for this success. This pride of historians published their first major works soon after the close of World War I. A rich outpouring of books, articles, papers, and students followed for the ensuing thirty years and is far from closed off.

Obviously, a happy longevity attended the careers of these historians. Of the men named, four were born between 1890 and 1899, and all in the decades 1881–1902. Death claimed Randall in 1953, Beale in 1959, and Hesseltine in 1963. Until each man died, he was busy at work, as Craven, Nevins, and Nichols are as this is written, and hopefully will remain for a long time to come. To further the effect of longevity, each of these distinguished historians brought forth disciples who in turn have taken places of leadership in the profession, as T. Harry Williams has complemented the work of his mentor, Hesseltine, and David Donald, the work of Randall.

A further factor in the revisionist triumph, adding to the effects of their diligence, lengthy careers, and superlative talents, is that fortunate timing attended them. They came to prominence when Americans were accepting as valid the proposition that intervention in World War I had been a tragic error. No doubt there was reciprocation here. The attitude spread because historians wrote on it so tellingly, and their writings spread because the climate of opinion was receptive. It is less important to worry the question of which came first than to point to the unusual coincidence that obtained in popular and scholarly assumptions on certain basic matters, especially on the nature of war in history—any war.

These scholars extrapolated from the picture they accepted of the "needless" war of 1917 and created a "repressible conflict" in 1861. Their works argued that war came at Sumter less from moral imperatives centering on slavery than from economic sectionalism; that hyperbolic, ambitious extremists among politicians failed to be statesmen and misguided the blundering generation of the 1850's to the fateful impasse at Charleston Harbor; and that reasonable men were subordinated by those of the fanatical cast of John Brown. The crises of Lincoln's America became in revisionist scholarship not products of nobility and progress but the results instead of demogoguery, propaganda, hysteria, and sordid conspiracies. Reconstruction, by these analyses, was as much of an irrelevance as the Versailles *diktat* that in the 1920's weighed so heavily (they felt) on Germany.

They felt—that is the point. Despite its preachments to objectivity, this body of scholarship reflected an emotional attitude, not a philosophical system; a prejudgment, not an injunction to intellectual neutrality; a sermon in monographic form. Arthur Schlesinger, Jr., properly described revisionism as historical sentimentalism.[39]

Chiefly, it was an attitude toward war. The revisionist presupposition was that of the romantic optimist who believed that progress had lifted modern man too high for him ever rationally to choose war as a means of solving international difficulties, because no moral evil was greater than that of war itself.

To be sure, these scholars did not recognize their penchant toward moralizing or their application to the past of present attitudes. Instead, they maintained a posture (not an imposture) of impressive objectivity in their scholarship.

Retrospectively, it is striking how completely these historians were accepted on their own terms. As has been mentioned, almost no reviewers of the 1920's or 1930's took issue with them to point out the subjective and intuitive approach that underlay their methodological practices.

One of the few critical commentators was the insightful Bernard DeVoto. In a 1946 review of Randall's *Lincoln the President*, DeVoto noted:

Historians who are now mature, the generation to which Mr. Randall belongs, happened to be young and impressionable at a

---

[39] Schlesinger, "The Causes of the Civil War: A Note on Historical Sentimentalism," *Partisan Review*, XVI (October 1949), 969–981.

time when an intellectual fashion was developing the (erroneous) thesis that the United States could have and should have stayed out of the First World War and the (false) theorem that we were betrayed into it by propaganda. . . . This generation of historians has built up a body of judgment [revisionism] about the Civil War. Some of it is certainly sound, some certainly unsound. . . . No historian, I suppose, accepts all of it, but every historian has incorporated a large or a small part of it into his thinking and assumes some of it as judgment on the way to form further judgments.[40]

DeVoto's criticism received little attention anywhere in academia. Certainly it failed to swerve leading historians from their courses. But not even the impact of World War II moved most of these scholar-teachers away from their set convictions. This four-decades-long consistency is another characteristic that helps to account for the success of these historians. Men of such continuing convictions impress by the strength of their beliefs, especially when it is joined by their other fine qualities of intellect and personality.

Avery Craven's adventures as an historian illustrate this striking tenacity in views. Craven's *The Coming of the Civil War*, published in 1942—note the year—provided a classic expression of the repressibility theme. According to DeVoto, Craven had wanted the title to be *The North's Mistake*, but the publisher won the less loaded one. DeVoto noted how, in the book, all the villains were "abolitionists, free-soilers, the Republican Party, more radical reformers, in short, everyone who thought that the slavery issue was in some degree a moral issue." Such extremists, according to Craven, prevented a rational solution of the 1860 crisis by men of good will and later were responsible for Reconstruction excesses.[41]

That was 1942. Craven's 1964 presidential address to the

---

[40] DeVoto, "The Easy Chair," *Harper's*, CXCII (February 1946), 123. See the entire review-article, pp. 123–126, and continuing into the March issue, pp. 234–237.

[41] *Ibid.*, p. 124.

major association of historians in the United States indicated
that he still defended the revisionists' lines against the incursions of newer views on the nature of war, on the role of
economic forces in history, and on the historian's responsibilities and capacities:

> What can the historian sitting on his impartial fence . . . write
> on the sand for his own generation. He will, of course, living in
> this day, be inclined to keep the Negro and slavery in the fore-
> front and to see the sectional struggle which ended in civil war
> as one of the conflicting values and ideologies. That much his
> age imposes on him. Yet it seems to me that if he will take a firm
> grip on the top rail of his fence so as not to fall to either side, he
> will begin to see that his own age has, to some degree, misled
> him. The really important point for the South, as well as for the
> North in the years before the Civil War, was that the Industrial
> Revolution with its opportunities and its spirit of enterprise was
> 'shaking to pieces the simpler economy of 18th century America.'
> . . . In fact, in matters economic, the South had drifted steadily
> towards a colonial status. . . . [B]y 1860, the political situation
> had become so desperate for the South that her . . . leaders were
> willing to risk their all in an effort to keep control of the rebel-
> lious Democratic party. The gamble failed and political impo-
> tence [for the South] was added to economic colonialism.[42]

Some commentators see progression in Professor Craven's
views. I do not. His rejection of slavery as a genuine issue
impelling men a century ago to demand swift solution is unchanged throughout the decades of rich professional activity
that have marked his distinguished career.

---

[42] Craven, "An Historical Adventure," *Journal of American History*,
LI (June 1964), 17–18, 19. Suggestions that Professor Craven has
adapted his revisionist views to the post-World-War-II scene are in John
Higham, "Beyond Consensus: The Historian as Moral Critic," *American
Historical Review*, LXVII (April 1962), 613; and T. N. Bonner, "Civil
War Historians and the Needless War Doctrine," *Journal of the History
of Ideas*, XVII (April 1956), 193–216. See also David M. Potter's review
of Craven's *An Historian and the Civil War* in *Journal of Southern History*, XXXI (May 1965), 207–210.

The work of Roy F. Nichols offers another example of this fruitful tenacity. His first book, published in 1923, examined closely and constructively the strains that in the early 1850's were tearing the Democratic party's organization and that by the end of that decade were to rip the nation apart.[43] Then in 1963 Nichols presented as capstone for his career a broad overview of American constitutional and institutional history, centering on the mid-nineteenth-century crossroads. He called it *Blueprints for Leviathan: American Style,* and as reviewers noted, it offered a canvas so wide, so deftly executed as to inspire analogies to Turner and Beard.

But because it left no new prints in the sands of history, *Blueprints* disappoints. In 1963 Nichols remained satisfied with his approaches of 1923. He wrote in *Blueprints* that there exists "some law of behavioral average" whereby for the historian there is always as much to praise as to blame in "the conduct of great masses of people." By the application of "dry scientific concepts of the behavioral sciences to an analysis of this [the Civil] War," Nichols continued, "it becomes difficult to assign praise or blame or to award victory or defeat."[44] Of course it is difficult—but worth the effort.

Nothing more vividly illustrates the Southern victory among historians than the sudden upward rise in the scholarly and popular estimations of Andrew Johnson that occurred at the close of the 1920's. Until then, Johnson in all accounts had been described as an inadequate man for the weights of his office. Most commentators agreed that his misfortunes leading to the impeachment were his own fault, rising from defects in his character, intelligence, and education. Even Dunning admitted that Johnson at best was simply not a statesman.

---

[43] Nichols, *The Democratic Machine, 1850–1854* (New York: Columbia University Press, 1923).

[44] (New York: Atheneum, 1963), pp. 259–260. Note that Nichols dedicated *Blueprints* to Dunning, and that the careers of these two men span all twentieth-century historiographical production.

Suddenly the Southern view of Reconstruction triumphed. As a consequence, by 1930 Andrew Johnson's reputation experienced the meteoric rise described in Castel's recent analysis:

> . . . [A]t the end of the 1920's, an historiographical revolution took place. In the brief span of three years five widely-read books, all extremely favorable to Johnson, appeared. First, in 1928, was Hobert W. Winston's *Andrew Johnson: Plebian and Patriot*. Next, in 1929, there was Lloyd Paul Stryker's *Andrew Johnson: A Study in Courage* and Claude G. Bowers' *The Tragic Era*. And finally, in 1930, there came Howard K. Beale's *The Critical Year* and George Fort Milton's *The Age of Hate*. . . . [A]ll combined to raise Johnson's reputation to a height which would have been inconceivable to James Ford Rhodes. No longer was Lincoln's successor deemed a stubborn, egotistical, ill-tempered demagogue whose maladroit policies and vulgar conduct needlessly antagonized Congress and led to the regrettable excesses of Radical Reconstruction. Now he was a humane, enlightened, and liberal statesman who waged a courageous battle in defense of the Constitution, the Union, and democracy against the scheming and unscrupulous Radicals, who for their part were motivated by a vindictive hatred of the South, personal ambition, and (in the eyes of Beale in particular) a desire to establish the national supremacy of Northern 'Big Business.' In short, rather than a boor, Johnson was a martyr; instead of a villain, a hero.[45]

An extraordinarily popular historical overview, Charles and Mary Beard's *Rise of American Civilization,* brought this inflated depiction of Johnson to the attention of tens of thousands of Americans during the ensuing decades. Millions who watched the now-classic film, *Gone with the Wind,* received similar impressions of Reconstruction's evils. Another less spectacular film, *Johnson of Tennessee,* was also widely viewed and in 1964 was reissued for television showing. The new look

[45] Albert Castel, "Andrew Johnson: His Historiographical Rise and Fall," *Mid-America,* XLV (July 1963), 178–179.

fitted perfectly with the revisionist morality play on the causation of the Civil War, of the repressible conflict moving logically to an unnecessary Reconstruction.

Matters had gone too far. Johnson's overblown stature troubled even Beale, who had helped to create it.[46] Onrushing events, centering on the domestic Depression and the mushrooming totalitarian growth abroad, brought some scholars to question the directions they had marked out in describing America's more distant past.

In striking contrast to the effects of World War I on American intellectuals, World War II was supportable on moral terms to many historians, especially younger men, some of whom had experienced the war in military or auxiliary services. The postwar effort to restructure conquered Germany and Japan into less bellicose postures was seen as necessary and proper. With respect to the war against Nazi Germany and her cohorts, an almost complete consensus obtained that no "conspiracies" shotgunned America into the fray or governed the postvictory occupation program. Scholars saw a difference between the combatants. It mattered who won. The upshot was to restore to respectability the study of good and evil as pre-eminent factors in the causes, conduct, and consequences of wars.[47]

As with the question of war, race as a moral factor received new attention in the years centering on World War II. In 1939 Simkins frankly admitted his judgment that race after all was the central question in Reconstruction. Adequately critical study on that period did not yet exist, he argued. His estimate

---

[46] Beale, *The Critical Year: A Study of Andrew Johnson and Reconstruction,* new ed. (New York: F. Ungar Pub. Co., 1958); Beale's article "On Rewriting Reconstruction History," *American Historical Review,* XLV (July 1940), 807–827.

[47] Louis Morton, "The Historian and the Study of War," *Mississippi Valley Historical Review,* XLVIII (March 1962), 599–612; Higham, "Beyond Consensus," pp. 609–625.

received reinforcement the following year from Beale, who asked colleagues to review Reconstruction without prejudgments as to the wickedness of the Radicals and their carpetbagger and scalawag cohorts.[48]

Unfortunately, the bright promise for a clarifying review of the Reconstruction, represented by 1940 in the Simkins and Beale articles, was not realized until very recently. Even in 1957, Weisberger, surveying "The Dark and Bloody Ground of Reconstruction Historiography," felt justified in expressing his disappointment that the profession had not used "the perspective gained at the end of one decade of swift social change [the 1930's] in the careful examination of an earlier period of upheaval. Yet now, twenty years after these premonitory signs [i.e., the Simkins-Beale plea], . . . the work still needs to be done. . . . It is more important than ever that progress be made towards understanding the issues raised in the 'old' Reconstruction of 1865 to 1877."[49]

Now, a quarter century after Beale and Simkins called for a re-evaluation of Reconstruction, it appears at last to be well under way. As example, David Donald, a front-runner in Civil War scholarship, suggested that the Radicals were merely one of the most "noisy and conspicuous" wartime factions within the Republican organization. Their wartime importance should not be exaggerated, he warned. And he advised, rightly, that historians might pay attention to the Radicals' principles as well as to their politics.

The suggestion that the Radicals enjoyed possession of principles is startling, and Donald took care to hold it within bounds. Except for "simple antislavery zeal," he wrote, the Radicals "held few ideas in common." Only with Lincoln's

---

[48] Simkins, "New Viewpoints of Southern Reconstruction"; Beale, "On Rewriting Reconstruction History," pp. 807–827.

[49] Weisberger, pp. 428–429.

death and with emancipation virtually achieved did the Radicals become "a unified political group."[50]

This is a long step forward from the older condemnation of the Radicals as villains during the Civil War as after. Donald grants to the Radicals the principle of emancipation, at least until Appomattox. He casts them in roles of lesser significance within the Republican organization, and of lesser vindictiveness than the earlier consensus had assigned.[51]

What, then, of Reconstruction after Lincoln's murder and Lee's surrender? Do the Radicals return, after Appomattox, to the old casting as unprincipled villains—a stock-typing against which even Beale protested? Is Appomattox to remain the incontinent divide, on one side of which the Radicals, having won emancipation, thereafter seek power only, and in the process exploit freedmen and flood the prostrate South with carpetbaggers, troops, and complaisant puppets, the scalawags?

A possibility exists that this sharp division will mark most writing on the Radicals and Reconstruction. Vincent P. De Santis' survey of the Republican party organization in the South after Hayes's inauguration, in harmony with Donald's analysis, concluded that the only real reformers in the party were the old abolitionists. Appomattox and, nine months later, the ratification of the Thirteenth Amendment satisfied most of these antislavery veterans. Spoilsmen took over after the reformers left politics, and, keeping the reformers' rhetoric,

---

[50] "The Radicals and Lincoln," in *Lincoln Reconsidered*, ed. David Donald (New York: Vintage, 1961), p. 126 and *passim*.

[51] Donald, "Devils Facing Zionwards," in *Grant, Lee, Lincoln and the Radicals: Essays on Civil War Leadership by Bruce Catton, Charles P. Roland, David Donald, and T. Harry Williams*, ed. Grady McWhiney (Evanston: Northwestern University Press, 1964), pp. 72–91, should be compared to T. Harry Williams' contribution to that volume, "Lincoln and the Radicals: An Essay in Civil War History and Historiography," pp. 92–117. Agreement between the two men appears to be less complete than Professor Donald suggests on page 88. See Donald's exchange with Professor T. Harry Williams in the same volume.

they kept as much of the great barbecue going as they could.[52]

John Hope Franklin's survey of Reconstruction agrees with Donald and De Santis that the postwar Radicals were a different and less exalted breed than the wartime reformers.[53] Because the postwar Radicals had selfish purposes, they failed to achieve the true reconstruction of Southern society made possible by the Confederate defeat and the Northern Democratic party's disorganization. The postwar Radicals were not so radical after all, and in truth were little different from the opportunists portrayed in our literature since the century's turn.

But there is another branch of this interpretive stream to travel. Recent work on Ben Butler, Andrew Johnson, Thad Stevens, Edwin Stanton, and Ben Wade has taken issue with such implications. The most insightful inquiry to date on the relationships between the Republicans and Northern businessmen, by Stanley Coben, suggests that "factors other than the economic interests of the Northeast must be used to explain the motivation and aims of the Radical Republicans."[54]

What factors? It appears that the relevant ones are precisely those denied in the Donald-Franklin approach—those of

---

[52] De Santis, pp. 22–23; and see his "The Republican Party and the Southern Negro, 1877–1897," *Journal of Negro History*, XLV (April 1960), 71–87.

[53] Franklin, *Reconstruction: After the Civil War* (Chicago: University of Chicago Press, 1961), pp. 232–242 (hereafter cited as Franklin, *Reconstruction*); and see too his "Whither Reconstruction Historiography?" *Journal of Negro Education*, XVII (Fall 1948), 446–461.

[54] Coben, "Northeastern Business and Radical Reconstruction: A Re-Examination," *Mississippi Valley Historical Review*, XLVI (June 1959), 67, 90. Other works mentioned are Fawn Brodie, *Thaddeus Stevens: Scourge of the South* (New York: Norton, 1959); Eric McKitrick, *Andrew Johnson and Reconstruction* (Chicago: University of Chicago Press, 1960); Benjamin P. Thomas and Harold M. Hyman, *Stanton: The Life and Times of Lincoln's Secretary of War* (New York: Knopf, 1962); and Hans Trefousse, *Ben Butler: The South Called Him Beast!* (New York: Twayne, 1957); *Benjamin Franklin Wade: Radical Republican from Ohio* (New York: Twayne, 1963).

principled postwar Radical Republicanism. Patrick W. Riddleberger has offered his opinion that at least some of the leading
Radicals even after Appomattox were motivated by theoreti-
cal and intellectual convictions transcending merely material
goals. Evaluations of Andrew Johnson and of his political
purposes and opponents by Eric McKitrick and John and
LaWanda Cox lend support to Riddleberger's thesis.[55]

And so at last the tide is turning in the direction of fairer
interpretations, so long overdue, of the men and measures
of 1861–1865, if not of the postwar years; and the result is
to decrease the South's customary advantage.[56] To be sure, the
amassing weight of the newer scholarship bothers some historians who apparently had assumed that most of the basic
questions about Civil War America had been not only asked
but answered. Though hardly of this imperceptive point of
view, Professor Woodward recently confessed his uneasiness
because "Our Past Isn't What It Used To Be." In his article
of this title, Woodward worried that

> the political historians [of the Civil War and Reconstruction]
> have dug up the hatchet again. Northerners complain that the
> Rebels have won the battle of books. Rejecting the concept of a
> 'needless war' brought on by blunderers, and discarding the
> economic interpretation, which played down slavery, they have
> revived the moral interpretation and applied it sweepingly. . . .
> Detachment is frowned upon, and history becomes the continua-
> tion of war by other means. As a consequence there is far less

[55] Riddleberger, "The Radicals' Abandonment of the Negro During
Reconstruction," pp. 88–102; McKitrick, *Andrew Johnson and Reconstruction;* LaWanda Cox and John H. Cox, *Politics, Principle, and Prejudice, 1865–1866: Dilemma of Reconstruction America* (New York: Free
Press of Glencoe, 1963).

[56] Frank E. Vandiver, "The Confederacy and the American Tradition," *Journal of Southern History*, XXVIII (August 1962), 277–286.
Note that seven years earlier, Vandiver felt able to write on "How the
Yankees Are Losing the War," *Southwest Review*, XL (Winter 1955),
62–66.

agreement over the interpretation of the Civil War than there was half a century ago.[57]

Professor Woodward is somewhat overconcerned with the immediacy of the impact of newer interpretations. After all, a long time must pass before the more recent and more favorable evaluations of Republican political leaders such as Stanton, Stevens, and Wade, of Northern generals such as Grant, and of the North's political morality during wartime and in the Reconstruction are widely disseminated. Such novel estimates are still in the main restricted in expression to small-sale biographies, to the cloistered pages of scholarly monographs and periodicals, and to graduate seminars. These researches may eventually trickle down into high school and college textbooks to be written someday and thus may gain large captive audiences in their turn. But this process will take time. Further, to make more glacial the diffusion of new views, many of today's classroom instructors, trained in and believing in older modes and with decades of teaching ahead of them as well as behind, will abandon cherished lecture notes only reluctantly. When the television scriptwriters will find adequate inspiration in this recent scholarship to better balance their products, only Trendex knows.

In sum, old errors in historical attitudes will persist more tenaciously than newer correctives can remove them. Mrs. Brodie was not beating a dead horse in worrying that the South still wears the victor's laurels, especially in estimations of the Reconstruction era.

Although he is critical of the new scholarship, Professor Woodward has again placed the fraternity of historians in his debt, in pleading that the former victim of the war and of the Reconstruction—the Southern white—should not merely be shifted to a villain's corner, while the Radical Republican

---

[57] *New York Times Book Review,* July 28, 1963, pp. 1 ff.

takes on, in the newer estimations, the hero's garb so long denied him. Returning to the challenging question that Mrs. Brodie posed—"Who won the Civil War, anyway?"—it appears appropriate to consider the intimately related question of what was won by the Northern victory of arms. If this can be ascertained, perhaps when the victor's crown leaves the South, we may know where it should properly go.

What did Americans win at Appomattox that was worth the cost of the longest, bloodiest war fought anywhere in the world between Napoleon's surrender in 1815 and the terrible attritions of World Wars I and II? First and foremost, the Union soldiery who cheered Lee at his surrender won a chance to have a national future, by closing off forever the appeals to dismemberment that had so marred the pre-1860 years. Adverting in 1866 to this happy fruit of the war, John A. Dix, a veteran of Buchanan's ill-fated cabinet as well as of Lincoln's army, told his fellow campaigners of New York's Seventh Regiment that their efforts had settled forever the prickly poison of secession, which had "vanished as a disturbing dream."[58]

Disturbing indeed. Before secession cast its pall on progress, a vibrant optimism had marked American institutions, and it was justified by spectacular growth in every aspect of life. Millions of immigrants flocked here from Europe in the greatest mass movement of people in history to that time. Before secession cast its pall on progress, great cities had rooted on the Eastern seaboard and were rising on the Midwestern plains. Settlers tried to tame the Mississippi Valley. Canals, railroads, and turnpikes connected the old and the new. Political institutions developed during the early years of the century flowered into more adequate forms. To almost all onlookers, the burgeoning nation seemed to be adequately and well

---

[58] Dix, *Address at the Reception of the Seventh Regiment, National Guard, State of New York, January 31, 1866* (New York: Francis & Loutrel. 1866), pp. 16–17.

governed—or rather, to be governed very little indeed. The future appeared to be open and limitless.

But the slavery issue defeated politics and halted progress. In the winter of 1860–1861, Southerners proclaimed by secession that American democratic practices were unsuitable for their slave institutions, and that democratic aspirations were foolish and futile.

Despair born of Northern weakness appeared to validate the Southern judgment. Unopposed secession seemed to doom forever the idea of the workability of political democracy and of a federal system as the governmental frame for any territory larger than a Swiss mountain canton or a Dutch lowland province. Little wonder that a son of the historian George Bancroft, observing the unopposed secession of the Southern states, wrote on December 18, 1860: "What will become of Father? His occupation will certainly be gone. Nobody will want to read in the history of the formation of a government by our forefathers which we have let fall to pieces."[59]

Then, slowly and with great pains, after the attack on Sumter, drift gave way to decision. Despairing counselors of constitutional limitations were succeeded by champions of adequate constitutional powers who inspired exertions and functions on the part of national and state governments such as Americans had never known. The North found in itself the vigor, strength, patience, and passion, and the men and measures, to gain finally the Appomattox capitulation. The accelerating power of Northern armies and the augmenting vision of the nation's purpose, climaxing in emancipation, thrilled the generation, so that much-wounded Oliver Wendell Holmes, Jr., remembered years later how he and his fellows were touched with fire in the nation's service.

It is very doubtful that Holmes and his comrades of the Union Army, or that Lincoln and his coadjutors in the civilian branches, deceived themselves with respect to what the war

---

[59] Bancroft-Bliss Papers, Manuscripts Division, Library of Congress.

had accomplished and what they had won. Rather, it appears reasonable to say that the Americans who after four years of agony cheered the news of Lee's surrender knew that they had achieved the deaths of slavery and secession and thereby gained a future for themselves and for their nation.

By this measure alone, the American nation of 1865 was a far finer one than had been the case in 1861. Emancipation and reunion were majestic fruits of the war. To add to the sweetness of this victory, they were not won at the cost of American liberty. Quite the opposite, the war expanded the theory and practice of American democracy and the reality of American liberty and opportunity.

In part this astonishing and unanticipatable expansion was a factor of emancipation. Because of the war, ten per cent of Americans were no longer property but were freed, if not yet free and equal; and because of the Reconstruction, the freedmen remained free and for a while moved nearer toward equality. Instead of slavery continuing its territorial expansion westward, as it had for thirty years before the war, freedom expanded southward to encompass finally the entire nation, and in the Reconstruction the theory and practice of enlarged liberty followed hard on freedom's out-thrusting ways.

Freedom and liberty required political machinery to plot their courses and carry them forward. As a magnificent result of the war, the conflict ended with Americans in possession of a political apparatus vastly better based than had been true in 1860.[60] Seemingly shattered forever during the secession winter, the two-party system rebuilt itself in the North during the

---

[60] The Ohioan Henry Stanbery, later President Andrew Johnson's Attorney General and his defender in the impeachment, stumped for Lincoln during the 1864 campaign. He noted in one speech that it was fortunate for the Union that the war ". . . began when a Presidential election was as remote as possible. I had seen too much of our [1860] Presidential contest not to dread the fierce party strifes which they engender." Stanbery, *The Ballot and the Bullet: How to Save this Nation. Address, Newport, Kentucky, Sept. 17, 1864* (Cincinnati: *Gazette,* 1864), p. 2.

terrible strains of war, and with incredible swiftness and vigor. Long before Lee surrendered, the North's armies brought balloting booths to occupied portions of the Confederacy, and soon after Appomattox political parties flourished everywhere in the South as well as in the victorious North. Indeed, the judgment appears to be reasonable that the Reconstruction rewon the South for the forms of political democracy that Southerners had viewed with such contempt during the halcyon days of secession.

The North's political machinery was able to export its ways after victory only because before Appomattox it functioned superbly and took deadly risks in the face of defeat. Remarkably—but too rarely remarked during the 1860's or since—in the North regular, free, and open elections were held all during the war, and without serious suggestion, no matter how dismal the prospects, that canvasses be delayed or canceled.

It amazed European onlookers (though Americans took the event matter-of-factly) that national, state, and local governments should in the midst of crisis permit deadly opponents of the war to run for office, and should see them seated when they won.[61] Samuel Osgood, a *Harper's Monthly* correspondent, wrote that the American wartime generation was "learning statesmanship" by this marvelous exercise in democratic practice, represented by free balloting during wartime, from 1862 onward. Observing New Yorkers voting in 1864, he saw ". . . something in the look and manner of the crowd there gathered [to vote] that was peculiar and most impressive. Nothing, or next to nothing was said, but the great thing was taken for granted." Osgood watched a long queue of citizens wait at least two hours to reach the polls, and the line was as long at noon as it had been at sunrise when the booths opened.

---

[61] See, as only one example of European reaction, Auguste Laugel, *The United States During the Civil War,* ed. Allan Nevins (Bloomington: Indiana University Press, 1961), pp. 20, 23, 29, 35, 180, 186–189, 225–226.

"What memorable demeanor in that whole company!" he marveled. Despite the bloody draft riots of the preceding year, not a soldier was in sight. The destiny of the war was in each voter's hands, and everyone knew that the war would end in a negotiated armistice if McClellan won; his election would thereby acknowledge that the Confederacy was an independent slave-owning victor, and that slavery was forever untouchable by political processes or by military effort.

Ennobled by their millions and by the fact that they were employing their suffrage, the voters of 1862, 1863, and especially of 1864 "were transformed from partisans into patriots," Osgood wrote. To be sure, he worried in 1864 that McClellan might win. Such a verdict would represent failure for America's whites with respect to maintaining the Union and would ensure eternal slavery for America's blacks. But Osgood and his countrymen of the North apparently assumed that even if "Little Mac" became President of the United States, then that judgment by ballot would have to be honored.[62]

If it was marvelous that civilians voted freely, how much more surprising and inspiring it was that the North's soldiers also cast their ballots, with freedom to choose between issues and candidates. The soldier vote was significant in 1864 in winning Lincoln's re-election. In essence this uniformed vote meant that Northern soldiers believed that the war should go on and that they should remain in the Army, to risk death, to suffer, and to sacrifice, until their task was completed. Perhaps the best expression of the assumption that American democracy alone in the world was strong enough to permit soldier voting, especially in the midst of a great war, was offered by George F. Noyes, chaplain to Doubleday's tough brigade, at a July Fourth commemoration in 1862. "In a Republic like

---

[62] Osgood's articles from *Harper's* are reprinted in his *American Leaves: Familiar Notes of Thought and Life* (New York: Harper's, 1867), pp. 168–171.

ours," Noyes told the attentive soldiers, "bayonets may safely be allowed to think."[63]

Some contemporary commentators disagreed. An Englishman, James Dawson Burns, who spent *Three Years Among the Working Classes in the United States during the [Civil] War,* estimated that the soldier vote of 1864 was "a very dangerous expedient." Recalling the history of Rome's legions, Burns warned Americans that "the exercise of the franchise by the Army of a country is incompatible with good government and the civil liberty of a people. Soldiers . . . cannot be free agents."[64]

Burns's analysis of ancient history simply did not fit American conditions. In a Christmas 1864 address delivered to Americans resident in Montreal, Reverend John Cordiner of Boston extolled American voters, soldiers, and civilians alike for presenting "a spectacle for the world to admire" on the preceding November election day. The balloting for President in 1864, Cordiner asserted, "bears more emphatic witness for the stability of popular government than all the victories of Grant and Sherman."[65]

Stressing the theme that the ballot could be safely trusted to all Americans because the nation was growing strong through the war, newsman Osgood defended the propriety of soldiers voting. "The sword is in the hands of men who know and love the law, and will not see it trodden under foot," he wrote. More important still, in the thinking of Congregationalist minister George E. Ellis, was that the law was in the hands of men who, knowing the terrors of the sword, were firm in determination to carry on with war in order to

---

[63] *Celebration of the National Anniversary by Doubleday's Brigade, at Camp Opposite Fredericksburg, Virginia, July 4, 1862* (Philadelphia, 1862), p. 7.

[64] (London: Smith Elder, 1865), pp. 250–251.

[65] Cordiner, *The American Conflict: An Address Before the New England Society of Montreal . . . December 22, 1864* (Montreal, 1865), p. 33.

strengthen the law. In a sermon delivered a week after the balloting, Ellis exulted that "we can scarce deny or depreciate the weight of that decision now. Those who, after experience of war, resolve to continue it, must, at least, be regarded as more resolute than those who begin a war." Resolute for what? The election ". . . avows what we purpose to do, and then it throws us back on our ways and means," Ellis stated.[66]

Improved democracy was the ultimate source of the "ways and means" to which Ellis referred. Proof of that pudding, in the thinking of numerous commentators, was the fact that the United States emerged from the Civil War unsullied even by a threat of military dictatorship. Yet almost two million men out of the nation's ten million had been in uniform. In 1860 the American society, seemingly collapsing, had quivered in helpless weakness as the South seceded. In 1865 the rewon nation gloried in its amassed power as its victorious armies paraded in grand reviews and then, to the amazement of on-lookers over the world, hurried back to civilian pursuits as swiftly as its hundreds of thousands of veterans could shuck off uniforms, and despite the shock of Lincoln's murder.

The ease, security, and necessity of these wartime elections and of military demobilization made the initiation of postwar political contests peaceful, simple, and inevitable. Davis Thomas, an English visitor to Connecticut in October 1865, where a vote was in progress on a state constitutional amendment granting suffrage to Negroes, expected violence to occur. Instead:

> everything was conducted in the most orderly manner. . . .
> There was no excitement whatever, and not the least obstruction in the way of voters, for every man could vote as he liked without being questioned upon it. . . . The vote by ballot is evidently

---

[66] Osgood, p. 171; Rev. George E. Ellis, *The Nation's Ballot and its Decision: A Discourse Delivered at the Austin Street Church, Cambridgeport [Massachusetts] . . . November 13, 1864* (n.p., n.d.), pp. 7, 10. This is a pamphlet reprint of Ellis's sermon as it appeared in the *Monthly Religious Magazine,* probably in December 1864.

very popular here, for I conversed with persons belonging to different political parties but they were all satisfied with the opinion of the ballot.[67]

The state elections of 1865 and the Congressional contests of the critical year 1866 went off despite the increasing strains of the Reconstruction controversy. At the height of the crisis of Andrew Johnson's impeachment, the 1868 nominating conventions assembled and made the two parties' choices, the election was run, and the victor was inaugurated. The 1868 election was the living proof that the war had won for all Americans the opportunity to do with their future whatever their best or worst interests or instincts judged was opportune. After all, these were the same American political and constitutional institutions that had broken down at Lincoln's election in 1860, but that easily bore up under the simultaneous strains of Johnson's impeachment and near conviction, and of the Grant-Seymour contest. Never again would the verdict of the ballot result in a refusal to abide by whatever fine or poor decision had been made. Even the patchwork deal that in 1877 installed Hayes in the White House and abandoned the South's Negroes to the South's mercies was a struggle for control of the political mechanism, rather than an abandonment or a rejection of it. Commenting in 1868 on *The Presidential Issue*, a New York merchant, Elliot Cowdin, told members of the National Club of that city: "Happily, the glorious results of the late war . . . have relieved us, and we trust, posterity also, from many troublesome questions that were sources of vexation and alarm at every Presidential contest for thirty years previous to the Rebellion."[68]

Walt Whitman saw all this clearly almost a century ago. The real war would never get into books, he warned. But then,

---

[67] Davis Thomas, *My American Tour: Being Notes Taken during a Tour Through the United States shortly after the Close of the Late American War* (Bury [Eng.], 1868), p. 17.

[68] Cowdin, *The Presidential Issue: Speech, National Club of N. Y., October 19, 1868* (New York: National Club, 1868), p. 3.

as if to see to it that men might one day understand the Civil War even to the point of capturing its reality, he left this estimation:

> The movements of the late Secession War and its results, to any sense that understands well and comprehends them, show that popular democracy, whatever its faults and dangers, practically justifies itself beyond the proudest claims and wildest hopes of its enthusiasts. . . . What have we seen here if not, towering above all talk and argument, the . . . last-needed proof of democracy. . . . That our national democratic experiment, principle, and machinery could triumphantly sustain such a shock, and that the Constitution could weather it, like a ship in a storm, and come out of it as sound and whole as before, is by far the most signal proof yet of the stability of that experiment—Democracy—and of those principles and that Constitution.[69]

These, then, are in part what we all won from the North's victories in the war. All Americans then and since were the victors. Admittedly, Negro Americans have had to wait a century in order even to claim a fair share in what Professor Woodward has described so well as a deferred commitment to equality. There can be no better time than these years of the centennial observation to regain sight of the fact that this commitment came into being only because of the Civil War *and* the Reconstruction. A great leap forward in the conditions of America and Americans is what we all won from what men fought for before Appomattox as well as after Lee surrendered.

In 1964 a volume by the Englishman W. R. Brock of Cambridge University, *An American Crisis: Congress and Reconstruction, 1865–1867*, came at once to the heart of matters:

> It is a great error to suppose that the ideals enunciated by people during war are insincere and that their force evaporates when

---

[69] *Walt Whitman's Civil War*, ed. Walter Lowenfels (New York: Alfred A. Knopf, 1961), pp. 283–290, *passim*.

the fighting ends. The catastrophe of war had cut deeply into the emotions and forced men to decide for themselves why, how, and with what objectives it was necessary to fight. Ideas which had been dimly perceived before the war emerged as clear-cut propositions, and views which had been held by small minorities suddenly became great national convictions. . . . The war had been started to preserve the Union, but for the majority in the victorious North it had become a war to create a more perfect Union. . . . It was not only necessary to defeat the South but also to democratize it, and of all needs the first was the abolition of slavery. . . . In fact negro status stood at the heart of the whole Reconstruction problem and presented a devastating challenge to American civilization.[70]

Brock's approach is moderate, restrained, sensitive, and sensible, and his book deserves close attention. But a major difficulty limits him, as it did the recent able re-evaluations of the Reconstruction that John Hope Franklin and John and La-Wanda Cox have offered. This difficulty grows out of the fact that in almost everything written on Reconstruction since 1865, only post-Appomattox events are considered in depth.

It is not surprising that this should be so. Men naturally divide peace from war. Lincoln's contemporaries were fond of employing the figure of a falling curtain to symbolize separation between events of wartime and problems of Reconstruction. As example, Goldwin Smith, the English historian who observed and wrote on American events with closest attention and with deep sympathy for the Union's cause, wrote after a visit here in 1866:

The curtain has fallen upon the great drama of war. It rises for a political drama almost as great. The work of reconstruction presents problems which will tax to the utmost the practical sagacity of the American people; but in that sagacity I have

[70] (New York: St. Martin's Press, 1963), pp. 2–4; and see the review by LaWanda Cox in *Journal of American History*, LI (June 1964), 108–109.

almost unbounded faith. It is the quality not of isolated statesmen, with difficulty dragging the dull masses after them, but of
a whole nation, capable of entering into political questions, and
at once supporting and correcting the action of the government,
which is in fact the only organ of the [whole] people.[71]

Lincoln also employed a before-and-after terminology in
responding to the happy news of Lee's surrender. But more
than the Confederate collapse, the President's murder appeared to contemporaries, and then to historians, to pull down
the curtain on the war and to raise it for another kind of time
—the Reconstruction.[72]

To leading Republicans in 1865, who proudly acknowledged
the adjective "radical" as an honorable identification, no sharp
line existed. Francis Lieber, one of the major theoreticians of
the Radical Republicans put the position succinctly later that
year, in an argument designed to evoke popular support for
proposed new amendments to the Federal Constitution that
looked toward guarantees of political rights of freedmen.
Never had any nation altered so much in five years as the
United States had done since 1861, Lieber wrote:

> The heat of a civil war of such magnitude would alone be suf-
> ficient to ripen thought and characteristics which may have been
> in a state of incipiency before; a contest so comprehensive and so
> probing makes people abandon many things, to which they had
> clung by mere tradition without feeling their sharp reality. . . .

[71] Smith, *The Civil War in America: An Address Read at the Last
Meeting of the Manchester Union and Emancipation Society* (London:
Simpkin, Marshall & Co., 1866), pp. 67–68.
[72] *Collected Works of Abraham Lincoln,* ed. Roy P. Basler (New
Brunswick: Rutgers University Press, 1953), VIII, 400–405. Hereafter
this collection is cited as Lincoln, *Works.* See too Jay Monaghan, "An
Analysis of Lincoln's Funeral Sermons," *Indiana Magazine of History,*
LXI (March 1945), 31–44. The most recent reconsideration of Recon-
struction, Kenneth M. Stampp, *The Era of Reconstruction* (New York:
Alfred A. Knopf, 1965), also follows the traditional division between
the war years and after, although Professor Stampp in all other matters
fruitfully maintains currency with the new scholarship.

And may not the question be put, whether ever a society has come out of a civil war without material changes in its fundamental law, or whether a civil war is of itself not sufficient proof that practical changes have taken place and require corresponding changes in the framework of society.[73]

Lieber made it clear that he was not suggesting that the task of reorganizing Southern society toward more democratic lines would be easy. Almost no Republican did. As example, Senator John Sherman advised General Manning Force, as Lee's capitulation became certain, that "he is looking at the difficulties which will spring up, after the war [ends]—questions as hard to determine as it was originally to make the Constitution."[74]

Difficult, yes; but never impossible, never unconstitutional, never separable from the causes or results of the War. "Gentlemen," said the federal attorney who in 1871 was prosecuting members of the South Carolina Ku Klux Klan, "we have lived over a century in the last ten years."[75]

The century since Appomattox has crowded into American life so many drastic and dramatic changes that it is little wonder why we return to the years of the Civil War and Reconstruction and find in its men and measures lessons and courage for our own time of troubles.[76] But it has been a very long time since any one accepted that "period" as a unity, save conversationally or as a title for a college course or textbook.[77]

---

[73] Lieber, *Amendments to the Constitution* (New York: Loyal Publication Society [No. 83], 1865), pp. 11–12.

[74] March 31, 1865, in Force's MS "Personal Record," 131, Force Papers (University of Washington).

[75] D. T. Corbin, *Argument in the Trial of the KKK before the United States Circuit Court, Columbia, South Carolina, November Term 1871* (Washington: *Chronicle*, 1872), p. 4.

[76] Oscar Handlin, "The Civil War as Symbol and as Actuality," *Massachusetts Review*, III (Fall 1961), 133–143.

[77] Inquiring into the reasons why the Reconstruction has appeared to be separable from other events, Woodward found a key in the imposition of Negro suffrage upon the defeated South. "By the operation of a sort

Yet there were numerous efforts during the four years of the war at reconstructing substantial portions of the South. Witness the fact that in 1864 the question of how wartime Reconstruction should further proceed almost split the Republican-Union party. Notwithstanding, the post-Appomattox years have so dominated the attention of investigators of the Reconstruction that it has been seventy years since anyone set out to survey the unfolding of Reconstruction policy between Sumter and Appomattox.

Until very recently, the last such deviationist was Eben Greenough Scott. In 1895, when his *Reconstruction during the Civil War in the United States*[78] appeared, Scott was sixty years old. He was a Pennsylvanian, a Yale graduate and a successful lawyer, and he had been a company officer of Union volunteers. In 1863 he was invalided out of the Army. Scott lived until 1919, combining his legal pursuits with literary and historical interests centering on the Civil War and on constitutional developments.

His scholarly efforts are in the mainstream of evolutionary thinking on the workings of history. Scott believed that institutions and policies flowered from earlier, simpler forms. Therefore his Reconstruction book allotted more than half of its four hundred pages to analyses of pre-1861 constitutional and institutional developments in the colonial and early na-

---

of historical color bar," he wrote, "the history of the Negro's political experience has been studied too much in isolation and pictured as unique." Then Woodward went on to suggest the utility of comparing the Negro's course as citizen during the Reconstruction with that of immigrants in from Europe, suddenly enfranchised and quickly boss-ridden. (Woodward, "Political Legacy of Reconstruction," p. 238 and *passim*.) However valuable, such a comparative view would continue to leave the Reconstruction dangling without adequate connections to the wartime past.

[78] (Boston and New York: Houghton, Mifflin and Co., 1895), pp. iv–v. *Who's Who*, 1900, offers biographical details. To be sure, Du Bois, in *Black Reconstruction*, surveyed the impact of the Civil War and Reconstruction upon Negroes and employed the years 1860–1880 as his stage.

tional periods of American history, an allocation of space that no modern publisher would consider even if an author suggested the ratio. Yet Scott was too good a student of the past to be completely a prisoner of the intellectual convictions of his own time. As a participant in the war, he remembered vividly how unprecedented everything seemed to be during the secession winter and after. Scott understood that Reconstruction policy evolved eclectically, not out of ideological structures, and that the Republicans were the popular party, not a conspiratorial junta.

If for nothing more than these "modern" insights, Scott deserves resurrection from the limbo into which he has fallen. More than this, however, he also realized, as his title suggests, that "reconstruction" began not the day after Appomattox but almost as soon as the guns around Charleston fired at Sumter.

It is a notable thing that, from the very beginning of the Civil War, the federal government never evinced a doubt of ultimate success, and it is significant that, even in moments of disaster which seemed irretrievable, it was occupied with the question, 'What is to be done with the revolted states when the fortunes of war shall have put their fate in our hands?'[79]

---

[79] Scott, pp. iii–iv. Willie Lee Rose, *Rehearsal for Reconstruction: The Port Royal Experiment* (Indianapolis: Bobbs-Merrill, 1964), has helped to redirect attention to pre-Appomattox events. See also David Brion Davis, "Abolitionists and the Freedmen: An Essay Review," *Journal of Southern History,* XXXI (May 1965), 164–170. Note that a recent documentary compilation on the Reconstruction obeys the traditional post-Appomattox beginning date: James P. Shenton, ed., *The Reconstruction: A Documentary History of the South after the War: 1865–1877* (New York: G. P. Putnam's Sons, 1963). Similarly, the very useful insight and improved balance on the subject offered in Richard N. Current's "Carpetbaggers Reconsidered," in *A Festschrift for Frederick B. Artz,* ed. David H. Pinckney and Theodore Ropp (Durham: Duke University Press, 1964), pp. 139–157, has a built-in limitation in its assumption that carpetbagging, whether evil, wholesome, or mixed in its morality, began only after Lee surrendered. David Donald's *The Politics of Reconstruction, 1863–1867* (Baton Rouge: Louisiana State University Press, 1965), unfortunately was not available when I completed writing this essay. His interest is clear in pushing Reconstruction

The uncommitted eclecticism of the Radicals was a fact of Civil War and Reconstruction life obvious to many onlookers. Young Georges Clemenceau, reporting on the Washington scene to readers in France, noted that ". . . most of the radicals of today embarked on the abolitionist sea without any clear idea of where the course would lead; that they arrived at their present position only after being forced from one reform to another."[80] Scott understood that the antislavery reformers formed the base of Republican strength, and he came to the correct conclusion that "the great change of opinion and sentiment which the people of the United States were then undergoing . . . at length found expression in three amendments to the Constitution." That is, the tide of public opinion was the cause and the result of Radical Republicanism. As cause, it forced Republicans generally into radical courses. And as effect, it guided Radicals in their efforts to move government into novel functional channels, devoted to the creation and protection of civil liberties, that the Reconstruction statutes and constitutional amendments had carved out. "The secret of this change in the temper and sentiment of the Republican party," Scott wrote, "is to be found in the temper and sentiment which the people themselves had undergone as the war continued."[81]

---

backward in time toward where it properly belongs. My argument remains that a study of Reconstruction requires a start in 1861, not in 1863 and certainly not in 1865.

[80] Clemenceau, *American Reconstruction,* ed. Fernand Baldensperger (New York: Dial, 1928), p. 278.

[81] Scott, pp. v, 390–391. Recent and useful efforts to tie together these factors over the whole period are available in Margaret Shortreed, "The Antislavery Radicals: From Crusade to Revolution, 1840–1868," *Past and Present,* No. 16 (November 1959), 65–87; and in James M. McPherson, *The Struggle for Equality: Abolitionists and the Negro in the Civil War and Reconstruction* (Princeton: Princeton University Press, 1964). Professor McPherson was kind enough to permit me to examine his doctoral dissertation, on which his volume is based.

It is time to go beyond Scott's 1895 insight and again to rejoin the Reconstruction to the Civil War. Perhaps through re-examination of relevant documents, fresh judgments may emerge on some of the men and measures who make the century-old story of the Civil War *and* Reconstruction worth commemorating. In 1866 Goldwin Smith presented us with an admirable injunction, which is still good advice.

> The Civil War in America is over . . . and though the ashes still glow, though the time when an impartial history can be written has not arrived, we may try to understand the real import of the conflict—the real significance of the victory—and to read, as far as mortal eyes may read, the counsels of Providence in this the great event of our age.[82]

---

[82] Smith, p. 1.

Bibliography

The Introduction in large part is an essay on sources. Therefore I have contented myself in this bibliography with a listing of the books, periodicals, pamphlets, and miscellaneous items that I employed. These printed materials divide by their essential characteristic into original or secondary sources.

Manuscripts include items as designated, from the Bancroft Papers at the Special Collections Library, Columbia University; the Charles Sumner Papers, Houghton Library, Harvard University; the Bancroft-Bliss, Salmon P. Chase, Giddings-Julian, Edward McPherson, and John G. Nicolay Papers, Manuscripts Division, Library of Congress; John A. Andrew Papers, Massachusetts Historical Society; House Committee on the Judiciary Records, Thirty-Ninth Congress, HR 39A-F 13.7 (with special permission of the Honorable Ralph Roberts, Clerk of the House of Representatives), and Army Command Records, Record Group 98, both at the National Archives; Timothy O. Howe Papers, State Historical Society of Wisconsin; William S. Rosecrans Papers, Special Collections Library, UCLA; and the Manning Force Papers, University of Washington Library.

Scattered printed items in addition to those listed below are drawn from the Chicago *Freedmen's Bulletin*, 1864 and 1865; London *Freed-Man*, 1865–1867; *The Nation*, 1865–1870; *North American Review*, 1862–1870; and the Philadelphia *Pennsylvania Freedmen's Bulletin*, 1865–1866. The footnoting will also indicate the employment of various official publications of the United States government, including the *Congressional Globe*, House and Senate reports of committees, the *Statutes at Large*, and the Supreme Court reports. Individual titles follow.

Printed Original Sources

Adams, Charles Francis, Jr. *The Double Anniversary, '76 and '63: Fourth of July Address, Quincy, Massachusetts.* Boston: Lunt, 1869.

Adams, Henry. "The Session," *North American Review*, CVIII (April 1869), 610–640.

———. "The Session, 1869–1870," *North American Review*, CXI (July 1870), 29–62.

[Amicus]. *The Rebel States, the President and Congress: Reconstruction and the Executive Power of Pardon.* New York: Dodge, 1866.

[Anonymous]. *Why Colored People in Philadelphia are Excluded from the Street Cars.* Philadelphia, 1866.

Banks, N. P. *Emancipation's Labor in Louisiana,* N.p., n.d.

Basler, Roy P., ed. *Collected Works of Abraham Lincoln.* 9 vols. New Brunswick: Rutgers University Press, 1953.

Beecher, Henry Ward. *Freedom and War: Discourses on Topics Suggested by the Times.* Boston: Ticknor and Fields, 1863.

"Beginning of the End," *American Freedman*, III (December 1868), 2–3.

Blaine, James G. *Political Discussions, Legislative, Diplomatic, and Popular 1856–1886.* Norwich, Conn.: The Henry Bill Publishing Co., 1887.

Blake, H. T. "Southern Regeneration," *New Englander*, XXVI (January 1867), 148–156.

Boutwell, George Sewall. *Reconstruction: Its True Basis, Speech at Weymouth, Massachusetts, July 4, 1865.* Boston: Wright & Potter, 1865.

Breck, Robert L. *The Habeas Corpus and Martial Law.* Cincinnati, 1862.

Broom, W. W. [alias Eboracus]. *Great and Grave Questions for American Politicians with a Topic for America's Statesmen.* New York, 1865.

Burns, James Dawson. *Three Years among the Working Classes in the United States during the [Civil] War.* London: Smith Elder, 1865.

Butler, Benjamin F. *The Present Relation of Parties, Address, Music Hall, Boston, November 23, 1870.* Lowell: Marden Co., 1870.

Byers, S. H. M., ed. "Reconstruction Days," *North American Review,* CXLIII (September 1886), 219–224.

Carpenter, Matthew. *The Powers of Congress. . . .* Washington *Chronicle,* 1868.

Chamberlain, Daniel. *The Facts and the Figures: The Practical and Truthful Record of the Republican Party of South Carolina, . . . Speech, October 4, [1870].* N. p., n. d.

Chase, Warren. *The American Crisis: or, Trial and Triumph of Democracy.* Boston: Marsh & Co., 1865.

Cheever, George B., Gilbert, Edward G., and Pillsbury, Parker, *et al. Petition and Memorial of Citizens of the United States to the Senate and House of Representatives in Congress Assembled: Adopted at a Public Meeting Held in the Church of the Puritans, New York City, November, 1865.* New York: Francis & Goutel, 1865.

———. *The Republic or the Oligarchy? Which? An Appeal Against the Proposed Transfer of the Right to Vote from the People to the State. By One of the People.* New York, 1866.

Christy, David. *Pulpit Politics: Or Ecclesiastical Legislation on Slavery in its Disturbing Influences on the American Nation.* Cincinnati: Faran & McLean, 1863.

Clark, Alexander. *Radical Reconstruction: and Radicalism.* Pittsburgh: Bakewell and Marthens, 1869.

Clemenceau, Georges. *American Reconstruction,* ed. Fernand Baldensperger. New York: Dial, 1928.

Colyer, Vincent. *Brief Report of the Services Rendered by the Freed People to the United States Army in North Carolina.* New York, 1864.

Conway, Moncure Daniel. *Autobiography, Memories, and Experiences.* 2 vols. Boston and New York: Houghton Mifflin & Co., 1904.

———. "Sursum Corda" ["Lift up your Hearts"], *The Radical,* I (April 1866), 291–294.

Corbin, D. T. *Argument in the Trial of the KKK before the United States Circuit Court, Columbia, South Carolina, November Term 1871.* Washington *Chronicle*, 1872.

Cordiner, Rev. John. *The American Conflict: An Address before the New England Society of Montreal, . . . December 22, 1864.* Montreal, 1865.

Cowdin, Elliot. *The Presidential Issue: Speech, National Club of N. Y., October 19, 1868.* New York: National Club, 1868.

DeWitt, William C. *Sundry Speeches and Writings: Driftwood from the Current of a Busy Life.* 2 vols. Brooklyn: Eagle Co., 1881.

Dix, John A. *Address at the Reception of the Seventh Regiment, National Guard, State of New York, January 31, 1866.* New York: Francis & Loutrel, 1866.

Dix, William Giles. *The American State and American Statesmen.* Boston: Estes and Lauriat, 1876.

Douglass, Frederick. *Narrative of the Life of Frederick Douglass, An American Slave. Written by Himself.* Boston: Anti-Slavery Office, 1845.

————. "Reconstruction," *Atlantic Monthly,* XVIII (December 1866), 761–765.

Drake, Charles. *Union and Anti-Slavery Speeches Delivered During the Rebellion.* Cincinnati, 1864.

Eaton, John. *Report of the General Superintendent of Freedmen, Department of the Tennessee and the State of Arkansas for 1864.* Memphis, 1865.

Ellis, George E. *The Nation's Ballot and its Decision: A Discourse Delivered at the Austin Street Church, Cambridgeport [Massachusetts] . . . November 13, 1864.* N. p., n. d.

Farley, Charles A. *The Crisis and its Lessons: An Address before an Encampment of the G. A. R. at Walnut Fork, Jones County, Iowa, November 29, 1866.* Dubuque, 1866.

Field, David Dudley. "Centralization in the Federal Government," *North American Review,* CCXCIV (May 1881), 407–426.

Frothingham, Octavius B. *The Religion of Humanity: An Essay.* 3rd ed. New York: Putnam, 1877.

Garrison, William Lloyd. *The Abolitionists, and Their Relation to the War. An Address . . . January 14, 1862, at the Cooper Institute, New York.* New York, 1862.

———. "Thirty-Five Years of Anti-Slavery Agitation Fittingly Rounded Out," Boston *Commonwealth*, April 23, 1870.

Giddings, Joshua. *History of the Rebellion: Its Causes and Cures.* New York: Follet, Foster & Co., 1864.

Grosvenor, William M. "The Law of Conquest the True Basis of Reconstruction," *New Englander*, XXIX (January 1865), 111–131.

———. "The Rights of the Nation, and the Duty of Congress," *New Englander*, XXIV (October 1865), 1–23.

"How Shall We Protect the Freedman?" *The American Freedman*, II (July 1866), 50–51.

Howard, Oliver Otis. "Address to a Convention of Midwestern Freemen's Aid Representatives," [Chicago] *Freedmen's Bulletin*, I (October 1865), 181–183.

———. *Autobiography of Oliver Otis Howard, Major General, United States Army.* New York: The Baker & Taylor Company, 1908.

Hurd, John Codman. "Theories of Reconstruction," *American Law Review*, I (January 1867), 237–264.

Jay, John. *Address of the President, Union League Club of New York, June 23, 1866.* New York, 1866.

Jenkins, Howard M. *Our Democratic Republic: Its Form—Its Faults—Its Strength—Its Need.* Wilmington, 1868.

Julian, George W. *Political Recollections, 1840–1872.* Chicago: Jansen, McClurg, 1884.

———. *Speeches on Political Questions.* New York: Hurd and Houghton, 1872.

Kendrick, Benjamin B., ed. *The Journal of the Joint Committee of Fifteen on Reconstruction, 39th Congress, 1865–1867.* New York: Columbia University Press, 1914.

[Kroeger, Adolph Ernst]. *The Future of the Country. By a Patriot.* Chicago, *ca.* 1883.

Laugel, Auguste. *The United States during the Civil War,* ed. Allan Nevins. Bloomington: Indiana University Press, 1961.

"The Lesson from Jamaica," [Philadelphia] *Pennsylvania Freed-men's Bulletin,* I (December 5, 1865), 88–89.

Lieber, Francis. *Amendments to the Constitution.* New York: Loyal Publication Society [#83], 1865.

Loring, George B. *The Present Crisis: A Speech . . . at Lyceum Hall, Salem, . . . April 26, 1865, on the Assassination of Abraham Lincoln.* South Danvers [Mass.]: Howard, 1865.

Lowell, James Russell. "Education of the Freedman," *North American Review,* CI (October 1865), 528–549.

———. "Loyalty," *North American Review,* XCIV (January 1862), 163–174.

McKaye, Colonel James. *The Mastership and its Fruits: The Emancipated Slave Face to Face with His Old Master.* New York: Bryant, 1864.

Massie, James William. *America: The Origin of Her Present Conflict: Her Prospect for the Slave, and Her Claim for Anti-Slavery Sympathy.* London: Snow, 1864.

Miller, Edwin H., ed. *Walt Whitman, The Correspondence, 1868–1875.* 2 vols. New York: New York University Press, 1961.

Morse, S. H. "Concerning the Nation's Soul," *The Radical,* I (April 1866), 281–290.

National Union Republican Convention. *Proceedings, Chicago, May 20–1, 1868.* Chicago *Journal,* 1868.

Norton, Charles Eliot, ed. *Letters of James Russell Lowell.* 2 vols. New York: Harper & Bros., 1894.

Noyes, George F. *Celebration of the National Anniversary by Doubleday's Brigade, at Camp Opposite Fredericksburg, Virginia, July 4, 1862.* Philadelphia, 1862.

Osgood, Samuel. *American Leaves: Familiar Notes of Thought and Life.* New York: Harpers, 1867.

Phillips, Wendell. "The Policy," *The Radical,* I (April 1866), 295–296.

———. "What We Ask of Congress," Boston *Commonwealth,* December 4, 1869.

Pierce, Edward Lillie. *Enfranchisement and Citizenship,* ed. A. W. Stevens. Boston: Roberts Brothers, 1896.

Plumb, David. "Citizenship and Suffrage: The Right and Duty of Congress to Enfranchise the Nation," *The Radical*, III (February 1868), 389–401.

Pollard, Edward. *The Lost Cause Regained*. New York: Carleton, 1868.

Prentiss, George L. "The Political Crisis," *American Presbyterian and Theological Review* (October 1866). [Pamphlet reprint; New York: Somers, 1866].

Rawlins, General John A. *General Grant's Views in Harmony with Congress: Speech, Galena, Illinois, June 21, 1867*. Washington *Chronicle*, 1868.

Richardson, James D., ed. *A Compilation of the Messages and Papers of the Presidents*. 10 vols. Washington: Government Printing Office, 1897.

Schurz, Carl. *Speeches, Correspondence, and Political Papers of Carl Schurz*, ed. Frederick Bancroft. 6 vols. New York: Putnam's, 1913.

Shenton, James P., ed. *The Reconstruction; A Documentary History of the South after the War: 1865–1877*. New York: G. P. Putnam's Sons, 1963.

Skinner, J. E. Hillary. *After the Storm: Jonathan and his Neighbours in 1865–1866*. 2 vols. London: Bentley, 1866.

Smith, Goldwin. *The Civil War in America: An Address Read at the Last Meeting of the Manchester Union and Emancipation Society*. London: Simpkin, Marshall & Co., 1866.

Spear, Samuel. *Radicalism and the National Crisis: A Sermon delivered at the South Presbyterian Church, Brooklyn, October 19, 1862*. Brooklyn, 1862.

Stanbery, Henry. *The Ballot and the Bullet: How to Save this Nation. Address, Newport, Kentucky, Sept. 17, 1864*. Cincinnati *Gazette*, 1864.

Stearns, Frank Preston. *True Republicanism or the Real and Ideal in Politics*. Philadelphia: Lippincott, 1904.

Stearns, George L., comp. *The Equality of All Men before the Law Claimed and Defended: In Speeches by William D. Kelley, Wendell Phillips, and Frederick Douglass*. Boston: Rand & Avery, 1865.

Stevens, Thaddeus. *The Present Canvass! Speech . . . at Bedford, Pa., . . . September 4, 1866*. Lancaster, Pa., 1866.

Sumner, Charles. *Works*. 15 vols. Boston: Lee & Shepard, 1870–1883.

Third Report of a Committee of the Representatives of the New York Yearly Meeting of Friends Upon the Condition and Wants of the Colored Refugees. N. p., 1864.

Thirty-Nine Articles of Faith of the New Party to be Organized at Philadelphia in August, 1866. N.p., n.d.

Thomas, Davis. *My American Tour: Being Notes Taken during a Tour through the United States shortly after the Close of the Late American War*. Bury [Eng.], 1868.

Trumbull, Lyman. "Can Congress Regulate Suffrage in the States?" Chicago *Advance*, September 5, 1867.

Twining, Alexander Catlin. "President Lincoln's Proclamation of Freedom to the Slaves," *New Englander*, XXIV (January 1865), 186.

United States, War Department. *The War of the Rebellion: A Compilation of the Official Records of the Union and Confederate Armies*. 128 vols. Washington: Government Printing Office, 1880–1901.

Vinton, Alexander H. *The Duties of Peace: Sermon, St. Mark's Episcopal Church, The Bowerie, New York, February 5, 1865*. New York: Gray & Green, 1865.

"A Voice from the Army on the Opposition to the Government," in *The Loyalist's Ammunition*. Philadelphia: Ashmead, 1863.

Wakefield, E. I., ed. *Letters of Robert G. Ingersoll*. New York: Philosophical Library, 1951.

Ward, Durbin. *Life, Speeches, and Orations of Durbin Ward of Ohio: Compiled by Elisabeth Probasco Ward*. Columbus: Smythe, 1888.

Whiting, William. *War Powers under the Constitution of the United States*. 1871 ed. Boston and New York: Lee & Shepard, 1871.

Wickersham, J. P. "Education as an Element in Reconstruction," National Teacher's Association *Proceedings and Lectures*, VI (August 1865), 283–310.

Secondary Materials

Allis, Frederick S., Jr. "The Handling of Controversial Material in High School Textbooks in American History," Massachusetts Historical Society *Proceedings,* LXXII, 323–329.

Bardolph, Richard. *The Negro Vanguard.* New York: Vintage Books, 1961.

Beale, Howard K., ed. *Charles A. Beard: An Appraisal.* Lexington: University of Kentucky Press, 1954.

————. *The Critical Year: A Study of Andrew Johnson and Reconstruction.* New ed. New York: Ungar, 1958.

————. "On Rewriting Reconstruction History," *American Historical Review,* XLV (July 1940), 807–827.

————. "What Historians Have Said About the Causes of the Civil War," Social Science Research Council *Bulletin,* 54 (1946).

Bentley, George R. *A History of the Freedmen's Bureau.* Philadelphia: University of Pennsylvania Press, 1955.

Bernstein, Barton J. "Case Law in Plessy v. Ferguson," *Journal of Negro History,* XLVII (July 1962), 192–198.

Bonner, T. N. "Civil War Historians and the Needless War Doctrine," *Journal of the History of Ideas,* XVII (April 1956), 193–216.

Bowers, Claude G. *The Tragic Era: The Revolution After Lincoln.* Cambridge: Houghton Mifflin Company, 1929.

Brock, W. R. *An American Crisis: Congress and Reconstruction, 1865–1867.* New York: St. Martin's Press, 1963.

Brodie, Fawn M. "A Lincoln Who Never Was," *The Reporter,* 20 (June 25, 1959), 25–27.

————. *Thaddeus Stevens: Scourge of the South.* New York: Norton, 1959.

————. "Who Won the Civil War, Anyway?" *New York Times Book Review,* August 5, 1962, pp. 1 ff.

Buck, Paul H. *The Road to Reunion, 1865–1900.* Boston: Little, Brown, 1947.

Burgess, John W. *Reconstruction and the Constitution, 1866–1876.* New York: Charles Scribner's Sons, 1902.

Castel, Albert. "Andrew Johnson: His Historiographical Rise and Fall," *Mid-America,* XLV (July 1963), 175–184.

Chidsey, Donald B. *The Gentlemen from New York: A Life of Roscoe Conkling.* New Haven: Yale University Press, 1935.

Coben, Stanley. "Northeastern Business and Radical Reconstruction: A Re-Examination," *Mississippi Valley Historical Review,* XLVI (June 1959), 67–90.

Cole, Charles C. *The Social Ideas of the Northern Evangelists, 1826–1860.* New York: Columbia University Press, 1954.

Commager, Henry Steele. *The American Mind: An Interpretation of American Thought and Character Since the 1880's.* New Haven: Yale University Press, 1950.

Cornish, Dudley T. "The Union Army as a Training School for Negroes," *Journal of Negro History,* XXXVII (October 1952), 368–382.

Coulter, E. Merton. *The South during Reconstruction, 1865–1877. A History of the South,* ed. Wendell Holmes Stephenson and E. Merton Coulter, Vol. VIII. Baton Rouge: Louisiana State University Press, 1947.

Cox, LaWanda, and Cox, John H. *Politics, Principle, and Prejudice, 1865–1866: Dilemma of Reconstruction America.* New York: Free Press of Glencoe, 1963.

Craven, Avery. "An Historical Adventure," *Journal of American History,* LI (June 1964), 5–20.

Current, Richard N. "Carpetbaggers Reconsidered," *A Festschrift for Frederick B. Artz,* ed. David H. Pinchney and Theodore Ropp. Durham: Duke University Press, 1964.

Degler, Carl N. "The South in Southern History Textbooks," *Journal of Southern History,* XXX (February 1964), 48–57.

De Santis, Vincent P. *Republicans Face the Southern Question— The New Departure Years, 1877–1897.* Baltimore: Johns Hopkins Press, 1959.

———. "The Republican Party and the Southern Negro, 1877–1897," *Journal of Negro History,* XLV (April 1960), 71–87.

DeVoto, Bernard. "The Easy Chair," *Harpers,* CXCII (February 1946), 123–126; (March 1946), 234–237.

Donald, David. "American Historians and the Causes of the Civil War," *South Atlantic Quarterly,* LIX (Summer 1960), 351–355.

———. *Charles Sumner and the Coming of the Civil War.* New York: Knopf, 1960.

————, ed., *Lincoln Reconsidered*. New York: Vintage, 1961.

Drake, Richard S. "Freedmen's Aid Societies and Sectional Compromise," *Journal of Southern History*, XXIX (May 1963), 175–186.

Du Bois, W. E. B. *Black Reconstruction: An Essay Toward a History of the Part Which Black Folk Played in the Attempt to Reconstruct Democracy in America, 1860–1880*. New York: Harcourt, Brace and Company, 1935.

————. "Reconstruction and its Benefits," *American Historical Review*, XV (July 1910), 781–799.

Dunham, Chester F. *The Attitude of the Northern Clergy towards the South, 1861–1865*. Toledo: Gray, 1942.

Dunning, William A. *Reconstruction, Political and Economic*. New York: Harper Brothers, 1907.

Foner, Philip S., ed. *The Life and Times of Frederick Douglass*. 4 vols. New York: International, 1955.

Forcey, Charles. *The Crossroads of Liberalism: Croly, Weyl, Lippmann, and the Progressive Era, 1900–1925*. New York: Oxford University Press, 1961.

Frank, Jerome. *Fate and Freedom: A Philosophy for Free Americans*. New York: Simon and Schuster, 1945.

Frank, John, and Monro, Robert F. "The Original Understanding of Equal Protection of the Laws," *Columbia Law Review*, L (February 1950), 131–169.

Franklin, John Hope. "A Century of Civil War Observance," *Journal of Negro History*, XLVII (April 1962), 97–107.

————. *Reconstruction: After the Civil War*. Chicago: University of Chicago Press, 1961.

————. "Whither Reconstruction Historiography?" *Journal of Negro Education*, XVII (Fall 1948), 446–461.

Gambill, Edward L. "Who Were the Senate Radicals?" *Civil War History*, XI (September 1965), 237–244.

Gillette, William. *The Right to Vote: Politics and the Passage of the Fifteenth Amendment*. Baltimore: The Johns Hopkins Press, 1965.

Gottschalk, Louis, ed. *Generalizations in the Writing of History: A Report of the Committee on Historical Analysis of the Social Science Research Council.* Chicago: The University of Chicago Press, 1963.

Griffin, Clifford. *Their Brother's Keeper: Moral Stewardship in the United States, 1800–1865.* New Brunswick: Rutgers University Press, 1960.

Groff, Patrick J. "The Abolitionist Movement in High School Texts," *Journal of Negro Education,* XXXII (Winter 1963), 43–51.

Gross, Theodore L. *Albion W. Tourgée.* New York: Twayne, 1963.

Hamilton, Peter Joseph. *The Reconstruction Period.* Philadelphia: United States Ed., 1905.

Handlin, Oscar. "The Civil War as Symbol and as Actuality," *Massachusetts Review,* III (Fall 1961), 133–143.

Harper, Alan D. "William A. Dunning: The Historian as Nemesis," *Civil War History,* X (March 1964), 54–66.

Herberg, Will. "The Civil War in New Perspective," *Modern Quarterly,* VI (Summer 1932), 54–61.

Hesseltine, William B. *Lincoln's Plan of Reconstruction.* Tuscaloosa: Confederate Publishing Co., 1960.

Higham, John. "Beyond Consensus: The Historian as Moral Critic," *American Historical Review,* LXVII (April 1962), 609–625.

————, ed. *The Reconstruction of American History.* New York: Harper Brothers, 1962.

Hirshsohn, Stanley P. *Farewell to the Bloody Shirt: Northern Republicans and the Southern Negro, 1877–1893.* Bloomington: Indiana University Press, 1962.

Hofstadter, Richard. *The Age of Reform: from Bryan to F. D. R.* New York: Alfred A. Knopf, 1955.

————. *Social Darwinism in American Thought.* Rev. ed. Boston: Beacon Press, 1955.

Hyman, Harold M. "Deceit in Dixie," *Civil War History,* III (March 1957), 65–82.

————. "Johnson, Stanton and Grant; A Reconsideration of the Army's Role in the Events Leading to Impeachment," *American Historical Review,* LXVI (June 1960), 85–100.

————. "Second Look at Stanton," *Columbia University Forum*, VI (Spring 1963), 43–45.

————. *To Try Men's Souls: Loyalty Tests in American History.* Berkeley and Los Angeles: University of California Press, 1959.

Jacobs, Clyde E. *Law Writers and the Courts.* Berkeley and Los Angeles: University of California Press, 1954.

James, Joseph B. *The Framing of the Fourteenth Amendment.* Urbana: University of Illinois Press, 1956.

Jellison, Charles A. *Fessenden of Maine: Civil War Senator.* Syracuse: Syracuse University Press, 1962.

Kelly, Alfred H. "The Congressional Controversy over School Segregation, 1867–1875," *American Historical Review*, LXIV (April 1959), 537–563.

Kirkland, Edward Chase. *Dream and Thought in the Business Community, 1860–1900.* Ithaca: Cornell University Press, 1956.

Krug, Mark M. "On Rewriting of the Story of Reconstruction in the U. S. History Textbooks," *Journal of Negro History*, XLVI (July 1961), 133–153.

Kutler, Stanley. "Radical Reconstruction and Reverse 'Court-Packing,' 1866: A Reconsideration." Unpublished paper, 1964 Used with permission.

Lee, Gordon Canfield. *The Struggle for Federal Aid, First Phase: A History of the Attempts to Obtain Federal Aid for the Common Schools, 1870–1890.* New York: Teacher's College, Columbia University, 1949.

Lerche, Charles O., Jr. "Congressional Interpretations of the Guarantee of a Republican Form of Government during Reconstruction," *Journal of Southern History*, XV (May 1949), 192–211.

Link, Arthur. "What Happened to the Progressive Movement in the 1920's?" *American Historical Review*, LXIV (July 1959), 833–851.

Long, Margaret. "The Imperial Wizard Explains the Klan," *New York Times Magazine*, July 5, 1964.

Lowenfels, Walter, ed. *Walt Whitman's Civil War.* New York: Alfred A. Knopf, 1961.

Lynch, John R. *The Facts of Reconstruction.* New York: Neale, 1913.

McCloskey, Robert Green. *American Conservatism in the Age of Enterprise, 1865–1910: A Study of William Graham Sumner, Stephen J. Field, and Andrew Carnegie.* Cambridge: Harvard University Press, 1961.

McKitrick, Eric. *Andrew Johnson and Reconstruction.* Chicago: University of Chicago Press, 1960.

McPherson, James M. *The Struggle for Equality: Abolitionists and the Negro in the Civil War and Reconstruction.* Princeton: Princeton University Press, 1964.

May, Amory D. "The Work of Certain Northern Churches in the Education of the Freedmen, 1861–1900," Department of the Interior *Annual Report,* I (1902), 285–314.

May, Henry F. *The End of American Innocence: A Study of the First Years of Our Own Time, 1912–1917.* New York: Alfred A. Knopf, 1959.

Mayer, George H. *The Republican Party, 1854–1964.* New York: Oxford University Press, 1964.

Merrill, Walter M. *Against Wind and Tide: A Biography of William Lloyd Garrison.* Cambridge: Harvard University Press, 1963.

Monaghan, Jay. "An Analysis of Lincoln's Funeral Sermons," *Indiana Magazine of History,* LXI (March 1945), 31–44.

Montgomery, David. "Radical Republicanism in Pennsylvania, 1866–1873," *Pennsylvania Magazine of History and Biography,* LXXXV (October 1961), 439–457.

Morgan, H. Wayne, ed. *The Gilded Age: A Reappraisal.* Syracuse: Syracuse University Press, 1950.

Morrow, Ralph E. *Northern Methodism and Reconstruction.* East Lansing: Michigan State University Press, 1956.

Morton, Louis. "From Fort Sumter to Poland: The Question of War Guilt," *World Politics,* XIV (January 1962), 386–392.

———. "The Historian and the Study of War," *Mississippi Valley Historical Review,* XLVIII (March 1962), 599–612.

Mowry, George F. *The Era of Theodore Roosevelt: 1900–1912.* New York: Harper, 1958.

Murray, Robert K. *Red Scare: A Study in National Hysteria, 1919–1920.* Minneapolis: University of Minnesota Press, 1955.

Nichols, Roy F. *Blueprints for Leviathan: American Style.* New York: Atheneum, 1963.

————. *The Democratic Machine, 1850–1854.* New York: Columbia University Press, 1923.

————."The Problem of Civil War Historiography: A Discussion of the Points of View of Professors [D. W.] Brogan, [J. B.] Duroselle, and [Pieter] Geyl," *American Philosophical Society Proceedings,* CVI (February 1962), 36–40.

Paul, Arnold M. *Conservative Crisis and the Rule of Law: Attitude of Bar and Bench, 1887–1895.* Ithaca: Cornell University Press, 1960.

Potter, David M. "Explicit Data and Implicit Assumptions in Historical Study," *Generalizations in the Writing of History: A Report of the Committee on Historical Analysis of the Social Science Research Council,* ed. Louis Gottschalk. Chicago: The University of Chicago Press, 1963.

Pressly, Thomas J. *Americans Interpret Their Civil War.* New York: Collier Books, 1962.

Randall, James G., and Donald, David. *The Civil War and Reconstruction.* Boston: D. C. Heath & Co., 1961.

Rawley, James A. "The Nationalism of Abraham Lincoln," *Civil War History,* IX (September 1963), 283–298.

Resek, Carl, ed. *War and the Intellectuals: Essays by Randolph S. Bourne, 1915–1919.* New York: Harper Torchbooks, 1964.

Riddleberger, Patrick. "George W. Julian: Abolitionist Land Reformer," *Agricultural History,* XXIX (July 1955), 108–115.

————. "The Making of a Political Abolitionist: George W. Julian and the Free Soilers, 1848," *Indiana Magazine of History,* LI (September 1955), 221–236.

————. "The Radicals' Abandonment of the Negro during Reconstruction," *Journal of Negro History,* XLV (April 1960), 88–102.

Roche, John D. *The Quest for the Dream: The Development of Civil Rights and Human Relations in Modern America.* New York: The Macmillan Company, 1963.

Rockwood, George I. "George Barrell Cheever: Protagonist of Abolition," *American Antiquarian Society Proceedings,* n. s., XLVI (April 1936), 82–113.

Rose, Willie Lee. *Rehearsal for Reconstruction: The Port Royal Experiment*. Indianapolis: The Bobbs-Merrill Company, Inc., 1964.

Roske, Ralph J. "The Post Civil War Career of Lyman Trumbull." Unpublished doctoral dissertation, University of Illinois, 1949.

——. "The Seven Martyrs?" *American Historical Review*, LXIV (January 1959), 323–330.

Ruchames, Louis. "The Historian as Special Pleader," *Nation*, 195 (November 24, 1962), 353–357.

——. "The Pulitzer Prize Treatment of Charles Sumner," *Massachusetts Review*, II (Summer 1961), 749–769.

Russ, William A., Jr. "Administrative Activities by the Union Army during and after the Civil War," *Mississippi Law Journal*, XVII (May 1945), 71–89.

——. "Was There a Danger of a Second Civil War during Reconstruction?" *Mississippi Valley Historical Review*, XXV (June 1938), 39–58.

Saloutos, Theodore. "Southern Agriculture and the Problems of Readjustment: 1865–1877," *Agricultural History*, XXX (April 1956), 58–76.

Scheiber, Harry N. *The Wilson Administration and Civil Liberties, 1917–1921*. Ithaca: Cornell University Press, 1960.

Schlesinger, Arthur M., Sr. *New Viewpoints in American History*. New York: Macmillan, 1926.

Schlesinger, Arthur M., Jr. "The Causes of the Civil War: A Note on Historical Sentimentalism," *Partisan Review*, XVI (October 1949), 969–981.

—— and White, Morton, eds. *Paths of American Thought*. Boston: Houghton Mifflin Company, 1963.

Schwartz, Harold. *Samuel Gridley Howe, Social Reformer, 1801–1876*. Cambridge: Harvard University Press, 1956.

Scott, Eben Greenough. *Reconstruction during the Civil War in the United States*. Boston and New York: Houghton, Mifflin and Co., 1895.

Scroggs, Jack B. "Carpetbagger Constitutional Reform in the South Atlantic States, 1867–1868," *Journal of Southern History*, XXVII (November 1961), 475–493.

——. "Southern Reconstruction: A Radical View," *Journal of Southern History*, XXIV (November 1958), 407–429.

Semmel, Bernard. *Jamaican Blood and Victorian Conscience: The Governor Eyre Controversy.* Boston: Houghton Mifflin Company, 1963.

Shortreed, Margaret. "The Antislavery Radicals: From Crusade to Revolution, 1840–1868," *Past and Present,* No. 16 (November 1959), 65–87.

Simkins, Francis B. "New Viewpoints of Southern Reconstruction," *Journal of Southern History,* V (February 1939), 49–61.

Smith, Timothy L. *Revivalism and Social Reform in Mid-Nineteenth Century America.* New York: Abingdon Press, 1957.

Sproat, John G. "Blueprint for Radical Reconstruction," *Journal of Southern History,* XXIII (February 1957), 25–44.

Stampp, Kenneth M. *The Era of Reconstruction, 1865–1867.* New York: Alfred A. Knopf, 1965.

———. "The Tragic Legend of Reconstruction," *Commentary,* XXXIX (January 1965), 44–50.

Stanton, William. *The Leopard's Spots: Scientific Attitudes Toward Race in America, 1815–59.* Chicago: The University of Chicago Press, 1960.

Sterne, Richard Clark. "Political, Social, and Literary Criticism in the New York *Nation,* 1865–1881; A Study in a Change of Mood." Unpublished doctoral dissertation, Harvard University, 1957.

Swinney, Everette. "Enforcing the Fifteenth Amendment, 1870–1877," *Journal of Southern History,* XXVIII (May 1962), 202–218.

ten Broek, Jacobus. *The Antislavery Origins of the Fourteenth Amendment.* Berkeley: University of California Press, 1951.

Thomas, Benjamin P., and Hyman, Harold M. *Stanton: The Life and Times of Lincoln's Secretary of War.* New York: Knopf, 1962.

Timberlake, Richard H. "Ideological Factors in Specie Resumption and Treasury Policy," *Journal of Economic History,* XXIV (March 1964), 29–52.

Trefousse, Hans. *Ben Butler: The South Called Him Beast!* New York: Twayne, 1957.

———. *Benjamin Franklin Wade: Radical Republican from Ohio.* New York: Twayne, 1963.

————. "The Joint Committee on the Conduct of the War; A Reassessment," *Civil War History*, X (March 1964), 5–19.

Ulrich, William J. "The Northern Military Mind in Regard to Reconstruction, 1865–1872." Unpublished doctoral dissertation, Ohio State University, 1949.

Vandiver, Frank E. "The Confederacy and the American Tradition," *Journal of Southern History*, XXVIII (August 1962), 277–286.

————. "How the Yankees Are Losing the War," *Southwest Review*, XL (Winter 1955), 62–66.

Wagandt, Charles L. "The Army Versus Maryland Slavery, 1862–1864," *Civil War History*, X (June 1964), 141–148.

Weinberg, Gerhard L. "Hitler's Image of the United States," *American Historical Review*, LXIX (July 1964), 1006–1021.

Weisberger, Bernard. "The Dark and Bloody Ground of Reconstruction Historiography," *Journal of Southern History*, XXV (November 1957), 427–447.

Welter, Rush. *Popular Education and Democratic Thought in America*. New York: Columbia University Press, 1962.

Williams, T. Harry. "An Analysis of Some Reconstruction Attitudes," *Journal of Southern History*, XII (November 1946), 469–486.

Wish, Harvey. *The American Historian: A Social-Intellectual History of the Writing of the American Past*. New York: Oxford University Press, 1960.

Wolgemuth, Kathleen L. "Wilson and Federal Segregation," *Journal of Negro History*, XLIV (April 1959), 158–173.

Woodward, C. Vann. "Our Past Isn't What It Used to Be," *New York Times Book Review*, July 28, 1963.

————. "The Political Legacy of Reconstruction," *Journal of Negro Education*, XXVI (Summer 1957), 231–240.

————. *The Strange Career of Jim Crow*. New York: Oxford University Press, 1955.

York, Robert M. *George B. Cheever, Religious and Social Reformer, 1807–1890*. Orono, Me.: University of Maine Press, 1955.

Zoellner, Robert H. "Negro Colonization: The Climate of Opinion Surrounding Lincoln," *Mid-America*, XLII (July 1960), 131–150.

The Radical Republicans

and Reconstruction, 1861–1870

PART ONE

The Year Before Sumter:

Radicals on the Defensive

---

1. BEN WADE, SENATE SPEECH

March 7, 1860

During the heated 1866 election campaign, a conservative New York Democrat offered one of the best descriptions on record of the nature of Radical Republicanism. "The Radicals . . . look exclusively to the future," he charged. "Their policy is purely present and original. They are a band of reformers, with new schemes, new doctrines, and new purposes to promulgate and establish."[1]

Only the war and the unprecedented opportunities it opened to the discerning for the better reconstruction of American society, especially in the South, could have developed these characteristics into dominant political motifs. The diverse personalities who in the late 1850's moved into the infant Republican organization had the lone

---

[1] William C. DeWitt, *Sundry Speeches and Writings: Driftwood from the Current of a Busy Life* (Brooklyn: Eagle Co., 1881), I, 74–76. DeWitt noted that Democrats looked to the past and clung to conservative constitutional doctrines, unlike the "political vagabonds" of the Republican party.

common goal of containing slavery. Before 1860–1861, men known as Radical Republicans employed a rhetoric of greater immediatism on this score than their party fellows, and they were defensive in this exposed position.[2]

The career of Benjamin Franklin Wade, and his speech in the United States Senate on March 7, 1860, illustrate the limitations of the Republicans' vision as of that time, and suggest the long road Radicals had to travel before they deserved the description of their Democratic opponent in 1866. Ben Wade once admitted that on matters of principle he found it "impossible . . . to sit still."[3] This inner itch lent form to his turbulent political career. There were in the mid-nineteenth century many opportunities for battle to a man like Wade, committed to combat on behalf of the good as he saw it. He entered the political ring well armed, with weapons developed in a tough school.

His family abandoned its hardscrabble Massachusetts farm and brought him as a youth to the semifrontier of Ohio. By the mid-1820's Wade completed the on-job training that sufficed then for education in the law, hung out his shingle, and entered the bottom ranks of the state's Whig party. Here, rasping Democratic opponents in rough-and-tumble campaigns, Wade found that Nature had endowed him generously for such frays. Even as a young man he was sturdy and muscular, and advancing years added impressive bulk to his heavy frame. Mastiff-like jaws, heavy lips, sharp eyes, and unruly hair turning iron gray as years passed fitted Victorian stereotypes of powerful masculinity. This was a time when effective speaking ability was of paramount importance, and Wade possessed a penetrating, raucous voice to add to the assets of his commanding presence, backed by a sharp intelligence, hair-trigger temper, and a rare command of vituperation.

The westward march of slavery turned Wade into a "conscience Whig," and he was an early convert to the new Republican organi-

---

[2] Arthur M. Schlesinger, Sr., *New Viewpoints in American History* (New York: Macmillan, 1926), p. 119; Benjamin F. Butler, *The Present Relations of Parties, Address, Music Hall, Boston, November 23, 1870* (Lowell: Marden, 1870), p. 4.

[3] *Congressional Globe,* 34 Cong., 1 sess., p. 1304 (hereafter cited as *CG*).

zation. Blunt, frank, and combative, this roughhewn Midwesterner became the conscience of the Republicans and a prod to Democrats.[4] By 1860 he was a veteran of the antislavery Republicans in the United States Senate and suffered with them the backlash of the John Brown raid. Democrats were tarring all Republicans with the brush of abolitionism, thereby dimming the prospects for Republican successes at the polls later that year. A sharp reverse in the 1860 balloting would likely destroy, or at least cripple, the young, unsure, faction-ridden Republican organization.

Most dangerous to the nation's and the party's future was the possibility that Democrats might squeeze conservatives in both parties with threats of secession and the heavy weight of the *Dred Scott* decision, in order to win Congressional guarantees for slavery everywhere in American territories. If this were gained for Southerners, Republicans would lose the single tie binding them together —the assumption that the national government had the duty and the power to deny the territories to slavery and thereby to preserve the future for free labor and capital.

After weeks of contention in Congress, Senator Toombs of Georgia spoke out to charge that Republicans—especially Radicals —and abolitionists were the cause of the increasingly tense sectional discontentment. Wade prepared to defend his party. Typically, he planned his strategy carefully. Months earlier he had advised his Ohio comrade in antislavery extension efforts, Benjamin Stanton, that he intended to capture the Democrats' pet argument, states' rights, for the Republicans' purposes, and that he would "invoke the [Virginia and Kentucky] Resolutions of [17]98–9 as containing the proper remedy for cases like the present . . . to [oppose] the execution of the 'Fugitive [Slave] Law' as they were [the proper remedy to oppose] to the old 'Alien and Sedition' Law." To resurrect now the original purposes of the Virginia and Kentucky Resolutions as defenses of individual rights, not states' rights, and to depict Republicans as strict constructionists "is only compelling them [Southerners] to take their own physic," Wade gloated.[5]

---

[4] Trefousse, *Wade*, ch. 1, has biographical details.

[5] May 30, 1859; owned by and used with permission of Stanton B. Allison.

Yet Wade in 1860 was not a Negrophile or an abolitionist, though he was properly accounted a Republican Radical. He frankly advocated that Negroes must colonize somewhere—any-where—abroad when someday they should be free. The most stinging description Wade conjured up of some lackadaisical Republican party workers was "understrappers and bootblacks, niggers in soul and spirit."[6]

Wade was a radical of 1860, not 1960. Negroes in his view were not white men, but they were God's handiwork. Therefore slavery violated divine law, and it also threatened to choke off the American dream. Wade's plea was to keep the future open. His biographer rightly concluded that "these principles were to remain the unchallenged platform of the radical wing of the Republican party."[7]

Wade's speech of March 7, 1860, is offered as an encapsulation of advanced Republican doctrine. It also represented (and this is too often forgotten) popular Northern sentiment. That it was radical for its time is the measure of how far ensuing events were to push all Americans who were not completely insensitive to the impact of the Civil War on their society.[8]

The Republican party [Wade said] has been always, as it is now, absolutely powerless to impress its principles on the administration of the Government. It stands by and looks on, wondering at the progress of the Democratic administration; and wondering, most of all, at hearing those who have conducted it entirely in their own way now threatening to pull down the pillars of the Union, and involve them all, with themselves, in a common ruin. In the name of God, . . . what does all this mean? . . . What, . . . could be more unreasonable and absurd than these whinings and complaints of northern aggres-

---

[6] *Ibid.* See too Robert H. Zoellner, "Negro Colonization: The Climate of Opinion Surrounding Lincoln," *Mid-America,* XLII (July 1960), 131–150.

[7] Trefousse, *Wade,* p. 116.

[8] *CG,* 36 Cong., 1 sess., Appendix, pp. 150–155.

sions and oppressions by the great and prosperous South, when the North is entirely out of power? . . . Property in slaves was never so prosperous as today. Look into the slave market; you will find that slaves never brought higher prices than now. Of course slave labor is more profitable to the owner now than it has ever been. Sir, these southern gentlemen are inconsistent and contradictory; in one breath they are all boast and glory; in the next it is all despair and destruction. Please reconcile some of these contradictions.

If the North has, by means of its underground railroads, fatally and treacherously sapped and undermined the foundations of your whole system of labor, how is it that your property has risen in value, and your prosperity culminated during all the time it has been going on? . . .

The Senator [Toombs] charges us all with perjury and disloyalty to the Constitution. Just see, now, how inconsistent a gentleman, in the heat of argument, may become. He has taken here an oath to support the Constitution; the same oath which we have taken, and which he accuses us of breaking; and yet he announced to us that he is impatient, nay eager, for a symbol of war from the Old Dominion [Virginia] against the Constitution and the Union. . . . He is ready and eager to second her motion. "One blast from her bugle horn," he said, "would call to their feet a million men." A million of men, sir! A million of men for what? Why, a million of men to topple down the pillars of this Republic, and overwhelm the whole country in one universal ruin. . . . Does he not stand on high ground, sir? I ask him to say, for himself, that he occupies high vantage ground, while charging us with treason and violation of our oaths, when he is with the same breath threatening to pull down the pillars of the Union. Sir, if this is not treason, then I do not know what it is. If this is not a violation of the oath to support the Constitution, then I do not understand the import of the words. . . .

I come now to your . . . fugitive [slave] bill. . . . It is not, however, my purpose to argue its constitutionality. I meet in this case, . . . the vague charge of unfaithfulness on our part [in enforcement of the 1850 fugitive slave law] with a general denial. I call your attention, sir, to the fact that there prevails among the people very generally an idea that many of the provisions of that law are unconstitutional. . . . Why do the people adopt the idea that it is unconstitutional? . . . I will only allude to that section of the law which confers judicial powers on commissioners appointed by the courts, who are not, and cannot, thus appointed, be judges. The people believe this provision unconstitutional, and so do I. . . .

You are continually repeating the assertion that this fugitive slave law provision was deemed an important one by the fathers, and that the Union could not have been effected without it. On the contrary, sir, it . . . was put into the Constitution with very little deliberation; and those who put it there had no idea that, in doing so, they were taking away from the States the most important element of sovereignty, namely, their power to protect their own citizens against unlawful seizures and searches and extradition. The rights of the States, the only protection made against overpowering and concentrated despotism, were the one special object of preservation. The States battled inch by inch against the surrender of any State power. I judge, therefore, that they never intended to confer upon Congress or upon any one State, or any body, a right to enter another sovereign State and take away, in a summary and arbitrary manner, whomsoever he should choose to claim as a fugitive from another State. . . .

The third count in the Senator's indictment is, that we intend to prohibit slavery in the vast Territories of this Union. That charge, I confess, is true. We do so intend. If I understand the objects and purpose of the Republican party; if I understand the emergencies of the case that brought that great party into existence it was this very subject. The General Government, acting in Congress faithlessly to all that it had covenanted heretofore, had broken down every barrier and violated every pledge it had given of freedom in any of our Territories. These covenants being overthrown, the Republican party arose to rescue freedom. Had there been no violation of the Missouri compromise, it is very probable there would have been no Republican party here. We did embody ourselves into a party, in order to rescue, protect, and defend the free Territories of this country against the pollution of slavery. I have no concealments to make. There we now stand; this is our platform; on it we will stand forever. . . .

[Wade turned next to the *Dred Scott* decision of the United States Supreme Court.]

The moment a Federal court transcends its legitimate authority, for the purpose of effecting some political object, its interference is impertinent; it is of no validity; and . . . I hold it in utter contempt. . . . Well, sir, if there ever was a holding on God's earth that would warrant any judge, private man, or Senator, in saying that he held it in utter contempt, it is what is called the Dred Scott decision; so manifestly an usurpation of power, so manifestly done in order to give a bias to political action, that no man, though he be a fool, can fail to see it. . . .

Strange as it may appear, those who complain of northern aggression have not only every other department under their feet, but with less than one third of the population of the North, you happen to have a majority of the Supreme Court on your side, and always have had. I will not say that that is the reason why the decisions of courts of late are magnified into such importance. Immaculate their decisions are now, it seems. The very [Democratic] party who, a few years ago, within the memory of us all, held that their decisions were of no effect whatever on governmental action, when coming in conflict with the views of the President, or the coördinate branches of the Government, have turned around of late, and have found a virtue in that court that can ride triumphantly over every other department of this Government. It is a pal-

pable heresy, and must be abandoned. The liberties of this
nation cannot consist with the doctrine now s'et up on the
other side of this Chamber with regard to your Supreme
Court. . . .

God knows, if you once have it established and acquiesced
in by the people of this Union, that the *dicta* of the Supreme
Court—a political court by its very constitution, yea, packed
on this very subject, as every Senator here knows—are to be
the laws binding on every other department, we have the
meanest despotism that ever prevailed on God Almighty's
earth. But I have no fears of it, sir. You may effect a temporary
purpose by it; but a doctrine so absurd, so incompatible with
the minds of the Anglo-Saxon race, so inconsistent with the
great principles of free government, will never be permitted
to stand.

In the Dred Scott decision . . . they overturned every decision
their own court had made for more than seventy years; they
holding, prior to that time, that Congress had full and plenary
power over the Territories of the United States. Judge Marshall so decided, and the court had followed his decision, and
every other department of the Government was well satisfied.
Therefore, this infallible court can overturn the most settled
decisions of its own and of other courts, and nobody can question its acts! . . . This is a position that cannot outlive this
generation.

Where did these judges find the power in the Constitution
of the United States to carry slavery into the Territories? If
they had anything to ground their *dicta* upon, they had the
power to show it written in the Constitution of the United
States; but there is no such thing there. . . . They find no
warrant in the Constitution; they find none in legal logic or
reason. It is said now that the Territories being the common
property of the States, the citizens of each State have a right
to go into them with any property that they perchance may
have. I deny the postulate. These Territories do not belong to

the States, as States. They belong to the people of the United States. Congress is the trustee for them; but no State can claim any portion of them. . . .

May not the same ground be applied to other cases? Suppose we had annexed—as I presume we shall ultimately annex —the Fejee Islands to this nation. In those islands the people not only enslave each other, but they actually kill and eat each other up. Now, suppose a Senator from the State of Fejee should appear in this body; suppose that he should claim the right of his constituents to bring with them their chattels into any of our Territories, and claim the right of the law in that country to practice cannibalism upon them, that he might roast and boil them as well as enslave them. He would claim, if you did not permit this to be done, "that the State of Fejee has not equal rights with the other States of this Union; a gentleman owns this property; it is an undoubted law in my State that we may fatten men for the roast, and we have a right to bring them here for the same purpose; and if you do not permit us to do so, we will pull down the columns of the Republic, laying it outspread in one universal ruin." [Laughter.] I suppose the Senator from Illinois [Stephen A. Douglas] would say, "The Territories have a perfect right to vote cannibalism in or to vote it out; I do not care whether they vote it up or down; but they have the right, and shall be perfectly free to do it." [Laughter.] Another Senator would arise and say the people of Fejee not only have the right to bring them in, but they have the right to be protected in doing so there under the laws of Congress. Another one says that Congress has no power to pass laws on that subject whatever; but the courts, which are now omnipotent in all things, may, without law, declare what the law is, and we must all bow down to it. . . . Our safety, Mr. President, consists in keeping close to the Constitution. Whatever we claim let us find the direct warrant for it there, or the necessary implication to carry out some other power that is manifestly granted. The moment we go astray from this we are in the fog; we are in dispute; we endanger the harmony of our action, and it is done in this instance. In this great departure from the early principles of this Government, you have involved portions of the nation in almost irretrievable hostility to each other. Let us go back to the Constitution and follow it. . . .

Now, I do not care for what the Senator from Georgia and others have told us, that slaveholding was the basis on which society had been founded for thirty centuries. We, at least, have discovered that it is a sandy foundation. It is fast washing away; and in exact proportion to the advance of mankind in civilization and in knowledge, on all hands this old principle is deemed barbarous, and is wearing away. Upon that issue I will meet you; it is a fair one. If it is right, extend it; if it is wrong, let it die the death, as all error and falsehood must die. . . .

I know it is said that the African is an inferior race, incapable of defending his own rights. My ethics teach me, if it be so, that this fact, so far from giving me a right to enslave him, requires that I shall be more scrupulous of his rights; but I know that, whether he be equal to me or not, he is still a human being; negroes are still men. Senators will bear me witness that there are thousands now in bondage who are much more white than black—yea, tens of thousands of such; but, whether white or black, I say again, they are still human; they are animated by the same hopes, they are afflicted with the same sorrows, they are actuated by the same motives that we are. Like us, they may be deprived of every right; they may be treated like brutes; their souls may be ignored; you may whip, scourge, and trample them in the dust, if you will; but they, being human, will arise from the utmost degradation, and still stand forth in the image of God, the conscious candidates of immortal life. This gives them a full assurance of their manhood, and stands as an eternal prophecy that they are not always to be slaves. It is part and parcel of human nature. It is implanted in every human soul, by the finger of God. You cannot eradicate it; and yet, while it remains, your institution cannot be secure. . . .

Why? Because, although the Senator from Virginia [Mr. Hunter] said that slavery was the normal condition, and, if I understood him, that freedom was an experiment yet, and likely to come out second best, nevertheless everything around you shows the security of the North. The perfect contentedness of the North shows which is the normal and which the other condition. Look to the great Northwest, to which I belong. There is a white population to-day, northwest of the river Ohio, as great as that of all your slave States, so secure, so impassive, so conscious of their own strength, that they are an empire in themselves. I am here day after day, and my constituents ask nothing of me but to be let alone. Here we hear this clamor from the South about southern rights, day after day, year after year, disturbing elements in our political progress constantly; and yet you hear nothing from the security of freedom and free labor in those regions. All this goes to show that slavery is not the normal condition of man; that it is an institution which has survived the exigencies of the times which permitted it to be established, and now lives on the bare sufferance of mankind. . . .

All I say is, that in the vast Territories of this nation I will allow no such curse to have a foothold. If I am right, and slavery stands branded and condemned by the God of nature, then, for Heaven's sake, go with me to limit it, and not propagate this curse. . . . Our principles are only these: we hold that you shall limit slavery. Believing it wrong, believing it inconsistent with the best interests of the people, we demand that it shall be limited; and this limitation is not hard upon you, because you have land enough for a population as large as Europe, and century after century must roll away before you can occupy what you now have. The next thing which we hold, . . . is the great principle of the homestead bill . . .

the greatest measure I know of to mold in the right direction the Territories belonging to this nation; to build up a free yeomanry capable of maintaining an independent republican Government forever. We demand, also, that there shall be a protection to our own labor against the pauper labor of Europe. We have always contended for it, but you have always stricken it down. . . .

There is in these United States a race of men who are poor, weak, uninfluential, incapable of taking care of themselves. I mean the free negroes, who are despised by all, repudiated by all; outcasts upon the face of the earth, without any fault of theirs that I know of; but they are the victims of a deep-rooted prejudice, and I do not stand here to argue whether that prejudice be right or wrong. I know such to be the fact. It is there immovable. It is perfectly impossible that these two races can inhabit the same place and be prosperous and happy. I see that this species of population are just as abhorrent to the southern States, and perhaps more so, than to the North; many of those States are now, as I think, passing most unjust laws to drive these men off or to subject them to slavery; they are flocking into the free States, and we have objections to them. Now, the proposition is, that this great Government owes it to justice, owes it to those individuals, owes it to itself and to the free white population of the nation, to provide a means whereby this class of unfortunate men may emigrate to some congenial clime, where they may be maintained, to the mutual benefit of all, both white and black. This will insure a separation of the races. Let them go into the tropics. There, I understand, are vast tracts of the most fertile and inviting land, in a climate perfectly congenial to that class of men, where the negro will be predominant; where his nature seems to be improved, and all his faculties, both mental and physical, are fully developed, and where the white man degenerates in the same proportion as the black man prospers. Let them go there; let them be separated; it is easy to do it. I understand that negotiations may easily be effected with many of the Central American States, by which they will take these people and confer upon them great privileges, if they will settle there. They are so easy of access that, a nucleus being formed, they will go of themselves and relieve us of the burden. They will be so far removed from us that they cannot form a disturbing element in our political economy. The far-reaching sagacity of Thomas Jefferson and others suggested this plan. Nobody that I know has found a better. I understand, too, that in these regions, to which I would let them go, there is no prejudice against them. All colors seem there to live in common, and they would be glad that these men should go among them. . . . I hope, after that is done, to hear no more about negro equality or anything of that kind. Sir, we shall be as glad to rid ourselves of these people, if we can do it consistently with justice, as anybody else can be. We will not, however, perpetrate injustice against them. We will not drive them out, but we will use every inducement to persuade these unfortunate men to find a home there, so as to separate the races, and all will go better than it can under any other system that we can devise.

2. CARL SCHURZ, ST. LOUIS SPEECH

August 1, 1860

By August 1860 Republicans had nominated Abraham Lincoln, and all Republicans snapped to his support. To be sure, Radical Republicans who were abolitionists did so with some reluctance, out of uncertainty about his antislavery principles. But as Joshua Giddings recalled, ". . . from his [Lincoln's] candor, his frankness and integrity, the anti-slavery men had confidence that he would respect their principles in due time."[1]

Prominent among these Radical Lincoln men was Carl Schurz, "the most eloquent of the German-American Free Soilers," in the opinion of the latest historian of the Republican party.[2] In 1860 Schurz was only thirty-five years old, but he was accounted a heavyweight among Republican stumpers because of his influence among the numerous German-speaking settlers in the Ohio and Mississippi valleys. Settling in Wisconsin, he became an original Republican organizer there. He aided antislave Republicans everywhere, including Lincoln in the Illinois senatorial contest of 1858, and his effort was not forgotten.[3]

He deserved the gratitude of Republicans in 1860 for his indefatigable efforts in Missouri if for no other reason. The state was hemmed in by free soil on all fronts save the western, where in Kansas the bloody troubles of the 1850's kept alive the possibility of the further spread of slavery. If in 1860 Missouri decided in favor of conservative Democratic principles and candidates, then a new Western slaveholding arc might open to the Pacific itself, men feared. On the other hand, a decision, however unlikely, in favor of Missouri's Republicans and of Lincoln could alchemize into policy the basic Republican plank of containing slavery inside its existing bounds so that someday—a generation? three? a dozen? —it might perish of its inner contradictions.

Further to excite Republican efforts, St. Louis was that rarest political phenomenon of 1860, a center, behind slaveholding lines, of Republican party organization and of sentiment against the extension of slavery. Nowhere else in the South could Republicans aspire to electoral success or could reformers organize for political ends. What became after 1861 basic military strategy, in August 1860 headed all lists of political priorities: Missouri must be fought for.

Therefore Schurz went to St. Louis, and he confided to a friend: "It is to be the greatest speech of my life." At the Verandah Hall in

---

[1] Giddings, *History of the Rebellion: Its Causes and Cures* (New York: Follet, Foster & Co., 1864), p. 445.

[2] George H. Mayer, *The Republican Party, 1854–1964* (New York: Oxford University Press, 1964), p. 73.

[3] Lincoln, *Works*, IV, 78–79.

St. Louis on August 1, he spoke out bravely on "The Doom of Slavery," stressing concepts of self-interest familiar to his audience of recent Europeans, and ignoring the constitutional abstractions so common to the American scene.[4]

Your social system [Schurz said, addressing himself first to slaveowners] is founded upon forced labor . . . [which] demands the setting aside of the safeguards of individual liberty . . . ; free labor demands their preservation as essential and indispensable to its existence and progressive development. Slavery demands extension by an aggressive foreign policy; free labor demands an honorable peace and friendly intercourse with the world abroad for its commerce, and a peaceable and undisturbed development of our resources at home for its agriculture and industry. Slavery demands extension over national territories for the purpose of gaining political power. Free labor demands the national domain for workingmen, for the purpose of spreading the blessings of liberty and civilization. Slavery, therefore, opposes all measures tending to secure the soil to the actual laborer; free labor, therefore, recognizes the right of the settler to the soil, and demands measures protecting him against the pressure of speculation. Slavery demands the absolute ascendency of the planting interest in our economic policy; free labor demands legislation tending to develop all the resources of the land, and to harmonize the agricultural, commercial and industrial interests. Slavery demands the control of the general government for its special protection and the promotion of its peculiar interests; free labor demands that the general government be administered for the purpose of securing to all the blessings of liberty, and for the promotion of the general welfare. Slavery demands the recognition of its divine right; free labor

---

[4] *Speeches, Correspondence, and Political Papers of Carl Schurz,* ed. Frederic Bancroft (New York: Putnam's, 1913), I, 121, 132–137, 154–159 (hereafter cited as Schurz, *Speeches*).

recognizes no divine right but that of the liberty of all men.

With one word, slavery demands, for its protection and perpetuation, a system of policy which is utterly incompatible with the principles upon which the organization of free-labor society rests. There is the antagonism. That is the essence of the "irrepressible conflict." It is a conflict of principles underlying interests, always the same, whether appearing as a moral, economic, or political question. Mr. Douglas boasted that he could repress it with police measures; he might as well try to fetter the winds with a rope. The South means to repress it with decisions of the Supreme Court; they might as well, like Xerxes, try to subdue the waves of the ocean by throwing chains into the water. . . .

The predominance of interests determines the construction of the Constitution. So it was and it will ever be. Only those who remained true to the original program of the Fathers remained true to the original construction. Decide the contest of principles underlying interests, and the conflict of constitutional constructions will settle itself. This may seem a dangerous political theory. It is not an article of my creed, not a matter of principles, but a matter of experience; not a doctrine, but a fact.

Thus the all-pervading antagonism stands before us, gigantic in its dimensions, growing every day in the awful proportions of its problems, involving the character of our institutions; involving our relations with the world abroad; involving our peace, our rights, our liberties at home; involving our growth and prosperity; involving our moral and political existence as a nation.

How short-sighted, how childish, are those who find its origin in artificial agitation! As though we could produce a tempest by blowing our noses, or cause an earthquake by stamping our puny feet upon the ground. . . .

[Schurz moved on to prophesy the effects on slavery of a war between the free states and the South.]

The slave States . . . cannot expose their territory without leaving unprotected the institution for the protection of which the war was undertaken. They have to cover thousands and thousands of vulnerable points, for every plantation is an open wound, every negro cabin a sore. Every border or sea-board slave State will need her own soldiers, and more too, for the protection of her own slaves; and where then would be the material for the concentrated army?

Besides, the slave States harbor a dangerous enemy within their own boundaries, and that is slavery itself. Imagine them at war with anti-slavery people whom they have exasperated by their own hostility. What will be the effect upon the slaves? The question is not whether the North will instigate a slave rebellion, for I suppose they will not; the question is, whether they can prevent it, and I think they cannot. But the anticipation of a negro insurrection (and the heated imagination of the slaveholder will discover symptoms of a rebellious spirit in every trifle) may again paralyze the whole South. Do you remember the effect of John Brown's attempt? The severest blow he struck at the slave-power was not that he disturbed a town and killed several citizens, but that he revealed the weakness of the whole South. Let Governor Wise of Virginia carry out his threatened invasion of the free States, not with twenty-three, but with twenty-three hundred followers at his heels—what will be the result? As long as they behave themselves we shall let them alone; but as soon as they create any disturbance they will be put into the stationhouse; and the next day we shall read in the newspapers of some Northern city, among the reports of the police-court: "Henry A. Wise and others, for disorderly conduct, fined $5." Or, if he has made an attempt on any man's life, or against our institutions, he will most certainly find a Northern jury proud enough to acquit him on the ground of incorrigible mental derangement. Our pictorial prints will have material for caricatures for two issues, and a burst of laughter will ring to the skies from Maine to California. And there is the end of it. But behold John Brown with twenty-three men raising a row at Harper's Ferry; the whole South frantic with terror; the whole State of Virginia in arms; troops marching and countermarching, as if the battle of Austerlitz were to be fought over again; innocent cows shot as bloodthirsty invaders, and even the evening song of the peaceful whippoorwills mistaken for the battle cry of rebellion. And those are the men who will expose themselves to the chances of a pro-slavery war with an anti-slavery people! Will they not look upon every [Northern] captain as a John Brown . . . ? They will hardly have men enough to quiet their fears at home. What will they have to oppose to the enemy? If they want to protect slavery then, every township will want its home regiment, every plantation its garrison. No sooner will a movement of concentration be attempted, than the merest panic may undo and frustrate it. Themistocles might say that Greece was on his ships; a French general might say that the Republic was in his camps; but slavery will be neither on the ships nor in the camp; it will be spread defenseless over thousands of square miles. This will be their situation: either they concentrate their forces, and slavery will be exposed wherever the army is not; or they do not concentrate them, and their army will be everywhere, but in fact nowhere. . . . And thus it turns out that the very same thing that would be the cause of the war, would at the same time be indefensible by war. The same institution that wants protection will at the same time disable its protectors. Yes, slavery, which can no longer be defended with arguments, cannot be defended with arms.

There is your dissolution of the Union for the perpetuation of slavery. The Southern States cannot reasonably desire it, for it would defeat the very objects for which it would be undertaken; they cannot reasonably attempt it, for slavery would lie helpless at the feet of the North. Slavery, which may die a slow, gradual death in the Union, will certainly die an instantaneous and violent death if they attempt to break out of the Union. What then will the South do in case of a Republican victory? I answer that question with another one, What *can* the South do in case of a Republican victory? Will there be a disturbance? If they know their own interests, the people of the South themselves will have to put it down. Will they submit? Not to Northern dictation, but to their own good sense. They have considered us their enemies as long as they ruled us; they will find out that we are their friends as soon as we cease to be their subjects. They have dreamed so long of the blessings of slavery; they will open their eyes again to the blessings of liberty. They will discover that they are not conquered, but liberated. Will slavery die out? As surely as freedom will *not* die out.

Slaveholders of America, I appeal to you. Are you really in earnest when you speak of perpetuating slavery? Shall it never cease? Never? Stop and consider where you are and in what day you live.

This is the nineteenth century. Never since mankind has a recollection of times gone by, has the human mind disclosed such wonderful powers. The hidden forces of nature we have torn from their mysterious concealment and yoked them into the harness of usefulness; they carry our thoughts over slender wires to distant nations; they draw our wagons over the highways of trade; they pull the gigantic oars of our ships; they set in motion the iron fingers of our machinery; they will soon plow our fields and gather our crops. The labor of the brain has exalted to a mere bridling and controlling of natural forces the labor of the hand; and you think you can perpetuate a system which reduces man, however degraded, yet capable of development, to the level of a soulless machine?

This is the world of the nineteenth century. The last remnants of feudalism in the old world are fast disappearing. The Czar of Russia, in the fulness of imperial power, is forced to yield to the irresistible march of human progress, and abolishes serfdom. Even the Sultan of Turkey can no longer maintain the barbarous customs of the Moslem against the pressure of the century, and slavery disappears. And you, citizens of a Republic, you think you can arrest the wheel of progress with your Dred Scott decisions and Democratic platforms?

Look around you and see how lonesome you are in this wide world of ours. As far as modern civilization throws its rays, what people, what class of society is there like you? Cry out into the world your "wild and guilty fantasy" of property in man, and every echo responds with a cry of horror or contempt; every breeze, from whatever point of the compass it may come, brings you a verdict of condemnation. There is no human heart that sympathizes with your cause, unless it sympathizes with the cause of despotism in every form. There is no human voice to cheer you on in your struggle; there is no human eye that has a tear for your reverses; no link of sympathy between the common cause of the great human brotherhood and you. You hear of emancipation in Russia and wish it to fail. You hear of Italy rising, and fear the spirit of liberty may become contagious. Where all mankind rejoices, you tremble. Where all mankind loves, you hate. Where all mankind curses, you sympathize.

And in this appalling solitude you stand alone against a hopeful world, alone against a great century, fighting your hopeless fight—hopeless, hopeless as the struggle of the Indians against the onward march of civilization. Exhaust all the devices which the inventive genius of despotism may suggest, and yet how can you resist? In every little village schoolhouse, the little children who learn to read and write are plotting against you; in every laboratory of science, in every machine shop, the human mind is working the destruction of your idol. You cannot make an attempt to keep pace with the general progress of mankind, without plotting against yourselves. Every steam whistle, every puffing locomotive, is sounding the shriek of liberty into your ears. From the noblest instincts of our hearts down to sordid greediness of gain, every impulse of human nature is engaged in this universal conspiracy. How can you resist? Where are your friends in the North? Your ever-ready supporters are scattered to the winds as by enchantment, never to unite again. Hear them trying to save their own fortunes, swear with treacherous eagerness that they have nothing in common with you. And your opponents? Your boasts have lost their charm, your threats have lost their terrors, upon them. The attempt is idle to cloak the sores of Lazarus with the lion skin of Hercules. We know you. Every one of your boasts is understood as a disguised moan of weakness—every shout of defiance as a disguised cry for mercy. We will no longer be imposed upon. Do not deceive yourselves. This means not only the destruction of a party—this means the defeat of a cause. Be shrewder than the shrewdest, braver than the bravest—it is all in vain; your cause is doomed.

And in the face of all this you insist upon hugging, with dogged stubbornness, your fatal infatuation? Why not manfully swing round into the grand march of progressive humanity? You say it cannot be done to-day. Can it be done to-morrow? Will it be easier twenty, fifty years hence, when the fearful increase of the negro population will have aggravated the evils of slavery a hundredfold, and with it the difficulties of its extinction? Did you ever think of this? The final crisis, unless prevented by timely reform, will come with the inexorable certainty of fate, the more terrible the longer it is delayed. Will you content yourself with the criminal words, "after me the deluge"? Is that the inheritance you mean to leave to coming generations—an inheritance of disgrace, crime, blood, destruction? Hear me, slaveholders of America! If you have no sense for the right of the black, no appreciation of your own interests, I entreat, I implore you, have at least pity on your children!

PART TWO

War: The Concentration

of Extraordinary Power for

Beneficent Purposes—1862

---

3. THE REVEREND GEORGE

B. CHEEVER,

NEW YORK *INDEPENDENT*

January 16, 1862

Historians still worry the question whether Lincoln's election in November 1860 constituted enough of a threat to the South to justify secession. Whatever scholars decide now, a century ago Southerners replied in defiant affirmatives. The world watched incredulously as a great nation permitted its own dissolution without forceful resistance on the part of constituted authorities. Little wonder that when the Thirty-sixth Congress met on December 3, 1860, the Union appeared to be moribund. Outgoing President Buchanan, old, bitter toward Democrats for their failure to nominate him for a second term, passionately angry with Republicans for upsetting his administration, in his last "state of the Union" message loaded guns further on behalf of the South.

Buchanan counseled moderation, but he marked out a middle ground on Southern terms. No one had any right to interfere with slavery inside a state, he insisted, although this was not a Republican principle and was not an issue in 1860. Adverting to specific means of placating the South, Buchanan proposed an amendment to the Constitution that if passed would have cemented slavery into the federal territories and in the states to be made from them and would have rendered foolish the Republican aspiration of containing slavery, as well as the Douglas Democrat nostrum of popular sovereignty.

It horrified some Republicans to sense in the North a bent toward acquiescence in the astonishing Buchanan formulation. In the Congress the Radical Republicans formed one of the rare islands of uncompromising Unionism and thereby gained prestige in the estimation of many Northerners. At least the nation should bow out on a note of manly self-respect, not with a doughface's whimper, the Republicans insisted; and their steadfastness was appropriate to James Russell Lowell's concern, expressed in a letter of December 31, 1860:

Is it the effect of democracy to make all men cowards? An ounce of pluck just now were worth a king's ransom. There is one comfort, though a shabby one, in the feeling that matters will come to such a pass that courage will be forced upon us, and that when there is no hope left we shall learn a little self-confidence from despair. That in such a crisis the fate of the country should be in the hands of a sneak [Buchanan]! If the Republicans stand firm we shall be saved, even at the cost of disunion. If they yield, it is all up with us and with the experiment of democracy.[1]

Congressional Republicans stood firm. They provided the only focus of nationalist leadership available to Unionists during those shameful weeks of "the secession winter," and they set hard a tradition of Congressional leadership.

---

[1] To Charles Nordhoff, in *Letters of James Russell Lowell,* ed. Charles Eliot Norton (New York: Harper & Bros., 1894), I, 308.

Efforts at sectional conciliation, stretching on toward Lincoln's inauguration day, failed. New, staunchly Unionist cabinet officers kept Buchanan from backtracking further with respect to Forts Sumter and Pickens, and the Republican membership in Congress suspiciously watchdogged "Old Buck's" activities. But secession advanced without impediment. With a Southern Confederacy already in existence, Abraham Lincoln became President of the United (!) States. No one appeared to know what paths to follow even after war came at Fort Sumter.

Early the question loomed concerning the purpose for which the war was being waged, and it never backed off central stage for very long. The first formal utterance on this matter of aims arose out of the desperate need Lincoln felt to placate the ostensibly loyal slave-holding border states and to keep support of Northern conservatives, combined with the near-panic that swept the North after the fiasco at Bull Run in July 1861, the first large-scale encounter between the scratch armies of the Union and of the Confederacy. Obeying these imperatives, the Congress, with Republican support, declared in the so-called Crittenden Resolution of July that the aim of the war was reunion, not a reconstruction of race relations.[2]

Although no one could predict it in July 1861, the Civil War was to develop into the longest, bloodiest, costliest conflict fought anywhere in the world during the nineteenth century. Even after the educative opportunities of our own time, war as an evolutionary process is little understood. It appears to be clear, however, that a total war cannot help but alter men's purposes and politics; that the causes of wars differ from expressed aims; and that the results of war often, if not always, diverge from both causes and aims.

No statute, no constitutional amendment, straitjackets history. Congressional resolutions are weaker expressions of legislators' opinions and are less likely to hold events to prescribed courses. Appeals to a policy in the form of a resolution are naïve when they are made in the midst of a great war's unanticipatable impacts on men, measures, and institutions.

To be sure, in 1861 the vast majority of Americans *were* naïve with respect to the nature of war. Their happy continental isolation had exempted them from the dour introspection that less favored

---

[2] See *CG*, 37 Cong., 1 sess., p. 222; Lincoln, *Works*, IV, 262–271.

situations had forced on men in other lands. But to those who were willing to see, it quickly became obvious that the Civil War was stripping away this habitual immunity.

In the North, throughout the war political institutions and other channels of opinion were open and continued to offer real alternatives. Within the Republican party the Radical Republican left rubbed uneasily against the Lincoln center and the Blair-Welles right. Friction developed. But there was dialogue. In many senses the war took on characteristics of a tremendous forced-draft education.[3] A great, unending debate marked the Northern scene, and the Radical Republicans served admirably as goads and mentors.

Because the outstanding characteristic of Radical Republicans was their future-looking attitude, they were markedly more sensitive than other Republicans and Democrats to the altering nature of the war. Even Radicals continued at first to hold to the belief that the war might end on a Crittenden Resolution note, with slavery merely contained inside its 1860 boundaries, and perhaps with guarantees against its further growth. Then the voice of abolitionists was heard with increasing effect in Radical ranks, and the patchwork Republican organization added another shade to its spectrum.

---

[3] Late in 1861, remarkably early in the war, a Kentucky lawyer offered this succinct statement:

The American people are engaged in a great struggle in the process of which they begin to be, for the first time, thrown upon the serious discussion of the most fundamental and vital principles of enlightened and constitutional liberty. It is an evidence of their past happy exemption from tempests such as those which have rocked other great nations, that these very elementary principles, these rudiments of liberty, are so little known and so feebly apprehended by them. They have lived in the almost unparalleled enjoyment of liberty, but have realized no occasion to study it, and have not analyzed or defined it. They have sailed upon a smooth sea, without the experience of a single storm to awaken serious apprehension for their safety, and have never examined the vessel which has borne them, to understand the great timbers and braces that hold it together.

Robert L. Breck, *The Habeas Corpus and Martial Law* (Cincinnati, 1862), p. 10. This is a pamphlet version of Breck's article in the Danville, Ky., *Review*, December ?, 1861, inspired in opposition to United States Supreme Court Justice Roger B. Taney's judgment in *ex parte Merryman*.

Veteran abolitionists had long preached that all political organizations were impure vessels. Not even the secession crisis kept William Lloyd Garrison, for example, from sternly criticizing as hopelessly conservative the Republican party and its Presidential nominee. After Sumter, abolitionists found offensive Lincoln's border-state policy and the Crittenden Resolution. Nevertheless, many abolitionists began to bore into Republican echelons. The question was whether men of such turbulent and individualistic natures as the abolitionists possessed could work effectively as politicians.

Events were to prove that they could, under certain conditions. A worthwhile mission and a chance, however slim, for success were the needed ingredients. Their mission—immediate emancipation of Southern slaves in order to make the war worth the costs—could not be contemned. The war provided the opportunity and the Republican party the mechanism. Abolitionists became Radical Republicans in order to turn the Republican party away from the delusive Crittenden Resolution war aim, toward freedom, the only goal likely to lead to victory.[4]

In sum, few other Americans were as ready as the abolitionists with clear, simple, and reasonable explanations for questions that were tearing at the nation's heart. Sumter turned abolitionists into prophets, and soon after the war began, John Brown's body rose from its felon's grave to march proudly in martyr's rhythm. The same swift alchemy raised abolitionists to unfamiliar peaks of respectability, prominence, and influence. Their readiness for and effectiveness in their task are to be measured by the speed with which Northern war policy traveled the revolutionary road from the July 1861 Crittenden Resolution to Lincoln's Emancipation Proclamation in September 1862, and then to the ratification of the Thirteenth Amendment in December 1865. What began as a war to restore the seceded states to the Union, and with the understand-

---

[4] Garrison, *The Abolitionists, and their Relation to the War. An Address . . . January 14, 1862, at the Cooper Institute, New York* (New York, 1862); and see Henry Ward Beecher's prophetic essay of June 1861, "Energy of Administration Demanded," in his *Freedom and War: Discourses on Topics suggested by the Times* (Boston: Ticknor and Fields, 1863), pp. 157–173.

ing that restoration would not upset race relations in the South, became a war to purify all Americans, especially those in the South, through basic reforms to be won through military force.

Abolitionists and Radical Republicans becoming abolitionists must be credited with being among the first to understand that the augmenting Union Army was the key to political policy. To be sure, in 1861 and 1862, bluecoats ranged only the peripheries of Dixie. But in border states and on isolated offshore Atlantic islands, the mere presence of Yankee troopers snapped links of slavery, unless Army commanders chose to return fugitive Negroes to "loyal" masters as the hated Fugitive Slave Law required. Halleck and McClellan chose this latter conservative course. Frémont directly freed slaves of rebel owners in his jurisdiction by martial proclamation; Butler labeled fugitives "contrabands" and avoided the storm.

But storm there was, and though Lincoln tried to ignore its existence, the dark cloud of the relationship of the United States Army to slavery's existence would not fade away. In August 1861 the Congress, under leadership of Illinois Senator Lyman Trumbull, passed a Confiscation Act that theoretically libeled property, including slaves, employed on behalf of the rebellion. The law provided no enforcement mechanism, however, and did not specify that "confiscated" slaves should go free, even though it was obvious that the Confederacy lived off the fruit of black muscle. Nevertheless, Lincoln saw fit to modify Frémont's proclamation freeing rebels' slaves so far as it exceeded Congress' Confiscation law, seeing that proclamation as an unwarrantable political decision by a military subordinate and as an affront to border state Unionists.

Lincoln's action affronted abolitionists in turn. In the statement that follows, a leading spokesman for this view points up the Radical Republican–abolitionist stand as of the new year, 1862.

Less well-known than Garrison, Wendell Phillips, or Theodore Dwight Weld, George Barrell Cheever for fifty years exerted almost unremitting pressure on behalf of numerous reforms and was one of the most effective wartime protagonists of abolitionism as a necessary and proper element in the reconstruction of the Union. He brought from his Maine boyhood and Andover education a deep sense of the responsibility of society to provide for the earthly needs of man as a means of achieving Christian life, and out of that sense came a commitment against slavery. In the autumn of 1861, having returned to the United States from a trip abroad, he pressed on to take advantage of the opportunity for abolition that he felt the war had opened. There could be no victory, no reconstruction, without freedom.

A masterly orator and a powerful writer, Cheever blasted at Lincoln for his timid policy with respect to Frémont and insisted that the Army must become an abolitionist force. Although some newspaper columns and pulpits closed against him as a result of his unflinching forthrightness, Cheever, in the words of his most recent biographer, ". . . was not wholly dependent upon any one newspaper. From his pulpit at Union Square [New York City's fashionable Church of the Puritans], from the rostrum of the Cooper Institute, the Tremont Temple in Boston, the House of Representatives in Washington, and numerous other platforms throughout the North, he reached the ears of thousands with his pleas for emancipation and negro rights."[5] As matters worked out, it was Cheever who was the prophet, not his critics. Here is his article, "The Slaves are Free by Virtue of the Rebellion and the Government is bound to Protect Them," which appeared in the New York *Independent,* January 16, 1862.

A mistaken notion is still widely prevalent that notwithstanding the rebellion of the Southern slaveholding states against the United States Government, and the consequent forfeiture of all their rights and claims under that Government, and the duty of that Government to conquer those revolted states, and extend its authority over them as conquered territory,

---

[5] Robert M. York, *George B. Cheever, Religious and Social Reformer, 1807–1890* (Orono, Me.: University of Maine Press, 1955), pp. 189–190. On oratory, see George W. Julian, *Political Recollections, 1840–1872* (Chicago: Jansen, McClurg, 1884), p. 370; and George I. Rockwood, "George Barrell Cheever: Protagonist of Abolition," American Antiquarian Society *Proceedings,* N.S., XLVI (April 1936), 82–113. See too on all these matters, James B. McPherson, *The Struggle for Equality,* pp. 238–239.

their right of slavery, their right of property in man, their claim to the possession of near four millions of the inhabitants of those states as slaves, still remains to them inviolate, unbroken. It is even asserted that it would be a usurpation, a monstrous, unwarranted stretch of power on the part of our Government, to emancipate those slaves, to declare them free, even for the purpose of crushing the rebellion. It is unfortunate that such an error should prevail at a time when the Government needs to be strengthened and animated to strike this just and sure blow for conquering the rebellious Confederacy, and putting our cause unquestionably on the side of righteousness and God.

Even if the rebellious states ever had any claim on our Government for the protection of their assumed right of slavery, it must be admitted that they have themselves destroyed that claim and cut us loose from that obligation by the rebellion. . . . *The slaves are free by this rebellion, ipso facto;* and our Government, the Government of the United States, can exercise no power in regard to them, no authority over them, *but only as freemen.* The Government of the United States has no right to touch them, no right to lay its hand upon them, but in this category. So far, then, from its being an undue stretch of power or authority to declare them free, it is the unquestionable right, privilege, and duty of the United States Government to announce this fact to the whole world, and to protect the slaves themselves, in their freedom, from the power of the rebellion.

Let us examine the matter, first, as to the only possible ground of any authority whatever in regard to the slaves.

The only point at which the United States Government ever could touch the slaves is through the clause respecting fugitives, and even through that medium, at that point of contact, *only as fugitives,* and not as slaves, not as property. And only as fugitives from one state *into another state,* and only as fugitives from *service due*. Even if fugitives, yet not being fugitives from the state where the service is due, not escaping from one state to another, the U. S. Government can have nothing to do with them, cannot touch them, has no power over them.

Much less has it any power *against* them in consequence merely of the fact that the United States army has possession of the country where they are, and that they are seen within the lines, or claimed by their pretended owners. The United States can know no man as a slave, nor treat him as a slave, nor as property: but has authority in any way only in case he is a fugitive from service from one state to another state, and then as a fugitive from service only, and not as a slave.

It is only by local state laws, and not the laws or the power of the United States, nor anything in the Constitution or Government, that the slaves are or can be held as slaves: and consequently, if those local state laws fail, or are cut off from their relation to the United States Government, as they are by the rebellion, the state of slavery fails and falls. Consequently, whenever the slaves come directly into personal contact with the United States, and under the Government and laws of the United States, it must be as freemen, and can be *only* as freemen, there being no slave-code of the Government, nor any power by which the Government can hold a slave, nor any recognition of the state of slavery, nor any permission or possibility of it, under the Government, nor any way by which the Government can receive slaves, or make slaves, or legislate over slaves, or take care of slaves, as slaves, but only as freemen: no possibility of holding slaves as property, for others, no possibility of guaranteeing the security of such persons as property, no authority to make laws in regard to them, except as persons owing allegiance to the Government, and under its authority and protection as freemen.

Now by virtue of the rebellion, the slaveholding states engaged in it have withdrawn from their allegiance to the United States, and taken all their laws and institutions with them, away from all connection with or dependence upon the United States Government and laws, and have entered into a connection with and dependence upon another government, making such changes in their own general constitutions and state laws as were required for such new relation, and abrogating all laws and relations connecting them with the United States Government, all oaths of allegiance, all claims or acknowledgments of protective interference, guardianship, interest, advantage, execution of statutes, security of property, arrest and return of fugitives or of criminals, and in fine anything and everything formerly claimed or defended as owing to them from the United States Government, or from them to that Government.

They have, in fact, abdicated all governmental authority and existence in relation to the United States, have abdicated their state sovereignty as connected with the United States, and transferred it to the Confederate Government, a government at enmity against the United States, and not permitting any states thus acknowledging its authority to maintain any relation with the United States Government, or receive any protection from it, or acknowledge any dependence upon it. Consequently, by virtue of this rebellion, *the state of slavery falls and is annihilated,* with reference to the United States Government; all the right of slavery before pretended, as in relation to or dependence upon the United States Constitution and Government, having utterly gone, having no more existence, being transferred to the rebellious Confederate Government, so that the United States Government can no longer rightfully know or recognize, as having any authority, any of the municipal regulations or state laws of those rebellious states; especially cannot know or acknowledge or permit any laws or transactions as valid which take away from under the authority and right of the United States Government any of the inhabitants of those states, transferring their allegiance to the rebellious Government, and making rebels of them.

The United States Government cannot acknowledge or treat any of the inhabitants of those states as owing allegiance to those states, or to the Confederate Government of those states, or as belonging to those states or to that Government, or as being the property of any *other* inhabitant of those states acknowledging that Government, or as being the slaves and property of *any* of those inhabitants. All such claim, authority, and relation is annihilated, and all the relations of all persons in those states revert, by virtue of the rebellion and abdication of those states, directly to the United States, *as free persons,* there being no legal relation between the Government of the United States and any persons holding allegiance to it, or claimed by it as in such allegiance, and under its authority, *except as free persons,* and no possibility of any relation as slaves.

Consequently, all assumptions of authority by the United States Government over the slaves, or any of them, *as slaves,* all treatment of them as such, as illegal, is a cruel and monstrous usurpation, is an absolute and terrific transfer of the state of slavery from its exclusive and only possible tolerated place of existence, the bosom of slave states under slave law, to the bosom of the United States, and the possession of the United States Government.

The slaves of the rebellious slaveholding states are, by virtue of the rebellion, free, being discharged from all obligations before resting upon them of obedience to the laws of those states, and bound in obedience and allegiance to the United States. They must be in allegiance either to one Government or the other; but if we claim them, and claim authority over them, as owing allegiance to the United States Government, this can be only as freemen, for the United States have no authority over slaves, no laws by which they can hold or govern slaves, as slaves, nor transfer them as slaves from the Government of a rebellious state to the Government of the United States.

But if we say they are still slaves, and treat them as such, then they are in allegiance to the rebellious states, through their owners, and to the rebellious Confederate Government, and we have no authority over them.

But by virtue of the rebellion they are in reality FREE in every way and relation to the United States in which we can consider and examine them; and the United States Government can *treat* them as slaves only by *making* them slaves. The United States Government has no authority over them but by United States law, which is law solely for free persons and not for slaves. The United States Government kidnaps every person that it takes and treats as a slave. Every commander in our armies has kidnapped every person whom he has dared, under pretended authority of the United States, to return into slavery. Every such commander, in every such act, is a man-stealer. The President of the United States and every member of his Cabinet, is a man-stealer, a maker of slaves, and a usurper of the power of the United States Government for that purpose, if either of them, by proclamation or act, forbid the freedom of any person held as a slave in any of the rebellious slaveholding states, or declare or treat, or command to be treated, any such person as a slave coming from any of those states. Neither the President, nor the members of his Cabinet, nor General McClellan, nor any of the generals of the army, nor the whole army together, nor the United States Government, nor any of its officers, nor the Congress in any of its capacities, have the lead authority over any such person, black or white or olive-colored, *but as a free person, owing allegiance to the United States Government,* and entitled, as in such allegiance, and under such authority, to the protection of the United States Government, secured by the Constitution to every person, of the rights of life, liberty, and property, never to be taken away but by DUE PROCESS OF LAW.

4. GEORGE JULIAN, SPEECH

January 14, 1862

Men of Cheever's stamp found in George W. Julian a champion for many of their views. Julian, an Indianan, came to the tasks of war already a veteran of twenty years of reform agitation, having given special attention to the need for more equitable land distribution policies than American governments had followed. When the Thirty-seventh Congress began its 1861 sessions, Julian was one of the few Republicans who was clearly identifiable as a Radical, and he gloried in the description.

In prewar decades Julian had held unswervingly to the need for containing the expansion of slavery, and soon after Sumter, he accepted the need for abolition of slavery everywhere as a necessary war aim—indeed, as the only Union goal that was likely to reward its military effort with success. Like Cheever, he saw the war as an opportunity for liberty. No reunion of the states could be worth much unless it involved freedom for slaves, i.e., a reconstruction of Southern society.

Julian was no egalitarian pioneer. His deep fear was that if continued overlong, the war might damage beyond repair all democratic institutions. Therefore abolition was justified because it would advance the day of victory to safe margins.

Hardheaded in his view of the nature of the war, he was incurably incapable of effective cooperation with Republican colleagues, many of whom were as prickly and individualistic as himself. Julian was as one with his Radical brethren in his ardent belief in the need for abolition, however, and in his concern over the survival and vitality of political democracy.[1] His phrase, "free thought and its free utterance must be the condition precedent of all progress," aptly describes a basic tenet of Radical Republicans.

Julian later noted that

> the congressional speech, during the late war, was a power in the country. It was quite as much the educator as the reflex of the public mind. Very large editions of this speech ["The Cause and Cure of our National Troubles," January 14, 1862] were published; and whoever will recall the state of the country at the time, the extent to which "Border State" policy and Conservatism swayed the administration, and the Radicalism it finally accepted as a necessity, will be able to estimate the value and timeliness of its utterances.[2]

Mr. Chairman, the *cause* of this gigantic conspiracy against the Constitution and laws is the topic which meets us at the very threshold of any intelligent thought or action on our part. What produced this infernal attempt upon the nation's life? . . . What power is it that has run through the entire gamut of ordinary villainies, and at last turned national assassin? These questions demand an answer. Shall we postpone it, as some of our loyal men advise us, till peace shall be restored, and the Union reëstablished? Sir, this would be to affront common sense, and surrender our mightiest weapons to the rebels. . . . If we expect the favor of God we must lay hold of the *conscience* of our quarrel, instead of keeping it out of sight. The revolutionary struggle of our fathers was preceded by the most exhaustive discussion of the causes which produced it,

---

[1] See Patrick Riddleberger, "The Making of a Political Abolitionist: George W. Julian and the Free Soilers, 1848," *Indiana Magazine of History*, LI (September 1955); and by the same author, "George W. Julian: Abolitionist Land Reformer," *Agricultural History*, XXIX (July 1955), 108–115.

[2] Julian, *Speeches on Political Questions* (New York: Hurd and Houghton, 1872), pp. 154–179 (hereafter cited as Julian, *Speeches*).

and which "a decent respect for the opinions of mankind'
required them "to declare." . . . There was no vital question
which they sought to ignore or postpone. So should it be with
us to-day. Stern work has to be done, and our appeal must be
to the enlightened judgment and roused moral sense of the
people. The cause and the cure of our troubles are inseparably
connected. . . .

It is argued, in very respectable quarters, that the slavery
question has nothing to do with our present troubles. This
rebellion, we are told, is the crowning fruit of the heresy of
State Rights, as expounded by some of the leading statesmen
of our country, and the issue involved, therefore, is simply the
old one between the Federal and Democratic parties. Sir, I
hope we shall not be misled by this fallacy. I trust our detestation of this rebellion, and of the dogma on which it assumes
to be based, will not drive us into a false position. I think there
are such things as State Rights, notwithstanding the efforts of
rebels to make them a cloak for treason. I believe there is
such a principle as State Sovereignty, recognized, while limited, by the Federal Constitution itself. . . . Whether the Constitution has been made to dip towards centralization or State
Rights, the disturbing element has uniformly been slavery.
This is the unclean spirit that from the beginning has needed
exorcism. Without it there were not defects enough in the
system of government which our fathers left us to endanger its
success, or seriously to disturb its equilibrium. To charge this
rebellion upon secession, and not slavery, is like charging the
domination of slavery itself upon the invention of the cotton-
gin. . . .

Mr. Chairman, when I say that this rebellion has its source
and life in slavery, I only repeat a simple truism. No fact is
better understood throughout the country, both by loyal and
disloyal men. It is accepted by the people as if it were an
intuition. And the germ of our troubles, it must be confessed,
is in the Constitution itself. These may seem ungracious words,

and will certainly win no applause; but it is best to face the truth, however unwelcome, and, if possible, profit by its lesson. . . . South Carolina and Georgia loved slavery better than they loved the Union, and hence our Union with them has proved ill-matched, unnatural, and calamitous. The Constitution received its life in concessions which slavery *demanded* as conditions of union, and slavery, from that moment, has assumed to deal with the Constitution as its master. The rebels to-day in arms against the government are the fit representatives of the rebels whom our fathers sought in vain to make loyal by concessions in the beginning.

I do not say that the founders of our government are to be judged in the light of the terrible evils which have been the off-spring of their mistake. . . . They thought they were simply yielding to slavery a transient sufferance, a brief hospitality, so that it might die and pass away "decently and in order;" and they did not dream that the evil thus abetted would treacherously demand perpetuity, and bid freedom serve at its black altar. . . . The first fatal concession to this rebel power prepared the way for a second, and the history of its relations to the government is a history of persistent but unavailing endeavors to placate its spirit, and make it possible for the nation to live with it in peace. . . . Sir, it has ruled the Republic from the beginning. To pet and please it seems to have been the work of our lives, and upon its rebel altar our public men, through long years of devil-worship, have offered their sacrifices.

Nor has the Republican party, Mr. Chairman, been wanting in tokens of forbearance towards the slave interest. While emphatically avowing an anti-slavery policy [with respect to federal territories], to a certain extent, it has been still more emphatic in *disavowing* any purpose to go beyond its self-imposed limits. Nothing could exceed the persistency, emphasis, and fervor with which its editors, orators, and leaders have disowned the intention to interfere with slavery in the

States of the South. They have protested, perpetually, and with uplifted hands, against "abolitionism," as if slavery had the stamp of divinity upon its brow. Denials, disclaimers, deprecations, virtual apologies to slavery, have been the order of the day with very many of our leaders; and so perfectly have we understood the art of prophesying smooth things, that multitudes have joined our organization, less through its known anti-slavery purpose, than the disavowal of any such purpose by those who have assumed to speak in its name. Great forbearance, moderation, and a studious deference to the constitutional rights of slavery, have uniformly marked the policy of the Republican party, and would have prevented this rebellion, had it been possible through the spirit of conciliation. Its chosen President is a cool, cautious politician, of conservative antecedents and most kindly disposition. No fact was better known to the leaders of this rebellion than that their constitutional rights were perfectly safe in his hands. . . . So systematically did he seem to go down into the Valley of Humiliation, that some of his own party friends, yielding to their impatience, pronounced the first six weeks of his administration simply a continuation of the policy of his predecessor. Every conceivable expedient was resorted to to preserve the public peace, and with such ingenuity and steadfastness did the Executive pursue his policy in this direction, that the rebels were at last obliged to fire upon Fort Sumter for no better reason than the sending of provisions to prevent our garrison from starvation, which he kindly assured them was the sole purpose of the expedition.

Sir, this rebellion is a bloody and frightful demonstration of the fact that slavery and freedom cannot dwell together in peace. . . . Why is it, that in the great centres of slavery treason is rampant, while, as we recede into regions in which the slaves are few and scattered, as in Western Virginia, Delaware, and other border States, we find the people loyally disposed toward the Union? These facts admit of but one explanation. Kindred to them is the known character of the men who are conducting this rebellion. They tell us, as Vice President Stephens has done, that slavery is to be the corner-stone of the Southern Confederacy. Its leaders and their associates denounce Jefferson as a sophist, and the Declaration of Independence as "Red-Republican doctrine." They speak of the laboring millions of the free States as the "mud-sills of society," as a "pauper banditti," as "greasy mechanics and filthy operatives." They declare that "slavery, black or white, is right and necessary;" and this doctrine has been advocated by the Southern pulpit, and by the leading newspapers of Charleston, Richmond, and New Orleans. They believe with Calhoun, that slavery is "the most safe and stable basis for free institutions in the world." They agree with Governor Hammond, that "slavery supersedes the necessity of an order of nobility, and the other appendages of a hereditary system of government." They teach that "capital should own labor," and that "some men are born with saddles on their backs, and others booted and spurred to ride them by the grace of God." In the language of a distinguished rebel Senator, they "would spread the blessings of slavery, like the religion of our Divine Master, to the uttermost ends of the earth." By these atrocious sentiments they are animated in their revolt against the government. Sir, does any man doubt that, should the rebels triumph over us, they will establish slavery in every free State? Was not the immediate cause of the revolt their inability to diffuse this curse under the Constitution? They do not disguise the fact that they are fighting for slavery. They tender us that special issue, and have staked the existence of their Idol upon the success of their arms against us. If we meet them at all, we necessarily meet them on the issue they tender. If we fight at all, we must fight slavery as the grand rebel. . . .

I know it was not the purpose of this administration, at first, to abolish slavery, but only to save the Union, and maintain the old order of things. Neither was it the purpose of our fathers, in the beginning of the Revolution, to insist on independence. Before the first battles were fought, a reconciliation could have been secured simply by removing the grievance which led to arms. But events soon prepared the people to demand absolute separation. Similar facts may tell the story of the present struggle. In its beginning, neither the administration nor the people foresaw its magnitude, nor the extraordinary means it would employ in prosecuting its designs. The crisis has assumed new features as the war has progressed. The policy of emancipation has been born of the circumstances of the rebellion, which every hour more and more plead for it. "Time makes more converts than reason." I believe the popular demand now is, or soon will be, the total extirpation of slavery as the righteous purpose of the war, and the only means of a lasting peace. We should not agree, if it were proposed, to restore slavery to its ancient rights under the Constitution, and allow it a new cycle of rebellion and crime.

The rebels have demanded a "reconstruction" on the basis of slavery; let us give them a "reconstruction" on the basis of freedom. Let us convert the rebel States into conquered provinces, remanding them to the *status* of mere Territories, and governing them as such in our discretion. Under no circumstances should we consent to end this struggle on terms that would leave us where we began it. . . . Sir, let us see to it, that out of this war shall come a permanent peace to these States. Let us demand "indemnity for the past, and security for the future." The mere suppression of the rebellion will be an empty mockery of our sufferings and sacrifices, if slavery shall be spared to canker the heart of the nation anew, and repeat its diabolical deeds. No, Sir. The old dispensation is past. It served us as a schoolmaster, to bring us into a new and higher one, and we are now done with it forever. We determined, in 1860, that the domination of slavery should come to an end. . . .

Mr. Chairman, our *power* to destroy slavery now, I believe, is not questioned. The law of nations applicable to a state of war takes from this rebel power every constitutional refuge it could claim in a time of peace. . . .

This, Sir, is the grand weapon which the rebels have placed in our hands, and we should use it as a matter of clear and unhesitating duty. . . . So far as emancipation is concerned, constitutional difficulties, if any existed, are no longer in the way, since the Constitution itself recognizes the war power of the government, which the rebels have compelled us to employ against them. They have sown the wind, now let them reap the whirlwind. We have leave to do what the great body of the people have hitherto excused themselves from doing, on the ground of impassable constitutional barriers, and our failure to act will be as criminal as the blessings of universal freedom would be priceless. . . . Never, perhaps, in the history of any nation has so grand an occasion presented itself for serving the interests of humanity and freedom. And our responsibility, commensurate with our power, cannot be evaded. As we are freed from all antecedent obligations, we should deal with this remorseless oligarchy as if we were now at the beginning of the nation's life, and about to lay the foundations of empire in these States for ages to come. Our failure to give freedom to four millions of slaves would be a crime only to be measured by that of putting them in chains if they were free. If we could fully grasp this idea, our duty would become at once plain and imperative. We want not simply the military power to crush the rebellion, but the statesmanship that shall comprehend the crisis, and coin this "golden moment" into jewels of liberty and peace, for the future glory of the Republic. . . .

I waive none of my humanitarian grounds of opposition to slavery, but I prefer to deal with the practical issues of the crisis. I am for putting down slavery as a "military necessity," and as the dictate of the highest statesmanship. The immediate question before the country is the suppression of the rebellion, and the common laws which govern a war between nations apply to the conduct of a civil war. . . .

A right to subdue the rebels carries with it a right to employ the means of doing it, and of doing it effectively, and with the least possible cost. . . . As the most vulnerable point of the rebels, we should naturally have aimed at it our first and hardest blows; and I insist that we shall so far forget our party prejudices and the dread of "abolitionism," as to do what the dictates of common sense and a regard for our own safety so clearly demand. Facts, bloody and terrific, are every day proving that slavery, or the Republic, must perish. As the animating principle of the rebellion it stands between us and the Union, and we are compelled to smite it. To strike at it is to strike at treason; and to favor it in any way, however unwittingly, is to take sides with the rebels. . . .

Mr. Chairman, I need make no argument to prove that slavery is an element of positive strength to the rebels, unless we employ it in furthering our own cause. The slaves till the ground, and supply the rebel army with provisions. Those not fit to bear arms oversee the plantations. Multitudes can be spared for the army, since women overseers are as capable and trustworthy as men. Of the entire slave population of the South, according to the estimates of our last census returns, one million are males, capable of bearing arms. They cannot be neutral. As laborers, if not as soldiers, they will be the allies of the rebels, or of the Union. Count all the slaves on the side of treason, and we are eighteen millions against twelve millions. Count them on the loyal side, and we are twenty-two millions against eight. How shall this black power be wielded? A gentleman, occupying a very high official position, has said that it would be a disgrace to the people of the free States to call on four millions of blacks to aid in putting down eight millions of whites. Shall we then freely give the rebellion four millions of allies, at the certain cost to us of many millions of money and many thousands of lives? And, if so, may we not as well reinforce the rebels with such portion of our own armies as will make the contest equal in numbers, and thus save our cause from "disgrace?" Is the conduct of this war to be the only subject which requires men to discard reason and forget humanity? . . .

Sir, when the history of this rebellion shall be written, its saddest pages will record the careful and studious tenderness of the administration toward American slavery. I say this with the sincerest regret. I do not doubt the good intentions of the President, nor would I forget the trying circumstances in which he and his advisers have been placed. Upon them, to a very great extent, must the hopes of our country rest in this crisis. To sustain their policy, wherever I can honestly do so, as a representative of the people, is my first duty; and my second is, frankly to point out its errors, whilst avoiding, if possible, the attitude of an antagonist. Instead of making slavery the special object of attack, as the weak point of the enemy, and the guilty cause of the war, the policy of the administration has been that of perpetual deference to its claims. The government speaks of it with bated breath. It handles it with kid gloves. Very often has it spread its parental wing over it, as the object of its peculiar care. In dealing with the interests of rebels, it singles out as its pet and favorite, as the spared object of its love, the hideous monster that is at once the body, soul, and spirit of the movement we are endeavoring to subdue. While the rebels have trampled the Constitution under their feet, and pursued their purposes like Thugs and pirates, the government has lost no opportunity of declaring that the constitutional rights of slavery shall be protected by loyal men. . . .

Our soldiers have not only been compelled to take upon them the duties specially and exclusively belonging to the officers of law, provided by the Fugitive Act of 1850, but have been required to return fugitives when they had not passed out of the State in which they belonged, and where, of course, the law itself would furnish no remedy. Sir, our treatment of these fugitives has not only been disgraceful, but infamous. For the rebels, the Constitution has ceased to exist; but were it otherwise, it is neither the right nor the duty of our army to return their slaves. The Constitution deals with them as persons, and knows them only as loyal or disloyal. If they are disloyal, they are simply belligerents, and if found among us should no more be allowed to return than other rebels. If as loyal men they come to our lines, tendering us their aid, our commanders who return them to their rebel claimants should be summarily crowned with the honors of the gallows. . . .

The conduct of the administration toward General Fremont forms a kindred topic of criticism. When he proclaimed freedom to the slaves of rebels in Missouri, it was greeted with almost universal joy throughout the free States. The popular instinct at once recognized it as a blow struck at the heart of the rebellion. The order that rebels should be shot did not carry with it half the significance of this proclamation of freedom to their slaves. But the President at once modified it, so far as its anti-slavery features went beyond the Confiscation Act of July [passed in August 1861]. He had no objection to the shooting of rebels, though it was as unwarranted by the act of Congress as the emancipation of their slaves. Their slave *property* must be held as more sacred than any other property; more sacred than their lives; more sacred even than the life of the Republic. Could any policy be more utterly suicidal? . . .

The rebels may be shot, but while they keep up the fight against us their slaves shall supply them with provisions, without which their armies must perish, and the lives of loyal men might be spared. The Confiscation Act bribes all the slaves of the South to murder our people [i.e., to perform positive acts on behalf of the rebellion in order to become confiscable as a property employed in the insurrection], and the President refuses to allow the war power to go beyond it. The effect is, that if the slaves engage in the war at all, they must do so as our enemies, while, if they remain at home on their plantations, in the business of feeding the rebel army, they will have the protection both of the loyal and confederate governments. . . .

To this dread of offending slavery must be charged our loss of the sympathy and respect of the civilized world. We have no true battle-cry. We are fighting only for the Union, and taking pains to tell mankind that this does not mean liberty. We are the champions of "law and order," and by giving foreign nations to understand that we are making common cause with the rebels for slavery, or at least doing nothing to oppose it, we justify Lord John Russell in saying that this is simply "a war for independence on the part of the South, and for power on the part of the North." On the other hand, by assuming the attitude of revolutionists, the rebels appeal successfully to the sympathy of the millions in the Old World who love liberty, and whose zealous espousal of our cause could be secured by writing freedom on our banner. . . . We must let the world know that this is not a struggle for slavery in the border States, but for Liberty and Republicanism, and thus enlist the millions in the Old World in our cause, by fighting their battle as well as our own. If we fail to do this, and continue to carry on the war on the principle of "how not to do it," our grand armies will continue idle, our means of carrying on the war will be exhausted, the spirit of the people will at last give way, the power of the rebels will increase, foreign wars will be inevitable, and the cause of free government throughout the world will find a common grave with the institutions of our fathers. . . .

I must not conclude, Mr. Chairman, without noticing a further objection to the policy for which I contend. I refer to the alleged danger of this policy, and the disposition of the slaves after they shall be free. This objection, like the one just considered, invites several answers. . . .

It will not do to talk about consequences, for no possible consequences of emancipation could be worse than destroying the government and subverting our free institutions. Do you ask me if I would "turn the slaves loose?" I reply, that this rebellion, threatening to desolate our land with the grandest assemblage of horrors ever witnessed on earth, is not the consequence of "turning the slaves loose," but of holding them in chains. Do you ask me what I would do with these liberated millions? I answer by asking what they will do with us, if we insist on keeping them in bondage? Do you tell me that if the slaves are set free they will rise against their former masters, and pillage and lay waste the South? I answer, that all that, should it happen, would be far less deplorable than a struggle like this, involving the existence of a free nation of thirty millions of people, and the hope of the civilized world. If, therefore, our policy is to be determined by the question of consequences, the argument is clearly on the side of universal freedom.

I reply, in the second place, that emancipation will be wise, safe, and profitable to both master and slave. In this assertion I am sustained by all history and experience relating to the question. Most triumphantly can I refer to the case of the British West Indies. There, by an act of legislation, nearly a million of slaves within those narrow islands, and greatly outnumbering the white population, were in an instant made free. No act of violence followed. No white man suffered in person or estate, by reason of emancipation. In the island of Jamaica thirty insurrections occurred in the century which preceded emancipation, but not one has occurred since. . . .

I answer, next, that if the slaves of the South are set free they will not be pent up within the confines of a few small islands, like those subjected to the great British experiment referred to. They occupy a country stretching between two oceans, vast portions of which are yet a wilderness. There is not only abundant room for them, but abundant need of their labor. They are not unfamiliar with industrial pursuits, and if compensated for their labor, and acted upon by the renovating power of kindness, they will not only take care of themselves, but become a mighty element of wealth in the latitudes of our country peculiarly suited to their constitution. Their local attachments are remarkable, and but for slavery they would not be found either in Canada or the Northern States. But I would give them freedom, and then leave them to the law of their condition. Let them work out their own destiny, and let them have fair play in fighting the battle of life. Colonization is one of the great tidal forces of modern civilization, and the enslaved races can scarcely escape the appeal it will make to their approving judgment. Hayti, near our shores, stretches forth her hands to welcome them to happy homes among a kindred people, where they can enjoy the blessing of equal rights. Remove slavery, and I believe the negro race among us will naturally gravitate toward a centre of its own, and separate itself from the race of its former oppressors. Our prejudices, borrowed from slavery, and still continuing to hold their sway, may aid this result; but if from any cause whatever these people should seek their welfare in other lands, I would, while leaving them perfectly free in this respect, encourage them by all the reasonable means in our power. . . .

5. BEN WADE, SPEECH

April 21, 1862

Lincoln and conservative Republicans could not have risen to Radical heights without great pressure to push them there. Wartime America's strongest winds blew in from the numerous locations of the largest and swiftest-growing political institution in the nation, the United States Army.

The Army was in politics not because Billy Yank was a Negrophile humanitarian or was much interested in constitutional nu-
ances. He was intensely interested in his own survival, as was true
of his family and friends. Therefore the Union soldier and his endless numbers of home-front connections were intimately concerned
with the sources of the enemy's strength.

Doubtless combat soldiers have always thought first of surviving.
But Mr. Lincoln's army was the most literate the world had ever
known. Quickly professionalizing themselves in terms of combat
prowess, its officers and men remained incurably civilian in spirit.
They chewed endlessly among themselves over policy matters and
in letters home discussed public questions as twentieth-century
American soldiers rarely troubled to do. Soldiers' opinions flowed
directly to state and national legislators, or indirectly from their
families, to state capitals and Congress and White House, and to
ministers' pulpits and newsmen's desks. Nationwide reciprocation
existed as civilians and soldiers instructed and influenced each
other.

It appears to be clear that by the end of the first war year,
Union troopers had reached a consensus, agreeable to the Radical
Republicans, that slavery had caused the rebellion and nourished it.
Therefore slavery must give way.[1]

Naturally, Radical Republicans furthered such views among the
soldiery, their families, and their friends. Far more swiftly than
slower-moving moderate Republicans or antediluvian Democrats of
the Bayard-Vallandigham stripe, the Radicals understood that the
Union Army was the key not only to the survival of political democracy but also to its advancement. In the Congressional Joint
Committee on the Conduct of the War, the Radicals developed a
superb instrument of communication with field armies and with
home-front audiences and employed it with weighty effect, especially in 1862.

Allegations are common that the committee hamstrung General
McClellan and his subordinates, obstructed Lincoln, and operated
as a vicious Star Chamber. The rhetoric of leading committeemen

---

[1] The army as a political force is little studied, but see Charles L.
Wagandt, "The Army Versus Maryland Slavery, 1862–1864," *Civil
War History*, X (June 1964), 141–148.

lends itself to this interpretation, when it is examined by the standards of a century after the event.

As example, Wade in the following speech likened to traitors those Northerners who cloaked themselves in the Constitution as a defense for antiwar deeds or words. Yet the point must be made that loyal Northerners of the 1860's did not revere the Constitution as an abstraction. Millions of Northerners agreed with Wade that since 1800 it had fostered slavery more than liberty, and in 1860 it had produced weakness, not strength. Since Sumter, the Constitution had sheltered real or quasi-traitors and, as interpreted by the Chief Justice of the United States in the Merryman "case," had made impossible the maintenance of home-front security. Defenders of slavery and disloyalists, not victory-minded Union men, venerated the "old" Constitution in Lincoln's day. Radicals especially were coming to a vision of a refashioned Constitution in which the Bill of Rights would play a larger role than had been the case. All Republicans were bent upon winning the war, and increasing numbers of them were coming to the Radicals' view that victory was illusory without abolition. The committee was an essential instrument in the Radicals' hands, and with it they raised the nation's war aims.

In any case, recent scholarship seriously questions the validity of the older judgments on the alleged viciousness of the committee. Evidence indicates that it cooperated with Lincoln more than not, and that he employed it to hammer at McClellan, as example, when the President preferred to move secretly. Committeemen were civilian watchdogs over the bestarred galaxy, preventing dictatorship and pushing generals afflicted with "the slows" to greater vigor. The Committee was a goad, not a guillotine.[2]

Here are the words of a leading Radical and the committee's chairman to this effect. Speaking to the Senate on April 21, 1862, Wade came to the hearts of several matters involving the committee and the Union's survival.[3]

---

[2] Trefousse, "The Joint Committee on the Conduct of the War: A Reassessment," *Civil War History*, X (March 1964), 19.

[3] *CG*, 37 Cong., 2 sess., pp. 1735–1737.

We have assailed no man. We have gone forth in the spirit of the resolution that created us a committee to inquire into the manner in which this war has been conducted; to ascertain by the best evidence and the best lights we could wherein there was anything in which we could aid the Administration in the prosecution of this war, and wherever there was a delinquency, that we might ferret it out, apprize the Administration of it, and demand a remedy. I suppose it was for that purpose that the committee was created with the immense powers that were devolved upon it. I do not say whether it was wise or unwise to create such a committee. The Senator from New York [Mr. Harris] yesterday said he thought it exceedingly unwise, because the committee, as he supposed, were conducting the war; that is, placing the armies in the field, and dictating the policy of the war. We did not construe our powers in that way. We knew that in the vast business that pertained to the executive branch of the Government, it was impossible for them to look into everything connected with the conduct of the war which they would like to know and which it was most essential to the country that they should know. Therefore, having leisure to inquire into many alleged abuses that they had no power or no time to investigate, we took it upon ourselves to investigate them, and, I say here, with a discretion and with a solicitude to injure no man that has never been exceeded in any investigation of any committee on God's earth.

Sir, we have not published what we have ascertained to any mortal man except to those who were armed with the power of administering the remedy. No idle curiosity has prompted any member of that committee to proclaim to the world as idle gossip the testimony that was before it. I challenge the Senate, and every man of it, to tell me which member of the committee or where have we made known to the public what was going on before us. I admit that as we ascertained facts, the existence of malpractices, short-comings, and things incon-sistent with the proper and beneficial conduct of the war, we have sought interviews with the President of the United States, we have sought them with the Secretary of War, and on some occasions with the whole Cabinet, and there in secret have disclosed the testimony that has come to us, and we have endeavored to work out a redress, and in innumerable in-stances I know we have done it, where, had it not been for that so-much maligned committee, the Administration would have been entirely ignorant of what was going on. Patriotic as they are, vigilant as they are, anxious as they are to ascertain the truth on all subjects, they are not invested with omni-science, and with six hundred thousand men in the field and innumerable officers, it may sometimes happen that there may be an unworthy one in that number without their being aware of it. We have endeavored on all occasions to enlighten them, but not to stab any man in the dark, as I understood the gen-tleman [Senator McDougall, Dem., Calif.] to insinuate, but which he backs out of now, and says he did not intend any such thing or did not say any such thing. . . .

We are tyrannical—the nation is tyrannical, says the gentle-man; and he quotes authorities from nations at war with each other where there is no suspicion of treason; where all is loy-alty on both sides; where nations have national feelings suffi-cient to repress everything favoring the adversary, and to bring forward everything favoring their own nation. He cites these precedents to enlighten us in the midst of a civil revolution, where traitors are in our midst, where you cannot walk the streets without meeting men whose hearts are opposed to the prosecution of this war. No, sir; you cannot go through the Executive Departments but you meet with violent enemies of the Government you are endeavoring to maintain. He reads precedents from English history to show the forbearance of that nation in times of civil strife. I wonder that the reading of that did not carry him back to the time when England was involved in civil war. . . . Sir, if you look at the old records during those troublesome times, you will find that men on slighter evidence than would impeach the gentleman [from California] were hung up by the neck until they were dead, and yet he lauds the mildness of the British government. . . .

Sir, the man who invokes the Constitution in forbearance of the law to punish traitors is himself a sympathizer. There never was a man who stood up in this Senate from the time when Mr. Breckinridge preached daily in favor of constitutional guarantees [for slavery] until now, and set up constitutional barriers against punishment for treason, but what is in his innermost heart of hearts a traitor. I do not want to hear any more of a man than that he is invoking the forbearance of the Constitution and the great barriers in favor of American liberty to protect an infernal traitor in his course, to know that he is a sympathizer. Our Administration is assailed because, not having the technical evidence in their possession to bring a man to trial and judgment of death, they do not let him go at large to plot against the life of the Government. . . .

A tyranny exists here, it is said. Sir, is it not most manifest to everybody that from the time when this treason broke out, when we had traitors in this Senate proclaiming their treason on this floor, when they conspired to take the life of your President on his way to the capital, when they beset your regiments coming here for no other purpose than to defend your capital, until now, every scintilla of information that your Executive has is communicated to traitors on the other side of the river as soon as it is to the people on this side. The Administration have attempted to put that down; they have not succeeded; and yet the Senator stands there and says you should not arrest a scoundrel when you know his heart is with the enemy, but who meanly skulks from overt acts in their favor; you should not imprison him, you should not restrain him; but you must let it all go, and permit the enemy to be perfectly cognizant of every expedition and of every move you make. I am sorry that the Senator does not remain on this floor and meet the consequences of his insinuations against the Administration and against the committee.

Sir, it is perfectly manifest that if persons are shut up in dungeons, and restrained of their liberty, it is that the Constitution may live. I know it is not in accordance with the principles of our Constitution. In ordinary times it could not for a moment be tolerated; but when, with all your caution, and with all this pretended tyranny, you have not been able, as yet, to conceal a knowledge of the most important expeditions of your armies and your intended movements from the enemy as soon as your own people possess it, the man who stands up for a rigid execution of the *habeas corpus* and the law, as in time of peace, is but a sympathizer with them. While I am up, let me say that in times of revolution and rebellion like this, when whole States have come out and proclaimed their intention to destroy the life of our glorious Government, when they have their martial hosts in the field, bent on its destruction, I understand them to be entirely absolved from the protecting aegis of the Constitution. They have renounced it utterly. They have struck at your life. They would take your heart's blood. They proclaim themselves ready to do it. And yet, sir, you are to treat them with lenity! Your Constitution prescribes that no man shall be deprived of his life, or despoiled of his goods, without due process of law. It guarantees to every man the right of life, liberty, and property; but are you not compelled to advance into his country with your armies, to plant your cannon, and destroy him by whole armies together? Is that constitutional? My secession friend, if there is any such here, why do you not invoke the Constitution in opposition to our cannon and our musketry against these rebels? The Constitution protects their rights. You do not invoke it on the field of

battle. You do not summon a jury. You do not try him there
by jury, as the Constitution says you shall. Why do you not
carry your doctrines to their legitimate end? Why stop short?
Does the Senator from California pretend that when our hosts
march in battle array, and meet those of the enemy, and it is
life against life, we should summon a jury before we begin
to shoot, and see whether they had committed actual rebellion?
Your Constitution says their lives shall not be taken without
due process of law. I ask you, caviler about the Constitution,
where is the law for it? . . .

Sir, I am tired of hearing these arguments in favor of traitors.
The Constitution takes their lives, their property, their all.
Why shall we stop short? Are they not in quest of ours? If
there is any stain on the present Administration, it is that they
have been weak enough to deal too leniently with these traitors. I know it sprung from goodness of heart; it sprung from
the best of motives; but, sir, as a method of putting down this
rebellion, mercy to traitors is cruelty to loyal men. Look into
the seceded States, and see thousands of loyal men there
coerced into their armies to run the hazard of their lives, and
placed in the damnable position of perjured traitors by force
of arms. If there is a man there bold enough to maintain his
integrity in the face of these infernal powers, do they scruple
to take his life, his property, his all? Sir, by your merciful
course you have paid a premium to treason, and made it almost
impossible that a loyal man in the seceded States can maintain
himself at all. . . . Sir, the rule is as impolitic as it is unjust.
You should carry the avenging sword along with your armies,
and smite traitors and smite treason, and put it down, and
yield protection to honest, loyal men. Until you adopt that
course, you will war in vain. Mr. President, for one, I say let
us go forward against treason and traitors; let us put down this
rebellion at all hazards. If, in doing so, your darling institution
must go under, I shall not regret it. If it must come to this,

that the Union and slavery cannot live together, let slavery die the death, for the Constitution, the Union, and the time-honored old flag shall live forever. . . .

Those who assail the Administration on account of what they call tyranny to men sympathizing with traitors, never to my knowledge, open their mouths on this floor in condemnation of the men who have risen in arms and are endeavoring to murder your Constitution and your Government. Towards them they are as mild as sucking doves. . . . Sir, you may know all these men from this circumstance: they are the men who cry peace, peace, when they know there can be no honorable peace. . . . I am proud that we are assailed from that quarter. It shows that our shots sometimes tell. Who are they who rise up and assail the committee on the conduct of the war? Are they men who are eager to trample this rebellion under foot? Are they the men who have shown a disposition and a zeal to put down rebellion? No, sir. I am happy that we are assailed in such excellent company as that of the President and Secretary of War. I care not who they are, nor where they are; whoever shows a zeal for putting down this rebellion will find that he is in the category to be assailed by this new organization to reconstruct the Government. . . .

What have the committee, who have been thus assailed, done, that should call down upon them the anathemas of the Senator from California, or should compare them, as well as the President and Secretary of War, to grand inquisitors, sitting behind the backs of men to get up accusations by which they are to be tortured and destroyed at the stake? Sir, I grant you we have a zeal, yea, a determination, so far as it lies in our power, that this Government shall be maintained, that treason shall be put down at all hazards and by any means that God Almighty has put in our hands. [Applause in the galleries.] No accusation of tyranny, no comparing us with inquisitorial tribunals, no mawkish sensibility in behalf of

traitors, will have the effect to deter us from our resolute determination to put treason under our feet and bring back the
Government to its old glorious bearings. Notwithstanding all
the whining in this body or outside of it, in your courts or anywhere else, this will be done.

Sir, we have heard all these arguments before. We learned
this tune a year ago from those who are now in the so-called
Confederate States. They were always crying out about violations of the Constitution, and ever ready to invoke it in aid of
treason. That was the course of remark from the lips of every
one who deserted his post and went out an open enemy to your
Constitution and your laws. Sir, I remember well when Mr.
Breckinridge stood on the other side of the Chamber, day after
day, making this same kind of speeches, accusing us of being
violators of the Constitution of the United States; and inas-
much as we plainly had the right to coerce traitors, to put
down treason by force of arms, he stood there to deprecate it,
and to invoke the Constitution as a barrier against loyal men.
The argument we have heard to-day is but a repetition of
those we heard a year ago. I could bring the arguments made
then on this floor by traitors who are now in open rebellion;
and they would make no discord with the speech we have just
heard. . . .

Sir, early in this session it pleased both Houses of Congress
to raise a committee empowered and directed to inquire into
the conduct of this war. I sought no position upon that committee; I had nothing to do with getting it up; but when it was
raised, being placed at its head, I cast about as did the rest
of the committee, to ascertain how we could make ourselves
most useful to the Government in the exercise of the vast
power which it had been the pleasure of Congress to confer
upon us. We instituted a pretty broad inquiry into public
affairs, and especially in the manner in which this war had
been conducted. . . . I repeat again . . . that if there ever was

a committee that proceeded with discretion, with moderation, with a care and forbearance that man should be injured, it is the committee whom I am chairman, and of whose action I am proud. We are an inquisition forsooth! The gentleman assailed the committee long before he knew anything of its action. He accused us of proceeding *ex parte,* getting a kind of illegitimate testimony, going forward with that and presenting it to the Administration to the detriment of innocent men. . . .

I have listened to this kind of defence of traitors long enough. What has the Administration done that this gentleman should rise here in the Senate and brand them as tyrants and despots and inquisitors, and tell us he is going to run a parallel between the President and Secretary of War and the old inquisition? Why, sir, only think of the perfect burlesque! The President of the United States, who neither by word or deed or thought would harm a hair of any man's head, who, of all men I know, is the most reluctant to offend anybody, but who, as a patriot, is anxious to vindicate the Constitution of the United States and the Government he has sworn to support—and he does it with a toleration and a mildness towards these traitors that has met with the censure of many good men, who think he does not go far enough—this mild, equitable, just man is to be branded here, by a Knight of the Golden Circle, with being a grand inquisitor, armed with tyranny, whose purpose it is to destroy the rights and property and the lives of men! Sir, the thing is absolutely ridiculous. . . .

Mr. President, that man is not quite honest who thus argues constitutional questions in this Senate, and invokes the Constitution in behalf of the rights of every man precisely as he would in times of peace, where there were isolated cases of delinquency, and where it was safe to bring a man to trial. The man who says it, and would have you proceed with these traitors precisely as you would in time of peace, is endeavoring to deceive the public. Can you prosecute a traitor south of

Mason and Dixon's line? As the old saying is, you might as well try the devil in hell and summon as jurors his chief angels. It is impracticable; it cannot be done. Why, then, start up here contending that men should be tried by all the constitutional guarantees that are thrown around them in peaceful times? I repeat what I said: as no jurist has yet undertaken to define the limits to which a man might go in the honest defence of his life when assailed, so no statesman would undertake to limit the powers that the Government might use to preserve its life when assailed by traitors. I defy the gentleman to make an argument worthy of the name again in that proposition.

Do you think that we will stand by, yielding to your argument, while you fetter our legs and bind our arms with the Constitution of the United States that you may stab it to death? Is that your idea of the Constitution, that it is made to tie the hands of honest men from its defence while traitors may stab it to the heart? That is the use you would make of the Constitution of the United States. Sir, I say again, I have no scruples about the Constitution of the United States as wielded against traitors in this time of violent revolution. You have seen that the ordinary course of the common law and of the Constitution cannot be followed. Shall the Constitution lie down and die? Must we give up all our glorious principles that were defended by it because traitors have assailed it in such way that they have prevented its operation? Sir, folly like that would deserve the ignominious fate which would inevitably follow so foolish a course. . . .

It is to preserve these great barriers of American liberty that I am zealous in the defence of my country, when they are sought to be overthrown by these traitors with arms in their hands. But, sir, is it not marvelous that they who are so zealous of this Constitution, and of these time-honored guarantees, should not have a single word to say against those who are in open hostility to overthrow and destroy them all? . . .

6. THE REVEREND GEORGE

F. NOYES,

SERMON TO TROOPS

July 4, 1862

Educable Union soldiers required educators. A superb corps of
mentors was at hand, in the persons of numerous ministers of
"radical" Christian bent who, in the words of the Unitarian theo-
logian Octavius B. Frothingham,

> went into the regiments as army chaplains; they went as privates
> into the ranks; . . . they worked the associations which were
> organized for the soldiers' relief; they urged the policy of eman-
> cipation; they went among the blacks as teachers. Their pulpits
> were draped with the flag and resounded with war-sermons;
> their vestry rooms buzzed with the laborers for the Sanitary
> Commission. They were unwearied in their efforts and indomita-
> ble in their faith. They believed in the divine decree of the
> crisis and the divine inspiration of the crisis. They saw no issue
> possible but liberty, and liberty was the mend-all and cure-all—
> vindicator, consoler, regenerator, savior. They never felt discour-
> agement save when the cause of liberty trembled on the scale
> of fortune and that discouragement could not last, for they de-
> voutly believed that at last servitude and servility must kick the
> beam. The Army of the North was to them the church militant;
> the leader of the Army was the Avenging Lord; and the recon-
> struction of a new order, on the basis of freedom for mankind,
> was the first installment of the Messianic kingdom.[1]

Evidence is weighty that soldiers in great numbers came to see

---

[1] Frothingham, *The Religion of Humanity: An Essay* (3rd ed.; New
York: Putnam, 1877), pp. 19–20.

matters in similar vein. Bluecoats accepted leadership in political matters from chaplains of the character Frothingham described, because what these preachers said meshed in with the realities of the Army's life. Consider that Union soldiers went willingly even on secular holidays to hear chaplains preach—a phenomenon unheard of in World Wars I or II! Sermons by military chaplains became sources of Army opinion from which Radical Republicans, especially in the Congress and most particularly of the Committee on the Conduct of the War, drew strength, inspiration, and instruction.

On July 4, 1862, Baptist minister George F. Noyes preached the following sermon to the toughened footsloggers of Doubleday's brigade, bivouacked near Fredericksburg, Virginia. Note how he joined in a trinity the Army, the Republican Radicals, and political democracy. His firm rejection of any need for the establishment of a military dictatorship as a quick way to win the war reflects a confidence in the capacity of civilian institutions that grew out of the Jacksonian wellsprings of Radical Republicanism, and that was reflected in the suspicious attitude of members of the Joint Committee on the Conduct of the War toward McClellan especially.[2]

We are here, not as Northerners, but as citizens of that *United* States he [Washington] labored so hard to establish. We claim *national citizenship,* and *birth-right privilege* in every spot of ground in Virginia, as in New York or Pennsylvania. Every acre of it is part and parcel of the Union he so much loved; and we should be recreant to his memory, did we permit traitorous hands to rob a single acre from us. May his spirit of patriotic devotion, and all-comprehending patriotism be with us, and bless our Country to-day.

---

[2] Noyes, *Celebration of the National Anniversary by Doubleday's Brigade, at Camp Opposite Fredericksburg, Virginia, July 4, 1862.* David Christy, *Pulpit Politics: Or Ecclesiastical Legislation on Slavery in its Disturbing Influences on the American Nation* (Cincinnati: Faran & McLean, 1863), protested against the mixing of church and statecraft in the Union's armies. He was a defender of slavery who never altered his views.

Standing, as we do, in the very crisis of our National destiny, our theme springs naturally from the hour. That you value the democratic principle, which is the seed-grain of Republican Institutions; that you love the Union, which grew up from that seed-grain; that you revere the men who framed the Declaration of Independence, and made the Fourth of July a holy day for us; all this is made clear as the sunlight, by the fact that you are here. A smooth-tongued *hypocrite* may declaim, in honeyed words, about these great blessings; only a *patriot* leaves home and friends, ready, if need be, in this great cause, to suffer and to die. The man who has taken his life in his hands in a contest like this, needs no homily on patriotism from me. I greet you rather as the worthy successors of the heroes of 1776, brothers in sympathy with the men who wrote out a part of our country's history with shoeless and bleeding feet, on the white snow of Valley Forge. . . .

Let us come then directly to the questions and the duties of the present hour. In a Republic like ours, bayonets may safely be allowed to *think;* especially on this Anniversary the soldier, for a brief period at least, is allowed to put on over his uniform the toga of American citizenship. Among these privileges one stands pre-eminent, and that is the privilege of his own thinking, adopting his own political creed. In despotic Europe the troops are sometimes compelled to vote as their generals may dictate, but I know of nothing in the articles of war which permits an American officer to detail his soldiers to march to the polls and vote any political ticket. So long as the American confines himself to the honest use of the *ballot*, he is left free and untrammeled; it is only when he makes traitorous appeal to the *bullet*, that it becomes necessary to let loose the dogs of war. But, in these few remarks, I would seek to avoid any word which might disturb the slumbering ashes of old political controversies, or lead us for a moment to forget, that far away from home associations, surrounded by men who hate us, and by women who hide their faces as we pass, we stand together, shoulder to shoulder, devoted to a common cause, and marshalled against a common enemy. . . .

For one, I believe *absolutely* in a government of the people. I have heard, in these latter days, from some unable to bear up under the responsibilities of freedom, whispered desire for a monarchy or military dictatorship. I can regard the American who can entertain such an opinion, only with contempt and scorn. Like the foolish ostrich, he would bury his head in the sand, unconscious that he thus offers only a surer mark for his enemy. Such a man should be clad in crinoline, were it not that he would disgrace our noble, patriotic, self-sacrificing women of America. If he had presence of mind enough to make a fair examination, he would find that there is not a single evil in our present form of government which is not ten-fold enhanced even in England, the nation usually selected as a model, by the very few timid, half-fledged Americans among us. . . .

Is it complained that we have not a *strong* Government? A nation which arms and equips more than half a million of men in six months, builds a navy in the same time, blockades a long line of sea coast with a strictness never before known in the world's history, and projects, even in the midst of a rebellion like this, a railroad to the Pacific, is strong with the strength of a mighty people. England, you will remember, saw thousands of her troops perish in the Crimea from a defective commissariat, the Crimean army was indeed well nigh strangled with red tape, as is clearly shown by the Roebuck Committee, in the House of Commons. America, on the other hand, gives her soldiers more than they can eat, and has, considering all the circumstances, looked out for their comfort with a protecting care, never before known in war. The foreign press, ready to wound us in every vulnerable point of our national shield, have lately taken up a contrary accusation—they now say our Government is *too strong,* does not respect the habeas corpus, is too fond of inviting traitors to the hospitalities of Fort Lafayette. How these organs of a pampered aristocracy hate a government of the people, and how they would shout for joy could America wither and die! But the good cause prospers despite their howling, while we, who are most interested, could even spare from yonder City of Fredericksburg a *few traitors more* to be entertained within stone walls.

Those of you who have lived under monarchical or despotic rule, need no word of warning in this regard. You know too well the difference between a Republic and a Monarchy. In those countries of wealthy *thousands* and beggared *millions,* where the *few* own all the land, and the *many* glean by wearying toil a scanty subsistence; where the *few* do all the governing, and the many sit like dumb beasts obeying their orders; where a titled aristocracy monopolizes all that is most desirable of worldly position; let him, who will, find something to praise and imitate. I confess I find none. Every day's travel among the splendid cities of Europe has only made me more thankful, more proud to say, I am an American citizen. And never before had I so strong a faith in the great Republican idea, and in the Constitution given us by our Fathers. Exposed to a rebellion which would have torn in pieces any other nation, taken unawares, and where treachery had crippled and disarmed us, unprepared for war, we have found all the powers in the Constitution necessary for the most vigorous measures, and we have found money and men in abundance, nobly to sustain and carry these measures forward. A Constitution which will stand such a shock as this, a Union which will bear without ruin such a fearful strain as this, is well worth living for, nay, more, it is well worth dying for, if it be necessary; to this will we cling as our sheet anchor in every coming storm. Whatever of peril may be in the future, whatever the madness of treason may suggest or attempt, whatever the wicked ambition of any man, soldier or politician, may prompt, on this point we will stand forever firm. We came here to fight for the Union and the Constitution, and no matter what reverses may come, we will have no *suggestion even* of the one-man power. The man who hints at a dictatorship, or any approach to despotic rule, is a traitor, and should be treated as such. As Americans, we mean to do our own governing, we mean to be our own masters. We do not intend to lift upon our bayonets any man into the dictatorial throne. By the blessing of God, we have outgrown the despotic follies of the old world, and stand pledged to the Past and to the Future, to our fathers and to our children, to remain true to our birthright privilege. For one, I believe to-day, as never before, in the true democratic idea— in war, domestic or foreign, it has made us brave and powerful, in peace it has come to the mansion of the rich and to the cottage of the poor, with impartial blessing. . . .

Against this fundamental idea, the right of the majority of Americans to govern America, these Southern Rebels have declared open war. To them it means only this: that the majority have a right to rule when they will rule just as the minority shall dictate. In other words, they would transplant English aristocratic rule in America. . . .

But great and fearful was the mistake of the South when it arrogated to itself the right to eternal domination. That political heresy was exploded, that spell was broken by the guns of Sumpter. Amid the roar of that opening battle, the democratic idea was vindicated anew. In this dire extremity, some timid men declared that the Union must die. *Not so*, thank God! thought the people. *Sick, but not dead*, was the universal cry.

What the political doctors could not remedy with their compromise quackeries and conciliatory humbug, the *American people* undertook with their own strong arms. The pills they are using are made, not of *calomel*, but of *lead;* their lancets are good steel *bayonets,* with manly courage to *drive them well home.* . . .

And thus our Constitution follows the law of manifest destiny. Nature has made this Continent for one people, bracing it together by long ranges of mountains, wedding State to State by rivers, whose fountains are far up in the cold North; while down, almost under the tropics, they leap into the embrace of Ocean. What God has joined together let no man put asunder. Can we parcel out the Mississippi? Are we to have four thousand miles of border line ravaged with border wars, or dotted with custom-houses from the Atlantic across to the Pacific? If we could float little South Carolina up into the polar regions and anchor her to an iceberg, until her rebel crew could cool off and become sane again, all would be glad to do it; but even that privilege is denied us.

It is this belittling doctrine of State rights which is the mother of much of our present trouble. Men forget that they have a Country, and remember only that they have a State. The Southern vision is limited—petty, small, unable to see over their State boundary lines. The Rebel does not seem to have a brain large enough to grasp a Continent, or a soul big enough to thrill with broad national considerations. He sits forever, like Diogenes, in his little tub—its hoops the boundaries of his own State; its bottom-staves these Calhoun abstractions—these selfish phantasms, called State rights,—a very leaky tub, my friends, for it might as well have no bottom at all.

We are doing all we can to cure this occular disease of the South, and by-and-by, perhaps they may be able to see even across Mason and Dixon's line, and recognize that, instead of going round forever in their own little bark-mill, they have rights and duties as citizens of the whole country. When we remember her Washingtons and Jeffersons, her Marions and Sumpters, we pray that this good day may speedily come.

We hear ever and anon, from half traitors at heart, the

timid cry: "Be sure and take care of the peculiar institution."
Now, as I take it, we are here to put down treason—to fight
for the Constitution—to save the country. The peculiar institution must take care of itself as best it may. If, in the shock
of this contest, the slave-masters lose their live stock, the army
will not probably be ordered to stack arms, draw pocket hand-
kerchiefs, and join in their lamentations. The American soldier
did not leave his loved ones at home to become a Southern
slave-catcher, or to stand guard over a rebel slave-pen. I
value the life of a Union soldier more than all the boasted
wealth of all the Rebels; and if that wealth chooses to take
to itself legs and run away, I would not peril the life or even
the comfort of a single volunteer to stop the whole of it.

Another favorite cry with a few men is this: "Save the
Union just as it was." Put things just as they were before the
rebellion, admit South Carolina at once to all her old privileges, forgive and forget, and conciliate! I don't believe that
the army is anxious for any such child's play as this. If South
Carolina needs a few years of military governorship, a few
years of territorial rule to teach her better behavior in the
future, may she have it to her heart's content. She will have
a better acquaintance with Northern mud-sills, and profit,
perhaps, by their example.

When a man puts a knife at my throat, and I succeed in
conquering and hand-cuffing him, shall I be so foolish as at
once to restore him to his former position, knife and all? Let
every man's own common sense answer this question. The
idea with some even at the North is, that the South is to be
acknowledged as an equal nation if triumphant, while, if she
is subdued after the great and fearful struggle, she is at
once to be invited into a front seat, and at once admitted to
all her old privileges. This is too much after the principle
of "heads I win, tails you lose." This would be playing the
fearful game of war with loaded dice, in which the South is
sure to win whatever may be the chances of the throw. To

hear some men talk, one would suppose that this was only a *political campaign,* and *not a bloody and bitter war.* Treason, with poisoned dagger ready to murder us, is treated as a mere difference of opinion—is too often courted and fed with honey and sugar plums, protected and cossetted and guarded by the very Government which it has plotted to ruin and destroy.

In all seriousness, as one who desires that the blood and treasure expended in this war shall bring some good fruit, let me say, that this policy seems to me suicidal and vain. . . .

PART THREE

Radicalism

Takes the Offensive

7. THE REVEREND SAMUEL

SPEARS, SERMON

October 19, 1862

By terms of Lincoln's September 1862 proclamation regarding emancipation, the first day of 1863 was the deadline for a revolution. Under the commander-in-chief authority of the President, freedom for the slaves of rebels was in effect as soon as Union advances southward made the process possible. More radical still was Lincoln's approval of the recruitment of Negroes for combat service in the Army, which meant that black men were to be armed to kill whites. To be sure, Lincoln admitted that his executive proclamation was reversible. Nevertheless, most men of antislavery mind were jubilant. The United States government had finally taken on as a strategical policy and as a new war aim the Radical Republican cry of freedom.

Although the proclamation dissatisfied leading Radicals because it failed to touch the "loyal" slaveholding states and adverted again to Lincoln's pet schemes for compensated emancipation there, with colonization for freed Negroes, one unforeseen result of its issuance was to heighten the pride of many Radicals in their outthrust position, and to give coherence to what earlier had been excessive vagueness. Consider that back in the dark days of December 1861, Wisconsin's Senator T. O. Howe had advised a confidant:

Don't hitch yourself to any measure. Don't anchor yourself to any policy. Don't tie up to any platform. The very foundations of the Government are [c]racking. . . . No mere policy or platform can outlast this storm. Clutch hold with both hands and with your teeth also [to] that great electoral principle underlying all governments both of God and men—that authority is of men and Government is for their use—and that all Government is usurped and unconstitutional which does not seek their good. Keep your eye on this principle and you will come ashore somewhere, but whether in time or in eternity I am sure I don't know.[1]

Radicalism had come a long way since then. Although Radical Republicans had been unable to prevent Lincoln from rescinding an order of General David Hunter freeing and arming rebels' slaves within his jurisdiction, the party had pushed through Congress a bar against military personnel returning any fugitive slaves and a second, more stringent Confiscation Act that affected rebels' property, although it left unsettled the dreaded question of the Negro's postwar fate.

These developments find reflection in a perceptive analysis by the Reverend Samuel Spear, *Radicalism and the National Crisis: A Sermon delivered at the South Presbyterian Church, Brooklyn, October 19, 1862* (Brooklyn, 1862). Spear was one of the churchmen whose defense of Radical principles gave to reformist politics a greater dignity and a larger audience than could otherwise have been possible. Note his lofty pride in the evolving Radical credo, and his overconfidence that the question of reconstruction was not one requiring instant action.

There are many people, in whose minds the terms *radical* and *radicalism,* are about equivalent to the terms *fanatic* and

---

[1] To nephew James Henry Howe, December 31, 1861, Howe Papers (State Historical Society of Wisconsin).

fanaticism. To their understanding these words mean *evil,* and only evil, and that continually. Hence they are convenient terms to excite the prejudices of men, and awaken popular odium. Sometimes they are used as a substitute for ideas, and quite often as the slang phrases of those who have some interest in promoting error, or practicing iniquity. I have no desire to make a plea for extremists and fools; yet there is a grand and glorious meaning connected with these much abused terms, which I wish, if possible, to rescue from all misapprehension and evil associations. I very much doubt whether it is best to be frightened simply because somebody cries out *radical;* and I am equally clear, that the term *conservative* has no natural right to monopolize the claim to either purity or wisdom. The so called conservatives are sometimes the weakest and most selfish of men. . . .

The true meaning of the term *radical,* the one which its etymology authorizes, . . . simply means to lay the axe at the *root* of the tree; and this means to go down to the bottom of things, and keep going down till you strike what may be properly designated as the *hard-pan* of fundamental truth. . . .

Such in all ages has been the professed aim of the radical spirit. I am well aware, that the history of this spirit has not always been equal to its profession. Sometimes it has been rash, impetuous, impatient, intolerant, dictatorial; sometimes also it has torn up the very foundations of society, being so vehement and lawless as utterly to fail of its own end; and yet it is equally true, that this spirit proposes to realize one of the grandest theories that ever inspired the breast of humanity. Fixing its eye on truth, it designs to assert it fearlessly and boldly, launching its sharp and oft repeated thunders against sin and error. Not infrequently, yea, perhaps generally, it makes a commotion in the world. It stirs human society, and sets men to thinking. It is itself a very thinking spirit.

In relation to *humanity*—its facts, its conditions, its wants, its duties and its destiny,—this spirit is the bone and sinew, the life and impulse of all real *progress*, alike in the Church and the State. The truth is, since the fall of Adam this world has never been just right; it is not so now; and it will not be for some time to come. There is a vast accumulation of error among men, and also a vast accumulation of iniquity, in various forms pervading human society. Human nature wants improvement. Society wants it. Hence the practical question is this:—Shall we leave things as they *are*, because they *are?* Or shall we attempt to make them better, rooting out the error and the wrong, and introducing the truth and the right? This is the question with which we have to deal; and to it the radical spirit always returns but one answer. It clamors for correction, improvement, and progress. It is indeed the spirit of progress. The enlightened radical is the man of progress. The fact that things *are*, is not in his judgment conclusive proof that they *ought* to be. He takes the liberty of inquiring into their nature; and when he has reached a conclusion, he frankly and firmly tells the world of it. . . .

Such, in a word, is my analysis of the radical spirit, taken,—first, in its elementary meaning,—secondly, in its direct and specific aim,—thirdly, in its relation to the progress and development of man from an imperfect to a more perfect form of life. This is what I mean by the phrase. This I hold to be the true and proper import of the phrase. . . .

Doubtless, there are many who glorify Luther to-day, who, if living in the sixteenth century, would have passed him by as a radical. Some people are very bold in killing *dead* lions; but no motive can persuade them to touch a living question, till all doubt about the issue is removed. Then their courage comes up to the mark. You can never find them when you want them; and when you *do not* want them, they are quite ready to help on the good cause. They are too conservative to peril any thing. Their consciences are too elastic to have much force.

I really wonder what those newspapers, and those orators and those office-seekers can be thinking about, who denounce the radical spirit, as if it were the quintessence of all evil. Are they playing with words? Are they trying to deceive the people? Do they understand what they so freely denounce? Are they honest? Have they read history? I take the liberty of saying to them, that the facts do not justify the opprobrium they design. The word *radical,* analytically and historically expounded, is a *royal* term. In reference to the momentous questions of the Revolutionary age, George Washington was a radical; Thomas Jefferson, another; John Hancock, and John Adams, another. They lived in a radical age, and were as radical as the age. They were the men of the future, while the Tories in this country and George III in England were the conservatives, the men of the present. . . .

As I survey the matter, there are three *radical* principles, crowded by the God of Providence upon this nation, and demanding our solution. The first is one of *national life;* the second is one of *moral justice;* and the third is one of an enlarged and generous *Christian philanthropy.* On each of these points I wish to say a word, beginning—

First, with the question of national life. It would be folly either to underrate or misunderstand our foe. He means to destroy this noble Union of States. His plan if successful, is perfectly fatal. Secession is the theory; but destruction is the end. Rebellion and fighting, robbery and pillage are the means of this gigantic crime against the Constitution and peace of our common country.

What have we to do in such premises? Shall we talk about peace-measures, and compromise-measures in the presence of an armed rebellion? Shall we call those our political brethren who are our public enemies, who are traitors to the Constitution, and who are putting the knife to the very throat of our national existence? Shall we by party strife, and for party purposes, seek to foment discord in our own ranks?

No—*never*—NEVER. Our duty is to put down this rebellion, to crush it absolutely, using all the means which God and nature have placed in our hands for this purpose. Our duty is to blast and brand with eternal infamy the theory of secession, and prove to the world that this Union "is a *government* in the highest sense of the term, the enforcement of whose laws, at whatever cost, is a fundamental article of its creed, just as fundamental as liberty itself." This we must do, or die as a nation. I hence regard this war for the Union as an imperative necessity. I regard it as a *holy* war. The sword was never drawn in a more sacred cause, and should never be returned to its scabbard till the end is gained. What shall be done with the rebels when they are conquered, is an *after*-question. Let us first conquer them. Let us beat them on the battlefield, as we can do, and I believe, we will do, dispersing their armies, and bringing them to absolute submission. This, I know, is a very radical measure; the land groans under the tred of contending legions; blood flows, and families weep; yet, in the circumstances of our position, no other measure meets the case. No other measure will give the death-blow to the wicked theory of secession. No other measure will preserve the integrity, the dignity, and glory of this government. No other measure will prove, that we are what we claim to be—a *Nation*. No other measure will settle this controversy upon a lasting basis. We must conquer the rebels, or be conquered by them. We must lay the military axe at the root of the tree, with an earnestness and decision that leave no doubt as to our purpose.

The second point is one of moral justice. We have practiced a great iniquity in this land. We have continued to practice it year after year, and generation after generation. In the bosom of the freest government on which the sun ever shone, we have the institution of human slavery. We have tolerated it, fostered it, legislated for it, bought territory for its extension, till it has grown to its present fearful and appalling dimensions. Not a few in this country have gone so far as to call it *right*. And not a few who think it *wrong*, have desired to say but little about it. The Southern people by one of the most extraordinary apostacies in morals to be found in the history of man, and contrary to the faith of their fathers, have canonized the institution of slavery. . . .

I am in favor of employing the whole military strength of this nation, to carry into practical execution the purposes expressed by the President in his recent [Emancipation] Proclamation. The measure, I know, is radical; yet there are times, and we have fallen upon them, when radical measures are the wisest.

As a *war-measure*, as the means of reaching a Constitutional end, which is the only aspect of the case presented in the President's Proclamation, I do not see how any reasonable man can doubt his right to adopt it. He has a right as "the Commander-in-Chief of the army and the navy," to do any thing justified by the usages of civilized warfare, which, in his judgment, may be necessary to the conquest of the rebellion. This is involved in the very nature of the war-power; and surely it is Constitutional to use the whole strength of this power to maintain the government of the United States. I am not able to see what there is in slavery so sacred, that it should be exempted from the ordinary incidents of war, especially a war provoked by itself. Let it take the consequences of its own acts. . . .

If it be objected, that this Proclamation may take effect in emancipating the slaves of those who are loyal citizens in the rebellious States, then I answer—: first, that the number of these persons must be exceedingly small, as compared with the whole people—: secondly, that a measure demanded by a great public necessity for the suppression of the rebellion, is not to be balked in its course for the sake of this small minority of persons, who are not in active rebellion—: thirdly, that the theory of the President is, that these persons should receive compensation from the Federal Government for the loss of their slaves. I confess, that I do not see any force in the objection. The loyal people of the Free States are suffering most severely in consequence of this war; and why should not the loyal people, if any there be, in the rebellious States, be willing to accept a measure, not primarily aimed at them, but designed to crush this accursed treason, even though they may be sufferers in its practical execution by reason of their connection with traitors? Is slavery so dear to them that they cannot give it up even to save the Union? If truly loyal, they will welcome the blow, and trust to the government to do them justice afterwards.

Those who are very sensitive about the Constitution at this time, who want the war prosecuted, as they say, according to the Constitution, and doubt the constitutionality of this measure, seem to forget that this very Constitution bestows upon the Government the *war*-power, of which the President is the executive agent. In discharging the trusts committed to him, the Constitution makes it his duty to conquer the foe, and use all the means in his power for this purpose. Traitors against the Constitution have no rights under it, except to be conquered and hung. They surely are not the men to plead the Constitution in their own behalf. . . .

The third question growing out of the times, is one of enlarged and generous Christian philanthropy—. It is sometimes called the *negro*-question in distinction from that of slavery. If we put away slavery, as I pray God that we may, then we must not butcher the black man to get rid of him, but treat him in the sequel of his history according to the law of love. As the superior race, we have injured him quite long enough. Let us now try to do him good. . . .

We are in the mere dawn of this problem; we cannot see very far into it at present; and the dictate of philanthropy is that we should make ourselves attentive students of the facts as they may be developed by Providence, and then act accordingly. The President, I perceive, is strongly inclined to the theory, that as we remove the system of slavery, the black race must be separated from the whites, and settled else-where. Perhaps he is right in this opinion, and perhaps the facts will show that he is not right. It is high time that the best minds in the nation should be thinking upon the subject. We have the question on hand, or judging from the indica-tions of Providence, we soon shall have in a very practical form; and we ought to be making up our minds as to what is just, and wise, and humane, and Christian. The question as to what we shall do *with* the black man, and what we shall do *for* him, if released from the bondage of slavery, let me tell you, is one of the great questions of the age. In its solu-tion he is for the most part dependent upon the friendship, the kind regards, and Christian philanthropy of the white race. He has no power to solve it himself. As he merges into freedom, he must receive his destiny from those at whose hands he receives that freedom. They will fix his position and his home rather than himself. He cannot conquer his own destiny. His intelligence, powers of combination, and resources of action are not equal to the task. He appeals to us to think for him; and think we must, and act we must, as wise and good men, thinking and acting in the fear of God, endeavoring to carry out towards the black man the prin-ciples of a sound, impartial, Christian philanthropy.

It is quite possible, moreover, that we are seriously under-rating the capacities of the black man to help himself. Per-haps what he most wants from the white race, is that we should *let him alone,* and give him a chance to work out his own destiny. This we have not hitherto done. We have sub-jected him to great disadvantages in the Free States, and in the Slave States oppressed him by one of the most cruel des-potisms that human nature ever felt. We have not been con-tent to let the black man alone, and let him take his chances with other men on the field of life. If now we would practice this species of justice towards him, both North and South, perhaps the Providence of God, at least in the course of a few generations, would show that we are making more of the negro-question than really belongs to it. At any rate, a good beginning towards the end will be to *let the black man alone* in the sense of ceasing to do him harm, in the sense of putting away slavery, and discontinuing his oppressions; and whatever remains to be done after this to assist him in the recuperative struggle for a higher life, will thereby be greatly simplified.

I have thus, my brethren, given you my thoughts upon some of the radical questions of this most radical age. . . .

8. CHARLES DRAKE, SPEECH

September 1, 1863

As was true of all the border states, Missouri was tragically divided in the sectional allegiances felt by its people, and the state, a natural crossroads, was fearfully exposed to the incursions of rebel raiders, saboteurs, and guerrillas. These unhappy conditions produced in Missouri spectacular political personalities, especially of the Radical persuasion, who favored war to the uttermost on the political as well as on the military fronts. As example, Missouri's Republicans brought forth the most severe test oath and disfranchising statutes known in any state.

Missouri's Radical Republicans were taking every advantage of the opportunity that the war provided to build a firmly based state organization. On September 1, 1863, United States Senator Charles D. Drake spoke in Jefferson City to his fellow Missourians. He told them of his pride in his Radical persuasion and posited as the essence of Radicalism as of that moment the need to support the

President's emancipation policy, to prevent any retrogression [in its coverage] through the influence of conservatives [in the matter of race] (not an impossible turn of affairs) and instead to advance abolition further so that it embraced the loyal border states as well as the specified areas of Secessia.[1] Here is a secular counterpoint for Spear's sermon on the nature of Radical Republicanism, mid-1863.

We are loyal Union men without any qualifications or conditions, and are not afraid to declare that we are, RADICALS. That is, we are for going to the *root* of the infamous rebellion which has distracted our land for more than two years, and are for destroying that as well as the rebellion. That root is *the institution* of SLAVERY. From it the rebellion sprung, by it has been sustained, in it lives, and with it will die. And until that root is pulled up and destroyed, there is no hope of permanent peace in our country. Therefore I am for pulling it up, every fiber of it. And that is what I understand it is to be RADICAL. By that I stand or fall. The position is one which necessarily admits of no compromise. It is Country or Slavery; and he is a traitor who will compromise between them.

This, in a few words, is what I hold to be our character and position here to-day. I am not afraid to go before the world upon it. I should despise myself, if I took any other. It follows that I am for using every legitimate means to destroy the rebellion, and to crush down, wipe out, and utterly annihilate every development, form, and hue of disloyalty. I would pursue disloyalty through all its infinitive turnings and twistings, and hunt it down, ferret it out, and drive it forth, till throughout our State and our land no disloyal hand should be raised, nor disloyal tongue speak, against our glorious Union.

---

[1] Drake, *Union and Anti-Slavery Speeches Delivered during the Rebellion* (Cincinnati, 1864), pp. 337–341.

It follows, further, that I uphold the Proclamation of Emancipation issued by President Lincoln on the 1st of January, 1863. I believe that Proclamation to have been a Constitutional exercise of the war power of the Commander-in-Chief of the Army and Navy of the United States, against public enemies. Were they foreign enemies, no American would question his right to strike at their main support: I affirm his right to strike at any and every support of our domestic enemies—the worse, by far, of the two. And it was a righteous exercise of his power. Slavery assailed the nation of which he was the head, and he was bound to assail Slavery in turn, even to its very death. And I hold that his Proclamation did, in law, free every slave in all the region it covered, on the very day it was issued. Not one of them has been lawfully held in Slavery since that day; nor can one of them, in my opinion, ever be lawfully enslaved again. The Proclamation is irrevocable—as irrevocable as death. No attempt at its revocation can ever make slaves again of those it made free. I accept and uphold it as the end of Slavery in the rebellious States, and I demand its enforcement there by the whole warlike power of the loyal people of the nation, as the only means of restoring abiding peace to our bleeding country.

And holding it right to use every lawful means to overwhelm rebellion, I rejoice that the President is enrolling among our country's armed hosts those whom his proclamation freed. I have no squeamishness about arming the negro. I am no half-breed Unionist, sensitive about seeing white men fight alongside of the "American citizen of African descent." No traitor is too good to be killed by a negro, nor has any traitor a right to insist on being killed by a white man. If for the sake of Slavery he turns traitor, let former slaves be his executioners; it is a just and fit retribution. Disaffection, if not disloyalty, lurks in him who opposes the arming of the negro, let him call himself what he may. For my part, I say to the President, *Go on in this good work, till the army of blacks shall be large enough to hold every rebel in subjection;* and then rebellion is at an end for ever and ever in this land.

I have been thus plain in the expression of these views, because I believe them to be the views heartily entertained by the entire body of the Radical Union men of Missouri. I do not believe there is one such man in our State who does not hold them, and who is not determined to stand by them. They spring from the deepest convictions of stern duty to our country and to the cause of Liberty. With him who opposes them we have nothing to do but to oppose him, and by all rightful means put him down. And that, my friends, is just the work which the Radicals of Missouri have before them.

To us are opposed a portion of the people of Missouri, who style themselves *Conservatives.* And who are they? Let the plain truth be spoken. They embrace all the *disloyal.* Every rebel in the State is with them. Every open or secret Secessionist is with them. Every guerrilla and bushwhacker is with them. Every Copperhead is with them. Every man who opposes the radical policy of the Government against the rebellion is with them. Every man who is under bond for disloyal practices or sentiments, is with them. Every sympathizer with the rebellion is with them. Almost every pro-Slavery man is with them. And nine-tenths of the slaveholders, I believe, are with them. And along with this motley gang of open enemies to, or fainthearted friends of, the Union cause, are associated just enough of real Union men [Drake refers here to the potent Blair family] to save the concern from going down instantly under the weight of its inherent and envenomed disloyalty. Nothing keeps that party alive this day but the presence of those Union men in its ranks, and *the concentration of official patronage and influence, State and National, in their hands.* They are the sugar-coat to the poison-pill which is sought to be administered to the people of Missouri. They alone give character to Conservatism in Missouri. They have suffered themselves to be identified with that class of our population, which would drag Missouri out of the Union in a moment, if they could; and they are supported and urged on by every man in the State whose hand or heart has been or is against his country. I profoundly regret that any of them should ever have been found in such company; but they are there, and must share the fate which surely awaits every disloyal man, whenever Missouri's loyal people can once have access to the ballot-box.

Such, my fellow-citizens, is what you and I know to be the position of parties in Missouri this day. It is not a matter of conjecture or supposition; we *know* it. We know that throughout this whole State there is not one single disloyal man in the Radical ranks. We know that every disloyal man in the State is a Conservative. We know, and desire the whole world to know, that the struggle now going on here, though ostensibly connected with the subject of Emancipation, is, in reality, *between Loyalty and Disloyalty.* . . .

9. FREDERICK DOUGLASS, SPEECH

December 4, 1863

While he was a slave boy in Maryland, illegally learning to read and write, the Negro who after his successful flight from servitude took the name Frederick Douglass came to understand the only ". . . pathway from slavery to freedom."[1] Its constituent elements were nation-wide emancipation, then education, and in the rebel states, once conquered, equal access with loyal whites to the ballot

---

[1] See Douglass' moving *Narrative of the Life of Frederick Douglass, An American Slave Written by Himself* (Boston: Anti-Slavery Office, 1845), p. 36. The 1963 Dolphin reprint was employed in this instance.

box. Quickly gaining a prominent place among Northern antislavery activists, among whom he was by far the most prominent Negro, Douglass devoted himself for fifty years to efforts to gain these improvements for colored Americans.

After Sumter he helped immeasurably to raise the sights of Republicans and all except Copperhead Northerners to these war aims, loftier than that of reunion alone. Powerful and lucid in his oratory, Douglass deeply impressed his audiences. He never deluded himself that most whites, even Northerners and Radical Republicans, were Negrophiles. Instead, as in the speech that follows, Douglass pitched his appeal to the self-interests of whites as well as to justice to Negroes.

Douglass, along with most Radical Republicans, recognized that 1863 had been the crossroads, and that the close of that year represented a beginning of a new phase of reformist effort through politics. An Englishman, visiting here in mid-1863, was struck by "the extended influence of the anti-slavery movement," reaching the level of a revolutionary impact. "Nations do not leap into revolutions or become the theater of great events without preliminary and adequate causes," the visitor further remarked.[2] Douglass and other Radical Republicans, working through the political organization and the potent antislavery societies, wanted to be the "preliminary and adequate cause" of improvements in the conditions of America's freedmen.

Here is Frederick Douglass's speech of December 1863 to the assembled members of the American Anti-Slavery Society, meeting in Philadelphia. His theme was "Our Work Is Not Done," and in the speech he spelled out the work to come for the society.[3]

[This] . . . has been a meeting of reminiscences. . . . I desire to be remembered among those having a word to say at this

---

[2] James William Massie, *America: The Origin of Her Present Conflict: Her Prospect for the Slave, and Her Claim for Anti-Slavery Sympathy* (London: Snow, 1864), p. 79.

[3] *The Life and Times of Frederick Douglass*, ed. Philip S. Foner (New York: International, 1955), III, 378–383 (hereafter cited as Foner, *Douglass*).

meeting, because I began my existence as a free man in this country with this association, and because I have some hopes . . . that we shall never, as a Society, [need to] hold another decade meeting.

I well remember the first time I ever listened to the voice of the honored President of this association, and I have some recollection of the feelings of hope inspired by his utterances at that time. Under the inspiration of those hopes, I looked forward to the abolition of slavery as a certain event in the course of a very few years. So clear were his utterances, so simple and truthful, and so adapted, I conceived, to the human heart were the principles and doctrines propounded by him, that I thought five years, at any rate, would be all that would be required for the abolition of slavery. I thought it was only necessary for the slaves, or their friends, to lift up the hatchway of slavery's infernal hold, to uncover the bloody scenes of American thraldom, and give the nation a peep into its horrors, its deeds of deep damnation, to arouse them to almost phrensied opposition to this foul curse. But I was mistaken. I had not been five years pelted by the mob, insulted by the crowds, shunned by the Church, denounced by the ministry, ridiculed by the press, spit upon by the loafers, before I became convinced that I might perhaps live, struggle, and die, and go down to my grave, and the slaves of the South yet remain in their chains.

We live to see a better hope to-night. I participate in the profound thanksgiving expressed by all, that we do live to see this better day. I am one of those who believe that it is the mission of this war to free every slave in the United States. I am one of those who believe that we should consent to no peace which shall not be an Abolition peace. I am, moreover, one of those who believe that the work of the American Anti-Slavery Society will not have been completed until the black men of the South, and the black men of the North, shall have been admitted, fully and completely, into the body politic of America. I look upon slavery as going the way of all the earth. It is the mission of the war to put it down. But a mightier work than the abolition of slavery now looms up before the Abolitionist. This Society was organized, if I remember rightly, for two distinct objects; one was the emancipation of the slave, and the other the elevation of the colored people. When we have taken the chains off the slave, as I believe we shall do, we shall find a harder resistance to the second purpose of this great association than we have found even upon slavery itself.

I am hopeful; but while I am hopeful, I am thoughtful withal. If I lean to either side of the controversy to which we have listened today, I lean to that side which implies caution, which implies apprehension, which implies a consciousness that our work is not done. Protest, affirm, hope, glorify as we may, it cannot be denied that Abolitionism is still unpopular in the United States. It cannot be denied that this war is at present denounced by its opponents as an Abolition war; and it is equally clear that it would not be denounced as an Abolition war, if Abolitionism was not odious. It is equally clear that our friends, Republicans, Unionists, Loyalists, would not spin out elaborate explanations and denials that this is the character of the war, if Abolition were popular. Men accept the term Abolitionist with qualifications. They do not come out square and openhanded, and affirm themselves to be Abolitionists. As a general rule, we are attempting to explain away the charge that this is an Abolition war. I hold that it is an Abolition war, because slavery has proved itself stronger than the Constitution; it has proved itself stronger than the Union; and has forced upon us the necessity of putting down slavery in order to save the Union, and in order to save the Constitution. [Applause.]

I look at this as an Abolition war instead of being a Union war, because I see that the lesser is included in the greater, and that you cannot have the lesser until you have the greater.

You cannot have the Union, the Constitution, and Republican institutions, until you have stricken down that damning curse, and put it beyond the pale of the Republic. For, while it is in this country, it will make your Union impossible; it will make your Constitution impossible. . . .

I know it will be said that I ask you to make the black man a voter in the South. . . . It is said that the colored man is ignorant, and therefore he shall not vote. In saying this, you lay down a rule for the black man that you apply to no other class of your citizens. I will hear nothing of degradation or of ignorance against the black man. If he knows enough to be hanged, he knows enough to vote. If he knows an honest man from a thief, he knows much more than some of our white voters. If he knows as much when sober as an Irishman knows when drunk, he knows enough to vote. If he knows enough to take up arms in defence of this Government, and bare his breast to the storm of rebel artillery, he knows enough to vote. [Great applause.] . . .

All I ask, however, in regard to the blacks, is that whatever rule you adopt, whether of intelligence or wealth, as the condition of voting [for whites], you shall apply it equally to the black man. Do that, and I am satisfied, and eternal justice is satisfied; liberty, fraternity, equality, are satisfied; and the country will move on harmoniously.

Mr. President, I have a patriotic argument in favor of insisting upon the immediate enfranchisement of the slaves of the South; and it is this. When this rebellion shall have been put down, when the arms shall have fallen from the guilty hands of traitors, you will need the friendship of the slaves of the South, of those millions there. Four or five million men are not of inconsiderable importance at any time; but they will be doubly important when you come to reorganize and reestablish republican institutions in the South. Will you mock those bondmen by breaking their chains with one hand, and with the other giving their rebel masters the elective franchise, and robbing them of theirs? I tell you the Negro is your friend. You will make him your friend by emancipating him. But you will make him not only your friend in sentiment and heart by enfranchising him, but you will make him your best defender, your best protector against the traitors and the descendants of those traitors, who will inherit the hate, the bitter revenge which will crystallize all over the South, and seek to circumvent the Government that they could not throw off. You will need the black man there, as a watchman and patrol; and you may need him as a soldier. You may need him to uphold in peace, as he is now upholding in war, the star-spangled banner. [Applause.] . . .

For twenty-five years, Mr. President, you know that when I got as far South as Philadelphia, I felt that I was rubbing against my prison wall, and could not go any further. I dared not go over yonder into Delaware. . . . I can go down there now. I have been down there to see the President; and as you were not there, perhaps you may like to know how the President of the United States received a black man at the White House. I will tell you how he received me—just as you have seen one gentleman receive another [great applause]; with a hand and a voice well-balanced between a kind cordiality and a respectful reserve. I tell you I felt big there! . . .

10. WILLIAM WHITING,

POLICY MEMORANDUM

July 28, 1863

By December 1863, when Frederick Douglass argued that "Our Work Is Not Done" until Negroes voted, the nation had already traveled a very long way since Sumter in consequence of its military effort. "Do we undervalue the liberation of the slaves?" demanded the radical Boston *Commonwealth*. "God forbid. Still less the arming of the slaves, . . . But all this is not peace! . . . [A]ll this liberating and arming the oppressed black people only ensures [the] future [of the] war with certain advantages to the right side."[1] And here was the kernel of difference between Lincoln and the Radicals. For Lincoln, military advantage was its own goal. But by the end of 1863, the great advances that the nation had made since Republicans had taken seriously the wretched Crittenden Compromise proposals two years earlier whetted the appetites of some men for achieving greater permanent gains in the practice of American democracy, as well as for continuing to forward the Union's military fortunes by enlarging the character of the war as an opportunity for liberty.

Regardless of anyone's desires, the war erected some issues that American society had to face. Emancipation forced forward the long-dreaded specter of the future of the freedmen in a white society as an issue that could not be downed or sidetracked. "A million . . . armed soldiers are debating it," Ohio's Republican congressman Albert Gallatin Riddle told his fellow representatives. "It is the argument of every red field of conflict. . . . It must be solved *and* settled. It must be talked about; all that everybody knows of, or can think about it, had better straightaway be said— said as well as men can say it; with good intent and for good purposes."[2] And so the great debate moved to another phase, from the prewar, decades-long arguments over the extension of slavery, to the issue of abolition, and then to the freed Negro's postwar status.

Very early in the war, Lincoln had worked out, in rough harmony to the rhythms set by the advances of the Union's armies, a process of re-establishing loyal civil governments in those parts of Dixie where Yankee troopers had ousted rebel authorities. The general procedure was to appoint a "military governor" of Lincoln's nomination. These officials, of unprecedented and vague powers, were charged with encouraging a return to Unionist allegiance among Southern whites in areas of Missouri, Tennessee, Louisiana, and

---

[1] March 4, 1864.
[2] January 27, 1862, in *CG,* 37 Cong., 2 sess., p. 497.

Arkansas, and on Atlantic coastal fringes where Northern military power pressed back overextended Confederate lines. The experience that Lincoln and Army occupation forces gained in these border regions developed into a formal plan for the reconstruction of presumably all the rebel states, which he presented to the Congress on December 8, 1863.

In that plan, Lincoln offered executive forgiveness, with few exceptions, to rebels who swore to a prescribed oath of future loyalty to the Union. When the number of subscribers to the oath in a state exceeded one tenth of the total of state voters in the 1860 election who otherwise qualified as voters by local ordinances, then the President, his military governor, and the Army would assist the tithe in creating a new state government, which would include abolition in its constitution. This done, the President would recognize the new state; and if Congress would admit its representatives, then "reconstruction" was completed.[3]

Lincoln's plan was built on a concept of a wartime President's powers so extended as to transcend the points of reference of earlier chief executives. It was military reconstruction, and it was the most direct imaginable intervention of the will of the national government into the internal structures of states. In terms of power, Lincoln's reconstruction plan was radical indeed.

The fact is that Lincoln enjoyed the services as mentor—with respect to the war-swollen power potentials of his office—of a prominent champion of Radical Republicanism, an old-line Boston abolitionist, William Whiting. Brought into the War Department as its solicitor—primarily in order to prepare briefs that the government employed to fend off suits, in Northern states and in border areas, alleging the unconstitutionality of conscription and internal security measures—Whiting was the most learned lawyer in the United States in matters of the international laws of war. He became the natural source of legalisms in support of the reconstruction program that the President was gradually evolving out of

---

[3] Lincoln, *Works*, VII, 53–56; William B. Hesseltine, *Lincoln's Plan of Reconstruction* (Tuscaloosa: Confederate Publishing Co., 1960), p. 25 and *passim;* W. A. Russ, Jr., "Administrative Activities by the Union Army during and after the Civil War," *Mississippi Law Journal*, XVII (May 1945), 71–89.

information he gained primarily from Army and War Department sources.

Here is Whiting's prophetic essay of July 28, 1863, issued as a letter to the Philadelphia Union League, under the title, "The Return of the Rebellious States to the Union."[4] Note its harmony with the Lincoln plan as issued the following December, so far as the assumption of national powers is concerned, as well as its expression of concern with respect to the untrustworthiness of a conquered South.

As the success of the Union cause shall become more certain and apparent to the enemy, in various localities, they will lay down their arms, and cease fighting. Their bitter and deep-rooted hatred of the Government, and of all Northern men who are not traitors, and of all Southern men who are loyal, will still remain interwoven in every fibre of their hearts, and will be made, if possible, more intense by the humiliation of conquest and subjugation. The foot of the conqueror planted upon their proud necks will not sweeten their tempers; and their defiant and treacherous nature will seek to revenge itself in murders, assassinations, and all under-hand methods of venting a spite which they dare not manifest by open war, and in driving out of their borders all loyal men. To suppose that a Union sentiment will remain in any considerable number of men, among a people who have strained every nerve and made every sacrifice to destroy the Union, indicates dishonesty, insanity, or feebleness of intellect.

The slaveholding inhabitants of the conquered districts will begin by claiming the right to exercise the powers of government, and, under their construction of State rights, to get control of the lands, personal property, slaves, free blacks, and poor whites, and a legalized power, through the instrumentality of State laws, made to answer their own purposes, to oppose and prevent the execution of the Constitution and

---

4 In Whiting, *War Powers under the Constitution of the United States* (Boston and New York: Lee & Shepard, 1871 ed.), pp. 229 ff.

laws of the United States, within districts of the country in-
habited by them. . . .

Eastern Virginia, Florida, and Louisiana are now knocking
at the door of Congress for admission into the Union. Men
come to Washington, chosen by a handful of associates, elevated by revolution, to unaccustomed dignity, representing
themselves as Union men, and earnest to have State rights
bestowed on their constituents.

If their constituents are clothed with the power to constitute a State, into whose hands will that power fall?

Beware of committing yourselves to the fatal doctrine of
recognizing the existence, in the Union, of States which have
been declared by the President's proclamation to be in rebellion. For, by this new device of the enemy—this new version
of the poisonous State rights doctrine—the Secessionists will
be able to get back by fraud what they failed to get by fighting. Do not permit them, without proper safeguards, to resume
in your counsels, in the Senate and in the House, the power
which their treason has stripped from them.

Do not allow old States, with their Constitutions still un-
altered, to resume State powers.

Be true to the Union men of the South; not to the designing
politicians of the Border States. The rebellious districts contain ten times as many traitors as loyal men. The traitors will
have a vast majority of the votes. Clothed with State rights
under our Constitution, they will crush out every Union man
by the irresistible power of their legislation. If you would
be true to the Union men of the South, you must not bind
them hand and foot, and deliver them over to their bitterest
enemies.

State Rights in Civil War.

Beware of entangling yourselves with the technical doctrine
of forfeitures of State rights, as such doctrines admit, by
necessary implication, the operation of a code of laws, and

of corresponding civil rights, the existence of which you deny.

The solution of all our difficulty rests in the enforcement against our public enemy of our belligerent rights of civil war.

Attitude of the Government, in the Beginning of the War, towards the Rebels, and towards Loyal Men in Rebel Districts.

When the insurrection commenced by illegal acts of Secession, and by certain exhibitions of force against the Government, in distant parts of the country, it was supposed that the insurgents might be quelled, and peace restored, without requiring a large military force, and without involving those who did not actively participate in overt acts of treason.

Hence the Government, relying upon the patriotism of the people, and confident in its strength, exhibited a generous forbearance towards the insurrection.

When, at last, 75,000 of the militia were called out, the President, still relying upon the Union sentiment of the South, announced his intention not to interfere with loyal men; but, on the contrary, to regard their rights as still under the protection of the Constitution. The action of Congress was in accordance with this policy. The war waged by this Government was then a personal war, a war against rebels; a war prosecuted in the hope and belief that the body of the people were still friendly to the Union, who, temporarily overborne, would soon right themselves by the aid of the army. Hence Congress declared and the President proclaimed that it was not their object to injure loyal men, or to interfere with their rights or their domestic institutions.

The Progress of Events Changed the Character of the War, and Required the Use of More Effective War Powers.

This position of the Government toward the rebellious States was forbearing, and magnanimous, and just, while the citizens thereof were generally loyal. But the revolution swept on-ward. The entire circle of the Southern States abandoned the Union, and carried with them all the Border States which they could influence or control.

Having set up a new government for themselves; having declared war against us; having sought foreign aid; having passed acts of non-intercourse; having seized public property, and made attempts to invade States which refused to serve their cause; having raised and maintained large armies and an incipient navy; assuming, in all respects, to act as an independent, hostile nation at war with the United States—claiming belligerent rights as an independent people alone could claim them, and offering to enter into treaties of alli-ance with foreign countries, and treaties of peace with ours—under these circumstances they were no longer merely insur-gents and rebels, but became a belligerent public enemy. The war was no longer against "certain persons" in the rebel-lious States. It became a territorial war; that is to say, a war by all persons situated in the belligerent territory against the United States.

Consequences Resulting from Civil Territorial War.

If we were in a war with England, every Englishman would become a public enemy irrespective of his personal feelings towards the United States. However friendly he might be to us, his ships on the sea would be liable to capture; himself would be liable to be killed in battle, or his property, situated in this country, would be subject to confiscation.

By a similar rule of the law of nations, whenever two nations are at war, every subject of one belligerent nation is a public enemy of the other.

An individual may be a personal friend, and at the same time a public enemy to the United States. The law of war defines international relations.

When the civil war in America became a territorial war, every citizen residing in the belligerent districts became a public enemy, irrespective of his private sentiments, whether loyal or disloyal, friendly or hostile, Unionist or Secessionist, guilty or innocent.

As public enemies, the belligerents have claimed to be exchanged as prisoners of war, instead of admitting our right to hang them as murderers and pirates. As public enemies they claim the right to make war upon us, in plain violation of many of the obligations they would have admitted, if they acknowledged the obligations or claimed the protection of our Constitution.

If they had claimed any State rights, under our Constitution, they would not have violated every one of the provisions thereof, limiting the powers of States. Asserting no such rights, they claim immunity from all obligations as States, or as a people—to this Government or to the United States.

When did the Rebellion become a Territorial War?

This question has been settled by the Supreme Court of the United States, in the case of the Hiawatha; decided on the 9th of March, 1863. In that case, which should be read and studied by every citizen of the Union, the members of the Court differed in opinion as to the time when the war became territorial. The majority decided that, when the fact of general hostilities existed, the war was territorial, and the Supreme Court was bound to take judicial cognizance thereof. The minority argued that, as Congress alone had power to declare war, so Congress alone has power to recognize the existence of war; and they contended that it was not until the act of Congress of July 13, 1861, commonly called the Non-Intercourse Act, that a state of civil, territorial war was legitimately recognized. All the Judges agree in the position, "that since July 13, 1861, there has existed, between the United States and the Confederate States, civil, territorial war."

What are the Rights of the Public Enemy since the Rebellion became a Territorial Civil War?

The Supreme Court have decided, in the case above-named, in effect:

"That since that time the United States have full belligerent rights against all persons residing in the districts declared by the President's proclamation to be in rebellion."

That the laws of war, "whether that war be civil or inter gentes, converts every citizen of the hostile State into a public enemy, and treats him accordingly, whatever may have been his previous conduct."

That all the rights derived from the laws of war may now, since 1861, be lawfully and constitutionally exercised against all the citizens of the districts in rebellion.

Rights of Rebels as Persons, as Citizens of States, and as Subjects of the United States, are, according to the Constitution, to be Settled by the Laws of War.

Such being the law of the land, as declared by the Supreme Court, in order to ascertain what are the legal or constitutional rights of public enemies, we have only to refer to the settled principles of the belligerent law of nations or the laws of war.

Some of the laws of war are stated in the dissenting opinion in the case above-mentioned.

A state of foreign war instantly annuls the most solemn

treaties between nations. It terminates all obligations in the nature of compacts or contracts, at the option of the party obligated thereby. It destroys all claims of one belligerent upon the other, except those which may be sanctioned by a treaty of peace. A civil territorial war has the same effect, excepting only that the sovereign may treat the rebels as subjects as well as belligerents.

Hence civil war, in which the belligerents have become territorial enemies, instantly annuls all rights or claims of public enemies against the United States, under the Constitution or laws, whether than Constitution be called a compact, a treaty, or a covenant, and whether the parties to it were States, in their sovereign capacity, or the people of the United States as individuals.

Any other result would be as incomprehensible as it would be mischievous. A public enemy cannot, lawfully, claim the right of entering Congress and voting down the measures taken to subdue him.

Why not? Because he is a public enemy; because, by becoming a public enemy, he has annulled and lost his rights in the Government, and can never regain them, excepting by our consent.

If the inhabitants of a large part of the Union have, by becoming public enemies, surrendered and annulled their former rights, the question arises, can they recover them? Such rights cannot be regained by reason of their having ceased to fight. The character of a public enemy, having once been stamped upon them by the laws of war, remains fixed until it shall have been by our consent removed. . . .

It must also be remembered that the right of Secession is not conceded by enforcement of belligerent law, since in civil war a nation has the right to treat its citizens either as subjects or belligerents, or as both. Hence, while belligerent law destroys all claims of subjects engaged in civil war, as against the parent government, it does not release the subject from his duties to that government. By war, the subject loses his rights, but does not escape his obligations.

The inhabitants of the conquered districts will thus lose their right to govern us, but will not escape their obligations to obey us. Whatever rights are left to them beside the rights of war will be such as we choose to allow them. It is for us to dictate to them, not for them to dictate to us, what privileges they shall enjoy.

The Pledge of the Country to its Soldiers, its Citizens, and its Subjects must be kept inviolate.

Among the war measures sanctioned by the President, to which he has more than once pledged his sacred honor, and which Congress has enforced by solemn laws, is the liberation of slaves. The Government has invited them to share the dangers, the honor, and the advantages of sustaining the Union, and has pledged itself to the world for their freedom.

Whatever disasters may befall our arms, whatever humiliation may be in store for us, it is earnestly hoped that we may be saved the unfathomable infamy of breaking the nation's faith with Europe, and with colored citizens and slaves in the Union.

Now, if the rebellious States shall attempt to return to the Union with constitutions guaranteeing the perpetuity of slavery,—if the laws of these States shall be again revived and put in force against free blacks and slaves, we shall at once have reinstated in the Union, in all its force and wickedness, that very curse which has brought on the war and all its terrible train of sufferings. The war is fought by slaveholders for the perpetuity of slavery. Shall we hand over to them, at the end of the war, just what they have been fighting for? Shall all our blood and treasure be spilled uselessly upon the ground? Shall the country not protect itself against the evil which has caused all our woes? Will you breathe new life into the strangled serpent, when, without your aid, he will perish?

If you concede State rights to your enemies, what security can you have that traitors will not pass State laws which will render the position of the blacks intolerable; *or reduce them all to slavery?*

Would it be honorable on the part of the United States to free these men, and then hand them over to the tender mercy of slave laws?

Will it be possible that State slave laws should exist and be enforced by Slave States without overriding the rights guaranteed by the United States law to men, irrespective of color, in the Slave States?

Will you run the risk of these angry collisions of State and National laws while you have the remedy and antidote in your own hands?

Plan of Reconstruction.

One of two things should be done in order to keep faith with the country and save us from obvious peril.

Allow the inhabitants of conquered territory to form themselves into States, only by adopting constitutions such as will forever remove all cause of collision with the United States, by excluding slavery therefrom, or continue military government over the conquered district, until there shall appear therein a sufficient number of loyal inhabitants to form a Republican Government, which, by guaranteeing freedom to all, shall be in accordance with the true spirit of the Constitution of the United States. These safeguards of freedom are requisite to render permanent the domestic tranquillity of the country, which the Constitution itself was formed to secure, and which it is the legitimate object of this war to maintain.

11. CHARLES SUMNER,

SENATE SPEECH ON RECONSTRUCTION

July 7, 1862

But what was "a sufficient number" of loyal persons in a conquered rebel state, and should this minimum include Negroes? Lincoln's solution as of December 1863 was to accept a white man's South. The point should again be made that Lincoln and his party colleagues in Congress agreed that there was to be an imposition of national demands on the Southern states once they were subdued, and that the Army must be the instrument of executing whatever policy obtained. Departure of views between the President and Radical Republican leaders in Congress and in the Northern states centered on the worthwhileness of a reconstruction policy that did not expand the practice of political democracy in the South to include Negroes.

Stated another way, Lincoln's thinking was geared to immediate wartime needs, essentially military and strategic. His reconstruction plan in effect was a weapon of psychological warfare. It seduced Southern whites away from Confederate allegiance by promising remission of punishment for treason, save for loss of slaves. This was a large advance in Lincoln's thinking since 1861.

Radical Republicans had progressed further and more swiftly than the President. A consensus was growing among many Northerners that a reconstruction should transcend reunion plus emancipation. By no means was such thinking restricted to prominent Radical congressmen. Here, as example of more homespun concern, are the words of a quite obscure Illinois lawyer, Adolph Ernst Kroeger, of Chicago. Under the pseudonym of "A Patriot," he published in mid-1863 a pamphlet in which he considered the conservatives' argument that once a rebel state gave up its fight

against the Union and renounced secession, then all wartime punitive statutes of Congress and proclamations of the President,
including that on emancipation, were void. "It seems almost superfluous to argue such a preposterous proposition," Kroeger wrote.
. . . [W]e consider the status of the rebel States after the war
indefinable and varied, to be settled by the Congress and according to circumstances, and the contingencies of the future. In the
same way, that we hold the rebel States at present, constitutionally under military rule, we can hold the[m] thereafter; and circumstances must decide when any of the[m] may be safely entitled to representation [in Congress]. The "when," it is, of
course, impossible to determine beforehand.
As for the South's Negroes, suffrage appeared to Kroeger to be in
the cards. "Of course," he admonished, "as soon as the slaves are
emancipated, they can not be excluded from political action; the
distinction of color ceases altogether and forever."[1]

That was the base of Radicalism, already well developed by 1863.
Beyond this enlarging core of agreement, wide differences obtained.
Some Radicals desired to implant greater economic democracy
throughout a conquered South through distribution of confiscated
rebel lands to Negroes and Unionist whites. Others stressed enforcement by the national government of augmented educational
opportunities southward for both races. But on these scores, Radi-
cal-minded men did not battle one another. "There is abundant
work for reformers," wrote one. "When one point is gained, others
are to gain."[2]

Early in the war, Republican Radicals realized that the essential
"one point" without which no advances were possible was the
maintenance over the rebel states of national authority, whether
executive or congressional, as they knuckled under. Way back in
July 1862, in a dodge to fend off emancipation, a coalition of
conservative Republicans and War Democrats tried to slip through
Congress a bill establishing civil governments in areas of Dixie

---

[1] [Kroeger], *The Future of the Country. By a Patriot* (Chicago: n.d.
[1863 publication date ascertained by marginal notations on copy em-
ployed]), pp. 22–24.
[2] Warren Chase, *The American Crisis: or, Trial and Triumph of Democracy* (Boston: Marsh & Co., 1865), p. 80.

some day to be overrun, and recognizing existing law codes of those states except for secession statutes. In successful opposition to the proposal, Senator Charles Sumner of Massachusetts illustrated its defects by quoting from the law codes of a Southern state—a tactic repeated in 1865 and 1866 with reference to the "black codes" of former slave and ex-rebel states.

Elegant, learned, and austere, Sumner enjoyed an international reputation as a reformer in politics. Two years younger than Lincoln, he had matured in such urban cosmopolitanism as Boston and Harvard afforded. By the middle 1840's he was embarked upon a career as a politician of a spectacular character, centering his attention on goals ranging from advocacy of international peace to antipathy to slavery. Sumner helped to organize the Republican organization, and he spearheaded the anti-Kansas bloc in Washington.

By the time Lincoln became President, the Massachusetts Senator was the center of Radical sentiment in the Republican party. He and Lincoln established cordial personal and effective official relationships between White House and Capitol Hill, and Sumner served as a bridge all during the war between the accelerating Radical ranks and the slower-moving but rarely immobile center of the party Lincoln represented. It may have been true, as Charles Francis Adams, Jr., suggested, that Sumner was a "statesman *doctrinaire*," and, in the words of his recent biographer, David Donald, "a man inflexibly committed to a set of moral ideas as basic principles."[3] But it was also true that in wartime matters Sumner was an immensely effective and intensely practical politician. As a combination, zeal and expertness are difficult to beat.

Here is Sumner's speech on "Provisional Governments and Reconstruction," July 7, 1862.[4]

Mr. President,—I cannot consent. . . . A government organized by Congress and appointed by the President is to enforce

---

[3] Donald, *Charles Sumner and the Coming of the Civil War* (New York: Knopf, 1960), pp. vii–viii.

[4] Sumner, *Works* (Boston: Lee & Shepard, 1870–1883), VII, 162–164.

laws and institutions, some of which are abhorrent to civilization. Take, for instance, the Revised Code of North Carolina,
which I have before me. Here is a provision which the Governor, under this Act, must enforce . . . that there shall be "no
interference with the laws and institutions existing in such
State at the time its authorities assumed to array the same
against the Government of the United States." Therefore they
must be enforced. And now, if you please, listen to one of
them.

"Any free person, who shall teach, or attempt to teach, any
slave to read or write, the use of figures excepted, or shall give
or sell to such slave any book or pamphlet, shall be deemed
guilty of a misdemeanor, and upon conviction thereof, if a
white man or woman, shall be fined not less than one hundred
nor more than two hundred dollars, or imprisoned, and if a
free person of color, shall be fined, imprisoned, or whipped,
not exceeding thirty-nine nor less than twenty lashes."

That abomination, Sir, is set forth in the Revised Code of
North Carolina, chap. 34, sec. 82. But lest it should fail by the
employment of slaves as school-teachers, we have the following prohibition.

"It shall not be lawful for any slave to teach, or attempt to
teach, any other slave or free negro to read or write, the use
of figures excepted."[5]

The punishment of slaves for this offence is whipping, repeated for every act. But, Sir, here is another specimen.

"If any person shall wilfully bring into the State, with an
intent to circulate, or shall wilfully circulate or publish within
the State, or shall aid or abet the bringing into, or the circula-
tion or publication of within, the State, any written or printed
pamphlet or paper, whether written or printed in or out of
the State, the evident tendency whereof is to cause slaves to
become discontented with the bondage in which they are held

---

[5] Chap. 107, sec. 31.

by their masters and the laws regulating the same, and free negroes to be dissatisfied with their social condition and the denial to them of political privileges, and thereby to excite among the said slaves and free negroes a disposition to make conspiracies, insurrections, or resistance against the peace and quiet of the public, such person so offending shall be deemed guilty of felony, and on conviction thereof shall, for the first offence, be imprisoned not less than one year, and be put in the pillory and whipped, at the discretion of the court, and for the second offence *shall suffer death.*"[6]

Here is yet another.

"If any free person of color shall preach or exhort in public, or in any manner officiate as a preacher or teacher in any prayer meeting, or other association for worship, where slaves of different families are collected together, he shall be deemed guilty of a misdemeanor, and, on conviction, shall, for each offence, receive not exceeding thirty-nine lashes on his bare back."[7]

And now one more.

"If any person shall wilfully carry or convey any slave, the property of another, without the consent of the owner or the guardian of the owner, with the intent and for the purpose of enabling such slave to escape out of this State, from the service of his owner, or any one having an interest in such slave, present or future, vested or contingent, legal or equitable, or if any person shall wilfully conceal any slave, the property of another, with such intent and purpose, the person so offending shall suffer death."[8]

I have read enough, Sir. These passages show you the statutes to be enforced in the name of the National Union, by its constituted authorities, in courts organized by Congress. And behind all these is Slavery itself to be enforced also.

---

[6] Chap. 34, sec. 16.
[7] Chap. 107, sec. 59.
[8] Chap. 34, sec. 11.

Sir, such an exhibition is more than sufficient. You cannot consent to any such thing. In organizing these governments, all that we can do is to protect life and property, and generally to provide the machinery of administration. Further we cannot go, and protect institutions in themselves an outrage to civilization.

12. RESOLUTION OF SOLDIERS OF THE

150TH PENNSYLVANIA VOLUNTEERS

March 11, 1863

Were Sumner and other Radical Republicans qualified to be critics of Lincoln's evolving reconstruction efforts or architects of superior alternative modes? There is no arithmetic scale to tip in absolute favor of either end of Pennsylvania Avenue. Everything in Civil War America was unprecedented. Historians then and since, who have marked out sharp justification for President or Congress to take sole hold of reconstruction reins, have been more certain than the facts allow.

It is clear that Sumner and other Republican legislators were as well informed as any one else about developments in the occupied South, and better informed than the White House on home-front sentiment. This edge resulted from the manifold connections that the congressmen enjoyed with their state and local organizations, with constituents at home and in the military services, and with patriotic and reform organizations.

As was true of Lincoln, congressmen understood that the Army was the key to everything. To illustrate, consider the increasingly rigorous home-front internal security policies that the President had seen fit to impose, including arrests of civilians by soldiers and temporary suspensions of traditional civil liberties. Democrats had hammered hard at these policies during the 1862 Congressional and state elections, and the Republicans had suffered thumping defeats in scores of contests. Therefore it was immensely significant that Republican congressmen were able to draw out of the Union Army statements such as the one following, to counter, as it were, the slings and arrows of the outraged Democracy. Here is "A Voice from the Army on the Opposition to the Government," printed as a letter dated March 12, 1863.[1]

A meeting of the officers and soldiers of the One hundred and fiftieth Regiment Pennsylvania Volunteers was held at the regimental headquarters on the 11th day of March, 1863, in pursuance of the following call signed by all the officers of the regiment:

"The undersigned, officers of the One hundred and fiftieth Regiment Pennsylvania Volunteers, respectfully request Colonel Wister, commanding the regiment, to call a meeting for the purpose of expressing our earnest loyalty and devotion to our country, and our detestation of the Northern traitors now endeavoring to paralyze the efforts of the army in the field, and insidiously to overthrow their country's cause."

Lieutenant-Colonel Huidekoper was called to the chair, and Adjutant R. L. Ashhurst appointed secretary.

The object of the meeting having been stated by Major Chamberlin, after appropriate and patriotic remarks by Colonel Wister, Adjutant Ashhurst, Lieutenant-Colonel Huidekoper, Private Philip Hammer, Co. A., Lieutenant William P. Dougal, Co. D., and Quartermaster A. S. Voorhis, the following preamble and resolutions, offered by Major Chamberlin, were unanimously adopted amid great enthusiasm:

Whereas, After nearly two years of the most patriotic sacrifices on the part of our people, and the most desperate trials

---

[1] In *The Loyalist's Ammunition* (Philadelphia: Ashmead, 1863), pp. 7–9.

and struggles on the part of our army to restore our shattered Union and maintain our national honor, our Government finds itself assailed by a class of persons at home who would yield it, Judas-like, into the hands of the enemy, or sully it by a dishonorable compromise with the hosts of treason, and who are even now trying to induce the masses to resist its lawful authority in order the sooner to gain their hellish ends; therefore,

Resolved, That we hereby express our firm and unalterable devotion to our Government and its laws, and declare our determination to stand by it at all hazards, pledging to the restoration of its entire authority, "our lives, our fortunes, and our sacred honor."

Resolved, That we look upon all proposals, from whatever source, to give up this struggle on any other terms than the unconditional submission of the traitors in arms against their country, as disgraceful to those who originate, and to those who, for a moment, lend an ear to them.

Resolved, That we condemn and repudiate as unworthy sons of their country those who, staying at home in the North, are striving to cripple the hands of their country's defenders; who, under the garb of a false patriotism, and an assumed zeal for the Constitution, cavil at all measures calculated to prostrate the rebellion, and who endeavor to hold back and paralyze the strong arm of right, now outstretched to crush the foul treason which attacks the life of the nation.

Resolved, That we have no sympathy or feeling in common with those who, from real or pretended admiration of any man or general, would make their earnestness in their country's cause, or perhaps their loyalty, dependent on, or subordinate to, their personal feelings; that we are ready and anxious to fight for our country under whatever commander we may be placed, and under none with greater alacrity than our present commander-in-chief.

Resolved, That as we believe that "fighting for Southern rights" means nothing more than warring for the extension of slavery, which we regard alike as a *curse to the land,* and a *great moral wrong,* we hail with joy the President's proclamation doing away with that institution in every State in which rebellion exists, and hope soon to see it forever blotted from our soil.

Resolved, That our feeling towards traitors, both North and South, is one of implacable hatred, and that, while this army has bullets for those at the South, it has also heels broad enough and heavy enough to crush the vile "copperheads" of the North if they persist in their insidious attempts to weaken and overthrow the Government.

Major Chamberlin, Captain Widdis, Co. A., Captain Reisinger, Co. H., Quartermaster Voorhis, and Adjutant Ashhurst, were appointed a committee for the publication of these resolutions.

On motion, adjourned.

H. S. HUIDEKOPER,
Lieutenant-Colonel 150th Regiment P. V., Chairman.
R. L. ASHHURST.
Adjutant 150th Regiment P. V., Secretary.

13. AMERICAN FREEDMEN'S INQUIRY COMMISSION, PRELIMINARY REPORT

June 30, 1863

The Republicans' intimate pipelines to the Army allowed few military developments to go forward behind veils. Congressmen knew that as colored soldiers enlisted after January 1, 1863, into blue-coated ranks, the service itself took on characteristics of a vast educational system for the sable arm. Earlier than this, experiments were under way in quiet backwaters of occupied Dixie, involving efforts by the Army and/or civilian reform organizations to bridge the gap between slavery and whatever new status would develop for Negroes from the ongoing war, and to relieve combat commands of the burden of supporting the swelling numbers of colored refugees who attached themselves to Yankee columns. Pockets of military jurisdiction, including offshore islands and coastal strips of the Carolinas, parcels of northern and western Virginia, and Gulf and Mississippi Valley enclaves, became laboratories where for the first time the reformers' belief that Negro slaves could jump at once to the heights of free worker and citizen was tested. The seed of trouble lay in that these same areas also became the centers of Lincoln's nuclei of Southern white Unionism.

Although the Army was involved in all these developments, along with other Federal agencies, notably the Treasury Department because of the confiscation laws, the major reform effort was of civilian inspiration.[1] The primary financial burden of applying direct relief for freedmen and of supporting teachers, missionaries, and other on-scene personnel fell largely on the numerous freedmen's aid societies that the North generated, often from former abolitionist groups. Many of these societies were tied in turn to a web of Protestant religious organizations and to secular reformist and war-work associations, including the Republican party. Radical Republicans especially were political beneficiaries of the endless interconnections that these numerous societies spread across the North and into the occupied South.

Consider as one example of this complex process the work of Vincent Colyer. Very early in 1862 General Burnside appointed him to the novel position within an Army command of Superintendent of the Poor, to cope with the refugee Negroes who encamped on the North Carolina coastal fringe wrested from the Confederacy. Among other activities, Colyer established schools for colored children. Lincoln meanwhile was working out means and ends toward a reconstruction policy, and he appointed the Unionist North Carolinian Edward Stanly military governor. Stanly closed the schools without consulting Colyer, offering as his reason

---

[1] Dudley T. Cornish, "The Union Army as a Training School for Negroes," *Journal of Negro History,* XXXVII (October 1952), 368–382.

that North Carolina's laws forbade the education of blacks, and indirectly explaining why Sumner in the foregoing speech singled out that state's laws to illustrate what was wrong with conservative ways in reconstruction.[2]

Even more exacerbating was the method of regulating freedmen's labor that the hapless General N. P. Banks later worked out in Louisiana, and which appeared to be barely better than slavery. Critical onlookers insisted that the Lincoln-supported civil government of "loyal" Louisiana whites was the beneficiary of the Banks code, not the freedmen. "Look at Louisiana and its workings under Banks's policy—or as I suppose President Lincoln's policy," complained a Michigan Baptist minister, on furlough from Army chaplain duty at New Orleans, to Sumner. "Government officers [are] playing Egyptian taskmasters while the employers task him [Negroes] to the extent of his powers. . . . Now I ask if Louisiana is received back as a state with such a policy, how can we ever be reunited [?]. . . . We have played Calhoun's fools."[3]

In sum, the consensus of reports from field operatives of the freedmen's aid societies and from sympathetic uniformed personnel ranging from enlisted chaplains to bestarred commanders such as Rufus Saxton, David Hunter, and Ulysses Grant, was that the President's military governors and dependent "loyal" whites deserved suspicion, not trust. The policy of the Republicans in Congress of holding off delegates-elect from "reconstructed" Southern areas who appeared on Capitol Hill at various times during the war therefore received widespread popular support. It is noteworthy that Lincoln chose not to make an intra-Republican fight even over the admission of one of his "pet" state delegations to

---

[2] Willie Lee Rose, *Rehearsal for Reconstruction: The Port Royal Experiment* (Indianapolis: The Bobbs-Merrill Company, Inc., 1964); John G. Sproat, "Blueprint for Radical Reconstruction," *Journal of Southern History*, XXIII (February 1957), 25–44. Colyer's complaints were spread among the freedmen's aid societies through his *Brief Report of the Services Rendered by the Freed People to the United States Army in North Carolina* (New York, 1864).

[3] Rev. Daniel Platt to Sumner, April 17, 1864; Sumner Papers (Houghton Library, Harvard University). Banks's apologia is in his *Emancipation's Labor in Louisiana* (n.p., n.d.); an address, October 30, 1864, at the Boston YMCA Commission Hall. See too McPherson, *The Struggle for Equality*, pp. 289–293.

the Congress, though he heard them knocking vainly at the door.

Inescapable in all this was the growing realization that novel relationships were in process of creation among the national government, the rebel Southern states as each was overcome, the millions of freedmen, and the hard-working freedmen's aid societies of the North. Some participants in events were optimistic that the lineaments of these relationships were already marked out. "The inferences are obvious," wrote Grant's Superintendent of Freedmen for a large share of the vast Mississippi Valley. "No one can apprehend them . . . without seeing, in the policy of the government, towards the Freedmen, the easy settlement of some of the most difficult questions of reconstruction."[4]

But instead of this prophesied "easy settlement," the question of what government policy should obtain with respect to reconstruction became a source of political conflict. Early in the course of the war, Radical Republicans had to their credit understood that a problem existed, and that *some* national policy was going to be necessary to effect the rehabilitation of rebel states as they were suppressed, and of Negroes as they were liberated. Way back in January 1862, very close to two years before Lincoln specified a road back into the Union for repentant Southern whites to take, Sumner had set down thoughts on the "Power of Congress over the Rebel States," which obviously argued for the legislature's natural priorities in this area. The Senator delayed presenting these views in public until the progress of battles and the evolution of Union Army occupation practices substantiated their premises. After bringing his argument up to date, Sumner published it in the October 1863 issue of the influential periodical, *Atlantic Monthly*.[5] At once conservatives blasted it, Montgomery Blair asserting that this "keynote of revolution" was an affront to the President. Certainly Sumner intended to influence Lincoln as well as to guide Congressional opinion.

As though directly to contradict Sumner, Lincoln on December 8

---

[4] Col. [Chaplain] John Eaton, Jr., *Report of the General Superintendent of Freedmen, Department of the Tennessee and the State of Arkansas, for 1864* (Memphis, 1865), p. 96.

[5] Reprinted in Sumner, *Works*, VII, 493 ff.

issued his reconstruction proclamation. Then, six days later, in Congress, Representative Thomas D. Eliot introduced a bill to establish a federal bureau of emancipation. Congress and reformers organized in the Republican party were going to be heard from on the interlocking matters of reconstruction and the freedmen's condition.

An alliance of old-line abolitionists early in 1862 had formed an Emancipation League, headquartered in Boston. Its initial goal gained when Lincoln in September 1862 declared for abolition, the league moved on to concern itself with the need to achieve decent treatment for the ever-growing number of freedmen. Understanding increased that the task was going to be beyond anything Americans had ever undertaken, surpassing the resources of private benevolent societies. At the same time, the conviction grew among the league's prominent leadership that alternatives were necessary to the patterns of reconstruction unfolding in the occupied Southern regions under inspiration of Lincoln's unpopular civilian appointees, and to the unsavory martial devices of the sort General Banks employed in Louisiana.

Lincoln and Stanton agreed that some of the league's criticisms were worth testing. Stanton authorized a vice-president of the league, Samuel Gridley Howe, the famed educator of the deaf-blind, along with Robert Dale Owen, the Indiana reformer, and Colonel James McKaye of New York, to form the American Freedmen's Inquiry Commission. The commissioners toured occupied zones of Dixie early in 1863 and subsequently reported on the unprecedented functions that they felt the war was forcing upon the national government. Here is the first plea in America's history for establishment even of a temporary guardian relationship between federal authorities and a specified class of persons, as contained in the commissioner's official "preliminary report" of June 30, 1863, to Lincoln and Stanton, and as broadcast privately through the web of freedmen's aid societies and to sympathetic Republican state and national legislators.[6]

---

[6] The "Preliminary Report" is in *The War of the Rebellion: A Compilation of the Official Records of the Union and Confederate Armies* (Washington: Government Printing Office, 1880–1901), Series 3, Vol. III, pp. 430–454. The "Final Report" is in *ibid.*, Series 3, Vol. IV, pp.

Character of Organization Proposed.

The researches and investigations of the commission have not yet been sufficiently extended and thorough to justify them in suggesting a definite system for the ultimate solution of one of the gravest social problems ever presented to a government. Certain measures, however, are, in the present emergency, evidently demanded, not merely from considerations of common humanity, to alleviate the sufferings caused to non-combatant laborers by the forced derangement of industry consequent upon military invasion, but also in virtue of the fact that a great and radical industrial and domestic change, every hour in progress, and ultimately involving the eradication of a labor system which has been the growth of more than two centuries, needs, for a time to which we cannot yet assign a definite limit, to be, to a certain extent, facilitated and directed by governmental assistance and control. The two labor systems—namely, that of enforced slave labor and that of free compensated labor—are, in spirit and result, so thoroughly at variance that the change from the one to the other by four millions of people cannot safely be left undirected and uncared for, to work itself out, drifting on at haphazard, according to the chance shiftings of the current of daily events. . . . The question remains open, whether, and how soon, the American freedman, with the dependence engendered by the slave system still clinging to him—and what is worse, weighted down in his efforts to rise by that prejudice which prompts men to despise whoever has long been their inferior—will be able peacefully to maintain his new rights, and to protect himself

289–382. (Hereafter this invaluable collection is cited as *OR*.) An alternative version of the final report is in McKaye's *The Mastership and its Fruits: The Emancipated Slave Face to Face with his Old Master* (New York: Bryant, 1864). Recent scholarship is in Harold Schwartz, *Samuel Gridley Howe, Social Reformer, 1801–1876* (Cambridge: Harvard University Press, 1956), pp. 256–267.

against undue ascendency and imposition from the white man. Coming into competition with another race—one among the most energetic in the world—for the first time in the history of our country, on something like equal terms, will he, if left to himself, be overborne and crushed? And if he should be, will he bear it as patiently in his capacity of freedman as he has borne it under subjection as a slave?

On one point the commission are already agreed, namely, that a scheme of guardianship or protection for one race of men against another race inhabiting the same country cannot become a permanent institution. If the necessity for the constant operation of such a scheme could be proved, the proof would amount to this, that the two races cannot in perpetuity inhabit the same country at all, and that the one must ultimately give way to the other.

The commission, therefore, adopt the opinion that all special governmental measures, particularly those involving continuous expenditure, whether for the relief of poor southern whites or of poor refugee blacks, or for the guardianship of such refugees, should be more or less temporary in their character, and should be prepared and administered in that idea and intent.

In this view of the case, the commission state, with satisfaction, that, in the course of their inquiries, they have found unmistakable indications that the negro slave of the south, though in some respects resembling a child from the dependence in which he has been trained, and the unreasoning obedience which has been exacted from him, and therefore, in many cases, seeking and needing, for a season, encouragement and direction, is by no means devoid of practical sagacity in the common affairs of life, and usually learns, readily and quickly, to shift for himself. This, the commission think, it is just and desirable that he should be led to do at as early a period as is practicable, without further reliance, for aid or guidance, on the government.

In this view, the commission recommend that all "contra-band camps" (as they are usually called) be regarded as places of reception and distribution only, and that the super-intendents be informed that it is the policy of the government not to continue the aggregation of these people in military villages a day longer than is necessary to dispose of them as military laborers or on plantations, or in other self-supporting situations. . . .

Upon the same principle, the working of plantations by gov-ernment should be undertaken as a temporary expedient, ren-dered necessary during the period of transition. But as soon as there are found loyal and respectable owners or lessees of plantations who will hire the freedmen at fair wages, this is to be preferred; or when the freedmen themselves have saved a little to start upon, or when they evince ability to manage a small farm or market garden of their own, such spots may be temporarily assigned to them, at a moderate rent, on forfeited estates, until Congress, which can alone originate a public policy in regard to such lands, shall make, if it sees fit to make, some permanent arrangement touching this matter. Ultimately, when these lands come into market, the desirable result is, that the freedmen should become owners in fee of the farms or gardens they occupy.

To the superintendent it must, in a measure, be left to select one or other of these plans, according to the varying circum-stances in different places. When freedmen are hired, in the neighborhood of the superintendent station, by the owners or lessees of plantations or of manufactories, it should be made the duty of the superintendent to keep an eye over them for the time being, so as to ascertain that they have fair treatment and prompt payment of wages earned. . . .

The commission believe it to be another important feature, in a plan of organization for the care of refugees, that such organization should be substantially separate from and (ex-cept when military exigencies intervene) independent of the ordinary military administration of the army; it being understood, however, that the refugees, on first entering our lines, come in charge of the provost marshal, who turns them over to the proper superintendent, and that every superintendent shall be required to meet, to the full extent of his ability, all requisitions made upon him by the proper authorities for military laborers; payments or other supplies to refugees not in military service to be directly through the department superintendents, who should be required to give bond as army paymasters do, and whose reports should be made directly to the superintendent general of freedmen.

The commission, specially desirous to propose no scheme which might endanger a conflict of authorities, have taken pains to submit this feature of their plan to generals commanding departments whenever they have had opportunity: as to General Schenck at Baltimore, to General Dix at Fortress Monroe, to General Viele at Norfolk, to General Peck at Suffolk, to General Hunter at Hilton Head, and to General Saxton at Beaufort. Each of these officers, when such a separation was suggested, approved it in unqualified terms, usually adding that it would be the greatest relief to themselves to be freed from all care and responsibility in regard to refugees. One of these officers remarked that he had rarely found military abilities and the special qualifications needed to superintend freedmen united in the same person, especially in subalterns.

Details of Organization Proposed.

The commission suggest a plan of provisional organization, for the improvement, protection, and employment of refugee freedmen, extending, for the present, over those districts of country only with the condition of which they have become acquainted, chiefly by personal inspection of the various locations, in part by reliable reports and depositions, namely, the District of Columbia, Eastern Virginia, North Carolina, South Carolina, and Florida. . . .

The commission propose—

1. That the above region of country constitute three freedmen's superintendencies or departments—the first comprising the District of Columbia and Eastern Virginia, the second extending over North Carolina, and the third embracing the States of South Carolina and Florida.

2. That there be appointed for each of these superintendencies a department superintendent, with the pay and allowances of colonel of cavalry.

3. That there be appointed as many resident superintendents in each department as there are important stations therein, with not less in each than from three to five thousand freedmen to care for; these resident superintendents to have the pay and allowances of captain of cavalry.

4. That where the number of freedmen at any station shall exceed seven or eight thousand, and it is the opinion of the department superintendent, expressed in writing, that an assistant superintendent is required, there be appointed such assistant, with the pay and allowances of lieutenant of cavalry.

In all cases necessary transportation to be allowed to such superintendents.

5. That there be appointed such clerks and foremen as may be necessary to carry out the details of this organization, with wages of from one to three dollars a day, graduated according to the character of their duties.

And, finally, that there be detailed, as superintendent general of freedmen, an officer of suitable qualifications, not under the rank of a brigadier general, to whom and to his staff be assigned an office in the War Department, his staff officers acting as secretaries, and otherwise aiding him in his duties of supervision.

It will be seen that this organization presupposes three grades of superintendents, besides a chief as central head, thus:

One superintendent general of freedmen for the United States.

Department superintendents: one for each superintendency, comprising not less than a State.

Resident superintendents: one for each residency, with not less than three thousand freedmen to care for.

Assistant superintendents: one to aid the resident superintendent when the number of freedmen within the residency exceeds seven or eight thousand.

Together with the needful clerks and foremen.

The plan will not, the commission believe, be deemed unnecessarily elaborate when the possibility is taken into account that the colored population, for whose supervision it is prepared, may reach the number of a million or a million and a half before the current year expires.

The commission further propose that to the general officer detailed as superintendent general of freedmen be committed, until Congress shall otherwise provide, the general supervision throughout the United States, of the colored population emancipated by the President's proclamation and by acts of Congress; and the duty of seeing faithfully carried out the plan of organization which may be adopted.

That to this officer, as head of the organization, all reports of department superintendents, and all requisitions by them for money or other supplies, be addressed; and that it be his duty to lay these, with such remarks thereon as he may deem proper, before the Secretary of War. . . .

A competent surgeon and hospital steward should be appointed for each residency, and an assistant surgeon added when the number of refugees attached to the residency requires it. It may be necessary at first to give these officers the pay and allowances of officers of the same rank in the army; but it is very desirable that, as soon as possible, the proper relation between physician and patient be, in a measure, at least, established, by causing these medical men to depend, in part, for support on those whom they attend.

The importance of enlightened instruction, educational and

religious, to these uneducated people cannot be overestimated. It is pleasant to the commission to be able to state their conviction, that the freedmen, in every district of country they have visited, eager to obtain for themselves, but especially for their children, those privileges of education which have hitherto been jealously withheld from them, may already be depended upon to support, in part, both teachers and pastors. The benevolent and religious societies of the north are aiding liberally in this good work; and the opinion of some of those who have taken a leading part in these philanthropic efforts (as expressed to the commission) is, that, with the aid of the freedmen themselves, they will be able, for the present, and until the number of refugee freedmen shall materially increase, to supply, in most cases, the necessary literary and religious instruction. If, in the organization of the various superintendencies, this opinion should prove to be correct, it is well. But organized efforts of private benevolence are usually uncertain in their duration, and a greatly increased immigration of refugees may so augment the number of freedmen needing instruction that the demand for school teaching and pastoral care will exceed the supply. In that case, it may be necessary, in certain locations, that government, for the time being, detail a chaplain to take the religious charge of a residency; and that it pay the salaries of the necessary teachers until the freedmen's schools become self-supporting.

As to these matters, it should be made the duty of the department superintendent specially to report.

Meanwhile, the government should afford transportation to any religious or secular teachers who are duly accredited by respectable societies, and supported, in whole or in part, from the funds of such societies.

As a general rule, the refugees will probably sooner be able to pay their clergymen than to provide the requisite number of teachers for their children. The freedmen of Newbern have recently invited a private of the forty-third Massachusetts volunteers, named Edward Fitz, of the Methodist persuasion, and having a license to preach, to become their pastor, at a salary of one thousand a year.

The organization proposed will be incomplete in those parts of the superintendencies here spoken of in which the ordinary courts of justice are suspended, unless temporary provision be made for a magistracy through whose action these people may learn the important lesson that the obedience which, as slaves, they paid to the will of a master, must now be rendered by them, as freedmen, to establish law—care being taken not to encourage them to become litigious. In this view, the commission recommend that wherever, throughout the superintendencies aforesaid, justices of the peace and circuit and other judges have ceased to hold their sessions, a provost judge, if he be not already appointed, should be. The lack of such an officer at Port Royal is very much felt.

They further recommend that the proper department superintendent be vested with authority to bring to conciliation and settlement all difficulties arising between freedmen, except where resort to a provost judge or other legal tribunal becomes necessary. Where a case of difficulty occurring between a freedman and a white man goes before a provost marshal or provost judge, or before any regularly established legal tribunal, it should be made the duty of the department superintendent so far to act as friend and adviser for the freedman as to see to it that his case is fairly presented and tried; and to this end, in important cases, where necessary, to employ legal counsel. In all these cases, the department superintendent should give such counsel and advice as shall tend to justice between the parties, acting in person when practicable; but, if necessary, he may be allowed to appoint the appropriate resident superintendent to act for him as deputy, during his absence, in the settlement of minor cases.

It should be specially recommended to the department superintendent, in the settlement of all personal difficulties between these people, to act as arbitrator rather than as formal judge, adopting the general principles governing courts of conciliation. And it is confidently believed by the commission that if he shall succeed in gaining the confidence of the freedman under his charge, he will, with rare exceptions, be able amicably and satisfactorily to adjust such difficulties without further resort to law.

As to the mode of appointment of superintendents and employés above proposed, the commission suggest as follows:

That the department superintendents be appointed by the Secretary of War. . . .

The commission here desire to record their profound conviction, that upon the judicious selection of department superintendents and of superintendent general of freedmen will mainly depend the successful practical workings of the above sketched plan of organization. The African race, accustomed to shield itself by cunning and evasion, and by shirking of work, whenever it can be safely shirked, against the oppression which has been its lot for generations, is yet of genial nature, alive to gratitude, open to impressions of kindness, and more readily influenced and led by those who treat it well and gain its confidence than our race, or perhaps than any other. The wishes and recommendations of government, if they are not harshly enforced, but quietly communicated by those who understand and sympathize with the African nature, will be received and obeyed as commands in almost every instance. It is highly important, therefore, that those who have in charge the interests of these freedmen shall be men not only of administrative ability, but also of comprehensive benevolence and humanitarian views.

On the other hand, it is equally desirable that these refugees, as readily spoiled as children, should not be treated with weak and injurious indulgence. Evenhanded justice, not special favor, is what they need. Mild firmness is the proper spirit in which to control them. They should find themselves treated, not as children of preference, fostered by charity, dependent for a living on government or on benevolent associations, but as men from whom, in their new character of freedmen, self-reliance and self-support are demanded.

Superintendents imbued with this spirit and the views here recommended will, if they possess a fair amount of executive talent, find little difficulty in managing refugee freedmen, and, with infrequent exceptions, will meet with no factious opposition on their part. . . .

PART FOUR

Reconstruction Policy and
Republican Crisis

---

14. WADE-DAVIS BILL

July 2, 1864

Despite the able character of the American Freedmen's Inquiry Commission's report, sympathetic congressmen had to labor intermittently for almost two years in order to build a bill acceptable to their colleagues. Priorities on the agenda of Senate and House and in congressmen's energies and attention went always to the war. And as 1864 moved on to its long, hot summer, the election whirligig dominated central stage.

Elements implicit in the commissioners' proposal for establishment of a national freedmen's bureau to meet the challenge of emancipation tangled inextricably with intra-Republican division of opinion with respect to Lincoln's adequacy as President. Many Republicans, especially Radicals, feared that his December 1863 proclamation on reconstruction and amnesty did not specify strongly enough that emancipation was irreversible. Doubters worried that Lincoln's obvious concentration on rebuilding the structures of the rebel states and fixing their ties to the national government might result in his cancellation of the Emancipation Proclamation in order the more swiftly to win the surrender of the bulk of Southern whites. These concerns underlay the animadversions on his "loyal" state-building in the South that sounded out from within his party, and the opposition from Republican ranks to his renomination.

With respect to setting reconstruction policy, Lincoln had on his side the advantage of his office. He could move first, and he courageously and imaginatively did so. His reconstruction plan was in action ahead of contenders; "first in the field," as Eben Greenough Scott noted shrewdly. But Lincoln's spurt into reconstruction leadership incurred heavy political costs. Again to quote Scott, ". . . it was satisfactory to nobody. . . . Democrats and Republicans joined in one cry, that it was a creature unknown to the Constitution, and both [parties], as if inspired with the same motive, fell upon it, stripped it of its raiment, and lashed it in mockery naked through the world."[1] To which it should be added that when chips came down, Lincoln did not fight very hard to maintain a monopoly for his curious creations in the South, the state governments that by his orders the United States Army was propping up with its bayonets. Chips came down in 1864, in one of the most direct confrontations between a President and unruly Congressional leaders of his own party in American history.

By the beginning of 1864 Congressional Radical Republicans had advanced to the commitment not to end the war until freedom was ineradicable. Therefore Radicals were suspicious of any move toward a negotiated peace with the Confederacy, an armistice, or a compromise, that might buy peace at the cost of emancipation. Certainly Radicals, Republicans generally, and most Northerners, for that matter, did not trust the mass of Southern whites to keep faith with oaths of future loyalty or with mere

---

[1] Scott, *Reconstruction During the Civil War in the United States,* p. 273.

promises of decent treatment to Negroes. This cynicism in the North was nourished far more by soldiers' reports of actual espionage, sabotage, and turncoating opportunism by Southern whites, than by anything Radical propaganda could achieve. A result was a growing conviction among Republican supporters that Lincoln's puny tithe of galvanized whites was simply inadequate for the task of reconstruction.[2]

So deep and general was Northern displeasure with the out-working of Presidential reconstruction that an intra-Republican revolt impended. Out of this a Democratic victory at the polls was likely, to be followed in turn by the equivalent of triumph for the Confederacy. Prospects of disaster of this magnitude pulled Republicans and War Democrats together in a Union coalition. At Baltimore in June, Lincoln was able to engineer for himself a unanimous renomination with such apparent ease as to be "a matter of wonder" to close students of his career.[3] But though he held party lines tightly at the convention, less than a month later Lincoln was unable to repeat the miracle in the Congress, where the reconstruction issue was up for grabs.

Political "pros" do not lightly risk schism. If Republican infighting over reconstruction policy continued too close to November, the unifying effects of the recent convention would likely go to waste. Nevertheless, Republicans in both houses of Congress, many of whom had barely returned from the Baltimore convention, on July 2, 1864, passed the Wade-Davis bill, knowing that it countered the policy of the man they had renominated for the Presidency. Surely a great many congressmen must have felt very deeply on this issue, to be willing to accept the political hazards involved. Equally clearly, a majority of Republicans and War Democrats agreed with the Radical premise that Congress had authority to set the conditions of reunion—including the guaranteeing of the permanence of emancipation and of republican forms of government in the Southern states—by specifying the qualifications

---

[2] Harold M. Hyman, "Deceit in Dixie," *Civil War History*, III (March 1957), 65–82.

[3] James G. Randall and David Donald, *The Civil War and Reconstruction* (Boston: D. C. Heath & Co., 1961), p. 468.

of voters and officeholders.[4] Here is the text of the Wade-Davis bill.[5]

[H. R. 244, Thirty-eighth Congress, first session.]

AN ACT to guarantee to certain States whose governments have been usurped or overthrown a republican form of government.

Be it enacted by the Senate and House of Representatives of the United States of America in Congress assembled, That in the States declared in rebellion against the United States the President shall, by and with the advice and consent of the Senate, appoint for each a provisional governor, whose pay and emoluments shall not exceed that of a brigadier-general of volunteers, who shall be charged with the civil administration of such State until a State government therein shall be recognized as hereinafter provided.

SEC. 2. *And be it further enacted,* That so soon as the military resistance to the United States shall have been suppressed in any such State and the people thereof shall have sufficiently returned to their obedience to the Constitution and the laws of the United States the provisional governor shall direct the marshal of the United States, as speedily as may be, to name a sufficient number of deputies, and to enroll all white male citizens of the United States resident in the State in their

---

[4] Charles O. Lerche, Jr., "Congressional Interpretations of the Guarantee of a Republican Form of Government during Reconstruction," *Journal of Southern History,* XV (May 1949), 195–196.

[5] James D. Richardson, *A Compilation of the Messages and Papers of the Presidents* (Washington: Government Printing Office, 1897), VI, 222–226. Hereafter this collection is cited as Richardson, *Messages and Papers.*

respective counties, and to request each one to take the oath
to support the Constitution of the United States, and in his
enrollment to designate those who take and those who refuse
to take that oath, which rolls shall be forthwith returned to
the provisional governor; and if the persons taking that oath
shall amount to a majority of the persons enrolled in the State,
he shall, by proclamation, invite the loyal people of the State
to elect delegates to a convention charged to declare the will
of the people of the State relative to the reestablishment of a
State government, subject to and in conformity with the Constitution of the United States.

SEC. 3. *And be it further enacted,* That the convention shall
consist of as many members as both houses of the last constitutional State legislature, apportioned by the provisional governor among the counties, parishes, or districts of the State, in
proportion to the white population returned as electors by the
marshal in compliance with the provisions of this act. The provisional governor shall, by proclamation, declare the number
of delegates to be elected by each county, parish, or election
district; name a day of election not less than thirty days thereafter; designate the places of voting in each county, parish,
or district, conforming as nearly as may be convenient to the
places used in the State elections next preceding the rebellion;
appoint one or more commissioners to hold the election at each
place of voting, and provide an adequate force to keep the
peace during the election.

SEC. 4. *And be it further enacted,* That the delegates shall be
elected by the loyal white male citizens of the United States
of the age of 21 years, and resident at the time in the county,
parish, or district in which they shall offer to vote, and enrolled as aforesaid, or absent in the military service of the
United States, and who shall take and subscribe the oath of
allegiance to the United States in the form contained in the
act of Congress of July 2, 1862; and all such citizens of the
United States who are in the military service of the United

States shall vote at the headquarters of their respective commands, under such regulations as may be prescribed by the provisional governor for the taking and return of their votes; but no person who has held or exercised any office, civil or military, State or Confederate, under the rebel usurpation, or who has voluntarily borne arms against the United States, shall vote or be eligible to be elected as delegate at such election.

SEC. 5. *And be it further enacted,* That the said commissioners, or either of them, shall hold the election in conformity with this act, and, so far as may be consistent therewith, shall proceed in the manner used in the State prior to the rebellion. The oath of allegiance shall be taken and subscribed on the poll book by every voter in the form above prescribed, but every person known by or proved to the commissioners to have held or exercised any office, civil or military, State or Confederate, under the rebel usurpation, or to have voluntarily borne arms against the United States, shall be excluded though he offer to take the oath; and in case any person who shall have borne arms against the United States shall offer to vote, he shall be deemed to have borne arms voluntarily unless he shall prove the contrary by the testimony of a qualified voter. The poll book, showing the name and oath of each voter, shall be returned to the provisional governor by the commissioners of election, or the one acting, and the provisional governor shall canvass such returns and declare the person having the highest number of votes elected.

SEC. 6. *And be it further enacted,* That the provisional governor shall, by proclamation, convene the delegates elected as aforesaid at the capital of the State on a day not more than three months after the election, giving at least thirty days' notice of such day. In case the said capital shall in his judgment be unfit, he shall in his proclamation appoint another place. He shall preside over the deliberations of the convention and administer to each delegate, before taking his seat in the convention, the oath of allegiance to the United States in the form above prescribed.

SEC. 7. *And be it further enacted,* That the convention shall declare on behalf of the people of the State their submission to the Constitution and laws of the United States, and shall adopt the following provisions, hereby prescribed by the United States in the execution of the constitutional duty to guarantee a republican form of government to every State, and incorporate them in the constitution of the State; that is to say:

First. No person who has held or exercised any office, civil or military (except offices merely ministerial and military offices below the grade of colonel), State or Confederate, under the usurping power, shall vote for or be a member of the legislature or governor.

Second. Involuntary servitude is forever prohibited, and the freedom of all persons is guaranteed in said State.

Third. No debt, State or Confederate, created by or under the sanction of the usurping power shall be recognized or paid by the State.

SEC. 8. *And be it further enacted,* That when the convention shall have adopted those provisions it shall proceed to reestablish a republican form of government and ordain a constitution containing those provisions, which, when adopted, the convention shall by ordinance provide for submitting to the people of the State entitled to vote under this law, at an election to be held in the manner prescribed by the act for the election of delegates, but at a time and place named by the convention, at which election the said electors, and none others, shall vote directly for or against such constitution and form of State government. And the returns of said election shall be made to the provisional governor, who shall canvass the same in the presence of the electors, and if a majority of the votes cast shall be for the constitution and form of government, he shall certify the same, with a copy thereof, to the President of the United States, who, after obtaining the assent of Congress, shall, by proclamation, recognize the government so established, and none other, as the constitutional government of the State; and from the date of such recognition, and not before, Senators and Representatives and electors for President and Vice-President may be elected in such State, according to the laws of the State and of the United States.

Sec. 9. *And be it further enacted,* That if the convention shall refuse to reestablish the State government on the conditions aforesaid the provisional governor shall declare it dissolved; but it shall be the duty of the President, whenever he shall have reason to believe that a sufficient number of the people of the State entitled to vote under this act, in number not less than a majority of those enrolled as aforesaid, are willing to reestablish a State government on the conditions aforesaid, to direct the provisional governor to order another election of delegates to a convention for the purpose and in the manner prescribed in this act, and to proceed in all respects as hereinbefore provided, either to dissolve the convention or to certify the State government reestablished by it to the President.

Sec. 10. *And be it further enacted,* That until the United States shall have recognized a republican form of State government the provisional governor in each of said States shall see that this act and the laws of the United States and the laws of the State in force when the State government was overthrown by the rebellion are faithfully executed within the State; but no law or usage whereby any person was heretofore held in involuntary servitude shall be recognized or enforced by any court or officer in such State; and the laws for the trial and punishment of white persons shall extend to all persons, and jurors shall have the qualifications of voters under this law for delegates to the convention. The President shall appoint such officer provided for by the laws of the State when its government was overthrown as he may find necessary to the civil administration of the State, all which officers shall be entitled to receive the fees and emoluments provided by the State laws for such officers.

SEC. 11. *And be it further enacted,* That until the recognition of a State government as aforesaid the provisional governor shall, under such regulations as he may prescribe, cause to be assessed, levied, and collected, for the year 1864 and every year thereafter, the taxes provided by the laws of such State to be levied during the fiscal year preceding the overthrow of the State government thereof, in the manner prescribed by the laws of the State, as nearly as may be; and the officers appointed as aforesaid are vested with all powers of levying and collecting such taxes, by distress or sale, as were vested in any officers or tribunal of the State government aforesaid for those purposes. The proceeds of such taxes shall be accounted for to the provisional governor and be by him applied to the expenses of the administration of the laws in such State, subject to the direction of the President, and the surplus shall be deposited in the Treasury of the United States to the credit of such State, to be paid to the State upon an appropriation therefor to be made when a republican form of government shall be recognized therein by the United States.

SEC. 12. *And be it further enacted,* That all persons held to involuntary servitude or labor in the States aforesaid are hereby emancipated and discharged therefrom, and they and their posterity shall be forever free. And if any such persons or their posterity shall be restrained of liberty under pretense of any claim to such service or labor, the courts of the United States shall, on *habeas corpus,* discharge them.

SEC. 13 *And be it further enacted,* That if any person declared free by this act, or any law of the United States or any proclamation of the President, be restrained of liberty with intent to be held in or reduced to involuntary servitude or labor, the person convicted before a court of competent jurisdiction of such act shall be punished by fine of not less than

$1,500 and be imprisoned not less than five nor more than twenty years.

Sec. 14. *And be it further enacted,* That every person who shall hereafter hold or exercise any office, civil or military (except offices merely ministerial and military offices below the grade of colonel), in the rebel service, State or Confederate, is hereby declared not to be a citizen of the United States.

15. ABRAHAM LINCOLN,

VETO MESSAGE ON WADE-DAVIS BILL

July 8, 1864

Why were Radical Republicans, and indeed most Republicans, willing in the face of terrible political consequences to support the Wade-Davis measure? The answer appears to be that a sizable majority of congressmen would not risk the greater risks they foresaw if too much leeway were left in the hands of unregenerate Southern whites. Noteworthily, Wade and Henry Winter Davis of Maryland, the bill's sponsors, held off an amendment requiring that Negroes vote in a Southern state as a condition of reconstruction. Instead, Congress, as Lincoln had done, accepted a white South rebuilding with the aid of the North's armies.

As to matters of difference between the President's and Congress' plans, they were large, though not fundamental. The Wade-Davis bill involved legislative, not executive, inspiration for reconstruction. Lincoln's specification was that a viable electorate could form in a conquered Southern state when ten per cent of the voters as of 1860 qualified by swearing future loyalty to the Union. The decision in Congress was that the President was not requiring enough democracy on which to build an adequate and dependably loyal base in a Southern state. Therefore the Wade-Davis bill ordained that a majority of white residents of a surrendered rebel state must qualify for voting and holding office by swearing to their intention of keeping future loyalty. These qualified citizens were then to choose delegates to a constitutional convention to rewrite their state's fundamental law, men who could also attest to their past loyalty to the Union, as formulated in an "iron-clad test oath."

Though both Lincoln's and Congress' reconstruction schemes had the national government specifying minimum qualifications for voting and officeholding to a dozen states, the Wade-Davis requirements obviously were more demanding. The Radicals intended to rely on the only Southern whites they felt were reliable, and thereby to guarantee republican forms of government in Southern states. These trustworthy souls were the Southern white Unionists. Ever since Sumter, tens of thousands of displaced persons had fled northward, especially from the border areas; and afterward, many had suffered grievously because their stubborn Unionism made them anathema to Confederate society. Whole regiments in the Union Army were made up of refugee Southerners and border state men who had risked awful consequences by their patriotism to the nation. Still other thousands of Southern white Unionists languished at one time or another in prisons spotted through the shrinking heartland of rebeldom, or endured the overseership of home guardsmen or vigilantes.

Once having returned to their conquered states, these exiles would form the clusters of population adequate in numbers to be the majority the Wade-Davis bill demanded, who without perjury could swear to unmarred past loyalty to the United States. At the same time, the amount of democracy in the South would enlarge, for many Unionists would never have qualified as voters or troubled to qualify under their state's prewar standards. The defeated rebel whites would remain disfranchised while Unionists built a better political society. With the smell of victory wafting closer, the North was in no mood to trust the professions of loyalty of Confederate supporters.

Of course, Lincoln understood all this. Advised that Congress had popular Northern sentiment in its favor with respect to the Wade-Davis bill, and anxious, as all Republicans were, to prevent a Democratic victory at the polls, Lincoln tried to side-step the issue. He took advantage of the almost-forgotten constitutional provision allowing the President to "pocket veto" a bill. The Wade-Davis proposal came to him during the last hour of the Congressional session; Lincoln withheld his signature but did not veto the bill. After Congress dispersed, he issued on July 8 a curious explanatory proclamation, the text of which follows.[1]

By the President of the United States.
A Proclamation.

Whereas at the late session Congress passed a bill "to guarantee to certain States whose government have been usurped or overthrown a republican form of government," and . . .

Whereas the said bill was presented to the President of the United States for his approval less than one hour before the *sine die* adjournment of said session, and was not signed by him; and

Whereas the said bill contains, among other things, a plan for restoring the States in rebellion to their proper practical relations in the Union, which plan expresses the sense of Congress upon that subject, and which plan it is now thought fit to lay before the people for their consideration:

Now, therefore, I, Abraham Lincoln, President of the United States, do proclaim, declare, and make known that while I am (as I was in December last, when, by proclamation, I propounded a plan for restoration) unprepared by a formal approval of this bill to be inflexibly committed to any single plan of restoration, and while I am also unprepared to declare that the free State constitutions and governments already adopted and installed in Arkansas and Louisiana shall be set aside and held for naught, thereby repelling and discouraging the loyal citizens who have set up the same as to further effort, or to declare a constitutional competency in Congress to abolish slavery in States, but am at the same

---

[1] Richardson, *Messages and Papers*, VI, 222–223.

time sincerely hoping and expecting that a constitutional amendment abolishing slavery throughout the nation may be adopted, nevertheless I am fully satisfied with the system for restoration contained in the bill as one very proper plan for the loyal people of any State choosing to adopt it, and that I am and at all times shall be prepared to give the Executive aid and assistance to any such people so soon as the military resistance to the United States shall have been suppressed in any such State and the people thereof shall have sufficiently returned to their obedience to the Constitution and the laws of the United States, in which cases military governors will be appointed with directions to proceed according to the bill.

16. THE WADE-DAVIS

MANIFESTO

August 5, 1864

Outraged by Lincoln's astonishing action, members of his party at first came close to mutiny. Wade and Davis spoke up for the Radicals in a fierce manifesto appearing in the influential New York *Tribune* on August 5. The following is the rarely reprinted full text of the Wade-Davis Manifesto.[1]

PROTEST OF SENATOR WADE AND H. WINTER DAVIS, M.C.
To the supporters of the Government:
    We have read without surprise, but not without indigna-

---

[1] *American Annual Cyclopaedia and Register of Important Events of the Year 1864* (New York: D. Appleton & Co., 1869), pp. 307-310n.

tion, the proclamation of the President of the 8th of July, 1864. . . .

The President did not sign the bill "to guarantee to certain States whose government have been usurped, a Republican form of government"—passed by the supporters of his Administration in both Houses of Congress after mature deliberation.

The bill did not therefore become a law; and it is, therefore, nothing.

The proclamation is neither an approval nor a veto of the bill; it is, therefore, a document unknown to the laws and Constitution of the United States.

So far as it contains an apology for not signing the bill, it is a political manifesto against the friends of the Government.

So far as it proposes to execute the bill which is not a law, it is a grave Executive usurpation.

It is fitting that the facts necessary to enable the friends of the Administration to appreciate the apology and the usurpation be spread before them.

The proclamation says:

"And whereas the said bill was presented to the President of the United States for his approval less than one hour before the *sine die* adjournment of said session, and was not signed by him—"

If that be accurate, still this bill was presented with other bills which were signed.

Within that hour the time for the *sine die* adjournment was three times postponed by the votes of both Houses; and the least intimation of a desire for more time by the President to consider this bill would have secured a further postponement.

Yet the committee sent to ascertain if the President had any further communication for the House of Representatives reported that he had none; and the friends of the bill, who had anxiously waited on him to ascertain its fate, had already been informed that the President had resolved not to sign it.

The time of presentation, therefore, had nothing to do with his failure to approve it.

The bill has been discussed and considered for more than a month in the House of Representatives, which it passed on the 4th of May. It was reported to the Senate on the 27th of May, without material amendment, and passed the Senate absolutely as it came from the House on the 2d of July.

Ignorance of its contents is out of the question.

Indeed, at his request, a draft of a bill substantially the same in material points, and identical in the points objected to by the proclamation, had been laid before him for his consideration in the winter of 1862-1863.

There is, therefore, no reason to suppose the provisions of the bill took the President by surprise.

On the contrary, we have reason to believe them to have been so well known that this method of preventing the bill from becoming a law without the constitutional responsibility of a veto, had been resolved on long before the bill passed the Senate. . . .

Had the proclamation stopped there, it would have been only one other defeat of the will of the people by the Executive perversion of the Constitution.

But it goes further. The President says:

"And whereas the said bill contains, among other things, a plan for restoring the States in rebellion to their proper practical relation in the Union, which plan expresses the sense of Congress upon that subject, and which plan it is now thought fit to lay before the people for their consideration—"

By what authority of the Constitution? In what forms? The result to be declared by whom? With what effect when ascertained?

Is it to be a law by the approval of the people, without the approval of Congress, at the will of the President?

Will the President, on his opinion of the popular approval, execute it as a law?

Or is this merely a device to avoid the serious responsibility of defeating a law on which so many loyal hearts reposed for security?

But the reasons now assigned for not approving the bill are full of ominous significance.

The President proceeds:

"Now, therefore, I, Abraham Lincoln, President of the United States, do proclaim, declare, and make known that, while I am (as I was in December last, when by proclamation I propounded a plan for restoration) unprepared by a formal approval of this bill to be inflexibly committed to any single plan of restoration."

That is to say, the President is resolved that people shall not *by law* take *any* securities from the rebel States against a renewal of the rebellion, before restoring their power to govern us.

His wisdom and prudence are to be our sufficient guarantees! He further says:

"And while I am also unprepared to declare that the free-State constitutions and governments already adopted and installed in Arkansas and Louisiana shall be set aside and held for naught, thereby repelling and discouraging the loyal citizens who have set up the same as to further effort—"

That is to say, the President persists in recognizing those shadows of governments in Arkansas and Louisiana which Congress formally declared should not be recognized—whose representatives and senators were repelled by formal votes of both Houses of Congress—which it was declared formally should have no electoral vote for President and Vice-President.

They are mere creatures of his will. They are mere oligarchies, imposed on the people by military orders under the form of election, at which generals, provost marshals, soldiers and camp-followers were the chief actors, assisted by a handful of resident citizens, and urged on to premature action by private letters from the President.

In neither Louisiana nor Arkansas, before Banks's defeat, did the United States control half the territory or half the population. In Louisiana General Banks's proclamation candidly declared: "The fundamental law of the State is martial law."

On that foundation of freedom he erected what the President calls "the free constitution and Government of Louisiana."

But of this State, whose fundamental law was martial law, only sixteen parishes out of forty-eight parishes were held by the United States; and in five of the sixteen we held only our camps.

The eleven parishes we substantially held had 233,185 inhabitants; the residue of the State not held by us, 575,617.

At the farce called an election the officers of General Banks returned that 11,346 ballots were cast; but whether any or by whom the people of the United States have no legal assurance; but it is probable that 4,000 were cast by soldiers or employés of the United States, military or municipal, but none according to any law, State or national, and 7,000 ballots represent the State of Louisiana.

Such is the free constitution and Government of Louisiana; and like it is that of Arkansas. Nothing but the failure of a military expedition deprived us of a like one in the swamps of Florida; and before the Presidential election like ones may be organized in every rebel State where the United States have a camp. . . .

Even the President's proclamation of the 8th of December formally declares that "whether members sent to Congress from any State shall be admitted to seats constitutionally rests exclusively with the respective houses, and not to any extent with the Executive."

And that is not the less true because wholly inconsistent with the President's assumption in that proclamation of a right to institute and recognize state governments in the rebel States, nor because the President is unable to perceive that his recognition is a nullity if it be not conclusive on Congress.

Under the Constitution, the right to senators and representatives is inseparable from a State Government.

If there be a State Government the right is absolute.

If there be no State Government there can be no senators or representatives chosen.

The two Houses of Congress are expressly declared to be the sole judges of their own members.

When, therefore, senators and representatives are admitted, the State Government under whose authority they were chosen is conclusively established; when they are rejected, its existence is as conclusively rejected and denied; and to this judgment the President is bound to submit.

The President proceeds to express his unwillingness "to declare a constitutional competency in Congress to abolish slavery in States" as another reason for not signing the bill.

But the bill nowhere proposes to abolish slavery in States.

The bill did provide that all *slaves* in the rebel States should be *manumitted*.

But as the President had already signed three bills manumitting several classes of slaves in States, it is not conceived possible that he entertained any scruples touching *that* provision of the bill respecting which he is silent.

He had already himself assumed a right by proclamation to free much the larger number of slaves in the rebel States, under the authority given him by Congress to use military power to suppress the rebellion; and it is quite inconceivable that the President should think Congress could vest in him a discretion it could not exercise itself.

It is the more unintelligible from the fact that except in respect to a small part of Virginia and Louisiana, the bill covered only what the proclamation covered—added a Congressional title and judicial remedies by law to the disputed title under the proclamation, and perfected the work the President professed to be so anxious to accomplish.

Slavery as an institution can be abolished only by a change of the Constitution of the United States, or of the law of the States; and this is the principle of the bill.

It required the new constitution of the State to provide for that prohibition; and the President, in the face of his own proclamation, does not venture to object to insisting on that condition. Nor will the country tolerate its abandonment—yet he defeated the only provision imposing it.

But when he describes himself, in spite of this great blow at emancipation, as "sincerely hoping and expecting that a constitutional amendment abolishing slavery throughout the nation may be adopted," we curiously inquire on what his expectation rests, after the vote of the House of Representatives at the recent session, and in the face of the political complexion of more than enough of the States to prevent the possibility of its adoption within any reasonable time; and why he did not indulge his sincere hopes with so large an instalment of the blessing as his approval of the bill would have secured?

After this assignment of his reasons for preventing the bill from becoming a law, the President proceeds to declare his purpose to execute it as a law by his plenary dictatorial power.

He says: "Nevertheless, I am fully satisfied with the system for restoration contained in the bill as one very proper plan for the loyal people of any State choosing to adopt it; and that I am, and all times shall be, prepared to give the Executive aid and assistance to any such people as soon as the military resistance to the United States shall have been suppressed in any such State, and the people thereof shall have sufficiently returned to their obedience to the Constitution and the laws of the United States—in which cases military governors will be appointed, with directions to proceed according to the bill."

A more studied outrage on the legislative authority of the people has never been perpetrated.

Congress passed a bill; the President refused to approve it, and then by proclamation puts as much of it in force as he sees fit, and proposes to execute those parts by officers unknown to the laws of the United States, and not subject to the confirmation of the Senate.

The bill directed the appointment of provisional governors by and with the advice and consent of the Senate.

The President, after defeating the law, proposes to appoint, without law and without the advice and consent of the Senate, military governors for the rebel States! . . .

Whatever is done will be at his will and pleasure, by persons responsible to no law, and more interested to secure the interests and execute the will of the President than of the people; and the will of Congress is to be "held for naught," "unless the loyal people of the rebel States choose to adopt it."

If they should graciously prefer the stringent bill to the easy proclamation, still the registration will be made under no legal sanction; it will give no assurance that a majority of the people of the States have taken the oath; if administered, it will be without legal authority and void; no indictment will lie for false swearing at the election, or for admitting bad or rejecting good votes; it will be the farce of Louisiana and Arkansas acted over again, under the forms of this bill, but not by authority of law.

But when we come to the guaranties of future peace which Congress meant to enact, the forms, as well as the substance of the bill, must yield to the President's will that none should be imposed.

It was the solemn resolve of Congress to protect the loyal

men of the nation against three great dangers: (1) the return to power of the guilty leaders of the rebellion; (2) the
continuance of slavery, and (3) the burden of the rebel debt.

Congress required assent to those provisions by the convention of the State; and if refused, it was to be dissolved.

The President "holds for naught" that resolve of Congress,
because he is unwilling "to be inflexibly committed to any
one plan of restoration," and the people of the United States
are not to be allowed to protect themselves unless their
enemies agree to it.

The order to proceed according to the bill is therefore
merely at the will of the rebel States; and they have the option to reject it, accept the proclamation of the 8th of December, and demand the President's recognition!

Mark the contrast! The bill requires a majority, the proclamation is satisfied with one-tenth; the bill requires one oath,
the proclamation another; the bill ascertains voters by registering, the proclamation by guess; the bill exacts adherence
to existing territorial limits, the proclamation admits of others;
the bill governs the rebel States *by law,* equalizing all before
it, the proclamation commits them to the lawless discretion of
Military Governors and Provost Marshals; the bill forbids
electors for President, the proclamation and defeat of the bill
threaten us with civil war for the admission or exclusion of
such votes; the bill exacted exclusion of dangerous enemies
from power and the relief of the nation from the rebel debt,
and the prohibition of slavery forever, so that the suppression
of the rebellion will double our resources to bear or pay the
national debt, free the masses from the old domination of
the rebel leaders, and eradicate the cause of the war; the
proclamation secures neither of these guaranties.

It is silent respecting the rebel debt and the political exclusion of rebel leaders; leaving slavery exactly where it was
by law at the outbreak of the rebellion, and adds no guaranty
even of the freedom of the slaves he undertook to manumit.

It is summed up in an illegal oath, without sanction, and therefore void.

The oath is to support all proclamations of the President, during the rebellion, having reference to slaves.

Any government is to be accepted at the hands of one-tenth of the people not contravening that oath.

Now that oath neither secures the abolition of slavery, nor adds any security to the freedom of the slaves the President declared free.

It does not secure the abolition of slavery; for the proclamation of freedom merely professed to free certain slaves while it recognized the institution.

Every constitution of the rebel States at the outbreak of the rebellion may be adopted without the change of a letter: for none of them contravene that proclamation; none of them establish slavery.

It adds no security to the freedom of the slaves; for their title is the proclamation of freedom.

If it be unconstitutional, an oath to support it is void. Whether constitutional or not, the oath is without authority of law, and therefore void.

If it be valid and observed, it exacts no enactment by the State, either in law or constitution, to add a State guaranty to the proclamation title; and the right of a slave to freedom is an open question before the State courts on the relative authority of the State law and the proclamation.

If the oath binds the one-tenth who take it, it is not exacted of the other nine-tenths who succeed to the control of the State government, so that it is annulled instantly by the act of recognition.

What the State courts would say of the proclamation, who can doubt?

But the master would not go into court—he would seize his slaves.

What the Supreme Court would say, who can tell?

When and how is the question to get there?

No *habeas corpus* lies for him in a United States Court; and the President defeated with this bill the extension of that writ to his case.

Such are the fruits of this rash and fatal act of the President—a blow at the friends of his Administration, at the rights of humanity, and at the principles of Republican Government.

The President has greatly presumed on the forbearance which the supporters of his Administration have so long practised, in view of the arduous conflict in which we are engaged, and the reckless ferocity of our political opponents.

But he must understand that our support is of a cause and not of a man; that the authority of Congress is paramount and must be respected; that the whole body of the Union men of Congress will not submit to be impeached by him of rash and unconstitutional legislation; and if he wishes our support, he must confine himself to his Executive duties—to obey and execute, not make the laws—to suppress by arms armed rebellion, and leave political reorganization to Congress.

If the supporters of the Government fail to insist on this, they become responsible for the usurpations which they fail to rebuke, and are justly liable to the indignation of the people whose rights and security, committed to their keeping, they sacrifice.

Let them consider the remedy of these usurpations, and, having found it, fearlessly execute it.

B. F. WADE,
Chairman Senate Committee.
H. WINTER DAVIS,
Chairman Committee House of Representatives on the Rebellious States.

Peace Will Soon Break Out

17. WILLIAM MASON GROSVENOR,

ARTICLE

January 1865

By the end of the summer of 1864, the intraparty stalemate at the Republican summit had paralyzed the creation of reconstruction policy but had not halted the ongoing process of rebuilding state governments in the South according to the terms Lincoln had set forth in his December 1863 statement. In the wakes of Union armies, galvanized Southerners continued to bring into being local and state governments that depended for survival on the Union Army's bayonets and the President's good offices. But though Southern whites accepted Lincoln's specifications for restoring civil government, they casually ignored his suggestion, made in his veto message on the Wade-Davis bill, that they consider the Congressional formulation to be as acceptable as his own. No Southern state saw fit to heed this wise counsel, nor did Lincoln press the matter.

Republican congressmen were hardly in a temper to temporize when delegates-elect from "ten per cent" states knocked at the Capitol doors, bearing certificates of election and of Lincoln's pardon for acts of rebellion. Instead, Republican majorities held them off. The score on completed state reconstructions was zero so far as admission to Congress was concerned.

Nevertheless, by September 1864 intra-Republican tensions had lessened from the ugly level of July. A rising swell of criticism swept the North, directed at Lincoln as well as against the Congressional front-runners, for risking electoral defeat in November over the reconstruction issue. After all, the war was still to be won. If McClellan could be downed at the polls, then Republicans had four years more in which to seek agreeable reconstruction modes. Since Sumter, the party leadership had worked effectively, and it likely would continue on with adequate rough harmony in a second Lincoln administration if intraparty discord did not give Democrats a free gift of ballot victory.

Lincoln's support for the proposed Thirteenth Amendment to the Constitution, leading to the same Radical goal of permanent abolition of slavery that some supporters of the Wade-Davis bill had sought to reach by a reconstruction process, helped to clear the air. To be sure, although the amendment proposal passed the Senate, it failed to gain the needed two-thirds vote in the House. Nevertheless, these factors combined to make clear the necessary Republican strategy for November 1864. It was to close ranks in order to defeat McClellan and the peace Democracy. Hopefully, Republicans would emerge from the electoral contest reinforced in numbers. Then the constitutional amendment, a Congressional statute on reconstruction policy, and a freedmen's bureau were in the cards.

Therefore Republicans of all shades of opinion dropped schemes to scuttle Lincoln and concentrated on defeating the greater evil that "Little Mac" represented. As example, although Sumner had vigorously supported the Wade-Davis bill and was approaching a new dimension of Radicalism involving Negro suffrage as well as freedom, he threw his heavy weight in support of Lincoln. Only Sumner's confidence that Lincoln, who had grown up to accept abolitionism, would continue to be educable, can explain the Senator's support of the President.[1]

Lincoln's victory at the polls in November, and its coattailing

---

[1] Sumner, *Works,* IX, 68–82.

effect on many Republican–War Democrat "Union" candidates for federal and state offices, ensured that the Northern elections would not result in a compromise victory for the South. Following the election and on into the new year, a stream of significant military news flowed northward. Grant's immense forces were keeping up unceasing pressures on Lee's contracting lines. Sherman was moving finally to close final pincers. At last, after so many bitter frustrations, an end was in sight. It was a time to take stock.

All this inspired musings on changes the war had wrought in American society, as symbolized especially by the 1864 election results. Few commentators failed to suggest the implications that the elections contained for politically acceptable reconstruction policy and for the future of black Americans in the white re-United States.

One unusually competent observer, William Mason Grosvenor, though a young man in 1865, was already mature in experience. A Yale graduate and a professional journalist when the war began, Grosvenor was an abolitionist long before it was popular to be one. News of Sumter inspired him to volunteer at once as a private soldier. A year later, field-commissioned, Captain Grosvenor was a combat veteran. In 1863 he became colonel of one of the first Negro units in the Union Army, a regiment formed primarily from among Louisiana freedmen.

Invalided home to Connecticut and discharged, Grosvenor returned to journalism early in 1864. His on-scene observations in Louisiana of Presidential reconstruction, and his freedom from political connections, enabled him to command widespread attention.

Despite his abolitionist past, in late 1864 Grosvenor was neither a Radical Republican nor a Negrophile egalitarian. As will be shown later, his Army service had left in him a temporary but strong anti-Negro prejudice, and he wrote the following article, "The Law of Conquest the True Basis of Reconstruction,"[2] while he suffered from this illiberal conviction.

Therefore Grosvenor's admission is particularly weighty that the

---

[2] *New Englander,* XXIX (January 1865), 111–131. Grosvenor lived until 1900, becoming one of the country's experts on tariff matters, adviser to Presidents, Congresses, and lobbyists, economic editor of the *New York Times,* publicist, and political reformer in the genteel tradition.

Radical Republicans were correct in requiring a reconstruction of the South's politics as a necessary means of making sense out of the war's sacrifices and of ensuring the future stability of the nation. A lucid and tough-minded analyst, Grosvenor as a recruit to Radical Republicanism represented secular, self-interested white opinion, which was concerned over the Negro's fate primarily as it affected the white man's future.

It is fortunate that the political victory achieved in the re-election of President Lincoln is generally received, not with noisy exultation, but with calm and thoughtful thankfulness. It gives ground for hope that in rejoicing over triumphs gained and dangers escaped, the nation will not be blind to the severer trial yet to be met, and the fearful responsibilities that will attend it. . . .

The crisis of the trial of arms was safely passed in July, 1863. Till then we had been organizing and learning to fight. Nor had our earlier efforts been unattended by most shameful failures—failures in battle, failures in generalship, and failures in administrative talent and energy, by which a vast superiority of force was neutralized. But the opening of the Mississippi river and the victory at Gettysburg gave proof that our days of pupilage in the art of war were over, and that at last we could develop and direct our forces. The rebellion as a military power culminated in the great invasion by Lee; at Gettysburg the mounting wave reached its highest point; and with the calm review that followed the tremendous achievements of that period there came to every thinking man, North and South, the conviction that in so far as the contest should be one of arms alone, the North was sure of ultimate success. From that day the apprehensions of the wisest loyalists and the hopes of the shrewdest rebels were alike turned to the political contests at the North, as affording to the rebellion a second chance of the victory which it could no longer hope to attain by triumphs in battle.

The trial by ballot reached its crisis in the presidential election. In that most exciting canvass, conducted with the utmost license of speech and of the press even in the face of a great civil war, all the influences which could pervert the judgment, sap the loyalty, or shake the purpose of the people, culminated in a final appeal against the war and the administration. Ignorance of our system of government, of the duties of citizens and the rights of States; gross misrepresentations of fact as to the events and results of the struggle; attachment to a General who had been the popular favorite in the days of our military babyhood; the conservative dry-rot, hostility to all reform, and especially hatred of the negro and the abolitionist; prices, taxes, and pecuniary burdens already more grievous to sordid souls than any national dishonor or calamity; dread of the phantom of usurpation and of the prospect of another draft; influence of foreign agents, of rebel sympathizers, and of secret organizations, whose machinery was north but whose motive power was south of the border; the magic spell of a party name, and the yet mightier power of a church and a foreign-born clan; all threatened to bring about the abandonment of a struggle, the sufferings and sacrifices of which had been brought home to every household by the new-made graves in all our church-yards, and the little mounds of earth on a thousand fields of conflict. It would not have been strange if a few thousand votes had changed the result. But though, as at Gettysburg, the victory was won only when almost the last brigade of reserve had been called to the front of the battle, it was complete and overwhelming; and the nation was saved in the trial of partiotism on the 8th of November, 1864, as decisively as on the 4th of July, 1863, it was assured of final victory in the trial of arms.

There remains the third and most serious test of all—the trial of wisdom and statesmanship. This is not merely a rebellion or a political contest with which we have to deal; it is a revolution. Our task is to obey and execute a fiat of the Almighty, written on the face of the Western hemisphere in the course of the Mississippi river: "There shall be, upon this broad domain, one nation and but one." The shock of arms revealed the fact that we had never been one people, and that a true nationality, embracing all States and sections, had never existed. Heterogeneous populations, hostile systems, and irreconcilable ideas had only been placed in contact, and held to bare juxta-position by a constitutional compact. No chemical union had ever taken place; for that the white-hot crucible of civil war was found necessary. To keep up the fire until antagonistic elements are refined away and a perfect union is effected is needful, and is the deliberate purpose of the nation, expressed in the late election; but that is not all. To direct the process of amalgamation, to determine the time for each step, and to give shape to the new substance, will demand the most exalted statesmanship. A single error may cause a flaw that shall send the whole work back to the furnace. . . .

To guide the resistless forces, and to shun dangers on either hand—as well the Scylla of a too timid conservatism as the Charybdis of an all-destroying radicalism—to settle the thousand questions and meet the thousand difficulties that will arise, will assuredly call for a higher wisdom, a wider knowledge, a profounder foresight than has yet been needed. If we were unused to war, and had to create an army and master the art; if we had hitherto found no need of self-sacrificing patriotism in the halcyon days when love of country was an undeveloped and untested force, so it may almost be said that no statesmanship yet made manifest among us is equal to the needs of the swiftly advancing emergency. All the maxims of the past are obsolete. The teachings of the great minds of other days will be, in this trial, of as little use as the old Constitution frigate with her carronades in a battle of iron-clads. The machinery and framework of government may not improbably be found all too slender and weak for the mighty forces now evolved. A statesmanship will be needed that can steer by the compass instead of the lead-line, and can push boldly out of the narrow range of precedents and established forms into the deep water of first principles and permanent truths. It is work for a discoverer rather than for a pilot. . . .

But whether the future nationality shall be equal to the glorious possibilities of free government, whether the harmony of forces and homogeneity of elements shall be complete, will depend upon the measure of statesmanship that may guide the work now close at hand. Already a great constitutional reform is demanded; and we are but dull scholars if we have not learned through all the severe experiences of this war, that no work of human device is perfect, and that nations, like children, will outgrow their clothes. Already the financial problem calls for something more than temporary expedients. Already questions of a standing army, of a permanent revenue, and of tariff or direct taxation, require reëxamination by the light of new events and needs. Already the problem of the future of the negro race assumes the gravest importance, and can be deferred but a little longer. Questions of amnesty or punishment of public enemies already engage the attention of rulers and people. Behind these there throng in the anteroom whole troops of problems new and strange—of interests needing protection and claims clamoring for adjustment. The offing is full of questions, fast anchored once, but now cast adrift by the storm. The change to which we are called is radical. It is the new-birth of the nation.

In such a crisis it may be well to remember that the nation that governs itself has to pay for its blunders, and that it will not do to play at politics. . . .

Of all the unsolved problems the most important, and the one that demands most urgently thorough examination and final settlement, is that which concerns the present status of the rebellious States and the proper mode of reconstruction. It is too momentous a subject to be left to chance. Future generations will consider with amazement that, instead of first ascertaining the true theory, and guiding by that the decisions that shall serve as precedents for the future, we permit local, temporary, and often personal considerations to determine the decisions. Thus blind and often conflicting precedents are established; and the theory is left to some era of leisure when the political geologist, by patient delving and much study of the fossil remains, may perhaps pick it out of the chaotic record. The organic law of ten future States ought to be arrived at in some different fashion. But this blindness of action, and the prevalence of views peculiarly chaotic and vague, are not without excuse. The question is one of no little difficulty; it goes deeper than all our statutes and deeper than the Constitution itself, and makes all precedents as useless as the trilobites. The very multitude of theories darkens counsel, and rarely, if ever, has the question been stripped of all extraneous matter and clearly stated. It has nothing to do with slavery or confiscation. It is simply this: "Do the civil rights under our government, once vested in certain States and the citizens of those States, still exist, and, if so, in whom are they vested?" To discuss particular measures of reconstruction and attempt partial reorganizations, without first giving to this question a final and formal answer, is to put up a frame and finish off a wing before the shape of the building is fixed or the foundation laid. . . .

It would surely be not a little to the credit of the nation to sweep away . . . all those paltry *simulacra* of elections and organizations which have hitherto started up like mushrooms in the track of our armies. . . . Have we not seen enough of these manufactured organizations, which "live, move and have their being" in the baggage wagons of our army? They afford excellent chances for political chicanery; nice honors and fat offices are recovered from "abeyance" by men whose surprising merit had not been discovered in times of peace; but is the Union cause materially helped or do the Union loving people of the South thereby obtain any substantial protection? Is it not time to ask if these sickly plants do not cost more than it is worth to rear them, and to look with favor on a theory, which, by removing all pretext for such premature growths, sweeps away the whole system of political jugglery so engendered?

Another consideration seems worthy of especial attention. Our law of treason is less effective or severe than that of other civilized nations. To the framers of the Constitution treason seemed a crime strangely horrid and improbable, and there doubtless appeared to be greater danger from an over rigorous loyalty, which, in times of excitement, might mistake reasonable freedom of thought and speech for hostility to the government. . . . But, were the South to lay down her arms to-day, and resume the rights which the abeyance theory concedes, there is no security that even these leaders would not find absolute immunity from punishment. Even the most notorious traitor could exercise every right of citizenship until he had been tried and convicted by a jury from his own State, and nothing in the laws of that State would exclude any other notorious traitor from the jury-box. What punishment would Davis fear from a jury of Mississippians, of whom perhaps half had just laid aside smoking muskets and dripping swords to enter the panel? To place such immunity within the reach of rebels, who may abandon the contest whenever they find it hopeless, is to put a premium on treason. We are cramped by no legal forms of constitutional obligations, unless we choose, in punishing this rebellion. Rising to the proportions of a civil war, it has placed in the hands of the nation not only the remedial agencies of the courts, but the torch and sword of the conqueror. Rebels are now not rebels only, but public enemies; Gettysburg's slaughter and Sherman's march have a broader sweep than any enacted penalties; and the right of conquest cuts deeper than any conceivable measure of confiscation. The law of war becomes supreme, and of that law "*Vae Victis*" is the epitome. We have only to apply the principles of the decision above quoted to the work of reconstruction, to make sure that the punishment, for leaders at least, shall be severe enough to prevent for all future time the recurrence of a crime so terribly destructive to the national prosperity and the national honor. . . . Schemes of reconstruction which make possible immunity for the great conspirators, or instant return to all political privileges for traitors as well as loyalists, will not be such as the people will approve or the nation can safely adopt. Nor will it answer, in overflowing leniency for past offenses, to neglect security for healthy political action in the future. Men who have deliberately betrayed trusts guarded by all the sanctity of an oath are not safely to be trusted as loyal and true citizens, whenever they may choose to renew an obligation once violated. But the state constitutions only can effectually debar any from suffrage, office, or trust; under the abeyance theory each State can demand recognition with her old constitution and laws; nor is it easy to find authority for requiring particular changes as conditions of recognition. Instead of retaining these old constitutions, redolent of the slave-pen, defiled in every part by the use of traitors, and infested in every joint and crevice by claims that loyal men must loathe but can never wholly extirpate, the erection and admission of new States demolishes all these relics of a shameful past, and secures new and spotless constitutions, each in harmony in every part with the spirit of the new era, and instinct and vital with freedom and loyalty. . . .

In this view all [reconstruction] action thus far taken in the case of Louisiana must be held premature and ill-considered. False in theory, it has been not less pernicious in its consequences. How much the "abeyance" theory has helped

Louisiana thus far, can be learned by a very slight examination of the character of the men brought to the surface of the political caldron. How much it has advanced military operations, let the Red River performances answer. What sort of a "State" has been produced by this hot-house culture, those can judge who know that its authority is bounded by the range of our cannon, and that the loyal districts are but islets in a wide circumambient ocean of disloyalty. The question is already before Congress, and it is to be hoped that not only its special merits and demerits, but the whole theory of reconstruction, may now receive thorough consideration. . . .

18. BEN WADE, SPEECH

January 9, 1865

Radical Republicans in and out of Congress agreed that the "thorough consideration" that Grosvenor asked for was necessary. To be sure, the sense of urgency on this score early in 1865 was far less than had been true six months earlier, during the angry exchanges on the Wade-Davis veto and the subsequent manifesto. The balmy effects of Lincoln's renomination and re-election, of his choice of Chase as Chief Justice of the United States, of his support for the freedmen's bureau and the Thirteenth Amendment proposals, and above all of Lee's declining fortunes southward, generated the softer mood. In a sense the North was entering springtime after a fearfully long and hazardous winter.

Even the siren song of spring softened craggy Ben Wade only a little. He spoke up in the Senate on January 9, 1865, to plead for nation-wide abolition, as envisaged in the Thirteenth Amendment, as a minimum for peace, instead of the Emancipation Proclamation, which embraced only the seceded states. Educated by the war, Wade no longer believed that Negroes were inferior to white men. His sense of outrage that conservative Northern Democrats were still bent somehow on retaining slavery, or at least on gaining financial compensation for masters of emancipated human property, even for the colored soldiers of the Union's armies and their families, manifested itself on January 9, 1865. After discounting rumors that Lincoln intended to retract the Emancipation Proclamation and to oppose the Thirteenth Amendment, Wade launched into a survey of the rise in Republicanism, leading to the present Radical moment.[1]

Whatever some men may say, Mr. Lincoln stands upright on the principle that I avow, that slavery shall be abolished before there can be peace. I know who they are that have . . . endeavored to explain it [Lincoln's Emancipation Proclamation] away, and their comments go to Europe and the ruling classes there are quick to seize these commentaries on the President's proclamation in order to deceive their own people, if they possibly can, with the idea that Mr. Lincoln is backing out of the great principles of liberty which endeared him to our people and secured his renomination and triumphant reëlection, and without which he would have had a millstone around his neck and could by no means have succeeded. Conservative gentlemen always suppose they are more numerous than the elections show them to be. They are about the poorest reliance a man ever found to lean upon at election time. For nearly ten years past no man has received any considerable promotion unless he won it at the hands of those who are called radicals. The radical men are the men of principle; they are the men who feel what they contend for. They are not your slippery politicians who

[1] *CG*, 38 Cong., 2 sess., p. 165.

can jigger this way or that, or construe a thing any way to suit the present occasion. They are the men who go deeply down for principle, and having fixed their eyes upon a great principle connected with the liberty of mankind or the welfare of the people, are not to be detached by any of your higgling. The sternness of their purpose has regenerated as it were this whole continent, has revolutionized it, at any rate.

Sir, the principles that I stand here to-day to contend for I contended for ten years ago in such a miserable minority in this body that those who concurred with me were not strong enough to be able to order the yeas and nays, and as we traveled up and down the streets of Washington we were in danger of being beset by the myrmidons of slavery. But where are you now, ye conservatives, that then stood with your heads so high? The radicals have their feet upon your necks; they stand now upon the principles they avowed at that day, and they are determined that their feet shall rest on the neck of this monster until he breathes his last. In the hour of victory, when we have the solution of the great question which we have so long contended for within our grasp, within our reach, do you suppose we are now to back down and to permit you to make a dishonorable pro-slavery peace after all this bloodshed and all this sacrifice of life and property? It cannot be. Such revolutions never go backwards, and if God is just, and I think He is, we shall ultimately triumph. Those who undertake to misconstrue the position of the President of the United States are acting without authority, I feel certain. If, however, the President does believe as they say, and dare take the position they would ascribe to him, it is so much the worse for the President. The people of the United States are greater than the President. The mandate they have sent forth for the death and execution of this monster, slavery, will be persisted in. The monster must die, and die he shall. . . .

19. GEORGE W. JULIAN,

SPEECH

February 7, 1865

Obeying imperatives similar to Wade's, Julian offered a reflective address to his fellow representatives on February 7, 1865, on "Radicalism and Conservatism—The Truth of History Vindicated."[1] Through his relationship to antislavery leader Giddings and because of his own forceful character and unflinching bravery, among Radicals Julian was accounted one of the men responsible for helping to guide the Union to a safe abolitionist harbor. His speech reflects the mood of confidence in the future of a slaveless, reunited America that so sweetened politics in that happiest of American new years, 1865.

Perhaps no task could be more instructive or profitable, in these culminating days of the rebellion, than a review of the shifting phases of thought and policy which have guided the administration in its endeavors to crush it. Such a retrospect, will help us vindicate the real truth of history, both as to measures and men. It will bring out, in the strongest colors, the contrast between Radicalism and Conservatism, as rival political forces, each maintaining a varying control over the conduct of the war. It will, at the same time, point out and emphasize those pregnant lessons of the struggle which may best supply the government with counsel in its further prosecution. The faithful performance of this task demands plain-

---

[1] In Julian, *Speeches on Political Questions,* pp. 229–238; and *CG,* 38 Cong., 2 sess., Appendix, pp. 65–68.

ness of speech; and I shall not shrink from my accustomed use of it, in the interests of truth and freedom.

At the beginning of this war, . . . neither of the parties to it comprehended its character and magnitude. Its actual history has been an immeasurable surprise to both, and to the whole civilized world. The rebels evidently expected to make short work of it. Judging us by our habitual and long-continued submission to Southern domination, and confiding in the multiplied assurances of sympathy and help which they had received from their faithful allies in the North, they regarded the work of dismemberment as neither difficult nor expensive. They did not dream of the grand results which have proceeded from their mad enterprise. Nor does their delusion seem to have been at all strange or unnatural. Certainly, it was not more remarkable than the infatuation of the administration, and its conservative friends. The government understood the conflict as little, and misunderstood it as absolutely, as its foes. This, sir, is one of the lessons of the war which I think it worth while to have remembered. This revolt, it was believed, was simply a new and enlarged edition of Southern bluster. The government did not realize the inexorable necessity of actual war, because it lacked the moral vision to perceive the real nature of the contest. To every suggestion of so dire an event it turned an averted face and a deaf ear. It hoped to restore order by making a show of war, without actually calling into play the terrible enginery of war. It trusted in the form, without the power of war, just as some people have trusted in the form, without the power of godliness. It will be remembered that just before the battle of Ball's Bluff, General McClellan ordered Colonel Stone to "make a slight demonstration against the rebels," which might "have the effect to drive them from Leesburg." The government seems to have pursued a like policy in dealing with the rebellion itself. "A slight demonstration," it was believed, would "have the effect" to arrest the rebels in their madness, and reëstablish order and peace in about "sixty days," without allowing them to be seriously hurt, and without unchaining the tiger of war at all. . . . Even the Commander-in-chief of our army and navy scouted the idea of putting down the rebellion by military power. He thought the country was to be saved by giving up the principles it had fairly won by the ballot in the year 1860, and to the maintenance of which the new administration was solemnly pledged. He believed in "conciliation," in "compromise,"—the meanest word in the whole vocabulary of our politics, except, perhaps, the word "conservative,"—and had far less faith in the help of bullets and bayonets in managing the rebels than in the power of our brotherly love to melt their susceptible hearts, and woo them back, gently and lovingly, to a sense of their madness and their crime. Our distinguished Secretary of State declared that "none but a despotic or imperial government would seek to subjugate thoroughly disaffected sovereignties." The policy of coercing the revolted States was disavowed by the President himself in his message to Congress of July, 1861.

Nor did the Legislative Department of the government, at that time, disagree with the Executive. On the 22d day of July of the same year,—and I say it with sorrow and shame,—on the very morning following the first battle of Bull Run, the House of Representatives, speaking in the form of solemn legislative resolves, as did the Senate two days later, declared [in the Crittenden Resolutions] that it was not the purpose of the government to "subjugate" the villains who began this work of organized and inexcusable rapine and murder. Indeed, it was not then the fashion to call them villains. In the very polite and gingerly phrase of the times they were styled "our misguided fellow-citizens," and "our erring Southern brethren," while the rebel States themselves were lovingly referred to as "our wayward sisters." The truth is, that for about a year and a half of this war the policy of tenderness to the rebels so swayed the administration that it seemed far less intent upon crushing the rebellion by arms, than upon contriving "how *not* to do it." General McClellan, who so long palsied the energies and balked the purpose of the nation, would not allow an unkind word to be uttered in his presence against the rebel leaders. If an officer or soldier was heard to speak disrespectfully of the great Confederate chief, he was summarily reprimanded, while the unrivaled reprobate and grandest of national cut-throats was pronounced a high-souled gentleman and man of honor! Not the spirit of war, but the spirit of peace, seemed to dictate our principles of action and measures of policy toward the men who had resolved, at whatever hazard or sacrifice, to break up the government by force. . . .

That this sickly policy of an inoffensive war has naturally prolonged the struggle, and greatly augmented its cost in blood and treasure, no one can doubt. That it belongs, with its entire legacy of frightful results, exclusively to the conservative element in our politics, which at first ruled the government, is equally certain. The radical men saw at first, as clearly as they see to-day, the character and spirit of this rebel revolt. . . .

But a time came when its lessons had to be unlearned. In the school of trial it was forced to admit that war does not mean peace, but exactly the opposite of peace. Slowly, and step by step, it yielded up its theories and brought itself face to face with the stern facts of the crisis. The government no longer gets frightened at the word subjugate, because of its literal etymology, but is manfully and successfully endeavoring to place the yoke of the Constitution upon the unbaptized necks of the scoundrels who have thrown it off. The war is now recognized as a struggle of numbers, of desperate physical violence, to be fought out to the bitter end, without stopping to count its cost in money or in blood. Both the people and our armies, under this new dispensation, have been learning how to hate rebels as Christian patriots ought to have done from the beginning. They have been learning how to hate rebel sympathizers also, and to brand them as even meaner than rebels outright. They regard the open-throated traitor, who stakes his life, his property, his all, upon the success of his conspiracy against the Constitution and the rights of man, as a more tolerable character than the skulking miscreant who in his heart wishes the rebellion God-speed, while masquerading in the hypocritical disguise of loyalty. Had the government been animated by a like spirit at the beginning of the outbreak, practically accepting the truth that there can be no middle ground between treason and loyalty, rebel sympathizers would have given the country far less trouble than they have done. A little wholesome severity, summarily administered, would have been a most sovereign panacea. On this point the people were in advance of the administration, and they are to-day. . . . The times of brotherly love toward rebels in arms have gone by forever. Such men as McClellan, Buell, and Fitz-John Porter, are generally out of the way, and men who believe in *fighting* rebels are in active command. This revolution in the war policy of the government, as already observed, was absolutely necessary to the salvation of our cause; and the country will not soon forget those earnest men who at first comprehended the crisis and the duty, and persistently urged a vigorous policy, suited to remorseless and revolutionary violence, till the government felt constrained to embrace it. . . .

But, here, again, Mr. Chairman, the government had to unlearn its first lessons. Its purpose to crush the rebellion and spare slavery was found to be utterly suicidal to our cause. It was a purpose to accomplish a moral impossibility, and was therefore prosecuted, if not conceived, in the interest of the rebels. It was an attempt to marry treason and loyalty; for the rebellion *is* slavery, armed with the powers of war, organized for wholesale schemes of aggression, and animated by the overflowing fullness of its infernal genius. . . . Congress took the lead in ushering in the new dispensation. A new article of

war was enacted, forbidding our armies from returning fugitive slaves. Slavery was abolished in the District of Columbia,
and prohibited in our national Territories, where it had been
planted by the dogma of popular sovereignty and the Dred
Scott decision. Our federal judiciary was so reorganized as to
make sure this anti-slavery legislation of Congress. The confiscation of slaves was provided for, and freedom offered to all
who would come over and help us, either as laborers or soldiers. . . . The [1850] Fugitive Slave Law was at first made
void as to the slaves of rebels, and finally repealed altogether,
[along] with the old [fugitive slave] law of 1793. The coast-
wise slave-trade, a frightful system of home piracy, carried on
by authority of Congress since the year 1807, was totally
abolished. The right of testimony in our federal courts, and
to sue and be sued, was conferred upon negroes. Their employment as soldiers was at last systematically provided for,
and their pay at length made the same as that of white soldiers. The independence of Hayti and Liberia was recognized,
and new measures taken to put an end to the African slave-
trade. In thus wiping out our code of national slave laws,
acknowledging the manhood of the negro, and recognizing
slavery as the enemy of our peace, Congress emphatically re-
buked the policy which had sought to ignore it, and to shield
it from the destructive hand of the war instigated by itself;
while it opened the way for further and inevitable measures of justice, looking to his complete emancipation from the
dominion of Anglo-Saxon prejudice, the repeal of all special
legislation intended for his injury, and his absolute restoration
to equal rights with the white man as a citizen as well as a
soldier.

Meanwhile, the President had been giving the subject his
sober second thought, and reconsidering his position at the
beginning of the conflict. Instead of affirming, as at first, that
the question of slavery was not involved in the struggle, he
gradually perceived, and finally admitted, that it was at once

the cause of the war and the obstacle to peace. Instead of resolving to save the Union *with* slavery, he finally resolved to save the Union without it, and by its destruction. Instead of entertaining the country with projects of gradual and distant emancipation, conditioned upon compensation to the master and the colonization of the freedmen, he himself finally launched the policy of immediate and unconditional liberation. Instead of recoiling from "radical and extreme measures," and "a remorseless revolutionary conflict," he at last marched up to the full height of the national emergency, and proclaimed "to all whom it may concern," that slavery must perish. Instead of a constitutional amendment for the purpose of eternizing the institution in the Republic, indorsed by him in his inaugural message, he became the zealous advocate of a constitutional amendment abolishing it forever. Instead of committing the fortunes of the war to pro-slavery commanders, whose hearts were not in the work, he learned how to dispense with their services, and find the proper substitutes. These forward movements were not ventured upon hastily, but after much hesitation and apparent reluctance. Not suddenly, but following great deliberation and many misgivings, he issued his proclamation of freedom. Months afterward he doubted its wisdom; but it was a grand step forward, which at once severed his relations with his old conservative friends, and linked his fortunes thenceforward to those of the men of ideas and of progress. Going hand in hand with Congress in the great advance measures referred to, or acquiescing in their adoption, the whole policy of the administration has been revolutionized. Abolitionism and loyalty are now accepted as convertible terms, and so are treason and slavery. Our covenant with death is annulled. Our national partnership with Satan has been dissolved; and just in proportion as this has been done, and an alliance sought with divine Providence, has the cause of our country prospered. In a word, Radicalism has saved our nation from the political damnation and ruin to which Conservatism would certainly have consigned it; while the mistakes and failures of the administration stand confessed in its new policy, which alone can vindicate its wisdom, command the respect and gratitude of the people, and save it from humiliation and disgrace.

Mr. Chairman, these lessons of the past suggest the true moral of this great conflict, and make the way of the future plain. They demand a vigorous prosecution of the war by all the powers of war, and that the last vestige of slavery shall be scourged out of life. Let the administration falter on either of these points, and the people will disown its policy. They have not chosen the President for another term through any secondary or merely personal considerations. In the presence of so grand an issue, men were nothing. They had no faith in General McClellan and the party leaders at his heels. They had little faith in the early policy of Mr. Lincoln, when Democratic ideas ruled his administration, and the power of slavery held him in its grasp. Had his appeal to the people been made two years earlier, he would have been as overwhelmingly repudiated as he has been gloriously indorsed. The people sustain him now, because of their assured faith that he will not hesitate to execute their will. In voting for him for a second term, they voted for liberating and arming the slaves of the South to crush out a slaveholders' rebellion. They voted that the Republic shall live, and that whatever is necessary to save its life shall be done. They voted that slavery shall be eternally doomed, and future rebellions thus made impossible. They voted, not that Abraham Lincoln can save the country, but that *they* can save it, with him as their servant. That is what was decided in the late elections. . . . They expect that Congress will pass a bill for the confiscation of the fee [i.e., landed property] of rebel landholders, and they expect the President will approve it. They expect that Congress will provide for the reconstruction of the rebel States by systematic legislation, which shall guarantee Republican governments to each of those States and the complete enfranchisement of the negro; and they will not approve, as they have not approved, of any executive interference with the people's will as deliberately expressed by Congress. They expect that Congress will provide for parceling out the forfeited and confiscated lands of rebels in small homesteads among the soldiers and seamen of the war, as a fit reward for their valor, and a security against the ruinous monopoly of the soil in the South; and they will be disappointed should this great measure fail through the default either of Congress or the Executive. They demand a system of just retaliation against the rebels for outrages committed upon our prisoners; that a policy of increasing earnestness and vigor shall prevail till the war shall be ended; and that no hope of peace shall be whispered save on condition of an absolute and unconditional surrender to our authority; and the government will only prolong the war by standing in the way of these demands. . . .

20. FREDERICK DOUGLASS,

SPEECH

April 1865

Not all Radical Republicans were willing to permit attention to center only on the future of white America. Notions had advanced during the war, with respect to the question of the Negro's future as a free man, to advocacy, by a minority of front-runners, of biracial democracy in voting, at least in conquered Secessia. With this appeal for mass democratization, at least in the South, of the machinery of decision-making, a new frontier of American political democracy opened.

Frederick Douglass pioneered the novel landscape. Speaking early in 1865 to members of the Massachusetts Anti-Slavery Society, he provided new goals for it to seek now that abolition was well on the road to achievement. Here is Douglass' statement on "What the Black Man Wants."[1] Note especially the agreeable response of his audience to his arguments, and the judgment Douglass offered that once freed and armed with the vote, Negroes would require little or no differential treatment from the national government.

I have had but one idea for the last three years to present to the American people, and the phraseology in which I clothe it is the old abolition phraseology. I am for the "immediate, unconditional, and universal" enfranchisement of the black man, in every State in the Union. [Loud applause.] Without this, his liberty is a mockery; without this, you might as well almost retain the old name of slavery for his condition; for in fact, if he is not the slave of the individual master, he is the slave of society, and holds his liberty as a privilege, not as a right. He is at the mercy of the mob, and has no means of protecting himself.

It may be objected, however, that this pressing of the Negro's right to suffrage is premature. Let us have slavery abolished, it may be said, let us have labor organized, and then, in the natural course of events, the right of suffrage will be extended to the Negro. I do not agree with this. . . . We all feel, in the existence of this Rebellion, that judgments terrible, wide-spread, far-reaching, overwhelming, are abroad in the land; and we feel, in view of these judgments, just now, a disposition to learn righteousness. This is the hour. Our streets are in mourning, tears are falling at every fireside, and under the chastisement of this Rebellion we have almost come up to the point of conceding this great, this all-important right of

---

[1] Foner, *Douglass*, IV, 158–165.

suffrage. I fear that if we fail to do it now, if abolitionists fail to press it now, we may not see, for centuries to come, the same disposition that exists at this moment. [Applause.] Hence, I say, now is the time to press this right.

It may be asked, "Why do you want it? Some men have got along very well without it. Women have not this right." Shall we justify one wrong by another? This is a sufficient answer. Shall we at this moment justify the deprivation of the Negro of the right to vote, because some one else is deprived of that privilege? I hold that women, as well as men, have the right to vote [applause], and my heart and my voice go with the movement to extend suffrage to woman; but that question rests upon another basis than that on which our right rests. We may be asked, I say, why we want it. I will tell you why we want it. We want it because it is our *right*, first of all. No class of men can, without insulting their own nature, be content with any deprivation of their rights. We want it again, as a means for educating our race. Men are so constituted that they derive their conviction of their own possibilities largely from the estimate formed of them by others. If nothing is expected of a people, that people will find it difficult to contradict that expectation. By depriving us of suffrage, you affirm our incapacity to form an intelligent judgment respecting public men and public measures; you declare before the world that we are unfit to exercise the elective franchise, and by this means lead us to undervalue ourselves, to put a low estimate upon ourselves, and to feel that we have no possibilities like other men. Again, I want the elective franchise, for one, as a colored man, because ours is a peculiar government, based upon a peculiar idea, and that idea is universal suffrage. If I were in a monarchial government, or an autocratic or aristrocratic government, where the few bore rule and the many were subject, there would be no special stigma resting upon me, because I did not exercise the elective franchise. It would do me no great violence. Mingling with the mass I should partake of the strength of the mass; I should be supported by the mass, and I should have the same incentives to endeavor with the mass of my fellow-men; it would be no particular burden, no particular deprivation; but here where universal suffrage is the rule, where that is the fundamental idea of the Government, to rule us out is to make us an exception, to brand us with the stigma of inferiority, and to invite to our heads the missiles of those about us; therefore, I want the franchise for the black man.

There are, however, other reasons, not derived from any consideration merely of our rights, but arising out of the conditions of the South, and of the country . . . which must arrest the attention of statesmen. I believe that when the tall heads of this Rebellion shall have been swept down, as they will be swept down, when the Davises and Toombses and Stephenses, and others who are leading this Rebellion shall have been blotted out, there will be this rank undergrowth of treason, to which reference has been made, growing up there, and interfering with, and thwarting the quiet operation of the Federal Government in those States. You will see those traitors, handing down, from sire to son, the same malignant spirit which they have manifested, and which they are now exhibiting, with malicious hearts, broad blades, and bloody hands in the field, against our sons and brothers. That spirit will still remain; and whoever sees the Federal Government extended over those Southern States will see that Government in a strange land, and not only in a strange land, but in an enemy's land. A post-master of the United States in the South will find himself surrounded by a hostile spirit; a collector in a Southern port will find himself surrounded by a hostile spirit; a United States marshal or United States judge will be surrounded there by a hostile element. That enmity will not die out in a year, will not die out in an age. The Federal Government will be looked upon in those States precisely as the Governments of Austria and France are looked upon in Italy at the present moment. They will endeavor to circumvent, they will endeavor to destroy, the peaceful operation of this Government. Now, where will you find the strength to counterbalance this spirit, if you do not find it in the Negroes of the South? They are your friends, and have always been your friends. They were your friends even when the Government did not regard them as such. They comprehended the genius of this war before you did. It is a significant fact, it is a marvellous fact, it seems almost to imply a direct interposition of Providence, that this war, which began in the interest of slavery on both sides, bids fair to end in the interest of liberty on both sides. [Applause.] It was begun, I say, in the interest of slavery on both sides. The South was fighting to take slavery out of the Union, and the North fighting to keep it in the Union; the South fighting to get it beyond the limits of the United States Constitution, and the North fighting to retain it within those limits; the South fighting for new guarantees, and the North fighting for the old guarantees;—both despising the Negro, both insulting the Negro. Yet, the Negro, apparently endowed with wisdom from on high, saw more clearly the end from the beginning than we did. When Seward said the status of no man in the country would be changed by the war, the Negro did not believe him. [Applause.] When our generals sent their under-lings in shoulder-straps to hunt the flying Negro back from our lines into the jaws of slavery, from which he had escaped, the Negroes thought that a mistake had been made, and that the intentions of the Government had not been rightly understood by our officers in shoulder-straps, and they continued to come into our lines, threading their way through bogs and fens, over briers and thorns, fording streams, swimming rivers, bringing us tidings as to the safe path to march, and pointing out the dangers that threatened us. They are our only friends in the South, and we should be true to them in this their trial hour, and see to it that they have the elective franchise.

I know that we are inferior to you in some things—virtually

inferior. We walk about among you like dwarfs among giants. Our heads are scarcely seen above the great sea of humanity. The Germans are superior to us; the Irish are superior to us; the Yankees are superior to us [laughter]; they can do what we cannot, that is, what we have not hitherto been allowed to do. But while I make this admission, I utterly deny, that we are originally, or naturally, or practically, or in any way, or in any important sense, inferior to anybody on this globe. [Loud applause.] This charge of inferiority is an old dodge. It has been made available for oppression on many occasions. It is only about six centuries since the blue-eyed and fair-haired Anglo-Saxons were considered inferior by the haughty Normans, who once trampled upon them. If you read the history of the Norman Conquest, you will find that this proud Anglo-Saxon was once looked upon as of coarser clay than his Norman master, and might be found in the highways and byways of old England laboring with a brass collar on his neck, and the name of his master marked upon it. *You* were down then! [Laughter and applause.] You are up now. I am glad you are up, and I want you to be glad to help us up also. [Applause.] . . .

I look over this country at the present time, and I see Educational Societies, Sanitary Commissions, Freedmen's Associations, and the like,—all very good: but in regard to the colored people there is always more that is benevolent, I perceive, than just, manifested towards us. What I ask for the Negro is not benevolence, not pity, not sympathy, but simply *justice*. [Applause.] The American people have always been anxious to know what they shall do with us. . . . Everybody has asked the question, and they learned to ask it early of the abolitionists, "What shall we do with the Negro?" I have had but one answer from the beginning. Do nothing with us! Your doing with us has already played the mischief with us. Do nothing with us! If the apples will not remain on the tree of their own strength, if they are wormeaten at the core, if they are early ripe and disposed to fall, let them fall! I am not for tying or fastening them on the tree in any way, except by nature's plan, and if they will not stay there, let them fall. And if the Negro cannot stand on his own legs, let him fall also. All I ask is, give him a chance to stand on his own legs! Let him alone! If you see him on his way to school, let him alone, don't disturb him! If you see him going to the dinner-table at a hotel, let him go! If you see him going to the ballot-box, let him alone, don't disturb him! [Applause.] If you see him going into a workshop, just let him alone,—your interference is doing him a positive injury. . . . Let him fall if he cannot stand alone! If the Negro cannot live by the line of eternal justice, . . . the fault will not be yours, it will be his who made the Negro, and established that line for his government. [Applause.] Let him live or die by that. If you will only untie his hands, and give him a chance, I think he will live. He will work as readily for himself as the white man. . . .

21. ELIZUR WRIGHT, LETTER

March 1865

The Douglass position among Radical Republicans—advocacy of Negro suffrage as a base of reconstruction—commonly received justification as a step whites should favor out of sectional, patriotic self-interest. Elizur Wright early in 1865 offered a capsule statement of a derivative theme that Radical Republicans were to repeat for the ensuing five years: that if Negroes did not vote, then the white, ex-rebel, untrustworthy South's strength in the House of Representatives must rise because the old three-fifths clause would be canceled once the Thirteenth Amendment gained ratification. Surely no rebels in history ever received a bonus for failing in their treason!

A pioneer abolitionist who had made a reputation by reforming corrupt practices of New England insurance corporations, Wright argued in this letter to the Boston *Daily Advertiser* that Northern white men should favor the black man's vote in the South as mere common sense. Because Wright was not connected with the militant New England Radicals, his dry, actuarial presentation had considerable impact. He entitled this essay, "Suffrage for the Blacks Sound Political Economy."[1]

On the heels of victory comes a question which no tax-payer can afford to neglect a moment. If the public mind is not made up on it by the time victory is fully ours, we might almost as well be defeated—that is, considering ourselves merely as property-holders and tax-payers. The question is that of reconstruction.

Opinions may differ, according to the degree of information, as to facts; but I think all will agree that there is little use and much waste of power in working a State government *by Federal machinery.*

Till the *enfranchised* population of a rebel State is so far reclaimed from the secession heresy that a *majority* of it can be relied on to protect itself and maintain its authority as an organized loyal State government, such organization is worse than superfluous, for the national power must be present in force, and to make that force efficient must be supreme. As to the white population of the rebel states, nothing is more certain than that it will take a long period of military subjugation, after the overthrow of the rebel armies, to educate out of it its rebel propensities, so that a majority of it can be relied on for loyal State government. It is certainly true that powerful interests are on the right side, and the thing would come about

---

[1] Reprinted and widely distributed in George L. Stearns, comp., *The Equality of All Men Before the Law Claimed and Defended; In Speeches by William D. Kelley, Wendell Phillips, and Frederick Douglass* (Boston: Rand & Avery, 1865), pp. 40–41.

in time. But in the meantime two things inevitably go on:—

1st. The public debt accumulates, for a military occupation never pays as it goes.

2d. The blacks are largely trained to arms, for they are the cheapest and best troops we can have under the circumstances.

Hence, when we arrive at the period when loyal State governments—*that will go alone*—can be set up, the blacks must be enfranchised or they will be ready and willing to fight for a government of their own; and here is more war, and more public debt, and more taxation.

Observe how we have put one foot in by enlisting colored troops. Perhaps we couldn't help it. We certainly cannot withdraw it. Now we are putting in the other, by passing the [Thirteenth] amendment to the Constitution.

The effect of this, when passed, is to take away about 1-27th of the power of the loyal States in the lower house of Congress, and give it to the reconstructed rebel States, provided all are restored. This comes of counting into the representative population two-fifths of certain persons who were before counted out. To be more exact, suppose the amendment passed, all the rebel States restored, and the 24 members of the House of Representatives to be apportioned among the several States by the rule adopted for the 38th Congress, members would be gained and lost as follows:—

Gain.		Loss.	
Alabama ....1 Member.		Illinois ....1 Member.	
Georgia ....1 "		Indiana ....1 "	
Louisiana ....1 "		Iowa ....1 "	
Mississippi ......1 "		Minnesota ....1 "	
N. Carolina ......1 "		New York ....1 "	
S. Carolina ......1 "		Ohio ....1 "	
Tennessee ....1 "		Rhode Island .....1 "	
Texas .... "		Pennsylvania .....2 "	
Virginia ....1 "		—	
—		Total .... "	
Total 9			

If the franchise in the reclaimed States is to be restricted to the white population, this giving them the advantage of eighteen votes when readmitted, puts off the day when such a thing can be safely done. If done too promptly, before secession theories and confederate bonds shall have gone back into nothingness, we may find that by the very act of amending the Constitution we have brought ourselves to the unpleasant dilemma of having either to pay the rebel debt or borrow the rebel theory and secede from the very Union we have restored by conquering the rebels.

There is only one way to avoid this and make our victory immediately fruitful. In two States a decided majority of the population is black, and, by necessity, loyal. In five others, the black element is more than one-third; and it is strong enough to make an effective balance of power in every State where the rebellious element is of any serious magnitude. Again, the particular chivalry which got up and engineered the Rebellion has such a horror of sharing political power with its former chattels, that when the enfranchisement of the blacks is determined on as the *sine qua non* of reconstruction, and its own military power is overthrown, it will emigrate to a more congenial political atmosphere. We have then nothing to do but convert whites enough to make a majority, when added to the enfranchised blacks, to have State governments that can be trusted to stand alone.

I think I could easily convince any man, who does not allow his prejudices to stand in the way of his interests, that it will probably make a difference of at least $1,000,000,000 in the development of the national debt, whether we reconstruct on the basis of loyal white and black votes, or on white votes exclusively, and that he can better afford to give the Government at least one-quarter of his estate than have it try the latter experiment.

I am not disputing about tastes. A negro's ballot may be more vulgar than his bullet. Being already in for it, the question with me is, how the one or the other can be made to protect my property from taxation; and I am sure I would rather give away half the little I have, than to have the victories of 1865 thrown away, as I am sure they will be, if, endeavoring to keep the South in subjugation by black armies, the Government allows four millions of black population to continue disfranchised.

22. ABRAHAM LINCOLN, SPEECH

April 11, 1865

Implicit in these arguments is a conviction that equal access to the ballot in effect ended the nation's responsibility for the millions of Negroes freed because the nation needed to deny their muscles to the Confederacy. Armed with the ballot, Southern freedmen became in truth free men. Thereupon they required no further paternalistic protection from the government. Further, if Southern Negroes participated as voters or even as officeholders in restored state governments of defeated Dixie, then intra-Republican splits over reconstruction policy, as in the Lincoln versus Wade-Davis imbroglio, were made unnecessary. President and Congress need create no formal reconstruction policy at all. Biracial politics in the South would reflect fairly the region's war-swollen number of seats in the lower house of Congress. The Southern white Unionists thereby would receive the nation's support, and thereafter even the South presumably would vote Republican. A viable two-party system could rise. More, the disagreeable question of disfranchisement could be avoided. Ex-rebels would require only temporary second-placing until they should, if they could, regain top spot, with the understanding that never again would they reinstate slavery or threaten secession. Indeed, the argument for Negro suffrage boiled down to a conviction that postwar biracial democracy in Dixie best could cure the Southern ills that resulted from too little prewar democracy.

Abraham Lincoln was only the most prominent recruit to these views. He announced his conversion publicly on April 11, 1865. That softly twilighted evening, a crowd of gay celebrants wove an erratic course to the White House in order to cheer the President who had led them to this happy moment of Lee's surrender. Their calls drew Lincoln out into the sweet spring evening.

The occasion was hardly usual for airing a controversial question. Nevertheless, the President had something to say beyond offering heartfelt thanks to the armed services that had won the victory. The inextricably intertwined questions of the reconstruction of the South and the fates of the millions of the South's Negroes were matters so important to Lincoln that he was impelled to bring them before this adventitious audience, perhaps in order to clarify his own thinking by stating the problem, to gain the unstudied reaction of the crowd as a gauge to public opinion, and certainly in order to inform Congressional leaders of both parties how he felt on certain questions.

Of course Lincoln was immensely proud that he was the first President since Jackson to receive the accolade of election to a second term. From his anticipation that he had four years at his disposal in which to apply the lessons of the past to present and future needs, and from his buoyant optimism concerning the health of America's political institutions and moral standards now that secession was reversed and slavery was doomed, Lincoln spoke candidly to his attentive audience:

By these recent successes the re-inauguration of the national authority—reconstruction—which has had a large share of thought from the first, is pressed much more closely upon our attention. Unlike the case of a war between independent nations, there is no authorized organ for us to treat with. No one man has the authority to give up the rebellion for any other man. We must simply begin with, and mold from, disorganized and discordant elements. Nor is it a small additional embarrassment that we, the loyal people, differ among ourselves as to the mode, manner, and means of reconstruction.[1]

Clearly there was no fixed "presidential plan of reconstruction."

---

[1] Lincoln, *Works,* VIII, 400–405.

Lincoln understood what historians later forgot—that "so great peculiarities pertain to each [rebel] state; and such important and sudden changes occur in the same state; and, withal, so new and unprecedented is the whole case [of reconstruction], that no exclusive, and inflexible plan can safely be prescribed as to details and collaterals."[2]

Still, Lincoln believed that essential minimum standards must exist in any reconstruction effort, if the North was to accept it, and if obvious injustice was to be avoided. "Important principles may, and must, be inflexible," he insisted.

The primary clue as to what Lincoln believed were "important principles" that must be "inflexible" emerged as he discussed the Unionist state government in Louisiana, long the showpiece of executive reconstruction in the occupied South. The Louisiana experiment, under way since New Orleans had fallen three years earlier, had built itself, with the essential support of the United States Army, into a revamped state government. A minority (twelve thousand) of white Louisianans had sworn future loyalty to the Union, accepted Lincoln's pardon for their past participations in rebellion, and crafted a new constitution for that state. Lincoln noted approvingly that this reformed constitution embraced the abolition of slavery and contained clauses "giving the benefit for public schools equally to black and white, and empowering the [state] Legislature to confer the elective franchise upon the colored man."[3]

Nevertheless, Louisiana was under fire from northern humanitarians and Radical Republican political spokesmen, as being a hypocritical subterfuge barely concealing renascent servitude for that state's colored people. As proof, critics correctly charged that the "loyal" whites in Louisiana, despite the permissive clause in their constitution, kept the polls closed to Negroes. Lincoln wished that Louisiana whites would alter and broaden the electoral base. "I would myself prefer that it [the suffrage] were now conferred on the very intelligent [Negroes], and on those who serve our cause as soldiers," he said. And he warned: "What has been said

---

2 *Ibid.*
3 *Ibid.*

of Louisiana will apply generally to other [Southern] States." He
expected to have to "make some new announcement to the people
of the South. I am considering [one], and shall not fail to act, when
satisfied that action shall be proper."[4]

This was not Lincoln's first leaning toward the growing Radical
sentiment in favor of Negro suffrage. A year earlier, on March 13,
1864, Lincoln had written confidentially to Louisianan Michael
Hahn, his newly designated governor of that "reconstructed" state.
"I barely suggest for your private consideration, whether some of
the colored people may not be let in [to the exercise of the suf-
frage]—as, for instance, the very intelligent, and especially those
who have fought gallantly in our ranks. They would probably
help, in some trying time to come, to keep the jewel of liberty
within the family of freedom."[5]

To be sure, even this flaccid suggestion, given without hint of
command, was advanced for the time. How much further had
Lincoln traveled by April 1865, when he stated publicly, not in a
private letter, that he intended to see to it that at least some
Negroes voted in every Southern state as one of the minimums of
principle to which he adverted in his speech.

23. WHITELAW REID, ARTICLE ON

LINCOLN AND NEGRO SUFFRAGE

July 23, 1865

Nothing in Lincoln's career suggests that he championed causes
in which he did not believe or that he felt were beyond the realm
of probable attainment through political action. He regarded Presidential speeches and state papers as opportunities to preach to, and

[4] *Ibid.*
[5] Lincoln, *Works*, VII, 243; see Fawn M. Brodie, "A Lincoln Who
Never Was," *The Reporter* (June 25, 1959), pp. 25–27.

to teach, his countrymen. In 1862 he had employed such an occasion with respect to emancipation. At Gettysburg a year later he tied the war's unfolding meaning to the nation's history. On the occasion of his second inauguration in March 1865, Lincoln spoke out feelingly for a reconstruction without rancor.

His speech five weeks later on April 11 made clear his belief, newly achieved, that Negro suffrage was the way for white Southerners to prove that they deserved such treatment. Of course Lincoln thought he had until March 1869 to prod sluggish ex-rebels toward new biracial high-water marks of democratic practice. But only three days, not four years, remained to him.

In later months and years, conservatives denied that Lincoln had ever declared for Negro suffrage or intended the novelty to apply across the crumpled Confederacy. Men close to events knew better.

Replying in July 1865 to the canard that Lincoln had not advocated Negro suffrage as the best road for the white South to take, Ohio journalist Whitelaw Reid revealed that Salmon P. Chase, former Treasury head and recently Chief Justice of the United States, was a source of Radical ideas commanding respect in high places. The selection that follows appeared July 23, 1865, in the Cincinnati *Gazette* under Reid's by-line, "Agate." It reflects the confidence both of Chase and of Reid in Lincoln's determination and sincerity on this score. Neither man was likely to be fooled.[1]

President Lincoln on Negro Suffrage.

Efforts have recently been made to prejudice the dispassionate argument of the question of Universal Suffrage on its merits, by bringing the weight of a great name to bear against it. Whether it is right is, it is true, a much more important question than whether Mr. Lincoln was in favor of it; but, while the world stands, we shall always have large numbers whose principles are adopted, rather because great men have be-

---

[1] See alternative text for Chase's letter in Lincoln, *Works*, VIII, 399–401n.

lieved them, than because of any logical conviction of their truth.

Lately published extracts have shown, in part, what Mr. Lincoln thought it politic to say of Negro Suffrage in the campaigns of 1858–9. Men who are ready to accord weight to his opinions then will not hesitate to give greater weight to opinions formed in the light of larger experience, and held down to the morning of the day of his assassination.

Yesterday's *Gazette* brought to light a letter from Mr. Lincoln, written [to Hahn] as long ago as March, 1864, when Negro Suffrage was a thing to speak of in bated breath, and with many a shudder. Even then, in advance of almost every leading man of the party which supported him, Mr. Lincoln was found inquiring—in a quarter where he knew inquiry to be almost equal to command—whether the very intelligent negroes, especially those who had fought gallantly in our ranks, might not be "let in."

. . . A year later this suggestive inquiry deepened into a settled conviction. On the evening of 11th April, 1865, in response to the congratulations of the citizens of Washington over the fall of Richmond, the President read from the portico of the White House a carefully written speech, in which, referring to the Louisiana reorganization, he used these words:

'It is unsatisfactory to some to know that the elective franchise is not given to the colored man. I would myself prefer that it were now conferred on intelligent colored men, and on those who serve our cause as soldiers.'

Such were Mr. Lincoln's views, expressed with all the deliberation of a grave political manifesto, three days before his death. Fortunately there is authentic evidence that they remained unchanged to the end.

In the midst of the general ecstasy of rejoicing over the surrender of Lee's army, the following letter, never before published, was addressed by Chief Justice Chase to the President: . . .

'Baltimore, April 12.

DEAR SIR:

The [Baltimore] American of this morning contains your speech of last evening. Seeing that you say something on the subject of . . . reorganization—and refer, though with out naming me, to the suggestions I made [in a letter of the preceding day] in relation to the [December 1863 reconstruction and] amnesty proclamation, when you brought it before the heads of Departments, I will add some observations to what I have already written.

I recollect . . . an objection to the restriction of participation in reorganization to persons having the qualifications of voters under the laws [of Southern states] in force just before rebellion. Ever since questions of reconstruction have been talked about, it has been my opinion that colored loyalists ought to be allowed to participate in it; and it was because of this opinion that I was anxious to have this question left open. I did not, however, say much about the restriction [in Cabinet]. I was the only one who expressed a wish for its omission, and did not desire to seem pertinacious.

You will remember, doubtless, that the first order ever issued for enrollment [of voters], with a view to reorganization, went to Gen. Shepley, and directed the enrollment of all loyal [Louisiana] citizens; and I suppose that . . . no one connected with your Administration has questioned the citizenship of free colored men, more than that of free white men. The restriction in the amnesty proclamation operated as a revocation of the order to Gen. Shepley; but as I understood you not to be wedded to any particular plan of reconstruction, I hoped that reflection and observation would satisfy you that the restriction should not be adhered to. I fully sympathized with your desire for the restoration of the Union by the change of rebel slave States into Union free States, and was willing, if I could not get exactly the plan I thought best, to take the plan you thought best and trust to the future for modifications.

I know you attach much importance to the admission of Louisiana, or rather to her right to representation in Congress, as a loyal State in the Union. If I am not misinformed, there is nothing in the way except the indisposition of her Legislature to give proof satisfactory of loyalty by a sufficient guarantee of safety and justice to colored citizens, through the extension to loyal colored men of the right of suffrage. Why not, then, as almost every loyal man concurs with you as to the desirableness of that recognition, take the shortest road to it, by causing every proper representation to be made to the Louisiana Legislature, of the importance of such extension?'

Mr. Chase entered more in detail into a discussion of the question, covering in the main his often expressed views, and concluded thus:

'Once I should have been, if not satisfied, partially, at least, contented with suffrage for the intelligent and those who have been soldiers; now I am convinced that Universal suffrage is demanded by sound policy and impartial justice. I have written too much already, and will not trouble you with my reasons. I shall return to Washington in a day or two, and perhaps it will not be disagreeable to you to have the whole subject talked over.

Truly and faithfully yours,

S. P. CHASE'

That conversation never came. The shot which struck down the Martyr-President in the midst of splendid success and noble purposes, left the Chief Justice on his return no other duty than that of swearing into office Mr. Lincoln's successor.

The last of these letters, however, was received by the President on the evening before his assassination. It happens to be within my personal knowledge that on the next morning he showed it to a leading member of the Cabinet; and it was so well known as to have been currently talked of among Administration leaders at Washington that at the Cabinet meeting that day, which followed, Mr. Lincoln's expressions in favor of the liberality toward negro citizens in the reorganization which Mr. Chase had urged, were fuller and more emphatic than in either of the instances already quoted.

Never were the hopes of the progressive loyalists of the country in Mr. Lincoln stronger; never was their confidence in him more perfect; never was the assurance that his wisdom, benevolence and power would secure perfect protection to the rights of all men so complete, as on the day when he was lost to the Nation and to Mankind. The Country can judge with what lack of reason *his* authority is now invoked against these latest expressions of his faith and wish.

PART SIX

The Freedmen's Bureau:

Self-Help Versus Paternalism

---

24. CHARLES SUMNER, SPEECH

June 8, 1864

On April 11, 1865, when Lincoln advocated biracial suffrage as a condition for reconstruction, he had at hand an administrative instrument through which he and other Republicans expected to achieve acceptance in the South of Negro voting, thus to avoid repetition of the intraparty disputes so frequent in 1864. At last Congress had passed the laggard statute that created in the War Department a temporary Bureau of Freedmen, Refugees, and Abandoned Lands. Lincoln had agreeably signed it into law the same day it emerged from Congress, March 3, 1865.

The Bureau act ignored the prickly question of whether President or Congress had a monopoly over reconstruction. Instead of ruinous Republican cross-purposes over the outward forms of loyalty in the South, the Bureau hoped to build better inward practices of democracy. Once the familiar machinery of Northern democracy —free schools especially, and loftier versions of Christian morality—was rooted in Dixie, the optimistic assumption was that an enlarged, piebald, and trustworthy electorate would follow.

As James Russell Lowell noted, Lincoln's Republicans were not in search of "abstract ideal[s]" but were seeking "adaptation [of government] to the wants of the governed." He argued that Congress' performance must be judged by its "capacity to shape itself to the demands of the time. It is not to be judged by its intention but by its results, and those will be proportioned to its practical, and not its theoretic excellence." Most notably, the Radical Republicans sought "the practical comfort of a system that works," Lowell wrote.[1]

What, practically, would "work" to alter Southern society and to make that contumacious section more harmonious with and conformable to the ways of the North? For many concerned Americans, the answer was simple and obvious. Free schools would be the carpet magically transforming the South's aristocratic tradition into democratic practices. "The line of free schools marked the line of loyalty to the [national] Government," a Pennsylvania educator told an audience at a professional convention held early in 1865. "We must push that line to the Gulf. Free schools are needed not only as an element in the reconstruction of the Union, but as a means of preserving it when reconstructed."[2]

An effort today equivalent to that the Republicans planned for the Bureau would involve many government agencies, ranks of experts drawn from universities and industries, and staffs from prestigious philanthropic foundations. Vast budgets would bring forth, in predictable first order of priority, "studies" of the problem. Statutes built on this accumulation presumably would call for large money appropriations, to run for years, and for creation of an administrative staff of impressive proportions.

To be sure, the framers of the Bureau bill were unfamiliar with "Parkinson's Law." But they were not fools. Awareness in Congress was clear and general that a titanic job impended. Four million Negroes were to ascend what Sumner described in a speech,

---

[1] Lowell, *Works*, V, 217–218.
[2] J. P. Wickersham, "Education as an Element in Reconstruction," National Teacher's Association *Proceedings and Lectures* (August 1865), p. 296.

June 8, 1864, as a "Bridge from Slavery to Freedom"—the Freedmen's Bureau.[3]

In America's earlier history, organized charity had been private, usually church-connected. Sumner's major argument in this speech centered on the need for the national government to assume the major burden in leading freedmen to freedom. A social change so vast was beyond the capacity of private humanitarian enterprise to handle, he argued. Only the resources of the nation, which had been hugely enlarged since 1861, and which already provided assistance to transcontinental railroad corporations and to states' universities, could bear the load or

. . . supply the adequate machinery, and extend the proper network of assistance, with the proper unity of operation. The National Government must interfere in the case, precisely as in building the Pacific Railroad. Private charity in our country is active and generous; but it is powerless to cope with the evils arising from a wicked institution; nor can it provide a remedy, where society itself is overthrown.

There are few who will not admit that something must be done by the Government. Cold must be the heart that could turn away from this call. But whatever is done must be through some designated agency; and this brings me to another aspect of the question.

The President in his Proclamation of Emancipation has used the following language: "I recommend to them,"—that is, to the freedmen,—"that in all cases, when allowed, they labor faithfully for reasonable wages." Such is the recommendation from that supreme authority which decreed Emancipation. They are to labor, and for reasonable wages. But the President does not undertake to say how this opportunity shall be obtained,—how the laborer shall be brought in connection with the land, how his rights shall be protected, and how his new-found liberty shall be made a blessing. It was enough, perhaps, on the occa-

---

[3] Sumner, *Works*, VIII, 480–481. Note that even at this late date, Sumner felt it necessary to calm fears of "loyal" border-state slaveowners and of Northern entrepreneurs who planned to employ freedmen in large-scale cotton production schemes, by stressing that the Bureau would have jurisdiction only over Negroes whom the war had liberated.

sion of the Proclamation, that the suggestion should be made. Faithful labor and reasonable wages: let these be secured, and everything else will follow. But how shall they be secured?

Different subjects, as they become important, are committed to special bureaus. I need only refer to Patents, Agriculture, Public Lands, Pensions, and Indian Affairs,—each under the charge of a separate Commissioner. Clearly, the time has come for a Bureau of Freedmen. In speaking of this agency, I mean a bureau which will be confined in operation to the affairs of freedmen, and not travel beyond this increasing class to embrace others, although of African descent. Our present necessity is to help those made free by the present war; and the term "freedmen" describes sufficiently those who have once been slaves. It is this class we propose to help during the *transition period* from Slavery to Freedom. Call it charity or duty, it is sacred as humanity.

25. FREEDMEN'S BUREAU LAW

March 3, 1865

In view of this awareness of the immensity of the work before them, it is astonishing that the congressmen who shaped the Bureau should have specified for it a life of only one year after armed hostilities ceased. Further, the initial money appropriation for the Bureau's operations was—nothing at all.

Among historians, the consensus has been that the Bureau was a sham, and many of its Republican backers, hypocritical exploiters of the Negro's needs. The eminent historian W. E. B. Du Bois, a Negro, concluded in 1910 that "a Freedman's Bureau [should have been] established for ten twenty or forty years with a careful distribution of [rebel's] land and capital [among Negroes and Unionist whites] and a [national, unsegregated] system of education for the [South's] children."[1] Closing the most complete inquiry available into the Bureau's origins and operations, George

---

[1] Du Bois, "Reconstruction and its Benefits," *American Historical Review*, XV (July 1910), 785.

R. Bentley in 1955 estimated that "what the freedmen . . . needed in 1865 was not just an act of Congress and the guardianship of a federal agency, but a change in the mores of a nation."[2]

Du Bois condemned the Bureau's architects for attempting too little; Bentley, for essaying too much. In 1964 Henry Steele Commager added other measures by which to criticize the conceptual adequacy of the Bureau:[3]

> The Government—Congress, Executive, Army—failed to work out a consistent policy and, in the end, failed the Negro. At a time when Congress set aside millions of acres for homesteaders in the West and gave over a hundred million acres to railroad corporations, it could not summon up either generosity or vision enough to give land to the freedmen. It was this . . . that was most ominous, for it revealed not a deliberate decision to repudiate the Negro but the absence of any sense of obligation and any imagination where the Negro was concerned. The Government, which spent hundreds of millions to free the Negro and eagerly availed itself of the services of a quarter of a million Negro soldiers, did next to nothing to take care of the freedmen once the war was over.
>
> This lack of imagination in the victorious North was paralleled by an equally ominous lack of imagination in the defeated South: an assumption by members of the planter class that slavery, secession, war and defeat should not be held against them in the final reckoning. They acknowledged that they had been defeated. They were not prepared to admit that defeat should have unpleasant consequences for them. A kind of modified feudalism would now be substituted for slavery, and they expected things to go on just as they had in the past.
>
> Because few Northerners had any interest in the Negro, and fewer still any real understanding of the race problem in the South, and because most Northerners were far too eager to return to normalcy to persist in the effort to impose an unpopular policy upon the South, Northern opinion and Government acquiesced in the Southern view of the Negro and, finally, of the

---

[2] George R. Bentley, *A History of the Freedmen's Bureau* (Philadelphia: University of Pennsylvania Press, 1955), p. 214.

[3] In a review of Rose, *Rehearsal for Reconstruction,* in *New York Times Book Review,* September 13, 1964, p. 6.

war itself. That acquiescence—dramatized in the Compromise of 1876 and rationalized in the judicial emasculation of the 14th and 15th Amendments—was to stretch out across American history for a hundred years.

Of this much-maligned law, Attorney General James Speed was moved in mid-1865 to complain, "There are few statutes that are disfigured by loose and indefinite phraseology to a greater extent than the act of 1865, establishing this Bureau. . . . [N]o man can . . . be certain that any construction of the words employed reaches the true meaning of the Legislature."[4]

Du Bois' criticisms are justified if the possibility existed in 1865 to arm the Bureau with war-scale powers, functions, and budgets, and to provide it with indefinite or even permanent tenure. Bentley's conclusion is relevant if the Bureau's Congressional architects intended to alter Northern mores, not Southern. Commager's suggestion that the national government fell short in what it did for Negroes, in comparison to what businessmen received, is applicable if the two scales are interchangeable. But none of these conditions obtained a century ago. Instead, the now curious features of the Freedmen's Bureau reflected imperatives of that time, not of ours, and represented what was possible as well as what most Republicans believed was desirable.

Stated otherwise, wartime Radical Republicanism was not focused wholly on the Negro, although many Radicals were turning that way, as Lincoln was. Other factors took precedence during 1864 and 1865. The overriding fact is that the question of morality is common to all these considerations.

Fear even among Radical reformers for the government's fiscal health was a prominent bar to braver leaps than the Freedmen's Bureau promised. Men hag-ridden by Victorian notions of fiscal economy, though of good will toward the Negro, agreed with the 1862 statement of William Pitt Fessenden of Maine that "the present of all times in the world is the last when we ought to enlarge the organization of the government."[5] Fessenden left Congress to

---

[4] Speed to Stanton, June 22, 1865, quoted in Bentley, p. 49; and see pp. 1–49.

[5] May 1862, in opposition to the proposed department of agriculture; *CG*, 37 Cong., 2 sess., p. 2016. Probably he would have voted against

succeed Chase as Secretary of the Treasury, and in Congress and Cabinet he had decisive influence on the curiously flat budget of the Bureau law.

The economy goad, among other reasons, justified locating the Bureau in the War Department. With war still on and rebel lines shrinking, many Army officers were becoming surplus and without budget increases could be assigned to Bureau work. Numerous officers during the war had experience in occupation duties. If armed resistance developed to Bureau operations, combat units would reply quicker if called by familiar voices. Vast quantities of noncombatant Army matériel could be used in the Bureau's relief and educational functions without incurring new tax burdens.

Indeed, in administrative terms it would have been simplest to make the Bureau entirely an Army show. Pious combat veteran Oliver O. Howard, the "Christian general" whom Lincoln named to head the Bureau, admitted that "it was very tempting to put the strong hand of the military power on the freedmen, but we had other trings to think of."[6]

These "other things" included certain facts of life obvious to career officers. Once shooting stopped, the mass citizen's armies would quickly demobilize. Most of the regular regiments would go westward to suppress war-restive Indians and to contain the French adventurers in Mexico. A wholly military Freedmen's Bureau, competing for a share of predictably tiny peacetime appropriations against the entrenched traditional departments and the combat field commands, would stand little chance to grab enough to reach its goals.

Therefore the Bureau's framers intended it to be a hybrid civil-military, budgetless organization. Uniformed officers were to gild its command posts and wrap the Bureau in the flag. But almost all

the Bureau; see Charles A. Jellison, *Fessenden of Maine: Civil War Senator* (Syracuse: Syracuse University Press, 1962), pp. 178–179. Although dealing with slightly later events, the following attend to the moral issue in the fiscal question: Richard H. Timberlake, Jr., "Ideological Factors in Specie Resumption and Treasury Policy," *Journal of Economic History*, XXIV (March 1964), 29–52; Irwin Unger, "Business Men and Specie Resumption," *Political Science Quarterly*, LXXIV (March 1959), 46–70.

[6] Quoted in *DeBow's Review*, N.S. I (March 1866), 324.

personnel and financial support were to come from volunteer civilian sources.

The understood goal of the Bureau—education for the South's whites and Negroes, to result in suffrage for the latter—also mitigated against military monopoly in the effort. The Regular Army had traditionally been proslavery, antiabolitionist, and antireform. These attitudes infested even wartime volunteers of humanitarian bent and Radical Republican politics. William Grosvenor, whose trenchant article appeared earlier, recalled to Sumner that when he was invalided out of the Army and ". . . came back [to Connecticut] from the South I was strongly under the influence of that same strange prejudice which leads so many of our officers and soldiers to oppose negro suffrage. . . . I came home very reluctant to extend to negroes the election franchise. Even to myself this feeling is still a mystery; I got over it soon, but can never tell when or how I imbibed it."[7]

What, then, of the provision of the 1865 Bureau law that it was to have only one year after hostilities closed in which to work? Congress was not being naïve, foolish, or cynical. Again employing Howard's trustworthy explanation, "It would have required more than human foresight to have wholly met [i.e., foreseen] the difficulties of this dark period of our Governmental history, but the friends of the measure hoped that . . . the experiences of one year of active operation under the eye of our most energetic and able Secretary of War [Edwin M. Stanton] would demonstrate the value of the Bureau sufficiently to warrant at least another year's trial."[8]

A year later the unanticipatable duel between Andrew Johnson and the Republican party was under way. The Bureau's terminal date nearing and its extension having been requested, Howard confessed that experience had illuminated a more realistic target date. "If we can hold a steady hand now, in five years there will be no need of a Government control over these people [Negroes]," he told a Cooper Union audience. "The military power can make

[7] To Sumner, September 5, 1865, Sumner Papers (Houghton Library, Harvard University).

[8] *Autobiography of Oliver Otis Howard, Major General, United States Army* (New York: Baker & Taylor, 1908) II, 205.

it [work]. I have said to Congress that education will go far towards it. . . . Education should, however, be placed there [in the ex-rebel states], as here, beyond the peradventure of failure. Some [more] time [beyond the initial one-year allotment] will be needed, but the leaven is working. The influx [into the South] of men who believe in education, and the negroes who so greatly need it, will doubtless secure the desired end."[9]

Stanton played a significant role in directing both Presidential and Congressional opinions on the shape the Bureau should assume and what it should do. He and Howard were a perfect team, which explains why Lincoln chose Howard. Neither man had political followings. Both were fearful of the decline in America's morality if the Treasury was overtasked. They believed also that patriotism as of 1865 required extension of governmental function to include the provision of suitable care for Southern Negroes, since the nation had used the blacks for war purposes.[10]

After three years' unresting service as Lincoln's "Mars," Stanton was the best-informed American on the deficiencies of the President's "ten per cent" state restorations in the South, getting his information from reports from Grant and from Congressional and War Department investigating commissions. His support for the Bureau, then, was as much to correct the white men's ways in state politics southward, as to raise the condition of freedmen. Simultaneously, as he admitted to Francis Lieber, Stanton had grown fearful of "the dangerous tendency of power concentrated in military hands." Therefore he wanted the Bureau to have only a brief life and to be hybrid rather than wholly uniform.[11]

[9] Howard in *DeBow's Review,* N.S. I (March 1866), 324–325. See also Howard's speech of August 28, 1865, in Chicago *Tribune,* August 29, 1865.

[10] See General H. W. Halleck to W. T. Sherman, August 27, 1863, in S. H. M. Byers, ed., "Reconstruction Days," *North American Review,* CXLIII (September 1886), 220; same to same, October 1, 1863, in "Some War Letters," *ibid.* (November 1866), pp. 499–500; and Benjamin P. Thomas and Harold M. Hyman, *Stanton: The Life and Times of Lincoln's Secretary of War* (New York: Knopf, 1962).

[11] Francis Lieber's memoir, Boston *Evening Transcript,* January 13, 1870; T. P. Atticus Bibbs to Sumner, April 18, 1866, Sumner Papers (Houghton Library, Harvard University).

Stanton and a few others briefly advocated having a permanent civilian agency come forth from Congress, to guard the rights of Negroes in the South when one day reconstruction should end. But this was too novel a conception to gain Republican support. Stanton and others abandoned it because conservative, anti-Negro Democrats distorted the goal from one of national protection of political rights in Southern states, to creation of a primitive apartheid policy. As example, Democratic congressman John Winthrop Chanler of New York told the House, during later debate on extending the life of the Freedmen's Bureau, that "I am in favor of some sort of [permanent] bureau for the negro, who is a foreigner and a ward of our Government, just as the Indian tribes have [a bureau], to regulate their relations with this [national] Government."[12] Republicans, aware of the easy tendency of Democrats to twist a permanent freedmen's agency into illiberal pathways, dropped the idea in favor of a bureau of brief life.

Some Radical Republicans of Sumner's stature shared a passionate belief in the social benefits the nation would win from a national, unsegregated educational system. Later Sumner and others tried to incorporate these notions into the Freedmen's Bureau statute as amended, then into the Bureau of Education, and finally into acts to enforce the war-born amendments to the Constitution— all unsuccessfully.[13]

The rapidly enlarging consensus among Republicans on the need for Southern Negroes to vote drew heavy support from evangelical, militant Christian humanitarians, men of good will to man. Another weighty phalanx, enlisted from among political champions of the precepts of the new Darwinian "science" then sweeping America, was to be vastly augmented in strength and numbers.[14] Social

---

[12] February 3, 1866, *CG*, 39 Cong., 1 Sess., Appendix, p. 85; and see J. W. Phelps to Sumner, October 23, 1864, Sumner Papers (Houghton Library, Harvard University).

[13] Rush Welter, *Popular Education and Democratic Thought in America* (New York: Columbia University Press, 1962), pp. 124–155; Alfred H. Kelly, "The Congressional Controversy over School Segregation, 1867–1875." *American Historical Review*, LXIV (April 1959) 537–563.

[14] Robert Green McCloskey, *American Conservatism in the Age of Enterprise, 1865–1910: A Study of William Graham Sumner, Stephen J. Field, and Andrew Carnegie* (Cambridge: Harvard University Press, 1961); Hofstadter, *Social Darwinism, passim.*

Darwinism was an ethic, an idealism, and a constitutional view that proponents dignified as an unalterable stricture on American governments.[15] Radical Republicans were no more able than anyone else to avoid immersion in the Darwinian climate of opinion. Appomattox proved the triumph of the virtuous, especially considering the terribly uneven start of Fort Sumter. The postwar task was to see to the permanence of the victory. Negro ballots in the South were the best, quickest way to that end, requiring the least and briefest involvement by government.

Men boosted the laissez-faire aspect of "Social Darwinism" as passionately as ever they championed abolitionism and reunion. In contrast to prewar transcendentalist abolitionists, who had preached the divine equality of all men and therefore the need to end slavery's expansion and career, the new Radicals of Darwinian inspiration (sometimes the same men, who moved to newer sources of ideas and ideals) saw man's inequalities. Reconstruction would bring whites and Negroes in the South to equality with respect only to suffrage; then the national government could withdraw and permit what would to develop.

26. AMERICAN FREEDMEN'S

INQUIRY COMMISSION,

FINAL REPORT

Mid-1864

To sum up, the Freedmen's Bureau was never a fraud. Its goal was not a welfare state for freedmen but better welfare, leading to

---

[15] Edward Chase Kirkland, *Dream and Thought in the Business Community, 1860–1900* (Ithaca: Cornell University Press, 1956).

self-help through access to the ballot and the influence of Christian morality. Though poorly phrased, the Bureau law accurately reflected the amalgam of ideas and ideals that formed Republican principles in 1864 and 1865 (especially among Radicals), of which Professor David Montgomery recently said: "The Radical ideology . . . placed its faith in political democracy based on universal suffrage and [in] a Republican party closely allied to the independent entrepreneurs of the nation."[1]

In one sense this is, obviously, innately limited radicalism. Certainly the Bureau law, though based on the Republican assumption that Congress and President constitutionally enjoyed plenary powers in defeated Dixie, envisaged no mass upsettings of private property titles in the South except in regard to slaves. Moral limits checked limitless constitutional views. Most Republicans stood foursquare against the bogey of centralization in government. Mid-nineteenth-century Americans believed that property, especially land, was simply too sacred to trifle with, even to punish rebels.[2] The Bureau's approach better fitted Victorian and Spencerian modes. It restrained excess in property matters by providing access to voting booths for freedmen.

Men of this laissez-faire mind were little interested in affording the Bureau long-term control over the South's labor-management relationships. Initiation in the Southern states of a permanent system of nationally directed, racially integrated public schools under Bureau direction was not in the cards.[3]

---

[1] Montgomery, "Radical Republicanism in Pennsylvania, 1866–1873," *Pennsylvania Magazine of History and Biography*, LXXXV (October 1961), 451.

[2] LaWanda Cox, "The Promise of Land for the Freedmen," *Mississippi Valley Historical Review*, XLV (December 1958), 413–440.

[3] Gordon Canfield Lee, *The Struggle for Federal Aid, First Phase: A History of the Attempts to Obtain Federal Aid for the Common Schools, 1870–1890* (New York: Teacher's College, Columbia University, 1949), pp. 23–26. Also, see David Dudley Field, "Centralization in the Federal Government," *North American Review*, CCXCIV (May 1881), 407–426; Arnold M. Paul, *Conservative Crisis and the Rule of Law: Attitudes of Bar and Bench, 1887–1895* (Ithaca: Cornell University Press, 1960); Clyde E. Jacobs, *Law Writers and the Courts* (Berkeley· and Los Angeles: University of California Press, 1954).

But it should also be clear that the Bureau's framers intended permanently to alter and to improve patterns of life and labor, especially involving race, in the new South. Champions of the Bureau correctly saw themselves as torchbearers of revolution, not as profiteering adventurers—both terms understandable then. Without provable hypocrisy, businessman-abolitionist-reformer Edward Atkinson advised congressmen who were considering the Bureau law, ". . . [A]void over-legislation, too much guardianship, too much taking care, but recognize in the negro a man fully competent to make his own contracts, if protected from injustice and abuse, and for whom the only compulsion is to be paid fair wages for a fair day's work."[4]

Agreeably to these sentiments, the American Freedmen's Inquiry Commission's "final report"[5] in mid-1864, which became the bedrock of the Bureau statute, warned:

We must not treat them [Negroes] as stepchildren; there is too much danger in doing too much as in doing too little. For a time we need a freedmen's bureau, but not because these people are negroes, only because they are men who have been, for generations, despoiled of their rights. . . . The freedman should be treated at once as any other free man. . . . The natural laws of supply and demand should be left to regulate rates of compensation and places of residence. . . . The Commission is confirmed in the opinion that all aid given to these people should be regarded as a temporary necessity; that all supervision over them should be provisional only, and advisory in its character. The sooner they shall stand alone and make their own unaided way, the better both for our race and for theirs. The essential is that we secure to them the means of making their own way; that is, that we give them, to use the familiar phrase, "a fair chance." . . . If, like whites they are to be self-supporting, then, like whites, they ought to have those rights, civil and political, without which they are but laboring as a man labors with hands bound. There will for some time to come be a tendency on the

---

[4] Quoted in Bentley, p. 34.
[5] United States, War Department, *War of the Rebellion: . . . Official Records of the Union and Confederate Armies* (Washington: Government Printing Office, 1880–1901), Ser. III, Vol. 4, pp. 381–382.

part of many among those who have heretofore held them in bondage still to treat them in an unjust and tyrannical manner. The effectual remedy for this is, not special laws or a special organization for the protection of colored people, but the safeguard of general laws, applicable to all, against fraud and oppression. . . . The sum of our recommendations is this: Offer the freedmen temporary aid and counsel until they become a little accustomed to their new sphere of life; secure to them, by law, their just rights of person and property; relieve them, by a fair and equal administration of justice, from the depressing influence of disgraceful prejudice; above all, guard them against the virtual restoration of slavery in any form, under any pretext, and then let them take care of themselves. If we do this, the future of the African race in this country will be conducive to its prosperity and associated with its well-being. There will be nothing connected with it to excite regret to inspire apprehension.

27. FREEDMEN'S BUREAU, CONTINUED:

CHURCHMEN, SOLDIERS,

REFORMERS

Late 1864

In another sense, the Freedmen's Bureau was the most radical of Radical institutions. Prewar abolitionist humanitarians were its chief backers. They were primarily concerned not with the Negro but with slavery. Decades-long efforts on the part of the organized abolitionists had brought the Negro to freedom. Slavery's chief victim, he deserved pity. A prop to the Union's sagging fortunes in terms of supply of military manpower, the Southern Negro also deserved the nation's gratitude and the limited and transient aids

the Bureau promised to supply. Employing these aids, the freedman would raise himself up as far and as fast as he could or would,
with his ballot as his primary device of self-help. The assumption
obtained among abolitionists that once the Negro freedman was
made literate and moral through the Bureau's classrooms and
prayers, he would prove the truth of the contention that humanity
transcended degradation. Once he became established sure-footed
in freedom, equality would become the Negro's business.

By this estimation the Bureau was a testament to faith, not a
fraud, an end to the need for a reconstruction, not its inadequate
beginnings. Of course the Bureau's framers intended that Negro life
and labor in the new South should never return to the unpalatable
characteristics of the old. But if Negroes voted, then improvement
in Southern society would work itself out in comfortable obedience
to laws natural and divine, and without need for unpalatable
bureaucratic effort. Summed up, the Freedmen's Bureau was built
to create a revolution, not to be a beachhead for a profiteering
foray. Christian ethics were at the heart of the Bureau's methods
and goals, inspiring its stay-at-home supporters and the volunteers
who staffed its field operations.

The Freedmen's Bureau was an optimistic and inspiring opportunity. Recalling decades later these halcyon times, Albion Tourgée
offered this stirring testament to the power of the Bureau's idea to
move men to action:

> I believed in many things then such as the Fatherhood of God
> and the brotherhood of Man. I believed in Christianity. . . . I
> believed in the United States and the flower of liberty, security,
> and equal right for all. I believed that the abolition of slavery
> was all that was required to establish security [for all men]
> before the law. I was so proud of our government and civilization
> that I could not endure the thought that it should be stained
> with injustice and oppression. I believed in that curious fetish
> of our modern thought "Education" as a remedy for wrong. . . .
> I wrote "The remedy for Wrong is Righteousness; for Darkness,
> Light. Make the spelling-book the scepter of national power!"[1]

Similar imperatives of motivation are at the heart of a plea of

---

[1] Theodore L. Gross, *Albion W. Tourgée* (New York: Twayne, 1963),
pp. 143–144.

an obscure and terribly war-weary Army captain. A Quaker despite his martial occupation, and on duty in Virginia, this officer enjoined his coreligionists in New York:

> The work of preparing an enslaved race for liberty and freedom is second only in importance to the work of liberating it. . . . It is a sad mistake to suppose that all they [the freedmen] need is to be set at liberty, without the fostering help of friends. . . . While the army is breaking Satan's instrumentality of degradation, the army of Christ should be erecting the structure of freedom in the hearts and lives of the [freed] people, so that the influence of education and the Gospel of the Son of God, shall ere long restore them in the scale of being to their true position among the families of the earth.[2]

Christian ethics underlying the Freedmen's Bureau merged neatly with the Spencerian upswell in laissez-faire business ethics. Of this period Octavius Frothingham wrote:

> In Social Science the popular theories favor the largest play of the social forces—the most unrestricted intercourse, the most cordial concurrence among men, free competition, free trade, free government, free action of the people in their own affairs—the voluntary system. The community, it is felt, has a self-regulating power, which must not be obstructed by toll gates, or diminished by friction, or fretted away by the impertinent interference of officials. Ports must be open; customs-houses shut; over-legislation is the bane.[3]

Veterans of the abolitionist crusade took it for granted that the Freedmen's Bureau would avoid what one British antislavery spokesman called "a poor law"—i.e., a dole. After returning to England from a visit to the occupied South in very early 1865, Anglican priest Samuel Garrett comforted representatives of asso-

---

[2] In *Third Report of a Committee of the Representatives of the New York Yearly Meeting of Friends Upon the Condition and Wants of the Colored Refugees* (n.p., 1864), p. 21.

[3] Frothingham, *The Religion of Humanity,* p. 9; and see Charles C. Cole, Jr., *The Social Ideas of the Northern Evangelists, 1826–1860* (New York: Columbia University Press, 1954), pp. 221–228; Timothy L. Smith, *Revivalism and Social Reform in Mid-Nineteenth Century America* (New York: Abingdon Press, 1957), pp. 232–237.

ciated antislavery organizations of England and France with the assurance that the Congress of the United States was determined to avoid involvement in direct relief activities.[4]

The opportunity at hand for Christian effort was a public duty, however, beyond the capacity of any private association to fulfill, as some clerical spokesmen realized. Episcopal minister Alexander H. Vinton argued that reunion plus abolition equaled a new America, improved by the social revolution implicit in five million people coming up from slavery. "It belongs to the North to expound the deep and radical significance of the war," Vinton preached early in 1865, "[and] to interpret the new social and political facts that are to form the platform of Southern life hereafter and always . . . namely, that secession is a heresy and slavery an outrage upon our national life, both divinely demonstrated to be such by the wager of battle." Moving in the mainstream of religious Radical Republicanism, Vinton spoke of the freedmen as only "a manhood of capabilities," whose potentialities required the exportation southward of free schools, which were "the honor of our land and the security and guarantee of our freedom, [and which] must in some way be extended to the South . . . for they will not originate there."[5]

Churchmen's views, more than those of politicians, shaped the Bureau. Almost since Sumter, relief activities in aid of fugitive or refugee Negroes, white wanderers, and straitened Union soldiers and their families, had been in the charge of affiliated volunteer organizations linked to a congeries of church congregations, usually Protestant. By 1864 these relief and missionary societies were the country's experts in matters of mass relief, education, and social engineering. They sponsored the Yankee schoolmarms at Port Royal and New Orleans, sustained the Army's superintendents of freedmen of the character of Vincent Colyer and John Eaton, and lambasted General Banks for leaning too heavily on coercive labor regulations for Louisiana's freedmen.

---

[4] "Poor law" phrase in, London *Freed-Man*, September 1, 1865, p. 23; *ibid.* (Oct. 1, 1865), p. 44, quotes Garrett.

[5] Vinton, *The Duties of Peace: Sermon, St. Mark's Episcopal Church, The Bowerie, New York, February 5, 1865* (New York: Gray & Green, 1865), pp. 15, 23.

No groups in the North knew better than the field workers of these organizations how tough and large a task the nation faced if it tried to meet its debts to the freed Negroes of the South. Keeping in mind that the war was still on in March 1865, the following description by a Chicago-based coalition of freedmen's aid societies accurately outlines the height of obstacles in the way of success:

At every stage of this rough experience [coming up from slavery] the [volunteer] Commission finds . . . work. The protection of the newcomers [to freedom] from the cruelty of bad men in the army; the defense of the virtue of the hapless but often comely women; the creation of sentiment among the [white] officers and men [of the Union Army] which shall securely establish relations wholesome for both [races]; the instruction of the new made [Negro] soldier in the mysteries of reading and writing, that he may become fit to take his turn upon picket and sentry duty; . . . the protection of the laborer against an unprincipled employer; the instruction of parents in their duties to each other and to their offspring, and (the most promising labor of all) the education of the young in all the wholesome truths which their parents had no opportunity to learn. . . . If these duties are neglected, the condition of the Freedmen becomes, if possible, more deplorable than the condition of the slave. If they are promptly and generously performed, he rises to the civilization of the [white] citizen.[6]

Representatives of freedmen's aid societies often were disgusted and enraged at the Union Army's ways with Negroes. Prejudices against color erupted distressingly frequently in bluecoated ranks. Egregious excesses such as the labor code drawn up by General N. P. Banks in Louisiana alerted freedmen's aid field workers, who signaled warnings back to church headquarters, thence to Capitol Hill.

The upshot was that men of a missionary impulse in 1864 and later centered attention on workaday questions of wage scales as well as on broad constitutional and ethical issues of reconstruction. They did not have to look far southward to realize the propensity

---

[6] Chicago *Freedmen's Bulletin*, I (March 1865), 74.

that existed for white men in the occupied South to exploit freed Negroes unless civilian watchdogs remained on guard.

To illustrate the extent of the Army's involvement on its own in restructuring social conditions for freedmen, here are regulations that a lowly major issued in November 1864. The major was a provost marshal in the Army of the Potomac. His unit was almost in the shadow of the Capitol at Washington. Election issues and the Wade-Davis standoff were at heights of passion. Yet this officer without visible tremor published a labor code that for ruggedness overmatched the worst Banks issued.[7]

[Headquarters, Provost Marshal's Office]

SPECIAL ORDER NO. 81   Eastville, Va., Nov. 4th. 1864.

Complaints have been made at this Office that many of the Freed Slaves and Colored inhabitants of the Eastern Shore of Virginia are living in idleness, refusing to labor for their livelihood, and subsisting in great part by depredating upon the property of others.

In order to correct the above evils and to provide a sufficiency of labor for the farmers of this District, it is ordered:

I. That a Census of all Colored persons over the age of Fourteen be at once made by the Assistant Provost Marshals of the Eastern Shore of Virginia, and that the following facts be ascertained viz: Their condition, residence and occupation; in the case of women, the number of children depending on them for support. This census will be used by Assistant Provost Marshals in providing labor for those negroes not engaged in some steady employment. All citizens are requested to report any colored persons living on their lands or who may have been formerly owned or hired by them.

---

[7] In Provost Marshal Records, Eastern Shore of Virginia, Army Commands, Virginia and North Carolina, Vol. CCXLVI, Record Group 98, National Archives.

II. All Colored persons able to work and not engaged in steady employment by which they can earn a full support will be required to engage themselves under a written contract to some employer at a fair remuneration.

III. Assistant Provost Marshals will appoint in their districts a loyal responsible citizen as Superintendent of Labor, whose duty it shall be to carry out under the instructions of the Assistant Provost Marshal the provisions of this order. Such Superintendents shall be paid a monthly salary of Seventy-five dollars; the expenses of such office to be provided for by a fee of fifty cents, to be paid by the employer for each laborer hired.

IV. All persons desiring to procure field or house servants can do so by making proper application at the office of the Superintendent of Labor and filing in such office a written contract.

V. *Labor by the day or week need not be contracted for at the Office of the Superintendent of Labor.*

VI. Asst. Provost Marshals will see that all Colored persons male or female able to work steadily, contract for labor, by the month, season or year.

VII. Any violation of contract upon the part of employer or employee shall be a matter of adjudication and punishment in the Provost Court of this District. Bad or cruel treatment upon the part of employers, and insolence, insubordination or improper conduct upon the part of employees shall be considered a violation of contract. Any charge which could properly be brought against a white laborer shall be held tenable as against a negro laborer and upon the same principle treatment improper in the case of a white laborer shall be equally unjustifiable in the case of a hired negro. . . .

To all Colored persons who shall in pursuance of above orders lead a regular honest and industrious life, assistance in sickness, destitution or distress shall be given by the Government.

It is hoped that a strict compliance with the above regulations will result to the benefit of all concerned: furnishing to the farmers and residents of this Shore economical and regular labor, and to the colored population a lawful and profitable means of subsistence.

Dec. 23d 1864.

CIRCULAR:

Superintendents of Labor will hereafter carry out the following instructions in organizing the laboring population of the Shore under Special Order No. 81:

I. On and after the 1st day of January, 1865 all colored persons remaining unemployed will be reported to this Office.

II. All colored persons able to *work* must engage themselves at some steady labor, except those hereinafter enumerated.

III. No person will be allowed to engage more laborers than he can furnish with steady employment.

IV. Where either party to a contract for labor shall violate such contract, upon complaint being made to the Superintendent of Labor, he shall investigate carefully into the matter and forward to this Office a full written statement of the facts.

V. If any colored persons shall have more children helpless from infancy or disease than they can support by their labor, the Superintendent of Labor shall report to this Office the necessary amount of assistance which in his judgment the Government should render to such persons. Any colored person in like manner helpless from age or disease shall also be reported.

VI. Employers can rent to their employees such houses or lands as they may desire.

VII. Any person renting to a colored person a house and farm must, by a bond, bind himself to report to the Superintendent of Labor, any continued idleness or improper conduct upon the part of the tenant. In no case must more persons able to labor be allowed to live in such house than are provided with steady employment upon the farm or otherwise.

VIII. The conditions of a contract between employer and employee must be entirely agreed upon between the parties concerned without any interference on the part of Superintendents.

IX. Contraband rations will be issued to those deserving of them by the commanding officers of posts upon the certificate of a Superintendent of Labor.

X. Two asylums for the old, infirm and diseased will be established; one in ACCOMAC COUNTY, and one in NORTHAMPTON COUNTY, to which all such persons will be forwarded.

XI. Assistant Superintendents will select one-tenth of the laboring population in each sub district to remain as day laborers, such persons being furnished with a certificate from four responsible citizens that they have hitherto borne a good character for honesty and industry. *The provisions of this order shall not in any way affect such day laborers.*

In addition to such persons, the following will be permitted to follow their usual avocations: *Blacksmiths, Carpenters, Shoemakers* and *skilled hewers of wood.* All persons above enumerated will be permitted to work at such times and places as they may desire during good conduct, and no persons, employers or otherwise, will be held responsible for them.

XII. Oystermen, during the oystering season, can continue their business, but on the expiration of the oystering season shall engage in other steady employment.

XIII. Persons renting land to colored persons on shares will not be obliged to give any bond for the good conduct of the tenant.

XIV. Employers will not be permitted to inflict corporeal punishment upon their colored employees.

XV. No contracts for labor, except for day labor, shall be

made for a less period than *three months*, nor more than *one year.*

XVI. Upon the expiration of contracts employers must report the fact to the Superintendent of Labor, in whose office such contracts have been made.

XVII. To create a fund for the support of those that would otherwise be thrown upon the community, for the payment of Superintendents of Labor, and for other contingent expenses, the following fees will be charged by the Superintendents of Labor for each contract filed or certificate issued:—

For each contract for three months or over the sum of fifty cents.

For each contract for six months or over the sum of one dollar.

For each contract for one year the sum of two dollars. Such fees to be paid by employers.

For each certificate given to those exempt from Order No. 81 the sum of fifty cents. The fund thus created will provide for the poor and infirm of this District, and will be re-paid to those furnishing it by a reliable and economical system of labor.

XVIII. Superintendents of Labor will forward to this Office on the 15th and 30th of each month full reports of all contracts made by them and funds received.

Superintendents are required to use judgment and discretion in the execution of this order. Their main duties are to see that labor is furnished to all colored persons seeking it; that no idleness or the demoralization inevitable upon it be permitted; that all contracts filed by them are strictly enforced, and that colored persons be protected in all of their rights and punished for any wrong doing.

FRANK J. WHITE,
Lt. Col. and Provost Marshal.

28. LYMAN ABBOTT,

SURVEY OF THE FREEDMEN'S

BUREAU'S WORK

August 1867

Suspicious of a totally Army show in aid of freedmen, yet keenly aware that the Army must be the primary instrument of Reconstruction, freedmen's aid societies worked out the curious features of the Bureau by which they themselves were involved as civilian volunteers in the ostensibly military operation the Bureau carried on. The prestige of the philanthropic societies was enormous. Few Republican congressmen could stand in their way. In terms of political muscle, the aid societies enjoyed intimate connections to Protestant church bodies and communicants, to journalists and veterans' groups, and to state and national legislators. To be sure, many members of these organizations prepared to "demobilize" as armed hostilities ended. But thousands more came on deck to bear fair shares of Christian responsibility and civic duty. Their spokesmen demanded, and obtained, a lion's share of the functional load of the Bureau and regeared the volunteer organizations to provide necessary funds and field personnel.

Justification for the involvement of private humanitarian associations with the Army's Freedmen's Bureau required little effort. When called on, spokesmen for the associations had ready to hand this explanation: "With a colossal war on its hands, taxing every resource, our Government is entitled to all the help that can be given to it from voluntary, outside assistance. . . . Our governmental machinery, as it came from the hands of our fathers, was not adopted to such exigencies. Resort, therefore, must be had to extemporized and voluntary action. Hence our Volunteer Soldiery to supply the deficiency of our regular army and enrolled militia; hence our Sanitary Commissions, to supplement the defects of our [Army] Medical Bureau; and hence our voluntary Relief Associations, to meet the wants—now for the first time felt—of a Bureau to cover the case of the freedman. The . . . Freedmen's Relief Association[s], therefore, besides relieving the freedman, relieves also the Government."[1]

The Bureau provided the philanthropic welfare groups with a watchdog within the Army, over the Army, and of a nature agreeable to men of Christian purposes and Spencerian convictions. John Eaton, to whom Grant had given rank as colonel to supervise the ever-augmenting numbers of freedmen in the imperial domain stretching from Cairo, Illinois, to the Red River, added his influential voice in agreement that a government bureau should be "lifting not carrying" freedmen. Any official agency touching the ex-slaves must bend efforts toward "enabling them to vindicate their capacity to be free, by relieving Government and [private] charity of all expense, and supplying themselves with shelter, clothing, food, and education." This was what had been occurring, Eaton stated, and alternatives looking toward greater paternalism and responsibility on the part of the government were "prejudice or fancy." Reformers must "hold fast to common sense, and Christian principles; to keep the eye on the lessons of history & to seek there for just teachings in regard to present times and emergencies; in a word, to make all governmental action to be simply the administration of justice towards them [Negroes] as free people. This has been allowed to parade. . . ."[2]

A series of regional alliances in the first half of 1865 permitted the numerous freedmen's aid groups to streamline themselves for the vast work of educating six million people (including whites) in quick time. Remarkable consensus existed among these normally

---

[1] [Philadelphia] *Pennsylvania Freedmen's Bulletin,* I (February 1865), 12.

[2] Quoted in the Chicago *Freedmen's Bulletin, Supplement,* I (September 1864), 34–35. In later years Eaton became a Freedmen's Bureau commissioner, then was appointed to head the new Federal Bureau of Education.

disputatious sectarians, and in Congress and the Army, on what they and the government should and should not do.[3] General O. O. Howard expressed it in an August 1865 address to a convention of Midwestern freedmen's aid representatives:[4] "A great many fanatics and, as I call them, fools, go down [South] from the North to teach them [freedmen] wrong things, telling them that they have possessions which they have not got," Howard complained.

We have left, whether it was strictly right or not, the title of [Southerners'] property where it was, and I believe it is better that it should be so. It is better for the freedman to begin at the bottom and work up, that he may learn how to preserve the property he acquires. He has never been able to hold anything, and now that we have freed him, we want him to learn how to husband his resources. . . . Now, with regard to this matter of schools [for Negroes], the Government made no appropriation for the Freedmen's Bureau . . . to accomplish any general purpose. Then again, it is not desirable to do it. You do not want to run an immense machine like this from Washington. You do not want your schools in Illinois to be run and controlled by any one at Washington, but you want to run and control your own schools. And we wish, on the same principle, schools to be established in each of these [Southern] States. "Then," you may say, "why do you interfere [there]?" Simply because we are trying to guarantee to these people the promise of the Government. Just as soon as the State authorities are ready and willing to do what is right and just, then they shall do it [have charge of the schools and related matters]. The Government did not establish the Freedmen's Bureau in order to put [Army] officers . . . in fat places. It does not wish to multiply positions. . . . The object of the Bureau is to aid these people in their transition from the

---

[3] McPherson, *The Struggle for Equality*, p. 398; Amory D. May, "The Work of Certain Northern Churches in the Education of the Freedmen, 1861–1900," in Department of the Interior *Annual Report* (1902), I, 285–314; Richard S. Drake, "Freedmen's Aid Societies and Sectional Compromise," *Journal of Southern History*, XXIX (May 1963), 175–186.

[4] Howard, August 28, 1865, in [Chicago] *Freedmen's Bulletin*, I (October 1865), 181, 183.

darkness of slavery to the light, to the privileges and the enjoyments of freedom. I have proposed all the time to myself . . . to be always looking forward to the end of it [the Bureau]; and just as soon as any State will show by the action of its officers, by the action of its people, by the sentiments put forth, that they are ready and willing to keep the promise and pledge of our beloved President, endorsed by our Congress, to our freedmen . . . then they may have the privilege of doing it, and it will relieve me from the responsibility. . . . My friends, I am only one amongst you—the centre as I think—placed at Washington, of Christian churches, Christian people, Christian associations, benevolent associations of every kind in this country. The matter is so arranged—the work is your own.

American and European militant Protestant church groups, old antislavery associations, and other private philanthropic sources readied themselves for this unparalleled opportunity and unprecedented task. Without question, the Bureau's curious characteristics received unstinted approval from these adventurers in good works, as is witnessed in this editorial from a British benevolent organization:

We now understand what we are expected to do, and what the [U.S.] Government and the [Freedmen's] Bureau will do for us. The Bureau accepts the care of four million of emancipated slaves, and will endeavour to provide for their wants, socially, intellectually, and religiously. To do this successfully the Bureau will throw a large share of the work upon the various Freed-Men's Associations. Congress gave the Bureau no money, but in lieu of money, connected it with the Army.[5]

Similarly, a Philadelphia freedmen's aid society, Quaker-oriented, promised Howard its cooperation and revealed its consensus on the incapacity of government for the job: "How much soever good may be done by the Government [Freedmen's] Bureau, . . . the chief work in the way of the black man's elevation will have to be done by the voluntary . . . popular associations, outside of the Government. . . ."[6]

---

[5] London *Freed-Man* (October 1, 1865), p. 58.
[6] Philadelphia *Freedmen's Bulletin*, I (February 1865), 12.

The varieties of work the Freedmen's Bureau undertook, and the Bureau's relationships to private organizations, are best encapsulated in the report that Lyman Abbott offered in August 1867 to the Paris international antislavery conference. That report also reflects the optimistic spirit and generous nature of the Bureau effort, and the impressive character of the Bureau's achievements.[7]

Emancipation in the United States was a growth rather than an enactment. The first act of war gave new vigour to the already strong anti-slavery sentiment of the North. . . .

These successive steps were taken in compliance with the progressive demands of the people. Petitions from public meetings, from political caucuses, from ministers, churches and ecclesiastical assemblages, poured in upon the President; newspapers and pulpits proclaimed at first the necessity and then the duty of universal emancipation. The varying fortunes of the war proved the work of quelling the rebellion to be even more difficult than had been anticipated; and, at length, in September 1862, President Lincoln declared his purpose to proclaim the abolition of Slavery throughout all the rebel States, after the lapse of a limited number of days, unless they should previously have laid down their arms and returned to their allegiance. This purpose he carried into effect; and on the first day of January 1863,—thenceforth for ever memorable in the annals of this country—issued his proclamation freeing, except in specified localities, all slaves within the region still in rebellion against the United States.

The full operation of this act was, of course, limited to non-excepted territory actually occupied by our armies, and that immediately contiguous; but in effect it invited the slaves

---

[7] Abbott's report is in Committee of the British and Foreign Anti-Slavery Society, *Special Report of the Anti-Slavery Conference held in Paris . . . on the 26th and 27th August 1867* (London, 1867) pp. 80–93; and see Ira V. Brown, "Lyman Abbott and Freedmen's Aid, 1865–1867," *Journal of Southern History*, XV (February 1949), 22–38.

to seek freedom within our lines, and unquestionably disturbed and disorganized labour in the interior of the South. Still the bondage in which the mass of the negroes were held, was rendered perhaps even more intolerable because of the prospect of their future liberation.

Not until the final defeat of the rebel armies, in the spring of 1865, did the proclamation of freedom become effective throughout the South; nor till six months later did the South formally accept the fact of emancipation, under the reconstruction measures of President Johnson, who demanded their assent to the abolition of Slavery as a condition preliminary to readmission. Finally, on the 18th day of December 1865, the Secretary of State announced the adoption, by two-thirds of the States, of that amendment to the Constitution of the United States, which for ever prohibits the existence of Slavery throughout the whole country.

But the abolition of Slavery and the establishment of freedom are not one and the same thing. The emancipated negroes were not yet really freemen. Their chains had indeed been sundered by the sword, but the broken links still hung upon their limbs. They were no longer "chattels," but their proper position in the body politic was not determined.*

The question, "What shall be done with the negro?" agitated the whole country. Some were in favour of an immediate recognition of their equal civil and political rights, and of conceding to them at once all the prerogatives of citizenship. But only a few advocated a policy so radical, and, at the same time, generally considered revolutionary, while many, even of those who really wished well to the negro, doubted his capacity for citizenship, his willingness to labour for his own support, and the possibility of his forming, as a freeman, an integral part of the Republic. The plans of the colonizationists were reproduced. Propositions were submitted to provide a

---

* As late as the Spring of 1867 a writ of Habeas Corpus was resorted to, to free a negro in Kentucky from Slavery.

home for the freedmen in Africa, in Mexico, in Central America, or in one of our own States—Texas or South Carolina, for instance—which should be set apart for their occupancy. Some, who hold colonization to be impossible, proposed that they should be kept in a state of legal tutelage, or, more properly, serfdom. No policy commanded the general assent; and it seemed to those who lacked faith in popular Government and in Divine Providence, as if the United States, having been compelled by the exigencies of war to emancipate the negro, would prove unequal to the situation, would fail to accept the only true solution of the problem, the absolute equality of all men before the law, and would leave the freedman in a position worse, if possible, than that from which they had taken him, subject to the tyranny of a dominant class, and without the protection which the selfish interest of his former master had afforded.

In republics, the laws are a fair indication of the prevailing public sentiment. Those enacted in the Southern States shortly after the war, afford an interesting indication of the spirit which prevailed there, and of the condition to which the freedmen would have been reduced if left to the sole control of their former masters.*

The fact that the negro, as a slave, worked under compulsion, was generally held to indicate in him an unusual dislike to labour, and to prove the necessity of peculiar special legislation in order to prevent him from becoming a pauper to be supported by the more industrious whites, or an outcast who would supply his wants only by depredation on the property of others. Hence, various forms of class, and therefore inequitable, legislation—in some States palpably unjust—and dictated by the hatred and irritation which had accompanied the war, and not been diminished by defeat and compulsory

---

* For these laws see letter of the Secretary of War to the Senate, January 3, 1867; 39th Congress, 2nd Session, Ex. Doc. No. 6, and abstract of them in the *American Freedman,* July, 1866, p. 57.

emancipation; in others, framed perhaps with a desire for justice, which was rendered futile however by the fundamental error which underlies all such legislation.

The idea of admitting the freedmen to an equal participation in civil and political rights was not entertained in any part of the South. In most of the States they were not allowed to sit on juries, or even to testify in any case in which white men were parties. They were forbidden to own or bear firearms, and thus were rendered defenceless against assault. Vagrant laws were passed, often relating only to the negro, or, where applicable in terms to both white and black, seldom or never enforced except against the latter. Under these laws, persons assumed to have no visible means of support,— which, in the case of a former slave, might be held to mean that he was not in the employ of any master,—could be arrested, fined, sold for a limited time to pay the fine,* hired out at the will of the court,† or put to work under overseers appointed by the authorities.‡ Special acts were passed to provide for and regulate labour contracts, required to be made in writing. The hours of labour were fixed, and the duties of master and servant defined in detail. A violation by the servant, such as an abandonment of the plantation before the expiration of his term of service, was made a misdemeanour, for which he was liable to be arrested and returned to his master like a fugitive slave;‖ while if the master violated the contract, the servant must seek his remedy through the slow process of a suit at law. In South Carolina the freedman was forbidden to exercise any trade or mechanical pursuit without a special license, for which he was required to pay an annual fee of from ten to one hundred dollars. Agricultural and domestic service only were free to him. The laws relating to

---

* In Mississippi.
† In Virginia.
‡ In Alabama.
‖ In Mississippi.

apprenticeship, when in form applicable to all classes, were in fact employed only to compel the labour of freed people. In some States any court—that is, any local Justice of the Peace—could bind out to a white person any negro under age, without his own consent or that of his parents.¶ The freedmen were subjected to the punishments formerly inflicted upon slaves.°° Whipping especially, which in some States disfranchised the party subjected to it, and rendered him for ever infamous before the law, was made the penalty for the most trifling misdemeanour. In short, it seemed as if no means were left untried to manifest the exasperation of the ex-slaveholders towards those whose nominal freedom they were compelled to acknowledge, and their determination to cause those freedmen to look back upon their former condition, as slaves, with regret.

These legal disabilities were not the only obstacles placed in the path of the freed people. Their attempts at education provoked the most intense and bitter hostility, as evincing a desire to render themselves equal to the whites. Their churches and schoolhouses were in many places destroyed by mobs.° In parts of the country remote from observation, the violence and cruelty engendered by Slavery found free scope for exercise upon the defenceless negro. In a single district, in a single month, forty-nine cases of violence, ranging from assault and battery to murder, in which whites were the aggressors and blacks the sufferers, were reported. Most of this violence was the act of the lower class of poor whites. In the disordered state of the country, consequent upon the war, there was no civil authority competent to preserve peace or to punish crime. But, in addition, underlying and pervading the whole legal and social situation, was the conviction

---

¶ Maryland.

°° As in Florida, whipping and the pillory; in Maryland freedmen were sold into Slavery for a term of years, as a punishment for petty offences.

° In Mobile, three coloured churches were burned in six months.

of most of the Southern people, that Slavery was right and a blessing; emancipation wrong and a curse. They had acquiesced in the latter, because they could not prevent it; but their convictions remained unchanged. "Overpowered, but not subdued," was a favourite expression of their orators and the press; and their entire legislative and social action was an unconscious attempt to apply to a state of freedom the political maxims and methods of Slavery, which alone they comprehended.

These acts of violence and outrage culminated in the bloody riots of Memphis and New Orleans. Then the excitement thereby produced in the North, the indignation of the better classes in the South, and the natural reaction even among those most prejudiced against the coloured people, worked together to provide the necessary remedy.

Such, in brief, and viewed in the Southern aspect alone, was the condition in which the abolition of Slavery left the freedmen. It was virtually a state of serfdom, in which they were subjected to heavy legal and social disabilities; a state in which they were without civil or political rights, and with few, if any, friends in the South to advocate their elevation to the rank of citizenship, or their education into the fulness of manhood.

In this condition, however, they were not allowed to continue. From the beginning, as opportunity offered, means were employed to relieve their wants and improve their situation. As time wore on, and the public interest increased in the work, these means were enlarged in extent and increased in effectiveness. What they were, and what have been their results, it is our business here to indicate.

The means employed for the relief and improvement and complete enfranchisement of the freed people have been of a twofold character, voluntary and governmental. . . .

With the inception of the war, efforts were commenced looking to the relief and ultimately to the education of the freed people. The first considerable public movement of this kind was made in February 1862. At that time the Proclamation of Emancipation had not been issued, those of Generals Fremont and Hunter had been rescinded, and the policy of the nation in respect to slaves had not been framed. General T. W. Sherman and Commodore Dupont, having captured the forts at the entrance of Port Royal and taken possession of the Sea Islands, found themselves surrounded by a crowd of ignorant, half-clad, half-famished negroes. Hon. S. P. Chase, then Secretary of the Treasury, learning that there was a large amount of cotton upon the captured islands, selected an officer of the army as agent of the Treasury Department to proceed thither and collect it. The reports which were received from this agent satisfied him that it was necessary, not merely to collect the ungathered cotton, but to provide in some way for the welfare of the labourers and for the culture of the land. No provision had been made by Congress on this subject. He sent thither Mr. E. L. Pierce, of Massachusetts, to survey the field and report. His reports, an official order from General T. W. Sherman, and private and personal letters from Commodore Dupont, called the attention of the North to the needs of the freed people. Public meetings were at once held in Boston, New York, and Philadelphia, and Societies nearly simultaneously organized at those points, first for the relief, and next for the education of these people, and the reorganization of their industry.

A similar Society was organized at the capital, under the immediate sanction and approval of the Government, which first took under its especial supervision the contrabands in the district of Columbia, but subsequently extended its operations to Fortress Monroe and the adjacent country.

A few months later, "The Contraband Relief Association" was organized in Cincinnati, subsequently reorganizing as the Western Freedman's-Aid Commission. In the fall of 1863, "The North-western Freedman's-Aid Commission" was established at Chicago, and still later were formed others at different points in the West.

At first, the objects to be accomplished and the methods to be employed, were but vaguely understood. Yet in the outset, along with that provision which simple humanity made for the physical wants of the houseless, the naked and the starving, Christian faith clearly perceived deeper needs. The first persons who were sent out carried, with clothes and provisions, also the Primer and the Bible. The earliest plans of the New-York Society provided for a temporary regulation of labour. The first name of the New-England Society—the Educational Commission—indicated its ulterior purposes. But the apparent beginning did not foretoken to the multitude the ultimate result. Labouring under difficulties, not easy to describe, and scarcely possible to exaggerate, in the utmost harmony of feeling, but without unity of organization, after six months of desultory and ill-regulated, but earnest and, on the whole, successful labour, the entire number of teachers and missionaries in the field, as reported to the Treasury Department, under whose supervision they then were, consisted of seventy men and sixteen women.

These figures do not, however, indicate the real results of that first six months work. They proved the capacity of the negro for free-labour and for education, and are understood to have exerted a very considerable influence upon the mind of President Lincoln in inducing him to adopt, at a later period, the policy of universal emancipation.

From the first, a desire for unity of effort among the philanthropic and Christian friends of the freedmen was felt, and earnest efforts were made to secure it.

Early in the year 1862, at the request of the Secretary of the Treasury, a meeting was held of representatives from New England, New York, and Philadelphia, to form a union, but although cordially cooperating in their common work, they were not finally and organically united in one Society until March 1865, when the American Freedmen's-Aid Union was formed. In the fall of the same year the Western Associations joined the Union, constituting the American Freedman's-Aid Commission. Later, its scope was enlarged, and its working-force increased by junction with the American Union Commission, a Society formed towards the close of the war, to aid in the establishment of free republican institutions in the South; and in May 1866, at a Convention of all the different Freedmen's-Aid Societies, the American Freedman's Union Commission, with its present Constitution, was finally and completely organized; and its motto, "No distinction of race or colour," was chosen as the distinguishing principle of the Society. This Commission now embraces nearly all the unecclesiastical agencies employed in the education of the coloured people.

From the beginning of the war, however, the churches also engaged, in their denominational capacity, and through their Missionary boards, in the work, not only of evangelization, but of education among the freed people. The Friends, the Old-School Presbyterians, the United Presbyterians, the Methodists, and the Congregationalists or Independents, have all had their special freedmen's organizations, through whom they have not only sent missionaries to preach, but also teachers to educate. One of the Tract Societies has engaged largely in the work of colportage among the freedmen. The Bible Society has distributed over a million copies of the Scriptures in the South, chiefly among the freed people. In brief, nearly every philanthropic, Christian and religious organization has received a new impetus, and has given its energies new direction, because of the opening of the Southern field by the act of emancipation. Of the missionary agencies, the largest, as it was one of the first in the field, is the American Missionary Association, the chosen organ of the Congregationalists. Combining missionary, educational, and physical relief work in one, its energies have largely contributed to the establishment of schools among the freed people, and the number of teachers and missionaries whom they employ is about the same as the number of teachers employed by the American Freedman's Union Commission. It is impossible to give in this report detailed and accurate statistics of the work accomplished by each separate agency. Instead of attempting this, we shall rather essay to describe its general aspects and results.

The whole work of education, as described hereafter, has been carried on through the instrumentality of these benevolent and religious organizations. The Government has aided in securing schoolhouses, has generally furnished transportation; and during the war, rations to the teachers, and, in a few localities, by special military tax, has even provided their salaries. This, however, has been exceptional, and the work of local commanders, rather than of the Government.

Of the thirteen hundred teachers who have been sent to the South, nearly all have been sustained by voluntary Societies. The books have been furnished, the school apparatus has been provided, the ground has been surveyed, and the wants ascertained by them. In the various cities, towns and villages of the North, local Societies have been organized, chiefly among the ladies, who, by sewing Societies, fairs, church contributions, and other instrumentalities, obtain the money to carry on this work. As a general rule, it has cost from three to six hundred dollars to support a single teacher for a year. In many instances, the local Society has assumed the support of a teacher, selected one known to them, and by that teacher's correspondence their interest has been stimulated and maintained. In some instances the auxiliary Society has undertaken to establish and carry on an entire school, and many of the Northern churches are represented in the South by one or more of their number, who have gone out, sustained not only by their prayers, but by their pecuniary contributions.

The amount contributed from the beginning, from all sources, for the relief and education of the freedmen, it would be impossible accurately to estimate. An officer of the Bureau, to whom a request for an approximate estimate was referred, has set down the cost to the Government, for the freedmen and refugees, for the two years ending July 14, 1867, "as nearly as he could compute it from statistics found in the office," at 5,278,363 dollars. From data afforded by annual reports, and other sources of information, the total amount in money and kind contributed through the various Freedmen's, Missionary and Church Associations, and by private benevolence, from the beginning of the movement, in February 1862, up to July 1, 1867, is set down in round figures at 5,500,000 dollars. Of this five million five hundred thousand dollars, fully one-fifth has come from abroad. England has contributed 80,000*l.*, and France, Germany, Switzerland and other countries have manifested in a substantial manner their sympathy in the work.

Freedmen's Bureau.

The governmental care of the freedmen was at first assumed by the Treasury Department. It was subsequently transferred to the War Department, as more able, from its military power, to extend the necessary protection and aid. But at an early day, immediately, in fact, after emancipation, the friends of the freedman felt that there was need of a special governmental organization to protect the rights and provide for the wants of the freed people, and an effort was made to obtain the passage of a Bill establishing a Freedman's Bureau. Such, however, was, even then, the prejudice existing, that at first the Bill failed; but having been broadened in its scope, so as to include poor white refugees, many of whom fled from Southern persecution because of their union sentiments, it finally passed the House of Representatives, and received the sanction of the Senate and the approval of the President. It is safe to say that the creation of the Freedmen's Bureau, which followed long after the organization of the Freedman's Associations, was largely due, indirectly, to their influence in awakening a public interest on behalf of the freedman, and directly to their labours with the public authorities in Washington. By this Bill, a "Bureau of Refugees, Freedmen and Abandoned Lands" was created as a branch of the War Department, under the management and control of a Commissioner appointed by the President, aided by Assistant Commissioners, not exceeding ten, for the States declared to be in insurrection. This Act passed in March 1865, and in May following, Major-General O. O. Howard, having received the appointment of Commissioner, assumed the duties of his office. By the terms of the Act creating it, this Bureau was to exist only for one year after the expiration of the war. At a later period, and by special Act, it was continued and its powers enlarged. It is still in active and most efficient operation, under the same Commissioner.

Before the organization of the Bureau the freedman's affairs had been entrusted to department commanders, treasury agents and other governmental officers. No uniform system had characterized their methods. Large numbers, accumulated in camps and barracks, were living in enforced idleness at various points occupied by our troops, and much of the voluntary labour which had been expended to prevent suffering and to establish schools, had been misspent, through the absence of any general, efficient direction. General Howard issued his first order defining the general policy of the Bureau on the 19th day of May 1865, at once appointed his Assistant Commissioners, and entered upon the work assigned to him. In this work he was greatly embarrassed by the lack of any governmental appropriations for his Bureau, by the opposition in the South to any measures looking towards the elevation of the freed people, and by the very widespread distrust in the North of their capacity for improvement.

Through the instrumentality of the Bureau, in co-operation with the voluntary agencies already referred to, labour has been reorganized, justice has been secured, systems of education, temporary or permanent, partial or complete, have been established, the transition period from Slavery to liberty has been safely passed, and the freed people have emerged from their state of bondage into that of the liberty of American citizenship. . . .

General Results.

Such has been the work of the two agencies, whose direct action upon the freedman we undertook to delineate, aided by the third and more potent influence referred to, the co-operation of natural causes and of revolution in political sentiment.

What is to be the effect of emancipation upon the industry of the community at large, upon the amount of production, upon the intelligence and morals of the people, upon commerce, trade, manufactures, agriculture and population, can as yet be only a matter for conjecture; and yet such and so marked even in these respects have been the results already, that probably few, if any, of the intelligent portion of the Southern people would desire to see Slavery re-established. Wherever the planter has honestly and intelligently accommodated himself to the system of free-labour, freedom has reaped a larger harvest than ever was garnered by Slavery.

But the effect upon the freed people is no longer a matter of question. They have refuted Slavery's accusation of idleness and incapacity. They have not only worked faithfully and well under white employers, but, when facilities have been accorded them, have proved themselves capable of independent and even self-organized labour. They are not generally extravagant or wasteful. Out of their meagre earnings they deposited in the Savings and Trust Company for Freedmen, in a little over a year after its organization, 616,802.54 dollars. In addition, a considerable number of them have purchased homesteads. They have manifested a wonderful appreciation of the political issues of the day, and a patience and faith no less wonderful in waiting for the consummation of their freedom; while the brightest feature of the present, and the most hopeful indication for the future, is the ambition and capacity for improvement which they have demonstrated. The church and the schoolhouse are alike crowded with eager, expectant people, the rapidity of whose development under these fostering influences has amazed both foes and friends, and contributed more, perhaps, than any other cause to mitigate the prejudice which survived Slavery, and make the work of enfranchisement complete.

> S. P. CHASE,
> O. O. HOWARD,
> JOSEPH P. THOMPSON,
> LYMAN ABBOTT,
> J. MILLER McKIM,
> FRANCIS GEORGE SHAW.
>   *Committee.*

PART SEVEN

The Critical Year—1865

---

29. DR. GEORGE B. LORING,

SPEECH AND LETTER

April 26, May 15, 1865

Optimism flowered, at Appomattox, that the reconstruction task (as distinguished from physical relief and rebuilding) was well in hand. Although no formal plans for reconstruction had received approval both by President and Congress, all the signs were that Lincoln and his Republicans on Capitol Hill were in happy accord. In early 1865, as the Thirty-eighth Congress readied to close its sessions, interest flagged in further efforts of the Wade-Davis type. Why bother?[1] With the war won, and the postwar period provided for by the Thirteenth Amendment and the Freedmen's Bureau, there remained no reasons for intra-Republican discord over reconstruction. An era of good feelings was in the making.

Lincoln's murder briefly checked the holiday mood. News of the assassination evoked some comments in poor taste from men of poor

---

[1] Antislavery veterans who tried (not very hard) to create a reconstruction inquiry commission, to do on that subject what the Freedmen's Inquiry Commission had done for the question of Freedmen's Bureau legislation, received no support. Schwartz, *Howe*, p. 267 and n.

taste, some of them Radical Republicans. Still, the auguries appeared to be clear that Booth's one mad act did not unsettle the Republican consensus on reconstruction.

This opinion emerges from a speech, April 26, 1865, by Dr. George B. Loring. He was a Massachusetts physician and humanitarian reformer, a Radical Republican in political sympathies, and a shrewdly effective political lobbyist. Loring's speech is of particular importance because he is one of the older prewar abolitionists who, unlike William Lloyd Garrison, refused to be satisfied with the Appomattox triumph plus abolitionism as fruits of the war. Instead, early in 1865 Loring made a transition and further advance. He centered his former general humanitarian concerns on Negrophilism and became a front-runner among the new Radical Republicans, who insisted that Negro suffrage in the South was the only way to keep the war's fruits from rotting.

Loring's speech in April illustrated that Lincoln had already ascended to the popular pantheon. Further, it set the Radical theme that clemency to the white South required balancing with justice toward the black.[2]

[Lincoln] seemed to be guided by instinct, and yet he had great wisdom. We all know he had a kind and generous heart, and his enemies came to know it too. He was not a great statesman, for he had not been educated as such; he was not a great lawyer, for his professional career was spent in the inferior courts of Illinois; he was not a great scholar, for books had been but a small part of his early possessions; he was not a great warrior, for he had no experience on the battle-field, no culture in military schools, but he was a great man—a great man—able to grapple with any subject that rose before him and to deal with it according to the exigencies of the times. Mark how he went through all those troubles. He began no wiser than you or I. He declared to congress that this war was

---

[2] Loring, *The Present Crisis: A Speech . . . at Lyceum Hall, Salem, . . . April 26, 1865, on the Assassination of Abraham Lincoln* (South Danvers [Mass.]: Howard, 1865), pp. 4–9.

not for the extinction of slavery, and he never conceived in the
outset that this was a war for emancipation. Was it not a great
deed, therefore, when the conservative forces of the country
stood trembling, when we were told that bankruptcy would
fall upon us, that anarchy and ruin would overspread the
land, and servile insurrection would lay waste one half of the
republic, was it not a great deed for him to obey the largest
impulses of his nature, and in an hour to change his convictions and come boldly and uncompromisingly up to the principle, that this land should be free so far as his proclamation
could make it free? Yes, my friends, it was a great deed—
greater than lawyers do,—your Websters and your Choates,
great as they are—a greater deed than is done in your courts
—a greater deed than Generals do—a greater deed than politicians generally do. (Applause.) And it was because, while all
the responsibility and the consequences rested upon him, he
rose above the surrounding level, and made that declaration of
freedom, that he made himself truly great.

I said he was kind-hearted; and you know there are many
men abroad in this land, pursuing their peaceful avocations,
through the forbearance of Abraham Lincoln, who by their
own showing are entitled to a life-punishment in the penitentiary. And you know, and I know, that when those men
who had undertaken to destroy the government, and had
deluged this land in blood, came forward but half-penitent,
half-clothed in sackcloth and ashes for their sins, his arms
were ever open to receive them, and no bosom was broader
than his. My friends, his clemency was his danger. And now
that he has laid down his life, let us remember that danger and
be warned by it. (Great applause.) I insist upon it that the
great end for which this war has been fought, the great business of his life, will never be accomplished by what is usually
called clemency—mercy not directed by justice. (Applause.)
If, after having done his duty so faithfully in this life, he has,
by his blood, cemented the hearts of the American people and

enlightened their minds in the work of elevating and purifying the land, this last act is his greatest. . . .

I know I used a strong expression when I said we must beware of clemency. I do not desire vengeance. I would not have the North imitate the example of those who dishonored our noble dead, and starved our imprisoned soldiers to decimate our armies. I would not have a free and gallant people vengeful and blood-thirsty—but I would have them just, prudent and wise. Can not we add wisdom to prudence, and accord strict justice to those who have taken up arms against our government? Shall we restore them to the fullness of their former rights? Never. They have taken their chances, and now let them abide by the result. (Great applause.) They have declared that they were independent, now let them remain independent. (Applause.) The world is wide, and all lands, and all oceans, and the islands of the sea are open to receive them. (Applause—amen.) Some of them have taken care to provide the necessary comforts for their journey. (Laughter.) And what a contrast we have before us—your eulogized and sainted President, known through all the world as the friend of freedom and a free government, who has written his name among the stars—and his opponent [Jefferson Davis] flying in the darkness before an indignant people, branded and despised, bearing his ill-gotten treasure if possible to that safety which a foreign land alone can give him, an outlaw and fugitive. What a contrast—the one a martyr in heaven—the other a felon sunk into the lowest pit of infamy on earth. (Applause.) This, my friends, impersonates the contest which has been going on between slavery and freedom. In the history of Abraham Lincoln I read the refulgence of American freedom —in the history of the great leader of the rebellion, I read the fate of American slavery—sunk to that lower deep which the imagination of man alone has reached.

I now desire to say a word upon the matter of reconstruction, but I fear I may weary you. (Go on, go on.) In all this question of reconstruction there is but one star that should guide us—and that star is the largest and broadest truth laid down and defended by Abraham Lincoln—the star he has set in the firmament of our heavens. We must not be led away from the issue, either by the blandishments of our foes or by our desire for peace. The American people must have the great principle of human freedom established, and they will never be satisfied until this is done, war or no war. (Great applause.) Starting from this point, from this great principle, I insist upon it *that it is impossible to treat with traitors who have taken up arms against this government, for the express purpose of blasting it and all hopes of freedom with it.* We cannot restore our government in this way. I feel it to be impossible, and would never, so long as I had the power of an American citizen, I would never agree to the restoration of the old state organizations among the revolted states, or to any state governments manufactured for the occasion. I would as soon invite Jefferson Davis to come to Washington and take his seat by the side of President Johnson, as I would allow Extra Billy Smith to reorganize the state government of Virginia. So I say of all the states which have destroyed their "practical relations" to the general government by rebellion. When *all the citizens* of a state reach that point at which they are ready to return, upon the basis of government which the war has made for us all, let them return. But not until this is accomplished—not until free suffrage is established—not until the institutions of these states conform to the highest civilization of the land—would I place them on an equality with the loyal states. No twelve nor twelve thousand men in any state can do this—but a free people regenerated by the efforts of the general government. Until this is done how can members of Congress be returned, whose principles shall render them fit to sit by the side of men from Massachusetts? (Great applause. Hurrah.) . . .

No oath of allegiance can purify them [prominent Confederate leaders who had once held high elective or appointive federal offices]. Our country—the civilized world, does not want their counsels. Their return would be an eternal disgrace to us. It would humiliate us in the eyes of all foreign powers. It would bring back all our controversy, paralyze all our efforts, overthrow all that we have accomplished, dishonor the white man, and enslave the black man. The freemen of the North and the bondmen of the South protest against it. May we forever avoid this snare. (Applause.)

Now, what is there on the other side? It is simply this. I would hold the revolted states by the power of the Federal authority,—that power which we have strengthened and confirmed by this war. The first gun fired at Sumter knocked down the institution of slavery, and dispelled forever all the fallacies and sophistries accumulated for years under the names of State Rights and State Sovereignty. I do not mean any invasion of the legitimate rights of a state,—but of that superlative folly which has been represented by the flag of South Carolina and the sacred soil of Virginia. The Federal authority has now become powerful, and is the supreme power in the land. When the revolted states are ready to recognize that authority, when they are ready to bear their proportion of the national debt, when they are ready to make common cause with the loyal North in their systems of education and laws and religion, when their citizens are ready to sacrifice their lives in support of the Union as the North has done for the last four years, then and not till then would I allow them to return. (Applause.) It has been said that the great contest has been between Massachusetts and South Carolina. Be it so. And as Massachusetts has carried the day, I would have South Carolina submit wisely and gracefully to the consequences of the defeat. (Applause and hurrahs.)

Let us see then, if we cannot adopt some system by which our schools, and all our institutions can be planted and nurtured upon their soil. I think we can. I think the American people are equal to this issue, and that they will never be satisfied until the Federal arm is stretched over the revolted states, holding them firmly in obedience, in its powerful grasp, until they shall have learned the lesson of freedom, which the North has furnished them. This would give us a government and a country worth having, worth living for and worth dying for. Accomplish this, and we can say that we have carried our country safely through this field of blood, and firmly established the great principles for which this war has been fought; and that we have proved ourselves not only brave in battle, but in peace and in war a Christian, and high-toned and moral people. For the accomplishment of this, there must be a period of pupilage, in which the social transformation may go on in safety to those who have been hitherto oppressed—in which the down-trodden there may work up to the standard of freedom—and in which they will acquire ability to defend themselves, when their freedom and social position shall be perfected. And during this period of pupilage let us exercise such military sway as will secure the great objects of the war.

My friends, I have often said, in view of the distressing events of these times, that I was born either too early or too late; but if in my day the regeneration of this people and nation shall be perfected, and they shall prove themselves to be valiant in the field, and wise, religious, Christian in council and aims, I shall feel that I was born in a blessed hour. It is indeed amazing to see how the people have been elevated by the contest, it is marvellous how self-sacrificing and courageous and lofty they have become under its trials and responsibilities. They have been equal to the occasion. When, therefore, I am warned that a free exercise of their powers is dangerous and subversive;—that no safety can exist in a community where the ballot is free, I can turn with pride and satisfaction to this chapter in the history of popular government. I have entire faith in the people, in the free ballot as an instrument of power which the people shall use, and use well in deciding all the great questions of the day. I know that these questions will be judged and settled in our homes and schoolhouses and pulpits—the very places of all others where they should be brought to judgment. And I have yet to see or read of the event in which the ruling and inevitable question of the day, the issue of the time, the controlling thought of the hour has not met with a response in the popular heart. There is a great, almost unknown, inestimable power, that sends truth into the hearts of the people; and the grander the truth the more quickly will their instincts run to it. The history of the war teaches us this lesson also. It is on this estimate of popular intelligence and right, that we of the North have established the exercise of free ballot—of universal suffrage. There is no distinction here among citizens; no one is deprived of the right to cast his ballot, if he pays his taxes and can read the law. Why should there be any other condition of affairs at the South? And above all things, should there be no discrimination against those who have toiled so faithfully for us and our cause. Shall not they at least exercise the right which they have defended—without distinction of race or complexion? I have yet to learn what living, mortal, conceivable attribute there is wrapt up in a man's skin, that shall prevent him from voting, if he shall pay his taxes and read his spelling book.—(Great applause.) I do not believe there is any danger in it. But I do believe that by the extension of the free ballot, and by that alone the permanency and security of our free institutions, will be secured. (Applause.) It is not written that this great war shall close with a great injustice unredressed. It is not written in the heavens that the American people shall now, at the end of this strife, commit another great wrong. And the strife will never cease until it shall be established that the principles of the Declaration are, and shall ever be, the law of the land. Those [Negro] men who have fought side by side with us in this war, who have perished on our hard-fought fields, and in our trenches, and who have guided our captured soldiers through the intricate paths of the enemy's country into the open air of freedom, always faithful, never flinching, must and shall now enjoy the privileges of free men. When you have established your government on this basis, then will the desire of your fathers be fulfilled and realized. Then will you have the Constitution which Washington and Jefferson proposed. Then will you stand before all nations of the earth, free indeed. Then will your power extend with benignant influence over this whole land. Then will the American people stand in the front rank of the nations, leading them on with the principles of free popular education and law, which they have laid down and fixed by this strife.

My friends, I hardly know how or when or by whom, the history of this great struggle shall be written. No man living to-day can write it as it should be. The events of the times have swept us on, and have carried our rulers along, until the mind of man becomes almost powerless in its efforts to estimate the consequences. When however in the future some wise and profound historian shall look back and record this chapter on his pages, he will at least be compelled to acknowledge that never before has a people risen in its might and stricken down all political heresy, all social wrong, and moral iniquity, and obtained by an overpowering impulse that lofty eminence which an enlightened and faithful, and intelligent people ought to possess. Let us then thank God that we have lived to see this day, and do not let us flinch now that the power is in our hands. Let us do our duty here. This is not a large assembly; and yet you can have but small idea of the power of such an assembly of earnest men, gathered together for the purpose of ascertaining the truth and pressing it home to the minds of their rulers. Our country is in confusion. The ideas of those who are to guide us through this crisis are yet to be moulded by the presentation from every quarter, of the great all-pervading truths which have grown out of the occasion. They do not, they cannot tell you how the mass is to crystallize—this turbid liquor is yet to be thrown into that condition from which forms and shapes may be taken. From such assemblies as these may go forth courage and wisdom, to teach our rulers and guide their councils. In the views expressed here you are not alone. When I tell you that the Chief Justice of the United States will sanction no law that is not based on the eternal principles of freedom and justice, and the mind of Salmon P. Chase is devoted to the solution of the problem upon which a lasting and honorable peace can be obtained, in which no man shall be deprived of his God-given prerogatives, you will know that the Supreme Court is at last a pillar upon which every man who would be free can lean for succor and support. (Prolonged applause.) I say this because I know it; and when I tell you that the Attorney General of the United States stands upon the same platform, that the Union men of the middle states cry out for the aid of the Federal Government in opening the revolted districts to free labor and free ballot, that your own Sumner has taken this ground and will not surrender, and that the best intelligence of the land is assuming this attitude, you will then feel how cordial should be our labor in strengthening the hands of those to whom this great work has been entrusted. . . .

[*In a letter to the Salem* Gazette *three weeks later, Loring reaffirmed his confidence that a just reconstruction was at hand. Through the 1864 elections and related appointments to high-level offices (as with Chase to the Chief Justiceship of the United States), all branches of the national government at last were synchronized with respect to reconstruction, he believed. True, Lincoln was gone from his place. But Loring accounted Andrew Johnson, the successor President, worthy to walk in Lincoln's footsteps and in harmony with Congress and with Court.*[3]]

In all this I see no danger, but safety and honor to our nation rather. We have a Congress now elected for the purpose of

---

[3] *Ibid.,* p. 12.

extending free institutions and perpetuating them; a Congress representing the highest purposes of a high-toned, elevated, moral, and free people, a Congress which, if true to all its obligations, must wipe every vestige of slavery from the land, and carry free northern prosperity, and education, and suffrage, into that region which set at defiance every advancing thought of the age. And it cannot be that with the lesson of the last four years in their minds, the American people will ever absolve their representatives from these high obligations, until the work is fully accomplished. We have a Supreme Court now, whose distinguished Chief has shown, in another sphere, how well he comprehended the necessities of the times, and whose whole life gives us an assurance that constitutional law will now rest upon the foundations of freedom and justice, and will be interpreted in accordance with those principles of government, which we have secured by undying devotion to the Federal authority. We have a President now, who knows the heresies and the wrongs, out of which the rebellion sprang, and whose education and instincts would guide him in our new path of national trials, to an eminence as illustrious as that won by his predecessor while he opened the way to higher national glories.

I am apt to believe that our nation has entered upon a new career of greatness, a career which will be untrammeled by the difficulties and trials of the past, whatever may be its dangers and trials in the future. I think the States have learned at last what their proper place is under the government. I think they have learned that the constitution and the laws enacted under it are the supreme law of the land; and that in learning this lesson they have lost none of those functions by which they have always controlled their own internal economy, for the peace, good order, and elevation of their people. I trust they have learned also that free-citizenship for all races of men is to be hereafter the unalterable law of the American people, and that every revolted State shall be held in territorial subserviency to the General Government, until she is ready to adopt this policy as her own.

30. FREDERICK DOUGLASS, SPEECH

May 9, 1865

The optimism after Appomattox that Reconstruction was a closed chapter gradually gave way in the face of accumulating evidence of its unfinished nature. Instead of accord after the close of armed hostilities, there came what Carl Schurz was to call a ". . . time of disappointments and unexpected trials," with "new dangers looming up where there ought to have been a quiet and peaceable development."[1]

A few Northerners were not taken unawares by the generally unexpected, frustrating, and exacerbating turn of events. Events were to prove that the most prophetic Republicans were the most radical—men who doubted the willingness of ex-rebels to allow Negroes to vote or to advance to decent levels of livelihood. In early 1865 the theme of this minority was "wait and see."

It can occasion little surprise that Frederick Douglass was of this suspicious mind. On May 9, 1865, he pleaded with the directors of the American Anti-Slavery Society not to disband, as William Lloyd Garrison and other abolitionist trail blazers wished to do. His speech was titled "The Need to Continue Anti-Slavery Work"[2] —a need, he insisted, that remained a cross for Christians to bear. Like the war, Reconstruction was opportunity. With freedom won, equality was to follow. Douglass wanted abolitionists to become racial egalitarians with respect to the North as well as the South. He pleaded for the antislavery movement to keep applying, in

---

[1] In *Proceedings of the National Union Republican Convention, Chicago, May 20–1, 1868* (Chicago: *Journal*, 1868), p. 9.
[2] In Foner, *Douglass*, IV, 166–169, from *The Liberator*, May 26, 1865.

search of these goals, their war-tested pressure techniques of lobbying and public education.

Many members of the society did resign. Others relaxed their efforts. But a core remained on deck. This cadre soon received heavy reinforcements as political events re-turned the North's attention southward, to focus ever more sharply on the Negro's condition there. Through efforts of this minority, the talents, training, and prestige of the abolitionist pioneers did not dissipate after Appomattox. Instead, they helped to give new meaning to the radical content of Radical Republicanism.

When I came [out of slavery] Abolitionists [wanted] to put the State of Massachusetts in harmony with the platform of the American Anti-Slavery Society. They said charity began at home. They looked over their statute-book, and whenever they found the word "white," there they recognized slavery, and they made war upon it. The anti-slavery ladies made themselves of no reputation by going about with petitions, asking the Legislature to blot out that hated word "white" from the marriage law. That was good anti-slavery work twenty years ago; I do not see why it is not good anti-slavery work now. It was a part of anti-slavery work then; it is a part now, I think.

I do not wish to appear here in any fault-finding spirit, or as an impugner of the motives of those who believe that the time has come for this Society to disband. I am conscious of no suspicion of the purity and excellence of the motives that animate the President of this Society [Garrison], and other gentlemen who are in favor its disbandment. I take this ground; whether this [Thirteenth] Constitutional Amendment is law or not, whether it has been ratified by a sufficient number of States to make it law or not, I hold that the work of Abolitionists is not done. Even if every State in the Union had ratified that Amendment, while the black man is confronted in the legislation of the South by the word "white," our work as Abolitionists, as I conceive it, is not done. I took the ground, last night, that the South, by unfriendly legislation, could make our liberty, under that provision, a delusion, a mockery, and a snare, and I hold that ground now. What advantage is a provision like this Amendment to the black man, if the Legislature of any State can to-morrow declare that no black man's testimony shall be received in a court of law? . . . Why, our Northern States have done it. Illinois, Indiana and Ohio have done it. Here, in the midst of institutions that have gone forth from old Plymouth Rock, the black man has been excluded from testifying in the courts of law; and if the Legislature of every Southern State to-morrow pass a law, declaring that no Negro shall testify in any courts of law, they will not violate that provision of the Constitution. Such laws exist now at the South. . . .

Slavery is not abolished until the black man has the ballot. While the Legislature of the South retain the right to pass laws making any discrimination between black and white, slavery still lives there. [Applause.] As Edmund Quincy once said, "While the word 'white' is on the statute-book of Massachusetts, Massachusetts is a slave State. While a black man can be turned out of a car in Massachusetts, Massachusetts is a slave State. . . ." Notwithstanding the provision in the Constitution of the United States, that the right to keep and bear arms shall not be abridged, the black man has never had the right either to keep or bear arms; and the Legislatures of the States will still have the power to forbid it, under this Amendment. They can carry on a system of unfriendly legislation, and will they not do it? Have they not got the prejudice there to do it with? Think you, that because they are for the moment in the talons and beak of our glorious eagle, instead of the slave being there, as formerly, that they are converted? I hear of the loyalty at Wilmington, the loyalty at South Carolina—what is it worth?

Not a straw. . . . They are loyal while they see 200,000 sable soldiers, with glistening bayonets, walking in their midst. [Applause.] But let the civil power of the States be restored, and the old prejudices and hostility to the Negro will revive. Aye, the very fact that the Negro has been used to defeat this rebellion and strike down the standards of the Confederacy will be a stimulus to all their hatreds, to all their malice, and lead them to legislate with greater stringency towards this class than ever before. [Applause.] The American people are bound—bound by their sense of honor (I hope by their sense of honor, at least, by a just sense of honor), to extend the franchise to the Negro; and I was going to say, that the Abolitionists of the American Anti-Slavery Society were bound to "stand still, and see the salvation of God," until that work is done. [Applause.] Where shall the black man look for support, my friends, if the American Anti-Slavery Society fails him? ["Hear, hear."] From whence shall we expect a certain sound from the trumpet of freedom, when the old pioneer, when this Society that has survived mobs, and martyrdom, and the combined efforts of priest-craft and state-craft to suppress it, shall all at once subside, on the mere intimation that the Constitution has been amended, so that neither slavery nor involuntary servitude shall hereafter be allowed in this land? What did the slaveholders of Richmond say to those who objected to arming the Negro, on the ground that it would make him a freeman? Why, they said, "The argument is absurd. We may make these Negroes fight for us; but while we retain the political power of the South, we can keep them in their subordinate positions." That was the argument; and they were right. They might have employed the Negro to fight for them, and while they retained in their hands the power to exclude him from political rights, they could have reduced him to a condition similar to slavery. They would not call it slavery, but some other name. . . . It has been called by a great many names, and it will call itself by yet another name; and you and I and all of us had better wait and see what new form this old monster will assume, in what new skin this old snake will come forth next.

31. ANDREW JOHNSON,

RECONSTRUCTION PROCLAMATION

May 29, 1865

As of the spring of 1865, the odds were very heavy against Douglass' successfully bringing to his position a majority of Republicans. By and large, Northern white society, though it hated slavery, did not love Negroes. The Southern slave was the focus of Northern prewar and wartime concern, not the free Negro. Men of Lincoln's stripe, who under the war's pressures had abandoned colonization chimeras and joined the abolitionist pioneers, were concerned less with the Negro as victim than with the degradation that slavery forced on all men, and with the strength that it gave to the Confederacy. Some of the staunchest wartime Radical Republicans never did see much point in pushing for political rights for freedmen. As example, Thaddeus Stevens and George Julian always insisted that the Negro would benefit more from provision for economic stability, especially through land ownership, than from exercise of political rights.

Recent scholarship, especially by W. R. Brock, John and La Wanda Cox, John Hope Franklin, Eric McKitrick, Kenneth Stampp, and Hans Trefousse impressively underscores the reluctance of most Republicans and Northerners to make the change to advocacy of political rights for freedmen. For the Negro to dominate the central stage in white politics required a pressure impossible for a Douglass or for the tiny cadre of like-minded Negrophile Radicals, such as Sumner, to achieve.

Yet within a shockingly short time after Appomattox, the white-centered politics of the North and of the restored nation focused on the Negro. First the Radical Republicans, then all Republicans, then a majority of Northerners advanced from the Lincoln position of April 1865 of advocacy of biracial coexistence and limited Negro suffrage in the South. During the advance, most Radicals temporarily became determined Negrophiles. They came finally to champion full, not limited, political equality for Southern Negroes. In pursuit of this egalitarian goal, Radicals grew to accept the Douglass position that abolition led to further national responsibilities.

In the words of Edward Pollard, a keen-minded Virginia journalist and chief literary mourner for the Lost Cause, the prewar abolitionists were inspired

> . . . from general motives of humanity; they desired to free . . . [the slave]; they desired to do for him such kindly offices as they would for any suffering people; but they pretended no special solicitude for him because he was a black man. . . . On the other hand, we find in the [postwar] Anti-Slavery [pro-equality, Radical Republican] party a positive and most offensive disease—manifesting for the Negro a singular affection . . . and intent upon making him the political pet and idol of America.[1]

Of course not all men moved reluctantly. Some old abolitionists gladly acceded to the Douglass appeal. As example, the editorial staff of the *Anti-Slavery Standard* in May 1865 announced happily: "Again we change front to fight [now] the battle of Suffrage, seeing that today the ballot-box is the only real charter of emancipation." Justice to the Negro, not vengeance against the South, must obtain; "No Reconstruction without Negro Suffrage" became the slogan of the *Standard* in July. Anything less would be a sham, a surrender to the slave power; for without the ballot, the freedman would descend again into slavery, and the war's sacrifices would become nullified.[2]

During the prewar decades and culminating in the war years, great debates had marked the American scene with respect to the extension of slavery, the enforcement of fugitive slave laws, and finally, the continuation of slavery itself. Another great debate

---

[1] Pollard, *The Lost Cause Regained* (New York: Carleton, 1868), pp. 130–131.
[2] May 27, July 27, 1865.

commenced in 1865. Out of it, by the close of 1866 a new Republican consensus to make firm the freed Negro's status in all states, without regard to race, had taken form. Republicans did not reach this decision casually; Democrats did not allow the program to succeed without tenacious opposition.

The astonishing renascence of the Northern Democratic party in 1865 requires more study than it has yet received. Phoenix-like in its capacity to rise out of Copperhead ashes, despite its taint from associative treason the Northern Democracy (i.e., Democrats) soon reached southward to realign with conservatives in the former rebel states. By late 1866 the unanticipatable reconversion of President Johnson to his prewar party affiliation heavily reinforced the rerisen Democracy with the weight of executive patronage. At least, the Republicans faced a tough rear-guard Democratic action that was as unexpected as it proved to be tenacious.

The upshot was that the Republican trend toward acceptance of universal suffrage in all states was never permitted to proceed without determined opposition and critical publicity. As one Radical Republican participant recalled fifty years later:

. . . it would be well to study the evolution of the subject . . . from February 1865 until the winter of 1869. It is safe to assert that no other measure has ever been so thoroughly discussed, debated, sifted, and examined from every point of the compass. The open debates upon it in the Senate and House only represented a portion of the consideration that was given to it. Many who had opposed it strenuously came to the conclusion that it was the only possible remedy . . . for existing conditions.[3]

In the spring of 1865, Republican leaders had no desire to reopen the reconstruction question at all. Party memories were raw of the encounter in 1864 between Lincoln and the Wade-Davis faction. How much better it would be on all counts to consider reconstruction a closed matter. Lincoln just before his murder had made clear the way to leave it quiet—to insure the participation of Negro voters in rebuilding Southern states. The Republican expectation was that his successor in the White House would hold to that minimal demand.

---

[3] Frank Preston Stearns, *True Republicanism or The Real and Ideal in Politics* (Philadelphia: Lippincott, 1904), pp. 213–215. He is the son of the abolitionist George L. Stearns.

First alarms commenced to spread as it grew obvious in the weeks after the assassination that Johnson did not intend to call the Congress into special session. The regular Congressional calendar had it that the legislature elected with Lincoln in November 1864 would not meet until December 1865. Yet its members believed that they, far more than Johnson, knew the desires of Northern voters. Some Republicans feared an eruption of violence approaching anarchy if another assassination took off Johnson. Who would succeed him?[4]

Deeper apprehensions grew from the announcement from the White House on May 29, 1865, of a reconstruction and pardoning policy similar in form to Lincoln's discredited one of December 1863. In mid-1864 Lincoln's party members in Congress had shown, by their support of the Wade-Davis bill and by their reaction to the dead President's veto of that act, what they thought of executive initiative in reconstruction. Plentiful evidence was on hand that Lincoln's way was not successful. Yet here was the new President repeating the pattern, though without the ability to claim, as Lincoln had, that executive reconstruction by proclamation was an effective war weapon.

Here is the text of the fateful May 29 orders. By the close of 1865, subsequent proclamations applied these stipulations to practically all the former Confederate states.[5]

By the President of the United States of America.

A PROCLAMATION.

Whereas the President of the United States, on the 8th day of December, A. D. 1863, and on the 26th day of March, A. D. 1864, did, with the object to suppress the existing rebellion,

---

[4] J. M. Stone to Governor John Andrew, April 15, 1865, Andrew Papers (Massachusetts Historical Society).
[5] Richardson, *Messages and Papers*, VI, 310–314.

to induce all persons to return to their loyalty, and to restore the authority of the United States, issue proclamations offering amnesty and pardon to certain persons who had, directly or by implication, participated in the said rebellion; and

Whereas many persons who had so engaged in said rebellion have, since the issuance of said proclamations, failed or neglected to take the benefits offered thereby; and

Whereas many persons who have been justly deprived of all claim to amnesty and pardon thereunder by reason of their participation, directly or by implication, in said rebellion and continued hostility to the Government of the United States since the date of said proclamations now desire to apply for and obtain amnesty and pardon.

To the end, therefore, that the authority of the Government of the United States may be restored and that peace, order, and freedom may be established, I, Andrew Johnson, President of the United States, do proclaim and declare that I hereby grant to all persons who have, directly or indirectly, participated in the existing rebellion, except as hereinafter excepted, amnesty and pardon, with restoration of all rights of property, except as to slaves and except in cases where legal proceedings under the laws of the United States providing for the confiscation of property of persons engaged in rebellion have been instituted; but upon the condition, nevertheless, that every such person shall take and subscribe the following oath (or affirmation) and thenceforward keep and maintain said oath inviolate, and which oath shall be registered for permanent preservation and shall be of the tenor and effect following, to wit:

I, ———— ————, do solemnly swear (or affirm), in presence of Almighty God, that I will henceforth faithfully support, protect, and defend the Constitution of the United States and the Union of the States thereunder, and that I will in like manner abide by and faithfully support all laws and proclamations which have been made during the existing rebellion with reference to the emancipation of slaves. So help me God.

The following classes of persons are excepted from the benefits of this proclamation:

First. All who are or shall have been pretended civil or diplomatic officers or otherwise domestic or foreign agents of the pretended Confederate government.

Second. All who left judicial stations under the United States to aid the rebellion.

Third. All who shall have been military or naval officers of said pretended Confederate government above the rank of colonel in the army or lieutenant in the navy.

Fourth. All who left seats in the Congress of the United States to aid the rebellion.

Fifth. All who resigned or tendered resignations of their commissions in the Army or Navy of the United States to evade duty in resisting the rebellion.

Sixth. All who have engaged in any way in treating otherwise than lawfully as prisoners of war persons found in the United States service as officers, soldiers, seamen, or in other capacities.

Seventh. All persons who have been or are absentees from the United States for the purpose of aiding the rebellion.

Eighth. All military and naval officers in the rebel service who were educated by the Government in the Military Academy at West Point or the United States Naval Academy.

Ninth. All persons who held the pretended offices of governors of States in insurrection against the United States.

Tenth. All persons who left their homes within the jurisdiction and protection of the United States and passed beyond the Federal military lines into the pretended Confederate States for the purpose of aiding the rebellion.

Eleventh. All persons who have been engaged in the destruction of the commerce of the United States upon the high seas and all persons who have made raids into the United States from Canada or been engaged in destroying the commerce of the United States upon the lakes and rivers that separate the British Provinces from the United States.

Twelfth. All persons who, at the time when they seek to obtain the benefits hereof by taking the oath herein prescribed, are in military, naval, or civil confinement or custody, or under bonds of the civil, military, or naval authorities or agents of the United States as prisoners of war, or persons detained for offenses of any kind, either before or after conviction.

Thirteenth. All persons who have voluntarily participated in said rebellion and the estimated value of whose taxable property is over $20,000.

Fourteenth. All persons who have taken the oath of amnesty as prescribed in the President's proclamation of December 8, A. D. 1863, or an oath of allegiance to the Government of the United States since the date of said proclamation and who have not thenceforward kept and maintained the same inviolate.

Provided, That special application may be made to the President for pardon by any person belonging to the excepted classes, and such clemency will be liberally extended as may be consistent with the facts of the case and the peace and dignity of the United States.

The Secretary of State will establish rules and regulations for administering and recording the said amnesty oath, so as to insure its benefit to the people and guard the Government against fraud.

In testimony whereof I have hereunto set my hand and caused the seal of the United States to be affixed.

[SEAL.]   Done at the city of Washington, the 29th day of May, A. D. 1865, and of the Independence of the United States the eighty-ninth.

ANDREW JOHNSON.

By the President:
WILLIAM H. SEWARD,
Secretary of State.

By the President of the United States of America.

A Proclamation.

Whereas the fourth section of the fourth article of the Constitution of the United States declares that the United States shall guarantee to every State in the Union a republican form of government and shall protect each of them against invasion and domestic violence; and

Whereas the President of the United States is by the Constitution made Commander in Chief of the Army and Navy, as well as chief civil executive officer of the United States, and is bound by solemn oath faithfully to execute the office of President of the United States and to take care that the laws be faithfully executed; and

Whereas the rebellion which has been waged by a portion of the people of the United States against the properly constituted authorities of the Government thereof in the most violent and revolting form, but whose organized and armed forces have now been almost entirely overcome, has in its revolutionary progress deprived the people of the State of North Carolina of all civil government; and

Whereas it becomes necessary and proper to carry out and enforce the obligations of the United States to the people of North Carolina in securing them in the enjoyment of a republican form of government:

Now, therefore, in obedience to the high and solemn duties imposed upon me by the Constitution of the United States and for the purpose of enabling the loyal people of said State to organize a State government whereby justice may be established, domestic tranquillity insured, and loyal citizens protected in all their rights of life, liberty, and property, I, Andrew Johnson, President of the United States and Commander in

Chief of the Army and Navy of the United States, do hereby appoint William W. Holden provisional governor of the State of North Carolina, whose duty it shall be, at the earliest practicable period, to prescribe such rules and regulations as may be necessary and proper for convening a convention composed of delegates to be chosen by that portion of the people of said State who are loyal to the United States, and no others, for the purpose of altering or amending the constitution thereof, and with authority to exercise within the limits of said State all the powers necessary and proper to enable such loyal people of the State of North Carolina to restore said State to its constitutional relations to the Federal Government and to present such a republican form of State government as will entitle the State to the guaranty of the United States therefor and its people to protection by the United States against invasion, insurrection, and domestic violence: *Provided,* That in any election that may be hereafter held for choosing delegates to any State convention as aforesaid no person shall be qualified as an elector or shall be eligible as a member of such convention unless he shall have previously taken and subscribed the oath of amnesty as set forth in the President's proclamation of May 29, A. D. 1865, and is a voter qualified as prescribed by the constitution and laws of the State of North Carolina in force immediately before the 20th day of May, A. D. 1861, the date of the so-called ordinance of secession; and the said convention, when convened, or the legislature that may be thereafter assembled, will prescribe the qualification of electors and the eligibility of persons to hold office under the constitution and laws of the State—a power the people of the several States composing the Federal Union have rightfully exercised from the origin of the Government to the present time.

And I do hereby direct—

First. That the military commander of the department and all officers and persons in the military and naval service aid and assist the said provisional governor in carrying into effect this proclamation; and they are enjoined to abstain from in any way hindering, impeding, or discouraging the loyal people from the organization of a State government as herein authorized.

Second. That the Secretary of State proceed to put in force all laws of the United States the administration whereof belongs to the State Department applicable to the geographical limits aforesaid.

Third. That the Secretary of the Treasury proceed to nominate for appointment assessors of taxes and collectors of customs and internal revenue and such other officers of the Treasury Department as are authorized by law and put in execution the revenue laws of the United States within the geographical limits aforesaid. In making appointments the preference shall be given to qualified loyal persons residing within the districts where their respective duties are to be performed; but if suitable residents of the districts shall not be found, then persons residing in other States or districts shall be appointed.

Fourth. That the Postmaster-General proceed to establish post-offices and post routes and put into execution the postal laws of the United States within the said State, giving to loyal residents the preference of appointment; but if suitable residents are not found, then to appoint agents, etc., from other States.

Fifth. That the district judge for the judicial district in which North Carolina is included proceed to hold courts within said State in accordance with the provisions of the act of Congress. The Attorney-General will instruct the proper officers to libel and bring to judgment, confiscation, and sale property subject to confiscation and enforce the administration of justice within said State in all matters within the cognizance and jurisdiction of the Federal courts.

Sixth. That the Secretary of the Navy take possession of all

public propery belonging to the Navy Department within said
geographical limits and put in operation all acts of Congress
in relation to naval affairs having application to the said State.

Seventh. That the Secretary of the Interior put in force the
laws relating to the Interior Department applicable to the
geographical limits aforesaid.

In testimony whereof I have hereunto set my hand and
caused the seal of the United States to be affixed.

[SEAL.]   Done at the city of Washington, this 29th day of
May, A. D. 1865, and of the Independence of the
United States the eighty-ninth.

ANDREW JOHNSON

By the President:
WILLIAM H. SEWARD,
Secretary of State.

32. GEORGE S. BOUTWELL, SPEECH

July 4, 1865

Though they were not called to Washington for a special session
of Congress during the months after Johnson's initiation of reconstruction in the South, the Republican leaders maintained close
watch on events. Probably puzzlement was their commonest
reaction.

George Sewall Boutwell was a Republican representative from
Massachusetts. In his middle years, Boutwell enjoyed a large reputation in the party as an original Republican and as an erstwhile
governor of his state. Young foreign newswriter Georges Clemenceau, commenting on the Washington scene for French readers,
thought Boutwell ". . . the last survivor of the puritans of a by-
gone age, a man after the heart of John Bunyan, and too much

fanatic to command . . . attention . . . , but too honest and sincere for his opinions to be ignored by his party."[1]

President Johnson should not have ignored the opinions of such a stalwart of the party as Boutwell. The Bay Stater spoke on July 4 on "Reconstruction: Its True Basis."[2] In this speech Boutwell admitted the uncertainty among Republicans as to the wisdom of the President's course in the South. He made clear to Johnson that the Negro was the central symbol of the white South's readiness for full readmission to the practices of citizenship.

If I understand President Johnson, he does not object to negro suffrage. It is, however, his desire that the right should be extended to the negroes of the once existing eleven States, recently in rebellion, by the white people of those States, who were authorized to vote when the rebellion commenced. If negro suffrage can be secured in that way, I shall, for one, readily accept the result without any inquiry as to the means. But if, on the other hand, as I expect, the attempt to secure negro suffrage, through the white people of the eleven rebel States, shall fail, I then expect that President Johnson and those who are co-operating with him, will accept the judgment of the country,—if it shall prove to be the judgment of the country,—that negro suffrage must be secured by some other means. Therefore, while I am content that these efforts should be made, and while I shall welcome the result, if it be favorable, I look upon the efforts as experiments, not binding upon President Johnson or upon his administration or on the country; and as was the fact in 1861 and '62, in reference to the expediency of emancipation, and the enrolment of colored soldiers in the army of the Republic, I now expect that the people will take this matter into their own hands. I

---

[1] Clemenceau, *American Reconstruction*, p. 178.

[2] Boutwell, *Reconstruction: Its True Basis, Speech at Weymouth, Massachusetts, July 4, 1865* (Boston: Wright & Potter, 1865), pp. 12–15, 24–33.

believe, with reference to President Johnson, as in 1861 and '62 I believed in reference to President Lincoln, that he will accept the judgment of the country, if, upon the whole, the public opinion shall be that negro suffrage is essential to the security of the Union as well as to the protection of the negroes themselves. Therefore I counsel discussion, argument, on the part of those who believe in negro suffrage; patience, that those in authority may have an opportunity to make this effort to secure the reconstruction of the government according to the ideas that have first presented themselves to them; that no one be committed to any particular line of policy, but all look to the grand result—the reconstruction of the government upon the principle of the equality of men. . . .

There was a Divine policy in our affairs which made emancipation a necessity; and we are now so subject to circumstances that all plans for the reconstruction of the government which do not recognize the political rights of the negro are sure to fail. The white men of the North must recognize the political rights of the black men of the South or surrender their own equality in the government of the country. They must decree political freedom for the blacks or accept political inferiority for themselves. Hence I well know in the beginning what their conduct will be. Nor do I underestimate the apparent difficulties in our way. There is first, the wide-spread and plausible error, which I shall attempt now to refute, that if we deny the existence of the eleven States as States, we admit the heresy of secession. There is next the prejudice against the negro race coupled with a sad misapprehension as to his capacity to take care of himself and to serve the country; and finally there is the difficulty, amounting to an obstacle in the estimation of some, that certain of the loyal States do even now deny to the negro the right of franchise. But all these are errors, misfortunes and wrongs, rather than serious difficulties in our way. When slavery existed, citizenship was of course denied to the slave class in all the slave States. It was also natural in States where slavery did not exist, but where its ideas were carried by immigrants or where its social and business influences prevailed, or, possibly, by mere comity in some cases, that the public policy should be fashioned upon the theory that slavery, or at least, a condition of political inferiority was the proper fortune of the black man. It is likely that the overthrow of slavery will be followed by a revision of this policy; but in any event the argument in favor of negro suffrage in the rebellious districts is as valid when addressed to Illinois or Indiana as when addressed to New York or Massachusetts.

The war for freedom and the Union has been carried on by the whites and negroes born on this continent, by the Irish and the Germans, and indeed by representatives of every European race. With this fresh experience we ought to make it a part of the organic government that no State shall make any distinction in the enjoyment of the elective franchise on account of race or color. . . .

We have carried on the war to a successful termination; we have subjugated the rebellious people; we have overthrown their military power; we have acquired jurisdiction over the territory, and consequently we have a right to demand,—as much as we should if, in a war with Mexico, we had acquired Chihuahua or Sonora,—that when these once existing States are reconstructed and admitted to the Union, they shall come with institutions which are in substantial harmony with the settled policy of the nation. And therefore, upon either of these theories,—upon the theory of the power of the people of the rebel States, or upon the theory of the war power of the Government,—we find sufficient reason and justification for what we propose. . . .

In passing, permit me to say that there are four methods or forms of government which might be established in the rebellious States. First, military governments, responsible to

the Executive of the country. Secondly, territorial governments, in which a law of Congress should define and prescribe the rights of the people in reference to suffrage, with
the power lodged in the President and Senate to appoint the
Governor, Secretary of State, District-Attorney and perhaps
some other officers. Thirdly, to recognize these States as States
in the American nation, and this without any inquiry and with
their old constitutions. And, fourthly, by treating the people
of these eleven States as within the jurisdiction of the General
Government, but without institutions of any sort, permit them
to frame a government and apply for admission to the Union.
A military government, being irresponsible, expensive, and,
for the most part, tyrannical, is unacceptable to the American
people. It can be continued for a short period of time only,
but ere long it would be compelled to give place to another
form. Probably, with reference to some of the States, as South
Carolina and Florida, a territorial government would be best
adapted to the existing condition of things. In Arkansas, Tennessee and Louisiana there is possibly so large a loyal sentiment, that if the colored people were allowed the right of
suffrage, those States might be safely restored to their ancient
relations to the Union. It therefore follows, as the practical
result, that it will be necessary to adopt different lines of
policy for different States. . . .

33. WILLIAM GROSVENOR, ARTICLE

September 1865

All during the summer and autumn of 1865, the unfolding pattern
of President Johnson's state rebuilding in the South offended increasing numbers of Northern whites. Prominent Republican lead-

ers, including Sumner and Stevens, felt impelled again to strain party lines and to speak out publicly against the drift of Southern affairs. Clearly, Negro suffrage was not going to come voluntarily from the hands of the white Southerners who swore future loyalty to the nation as the President required and, amnestied or pardoned, became qualified to vote and to hold office, whatever their past rebel records. The Republican dream grew dimmer of a swift, simple, inexpensive reconstruction built on the presence in each ex-Confederate state of a cadre of voting Negroes and white Unionists.

These events and consequent disappointments pushed William Grosvenor (and many other Northerners, undoubtedly) back into a Radical posture. Recall that Grosvenor had returned home from military service with an anti-Negro prejudice. He makes clear in the following article, written in September 1865, that the President's ways had stripped away that lingering racial antipathy. Now Grosvenor stands forth as a Negro-centered critic of racial conservatism in reconstruction, his attention focused on the question he asks: "Whether Emancipation shall prove a blessing or a curse?"[1]

We have conquered. Our vast armies, at the magic word of a citizen at Washington, melt away, not into nothingness, . . . but into intelligent and loyal citizens, industrious and enterprising. Hands that grasped the musket in the charge, now handle ledgers and direct pens. Brawny arms that pointed the great gun, now swing the scythe or the hammer. Voices that used to ring the word of command over smoky fields, are now modulated to the whispers of the professional office, or attuned to the ears of listening audiences in silk and broadcloth. Our great iron-clads rest at League Island. Mr. Stanton [Secretary of War] leaves Washington for the season of rest for which four years of herculean toil have given even him an appetite. In a word, we are at peace; and the flag of the

---

[1] Grosvenor, "The Rights of the Nation, and the Duty of Congress," *New Englander*, XXIV (October 1865), 1–23.

Republic, symbol now of a purer and worthier nationality than when first unfurled, springs from low earthworks to meet every eastern breeze that nears an Atlantic port, and hangs lazily in the perfumed air of the groves of orange and magnolia that border on the Gulf. Dusky forms, clad in blue, examine their passes for lordly Rhetts and Hammonds, or march them to the presence of a Yankee provost marshal. A pale, spare man [Jefferson Davis] at Fortress Monroe paces up and down the stone pavement of his casemate, and traces over, in long hours of unbroken meditation, the logical sequence from Calhoun's speeches, to the surrender of Lee and the capture of a half disguised fugitive in the gray dawn of a Georgia morning.

We have conquered, but among thoughtful men there is now the utmost anxiety regarding the future of the Republic. . . . The Union is saved, only to be handed over, men fear, to the charge of those who have been its most deadly enemies. Slaves are emancipated; but whether emancipation shall prove a blessing or a curse, to them and to the nation, depends altogether, it would seem, upon the voluntary conduct of those who have always said it would prove a curse. Slavery is abolished; but peonage, or some other plan of forced labor, hardly less unjust or dangerous to the nation than slavery itself, is the natural result of the present condition of affairs at the South, the only solution to which the mind or inclination of the land-owner turns, and the inevitable consequence of any early withdrawal of military control. Slave labor has ceased; and the masters, whose pride and honor are staked upon the claim that free labor must fail, combine to make it fail. Property in man has ceased; and Avarice no longer restrains Cruelty, Hate, or Passion from deeds of horror that would be incredible if the slave-pen and Andersonville were not fresh in memory. The freedman's bureau and the military power—these alone save the blacks today from a fight of extermination between them and their late oppressors. The military power must cease to protect when the work of reconstruction is complete, and that work is pressed with haste. In not a single state has adequate provision been made for the protection of the blacks by civil courts; in most of them such protection is plainly denied. Mississippi defeats all candidates who advocate negro testimony in courts; Alabama and South Carolina show the same spirit; the loyal legislature of Virginia (so-called) found time to relieve rebels of civil disabilities, but none to grant the slightest protection to loyal blacks; Louisiana, in her free-state constitution, grants no true equality before the law, and even Tennessee, the home of the President, denies the simplest justice to the hated race. Anxiety with regard to the treatment of the negroes is not confined to humanitarians nor philanthropists; business men know that the prosperity of the whole country depends now in no small degree upon the successful establishment of free labor at the South. . . .

Yet this is not the only cause of anxiety. For four years we have been learning to hate traitors. To see them shaping and controlling in many states the whole work of reconstruction is not pleasant. We look in vain, but too often, for those staunch and fearless loyal [Southern Union] men, who were to greet the return of the old flag, whose unforfeited rights as citizens have been the subject of so much keen metaphysical disquisition, and to whom belonged, we were told, those franchises and powers which active rebels had forever lost. South Carolina is searched for one, but only a [Benjamin F.] Perry is found [for appointment there as provisional governor]. Even in appointing Provisional Governors, it has been necessary, it seems, to take men who have held office under the rebellion. Instead of unflinching union men, confederate officers manage the business of reorganization. The roll of a Southern [state constitutional] convention, for titles, reads like a muster-roll of Lee's army. If elections are held, the staunch unionist is inevitably beaten by some man whose arm was carried away by a union bullet. In some places, as in Richmond and Norfolk, loyal votes are rejected, and rebel votes admitted. Everywhere, without exception, save in Tennessee, the work of reorganization falls to the hands of men whom, less than a year ago, it was lawful for any loyal man to shoot at sight.

But, by some people, the temper and conduct of these Southern managers are deemed highly satisfactory. "They accept defeat," it is said. So the culprit "accepts" imprisonment. They declare void the ordinances of secession. Then they have only ratified the acts of Grant and Sherman. South Carolina, however, refuses even by implication to admit that she had not the right to secede, and had not legally seceded; but she deliberately "repeals" her ordinance of secession, which is very kind of her. They also abolish slavery. But as they have been plainly told that without this all other action would be empty and fruitless, and military rule would be surely continued, we find in that act no especial merit or evidence of change of disposition; the less, as they all take pains to declare that this reform is effected, not by their own free choice, but by the military power of the United States. We are hardly left in doubt whether, if they should ever have the power, they would re-establish the system so reluctantly abandoned. . . .

The Southern men . . . tell us frankly that they submit, hold conventions, abolish slavery, and abrogate acts of secession, not because they are union men, but because they cannot help it. . . .

Those who have access to papers and constant intelligence from the South, know how truly this paints the spirit of Southern movements. Between the wary leader, who significantly urges a very submissive behavior "for the time," and the indiscreet disciple who threatens what shall be done when restoration is complete, the difference is one of reticence and cunning. In counting upon the aid of a Northern party, they do not reckon without their host. The speeches at Democratic [political] conventions, the New York [draft] riots, the Chicago plot, and the records of the Golden Circle [a Copperhead secret organization], show the spirit that animates the controlling men of that party. Through the thick darkness of their political infamy and ostracism, there gleams no ray of hope except in the final triumph of the rebels of the South. By that light they steer. With an energy that only new confidence of success could beget, they battle for immediate and unconditioned restoration of rebel states to their full political powers. Every measure or demand in behalf of the nation's honor or safety, they resist as one man. They denounce the punishment of traitors. They clamor for universal amnesty. The confiscation policy they term disgraceful. The constitutional amendment abolishing slavery is gall and wormwood to them. Test oaths, whether adopted by Congress or by states, they ridicule and will repeal if they can. The integrity of the national debt they already insidiously threaten under color of a demand for equal taxation by the states. The theory everywhere maintained by that party is that the Southern states have by rebellion forfeited no right whatever; that they are already states, in precisely the same sense and with precisely the same powers as those that have not rebelled; that neither President, Congress, nor People have any right to require of them any changes, or impose upon them any conditions; that if either of them refuses to abolish slavery or ratify the constitutional amendment, it cannot on that account be denied representation in Congress; that military control at the South is a usurpation which must cease at once; and that all these rebellious states must be restored to their full powers, no matter whether rebels or union men control them, and must be granted their full representation in Congress and the Electoral College, no matter what changes they may make or refuse to make in their constitutions or laws. In a word, this great party, still true as steel to its treasonable alliance, demands now, as it demanded [in 1864] at Chicago, that beaten rebels shall dictate terms to the nation, and that they shall be restored to all their rights and powers, not upon conditions that satisfy the nation, but upon such conditions as they may voluntarily offer!

Such willful treachery to the cause of the people would be incredible, if the last five years could be forgotten. These men, at least, have not been converted by the hallowing influences of defeat, and in their hands the great Democratic party is a perfect, well-oiled engine, obedient to the slightest touch upon the valves, and incapable of any principle or emotion except hunger. From that party, we may be sure, there will never come aid or protection for the blacks in any extremity of oppression. Men who called emancipation an act of robbery, will have little solicitude for the rights of freedmen. Men who rejoiced when Sumter fell or when Lincoln was assassinated, naturally long for the speedy restoration of such a South Carolina as Wade Hampton may represent. Men who declared the war a failure in 1864, are not resolute to make it a success in 1865. . . .

The war well over, the great mass of the people begin to turn a deaf ear to political discussions, and devote their energies to the making of money. Every day the magic shuttles of trade are weaving bands between Southern landowners and Northern voters—subtle threads that penetrate every work shop and counting room, that would have sacrificed right to convenience in 1860, and that will soon be felt once more in elections and in Congress. . . . The old prejudices of race and caste find new endorsement in a decision [early in 1865] of the people of a New England state [Connecticut, against Negro suffrage there]. The anxiety of loyal and thinking men, justified by the resolute bearing of the rebels and their Northern allies, finds little relief in the divided councils and faltering steps of those to whom the nation must look for aid in its time of peril.

It is most unfortunate that, rather by a few isolated expressions than by his general management, a President elected by loyal votes should give to the allies of rebellion some color of pretence for claiming him as their leader and chief. We cannot believe that Mr. Johnson, whose scathing denunciations of treason won him the confidence of the people, has for these tories, who have shown all the baseness and disloyalty with none of the pluck and manhood of rebels, any other feeling than unutterable loathing. It is impossible to believe that a President who retains Edwin M. Stanton in his cabinet, can really propose deliberate treachery to the cause by which he was elected to office. His heart must be right; but errors of the head are sometimes not less serious in their consequences than those of the heart. It cannot be more, and it surely is not less, than an error of judgment that has made the name of the President a tower of strength to those who clamor for the immediate restoration of rebels to full political rights on such terms as they may please. His admission of pardoned whites and exclusion of the loyal blacks, in prescribing the basis of reorganization, was not absolute justice, though in his judgment the best policy that the people would then sustain. And his reason for that course—that the regulation of their own policy of suffrage is a right which "the several states" have always "rightfully exercised"—a reason which applies with equal propriety to other steps in his own procedure, and which, by logical inference, condemns in advance every precautionary measure which Congress could adopt—has become the rallying cry of those whose political future depends upon the immediate and unconditional restoration of rebels to power. It impliedly answers—and answers not rightly—the first of the great questions before the country: "What can the nation lawfully do to protect itself and its honor?" It implies that the nation is confined, in its dealings with the rebellious communities, to the powers conferred upon it by the Constitution over organized and loyal states—a view not justified by sound reason nor by his own method in dealing with those communities, and which, if logically followed, would leave the nation wholly at the mercy of its conquered foes.

Either the states that have been in rebellion are now in such condition, notwithstanding that rebellion, as to be entitled to the rights and powers accorded to states in the Constitution, or they are not in such condition. If they are, then they are entitled to all the rights and powers of states. The Constitution either gives, or it does not give. Treason either forfeits all, or none. If, then, those communities are in such condition, they can elect their own Governors, retain their own constitutions if they choose, and claim, as of right, their seats in Congress as soon as men of legal qualifications are elected, and neither President nor Congress has any right to deny or delay that representation, or to require of them any changes whatever in their constitutions or laws. Whatever rights the constitution gives, it gives to all states alike. There is no such thing known to our constitution or system of government as a "state" which can exercise part of the rights of a state, but is not equally entitled to them all. . . .

President Johnson does not treat these communities as now entitled to all the rights of states. Except in the suffrage matter, his whole policy is in glaring contradiction to that theory. He appoints Provisional Governors, and invests them with executive functions. Does the Constitution empower a President to appoint Governors for "states"? He excludes from suffrage a large number of qualified electors under the laws of the former states, who have never yet been convicted of any crime against the United States. By what right could he disfranchise half the citizens of Massachusetts? Elections held under the authority of the only civil government in Virginia, were by his order set aside and pronounced void. Where does the Constitution empower the President to nullify the

elections in a state? Courts throughout the South are warned
that in a certain class of cases [i.e., those involving Negroes]
they shall not assume jurisdiction, and this, too, after those
courts have been reorganized under the authority of the
President. Military officers, the agents of the national Executive, try all cases in which negroes are concerned; set aside
state laws constantly, and in essential particulars, and no
state courts are permitted to review their decisions. What
color of authority does the Constitution give for such wholesale interference with the courts of "states"? But there are
even more striking proofs than these that the rebel communities are not regarded [even by the President] as now possessing the rights of constitutional states. There is no more
solemn act of sovereignty than the adoption or amendment of
a state constitution. There is no power belonging to a state
more important than that which is exercised in the final ratification of an amendment of the National Constitution. Yet
President Johnson has plainly declared to the rebellious communities that they must not only abolish slavery as a local
institution, by amendments of their state constitutions and
laws, but must give their formal assent to the anti-slavery
amendment of the National Constitution, or they will not be
restored to the power and representation of members of the
Union. No man pretends that a President can rightly impose
such conditions upon New Jersey or Delaware. Yet, if the
Constitution accords any rights or powers whatever to South
Carolina, it gives precisely the same as to Delaware or New
Jersey. If South Carolina is a state, within the meaning of
the Constitution, in such condition that she can claim as a
member of the Union any of the powers or rights accorded
by that supreme law to states, then she can claim them all;
can alter her constitution or not as she chooses, can elect her
own Governor, establish her own courts, and imprison military
officers who dispute or attempt to restrict their jurisdiction;

and, above all, can pronounce without fear or favor her own independent verdict of assent or rejection upon the amendment of the National Constitution.

The conclusion is one that no reasoning mind can evade. The rebel communities, call them by what name we please, are not now in such condition that they are entitled to rights or powers as states under the provisions of the Constitution. They have, at present, no constitutional rights whatever. . . .

Upon what conditions, then, is it the duty of Congress to insist? What practical policy will defeat the new schemes of unrepentant rebels and their allies?

We have, first, to protect the national honor. The faith of the nation is pledged to the abolition of slavery; and not only amendment of state constitutions, but, for full security, a ratification of the national amendment, will be required. But the freedom which the nation has solemnly promised is not a mere nominal emancipation. It involves full protection in all rights of person and property—absolute equality before the law.

No man will pretend that such protection is possible, after the withdrawal of bureau superintendence and military power, unless the testimony of the freedman is received in all the courts, and his rights of contract and property are placed upon the same basis as those of whites. Such provisions do not yet exist in any rebel state. Had the conventions which have been held incorporated provisions of this nature into the new constitutions, there would have been some security at least, that the rights of the loyal blacks would not be forever at the mercy of every state legislature. Every convention, as yet, has refused to do anything of the kind. The subject was not overlooked; the certainty that a just Congress would not overlook it seems to have been borne in mind; for ordinances were passed directing state legislatures to make provision for the protection of the freedmen, and "to guard the state against the evils which may result from their sudden emancipation." If it was thought that this vague but almost insulting formula would satisfy the just demands of a nation, whose faith is pledged to secure to these victims of oppression and hatred full and permanent protection in all their natural rights, surely Congress will not fail to teach the masters their error! . . .

While the present state of feeling lasts, to withdraw the protecting power of the nation, and restore the rebel states to full control over their domestic affairs, would be a deed of the most heartless cruelty. Indeed, it would be not only inhuman, but suicidal. It would end in anarchy, and a war of races.

For this difficulty there are but two remedies; to continue military or provisional government until a different state of feeling is developed, or to give to the blacks an invulnerable shield of self-protection in the right of suffrage. No man can logically deny the power of Congress to enfranchise the negroes, as the only sufficient guarantee of their true freedom and equality before the law. But there are many who doubt whether the negroes themselves should not have some opportunity of becoming familiar with their new rights and duties, before the best results can be expected from their exercise of the highest privilege of citizenship; whether any healthy political organization can be formed, until the labor problem has been practically solved, and its difficulties adjusted; whether, during the period of adjustment, the protective interference of the general government is not imperatively demanded, and whether, in any event, the immediate restoration of rebel states to political power would not be most dangerous to the nation. A term of probation will work no injustice to the whites. To the blacks, there are incalculable advantages in delay. . . .

Congress will then consider how to protect the truly loyal whites of those communities, and to secure for them in the management of affairs an influence of which, at present, they seem to have little. It will also have in mind the protection of the national credit, remembering that the public faith is pledged to those who have given of their substance to secure our victory. It is idle to say that no party will ever try to repudiate the national debt. So men said that no party would ever seek to destroy the Union. Join to the Northern Democracy the eleven states seeking restoration as now controlled, and repudiation, or division of the national and rebel war debts among the states, would almost surely follow. Nor is there any other matter of more lasting importance than provision for popular education at the South. Well filled school houses are a better pledge of loyalty than well manned forts. New England men, armed with muskets, have made the Southern people submissive; to make them loyal, prosperous, and fit to share in the glories of the future Union, send New England women armed with spelling-books. No truly republican form of government can succeed in states where the education of the people is forbidden by law or practice.

For each and all of these difficulties there is one ultimate remedy. To secure liberal provision for the education of the laboring class, give to the laboring class the ballot. To secure to the laborer sure protection in his rights of person and property—a protection more complete and permanent than any constitutional provision can give—put into his hands the ballot. To guard the national credit, arm with the ballot that class of whose freedom the national debt is the price. To crush forever the dominance of an aristocracy of purse or skin, make citizens of those who have been slaves. To build up loyal states at the South, trust not the absolute control to whites, known to be hostile in feeling, who still cherish theories which make oaths of allegiance a farce; trust rather the blacks, who are loyal, as the whites are disloyal, in obedience to prejudices and passions more potent than any logic or education. To reward fidelity, to punish treason, to save the nation, or to protect the rights of the blacks; the solution is ever the same. And then impartial suffrage is right. No man can make it anything but an outrage to deny civil privileges on the ground of color. No man can pretend that it is truly republican for a minority to control a majority, or truly safe to put loyal men at the mercy of rebels. . . .

It thrills one to think what a glorious nation care and patience will now give us. . . .

34. THE REVEREND GEORGE B. CHEEVER AND OTHERS, PETITION

November 30, 1865

Everyone understood that December 1865 might end reconstruction as a political issue or keep it open. Early that month the Thirty-ninth Congress as constituted by the 1864 elections would assemble for its first postwar session. If its members let in en bloc the delegates-elect from the recent Confederate states, rebuilt since Appomattox by Johnson's formulations on reconstruction, then all was ended.

Anticipating this easy way back to full participation in American government, delegates from the South headed toward Washington as December neared. Almost every one of the congressmen-elect carried a Presidential pardon for rebel activities as well as a certificate from his state confirming him as a senator or representative. Their consensus was that the President's pardon wiped out all penalties incurred through rebellion, including the need to swear to the "iron-clad" test oath requiring attestation to unsmirched past loyalty, which all members of Congress since 1864 had had to subscribe. Similarly, the Southern delegations assumed that their entrance into Congressional seats would face no bar from the parliamentary privilege the Congress enjoyed of determining, as the majority chose, qualifications of its membership.

Obviously, the Northern Democracy would support the returning Southerners in this contention. On the other hand, if the Thirty-ninth Congress could somehow keep the Southern delegations knocking on closed doors until Dixie rebuilt itself in harmony with precepts of minimal racial equity, then a truer reconstruction was still possible, though delayed by Johnson's "accidency."

At the White House the President secretly advised Southern whites to bend a little. Whatever his public constitutional abstractions, centering on the concept of a renascent state's rights, privately Johnson understood well enough that the post-Appomattox Southern states were his creations. Though he concealed the facts as best he could, he never deceived himself that the "provisional governors" of his nomination were in any way different from the "military governors" whom Lincoln had set up during the war to initiate state rebuilding (Johnson himself had held that position in his native Tennessee). The President knew that in 1865, as earlier, the Army was the primary instrument of social stability in the South. Therefore he confidentially recommended to prominent Southerners, during the summer and autumn weeks of 1865, that they open a few showpiece polling places and minor offices to a token cadre of compliant Negroes and white Unionists. This done, he anticipated that Republican thunder northward would dissipate.

Johnson was more sensitive to the impressive evidence of augmenting thunder than Southerners he advised. Revelations were becoming common of the wartime horrors that had taken place in Confederate prison camps. Less sophisticated than moderns concerning the barbarities of total war, men a century ago were nauseated by true accounts of what Andersonville and Libby had been like, and of what white Unionists had suffered in the South as a consequence of their loyalty. But the Southerners who were in charge of affairs southward under Johnson's program refused to listen to the suggestions of their benefactor. Becoming a prisoner of his own constitutional dogmas and of his personal commitment against a rise in Negro political status to equal that of whites, the President chose not to alter his advice into commands.

Johnson was also possessed of ambition. He was moving slowly in the direction of reshaping into conservative mold, and with Southern participation, the wartime Union coalition of Republicans and War Democrats. Success in this effort would have brought him a Presidential nomination in his own right, over a white man's country, in 1868—outcomes that he devoutly wished.

The point is that reconstruction was a political issue not because Radical Republicans wished it to be but because of a congeries of impulsions loose in the times and in the hearts of men. Events were to prove that Radical Republicans were continuing their wartime habit of expanding the theory and practice of democracy. As example, here is a petition directed to the oncoming Congress. Its authors were Rev. George Cheever, earlier introduced, and two close associates of several decades of reform activity, Edward Gilbert and Parker Pillsbury. As had been true during the war, the Radical drafters of this petition concluded that the Federal Constitution was a charter of power, not, as the President insisted, one of limitations on the national government. As though directly to counter Johnson's views, Cheever and his coadjutors ingeniously linked several constitutional segments to form restrictions on states in matters of race and political rights, adequate to adapt the 1787 document to the needs of 1865.[1]

This selection suggests that many prewar transcendentalist humanitarians were able successfully to make a transition from broad reformist goals to Negro-centered postwar politics. It is safe to say that none of the trio who signed this petition or the far larger number among Cheever's congregation who approved it wanted to concentrate primarily on the freedman. They were forced—as they estimated matters—into Negrophilism, and they resented the fact that the President's policies had levered them into the present unpleasantness.[2]

---

[1] See especially McKitrick, *Andrew Johnson and Reconstruction, passim;* Thomas and Hyman, *Stanton,* pp. 436–456; and John and LaWanda Cox, *Politics, Principle, and Prejudice, passim.*

[2] George B. Cheever, D.D., Edward Gilbert, Parker Pillsbury, *et al., Petition and Memorial of Citizens of the United States to the Senate and House of Representatives in Congress Assembled: Adopted at a Public Meeting held in the Church of the Puritans, New York City, November 30, 1865* (New York: Francis & Loutel, 1865).

To the Senate and House of Representatives:

1. Your memorialists respectfully represent that it is their desire to see the government of this country administered for the protection of the rights of all its citizens, without respect to persons. But respect to the color of the skin is, of all kinds of injurious partiality, the most cruel, unreasonable, and unjust; since under a dark complexion there may be found the brightest intelligence and highest moral worth. We pray your honorable body to deliver us as Americans from the shame of having our legislation ordered, and our justice administered, on such grounds as must make our republican government a reproach among civilized nations.

Constitutional Guarantee of the Right of Suffrage to the People.

2. Your memorialists would urge the second section of the first article in the Constitution of the United States, providing that the House of Representatives shall be composed of members chosen by the people of the several States. It is the same people, irrespective of color, whose unity and authority are set forth in the preamble, declaring that "We, the people of the United States, do ordain and establish this Constitution, to secure the blessings of liberty for ourselves and our posterity." The first security settled was this of the right of representation by the people of the several States. It is too plain for argument that all classes of citizens, from whom the Government of the United States requires allegiance, are the people of the several States: and it is the duty of the National Government, by proper legislation and action, to protect all its citizens in that right of representation, anything in the constitution or laws of any State to the contrary notwithstanding.

Furthermore, "The electors in each State shall have the qualifications requisite for electors of the most numerous branch of the State Legislature." These qualifications must be determined by the people themselves, who create the Legislature; and by the preceding guarantee of the right of representation to the people of the States, the same people who ordained and established the Constitution, the State itself is forever stopped from making the color of the skin a qualification or disqualification.

It would be the perfection of despotism if a single State could take away the right of representation from a class of citizens of the United States within its borders, the United States government being at the same time deprived of the right and power of interfering to protect that right. If that were State Sovereignty, and admitted, the United States would be simply a congeries of despotisms.

While, therefore, it is not within the competency of the government to withhold the right of suffrage from any class of the people, it is both in the power and obligation of the government to protect that right for all classes, and to prevent its being withheld from any class, by any State or any monopoly in the State.

Your memorialists cannot admit that the power to regulate a political franchise or natural right, as by conditions of age, or intelligence, or property, equally applicable to all classes, and pre-supposing the same right of all classes on arriving at those conditions, involves the right to destroy that franchise, or to exclude any class from it, especially by life-long and hereditary exclusion of color or race. The vote is a primal hereditary right of the sovereignty of the people; it may be regulated, but it cannot be destroyed. But to take it away from a whole class or race of millions of human beings on account of color is to destroy it; a power never committed by the Constitution to a State, nor by the people of the United States to Congress. No State Legislature has the power to destroy the right of voting. The right of a State to *prescribe* qualifications in all classes *for* suffrage, does not mean the right to *proscribe* the colored citizens of the State, as excluded *from* suffrage.

The same may be said as to the right of bearing witness. No State can possibly have the right to exclude any one class from that right; for it is a right of human nature, a natural right given by the Creator; and the invasion of it on the plea of the color of the skin is an attempt at moral assassination. The State has the right to regulate testimony, but not to destroy it; to enact laws against bearing false witness, but not to destroy the right of witnessing; to forbid falsehood and perjury in all classes alike, but not to forbid any class from giving evidence for truth, not to proscribe truth because of the color of the skin.

If this injustice is sanctioned in the Constitutions or laws of any of the States now suing for admission into the Union, and if they be received notwithstanding, then it is adopted and enacted by the government, and the millions thus defrauded of their rights could not hope to recover them. But the adoption of such injustice would be a governmental funded insurance of future anarchy and blood. So many of the races ostracized by penalty of the skin are nearly white, being Saxon, Celtic and Gallic, as well as African, and they are of such general and increasing intelligence, as well as numbers, that the attainder and outlawry of millions of such persons would be the fatal certainty of insurrections and bloody revolutions.

Your memorialists respectfully ask of Congress the prohibition of such injustice by enactments rendering it forever impossible.

Revolutionary Opinions and Articles of Government.

3. Against the adoption of color as a rule of disfranchisement, they would urge, besides its essential injustice and

cruelty, the opinions and practice of our Revolutionary Patriots and Statesmen; the principles laid down in the Declaration of Independence, and the Articles of . . . Confederation, including provisions rendering it impossible for any State to exclude any person from voting on account of color, securing all the privileges and immunities of free citizens in the several States to the free inhabitants of each of the States; the record of the fact of the Confederate Congress refusing to permit the State of South Carolina to introduce the word *white*, or any such principle of distinction and disfranchisement, and thus declaring that State Sovereignty, even before our present Constitution and Union, included no right of disfranchising any class or citizens on account of the color of the skin, and that no State should be suffered to exercise such a power; also the provisions of the Grand [Northwest] Territorial Ordinance of 1787, and the Second Section of the Fourth Article of our present Constitution, providing that "the citizens of each State shall be entitled to all privileges and immunities in the several States," permitting no disqualification on account of color.

Violation of the Contract Forbidden by the Constitution.

4. Your memorialists respectfully urge the provision of Section 10 in the first article of the Constitution, forbidding any State from framing any law impairing the obligation of contracts; as making it unconstitutional for any State then in the Union to take away the right to vote from any class of the inhabitants then possessing that right, or their posterity.

The Constitution was a contract entered into by all the States in behalf of all the free inhabitants of the land, that they should forever be the electors; representatives and taxes being apportioned among the several States according to the whole number of free persons, and the citizens of each

State being entitled to all privileges and immunities of citizens in the several States; meaning that the citizens of New York and Massachusetts are entitled in South Carolina and Georgia to all the privileges of United States' citizens which they enjoy in their own States, and that the citizens of South Carolina and Georgia are entitled likewise to all the privileges of the United States' citizens in New York and Massachusetts; so that a residence in one State or another cannot deprive any citizen or citizens of any right belonging to United States' citizenship any where in the Union; and any State laws, so depriving any class, are necessarily null and void, being a violation of contract, if passed since the adoption of the Constitution; and if in existence previously, then set aside by virtue of the Constitution as adopted.

Attainder of Color or Race Forbidden by the Constitution.

5. Your memorialists would urge that the taking away of the right of voting from any class of the inhabitants is equivalent to the passage of a bill of pains and penalties, and constitutes a bill of attainder forbidden in the ninth and tenth sections of the first article of the Constitution, equally to Congress and the States.

A bill, or law, or proclamation against the colored inhabitants of any State, depriving them of the rights of free citizens on account of their color, is precisely such forbidden legislation in its most offensive form. It is their moral assassination, for it strikes down all their liberties, and condemns them to a state of perpetual caste-degradation, which is a living death. It is a bill of pains and penalties for posterity, by corruption of blood. Justice Story remarks in regard to it, that "the existence of such a power is inconsistent with first principles, and incompatible with all just notions of the true ends and objects of a republican government." Not even the crime of treason is permitted by our government to destroy the right to vote, for the traitors or their children. Shall the color of the skin be permitted to destroy it for faithful, loyal citizens and their posterity?

The black codes of the Southern States are terrible examples of such illegal, unconstitutional and tyrannical bills of attainder. Enacted for the government of slaves, they are being renewed to create and perpetuate the state of slavery, under the law of reconstruction excluding the subjects of such tyranny from the right of the vote. Unusual pains and penalties have only to be added on account of color, and forms of colored crime ingeniously constructed, with statutes of forced labor for life, or imprisonment and sale of payment of jail fees, or even the boldly declared penalty of slavery, and the amendment of the Constitution, forbidding slavery except for crime, may legitimately and with perfect impunity be nullified. And that government which shall once have ratified the exclusion of this class of inhabitants in any State from the protection of the right to vote, will never interfere to protect or deliver them from such slavery.

Yet this very attainder of color against millions of innocent inhabitants is one of the laws of reconstruction proposed, and thus far enforced, by the President of the United States. And it adds an amazing exasperation to its cruelty, if appointed as the reconstructive law of the social system, that it is utterly impossible to graduate or establish such an attainder by any known standard of race, or law of evidence, or legal proof of what constitutes color. The range runs from shade to shade, as in a rainbow, from the complexion of Toussaint to the hue of Washington, and from the darkness of the Ethiopian wife of Moses to the whiteness of the leprosy of Miriam. Indeed, no language can describe the monstrous injustice and absurdity of such legislation. If it be appointed as a principle of law of reconstruction that none but whites shall vote, a color-meter of the *epidermis* should have been transmitted by the

President, together with instructions as to its use, for every State reached by his proclamations.

Ex Post Facto Laws inconsistent with the Constitution.

6. Your memorialists would urge the inconsistency and injustice of permitting to be adopted, for the government of persons who have become free, the statutes or customs of States where they had been held as slaves, and which were established for the purpose of perpetuating their condition of slavery. This would be an example of the iniquity of *ex post facto* laws, directly forbidden in the Constitution; oppressive statutes continued in existence, or renewed, after the oppression, which they were contrived to sustain, has itself been put away by the government. We call upon the authority which has put down slavery to obliterate and forbid the State codes that sustained it.

The President cannot throw back a free loyal population under the power of laws made by slaveholding and rebellious States for the purpose of enslaving them. He cannot be permitted to draw from the old Constitutions of those States precedents for the re-construction of free States, or Statutes to be set for the government of a free people. The Constitution and laws of the United States for the whole people are the only rightful authority and power; and we have no more right to govern the free loyal people of today by the State laws of their former enslaved condition, than by the laws of the kingdom of Dahomey.

Neither can the President be permitted to determine what rights they shall not have, or what they shall be deprived of, under the free Constitution of the United States, by what they were deprived of under the Slaveholding Constitutions and laws of Slaveholding States. They are a free people. Only the Constitution of the United States need be consulted in their behalf, and nothing can be consulted against them, or adopted for the purpose of taking away in the State the rights which they hold, or are entitled to hold, as free citizens under the Constitution.

Guarantee of a Republican form of Government in the Constitution.

7. Your memorialists would urge the guarantee of a Republican form of government for each State in the fourth section of the fourth article of the Constitution.

And as to the question, What constitutes a republican form of government, and what the people of the States have a right to demand of the United States under that guarantee, they refer to the Declaration of Independence, the Bills of Rights in the several States, and the recorded opinions and practice of our Revolutionary fathers. They held the essence of republicanism to consist in the security and enjoyment of representation by the whole body of the people as a personal right. When deprived of it themselves, they called it slavery, not republicanism, and maintained the war of the Revolution rather than relinquish it.

Your memorialists respectfully implore Congress to fulfil this guarantee of a republican form of government, with the freedom of the vote for all citizens of the United States without respect to color or race; and to refuse the admission of any State into the Union, until this condition of republican freedom be secured in the State Constitutions and laws. The common right of suffrage is one of those immemorial paths of common brotherhood in humanity and Christianity, that run across every State line and enclosure in this country. By our Constitution, the right of way in this path cannot be interrupted or shut up. In this thing consists the difference between our republican form of government, rightly administered, and any other in the world. Our citizens all have this common right of way, and the National Government is bound to protect it for all. No State, under pretence of sovereignty over its private enclosures, can shut up this path, or keep out any class of citizens from the right of way. It is the common law of the Constitution, anything in any State Constitution to the contrary notwithstanding.

A proclamation excluding all but *Albinos* and Protestants from the right of suffrage would be as rational and republican, as an edict declaring that none but whites shall vote. It is the creation of a ruling aristocracy of the skin; and the power being once again concentrated in their hands, and the militia of the States at their disposal, nothing short of a revolution could recover it.

In a republic the conditions of suffrage are the conditions of sovereignty, and they belong to the people themselves to settle. They are the conditions of freedom, for the people cannot be free if these conditions are out of their power. A free people exercise the primal elementary rights of self-government by voting in convention, and the right of voting belongs to every individual of the convention, as a primary assemblage of the people. This is the elementary condition of a free, popular, republican government.

Right of Blacks equal to that of Whites.
Testimony of Madison.

8. In the formation of our government, so unquestionably was the right of representation regarded as belonging to every free person, irrespective of color, that in the discussion as to the rule of suffrage, Governor Edmund Randolph, of Virginia, presented as a leading principle, "that the rights of suffrage ought to be proportioned to the number of free inhabitants." And Mr. Madison declared, speaking in behalf of the slaveholders, and presenting their own views, that if ever the slaves

were set free, the right of representation on their part would immediately follow.

The words of Mr. Madison are in the fifty-third number of the *Federalist,* as follows: "It is only under the pretext that the laws have transformed the negroes into subjects of property, that a place is disputed them in the computation of numbers; and it is admitted that if the laws were to restore the rights which have been taken away, the negroes could no longer be refused AN EQUAL SHARE OF REPRESENTA-TION WITH THE OTHER INHABITANTS."

By the abolition of slavery, the time having come of the restoration here referred to, of those rights of freedom which had been taken away, the negroes or colored citizens are entitled to the same right of representation as the white inhabitants.

This remarkable declaration of Madison, made with fore-sight of the abolition of slavery, and in prophecy of the rights that must ensue, was consistent with the affirmation in the Declaration of Rights prefixed to the Constitution of the State of Virginia, namely, that "All men having sufficient evidence of permanent common interest, with an attachment to the community, *HAVE THE RIGHT OF SUFFRAGE.*"

It deserves to be considered in connection with another prophetic paragraph in the writings of Madison on the Constitution of the United States, "I take no notice of an unhappy species of population abounding in some of the States, who, during the calm of a regular government, are sunk below the level of man; but who, in the tempestuous scenes of civil violence may emerge into the human character, and give a superiority of strength to any party with which they may associate themselves."

Emerging into the human character out of the tempest of the rebellion and war, they have proved themselves almost the only loyal class of citizens in the rebel States; and having allied themselves throughout with the party of loyalty and freedom in support of the United States government, they have given to us that superiority of strength, by which, under a guiding Divine Providence, the rebellion has been conquered and the government preserved.

Shall we now desert these faithful allies, and give them over into the hands of their former owners, under the grinding tyranny of black codes that will speedily reduce them to the condition of their former slavery? Your memorialists pray that by the prompt and decisive interposition of Congress in their behalf, they may be forever secured from the possibility of such oppression. And they would add the declaration of Madison as to the protection requisite equally for all classes, that "In a free government the security for civil rights must be the same as that for religious rights." This is what we demand for ourselves; we can ask nothing less for others, since religious rights are irrespective of the color of the skin, and we have the right to demand, in the name of God and justice, that the civil rights of all persons be guaranteed in the same manner.

Whatever prevents this is inconsistent with the nature and objects of a free and equitable government.

The Guarantee of Life, Liberty and Property, Irrespective of Color.

9. Your memorialists would urge the guarantee in the Constitution that no person shall be deprived of life, liberty or property without due process of law. The freedom of the vote is one of our liberties. No citizen can be disfranchised except for crime, with sentence by due process of law. Again, the vote is a property. That possession cannot be taken away except by crime, and with due process of law. But an Executive proclamation is not due process of law. Yet in the exclusion of the colored race from the right of suffrage, that property is taken away from the innocent and loyal, and bestowed upon criminals and traitors.

Meantime, pardon and property, liberty and suffrage, together with life, are bestowed upon rebels, the whole of whose estates, as well as life and liberty, are justly forfeited by crime. Property that belongs to the United States by two separate claims—namely, of statute justice for the crime of treason, and of public justice by the law of conquest, is given back to the rebels, amounting to hundreds of millions in value, property justly forfeited by their engaging in armed rebellion to overthrow the government, and compelling us into a war of self-defence against that piratical invasion, at the cost of a national debt of three thousand millions. Your memorialists pray that the claims of loyal citizens and soldiers be fulfilled, before the property belonging to the government, and which might be appropriated towards the payment of this vast national debt, is given back to unrepentant rebels. Your memorialists know of cases in which the widows of loyal soldiers slain in battle for the defence of their country against these rebels, have labored incessantly in vain to obtain the soldiers' pay due to them by law, while the requests of rebels have been immediately granted, and their confiscated properties restored to them. . . .

Supremacy of Congress.—The present the decisive Opportunity.

12. Your memorialists are aware that Congress have supreme authority in the government of the Rebel States; and Divine Providence has put into their hands at the present moment the power to decide for all time in the right. If the present opportunity be neglected, and a single State be admitted with the right to disfranchise colored citizens, then forever after, it will be too late to interfere. This injustice once received and sanctioned, the States that practice it will hold supremacy by it, and there will be no resistance against it. If not now required by the righteous authority of the gov-

ernment to put it away, by that authority they will claim and keep it. It will have been received into the government and made perpetual, and so far as any human agency is concerned, there is no hope of remedy.

Your memorialists therefore pray that no State may be admitted into the Union with the proscription of color in its Constitution or laws; neither Colorado, nor Tennessee, nor South Carolina, nor any other State now applying for admission.

Your memorialists pray that equality of all classes before the law, including the right of suffrage, the right of testimony, the right to bear arms, secured and protected for all classes as for the whites, may be required of the States in their constitutions and laws, before any of them are permitted to assume their former independent position in and under the Government of the United States.

That a renewal of the injustice for which the rebellion was undertaken may be rendered forever impossible, your memorialists further pray that an amendment be added to the Constitution, in the words or to the intent following,—"That no State shall make any distinction in civil rights and privileges on account of race, color, or parentage, among any of the citizens of the United States within its limits, either by classes or individuals."

35. CARL SCHURZ, REPORT

December 1865

Johnson also prepared for the opening of Congress. At his request Carl Schurz and other notables toured the South in the summer and autumn of 1865. The President expected that their observations would attest to the propensity of ex-rebel whites to deal justly with the freedmen. Conclusive evidence of returning loyalty in the South would make the Radical argument that reconstruction was still unfinished difficult to sustain.

Not a wealthy man, and anxious to build capital for his family, Schurz at first was reluctant to take on this new responsibility The President pressed him hard, and friends arranged insurance coverage for Schurz. Some of the money for the premiums came from Radical Republicans, Sumner among them. Although conservatives in 1865 and historians since jumped to a conclusion that Schurz slanted his conclusions in gratitude to the donors, no reliable evidence buttresses the implication. Probably Schurz was as honest and accurate in reporting his judgments as he had always been.

Having returned to Washington by mid-October, Schurz expected a swift summons from the President, who by logic should have been eager to get at him. Nothing happened. Then, on the seventeenth, Schurz wrote to Stanton that a meeting had occurred at last. At the White House, Schurz had encountered a distressingly chilly atmosphere.[1]

I waited long and patiently to be admitted—a circumstance somewhat extraordinary considering that I had just returned from a three months' journey made at his own request. At last the doors were thrown open and I entered with the crowd. The President received me with civility, indeed, but with demonstrative coldness. I was painfully surprised, and availed myself of the first lull in our conversation to withdraw from an interview which under such circumstances could lead to no satisfactory results. I left town the same evening to see my family. My duty to see the President before leaving was fulfilled.

To-day I find in the Washington correspondence of the New York *Herald* the following paragraph:

The latest explanation of the disfavor into which General Carl Schurz seems to have fallen with the President is that during his

[1] Schurz, *Speeches*, I, 273–277.

recent trip through the Southern States, ostensibly on freedmen's affairs, his time was largely spent in efforts to organize the Republican party in that section. He is accused of attempting to convince the people of the States he travelled through that their readmission would be determined thereby.

This story is simply absurd. But since the thing has got into the newspapers and people are speculating about the cause of my "disfavor" with the President, it seems to me that I should be the first man to know something about the matter. I raise no claim of consideration upon the services I have rendered the party to which the President owes his elevation. But the position I occupy entitles me, I believe, to a frank explanation of whatever differences or misunderstandings there may be between us. I examine my conduct in vain to discover anything that could have been personally offensive to the President. In my despatches, I gave him my views and impressions frankly and without reserve. It is quite possible that on some points the President's opinions and mine do not agree. I cannot suppose the President would make that the cause of a personal rupture. It may be that somebody has made some slanderous report about me. If so, I think they ought not to have been credited without my having been heard about it. Or if there be anything amiss of which I have at present no conception, the ordinary rules of propriety would serve to require that I should be asked what I have to say. I write to you about this matter because my appointment to the Southern mission passed through your hands; you encouraged me to take it, and our relations are—I have no reason to doubt—personally friendly. Will you be kind enough, as a mediator, to procure me the explanation to which I have, in my humble opinion at least, a just claim? After the reception I met with, I cannot apply to the President in person. I never received such treatment in my life. It is absolutely incomprehensible to me, and I should not like to expose myself to any more of it. I shall in all probability soon go West to take charge of a journalistic enterprise, and I am naturally anxious, before leaving the East, to have all these matters cleared up. By acceding to my request you will place me under great obligations. May I expect the favor of an early reply? It will find me here.

Schurz to Charles Sumner

Bethlehem, Pa., Oct. 17, 1865.

I returned from my Southern trip on Thursday night, last, and had an interview with the President, Saturday. The information I bring with me is of considerable interest and importance; it might become of value in your Congressional deliberations. I am engaged in writing out a general report which the President seems by no means anxious to possess.

You have, perhaps, seen statements in the newspapers that I am in "disfavor." I wish to tell you confidentially that I myself believe it is so. He received me not, indeed, without civility, but with great coldness, asked me no questions about the results of my investigations and seemed to desire not to have any conversation about them at all. I accommodated him in that respect, withdrew from the interview as soon as I saw that it became very irksome, and left town the same night to see my family.

What the President's reasons are for treating me in so strange a manner I am at a loss to understand. The explanation given in the Washington despatches of yesterday's *Herald* is absurd. I cannot imagine what it can be. . . . That the views expressed in my letters to the President were radically at variance with his policy, is quite probable, but I do not see how, as a sensible and fair-minded man, he could make that the occasion for a personal rupture. In one word, I am completely in the dark. To-day I have written to Stanton requesting him to give or procure me some explanation.

Meanwhile, I am composing my report; when it is ready I shall present it, and then we shall see. . . .

From Charles Sumner to Schurz

Boston, Oct. 20, 1865.

Private.

It is as I expected. It was so with the Chief Justice, who visited the South, by arrangement with the President, and who wrote to him from different places, until, at Mobile, he encountered proclamations, when he stopped. When he saw the President on his return nothing was said of his observation. It seems it was so with you.

I did not think the President in earnest when he invited you to make your tour. Since then he has been pushing forward his "experiment," and I doubt not, will push it further, if Congress does not assume jurisdiction of the whole subject.

Of course, you will make your report. But you ought as soon as possible to make a speech. . . .

I wish you could give me briefly an outline of your impressions. My own convictions are now stronger than ever with regard to our duty. *The rebel States must not be allowed at once to participate in our Government.* This privilege must be postponed. Meanwhile all parties will be prepared for the great changes in their political relations. *There must be delay.* The President does not see this and every step that he takes is toward perdition.

Never was the way so clear or the opportunity so great. The President might have given peace to the country and made it a mighty example of justice to mankind. Instead of this consummation, he revives the old Slave Oligarchy, envenomed by war, and gives it a new lease of terrible power. This Republic cannot be lost; but the President has done very much to lose it. We must work hard to save it. . . .

Schurz to Charles Sumner

Bethlehem, Nov. 13, 1865.

. . . My report is ready and is being copied. It is quite voluminous, very full in the discussion of all the important points and has cost me considerable labor. I shall go to Washington to present it to the President probably before the end of the week. I intend to ask his permission to publish it at once so that it may be before the country when Congress meets. I consider it somewhat doubtful whether he will give that permission. If he does not, it will have to be asked for by Congress. . . .

[Almost as soon as the Thirty-ninth Congress assembled, Sumner and others called for Schurz's report. The President had no wish to precipitate an argument across Pennsylvania Avenue at that moment and sent in the document. Here is the heart of the exacerbating portion of Schurz's observations, in the viewpoint of the President.[2] To most Republicans, to all Radicals, it was sound common sense.]

. . . Nothing can . . . be more desirable than that the contact between the Southern people and the outside world should be as strong and intimate as possible; and in no better way can this end be subserved than by immigration in mass. Of the economic benefits which such immigration would confer upon the owners of the soil, it is hardly necessary to speak.

Immigration wants encouragement. As far as this encouragement consists in the promise of material advantage, it is already given. There are large districts in the South in which an industrious and enterprising man, with some capital, and acting upon correct principles, cannot fail to accumulate large gains in a comparatively short time, as long as the prices of the staples do not fall below what they may reasonably be expected to be for some time to come. A Northern man has, besides, the advantage of being served by the laboring population of that region with greater willingness.

But among the principal requisites for the success of the immigrant are personal security and a settled condition of things.

---

[2] The report is most conveniently available in Schurz, *Speeches*, I, 362–367. The official form is in *House Reports* #11, 39 Cong., 1 sess., dated December 18, 1865.

Personal security is honestly promised by the thinking men of the South; but another question is, whether the promise and good intentions of the thinking men will be sufficient to restrain and control the populace, whose animosity against "Yankee interlopers" is only second to their hostile feeling against the negro. If the military forces of the Government should be soon and completely withdrawn, I see reasons to fear that in many localities immigrants would enjoy the necessary security only when settling down together in numbers strong enough to provide for their own protection. On the whole, no better encouragement can be given to immigration, as far as individual security is concerned, than the assurance that the National Government will be near to protect them until such protection is no longer needed.

The South needs capital. But capital is notoriously timid and averse to risk itself, not only where there actually is trouble, but where there is serious and continual danger of trouble. Capitalists will be apt to consider—and they are by no means wrong in doing so—that no safe investments can be made in the South as long as Southern society is liable to be convulsed by anarchical disorders. No greater encouragement can, therefore, be given to capital to transfer itself to the South than the assurance that the Government will continue to control the development of the new social system in the late rebel States until such dangers are averted by a final settlement of things upon a thorough free-labor basis.

How long the National Government should continue that control depends upon contingencies. It ought to cease as soon as its objects are attained; and its objects will be attained sooner and with less difficulty if nobody is permitted to indulge in the delusion that it will cease *before* they are attained. This is one of the cases in which a determined policy can accomplish much, while a halfway policy is liable to spoil things already accomplished. The continuance of the National control in the South, although it may be for a short period only, will cause some inconvenience and expense; but if thereby destructive collisions and anarchical disorders can be prevented, justice secured to all men, and the return of peace and prosperity to all parts of this country hastened, it will be a paying investment. For the future of the Republic, it is far less important that this business of reconstruction be done quickly than it be well done. The matter well taken in hand, there is reason for hope that it will be well done, and quickly too. In days like these great changes are apt to operate themselves rapidly. At present the Southern people assume that free negro labor will not work, and therefore they are not inclined to give it a fair trial. As soon as they find out that they must give it a fair trial, and that their whole future power and prosperity depend upon its success, they will also find out that it will work, at least far better than they have anticipated. Then their hostility to it will gradually disappear. This great result accomplished, posterity will not find fault with this Administration for having delayed complete "reconstruction" one, two, or more years.

Although I am not called upon to discuss in this report the Constitutional aspects of this question, I may be pardoned for one remark. The interference of the National Government in the local concerns of the States lately in rebellion is argued against by many as inconsistent with the spirit of our Federal institutions. Nothing is more foreign to my ways of thinking in political matters than a fondness for centralization of military government. Nobody can value the blessings of local self-government more highly than I do. But we are living under exceptional circumstances which require us, above all, to look at things from a practical point of view; and I believe it will prove far more dangerous for the integrity of local self-government if the National control in the South be discontinued— while by discontinuing it too soon, it may be rendered necessary again in the future—than if it be continued, when by continuing it but a limited time all such future necessity may be obviated. At present these acts of interference are but a part of that exceptional policy brought forth by the necessities into which the rebellion has plunged us. Although there will be some modifications in the relations between the States and the National Government, yet these acts of direct interference in the details of State concerns will pass away with the exceptional circumstances which called them forth. But if the social revolution in the South be now abandoned in an unfinished state, and at some future period produce events provoking new and repeated acts of direct practical interference,—and the contingency would by no means be unlikely to arise,—such new and repeated acts would not pass over without most seriously affecting the political organism of the Republic.

Negro Suffrage

It would seem that the interference of the National authority in the home concerns of the Southern States would be rendered less necessary, and the whole problem of political and social reconstruction be much simplified, if, while the masses lately arrayed against the Government are permitted to vote, the large majority of those who were always loyal, and are naturally anxious to see the free-labor problem successfully solved, were not excluded from all influence upon legislation. In all questions concerning the Union, the National debt, and the future social organization of the South, the feelings of the colored man are naturally in sympathy with the views and aims of the National Government. While the Southern white fought against the Union, the negro did all he could to aid it; while the Southern white sees in the National Government his conqueror, the negro sees in it his protector; while the white owes to the National debt his defeat, the negro owes to it his deliverance; while the white considers himself robbed and ruined by the emancipation of the slaves, the negro finds in it the assurance of future prosperity and happiness. In all the important issues the negro would be led by natural impulse to forward the ends of the Government, and by making his influence, as part of the voting body, tell upon the legislation of the States, render the interference of the National authority less necessary.

As the most difficult of the pending questions are intimately connected with the status of the negro in Southern society, it is obvious that a correct solution can be more easily obtained if he has a voice in the matter. In the right to vote he would find the best permanent protection against oppressive class-legislation, as well as against individual persecution. The relations between the white and black races, even if improved by the gradual wearing off of the present animosities, are likely to remain long under the troubling influence of prejudice. It is a notorious fact that the rights of a man of some political power are far less exposed to violation than those of one who is, in matters of public interest, completely subject to the will of others. A voter is a man of influence; small as that influence may be in the single individual, it becomes larger when that individual belongs to a numerous class of voters who are ready to make common cause with him for the protection of his rights. Such an individual is an object of interest to the political parties that desire to have the benefit of his ballot. It is true, the bringing face to face at the ballot-box of the white and black races may here and there lead to an outbreak of feeling, and the first trials ought certainly to be made while the National power is still there to prevent or repress disturbances; but the practice once successfully inaugurated under the protection of that power, it would probably be more apt than anything else to obliterate old antagonisms, especially if the colored people—which is probable, as soon as their own rights are sufficiently secured—divide their votes between the different political parties.

The effect of the extension of the franchise to the colored people upon the development of free labor and upon the security of human rights in the South being the principal ob-

ject in view, the objections raised on the ground of the ignorance of the freedmen become unimportant. Practical liberty
is a good school, and, besides, if any qualification can be
found, applicable to both races, which does not interfere with
the attainment of the main object, such qualification would in
that respect be unobjectionable. But it is idle to say that it
will be time to speak of negro suffrage when the whole colored
race will be educated, for the ballot may be necessary to him
to secure his education. It is also idle to say that ignorance is
the principal ground upon which Southern men object to negro
suffrage, for if it were, that numerous class of colored people
in Louisiana who are as highly educated, as intelligent and as
wealthy as any corresponding class of whites, would have been
enfranchised long ago. . . .

36. "THE LESSON FROM JAMAICA,"

EDITORIAL

December 1865

From a United States Army post near Jackson, Mississippi, the
youthful commanding officer wrote on December 3, 1865, to his
father, the distinguished archivist Peter Force. "I hope the Congress
which is to meet tomorrow will help to heal the wounds of the
country," the soldier prayed. But he worried that white Mississippians were becoming increasingly hostile to all national officers.
This coldness of attitude resulted from the President's removals of
restraints. "Black codes" passed in the state's legislature also
troubled the writer. Labor provisions in the Mississippi law with
respect to freedmen attempted ". . . to force them to go to work
at once, and to keep them on the same plantation [as under slav-

ery], turning the whole [white] population of the state into a posse to catch them when they stray and to heap up penalties so that they remain in debt."

This educated, literate, sensitive young man was by no means certain what solutions were useful. Primarily he feared that once they returned to Congress as representatives of States, the Southern delegations, linked with Northern Democratic friends, would demand payment for all damages the war had inflicted in rebel Dixie. The revulsion of loyal men against such a travesty in policy would unsettle the nation almost as severely as had been the case in 1861, he predicted.

> But I don't know that on the whole it would be a gain in the end, for Congress to keep these states out as territories or some nondescript condition, under constraint until they do pass laws which we consider just. In abolishing slavery, conferring upon freedmen the right to testify [in Freedmen's Bureau courts], and repudiating the rebel war debt, they have done a good deal. How far we are in honor bound to supervise their state laws upon the subject of freedmen is a nice point.[1]

Ambivalence on this "nice point" unsteadied Republicans and delighted alert Northern Democrats. Here was a way out for the latter from under the burdens of associative guilt that secession and Copperheadism had fastened on them, as well as an opportunity to reforge the tough links that traditionally had bound together the sectional wings of the party.

Democrats set out to make themselves the defenders of the Bill of Rights by insisting implicitly and often explicitly that it sustained only white rights. Conservatives revived traditional prewar theories on federal-state relationships in order to mask current concerns over wartime and postwar shifts in race relations, and they centered attention on demanding a halt to change. They seemed to have all the aces.

Shocking news in from the Caribbean island of Jamaica in the late autumn of 1865 further reinforced conservative-Democratic arguments. Bloody racial strife exploded there, after the Negro pop-

---

[1] Manning Force to Peter Force, December 3, 1865, Force Papers (Letter files, Boston University).

ulation had enjoyed emancipation but suffered inequality for thirty years.[2] Southern spokesmen and their Northern champions saw proof, in the ghastly episodes reported from the West Indies, of the dim results that must emerge from governmental tinkering and humanitarian experimenting. Therefore Democrats let it be known as they readied for the opening of the Thirty-ninth Congress that they were dead set against further disturbances emanating from Washington, in the South's racial equilibrium, symbolized by the famous—or better, infamous—"black codes."

By taking this stand, Democrats found themselves extolling, long after armed hostilities closed, precisely the employments of executive authority and military support for state rebuilding that during the war they had condemned as dictatorial and unconstitutional. It was a tortured twist of logic and a distortion of historical evidence for Democrats to claim, as they did in 1865 and later, that Johnson was following Lincoln's ways and seeking his goals. Nevertheless, had Democrats stood foursquare against all national reconstructing, they might have improved their appeal to Northerners who worried little about the Negro but feared the bogey of centralization. Instead, Democrats approved the activities in the South only of one branch of the national government—the President and the Army as his instrument—but condemned action by Congress or the Freedmen's Bureau. Reasonable men failed to see how one end of Pennsylvania Avenue enjoyed out of the Constitution the monopoly in reconstruction jurisdiction that the Democrats claimed for the White House.

Republicans would have been dull and inept not to see the incongruities in the Democrats' position on reconstruction. They were neither. Negrophile humanitarians who for four decades had endured the opposition of their communities and persevered in antislavery work were not to be frightened off from the new pursuit of racial equality before the law by scare stories from Jamaica. Instead, Republicans and their coadjutors among the organized philanthropic societies worked matters so that their combined purposes benefited from the opposition attacks.

---

[2] Bernard Semmel, *Jamaican Blood and Victorian Conscience: The Governor Eyre Controversy* (Boston: Houghton Mifflin Company, 1963).

First as to Jamaica, spokesmen for freedmen's aid societies read in the sorrowful news history's proof that emancipation was not enough. Here is "The Lesson from Jamaica," which in one form or another was common currency among Republicans assembled in Washington in the first week of December 1865.[3]

The Lesson from Jamaica.

The lesson which comes to us from Jamaica is two-fold. First, as to the freedpeople. When they were emancipated, neither equality before the law, nor the means of education, was secured to them—two grave mistakes on the part of the British government and people, which, it is to be hoped, will not be repeated by us. It is persistently asserted by some of our newspapers, that all classes in Jamaica are on a footing of entire political equality, and, therefore, that the late riot, on the part of the Blacks, was without excuse. Now, the population of Jamaica, in 1860, was 441,264, not far from three-fourths of that of Philadelphia in the same year, when the Presidential vote of the city was 77,247. Sewell and Underhill both state that the vote of Jamaica, for members of the House of Assembly, never exceeds 3,000. An annual registration fee of ten shillings per head causes, and was intended to cause, this great disproportion between the number of people and the number of voters. Men, whose daily wages on a plantation range from ninepence to a shilling, do not care to pay the earnings of ten or twelve days' work for the privilege of voting, the full importance of which to their interests they have never been taught to appreciate; and, therefore, they do not vote. "The vast mass of small occupiers of land," says Mr. Underhill, "are not represented. The voters are planters, attorneys, agents, clerks and shopkeepers." From this class constituency has naturally resulted a system of class legislation, involving many

<hr>

[3] "The Lesson from Jamaica," [Philadelphia] *Pennsylvania Freedmen's Bulletin,* I (December 5, 1865), 88–89.

special taxes which press with great weight on the unrepresented laboring population. And it is this class taxation without representation, combined with a two years' drought, which was the ultimate cause of the late riot. . . .

The truth is, only the body of slavery in Jamaica was destroyed at emancipation. The tree was cut down, not rooted up. And, while anything essential to the character of slavery remains in the condition of a people who have once been slaves, there will always be found a corresponding spirit of class domination in the hearts of those who were once their masters. This will descend from father to son. The fire will last as long as there is fuel to feed it. The embers and even the brands of slavery are still alive, and are sometimes seen to blaze in Pennsylvania.

The lesson from Jamaica, then, is this. There is not, as some men in high places seem to suppose, any safe, comfortable, halfway resting-place between slavery and freedom, any more than there is such between life and death, in the passage from this world to the next. And so long as there shall be anything short of complete equality before the law at the South—so long, if it is for a century to come, as any vestige of slavery remains there to call forth and tempt into exercise the evil passions and habits which slavery has engendered—so long we shall have our own special troubles with the late slaveholders and their descendants.

PART EIGHT

Fruits into Ashes

37. THE IMPERATIVES TO ACTION:

GENERAL ORDER NO. 3

A rhythm in reconstruction matters had earlier become discernible, consisting of an initial executive order for one state, followed by repetitions for all the former Confederacy. On December 1 President Johnson proclaimed the restoration of the privilege of the writ of habeas corpus in North Carolina. This executive order constrained the Army and the Freedmen's Bureau with respect to protecting Negroes and Unionist whites. Predictably, similar orders would soon follow for other Southern states.

Anticipating deliverance, delegates-elect to Congress were assembled in Washington from all ex-rebel states save Texas, where the President's program was delayed. Doors opened at the Capitol for Northern members of the Thirty-ninth Congress, but not for the Southerners. Presession Republican planning avoided direct clashes by arranging matters so that parliamentarians omitted the Southern states from the rolls of House and Senate.

Democrats cried "foul," as though the technique was novel, immoral, or a Republican invention. None of these accusations was true. As to novelty, it was common gossip in Washington that the Republicans were readying their plans. In May 1865 Henry Winter Davis had prepared a memorandum outlining ways and means to the end reached on December 4, and much of his suggestion had dribbled into newspapers. Farther back, in December 1863, Lincoln and House Speaker Schuyler Colfax had sniffed out a Democratic scheme to work analogous tricks on Republicans in Congress. The President and the congressman from Indiana spiked the Democrats' guns, and that scheme fizzled.[1]

It boils down to the fact that in December 1865 the Republicans were prepared for emergency and the Democrats were not. The Republicans gained their point of holding off the Southern delegations by moving as before in harmony with Northern public opinion and without overstraining their party's fabric. For these reasons, December 4, 1865, was a Republican triumph.

Their tactics having succeeded on the fourth, Republicans moved swiftly and surely ahead. Reflecting the wartime experience of members, they created a joint committee to oversee conditions in the Southern states precedent to judgment as to their restoration. Only three weeks after the opening of the Congressional session, this "reconstruction committee" was approved, staffed, and ready to work. The nine House members and the six senators came under the chairmanship of moderate, careful William Pitt Fessenden. The committee enjoyed the mandate of both houses of Congress to

> . . . inquire into the condition of the states which formed the so-called Confederate States of America, and report whether they, or any of them are entitled to be represented in either House of Congress, with leave to report at any time, by bill or otherwise.[2]

On December 18 the Thirteenth Amendment went into effect, votes of the Southern states being counted, but the amendment of undoubted ratification even without those assents. Slavery ended everywhere in America. Many antislavery war horses, including

---

[1] See unsigned memo, probably Colfax, to John Hay, December 6, 1863, John G. Nicolay Papers (Library of Congress); H. W. Davis to House clerk Edward McPherson, May 7, 1865, McPherson Papers (Library of Congress).

[2] *CG*, 39 Cong., 1 sess., pp. 29–30. See too Benjamin B. Kendrick, *The Journal of the Joint Committee of Fifteen on Reconstruction, 39th Congress, 1865–1867* (New York: Columbia University Press, 1914), pp. 17–145.

William Lloyd Garrison, felt that this was the signal to end their decades of reform activism. But this did not mean that abolitionist opinion, however happy to see slavery's end, thereby concluded that reconstruction also should close off. "I trust Congress will not re-admit any one of the late rebel States," Garrison wrote to Julian in February 1866. ". . . The [national] Government is solemnly bound to be omnipresent, omniscient, and omnipotent in every part of the South for a long time to come."[3]

Not so, President Johnson insisted in his message to the Congress during its opening days. Reconstruction was all but ended; the national authority must return to its pre-Sumter limits. "The public interest will be best promoted if the several States will provide adequate protection and remedies for the freedmen," he declared.[4]

No Republican would disagree with the President on this single sentence in his message. The rub came in evaluating how adequately the freedmen fared in the Southern states. Reconstruction committeemen would search out facts and then interpret them.

With the reassembly of Congress after the turn of the year, Republican leaders realized that they had to act at once on certain matters involved in reconstruction, beyond merely holding off the Southern delegates-elect until the new joint committee came to decisions. The first imperative to action came from the Army's peculiar situation.

The war having ended, damage suits in Northern state courts were initiated, directed against Army officers who during the war had executed conscription and internal security policies. Inquiry disclosed that almost all the plaintiffs were Democratic partisans and had been Copperhead activists. It also became notorious that the President and the Attorney General were not exerting their offices to shield former Army officers. Here is a heretofore-unpublished memorandum on this score from Provost Marshal General James B. Fry to Secretary of War Stanton, January 6, 1866:[5]

I deem it proper to invite your attention to the fact that the

---

[3] Garrison to Julian, February 11, 1866, Giddings-Julian Collection (Library of Congress).

[4] Richardson, *Messages and Papers,* VI, 361, and see 353–371.

[5] Records of the House Committee on the Judiciary, 39th Congress, HR39A-F13.7, National Archives. I thank Hon. Ralph Roberts, Clerk of the House, for his permission to examine and to use this document.

Officers and Employees of this Bureau are being subjected to civil prosecution for Acts done in their official capacity. In the States of New Hampshire, Vermont, New York, Pennsylvania, Indiana, Illinois, Kentucky and Wisconsin, actions of this character have been commenced, numbering more than Sixteen (16) Cases; in Twelve (12) of which, the Attorney General of the United States has been requested to instruct the proper District Attorney to conduct the defence; I am advised that a great number of other cases may be expected. In each of these cases application has been or will be made to this Bureau for re-inbursement of Expense incurred in defending them, and the payment of Judgments and Costs. I present the subject for such action as you may deem proper, respectfully submitting that Officers and Employees of the Government, who have faithfully discharged their duties, ought not to be subjected to harrassing litigation and Costs for their proper official acts.

So far as I have been able to ascertain, the mischief here complained of, is prompted mainly by that class of persons which labored to embarrass the Bureau and the Department in the efforts to raise troops during the War,—protect the honor and welfare of the Army, and prevent the practice of wrong and fraud upon the Recruits joining it.

In quiet meetings with Generals Grant and Howard, Secretary Stanton, and Solicitor Whiting, Congressional leaders learned that in the Presidentially reconstructed Southern states, American soldiers, Bureau officers, and Unionists were suffering even more exacerbating harassments. A spate of injunctions and ruinous damage suits impeded the officers' work. . . .

The upshot was that unwarranted insults and assaults committed on freedmen and soldiers went unpunished. Worse, ferociously disproportionate penalties awaited the luckless military functionary or the Negro who transgressed some local law or custom. With reconstruction declared closed by the President's orders, Army commanders felt helpless to interpose the military mantle against this vicious civilian onslaught. Army and Bureau operations slowed and promised to halt unless aid arrived.

Out of these conferences came an Army General Order, No. 3, January 12, 1866.[6] Grant's subscription to this extraordinary order provided a temporary bulwark of such weight that the President dared not openly denounce him or it. Meanwhile, Congress must take a hand.

GENERAL ORDERS, } WAR DEPARTMENT,
    No. 3.   }   ADJUTANT GENERAL'S OFFICE,
                    Washington, January 12, 1866.

To protect loyal persons against improper civil suits and penalties in late rebellious States.

Military Division and Department Commanders, whose commands embrace, or are composed of, any of the late rebellious States, and who have not already done so, will at once issue and enforce orders protecting from prosecution or suits in the State or Municipal Courts of such States, all officers and soldiers of the armies of the United States, and all persons thereto attached, or in any wise thereto belonging, subject to military authority, charged with offenses for acts done in their military capacity, or pursuant to orders from proper military authority; and to protect from suit or prosecution all loyal citizens or persons charged with offenses done against the rebel forces, directly or indirectly, during the existence of the rebellion, and all persons, their agents or employees, charged with the occupancy of abandoned lands or plantations, or the possession or custody of any kind of property whatever, who occupied, used, possessed, or controlled the same, pursuant to the order of the President, or any of the Civil or Military Departments of the Government, and to protect them from any penalties or damages that may have been or may be pronounced or adjudged in said Courts in any of such cases; and also protecting colored persons from prosecutions in any of

---

[6] U.S. Army, Adjutant General's Office, *General Orders, 1866* (Washington: Government Printing Office, 1867), No. 3.

said States charged with offenses for which white persons are not prosecuted or punished in the same manner and degree.

BY COMMAND OF LIEUTENANT GENERAL GRANT:

E. D. TOWNSEND,
Assistant Adjutant General

38. CIVIL RIGHTS BILL

April 9, 1866

General Order No. 3 presented for the first time on a high official level the expression of the Radical Republican goal, developed in the postwar months, that race not be a measure of civil rights. The concept and language derived primarily from Illinois Senator Lyman Trumbull, who participated in the December War Department conclaves. An antislave Democrat, in the late 1850's he and the "conscience" Whig Lincoln entered Republican ranks. During the war Trumbull was the powerful head of the Senate judiciary committee, and he sponsored the 1861 and 1862 confiscation laws and the Thirteenth Amendment.

On most counts Trumbull was properly accounted a Radical. Yet he sometimes exhibited opacity in perception. As example, he criticized internal security policies that even Lincoln insisted were barely minimal to prevent home-front holocausts. His biographer has noted that Trumbull ". . . acted with the so-called 'Radicals' in Congress on many occasions, but he was unique in at least one respect—his devotion to legal forms."[1]

Probably this aspect of personality inspired Trumbull early in 1866 to sponsor two extraordinary bills, affording regularization for the provisions of General Order No. 3. The first indefinitely ex-

---

[1] Ralph J. Roske, "The Post Civil War Career of Lyman Trumbull." Unpublished doctoral dissertation, University of Illinois, 1949, p. 41. See also Edward L. Gambill, "Who Were the Senate Radicals?" *Civil War History,* XI (September 1965), 237–244.

tended the life of the Freedmen's Bureau, expanded its powers and jurisdiction, and provided it with a budget appropriate to the magnitude of its task. Trumbull's second bill spelled out for the first time certain civil rights of American citizens that race must not measure. Stated briefly, Trumbull desired national provision for equality of an American's status in all matters before local, state, and national laws. Thus in making and enforcing contracts; in being parties to suits and offering testimonies in courts; in handling questions of property transfer by purchase, lease, rental or inheritance; and in suffering the penalties of laws as well as the protections, "make the penalty the same on all classes of the people for the same offense," Trumbull pleaded in the Senate in defense of his civil rights bill proposal.[2]

Among congressmen, Trumbull and Iowa's James Grimes, Indiana's Julian, Maine's Fessenden, Thaddeus Stevens of Pennsylvania, and Sumner of Massachusetts agreed that these two laws were to wipe out the last vestiges of slavery in state law codes and customary practices, and to provide equality in the protections citizens received from laws.[3] Passage of both bills was not difficult. Then came shocking setbacks. President Johnson vetoed these bills—the first employment of the executive veto power on substantive matters since Tyler's time.[4] Equally novel was the reflexive attempt by Congressional Republicans to overpass the vetoes. The attempt failed in March with respect to the Bureau extension bill (to succeed in mid-1866). The Civil Rights Act on April 9, 1866, did pass the veto obstacle—another constitutional first. Its text follows.[5]

CHAP. XXXI. — *An Act to protect all Persons in the United States in their* April 9, 1866. *Civil Rights, and furnish the Means of their Vindication.*

---

[2] *CG*, 39 Cong., 1 sess., p. 129; and see p. 322.

[3] John Frank and Robert F. Monro, "The Original Understanding of Equal Protection of the Laws," *Columbia Law Review*, L (February 1950), 131–169.

[4] See Richardson, *Messages and Papers*, VI, 398 ff., and 405 ff., for both veto messages.

[5] U.S. *Statutes at Large*, XIV, 27 ff.

Who are citizens of the United States;

Be it enacted by the Senate and House of Representatives of the United States of America in Congress assembled, That all persons born in the United States and not subject to any foreign power, excluding Indians not taxed, are hereby declared to be citizens of the United States; and such citizens, of every race and color, without regard to any previous condition of slavery or involuntary servitude, except as a punishment for crime whereof the party shall have been duly convicted, shall have the same right, in every State and Territory in the United States, to make and enforce contracts, to sue, be parties, and give evidence, to inherit, purchase, [lease,] sell, [hold,] and convey real and personal property, and to full and equal benefit of all laws and proceedings for the security of person and property, as is enjoyed by white citizens, and shall be subject to like punishment, [pains, and penalties,] and to none other, any law, [statute, ordinance, regulation, or custom,] to the contrary notwithstanding.

their rights and obligations.

Penalty for depriving any person of any right protected by this act, by reason of color or race, &c.

Sec. 2. *And be it further enacted,* That any person who, under color of any law, [statute, ordinance, regulation, or custom,] shall subject, [or cause to be subjected,] any inhabitant of any State or Territory to the deprivation of any right secured or protected by this act, or to different punishment, [pains, or penalties] on account of such person having at any time been held in a condition of slavery or involuntary servitude, except as a punishment for crime whereof the party shall have been duly convicted, or by reason of his color or race, than is prescribed for the punishment of white persons, shall be deemed guilty of a misdemeanor, and, on conviction, shall be punished by fine not exceeding one thousand dollars, or imprisonment not exceeding one year, or both, in the discretion of the court.

SEC. 3. *And be it further enacted,* That the district courts of the United States, within their respective districts, shall have, exclusively of the courts of the several States, cognizance of all crimes and offences committed against the provisions of this act, [and also, concurrently with the circuit courts of the United States, of all causes, civil and criminal, affecting persons who are denied or cannot enforce in the courts or judicial tribunals of the State or locality where they may be any of the rights secured to them by the first section of this act;] and if any suit or prosecution, [civil or criminal] has been or shall be commenced in any State court, against any such person, for any cause whatsoever, or against any officer, civil or military, or other person, for any arrest or imprisonment, trespasses, or wrongs done or committed by virtue or under color of authority derived from this act or the act establishing a Bureau for the relief of Freedmen and Refugees, and all acts amendatory thereof, or for refusing to do any act upon the ground that it would be inconsistent with this act, such defendant shall have the right to remove such cause for trial to the proper district or circuit court [in

Courts of the United States to have jurisdiction of offences under this act.

Suits commenced in State courts may be removed on defendant's motion.

1865, ch. 90. Vol. xiii. p. 507.

the manner prescribed by the "Act relating to habeas corpus and regulating judicial proceedings in certain cases," approved March three, eighteen hundred and sixty-three, and all acts amendatory thereof. The jurisdiction in civil and criminal matters hereby conferred on the district and circuit courts of the United States shall be exercised and enforced in conformity with the laws of the United States, so far as such laws are suitable to carry the same into effect; but in all cases where such laws are not adapted to the object, or are deficient in the provisions necessary to furnish suitable remedies and punish offences against law, the common law, as modified and changed by the constitution and statutes of the State wherein the court having jurisdiction of the cause, civil or criminal, is held, so far as the same is not inconsistent with the Constitution and laws of the United States, shall be extended to and govern said courts in the trial and disposition of such cause, and, if of a criminal nature, in the infliction of punishment on the party found guilty.

SEC. 4. *And be it further enacted,* That the district attorneys, marshals, and deputy marshals of the United States, the commissioners appointed by the circuit and territorial courts of the United States, with powers of arresting, imprisoning, or bailing offenders against the laws of the United States, the officers and agents of the Freedmen's Bureau, and every other officer who may be specially empowered by the President of the United States, shall be, and they are hereby, specially

1863, ch. 87.
Vol. xii. p. 755.
Jurisdiction to be enforced according to the laws of the United States, or the common law, &c.

District attorneys, &c., to institute proceedings against all violating this act.

authorized and required, at the expense of the United States, to institute proceedings against all and every person who shall violate the provisions of this act, and cause him or them to be arrested and imprisoned, or bailed, as the case may be, for trial before such court of the United States or territorial court as by this act has cognizance of the offence. And with a view to affording reasonable protection to all persons in their constitutional rights of equality before the law, without distinction of race or color, or previous condition of slavery or involuntary servitude, except as a punishment for crime, whereof the party shall have been duly convicted, and to the prompt discharge of the duties of this act, it shall be the duty of the circuit courts of the United States and the superior courts of the Territories of the United States, from time to time, to increase the number of commissioners, so as to afford a speedy and convenient means for the arrest and examination of persons charged with a violation of this act; and such commissioners are hereby authorized and required to exercise and discharge all the powers and duties conferred on them by this act, and the same duties with regard to offences created by this act, as they are authorized by law to exercise with regard to other offences against the laws of the United States.

Number of commissioners appointed by circuit and territorial courts to be increased; their authority.

SEC. 5. *And be it further enacted,* That it shall be the duty of all marshals and deputy marshals to obey and execute all warrants and precepts issued under the provisions of this act, when to them directed; and should

Marshals, &c., to obey all precepts under this act.
Penalty for refusal, &c.

any marshal or deputy marshal refuse to receive such warrant or other process when tendered, or to use all proper means diligently to execute the same, he shall, on conviction thereof, be fined in the sum of one thousand dollars, to the use of the person upon whom the accused is alleged to have committed the offence. And the better to enable the said commissioners to execute their duties faithfully and efficiently, in conformity with the Constitution of the United States and the requirements of this act, they are hereby authorized and empowered, within their counties respectively, to appoint, in writing, under their hands, any one or more suitable persons, from time to time, to execute all such warrants and other process as may be issued by them in the lawful performance of their respective duties; and the persons so appointed to execute any warrant or process as aforesaid shall have authority to summon and call to their aid the bystanders or posse comitatus of the proper county, or such portion of the land or naval forces of the United States, or of the militia, as may be necessary to the performance of the duty with which they are charged, and to insure a faithful observance of the clause of the Constitution which prohibits slavery, in conformity with the provisions of this act; and said warrants shall run and be executed by said officers anywhere in the State or Territory within which they are issued.

Sec. 6. *And be it further enacted,* That any person who shall knowingly and wilfully ob-

Commissioners may appoint persons to execute warrants.

Authority of such persons.

Warrants to run where.

Penalty for obstructing process under this act;

struct, hinder, or prevent any officer, or other person charged with the execution of any warrant or process issued under the provisions of this act, or any person or persons lawfully assisting him or them, from arresting any person for whose apprehension such warrant or process may have been issued, or shall rescue or attempt to rescue such person from the custody of the officer, other person or persons, or those lawfully assisting as aforesaid, when so arrested pursuant to the authority herein given and declared, or shall aid, abet, or assist any person so arrested as aforesaid, directly or indirectly, to escape from the custody of the officer or other person legally authorized as aforesaid, or shall harbor or conceal any person for whose arrest a warrant or process shall have been issued as aforesaid, so as to prevent his discovery and arrest after notice or knowledge of the fact that a warrant has been issued for the apprehension of such person, shall, for either of said offenses, be subject to a fine not exceeding one thousand dollars, and imprisonment not exceeding six months, by indictment and conviction before the district court of the United States for the district in which said offence may have been committed, or before the proper court of criminal jurisdiction, if committed within any one of the organized Territories of the United States.

for rescue, &c. ;

for aiding to escape ;

for haboring, &c.

SEC. 7. *And be it further enacted,* That the district attorneys, the marshals, their deputies, and the clerks of the said district and territorial courts shall be paid for their services

Fees of district attorneys, marshals, clerks, commissioner, &c. ;

the like fees as may be allowed to them for similar services in other cases; and in all cases where the proceedings are before a commissioner, he shall be entitled to a fee of ten dollars in full for his services in each case, inclusive of all services incident to such arrest and examination. The person or persons authorized to execute the process to be issued by such commissioners for the arrest of offenders against the provisions of this act shall be entitled to a fee of five dollars for each person he or they may arrest and take before any such commissioner as aforesaid, with such other fees as may be deemed reasonable by such commissioner for such other additional services as may be necessarily performed by him or them, such as attending at the examination, keeping the prisoner in custody, and providing him with food and lodging during his detention, and until the final determination of such commissioner, and in general for performing such other duties as may be required in the premises; such fees to be made up in conformity with the fees usually charged by the officers of the courts of justice within the proper district or county, as near as may be practicable, and paid out of the Treasury of the United States on the certificate of the judge of the district within which the arrest is made, and to be recoverable from the defendant as part of the judgment in case of conviction.

to be paid from the treasury of the United States, and to be recoverable from defendant when convicted.

President may direct the judge &c., to attend, &c., for the more speedy trial of persons charged with violating this act.

SEC. 8. *And be it further enacted,* That whenever the President of the United States shall have reason to believe that offences have been or are likely to be committed against the provisions of this act within any judicial district, it shall be lawful for him, in his discretion, to direct the judge, marshal, and district attorney of such district to attend at such place within the district, and for such time as he may designate, for the purpose of the more speedy arrest and trial of persons charged with a violation of this act; and it shall be the duty of every judge or other officer, when any such requisition shall be received by him, to attend at the place and for the time therein designated.]

Sec. 9. *And be it further enacted,* That it shall be lawful for the President of the United States, or such person as he may empower for that purpose, to employ such part of the land or naval forces of the United States, or of the militia, as shall be necessary to prevent the violation and enforce the due execution of this act.

may enforce the act with the military and naval power.

Sec. 10. *And be it further enacted,* That upon all questions of law arising in any case under the provisions of this act a final appeal may be taken to the Supreme Court of the United States.

Appeal to the supreme court of the United States.

SCHUYLER COLFAX,
Speaker of the House of Representatives.

LA FAYETTE S. FOSTER,
President of the Senate,
pro tempore.

39. THADDEUS STEVENS, SPEECH

May 8, 1866

Passage of the Civil Rights law, in the opinions of many Americans, represented the endlessly delayed but final closing off of the war's issues and a consequent finish to the need for concern over reconstruction or the freedman. John Jay proposed that the nation congratulate itself on this achievement ". . . as the last great victory in the war against slavery." Continuing, he offered the opinion that although

. . . the Supreme Court would have decided, whenever the question should have come before them, that the [Thirteenth] Amendment . . . made the freed slaves citizens ipso facto without the aid of Congressional legislation, I still deem the Civil Rights Act the proper complement of the Anti-Slavery amendment, since it relieves all misapprehensions as to the position which the American Republic is henceforth to occupy before the world, as regards the relationship of our people towards each other.

That law returned the United States to 1776, Jay exulted, and permitted national survival in "unity, freedom, and honor."[1]

Most Radical Republicans were less optimistic. They believed that the Civil Rights Act was none too sturdy a staff. What of its enforcement? The President was at best unsympathetic. Federal and state jurists were exhibiting increasingly conservative ways. And as one of Sumner's worried correspondents accurately noted, the Civil Rights Act, though as laudable, as sentiment, as the first Freedmen's Bureau statute, provided for no administrative apparatus to enforce its provisions:

I apprehend great difficulty, in rendering a statute efficient, in

---

[1] Jay, *Address of the President, Union League Club of New York, June 23, 1866* (New York, 1866), pp. 9–10.

the present condition of the machinery for its administration. . . . Deficiency [in enforcement provision] is their [Congressional Republicans'] worst fault, and that I suppose is incurable, though I think public opinion here is in advance of Congress.[2]

Increasing strain in political institutions and alignments followed. The whiplash critic of the Congressional Republican front-runners and especially of the Joint Committee on Reconstruction, President Johnson retained for as long as possible his titular headship of the Republican party. The Joint Committee continued its endless hearings. Committeemen gained acquaintance with Southern conditions mainly from informed men of good judgment and high principles. To keep lines taut against Southern intrusion, the committee on March 2, 1866, received reaffirmation from the whole Congress that former Confederate states would remain excluded from representation until the legislature admitted them. Precisely one month later, the President proclaimed that the insurrection was ended in all the ex-rebel states (excepting Texas, though it too soon met the President's standards). Next day the Supreme Court of the United States issued a decision clearly implying that perhaps even the President's ways in the South were excessive, since he had employed the United States Army there, after armed hostilities ended, as the key to reconstructing state governments.[3]

Confused and bitter at all this unexpected frustration after the long years of war, many persons became impatient that the Joint Committee did not hasten forth with its conclusions. On May 8, Thaddeus Stevens of Pennsylvania spoke up in the House of Representatives in defense of his Committee:[4]

The committee are not ignorant of the fact that there has been some impatience at the delay in making this report; that it existed to some extent in the country as well as among a few members of the House. It originated in the suggestions of faction, no doubt, but naturally spread until it infected some good men. This is not to be wondered at or complained of. Very few could

---

[2] T. Farrar to Sumner, May 11, 1866, Sumner Papers (Houghton Library, Harvard University).

[3] The case is *ex parte Milligan*, 4 Wallace, 2(1866). The opinion was to follow in the Court's December term.

[4] *CG*, 39 Cong., 1 sess., part 3, p. 2459.

be informed of the necessity for such delay. Beside, we are not all endowed with patience; some men are naturally restive, especially if they have active minds and deep convictions.

But I beg gentlemen to consider the magnitude of the task which was imposed upon the committee. They were expected to suggest a plan for rebuilding a shattered nation—a nation which though not dissevered was yet shaken and riven by the gigantic and persistent efforts of six million able and ardent men; of bitter rebels striving through four years of bloody war. It cannot be denied that this terrible struggle sprang from the vicious principles incorporated into the institutions of our country. Our fathers had been compelled to postpone the principles of their great Declaration, and wait for their full establishment till a more propitious time. That time ought to be present now.

It was. The committee had worked out a proposed Fourteenth Amendment to add to the national Constitution. Before moving on to consider the role this amendment played in the development of Radical Republicanism and reconstruction, a brief comment is in order on the committee itself. Thirty years ago the biographer of flamboyant Roscoe Conkling, United States Senator from New York and Reconstruction Committeeman, wrote:

The [Joint Congressional] Committee of Fifteen has been accused of the basest sort of partisanship, the most heinous offenses against justice. Thad Stevens has been called its master mind, the other fourteen members merely his puppets. Well, members of the committee made mistakes, but they were not devils intent upon doing wickedness just for the fun of it. Nor were they Thad Stevens' trained dogs, though that sardonic fellow was easily the most conspicuous among them and probably the most able. . . . The Committee *became* radical. At first, it was inclined to be conservative. The chairman, Senator Fessenden, was decidedly a conservative. Roscoe Conkling was rated as one, too, in the beginning. This Committee came to be Congress' army in its long, ungentlemanly war with the President.[5]

This statement retains its validity.

As to Thad Stevens, probably historians will never agree fully

[5] Donald B. Chidsey, *The Gentleman from New York: A Life of Roscoe Conkling* (New Haven: Yale University Press, 1935), pp. 64–65.

on his motivations and character. Evidence is impressive that he was sincere in his crusade for Negro rights and welfare and was neither a charlatan nor a psychopath. Certainly save for Sumner no tougher parliamentary fighter ranged Capitol Hill than this seventy-five-year-old Pennsylvanian. But unlike Sumner, Stevens was willing to accept what was possible and then to strike out again for better gains.

In his speech of May 8, Stevens surveyed for his fellow Representatives the piecemeal evolution of measures that came together in the final draft of the Fourteenth Amendment. He did not approve of all its features. Especially, he had hoped in the amendment's third section to keep the bulk of Southern whites disfranchised long enough—only four years—for Negroes and Unionists to root deeply into the South's political fabric. When this was denied in favor of far more lenient disfranchisement standards, Stevens acquiesced in order to save the whole.[6]

In rebuilding, it is necessary to clear away the rotten and defective portions of the old foundations, and to sink deep and found the repaired edifice upon the firm foundation of eternal justice. If, perchance, the accumulated quicksands render it impossible to reach in every part so firm a basis, then it becomes our duty to drive deep and solid the substituted piles on which to build. It would not be wise to prevent the raising of the structure because some corner of it might be founded upon materials subject to the inevitable laws of mortal decay. It were better to shelter the household and trust to the advancing progress of a higher morality and a purer and more intelligent principle to underpin the defective corner.

I would not for a moment inculcate the idea of surrendering a principle vital to justice. But if full justice could not be

---

[6] *CG*, 39 Cong., 1 sess., part 3, pp. 2459–2460. For text of the amendment in its present form, see any United States Constitution and Cheever's article in the next section.

obtained at once I would not refuse to do what is possible. The commander of an army who should find his enemy intrenched on impregnable heights would act unwisely if he insisted on marching his troops full in the face of a destructive fire merely to show his courage. Would it not be better to flank the works and march round and round and besiege, and thus secure the surrender of the enemy, though it might cost time? The former course would show valor and folly; the latter moral and physical courage, as well as prudence and wisdom.

This proposition is not all that the committee desired. It falls far short of my wishes, but it fulfills my hopes. I believe it is all that can be obtained in the present state of public opinion. Not only Congress but the several States are to be consulted. Upon a careful survey of the whole ground, we did not believe that nineteen of the loyal States could be induced to ratify any proposition more stringent than this. I say nineteen, for I utterly repudiate and scorn the idea that any State not acting in the Union is to be counted on the question of ratification. It is absurd to suppose that any more than three fourths of the States that propose the amendment are required to make it valid; that States not here are to be counted as present. Believing, then, that this is the best proposition that can be made effectual, I accept it. I shall not be driven by clamor or denunciation to throw away a great good because it is not perfect. I will take all I can get in the cause of humanity and leave it to be perfected by better men in better times. It may be that that time will not come while I am here to enjoy the glorious triumph; but that it will come is as certain as that there is a just God.

The House should remember the great labor which the committee had to perform. They were charged to inquire into the condition of eleven States of great extent of territory. They sought, often in vain, to procure their organic laws and statutes. They took the evidence of every class and condition of witness, from the rebel vice president and the commander-in-chief of their armies down to the humblest freedman. The sub-committees who were charged with that duty—of whom I was not one, and can therefore speak freely—exhibited a degree of patience and diligence which was never excelled. Considering their other duties, the mass of evidence taken may well be considered extraordinary. . . .

Let us now refer to the provisions of the proposed [fourteenth] amendment.

The first section prohibits the States from abridging the privileges and immunities of citizens of the United States, or unlawfully depriving them of life, liberty, or property, or of denying to any person within their jurisdiction the "equal" protection of the laws.

I can hardly believe that any person can be found who will not admit that every one of these provisions is just. They are all asserted, in some form or other, in our DECLARATION or organic law. But the Constitution limits only the action of Congress, and is not a limitation on the States. This amendment supplies that defect, and allows Congress to correct the unjust legislation of the States, so far that the law which operates upon one man shall operate *equally* upon all. Whatever law punishes a white man for a crime shall punish the black man precisely in the same way and to the same degree. Whatever law protects the white man shall afford "equal" protection to the black man. Whatever means of redress is afforded to one shall be afforded to all. Whatever law allows the white man to testify in court shall allow the man of color to do the same. These are great advantages over their present codes. Now different degrees of punishment are inflicted, not on account of the magnitude of the crime, but according to the color of the skin. Now color disqualifies a man from testifying in courts, or being tried in the same way as white men. I need not enumerate these partial and oppressive laws. Unless the Constitution should restrain them those States will all, I fear, keep up this discrimination, and crush to death the hated freedmen. Some answer, "Your civil rights bill secures the same things." That is partly true, but a law is repealable by a majority. And I need hardly say that the first time that the South with their copperhead allies obtain the command of Congress it will be repealed. The veto of the President and their votes on the bill are conclusive evidence of that. And yet I am amazed and alarmed at the impatience of certain well-meaning Republicans at the exclusion of the rebel States until the Constitution shall be so amended as to restrain their despotic desires. This amendment once adopted cannot be annulled without two thirds of Congress. That they will hardly get. And yet certain of our distinguished friends propose to admit State after State before this becomes a part of the Constitution. What madness! Is their judgment misled by their kindness; or are they unconsciously drifting into the haven of power at the other end of the avenue? I do not suspect it, but others will. . . .

If any State shall exclude any of her adult male citizens from the elective franchise, or abridge that right, she shall forfeit her right to representation in the same proportion. The effect of this provision will be either to compel the States to grant universal suffrage or so to shear them of their power as to keep them forever in a hopeless minority in the national Government, both legislative and executive. If they do not enfranchise the freedmen, it would give to the rebel States but thirty-seven Representatives. Thus shorn of their power, they would soon become restive. Southern pride would not long brook a hopeless minority. True it will take two, three possibly five years before they conquer their prejudices sufficiently to allow their late slaves to become their equals at the polls. That short delay would not be injurious. In the mean time the freedmen would become more enlightened, and more fit to discharge the high duties of their new condition. In that time, too, the loyal Congress could mature their laws and so amend the Constitution as to secure the rights of every human being, and render disunion impossible. Heaven forbid that the southern States, or *any one of them,* should be represented on this floor until such monuments of freedom are built high and firm. Against our will they have been absent for four bloody years; against our will they must not come back until we are ready to receive them. Do not tell me that there are loyal representatives waiting for admission—until their States are loyal they can have no standing here. They would merely *mis*represent their constituents. . . .

The third section may encounter more difference of opinion here. Among the people I believe it will be the most popular of all the provisions; it prohibits rebels from voting for members of Congress and electors of President until 1870. [Subsequently, especially by Fessenden's efforts, this clause received its present and even milder disfranchising form.] My only objection to it is that it is too lenient. I know that there is a morbid sensibility, sometimes called mercy, which affects a few of all classes, from the priest to the clown, which has more sympathy for the murderer on the gallows than for his victim. I hope I have a heart as capable of feeling for human woe as others. I have long since wished that capital punishment were abolished. But I never dreamed that all punishment could be dispensed with in human society. Anarchy, *treason,* and violence would reign triumphant. Here is the mildest of all punishments ever inflicted on traitors. I might not consent to the extreme severity denounced upon them by a provisional governor of Tennessee—I mean the late lamented Andrew Johnson of blessed memory—but I would have increased the severity of this section. I would be glad to see it extended to 1876, and to include all State and municipal as well as national elections. In my judgment we do not sufficiently protect the loyal men of the rebel States from the vindictive persecutions of their victorious rebel neighbors. Still I will move no amendment, nor vote for any, lest the whole fabric should tumble to pieces. . . .

Year of Decision—1866

---

40. WENDELL PHILLIPS, SPEECH

April 1866

Appeals such as those of Stevens helped immeasurably to maintain Republican accord in the face of the considerable pressure that the President was able to exert against it, and to confirm the increasing Northern popular consensus in favor of ratification of the Fourteenth Amendment. Agreement became general that the amendment went the proper middle way by limiting permissible arenas of states' actions in matters of political and civil rights. The understanding obtained that the amendment, though national in scope, pertained especially to Negroes and to the South. Probably most Republican rank and filers considered the amendment as the final necessary step in reconstruction. Depiction of the amendment as the Constitution's Appomattox was common, a figure popular among the Congressional Republican leaders.

Professor ten Broek has shown that the organized freedmen's aid societies, once antislavery in purpose, and the Congressional veterans of the abolitionist crusade were the major supporters of the Fourteenth Amendment.[1] But on the far left of the Republican spectrum, some Radicals had advanced to new frontiers of racial

---

[1] Jacobus ten Broek, *The Antislavery Origins of the Fourteenth Amendment* (Berkeley: University of California Press, 1951).

egalitarianism. To these front-runners, the amendment signified the Constitution's Sumter not its Appomattox; a beginning step toward racial justice instead of a finality; a defective opportunity for protecting democracy more than an effective opening for the enlargement of liberty. Most outrageous was the fact that the amendment's second section did not require states to allow all citizens to vote without regard to race. Instead, it merely penalized states for withholding suffrage. Doubt was immediate (and justified by events) that the penalty would ever find application.

Therefore the curious result was that humanitarian spokesmen who were not really Negrophile but were color-blind in attitude denounced the amendment because it failed to guarantee votes to Negroes. "There is but one vital point in the matter of reconstruction," the *Anti-Slavery Standard* editorialized on May 26, 1866; "—whether the Negro shall vote." The demand grew that Congress must provide specific guarantees for the Negro's access to balloting booths. Reconstruction was still to come as an opportunity to raise higher the level of political democracy and liberty.

Most Congressional Radicals, including Stevens and Sumner, understood better than these pioneers how sparse such sentiment was among Northerners generally. Both men had tried to alter the amendment to more courageous expression than it finally assumed. But both felt it necessary to acquiesce in what was artfully possible, in what their constituents would support. No one could know in the spring and summer of 1866 that the contumacy and wrongheadedness of President Andrew Johnson, of the Democratic organization nationally, and of enough Southern whites to justify the Radical claim of sectional unregeneracy, would bring the Congressional Radicals, along with a majority of Northerners, to seek at least for a while the same goal of Negro suffrage.

Approved in Congress by mid-1866 and thereafter out in the states seeking ratification, the Fourteenth Amendment represented the Republican consensus that Southern whites would not deal justly with Negroes. For the first time in America's history, the national government proposed limitations in the arena of state action on political rights. A basic alteration was approaching in federal-state-individual relationships, *if* enforcement provisions followed and found forceful application.

Advanced Radicals feared a sell-out, not a victory. In the following article, published in April 1866, Wendell Phillips gave pungent
expression to this concern. He disdained mine-run politicians and
the art of the possible. The Fourteenth Amendment was a conservative blind, he believed. Phillips distrusted the late-comers
from Democratic and Whig antecedents who had moved so quickly
into top Republican echelons, and he wanted to specify goals for
the party far beyond where its most influential members were willing to go.[2]

The worst evil of the past year has been our not knowing who
were our friends, and who were our enemies. The best result
of this winter's discussion has been the discovering where the
line runs between the two camps. No intelligent observer of
events needs to doubt that to-day the Head-quarters of the
Rebellion are in the White House at Washington. Andrew
Johnson is the leader of the present Southern effort to regain
by political management what the South lost in the battle-
field. He is therefore to be watched and opposed as the most
efficient servant of the still unchanged and rebellious South.
No fair words — no specious promises — are to lull again to
sleep this tireless and indispensable vigilance. Any journal
or man that tries to persuade us to trust him, must be branded
as treason's ally or tool.

In Congress, as representing the National sentiment and
purpose, is now our hope. While that stands, we have *political
machinery* to work with. Should that succumb to the Administration, we are thrown back upon mere public discussion,
and compelled to wait till other elections have replaced such
treacherous leaders. While holding office and representing
their party, members of Congress are the Nation's political
voice and teachers, whether in session or at home. Meanwhile
we are to remember that the North is already so far instructed

---

[2] Phillips, "The Policy," *The Radical,* I (April 1866), 295–296.

and convinced, that had the Administration stood by us, the whole perfect fruit of this National Victory might have been saved; and the nation remodelled, with absolute justice for its basis. As it is, we have the result perilled, if not lost, by the treachery of the Administration—by Mr. Johnson planning and straining every nerve, using all his power, and usurping more, to reconstruct the South as nearly as possible, just as she was before the war.

In such circumstances our effort should be to *avoid any settlement*. We should rejoice to recognize that the epoch is not ended, and that we have not yet reached dry, solid land. Some men are in haste to compromise in order to end this transition state. From Mr. Fessenden, of Maine, bred in the superficial and timid school of the Whig party nothing else could have been expected. No child of such a school could understand this era, much less be fit to lead in it. Mr. Wilson of Massachusetts, has studied for twenty years the history of slavery, and slavery compromises under this government; and his last speech shows that his twenty years study has taught him exactly nothing.

No compromise has ever been made, even in our dullest and weakest times, which has not hindered truth, postponed justice, and weakened freedom. Our fathers, in 1789, counted the slave as three-fifths of a man, affecting to believe,—perhaps believing,—that the selfish wish of the South to count the other two fifths would hasten emancipation. On the contrary, it led the South to intrigue for new territory to increase its relative weight; but it never gave rise to one, even the slightest effort, to secure more representative strength by freeing the negro. Meanwhile the compromise deadened the nation's conscience, strengthened slavery, and almost wrecked the government.

Just the same has been the history of all our compromises, made even in ordinary political times. Much more is it madness now in this formative hour of the nation's life,—when, if ever and more than ever, it can be taught and ripened, lifted up and on,—to shorten and surrender this our great opportunity, by a cowardly, distrustful, and ignorant haste to compromise.

Our true policy is this. Let Congress plainly announce its belief, that no state lately in rebellion, is fit to be readmitted to Congress. Let it lay down the principle that no one shall ever be admitted except it establishes universal or at least impartial suffrage: and then let Congress adjourn. Every day it continues in session jeopards this great cause. It may be bought, bullied, or deceived. All tends that way while it is in session, exposed to Administrative influence. Once adjourned, let the lines be distinctly drawn, and go to work to meet 1868 in earnest; the interval between now and the next elections, State, National, and Presidential, is none too long for the work. The treason of President Johnson and the impossibility of impeaching him, leaves no hope of any earlier settlement. It is just as well, and much safer to acknowledge this. To adjourn and go to the people on this issue is saving time. In this way, spite of the President, the whole fruit of the war may yet be saved. With the lines distinctly drawn; the fight above-board and acknowledged—the issue fairly presented, and every Congressman stumping his own State, the nation may yet be founded and built up on impartial and absolute justice. Our New England air will save some of our Senators at least from the compromise malaria of Pennsylvania Avenue.

Any other course, — drifting about in a storm of Constitutional Amendments, pilot blinded or drugged, and rudder unshipped — allows timid and heedless senators, to put us bound hand and foot into the hands of the enemy, under pretence of being *practical* statesmen. Any other course runs the risk of giving us another ten years of just such dislocated, discordant, and perilous national life as we have passed through since 1856. Adjourn Congress then. Let every member turn himself into witness, teacher, and drill master, and let our bugle call be, *No State admitted at present, and none ever admitted which has the word "WHITE," or the recognition of race in its Statute Books.*   Wendell Phillips.

41. THE REVEREND GEORGE

B. CHEEVER, PAMPHLET

1866

The most striking expression on record of the crossroads nature of the Fourteenth Amendment issue, in the eyes of zealous humanitarians, is in the publications during 1866 of George Cheever. Here are extracts from a consideration he offered, just after the 1866 Congressional elections, on the nature of the Fourteenth Amendment. He presented a constitutional view focused sharply and unswervingly on individual rights. Cheever was a poor politician, but in some matters he was a prophet, correctly foreseeing racial strife if justice failed in 1866.[1]

If the people of the United States examine the proposed [Fourteenth] Amendment to the Constitution in the light of their inalienable rights as citizens, they will find in the Second Section thereof the foundation not of a republican government, but a Confederacy of State Oligarchies.

That section proposes to submit the elective franchise, which is the primal and distinguishing right of American

---

[1] Cheever, *The Republic or the Oligarchy? Which? An Appeal Against the Proposed Transfer of the Right to Vote from the People to the State. By One of the People* (New York, 1866).

citizenship, to the will of each State Legislature, to abridge or take away at its pleasure.

It proposes to reconstruct the people for the States, not the States for the people. It is State reconstruction on the basis of popular disintegration; the reconstruction of States' rights, by taking away the people's rights.

The right to do this is assumed as a right of government. . . . But Congress might as well think fit not to bestow the right to life, liberty, and the pursuit of happiness. Where did Congress, or any branch of our government, ever get authority to withhold that right to vote? The inalienable possession of it by all the people is the foundation of the very existence and authority of the government, as the people's agent, but not the people's owner; the guardians in trust, but not the giver, of the people's rights. The right to vote belongs to the people, and can neither be withheld nor bestowed by the government; otherwise the people are slaves.

The Essence of an Oligarchy Is the Exclusion of Particular Classes from the Vote.

If it is intended to keep the blacks or any other class in serfdom, it is only necessary to exclude them from voting. If it is intended to return them by State law, under pretence of legal guardianship, into slavery, it is only necessary to exclude them from voting. . . . This is the perfection of State sovereignty as contended for at the South. This is the sovereignty that is being reconstructed in the Union, on any plan that excludes the colored race from the vote. It is the sovereignty of a white man's government, for the present limiting its exercise to the color of the skin, but including the power, which at any time may be developed, of a still more stringent despotism against any class that may become the object of hatred or jealousy.

The assumption of the right and power to bestow or withhold the right to vote, strikes at the foundation of our liberties. It is fraught with peril, and ominous of aristocratic sovereignty and usurpation.

Now, it is proposed to set the right of disfranchisement, for other causes than crimes, in the Constitution; but in doing this, the Government are deliberately taking from the people their sovereign rights as people, and putting them out of the citizens' power to recover, and out of the power of the United States to protect, by transferring them over to the States, as State rights. They are no longer the people's rights no longer rights at all—but conferred dignities, at the pleasure of the State sovereignties; mere trusts, to be resumed by the Government at pleasure—to be committed to as few as the Government please, or restricted to whatever conditions the Government may impose.

The proposed amendment says to the citizens of the United States—You have no right, in fee simple, to vote for representatives in your country's government; but it belongs to the State Legislature to say whether you shall be a voting citizen or not. A subject citizen, a taxed citizen, a soldier citizen, a mud-sill, you shall be at any rate, but not a free voting citizen, unless the State oligarchy chooses. Your sovereign right, as a citizen of the United States, to vote for representatives in Congress, is abdicated for you by this proposed amendment, and is transferred over into the power and at the disposal of the State Governments, thus constituted State sovereignties, that can at their pleasure forbid you from voting for the United States Government.

If this passes, then, in regard to the millions of free colored citizens in the rebel States, or any other classes obnoxious to the displeasure of the States, the Government will have abdicated its own power of protection, and transferred its loyal subjects to the will and disposal of rebel State oligarchies. But no State can disfranchise a citizen of the United

States. The right to do so for anything but crime would be the right to enslave him.

The demoralizing proposition is now made to the Legislature, and people of all the States of the Union, to alter the organic law of government, so as to disfranchise the whole colored race, so as to rob five millions of colored citizens of the United States and their posterity of their right of representation, if the States please—that is, if the white people of the States please. This question of the desolation of their own interests—the question of their own moral assassination—is not to be presented to the colored race themselves, as though they had any important concern in it, or any right to adjudicate upon it; but the white race are assumed and presupposed to be their supreme dictators, and the only judges. . . . We force upon an article in the Constitution which was intended to secure the right of representation as a right of citizenship, the conveyance of authority to destroy that right; for it is the enthronement of the Dred Scott decision that black men have no rights that white men are bound to respect. . . .

Shall their rights be protected, or shall they be taken away, without crime, by reason of the color of their skin? And shall rebels and rebel States be permitted to disfranchise them, to take away their right of representation, and make them serfs? And for this purpose shall the Constitution be so amended as to give to rebel States the power of disfranchising, without crime, on account of color or race?

The question involves the possibility of public and personal justice, the principles of a free government, of our own government, of the sacredness of covenants, of social, religious, and civil obligations, of regard to God's will, and of humanity, benevolence, and the law of mutual right among men.

European nations are watching the result. . . . Convocations of Christian Churches, the most illustrious in the world for

piety and patriotism, have addressed similar appeals, on religious grounds, to the people and Churches of this country.
The leading patriots of Great Britain and France—such men
as John Bright, Mill, Count Gasparin—have by letter, speech,
and public protest, implored in the name of humanity, and
for the sake of the possibility of anticipated impartial freedom in the Old World, the just and right decision of the
question here. They pray to be delivered from the shame
of beholding the first Republican power on earth authorizing
in its Constitution the right of despotism. The European
would be appalled at the phenomenon of the government
and Constitution of the United States reconstructed on the
foundation of the color of the skin, and human rights determined by that lowest and basest of all forms of tyranny in
respect of persons. Freedom, and the cause of free government, would be put back for ages. . . .

The question of impartial suffrage is, therefore, not only
the question of the age in Europe and in this country, but,
in laying anew the foundations of our government by reconstruction, it becomes a question for posterity as to the laws
and life of future ages, and the welfare of millions—industrial, social, civil, educational, religious. It can now be peacefully settled without revolution, without strife, for future
generations; preserving them from that possible conflict of
races which is inevitable, unless the rights of the blacks be
at this time established and secured.

The millions of to-day will be ten millions at another census, and fifteen millions at another. But if we take away
their rights now, they will have been educated by oppression
for revolution and revenge. We might keep down five millions, but we cannot keep down fifteen. Their number will
increase, for God has kept them increasing thus far, against
all the oppressive barbarities of slavery itself, and God has
given them freedom, and is making them to know that all
the privileges of free citizenship belong to them as to white

men. When they become fifteen millions, it will not be in
the power of fifty millions to keep them down; and when
they rise, then will come that terrible crisis, which God now
puts it in our power to prevent; a crisis of blood and desolation if we refuse, in reconstructing our foundations, to provide against it. This is what Divine Providence at this
moment gives us the power to do: putting a blank of reconstruction into our hands, and saying to us, "Fill it out, but
remember that as you sow, so shall you reap."

It is a question of Christian patriotism, of simple justice,
of love to our neighbor as ourselves, of doing to others as we
would have them do to us. These millions of human beings
that God has thrown upon us cannot be elevated religiously
under a law that takes away all their rights politically, and
consequently all their means of peaceful self-defence. It is a
false religion that consents to rob our fellow-creatures of
their rights and then pretends to make it up by missionaries
and teachers. We must first be just before we can be
generous. . . .

The just measures can be carried better by rejecting the
unjust, and no amendment is necessary for that purpose.

But it is said to be the best thing we could get, and that we
must accept the section disfranchising the colored race, because, if we reject that, we reject the whole. The support of
an iniquity is thus forced upon an unwilling people, because
its advocates affirm that if we do not sustain it, we endanger
the Republican party. The truth is, the party is damaged and
endangered more by the proposal of such iniquity than by the
whole force of rebel and treasonous enmity throughout the
country. Nothing injures the republican party so much as
the assumption and defence of an injustice so palpable, so
shameful, so unnecessary. . . . Better to lose a thousand such
amendments than accept the curse with them. Better no immediate reconstruction than one grounded on and governed
by such tyranny.

But the amendment is not at all necessary for the reconstruction, which will be accomplished better and more speedily without it than with it, by the exercise of the just powers of a Congress elected and supported by the people, for the re-establishment and security of the whole people's rights. Reconstruction by injustice is not what the people require, but reconstruction by the law of universal, impartial justice and liberty. The people create and endow their Congress for that purpose.

The Voice of the People is for Justice to All Classes, Injustice to None.

The uprising of the people in the recent [1866] elections is not because they desire the amendment, for they do not vote in regard to that, but because they mean to sustain their own Congress, and to put down the usurpation of the President. It is because they mean to have a Congress that shall put down the rebellion, and compel the rebel States to obey the Constitution and the laws, making all men equal before the law, and giving to all Citizens their rights, without respect to color or race. The people of the United States would vote against the second section of the proposed amendment if it were submitted to them. The people do not require the amendment, but they require a Congress that shall carry out the provisions of the Constitution for exact and equal justice to all men. . . .

But the authorization of this very crime is the essence of the proposed amendment. The only alteration of the Constitution is in the second section, which provides for the States the power and right to take away the right of suffrage from the people. . . . The other sections are measures already in the power of Congress to execute by simple enactment, as the welfare of the Union requires.

It is obvious then, at the outset, that the amendment is not necessary for any good purpose which cannot otherwise and more directly be accomplished. It is not requisite for the protection of loyalty, nor for the punishment of treason, nor for the establishment of Republicanism, nor for the peace and permanence of the Union, nor for the security of justice and liberty. It is not for speedy reconstruction, which can be accomplished more rapidly without it, by just laws of Congress according to the Constitution. . . .

Now, it would have been as easy to provide by amendment that colored citizens shall vote in reward for their loyalty, as that rebel white citizens shall have the right to deprive them of the vote, because of their unwillingness to relinquish a power they had always exercised, and for the perpetuity of which they had rebelled.

It is a question of the moral assassination of the whole colored race. It involves their interests, their happiness, their manhood, and to a large degree their morality and religion, for themselves and their posterity. For if the right to vote can be taken away, every other right will be seized whenever prejudice and cruelty and contempt indicate. . . .

No white man would give a fig for all his other rights if you make a *pariah* and a serf of him, by taking away his right to vote. The right to vote is the back-bone of all his other rights. A man crawls upon his belly in the dust the moment that right is taken away. So we propose to make worms of the black race, for the rebel white race to tread upon. The pretence of protecting their civil rights when taking away their political is base and hypocritical. No man's civil rights are or can be secured without his political. If civil rights are the flesh, political rights are the life-blood and organizing heart that sends the life-blood through the whole system. If you cut the flesh the wound will close and the blood will heal it, but if you take away the life-blood, if you cut the heart, the whole body dies. Secure a man's political rights and all his civil rights follow: deny his political rights and none of his civil rights can be secured. The right of representation is the root of the tree; if you cut that away the tree dies. A white man's tree will not live without that root, neither can a black man's. . . .

The Parties Appointed for Endurance of the Penalty.

The persons punished are the colored race, and none others. It is only the colored race that are deprived of the vote, being guilty of no crime. The whites cannot be disfranchised. The plan of reconstruction by which it is proposed to remedy the inequalities of white representation, is grounded on the disfranchisement of the colored race. The rebel States can not be disfranchised, but the loyal people can.

It is reconstruction by taking away the right to vote from the loyal and faithful inhabitants, and conferring it on the rebel and disloyal. It is reconstruction by giving to the rebel white population of the rebel States the right to take away the rights of the loyal colored population. It is reconstruction by making the rebel States each a white man's government, with the rule of justice that black men have no rights that white men are bound to respect. The State is only the white people of the State, and this amendment gives to the State thus constituted as a white State, the right of excluding blacks from representation, and when so excluded, the United States government excludes them from the census of representation, lest the whites, though not permitting them to vote, should count them in as white votes, and thus secure a larger white representation. The white men in each rebel State are invested, as a class by this amendment, with the right to disfranchise the black men, as a class. It is the reconstruction of a Union of white oligarchies.

And the advocates of this justice claim that it is beautifully and mildly just, because it makes every white man's vote at the North equal to every white man's vote at the South, and does not admit of the injustice of giving a three-fifths greater representation to a Southern than to a Northern one. The black man's personal rights are annihilated, in order that the white man's State rights may be equalized. Instead of giving the living child to the rightful mother, we propose, for the pleasure of the rebels and adjustment of our own claims, to cut him in two, and distribute the carcass North and South.

It is a partnership in fraud, and a bargain between the partners for a more equal division of the spoils than that which obtained under the system of slavery.

Heretofore, the rebel States, by means of slavery, counting three-fifths of their black chattels as white votes, have robbed the Free States of their rightful share of representation, taking themselves what belonged to the slaves. Now by the Constitution the slaves are freemen and have a right to their own vote. Instead of recognizing and maintaining this title, and giving them the right of suffrage which belongs to them, we propose to guarantee with their late masters, the white rebels of the South, to rob the whole free colored race of their right of representation, letting only the white population, both North and South, vote; thus reclaiming the political rights of which we have heretofore been defrauded as States, by both parties uniting in the robbery of the whole colored race as persons, for that purpose. In order to equalize the white representation North and South, in order to make a white Northern State equal to a white Southern State, we agree to reduce the whole colored race to serfdom, if the States please. Our republicanism is thus demonstrated as caring more for State monopolies, than for personal liberties.

Conclusion.

Such is the settlement which some men have the hardihood to praise as being a model of mild and simple justice.

Such is the scheme presented for the sanction of our legislatures, and demanding the people's approbation. It is proposed to amend the Constitution, not for any man's personal rights, or relief, or protection, but as an enabling act to enable

States to take away from large bodies of men the very right which is dearer to us all than any other, and on which, to a great degree, all our other rights depend.

An Amendment not to protect rights, but to take them away, not to enlarge the sphere and perfect the application of justice and liberty but to contract and corrupt it, ought to carry the certainty of its own defeat in its very nature. Every one of the amendments adopted in the time of Washington and our fathers, was an amendment for the enlargement and more infallible security of the rights of the people. This is for destroying the rights of more millions than the whole population then existing in the Union. This one fact ought to secure its rejection, namely, that is not *for* men's rights, but *against* them.

It is a revolution in which the corporate rights of States are preferred above the personal rights of citizens. We appeal against transferring our inalienable, primal rights to the possession of State Oligarchies, with power at their pleasure to confer upon us or withhold from us, what belongs only to ourselves.

And in the name of God, and for the safety of the Country, we appeal to the legislatures, the people, and the Congress against the proposed disfranchisement of the loyal blacks. The defeat of this invasion of the rights of the colored race to-day may prevent a San Domingo war of races as broad as this hemisphere, twenty years hence.

42. JOHN RICHARD DENNETT,

NATION REPORT

April 1866

On June 13 the proposed Fourteenth Amendment to the Constitution received approval in both Houses of Congress, and three days later it went out to the states for ratification. Chief Justice of the

United States Salmon Chase heard from his associate on the bench, the Californian Stephen J. Field:

The proposed amendment . . . appears to me to be just what we need. I think we members of the [Republican-] Union party can unite cordially in its support. If the President withholds his approval he will sever all connections with the Union party. Two things are certain—the American people do not intend to give up all that they have gained by the war—and they do intend that loyal men shall govern the country.[1]

Almost everything that occurred during the remainder of 1866 added strength to this position. President Johnson expressed disapprobation of the Fourteenth Amendment. News from Memphis of a terrible race riot in which pardoned ex-Confederates figured importantly and dishonorably (a situation later repeated on larger scale in New Orleans) added to Republican strength the support of men of many shades of opinion on political and racial matters. By midsummer 1866 some of the more critical onlookers from among the freedmen's aid fraternity, who earlier had found the Congressional Radicals inadequately radical, altered their tune. Reciprocally, Radical Republicans on Capitol Hill and across the nation began as never before to favor implicit enforcement of Negro suffrage at least in the South, instead of resting content with the vague formula that the Fourteenth Amendment prescribed nation-wide.

President Johnson's proclamation on August 20 that the insurrection was ended even in Texas, and that civil authority prevailed everywhere in the nation, further sharpened tempers. Army commanders and Freedmen's Bureau agents in the South had been depending on Grant's earlier General Order No. 3 and another, No. 44, of July 6, 1866, as protections for themselves and for Negroes against harassments by the "Johnson" state courts and local police officers.[2] Order No. 44 provided Grant's authority for military personnel in the former Confederacy

. . . to arrest all persons who have been or may hereafter be

---

[1] Field to Chase, June 30, 1866, Chase Papers, Vol. XCVII (Library of Congress).

[2] United States Army, Adjutant General's Office, *General Orders, 1866* (Washington: General Printing Office, 1867), No. 44; and see Thomas and Hyman, *Stanton,* pp. 471–491.

charged with the commission of crimes and offenses against officers, agents, citizens, and inhabitants of the United States, irrespective of color, in cases where the civil authorities have failed, neglected, or are unable to arrest and bring such people to trial, and to detain them in military confinement until such time as a proper judicial tribunal may be ready and willing to try them.

Grant let it be known that Johnson's peace proclamation did not destroy the protections of his general orders.

Terrific pressures were necessary to align a man of Grant's nature and ambitions openly against his President. Many thousands of Americans reacted to similar imperatives during the August-November months of 1866 and later.

As example, a June 1866 editorial from the *American Freedman*[3] supported the Fourteenth Amendment. Until this time, the writer had pressed the Congressional Republicans for stronger measures than the amendment's. Universal suffrage was his goal.

In sum, by mid-1866 Andrew Johnson was forcing together in a semblance of harmony mutually incompatible elements, not only mid-road and Radical Republicans, but also the fractious factions among the Radicals. The result of his concern to keep American government white was an augmenting demand to admit blacks to civil and political action, at least in the South. Fatefully, the impulsion toward racial equality emerged in many hearts from anti-Johnson and anti-Democratic anger more than from humanitarian goals.

America's peculiar constitutional structure, reaffirmed by free balloting in the free states even during the Civil War, required that elections proceed when specified, no matter how unsuitable the moment. Knowing the inevitability of the 1866 Congressional and state contests, politicians of all shades of opinion made careful preparations as the autumn season advanced. Though historians have made tradition of a contrary depiction, the conduct of the 1866 campaign was higher, not lower, than the nineteenth-century norm. National interest was too great, literacy too extensive, and comprehension of the basic issues too common for garish rhetoric

---

[3] "How Shall We Protect the Freedman?" *The American Freedman*, II (July 1866), 50–51.

to deceive, although audiences might enjoy its excesses and applaud its flourishes. Stated another way, "vote as you shot," was sound political science in the contexts of the nation's interests and democracy's advance, in the judgments of a decisive majority of Americans.

Reinforced heavily by the recruitment of the twice-turncoated President, Northern Democrats joined him in opposition to the proposed Fourteenth Amendment. Republican spokesmen approved it except for those among the most Radical, and they subdued criticism while the campaign lasted. To be sure, local and regional issues had impact, as is always true. But everywhere the dominant theme dividing men and parties was approval or disapproval of the amendment, and on this issue the 1866 campaign became a very great debate.

No doubt some men advocated support for the amendment out of selfish motives (although the old "conspiracy thesis" that the amendment was created in order to protect corporations against state regulations, not individuals against states' infringements of civil rights, is untenable). As example, Maryland's Henry Winter Davis was bent on humiliating Johnson and wanted an overwhelming popular vote in favor of Republicans and the amendment to stand as a slap in the President's face. No Negrophile, Davis supported Negro suffrage as a means to punish the South.

Nevertheless, during the campaign and in the Congressional sessions following, Winter Davis was a heavy weight in aid of men built of purer Radical metal—which is only to say that ignoble men for crass reasons may advance noble causes.

Sumner was the natural contrast to Winter Davis. Everyone knew where he stood. He was a moralist in politics and an effective politician with respect to marking out roads for men of slower moral imperatives to follow. But he was not a leader in the Senate. His personality and his commitment to humanitarian goals placed Sumner in the "loner's" position. There, exposed, taking pleasure in the role, Sumner was the party's mentor and hector, and during the campaign he enlarged his audience through a heavy writing and speaking schedule.

Surely the Winter Davis kind of Republican was more common

than the Sumner. Ben Wade, Jacob Howard of Michigan, and Sumner's Massachusetts colleague in the Senate, Henry Wilson, among other Republicans, hedged on whether ratification of the Fourteenth Amendment meant political rights or social equality everywhere for Negroes. Their regard for the constituents' sensibilities brought ordinary politicians to respond to political imperatives. Party lines were already badly askew from the President's defection. This was a generation that since the early 1850's had known little political party stability. The congruence of party collapse and the onset of war was terribly vivid. Prudence was a hallmark of most Republicans with respect to the Negro.

This being true, it does not follow that American voters were fooled at all by the thin disguises some Republican campaigners wore on the question of race, or that the "bloody shirt" was irrelevant to the issues in the election. Indeed, the very concept that disguises found wide employment requires examination. The Chicago *Tribune*, the voice of Midwestern Radicalism, in advocating equal suffrage for Negroes in the South instead of equality only in matters of law was frank enough. Its campaign support for the Fourteenth Amendment was a late-coming midsummer switch, brought about by repugnance for Johnson's ways. In its way, the *Tribune* was a model of moderate Republicanism, despite its categorization into Radical ranks.

That newspaper's editorial stand was a good deal like the position of Oliver Morton of neighboring Indiana. Since 1861 he had been governor of that state. He knew that Hoosiers hated slavery but were not overfond of Negroes. No Negrophile himself, Morton had become an abolitionist during the 1850's, had left the Democratic party for the new Republican organization, and had been an invaluable support for the Lincoln administration all through the war years. After Appomattox he had warmly sustained Johnson, and in Indiana Morton had spoken out frankly against Radicals, including Julian, who espoused biracial access to the polls.

But the course Johnson followed in the South, and the coarseness of Southern policies with respect to Negroes, white Unionists, and occupation troops, were altering Morton's views. During the 1866 campaign he was not yet ready to support Negro suffrage. Elected to the Senate as result of the campaign, he reached Capitol

Hill converted to Sumner's solution for the nation's and the party's ills.

In all these various ways and many more, Negro suffrage was an implicit and often an explicit issue in the critical 1866 campaign. For the first time in America's history, white men were even considering the advisability of democratizing the political process with respect to race, and at a time when white women could not vote (a fact that leaders of women's rights organizations pointed out with some asperity). Only five years earlier almost all Negroes were slaves, and most white men were content to buy peace at the price of perpetualizing slavery, as in the egregious Crittenden compromise proposal of 1861. By Appomattox, not only was the expansion of slavery halted, but freedom had almost everywhere been substituted for it in conformity with Lincoln's emancipation edict. Christmastime that year brought ratification of the Thirteenth Amendment. Now, less than a year later, white Americans were contemplating that Negroes vote and have equal protections in the practices of civil rights.[4]

In all this swift advance the Radical Republicans, whatever their individual motivations, had been leaders. They deserve credit less for altering the national climate of opinion on race, for with few exceptions they did not, than for understanding the nature and drift of the alteration. Sensitivity and educability mark the statesman, the effective politician, the moralist who understands how to complete his mission. Without this quality the American political system stumbles.

During the 1866 campaign Republican candidates received invaluable support from reports by journalists who after touring conquered Dixie, offered Northern readers their on-scene observations. In early March 1866, *Nation* correspondent John Richard Dennett sent from Vicksburg, Mississippi, this account of a conversation with an anonymous Ohioan who had traveled extensively in the postwar South. Printed in *The Nation* in its issue of April 5, 1866 (page 431) as part of a series on "The South as It Is," a description of Southern attitudes such as the following helps to

---

[4] I exploit here the researches of Professor Ernest Isaacs, who offered a paper on "The Radical Republicans and Negro Suffrage: An Interpretation," at the 1963 Mississippi Valley Historical Association.

explain why Northern public opinion supported the Radical Republicans in their developing Reconstruction policy.

"You must understand," said he, "that in 1860 I was a strong Douglas man. I didn't like Lincoln, and the abolitionists I hated; but, of course, I was Union. As the war went on I began to believe in Lincoln, and, by the time the Emancipation Proclamation was issued, I had been educated up to it and endorsed it. As a war measure, I mean; that was how Mr. Lincoln regarded it, and so did I. Well, since the war ended I've been a conservative; I've considered Stevens and Sumner dangerous men, who did n't understand the South, wanted to humble it and so on, and were standing in the way of peace. I believed what we used to hear, that the North did n't understand the South. I believe it yet, but in a very different sense. This journey has been the greatest that I ever experienced. I came out with the kindest feelings for these people down here; I wanted to see it made easy; we had whipped them, and I wanted it to rest there. I thought the South wanted it to end there. But I was tremendously mistaken. They hate us and despise us and all belonging to us. They call us cutthroats, liars, thieves, vandals, cowards, and the very scum of the earth. They actually believe it. They won't even allow that we won our own battles. 'We were overpowered by numbers,' they say; 'of course we could n't fight all Europe.' They've said that to me more than fifty times within the last few weeks. And they say that they are the gentlemen; we are amalgamationists, mudsills, vandals, and so forth. And I've heard and seen more brag, and lying, and profanity, and cruelty, down here, than I even saw or heard before in all my life. The only people I find that a Northern man can make a friend of, the only ones that like the Government and believe in it, are the negroes. I'm convinced they can vote just as intelligently as the poor whites. A Southerner would knock me down if I said that to him; but it's true. I tell you I'm going home to be a radical. Fight the devil with fire. I've learned to hate Southerners as I find them, and they can hate me if they want to. I'm a Sumner man after I get back, and I shall write out my experience for some of our papers. Every man that's seen what I've seen ought to let it be known. . . . I wish every county in the North would send out two men, who have the confidence of their fellow-citizens, and make them travel through the South and report the true condition of things. They could n't make a true report without changing every honest administration man into a radical."

43. GEORGE L. PRENTISS, ARTICLE

October 1866

Without coordination among themselves or with political professionals, Protestant ministers across the North continued for a while after Appomattox to play significant roles in clarifying public issues. It is not possible precisely to measure the impact of the pulpit in politics. Almost certainly it was very large. And certainly the ministers added fervor and flavor to campaign exchanges.

Minister in 1866 of one of New York City's most fashionable Presbyterian churches, George L. Prentiss was a consistent contributor to theological periodicals and newspapers. Back in April 1866 he had written in a popular sectarian periodical on "The Political Situation." His concluding wish had been

that Congress and the President might soon come to see eye to eye, and agree upon a joint policy which should be, like the wisdom from above, first pure, then peaceable, full of mercy and good fruits, without partiality, and without hypocrisy.

Six months later, in time and form to be of considerable if unmeasurable impact on readers (many of whom were ministers) in three dozen states, Prentiss surveyed the implications of what had become "The Political Crisis"[1]—and note the alteration of the title. Referring to the quoted hope of April 1866, Prentiss judged in October that:

We need not say how grievously this hope has been disappointed. The differences, which six months ago seemed not incapable of being reconciled, have since widened into an impassable chasm. The Executive and Legislative departments of the Government are arrayed against each other in open and determined conflict. Both have appealed to the country, and already the popular verdict has begun to utter itself. The nation is in the midst of a political crisis as momentous as any it has ever known. We propose to take a brief survey of the contest, and of the issues involved in it.

In our previous article we traced the President's policy down to the veto of the Civil Rights Bill. His message returning that bill left but little ground of hope that he would approve of any plan of restoration, which the wisdom of the National Legislature might devise. Everything, indeed, indicated that his mind was fully set in him to have his own way, in total disregard of the law-making power; and that his own way was to admit the States lately in insurrection to all their old rights and privileges, and to increased power in the Government, *without any further conditions or guarantees whatever.* He declared them (with the exception of Texas) to be already reconstructed, and as completely entitled to representation in either house of Congress as New York or Ohio. He had said, it is true, that they must present themselves *"in an attitude of loyalty"* as well as "in the persons of loyal representatives." But as he evidently considered himself the sole

---

[1] Prentiss, "The Political Crisis," *American Presbyterian and Theological Review* (October 1866 [pamphlet reprint; New York: Somers, 1866]).

judge of the first qualification, and loudly proclaimed their loyalty to be unimpeachable,* it only remained for Congress to look into the second. But here, again, there was an irreconcileable difference between the two branches of the Government. The word "loyal" was used by the President in a peculiar sense. He meant by it, as is now perfectly clear, anybody who, having been amnestied, or pardoned, professed approval of his "policy;" and this executive test Mayor Monroe, of New Orleans, or one of his "Thugs," could stand quite as well as Gov. Parsons and Gov. Orr. The Congressional test of a "loyal representative," on the other hand, was his ability to take the oath of office prescribed by the Constitution and the law of the land.† This oath, both in its letter

---

* "They (the late rebel States) are one and all in an attitude of loyalty towards the Government, and of sworn allegiance to the Constitution of the United States. In no one of them is there the slightest indication of resistance to this authority, or the slightest protest against its just and binding obligation. This condition of renewed loyalty has been officially recognized by solemn proclamation of the Executive department."— *Address of the Philadelphia Johnson Convention.*

† The oath is as follows: "I do solemnly swear (or affirm) that I have never voluntarily borne arms against the United States since I have been a citizen thereof; that I have voluntarily given no aid, countenance, counsel, or encouragement to persons engaged in armed hostility thereto; that I have neither sought nor accepted, nor attempted to exercise the functions of any office whatever, under any authority or pretended authority in hostility to the United States; that I have not yielded a voluntary support to any pretended government, authority, power, or Constitution within the United States, hostile or inimical thereto. And I do further swear (or affirm) that, to the best of my knowledge and ability, I will support and defend the Constitution of the United States, against all enemies, foreign and domestic; that I will bear true faith and allegiance to the same; that I take this obligation freely, without any mental reservation or purpose of evasion, and that I will well and faithfully discharge the duties of the office on which I am about to enter, so help me God."

"And why (it may be asked) did not Congress admit the few claimants who *could* honestly take this oath?" We reply, because it would have been a virtual abandonment of the vital point in dispute; it would have been giving up to the enemy the key to the whole position. Congress maintained the ground that no insurrectionary State was entitled

and spirit, is in utter antagonism to the policy of Mr. Johnson. Probably not half-a-dozen of all the claimants of seats from the South can take it without committing perjury; and yet not a single one of these claimants but is an enthusiastic supporter of the President; nor is there any reason to think that a single one of them all is regarded by him as disqualified to sit in the halls of National Legislation. How, then, can any loyal man be surprised that the breach between Congress and the Executive was not healed? It could have been healed only by the former consenting to abandon the whole question of reconstruction to the discretion of Mr. Johnson, to abdicate to this end its functions as the supreme law-making power of the Nation, and to admit to seats on its floor men whose hearts and lips were still envenomed with disloyalty, provided only they brought in their hands the pardon, and praised the "policy," of the Executive! Some have alleged, we are aware, that if Congress, early in the session, had decided upon the plan ultimately adopted, the President would, probably, have given it his approval; for he had again and again expressed himself as in favor of every one of its principles. We cannot concur in this opinion. We are constrained to believe that Mr. Johnson had already made up his mind not to agree with Congress, except on the condition of its first yielding to him all the vital points in controversy. If there were no other evidence of this, his speeches, and those of his Secretary of State, during their late electioneering tour to the grave of Douglas, leave no doubt on the subject. Whatever may have been thought before, we are at a loss to understand how anybody,

---

to representation in either house of the National Legislature, until, as a State, it gave adequate guarantees that it had abandoned the principles of the rebellion, and would henceforth abide by the amended Constitution, the Union, and the obligations of honor and justice contracted by the nation in putting down the rebellion. So long as such guarantees were not given, Congress would have stultified itself in admitting any man, however loyal; and so Horace Maynard, Senator Fowler, and Col. Stokes, the tried loyalists claiming seats from Tennessee, frankly acknowledged.

after reading these extraordinary effusions, can suppose for a moment that the dilatory action of Congress, or the "white-washing" epithet of Mr. Sumner, or even the sarcasms of that extremely "radical" but sturdy and whole-souled old patriot, Thaddeus Stevens, led Mr. Johnson to abandon the loyal cause. Is it not, alas! too plain that he had deserted it already in his heart; and that these things so offended him, because they helped to betray the fearful secret to the watchful eye of the country?

We are not disposed, therefore, to censure Congress for having delayed so long to decide upon a plan of reconstruction. This delay was highly salutary and needful. The task was one of the most difficult ever assigned to a legislative body. And for three months after Congress met, the country was far from being in the mood to break with the President and stand up in solid phalanx for its loyal Senators and Representatives. Thousands of patriotic and thoughtful citizens, who in July last were in full sympathy with Congress, in December, 1865, or even in February, 1866—at least before the 22d of that month—would have taken sides with the Executive; of this no other proof is needed than the memorable Cooper Institute meeting on the evening of Washington's birthday. So the final rupture came, probably, at the best time; neither too soon nor too late. It came just when public sentiment was ripe for the great issue. Instead of blaming Congress for not sooner agreeing upon a policy, we rather praise it for its wise delay. The policy was thus made far more perfect, and popular opinion was prepared to give it a much heartier and more intelligent support. However desirable it might have been to hasten the work of restoration, it was vastly more desirable that the work should be done well than done quickly. It is a thousand times better that the States lately in rebellion should be admitted in the right way one or two years hence, than that they should be admitted at once, or should have been admitted last winter, in a way dangerous to the future peace and safety of the country, or inconsistent with national honor and justice. And it seems to us that the future peace and safety of the Union, and not less the claims of honor and justice, are admirably provided for by the plan of settlement finally adopted by Congress. This plan is contained in a joint resolution proposing an amendment [the fourteenth] to the Constitution. . . .

This amendment speaks for itself and requires no interpreter. It is well entitled to the place in our American *Magna Charta,* which we trust it will soon occupy beside the great [Thirteenth] Amendment proposed by the Thirty-Eighth Congress. The more it is pondered, the more will it commend itself to the reason and conscience of the Nation as an eminently wise, just, and magnanimous basis for the settlement of the questions arising out of the rebellion. It is, surely, the very embodiment of national leniency and moderation, containing nothing vindictive, nothing harsh, even. Indeed, the only plausible ground of complaint against it is its extreme mildness. Where do the records of history afford another instance of a great and high-spirited nation dealing with a conquered rebellion, which had assailed and almost destroyed its life, on terms so considerate and merciful? Let us for a moment examine these terms. . . . [Here follows a description of the pending Fourteenth Amendment.]

Such is the plan of restoration devised by the patient, farseeing, and patriotic wisdom of the National Legislature. The Amendment has been ratified already by New Hampshire, Connecticut, Tennessee, New Jersey and Oregon. We cannot doubt that it will be ratified by all the other Northern States, and by a sufficient number of Southern States to make it valid as part of the Constitution. Nor do we doubt that it will confer imperishable honor upon its much-abused and calumniated authors—the faithful, fearless senators and representatives of the Thirty-ninth Congress. Compared with the insane policy of Mr. Johnson, it appears to us as the fine gold of sober, prudent, and high-toned American statesmanship—such statesmanship as sat in council in the renowned convention of 1787.

We are aware that some who acknowledge the Amendment to be essentially just and reasonable, still deny the right of the National Legislature to make its ratification a condition precedent to the admission of the late rebel States to representation in Congress. They are willing it should be urged upon the acceptance of the South, but only in the way of "moral agitation." This is the ground taken by Rev. Henry Ward Beecher in the deplorable letter which shot such a pang of grief through the hearts of millions of his old friends, and made so jubilant the hearts of millions of his old defamers. It is the ground taken by other honored citizens, whose purity of motive and sincere devotion to their country are unquestionable. But we cannot for a moment admit its validity. We yield nothing to these eminent men in our desire for a speedy and complete restoration of the Union. Nor are we willing to concede that our faith in the New Era, or in the beneficent and reconciling power of American and Christian ideas, is less strong than theirs. But this is not a mere question of "moral agitation," no more than was that of the adoption of the other great amendment abolishing slavery. Like that, it is pre-eminently a question of wise and practical statesmanship. It concerns not merely desirable things, but things absolutely vital to national honor, security and justice. Such, at least, is the deliberate conviction of myriads of the most thoughtful, sober-minded, and conscientious patriots in the land. Such is the solemn conviction of the overwhelming majority of the men and women, who sustained the country through the war, both at home and in the field. Nor have they the least misgiving as to the constitutional power, or the perfect historical and moral right of the American people, through their senators and representatives in Congress assembled, to require assent to the righteous provisions of the proposed amendment on the part of the late revolted States, as a condition precedent to their sharing again in the National Legislation and Government. No theory denying this power and right appears to them tenable; neither that which asserts the Nation to be pledged to the late rebel States by its public declarations during the war;* nor that of the transcendental and impeccable character of the States as States. This last doctrine, especially, as it is preached in support of Mr. Johnson's policy, they find it hard patiently to endure; the doctrine, we mean, that the Southern States could do no wrong and impair no right, or privilege, by the treason of the people and governments which constituted them States; that they could not go out of the Union, and never were out, either in law, or in fact; and that, therefore, they were fully entitled to representation in Congress, not only the instant the war ceased, but *all through the rebellion*—as fully entitled as Massachusetts

---

* On this point we think many have been misled by the language of the oft-cited [Crittenden] resolution on the object of the war, passed by the two houses of Congress in July, 1861, just after the battle of Bull Run. This resolution was a manifesto to the insurgent States, and was intended especially to allay their fears for the institution of Slavery. It embodied, no doubt, the loyal sentiment of the country at the time. But it seems to us that a most inordinate importance has been attached to it. It was passed by a Congress chosen before the war. It was no *law*. It did not bind the Executive, who never signed it, nor did it bind the next Congress chosen in the midst of the war and with exclusive reference to the new issues. When President Lincoln issued his Proclamation of Emancipation, the act was bitterly denounced as a violation of the letter and spirit of this Crittenden resolution; it was "overthrowing or interfering with the rights and established institutions of those States." But Mr. Lincoln did not consider that he was violating any pledge which bound either him or the Nation. The same charge was brought against the 38th Congress, for proposing the amendment abolishing slavery; it was an attempt to "overthrow an established institution, and impair the dignity, equality and rights" of the Southern States. But that noble Congress did not admit the charge to be just; nor did the loyal States who ratified that Great Amendment; nor did President Johnson, when he required the rebellious States to ratify it also. The Crittenden Resolution had no legal or constitutional force when it was passed; and it certainly has none now. Still, we see no real inconsistency between a vote for that resolution and a vote for the Constitutional Amendment. The object of the latter is simply to secure the great object of the war as declared by the former, and to fulfill the pledges given by the Nation in its successful prosecution.

or Illinois—and that to deny them this representation *until they give to the Nation proper guarantees of the loyalty of the people and governments which constitute them States, as also of its own future peace and safety*—is an act utterly unconstitutional, oppressive, and destructive of the Government. The overwhelming majority of those who sustained the country through the war, we repeat it, regard this doctrine as a monstrous sophism, repugnant alike to political reason, to fundamental principles of moral and social order, and to sound common sense. And their opinion of it seems to us entirely correct.

No fine-spun metaphysical theory of State rights, or of the Constitution, can serve as a just and proper basis for the settlement of such novel, momentous, and eminently practical questions as have sprung out of the Slaveholders' rebellion. The founders of the Republic never anticipated the occasion for such a settlement; just as little as they anticipated the breaking out, in 1861, of such a stupendous civil war; and they made special provisions for the one as little as for the other. In conducting the war to a successful issue, the Nation was compelled to adapt itself to the unparalleled exigency by creating, both on land ond water, its own military precedents; and it has the right to do a like thing in securing the fruits of its incomparable victory. When the Constitution and its own experience cast no sure light upon its "dim and perilous way," it must seek light elsewhere. Following its own Heaven-inspired instincts, and taking counsel at the oracles of Eternal Truth, why should it not create new political precedents in the interest of republican freedom, humanity and justice? Has it not already done so in devising and adopting the great Amendment? Nor have we any fear that such a course will lead it astray from the paths of a wise and genuine conservatism, or of Christian mercy and magnanimity. The loyal heart of the Nation is still disposed, as it has ever been, to the largest possible exercise of mercy and magnanimity towards those lately in arms against its life, that is consistent with the claims of public order, righteousness and good faith. It is afraid to exercise even the blessed quality of mercy at the expense of these sacred principles. And we believe the time is coming when even the South will fully understand this; when she will be willing to acknowledge that the great heart of the Nation, like the heart of its martyred President, was governed in its policy of restoration by no sentiment inconsistent "with malice toward none, with charity to all."

We have thus taken a brief view of the political crisis through which the country is passing; and what we have said might, for the most part, have been written as well before the adjournment of Congress as now. But since that date, public events have occurred of the gravest import, and bearing directly upon our subject. The nation has been in the midst of a severe moral, as well as political crisis. Its patience, its self-command, and its holiest convictions, have been tried and tested as hardly ever before. It has seen the boundless patronage of the Executive prostituted to the work of intimidating and corrupting popular opinion with open and shameless effrontery. Unscrupulous and ambitious, or disappointed, politicians, some of them veterans of half a century in the arts of party intrigue, and whose very names have become odious to the moral sense of the nation, have been seen conspiring together to thwart the righteous will of the people, and to betray the cause of Loyalty and Freedom into the hands of its worst foes. Deeds of savage butchery have been perpetrated at mid-day, in one of the chief cities of the Union [New Orleans], and in the sight of the Flag of our country, which find no parallel this side of the Sepoy massacres in the dark places of Oriental heathendom; and, to crown the horror, the Chief Magistrate of the Republic stands in such relations to them, both before and after, as to have impelled sober-minded, Christian citizens to turn deliberately to the Constitution and ponder, for the first time, the meaning of those "OTHER *high crimes and misdemeanors*" on impeachment for

and conviction of which "THE PRESIDENT . . . . SHALL BE RE-
MOVED FROM OFFICE." (ART. II. Sect. 4.)

And, as if this were not enough, the ear of the nation has
been assailed, week after week, by denunciations of its Supreme Legislature as a usurping, disunion body "hanging
upon the verge of the Government," and by dark threats of
a rival Congress to be made up of late rebels and their allies
from "the other end of the line," as also of another civil war,
to be carried on—not on Southern—but on Northern soil. Nor
have such threats and denunciations been uttered by reckless politicians alone; they have been scattered broadcast
over the land, like so many fire-brands, arrows and death, by
the lips of the Executive himself! Is it strange that these
things have filled the public mind with the deepest excitement and alarm? Is it strange that they have pressed, like
an incubus, upon all loyal hearts, keeping thoughtful men and
women awake at midnight? Is it strange that, in view of
them, the tide of popular sentiment is running with such resistless might in the direction indicated by the Vermont and
Maine elections?

It is not our purpose to discuss the New Orleans riot. The
end of that dreadful story is not yet. The American people are
still reading it; and they require no interpreter and no argument to explain to them its meaning, or to tell them who are
the responsible and guilty authors of it. They have studied
and compared the President's dispatches and every other dispatch, whether in its mutilated or unmutilated form; they
have read Mr. Johnson's apology for the massacre in his speech
at St. Louis; they have pondered Gen. Baird's report, and will
ponder every word of the Report of the Military Commission
when it sees the light. If any further evidence is needed, they
will demand that it be taken the moment Congress shall assemble. And we are very much mistaken if they do not also
demand in due time, and in a voice not to be trifled with,
that in some way the crime should be punished and the matchless infamy of it washed off from the American name. In dis-

missing the subject, we content ourselves with putting on record a single extract from one of Gen. Sheridan's dispatches to Gen. Grant; . . .

"The more information I obtain of the affair of the 30th in this city, the more revolting it becomes. *It was no riot. It was an absolute massacre by the police, which was not excelled in murderous cruelty by that of Fort Pillow. It was a* MURDER *which the Mayor and Police of the city perpetrated without the shadow of a necessity.*

"Furthermore, *I believe it was premeditated,* and every indication points to this. I recommend the removal of this bad man."

. . . We gladly leave a subject so ungrateful, and pass on to say a word of the other Philadelphia Convention, which met on the 3d of September.

The records of this remarkable gathering are before the country, and we need not go into details respecting it. The Northern people listened eagerly to its voice, have calmly pondered its statements, and will, in due time, make their own response to its pathetic and manly appeal. It was an assemblage as impressive as it was unique in American history. Its story sounded like a chapter from the old martyrologies of Christian faith and liberty, while its addresses and resolutions carried one back to the Declaration of Independence, and the "times that tried men's souls." . . .

There was only one point of serious difference among the members of the September Convention, viz., the question of impartial or negro suffrage; and even on that point the difference related rather to the time and mode than to the principle itself. Most of the delegates from the border States were unwilling to assert the principle at once, and put it into the platform; while most of the delegates from the "unreconstructed States" were not only ready to assert the principle and put it into the platform, but they maintained that their political salvation and that of the whole South which they represented—the Union men during the war, the poor whites, and the colored population—absolutely depended upon its bold assertion and early realization. And certainly no candid person can read their argument and statements in support of this opinion, without feeling their overwhelming force. Without approving of everything that was said, we believe the effect of the Convention will be to enlighten the public mind on this momentous question, to remove prejudice, and so to hasten the day when the mere color of his skin shall debar no American citizen from the right and privilege of the ballot-box. That day is sure to come. The logic of our democratic institutions, the inexorable logic of events, and the calm reason and justice of the nation will combine to bring it to pass without fail. And why should anybody be afraid of that day? Even President Johnson fully acknowledges the principle and the wisdom of putting it in practice, in his dispatch to Provisional Governor Sharkey, of Mississippi, dated August 15, 1865, in which, referring to the State Convention, he says: "If you could extend the elective franchise to all persons of color who can read the Constitution of the United States in English, and write their names, and to all persons of color who own real estate valued at not less than two hundred and fifty dollars, and pay taxes thereon, you would completely disarm the adversary and set an example the other States will follow. *This you can do with perfect safety.*" And if it could be done in Mississippi "with perfect safety" in August, 1865, when the war was hardly over, it certainly could be done now "with perfect safety" in every Southern State, and (alas! that it needs to be added) in every Northern State which is still enthralled to the cruel prejudices begotten of slavery and *caste.*

Let this question of impartial suffrage and the political rights of the colored citizen be settled in accordance with the fundamental principles of American society; and then—the Constitutional Amendment having been adopted, and enforced by appropriate legislation—we cannot doubt that peace and prosperity would soon prevail throughout all our borders, and that all classes and conditions and races of men among us would rejoice together in the blessings of a new era of Christian light and liberty. In the enjoyment of such blessings the bitter memories of the war would gradually fade away, the antipathies and rivalries of North and South would cease, and the whole nation, revering the merciful hand of God in the past, even in the bloody conflicts of the battle-field, would march forward on the line of its great destiny with exultant hope, trusting still to the guidance of that merciful and almighty Hand. A consummation so devoutly to be wished will not, indeed, come of mere legislation, however wise and beneficient; all the agencies of Christian faith and philanthropy, untiring prayers, every form of pious labor and self-sacrifice, the pulpit, the press, the church, the school, innumerable men, women and children even, who love Christ and His cause, must be added to complete and crown the glorious work. These heaven-born agencies are already busy with their part of the divine task. Let Christian patriotism and statesmanship do their part also, both at the ballot-box and in the council chamber; let political and religious wisdom and zeal thus conspire together; and who can refuse to believe that God, even our fathers' God, will be merciful unto us, and bless us, and make His face to shine upon us, as never before; or that the end thereof will be peace and assurance forever? Then shall come to pass in this great Republic the prophetic words, written thousands of years ago among the hills of Palestine: In righteousness shalt thou be established; thou shalt be far from oppression; for thou shalt not fear; and from terror, for it shall not come near thee. Thou shalt know that I, the Lord, am thy Saviour and thy Redeemer, the mighty One of Jacob. For brass I will bring gold, and for iron I will bring silver, and for wood brass, and for stones iron. I will also make thine officers peace and thine exactors righteousness; violence shall no more be heard in thy land, wasting and destruction within thy borders; but thou shalt call thy walls Salvation, and thy gates Praise.

PART TEN

Congress Acts on Reconstruction

1867

---

44. GEORGE W. JULIAN

ON THE 1866 ELECTIONS

December 1866

Despite pessimistic predictions of conservatives to the contrary, the 1866 Congressional elections went off without violence or fraud. The President's refusal to yield at all on the question of approving the Fourteenth Amendment added to the augmenting conviction northward that since Appomattox, the South had enjoyed every fair chance and had failed to offer satisfactory evidence of decent public behavior. As a result, Republicans gained election in numbers adequate to control two thirds of both houses of Congress.

The fact was that Radicals worried lest the Southern states ratify the Fourteenth Amendment. Doing so at that time, then unquestionably they would gain readmission into Congress. All possibility would end of new national prescriptions on race relations. In all likelihood Southern states, once readmitted, would ignore the Negro-centered purposes of the Fourteenth Amendment. The prospects would be dim indeed for Congress again to amass the will to

invoke against a "reconstructed" state even the puny punitive provisions of that amendment.

Then news came in that all states southward had rejected the
amendment. Left to themselves and encouraged by the President,
the states of the former Confederacy were going to remain white
man's political country. Therefore Republicans had new reconstruction proposals ready for the hopper as soon as the lame-duck session of the Thirty-ninth Congress assembled in December 1866.

Concerned that democracy build in the South not merely forms
but reality, some Radicals tried to brake the reconstruction tempo.
For their purposes the process might well continue for ten, twenty,
or more years. They feared that too swift a reconstruction rhythm
could not be adequate and would enable Southern whites to continue domination over enfranchised Negroes who lacked education
and economic independence. Recalling years later the sharpening
division among Republicans with respect to the desirable speed of
reconstruction, Julian offered the following description.[1]

On the meeting of Congress in December [1866] the signs of
political progress since the adjournment were quite noticeable.
The subject of impeachment began to be talked about, and
both houses seemed ready for all necessary measures. Since
mingling freely with their constituents, very few Republican
members insisted that the XIV Constitutional Amendment
should be accepted as a finality, or as an adequate solution of
the problem of reconstruction. The second section of that
amendment, proposing to abandon the colored race in the
South on condition that they should not be counted in the
basis of representation, was now generally condemned, and
if the question had been a new one it could not have been
adopted. This enlightenment of Northern representatives was
largely due to the prompt and contemptuous rejection by the
rebellious States of the XIV Amendment as a scheme of reconstruction, and their enactment of black codes which made

---

[1] Julian, *Political Recollections,* pp. 303–306.

the condition of the freedmen more deplorable than slavery itself. In this instance, as in that of Mr. Lincoln's Proclamation of Emancipation, it was rebel desperation which saved the negro; for if the XIV Amendment had been at first accepted, the work of reconstruction would have ended without conferring upon him the ballot. This will scarcely be denied by any one, and has been frankly admitted by some of the most distinguished leaders of the party.

The policy of treating these States as Territories seemed now to be rapidly gaining ground, and commended itself as the only logical way out of the political dilemma in which the Government was placed. But here again the old strife between radicalism and conservatism cropped out. The former opposed all haste in the work of reconstruction. It insisted that what the rebellious districts needed was not an easy and speedy return to the places they had lost by their treasonable conspiracy, but a probationary training, looking to their restoration when they should prove their fitness for civil government as independent States. It was insisted that they were not prepared for this, and that with their large population of ignorant negroes and equally ignorant whites, dominated by a formidable oligarchy of educated land-owners who despised the power that had conquered them, while they still had the sympathy of their old allies in the North, the withdrawal of Federal intervention and the unhindered operation of local supremacy would as fatally hedge up the way of justice and equality as the rebel despotisms then existing. The political and social forces of Southern society, if unchecked from without, were sure to assert themselves, and the more decided anti-slavery men in both houses of Congress so warned the country, and foretold that no theories of Democracy could avail unless adequately supported by a healthy and intelligent public opinion. They saw that States must grow, and could not be suddenly constructed where the materials were wanting, and that forms are worthless in the hands of an ignorant mob.

45. THADDEUS STEVENS, SPEECH

January 3, 1867

Whatever their differences, all Republicans agreed that Congress enjoyed plenary power to impose the nation's will upon the ex-Confederate states. Since William Whiting's advices to Lincoln four years earlier, Radical constitutional views to this effect had become common Northern currency.[1]

Naturally the renascent Northern Democracy supported Johnson's contrary view that by mid-1865 the national government had reached the end of its rope with respect to what it could do in the South. For men of conservative bent, the Constitution was a vital barrier against the rising Radical tide of color. The President also hoped that as champion of white-centered conservatism, he could springboard back into the White House for a full term on his own, to last until 1873, when surely the Radical impulse would have grown sluggish. His need was clear for a political ally of adequate respectability to clothe himself and the Northern Democratic spokesmen in new raiment, so to obscure the taints the latter bore from wartime behavior.

He found one close by. The Supreme Court of the United States chose this moment to enter the reconstruction ring. Doing so in a manner destructive of the Republicans' constitutional assumptions, the court forced Radicals to cooperate with the main body of Congressional Republicans in order to fend off this unexpected shaft, and slight as it was, the opportunity slid by for a patient regeneration of Southern society. A slightly more demanding rebuilding of Southern political structures, compared to what the President had established, was the best that came out of the Congress. In short, even Radicals accepted legislation in place of aspiration; they low-

---

[1] John Codman Hurd, "Theories of Reconstruction," *American Law Review*, I (January 1867), 237–264; Matthew Carpenter, *The Powers of Congress* . . . (Washington: Chronicle, 1868).

ered their sights from a reconstruction of politics to the politics of reconstruction.

The tradition among historians is that Congressional Republicans anticipated the judicial attack and in mid-1866, to blunt it, prevented the President from making appointments to the Supreme Court by limiting the number of its members. However, recent re-examination has disclosed that President Johnson signed the bill in question when at least he could have pocket vetoed it or vetoed it outright, as had become a habit. Further, several members of the court expressed approval of the limitation on numbers as a desirable reform.[2] The point is that the Supreme Court unleashed a massive onslaught in January 1867, and being unexpected, the impact on Republicans was the more dismaying.

Just as 1867 opened, the Court declared in the *Milligan* and Test Oath cases that the internal security policies that Lincoln and the Union Army had employed during the war in Indiana's critical Copperhead counties were excessive. It voided a rule Congress had set, requiring lawyers practicing before the Supreme Court to swear first to their past loyalty by means of the "iron clad test oath." And it condemned provisions of Missouri's Radical-written new constitution that excluded from licensed professions those unable to subscribe a similar past loyalty test.[3]

There were new beachheads of judicial review, surpassing even the functional outreaching of the disastrous *Dred Scott* decision just a decade—a lifetime—earlier. The *Milligan* and Test Oath cases form the most radical enlargement of the power of a branch of the national government known in America's history, second only to that which Johnson assumed with respect to his capacity as President to rebuild the South's state governments. Modern anti-totalitarian predilections against martial rule and loyalty tests have overlaid these decisions with an undeserved patina of liberalism. In 1867 Radical Republicans understood better that the only civil liberties the Court was actually defending (save rhetorically) in these cases were those of ex-rebels and recent traitors, white men

---

[2] Stanley Kutler, "Reconstruction and the Supreme Court: The Numbers Game Reconsidered," *Journal of Southern History*, XXXII (February 1966), 42–58.

[3] 4 Wallace 2; 277; 333.

exclusively. There were other Americans then, after all, whose liberties were also at stake.

On January 3, 1867, Thaddeus Stevens argued for Negro suffrage in the South, to be won through Congress' imposition of devices that the Court condemned. A bill Stevens introduced would have disfranchised for at least five years almost all former Confederates. His speech, a portion of which follows, comes unflinchingly to the core of issues.[4]

I desire that as early as possible, without curtailing debate, this House shall come to some conclusion as to what shall be done with the rebel States. This becomes more and more necessary every day; and the late decision of the Supreme Court of the United States has rendered immediate action by Congress upon the question of the establishment of governments in the rebel States absolutely indispensable.

That decision, although in terms perhaps not as infamous as the Dred Scott decision, is yet far more dangerous in its operation upon the lives and liberties of the loyal men of this country. That decision has taken away every protection in every one of these rebel States from every loyal man, black or white, who resides there. That decision has unsheathed the dagger of the assassin, and places the knife of the rebel at the throat of every man who dares proclaim himself to be now, or to have been heretofore, a loyal Union man. If the doctrine enunciated in that decision be true, never were the people of any country anywhere, or at any time, in such terrible peril as are our loyal brethren at the South, whether they be black or white, whether they go there from the North or are natives of the rebel States.

Now, Mr. Speaker, unless Congress proceeds at once to do something to protect these people from the barbarians who are now daily murdering them; who are murdering the loyal whites

---

[4] *CG*, 39 Cong., 2 sess., pp. 251–253.

daily and daily putting into secret graves not only hundreds but thousands of the colored people of that country; unless Congress proceeds at once to adopt some means for their protection, I ask you and every man who loves liberty whether we will not be liable to the just censure of the world for our negligence or our cowardice or our want of ability to do so?

Now, sir, it is for these reasons that I insist on the passage of some such measure as this. This is a bill designed to enable loyal men, so far as I could discriminate them in these States, to form governments which shall be in loyal hands, that they may protect themselves from such outrages as I have mentioned. In States that have never been restored since the rebellion from a state of conquest, and which are this day held in captivity under the laws of war, the military authorities, under this decision and its extension into disloyal States, dare not order the commanders of departments to enforce the laws of the country. One of the most atrocious murderers that has ever been let loose upon any community has lately been liberated under this very decision, because the Government extended it, perhaps according to the proper construction, to the conquered States as well as to the loyal States.

A gentleman from Richmond, who had personal knowledge of the facts, told me the circumstances of the murder. A colored man, driving the family of his employer, drove his wagon against a wagon containing Watson and his family. The wagon of Watson was broken. The next day Watson went to the employer of the colored man and complained. The employer offered to pay Watson every dollar that he might assess for the damage that had been done. "No!" said he, "I claim the right to chastise the scoundrel." He followed the colored man, took out his revolver, and deliberately shot him dead in the presence of that community. No civil authority would prosecute him; and, when taken into custody by the military authority, he is discharged by order of the President under this most injurious and iniquitous decision.

Now, sir, if that decision be the law, then it becomes the more necessary that we should proceed to take care that such a construction as that shall not open the door to greater injuries than have already been sustained. Thus much I have said at the outset of my remarks, which shall not be very long.

The people have once more nobly done their duty. May I ask, without offense, will Congress have the courage to do its duty? Or will it be deterred by the clamor of ignorance, bigotry, and despotism from perfecting a revolution begun without their consent, but which ought not to be ended without their full participation and concurrence? Possibly the people would not have inaugurated this revolution to correct the palpable incongruities and despotic provisions of the Constitution; but having it forced upon them, will they be so unwise as to suffer it to subside without erecting this nation into a perfect Republic?

Since the surrender of the armies of the confederate States of America a little has been done toward establishing this Government upon the true principles of liberty and justice; and but a little if we stop here. We have broken the material shackles of four million slaves. We have unchained them from the stake so as to allow them locomotion, provided they do not walk in paths which are trod by white men. We have allowed them the unwonted privilege of attending church, if they can do so without offending the sight of their former masters. We have even given them that highest and most agreeable evidence of liberty as defined by the "great plebian," the "right to work." But in what have we enlarged their liberty of thought? In what have we taught them the science and granted them the privilege of self-government? We have imposed upon them the privilege of fighting our battles, of dying in defense of freedom, and of bearing their equal portion of taxes; but where have we given them the privilege of ever participating in the formation of the laws for the government of their native land? By what civil weapon have we enabled them to defend themselves against oppression and injustice? . . . Think not I would slander my native land; I would reform it. Twenty years ago I denounced it as a despotism. Then, twenty million white men enchained four million black men. I pronounce it no nearer to a true Republic now when twenty-five million of a privileged class exclude five million from all participation in the rights of government. . . .

What are the great questions which now divide the nation? In the midst of the political Babel which has been produced by the intermingling of secessionists rebels pardoned traitors, hissing Copperheads, and apostate Republicans, such a confusion of tongues is heard that it is difficult to understand either the questions that are asked or the answers that are given. Ask, what is the "President's policy?" and it is difficult to define it. Ask, what is the "policy of Congress?" and the answer is not always at hand.

To reconstruct the nation, to admit new States, to guaranty republican governments to old States are all legislative acts. The President claims the right to exercise them. Congress denies it and asserts the right to belong to the legislative branch. They have determined to defend these rights against all usurpers. They have determined that while in their keeping the Constitution shall not be violated with impunity. This I take to be the great question between the President and Congress. He claims the right to reconstruct by his own power. Congress denies him all power in the matter, except those of advice, and has determined to maintain such denial. "My policy" asserts full power in the Executive. The policy of Congress forbids him to exercise any power therein.

Beyond this I do not agree that the "policy" of the parties are defined. To be sure many subordinate items of the policy of each may be easily sketched. The President is for exonerating the conquered rebels from all the expense and damages of the war, and for compelling the loyal citizens to pay the whole debt caused by the rebellion. He insists that those of our people who were plundered and their property burned or destroyed by rebel raiders shall not be indemnified, but shall bear their own loss, while the rebels shall retain their own property, most of which was declared forfeited by the Congress of the United States. He desires that the traitors (having sternly executed that most important leader, Rickety Weirze, as a high example) should be exempt from further fine, imprisonment, forfeiture, exile, or capital punishment, and be declared entitled to all the rights of loyal citizens. He desires that the States created by him shall be acknowledged as valid States, while at the same time he inconsistently declares that the old rebel States are in full existence, and always have been, and have equal rights with the loyal States. He opposes the amendment to the Constitution which changes the base of representation, and desires the old slave States to have the benefit of their increase of freemen without increasing the number of votes; in short, he desires to make the vote of one rebel in South Carolina equal to the vote of three freemen in Pennsylvania or New York. He is determined to force a solid rebel delegation into Congress from the South, and, together with Northern Copperheads, could at once control Congress and elect all future Presidents.

In opposition to these things, a portion of Congress seems to desire that the conquered belligerent shall, according to the law of nations, pay at least a part of the expenses and damages of the war; and that especially the loyal people who were plundered and impoverished by rebel raiders shall be fully indemnified. A majority of Congress desires that treason shall be made odious, not by bloody executions, but by other adequate punishments.

Congress refuses to treat the States created by him as of any validity, and denies that the old rebel States have any existence which gives them any rights under the Constitution. Congress insists on changing the basis of representation so as to put white voters on an equality in both sections, and that such change shall precede the admission of any State. I deny that there is any understanding, expressed or implied, that upon the adoption of the amendment by any State, that such State may be admitted, (before the amendment becomes part of the Constitution.) Such a course would soon surrender the Government into the hands of rebels. Such a course would be senseless, inconsistent, and illogical. Congress denies that any State lately in rebellion has any government or constitution known to the Constitution of the United States, or which can be recognized as a part of the Union. How, then, can such a State adopt the amendment? To allow it would be yielding the whole question and admitting the unimpaired rights of the seceded States. I know of no Republican who does not ridicule what Mr. Seward thought a cunning movement, in counting Virginia and other outlawed States among those which had adopted the constitutional amendment abolishing slavery. . . .

It is to be regretted that inconsiderate and incautious Republicans should ever have supposed that the slight amendments already proposed to the Constitution, even when incorporated into that instrument, would satisfy the reforms necessary for the security of the Government. Unless the rebel States, before admission, should be made republican in spirit, and placed under the guardianship of loyal men, all our blood and treasure will have been spent in vain. I waive now the question of punishment which, if we are wise, will still be inflicted by moderate confiscations, both as a reproof and example. Having these States, as we all agree, entirely within the power of Congress, it is our duty to take care that no injustice shall remain in their organic laws. Holding them "like clay in the hands of the potter," we must see that no vessel is made for destruction. Having now no governments, they must have enabling acts. The law of last session with regard to Territories settled the principles of such acts. Impartial suffrage, both in electing the delegates and ratifying their proceedings, is now the fixed rule. There is more reason why colored voters should be admitted in the rebel States than in the Territories. In the States they form the great mass of the loyal men. Possibly with their aid loyal governments may be established in most of those States. Without it all are sure to be ruled by traitors; and loyal men, black and white, will be oppressed, exiled, or murdered. There are several good reasons for the passage of this bill. In the first place, it is just. I am now confining my argument to negro suffrage in the rebel States. Have not loyal blacks quite as good a right to choose rulers and make laws as rebel whites? In the second place, it is a necessity in order to protect the loyal white men in the seceded States. The white Union men are in a great minority in each of those States. With them the blacks would act in a body; and it is believed that in each of said States, except one, the two united would form a majority, control the States, and protect themselves. Now they are the victims of daily murder. They must suffer constant persecution or be exiled. The convention of southern loyalists, lately held in Philadelphia, almost unanimously agreed to such a bill as an absolute necessity.

Another good reason is, it would insure the ascendency of the Union party. Do you avow the party purpose? exclaims some horror-stricken demagogue. I do. For I believe, on my conscience, that on the continued ascendency of that party depends the safety of this great nation. If impartial suffrage is excluded in rebel States then every one of them is sure to send a solid rebel representative delegation to Congress, and cast a solid rebel electoral vote. They, with their kindred Copperheads of the North, would always elect the President and control Congress. While slavery sat upon her defiant throne, and insulted and intimidated the trembling North, the South frequently divided on questions of policy between Whigs and Democrats, and gave victory alternately to the sections. Now, you must divide them between loyalists, without regard to color, and disloyalists, or you will be the perpetual vassals of the free-trade, irritated, revengeful South.

For these, among other reasons, I am for negro suffrage in every rebel State. If it be just, it should not be denied; if it be necessary, it should be adopted; if it be a punishment to traitors, they deserve it.

But it will be said, as it has been said, "This is negro equality!" What is negro equality, about which so much is said by knaves, and some of which is believed by men who are not fools? It means, as understood by honest Republicans, just this much, and no more: every man, no matter what his race or color; every earthly being who has an immortal soul, has an equal right to justice, honesty, and fair play with every other man; and the law should secure him those rights. The same law which condemns or acquits an African should condemn or acquit a white man. The same law which gives a verdict in a white man's favor should give a verdict in a black man's favor on the same state of facts. Such is the law of God and such ought to be the law of man. This doctrine does not mean that a negro shall sit on the same seat or eat at the same table with a white man. That is a matter of taste which every man must decide for himself. The law has nothing to do with it. If there be any who are afraid of the rivalry of the black man in office or in business, I have only to advise them to try and beat their competitor in knowledge and business capacity, and there is no danger that his white neighbors will prefer his African rival to himself. I know there is between those who are influenced by this cry of "negro equality" and the opinion that there is still danger that the negro will be the smartest, for I never saw even a contraband slave that had not more sense than such men.

There are those who admit the justice and ultimate utility of granting impartial suffrage to all men, but they think it is impolitic. An ancient philosopher, whose antagonist admitted that what he required was just but deemed it impolitic, asked him: "Do you believe in Hades?" I would say to those above referred to, who admit the justice of human equality before the law but doubt its policy: "Do you believe in hell?"

How do you answer the principle inscribed in our political scripture, "That to secure these rights governments are instituted among men, deriving their just powers from the consent of the governed?" Without such consent government is a tyranny, and you exercising it are tyrants. Of course, this does not admit malefactors to power, or there would soon be no penal laws and society would become an anarchy. But this step forward is an assault upon ignorance and prejudice, and timid men shrink from it. Are such men fit to sit in the places of statesmen?

There are periods in the history of nations when statesmen can make themselves names for posterity; but such occasions are never improved by cowards. In the acquisition of true fame courage is just as necessary in the civilian as in the military hero. In the Reformation there were men engaged as able and perhaps more learned than Martin Luther. Melanethon and others were ripe scholars and sincere reformers, but none of them had his courage. He alone was willing to go where duty called though "devils were as thick as the tiles on the houses." And Luther is the great luminary of the Reformation, around whom the others revolve as satellites and shine by his light. We may not aspire to fame. But great events fix the eye of history on small objects and magnify their meanness. Let us at least escape that condition.

46. GEORGE W. JULIAN

ON REPUBLICAN CROSS-PURPOSES

No one could say that Radical cards were not on the table. But Stevens and his fellows could not translate into statutes their fire, dedication, and concerns. The Republican majority shunted aside

Stevens' proposal in favor of a hotly contested measure that passed over the President's veto on March 2, 1867, the last day of the Congressional session, and became the basic Reconstruction Act. A complex interaction of personalities, purposes, and proposals on the Republican side of the Congress brought forth the historic statute. The lengthy debates reveal that many Republican legislators were still hesitant on the merits of imposing Negro suffrage, or if in favor, were uncertain how to initiate it in a manner to endure in the South and to be acceptable to constituents in the North. Julian's description follows of Republican cross-purposes.[1]

But the strange chaos of opinion which now prevailed was unfavorable to sound thinking or wise acting. Great and far-reaching interests were at stake, but they were made the sport of politicians, and disposed of in the light of their supposed effect upon the ascendancy of the Republican party. Statesmanship was sacrificed to party management, and the final result was that the various territorial bills which had been introduced in both Houses, and the somewhat incongruous bills of Stevens and Ashley, were all superseded by the passage of the "Military bill," which was vetoed by the President, but re-enacted in the face of his objections. This bill was utterly indefensible on principle. It was completely at war with the genius and spirit of democratic government. Instead of furnishing the Rebel districts with civil governments, and providing for a military force adequate to sustain them, it abolished civil government entirely, and installed the army in its place. It was a confession of Congressional incompetence to deal with a problem which Congress alone had the right to solve. Its provisions perfectly exposed it to all the objections which could be urged to the plan of territorial reconstruction, while they inaugurated a centralized military despotism in the place of that system of well-understood local self-government which the territorial policy offered as a preparation for restoration. The measure was analyzed and exposed with

---

[1] Julian, *Political Recollections,* pp. 306–309.

great ability by Henry J. Raymond, whose arguments were unanswered and unanswerable; but nothing could stay the prevailing impatience of Congress for speedy legislation looking to the early return of the rebel districts to their places in the Union. The bill was a legislative solecism. It did not abrogate the existing Rebel State governments. It left the ballot in the hands of white Rebels, and did not confer it upon the black loyalists. It sought to conciliate the power it was endeavoring to coerce. It provided for negro suffrage as one of the fundamental conditions on which the rebellious States should be restored to their places in the Union, but left the negro to the mercy of their black codes, pending the decision of the question of their acceptance of the proposed conditions of restoration. The freedmen were completely in the power of their old masters, so long as the latter might refuse the terms of reconstruction that were offered; and they had the option to refuse them entirely, if they saw fit to prefer their own mad ascendancy and its train of disorders to compulsory restoration. This perfectly inexcusable abandonment of negro suffrage was zealously defended by a small body of conservative Republicans who were still lingering in the sunshine of executive favor, and of whom Mr. Blaine was the chief; and it was through the timely action of Mr. Shellabarger, of Ohio, which these conservatives opposed, that the scheme of reconstruction was finally so amended as to make the Rebel State governments provisional only, and secure the ballot to the negro during the period, whether long or short, which might intervene prior to the work of re-admission. This provision was absolutely vital, because it took from the people of the insurrectionary districts every motive for refusing the acceptance of the terms proposed, and settled the work of reconstruction by this exercise of absolute power by their conquerors. It was this provision which secured the support of the Radical Republicans in Congress; but it did not meet their objections to this scheme of hasty military reconstruction, while these objections have been amply justified by time.

Thaddeus Stevens never appeared to such splendid advantage as a parliamentary leader as in this protracted debate on reconstruction. He was then nearly seventy-six, and was physically so feeble that he could scarcely stand; but his intellectual resources seemed to be perfectly unimpaired. Eloquence, irony, wit, and invective, were charmingly blended in the defense of his positions and his attacks upon his opponents. In dealing with the views of Bingham, Blaine, and Banks, he was by no means complimentary. He referred to them in his closing speech on the bill, on the thirteenth of February, when he said, in response to an interruption by Mr. Blaine, "What I am speaking of is this proposed step toward universal amnesty and universal Andy-Johnsonism. If this Congress so decides, it will give me great pleasure to join in the *io triumphe* of the gentleman from Ohio [Bingham] in leading this House, possibly by forbidden paths, into the sheep-fold or the goat-fold of the President." In speaking of the amendment to the bill offered by General Banks, he said, "It proposes to set up a contrivance at the mouth of the Mississippi, and by hydraulic action to control all the States that are washed by the waters of that great stream." He declared that, "The amendment of the gentleman from Maine lets in a vast number of Rebels, and shuts out nobody. All I ask is that when the House comes to vote upon that amendment, it shall understand that the adoption of it would be an entire surrender of those States into the hands of the Rebels." . . .

47. THE FIRST RECONSTRUCTION ACT

March 2, 1867

Here is the text of the law that occasioned so much heartburning a century ago, and that remains the center of historians' disagreements:[1]

---

[1] U.S. *Statutes at Large*, XIV, 428–429.

An Act to Provide for the more efficient Government of the Rebel States.

WHEREAS no legal State governments or adequate protection for life or property now exists in the rebel States of Virginia, North Carolina, South Carolina, Georgia, Mississippi, Alabama, Louisiana, Florida, Texas, and Arkansas; and whereas it is necessary that peace and good order should be enforced in said States until loyal and republican State governments can be legally established: Therefore,

Be it enacted by the Senate and House of Representatives of the United States of America in Congress assembled, That said rebel States shall be divided into military districts and made subject to the military authority of the United States as hereinafter prescribed, and for that purpose Virginia shall constitute the first district; North Carolina and South Carolina the second district; Georgia, Alabama, and Florida the third district; Mississippi and Arkansas the fourth district; and Louisiana and Texas the fifth district.

SEC. 2. *And be it further enacted,* That it shall be the duty of the President to assign to the command of each of said districts an officer of the army, not below the rank of brigadier-general, and to detail a sufficient military force to enable such officer to perform his duties and enforce his authority within the district to which he is assigned.

SEC. 3. *And be it further enacted,* That it shall be the duty of each officer assigned as aforesaid, to protect all persons in their rights of person and property, to suppress insurrection, disorder, and violence, and to punish, or cause to be punished, all disturbers of the public peace and criminals; and to this end he may allow civil tribunals to take jurisdiction of and to try offenders, or, when in his judgment it may be necessary for the trial of offenders, he shall have power to organize military commissions or tribunals for that purpose, and all interference under color of State authority with the exercise of military authority under this act, shall be null and void.

SEC. 4. *And be it further enacted,* That all persons put under military arrest by virtue of this act shall be tried without unnecessary delay, and no cruel or unusual punishment shall be inflicted, and no sentence of any military commission or tribunal hereby authorized, affecting the life or liberty of any person, shall be executed until it is approved by the officer in command of the district, and the laws and regulations for the government of the army shall not be affected by this act, except in so far as they conflict with its provisions: *Provided,* That no sentence of death under the provisions of this act shall be carried into effect without the approval of the President.

SEC. 5. *And be it further enacted,* That when the people of any one of said rebel States shall have formed a constitution of government in conformity with the Constitution of the United States in all respects, framed by a convention of delegates elected by the male citizens of said State, twenty-one years old and upward, of whatever race, color, or previous condition, who have been resident in said State for one year previous to the day of such election, except such as may be disfranchised for participation in the rebellion or for felony at common law, and when such constitution shall provide that the elective franchise shall be enjoyed by all such persons as have the qualifications herein stated for electors of delegates, and when such constitution shall be ratified by a majority of the persons voting on the question of ratification who are qualified as electors for delegates, and when such constitution shall have been submitted to Congress for examination and approval, and Congress shall have approved the same, and when said State, by a vote of its legislature elected under said constitution, shall have adopted the amendment to the Constitution of the United States, proposed by the Thirty-ninth Congress, and known as article fourteen, and when said article shall have become a part of the Constitution of the United States, said State shall be declared entitled to representation in Congress, and senators and representatives shall be admitted therefrom on their taking the oath prescribed by law, and then and thereafter the preceding sections of this act shall be inoperative in said State: *Provided,* That no person excluded from the privilege of holding office by said proposed amendment to the Constitution of the United States, shall be eligible to election as a member of the convention to frame a constitution for any of said rebel States, nor shall any such person vote for members of such convention.

SEC. 6. *And be it further enacted,* That, until the people of said rebel States shall be by law admitted to representation in the Congress of the United States, any civil governments which may exist therein shall be deemed provisional only, and in all respects subject to the paramount authority of the United States at any time to abolish, modify, control, or supersede the same; and in all elections to any office under such provisional governments all persons shall be entitled to vote, and none others, who are entitled to vote, under the provisions of the fifth section of this act; and no person shall be eligible to any office under any such provisional governments who would be disqualified from holding office under the provisions of the third *article* of said constitutional amendment.

> SCHUYLER COLFAX,
> > *Speaker of the House of Representatives.*
> LA FAYETTE S. FOSTER,
> > *President of the Senate, pro tempore.*

48. SUPPLEMENT TO

THE RECONSTRUCTION ACT

March 23, 1867

Without exterior pressure, Southern whites did not initiate the prescribed procedures. Therefore members of the Fortieth Congress in March 1867 took up the question of a supplement to the Reconstruction Act just passed.[1] Radicals employed the renewed debate as an opportunity again to seek high goals. Typical of much Radical expression is this plea by Sumner for provision of educational and landowning opportunities for Negroes, and for removal from the states of the power to employ race as a determinant for its citizens. Sumner spoke on such themes on March 7 and 11, 1867.[2]

Almost all Congressional Republicans except the Radicals were anxious to have reconstruction legislation drafted as swiftly as possible. The more quickly and inexpensively the Southern states could gain readmission, the better. In the interest of speed the Republican majority considered seriously no practical alternative to employment of military government in the South, to lead as rapidly as possible to formation of civil government. Despite their prophetic tone, Sumner's resolutions went into discard. The supplementary Reconstruction Act of March 23, 1867, reproduced below, passed easily over the President's expected and unavailing veto. It permitted Army commanders to initiate reconstruction processes that Southern whites would not begin, left to themselves.[3]

An Act supplementary to an Act entitled "An Act to provide for the more efficient Government of the Rebel States," passed March second, eighteen hundred and sixty-seven, and to facilitate Restoration.

Be it enacted by the Senate and House of Representatives of the United States of America in Congress assembled, That before the first day of September, eighteen hundred and sixty-seven, the commanding general in each district defined by an act entitled "An act to provide for the more efficient government of the rebel States," passed March second, eighteen hundred and sixty-seven, shall cause a registration to be made

---

[1] The Fortieth Congress met as soon as the Thirty-ninth Congress closed off, on a call from the latter, instead of waiting for the normal meeting time of December 1867 or for a Presidential summons to a special session, sure never to come.

[2] Sumner, *Works,* XI, pp. 129–133.

[3] U.S. *Statutes at Large,* XV, 2–5.

of the male citizens of the United States, twenty-one years
of age and upwards, resident in each county or parish in the
State or States included in his district, which registration shall
include only those persons who are qualified to vote for delegates by the act aforesaid, and who shall have taken and subscribed the following oath or affirmation: "I,——, do solemnly swear (or affirm), in the presence of Almighty God,
that I am a citizen of the State of ——; that I have resided
in said State for —— months next preceding this day, and
now reside in the county of ——, or the parish of ——,
in said State (as the case may be); that I am twenty-one
years old; that I have not been disfranchised for participation
in any rebellion or civil war against the United States, nor
for felony committed against the laws of any State or of the
United States; that I have never been a member of any State
legislature, nor held any executive or judicial office in any
State and afterwards engaged in insurrection or rebellion
against the United States, or given aid or comfort to the enemies thereof; that I have never taken an oath as a member
of Congress of the United States, or as an officer of the United
States, or as a member of any State legislature, or as an
executive or judicial officer of any State, to support the Constitution of the United States, and afterwards engaged in
insurrection or rebellion against the United States, or given
aid or comfort to the enemies thereof; that I will faithfully
support the Constitution and obey the laws of the United
States, and will, to the best of my ability, encourage others
so to do, so help me God"; which oath or affirmation may be
administered by any registering officer.

Sec. 2. *And be it further enacted,* That after the completion
of the registration hereby provided for in any State, at such
time and places therein as the commanding general shall appoint and direct, of which at least thirty days' public notice
shall be given, an election shall be held of delegates to a
convention for the purpose of establishing a constitution and

civil government for such State loyal to the Union, said convention in each State, except Virginia, to consist of the same number of members as the most numerous branch of the State legislature of such State in the year eighteen hundred and sixty, to be apportioned among the several districts, counties, or parishes of such State by the commanding general, giving to each representation in the ratio of voters registered as aforesaid as nearly as may be. The convention in Virginia shall consist of the same number of members as represented the territory now constituting Virginia in the most numerous branch of the legislature of said State in the year eighteen hundred and sixty, to be apportioned as aforesaid.

Sec. 3. *And be it further enacted,* That at said election the registered voters of each State shall vote for or against a convention to form a constitution therefor under this act. Those voting in favor of such a convention shall have written or printed on the ballots by which they vote for delegates, as aforesaid, the words "For a convention," and those voting against such a convention shall have written or printed on such ballots the words "Against a convention." The persons appointed to superintend said election, and to make return of the votes given thereat, as herein provided, shall count and make return of the votes given for and against a convention; and the commanding general to whom the same shall have been returned shall ascertain and declare the total vote in each State for and against a convention. If a majority of the votes given on that question shall be for a convention, then such convention shall be held as hereinafter provided; but if a majority of said votes shall be against a convention, then no such convention shall be held under this act: *Provided,* That such convention shall not be held unless a majority of all such registered voters shall have voted on the question of holding such convention.

Sec. 4. *And be it further enacted,* That the commanding general of each district shall appoint as many boards of registration as may be necessary, consisting of three loyal officers or persons, to make and complete the registration, superintend the election, and make return to him of the votes, list of voters, and of the persons elected as delegates by a plurality of the votes cast at said election; and upon receiving said returns he shall open the same, ascertain the persons elected as delegates, according to the returns of the officers who conducted said election, and make proclamation thereof; and if a majority of the votes given on that question shall be for a convention, the commanding general, within sixty days from the date of election, shall notify the delegates to assemble in convention, at a time and place to be mentioned in the notification, and said convention, when organized, shall proceed to frame a constitution and civil government according to the provisions of this act, and the act to which it is supplementary; and when the same shall have been so framed, said constitution shall be submitted by the convention for ratification to the persons registered under the provisions of this act at an election to be conducted by the officers or persons appointed or to be appointed by the commanding general, as hereinbefore provided, and to be held after the expiration of thirty days from the date of notice thereof, to be given by said convention; and the returns thereof shall be made to the commanding general of the district.

SEC. 5. *And be it further enacted,* That if, according to said returns, the constitution shall be ratified by a majority of the votes of the registered electors qualified as herein specified, cast at said election, at least one half of all the registered voters voting upon the question of such ratification, the president of the convention shall transmit a copy of the same, duly certified, to the President of the United States, who shall forthwith transmit the same to Congress, if then in session, and if not in session, then immediately upon its next assembling; and if it shall moreover appear to Congress that the election was one at which all the registered and qualified electors in the State had an opportunity to vote freely and without restraint, fear, or the influence of fraud, and if the Congress shall be satisfied that such constitution meets the approval of a majority of all the qualified electors in the State, and if the said constitution shall be declared by Congress to be in conformity with the provisions of the act to which this is supplementary, and the other provisions of said act shall have been complied with, and the said constitution shall be approved by Congress, the State shall be declared entitled to representation, and senators and representatives shall be admitted therefrom as therein provided.

SEC. 6. *And be it further enacted,* That all elections in the States mentioned in the said "Act to provide for the more efficient government of the rebel States," shall, during the operation of said act, be by ballot; and all officers making the said registration of voters and conducting said elections shall, before entering upon the discharge of their duties, take and subscribe the oath prescribed by the act approved July second, eighteen hundred and sixty-two, entitled "An act to prescribe an oath of office": *Provided,* That if any person shall knowingly and falsely take and subscribe any oath in this act prescribed, such person so offending and being thereof duly convicted shall be subject to the pains, penalties, and disabilities which by law are provided for the punishment of the crime of wilful and corrupt perjury.

SEC. 7. *And be it further enacted,* That all expenses incurred by the several commanding generals, or by virtue of any orders issued, or appointments made, by them, under or by virtue of this act, shall be paid out of any moneys in the treasury not otherwise appropriated.

SEC. 8. *And be it further enacted,* That the convention for each State shall prescribe the fees, salary, and compensation to be paid to all delegates and other officers and agents herein authorized or necessary to carry into effect the purposes of this act not herein otherwise provided for, and shall provide for the levy and collection of such taxes on the property in such State as may be necessary to pay the same.

SEC. 9. *And be it further enacted,* That the word "article," in the sixth section of the act to which this is supplementary, shall be construed to mean "section."

SCHUYLER COLFAX,
Speaker of the House of Representatives.
B. F. WADE,
President of the Senate pro tempore.

49. CHARLES SUMNER,
SPEECH ON EDUCATION
AND RECONSTRUCTION

March 16, 1867

Radical dissatisfaction with the military stress, and with the concentration on forms in the Reconstruction Act and its proposed supplement, found its spokesman in Sumner. Here is an excerpt from his speech on March 16, not in opposition to the supplemental measure, but in support of his doomed amendment to the supplement, which would have required new Southern state constitutions to provide color-blind educational opportunities to all.[1]

I shall vote for this bill,—not because it is what I desire, but because it is all that Congress is disposed to enact at the present time. I do not like to play the part of Cassandra,—but I

[1] Sumner, *Works,* XI, 146–147, 154–155.

cannot forbear declaring my conviction that we shall regret hereafter that we have not done more. I am against procrastination. But I am also against precipitation. I am willing to make haste; but, following the ancient injunction, I would make haste slowly: in other words, I would make haste so that our work may be well done and the Republic shall not suffer. Especially would I guard carefully all those who justly look to us for protection, and I would see that the new governments are founded in correct principles. You have the power. Do not forget that duties are in proportion to powers.

I speak frankly. Let me, then, confess my regret that Congress chooses to employ the military power for purposes of Reconstruction. The army is for protection. This is its true function. When it undertakes to govern or to institute government, it does what belongs to the civil power. Clearly it is according to the genius of republican institutions that the military should be subordinate to the civil. . . .

By the system you have adopted, the civil is subordinate to the military, and the civilian yields to the soldier. You accord to the army an "initiative" which I would assure to the civil power. I regret this. I am unwilling that Reconstruction should have a military "initiative." I would not see new States born of the bayonet. Leaving to the army its proper duties of protection, I would intrust Reconstruction to provisional governments, civil in character and organized by Congress. You have already pronounced the existing governments illegal. Logically you should proceed to supply their places by other governments, while the military is in the nature of police, until permanent governments are organized, republican in form and loyal in character. During this transition period, permanent governments might be matured on safe foundations and the people educated to a better order of things. As the twig is bent the tree inclines: you may now bend the twig. These States are like a potter's vessel: you may mould them to be vessels of honor or of dishonor. . . .

If this bill cannot be adopted, then I ask that you shall take at least one of its provisions. Require free schools as an essential condition of Reconstruction. But I am met by the objection, that we are already concluded by the Military Bill adopted a few days ago, so that we cannot establish any new conditions. This is a mistake. There is no word in the Military Bill which can have this interpretation. Besides, the bill is only a few days old; so that, whatever its character, nothing is as yet fixed under its provisions. It contains no compact, no promise, no vested right, nothing which may not be changed, if the public interests require. There are some who seem to insist that it is a strait-jacket. On the contrary, this very bill asserts in positive terms "the paramount authority of the United States." Surely this is enough. In the exercise of this authority, it is your duty to provide all possible safeguards. . . .

Sometimes it is argued that it is not permissible to make certain requirements in the new constitutions, although, when the constitutions are presented to Congress for approval, we may object to them for the want of these very things. Thus it is said that we may not require educational provisions, but that we may object to the constitutions, when formed, if they fail to have this safeguard. This argument forgets the paramount power of Congress over the Rebel States, which you have already exercised in ordaining universal suffrage. Who can doubt, that, with equal reason, you may ordain universal education also? And permit me to say that one is the complement of the other. But I do not stop with assertion of the power. The argument that we are to wait until the constitution is submitted for approval is not frank. I wish to be plain and explicit. We have the power, assured by reason and precedent. Exercise it. Seize the present moment. Grasp the precious privilege. There are some who act on the principle of doing as little as possible. I would do as much as possible, believing that all we do in the nature of safeguard must redound to the good of all and to the national fame. It is in this spirit that I now move to require a system of free schools, open to all without distinction of caste. For this great safeguard I ask your votes.

You have prescribed universal suffrage. Prescribe now universal education. The power of Congress is the same in one case as in the other. And you are under an equal necessity to employ it. Electors by the hundred thousand will exercise the franchise for the first time, without delay or preparation. They should be educated promptly. Without education your beneficent legislation may be a failure. The gift you bestow will be perilous. I was unwilling to make education the condition of suffrage; but I ask that it shall accompany and sustain suffrage.

50. GENERAL JOHN A. RAWLINS, SPEECH

June 1867

Most Republicans saw nothing wrong in having the Army serve as the key instrument of reform in the South (any more than after World Wars I and II, Americans objected to the Army's efforts to democratize Germany and Japan). Then, as now, the test was whether civilian overlordship directed the uniformed galaxy.

In any case, a century ago there was no alternative administrative agency in being that was anywhere near as capable as the Army trying to do the reconstruction job. Knowing this, President Johnson tried through indirection to force Army commanders in the South into on-scene policies contrary to the purposes and letter of the Congressional directives. He transferred out of Southern assignments generals of frank Republican sympathies. Obstructive interpretations from Henry Stanbery, the complaisant Attorney General of the United States, threatened to negate the disfranchising provisions of the Reconstruction Acts.

Too busy trying to ward off these counterblows from the White House to pay much serious heed to Sumner's proposals, Congressional Republicans during the middle months of 1867 worried more about whether the national hero, the Army's senior general, Grant, would obey the law or the President. The Army would go with him. Because the Army was the key to reconstruction out of the prescriptions of Congress' law, a sense of crisis attended any attempt by the President to bring the soldiery to heel. The Republicans insisted that as Commander in Chief, the President's constitutional duty was solely to enforce the legislative will.

Out of these imperatives the Republicans had stuck a rider to the March 2, 1867, Army Appropriations Act, the effect of which was to require the President to transmit all orders to lower echelons through Grant, who presumably would counter negative estimations on the powers of Southern commanders. Further, the rider locked Grant in Washington unless the Senate approved a transfer of location or a substitution in his lofty office, a stipulation made because Johnson had tried to get him out of the way on trumped-up missions abroad in order to slip in "Tecumseh" Sherman as his replacement. However, only Grant knew his own heart and mind. All through 1867 Republicans had to gamble on his bent toward their way.

To be sure, heartening evidence existed that he was so inclined. On June 21, Grant's devoted servitor, General John A. Rawlins, offered at Galena, Illinois, a speech well calculated to comfort Republican hearts.[1] Indeed, it is not hyperbolic to say that Grant's reliability provided such stability to American governmental relations at this crucial time as to warrant great praise. Little else could have held in check the increasingly indignant President.[2]

---

[1] Rawlins, *General Grant's Views in Harmony with Congress: Speech, Galena, Illinois, June 21, 1867* (Washington: *Chronicle,* 1868), pp. 11–16.

[2] William J. Ulrich, *The Northern Military Mind in Regard to Reconstruction, 1865–1872.* Unpublished doctoral dissertation, Ohio State University, 1949. See too my "Johnson, Stanton and Grant: A Reconsideration of the Army's Role in the Events Leading to Impeachment," *American Historical Review,* LXVI (June 1960), 85–100.

Obligation of the General Government to Guarantee Republican State Governments.

The Constitution guarantees to each State in this Union a republican form of government, and also provides that no person within this Union shall be deprived of life, liberty, and property without due process of law. That is to say, if any State in this Union, in its own wrong, ceases to be republican in form, the [national] Government will restore it to a republican form; or if a State fails or refuses to protect persons within its jurisdiction in their lives and property, the Government will give that protection. The manner in which, and the means to be used in executing these constitutional obligations are for the President and Congress to decide, and if they deem it necessary they may make use of the army. In fact, ever since those States withdrew their representation from Congress, and organized a government in hostility to the republican idea upon which the Union was founded, it has been deemed necessary by the President and Congress to use the army—first, to break down and destroy their governments in hostility to the Union, and secondly, to enable them to revive and put in motion the State governments they had when they attempted secession, and adapt them to the new condition of society. But as they, in their adaptation of these governments to the new state of society, failed to come up to the requirements of the republican form, and refused their assent to the amendments of the Constitution where its provisions had been affected or impaired by the war, and failed to properly enforce the civil rights bill for the protection of life and property, it was continued there.

The Military Reconstruction Bills.

The manner and means decided to be necessary for the execution of these constitutional obligations, and the restoration of these States to their proper relations with the Government, are set out in what is known as the military reconstruction bills. They are divided into five military districts, subjected to the military authority as prescribed in the bills, and each district is commanded by an officer of the army, whose duty is to protect all persons in their rights of persons and property, to preserve order, and cause criminals and disturbers of the peace to be punished; and to that end he is authorized to allow the local civil tribunals to try offenders, or when in his judgment it is necessary he may organize military commissions to try them, but no sentence of death can be carried into effect without the approval of the President.

To enable the people of each of these States to form a constitution in conformity with the Constitution of the United States in all respects, and extending the elective franchise to their male citizens twenty-one years old and upward, of whatever race, color, or condition, who have been one year resident of the State previous to any election—except such as may have been disfranchised for participation in the rebellion or for felony at common law—and to enable them to participate in the present governments in those States until the new constitutions shall go into effect, the right of suffrage is extended to all male citizens, irrespective of color or previous condition, who can take an oath that they have been, for one year previous to the election or registration, residents of the State, and twenty-one years old, and have not been disfranchised for participation in any rebellion or civil war against the United States, and have never been members of any State Legislature nor held any executive or judicial office in any State and afterward engaged in insurrection or rebellion against the United States, or given aid and comfort to the enemies thereof, and have never taken an oath as member of Congress or officer of the United States, or as member of any State Legislature, or executive or judicial office of any State to support the Constitution of the United States, and afterward engaged in insurrection and rebellion against the United States, or given aid and comfort to the enemies thereof; and to all who cannot take this oath the exercise of the elective franchise is denied, but the moment the new constitutions go into effect the denial of its exercises ceases. Because of their exercise of the offices they once held against the Government and their unfaithfulness to their oaths to support the Constitution, the right to exercise the elective franchise and to hold office is withheld from them until the will of the people of the States shall be made known through their constitutions respectively. When these States respectively shall have adopted their new constitutions and organized their governments under them, and the Legislatures of their new governments shall have ratified the constitutional amendment now pending, if Congress approves of their new government as republican in form, their representatives will be admitted to their seats in Congress.

These acts and the disabilities they impose are temporary, and are to end upon the accomplishment of their purpose, namely, the restoration to these States of republican forms of government, secure the protection of life and property, and settle the questions of the war affecting the Constitution and people of the United States.

The Elective Franchise

is the only sure protection to person and property. It gives one a voice in government, secures to him respect, and insures him the equal benefit of the laws. And when these acts have accomplished their purpose, there will be no male citizen in all these States, of the age of twenty-one years or upwards, except such as are disfranchised for rebellion, or felony at common law, who is not entitled to this right of suffrage, to this voice in their government. The only disability attaching to any such citizens will be that imposed by the third section of the constitutional amendment.

The Reconstruction Acts Constitutional.

That the objects and purposes of the acts are constitutional, there can be no reasonable question, nor do I think the manner and means adopted by the Government to secure these objects unconstitutional. They are in the nature of a writ or execution issued by a court upon a judgment or decree that it has arrived at after a full hearing of the facts and examination of the law in the case, in the hands of a sheriff to execute. If it is for the possession of houses and lands, he goes to the occupant, and if he gives up the possession to the person entitled to it peaceably and in obedience to the writ, that is the end of it; but if he refuses to give up the possession, in virtue of the authority of his writ of execution, he calls in the *posse comitatus*, or power of his county, and puts him out by force, and restores the possession to the rightful person, and that is the end of the writ and the authority of the officer under it.

So the Government having, with a full knowledge of the facts, and their constitutional obligations, determined the necessity of restoring to these States republican forms of government, and of securing to all the people thereof protection in their persons and property, and of settling the questions affecting the Constitution and people resulting from the war, issued its order, the purpose of which is fully set out therein, and placed it in the hands of officers of the army of the rank therein named, with authority to exercise such military power as was necessary to the execution of the purpose of their order, and the moment this purpose is executed their authority ceases. That the use of the military authority contained in these laws was necessary to enable the Government to perform its constitutional obligations, there is no doubt. In all its efforts through the civil authorities it had, we might say, wholly failed. And under the provision of the Constitution authorizing Congress to make all laws necessary and proper for carrying out the powers vested by the Constitution in the Government, the President and Congress are the judges of the necessity, and having determined it, the validity of their acts, being purely political, cannot be questioned. . . .

The Emancipation Amendment.

It may be asked what becomes of the constitutional amendment abolishing slavery which the Southern States have ratified, if they have illegal or anti-republican forms of government. The answer is they are governments *de facto,* nevertheless, and acts of theirs, especially those directly tending to the settlement of the questions involved in the war, or to render unquestionable the acts of the Government necessitated by the war, if accepted and ratified by the Government, as their action in this case has been, are binding and valid to all intents and purposes. Besides, it is not admitted that the amendment was not valid without their concurrence. To hold that it was not would be to admit a weakness in our Constitution inconsistent with the national life it is intended to perpetuate. . . .

Universal Suffrage.

It is to be hoped that all the States that have not conferred the right of suffrage on the emancipated race may deem it the part of wisdom, as well as justice, to do so at the earliest practical period, and not by delay in doing so compel an amendment of the Constitution for that purpose—an amendment which, with the aid of the eleven Southern States, in which it is extended to them, would be sure to be adopted. It may be thought by some that these States could not be relied on for such aid, because of the hope that may exist among their white citizens of securing at some time the disfranchisement of the colored citizens, as was once done in

North Carolina and Tennessee; but if there is any such hope it will be forever dissipated by a clause that I have no doubt will be inserted in all of their constitutions, providing that no amendment to them shall ever be made abridging the elective franchise as therein declared.

No Danger from Extension of the Elective Franchise.

There need be no apprehension of danger to our institutions from the extension of the elective franchise to the African race on account of their great number and ignorance. The love of liberty and of the forms of free government are too much a part of the American character ever to be affected in any such way. The men of the South who made the determined and desperate fight for the enslavement of the African because of his value as property, nevertheless love and appreciate liberty for themselves. And the African, elevated from the degradation of slavery, rendered respectable by his voice in government, admitted to all sources of intelligence, inspired by the same love of freedom, speaking the same language and worshipping the same God, will rise rapidly in the scale of knowledge and the cloud of ignorance that envelopes him will as rapidly pass away, and he will not fail "to help to keep the jewel of liberty in the family of freedom." And that peace so long desired, but which can never be had in a government like ours while a political right accorded to one is denied to another, will prevail through all the land.

No Danger from the Army.

Nor need fears be entertained of danger to the people's liberties from the army. The army is of the people, and has ever been with the Government, and no one has been, or ever will be, mad enough in their purpose to destroy the liberties of the country to rely upon its assistance. On the contrary, the first thing they would do would be to get rid of it. What did the leaders in the rebellion just closed do? With the Secretary of War, (Floyd,) the adjutant general of the army, (Cooper,) the quartermaster general of the army, (Joe Johnston,) and the chief of staff to the lieutenant general commanding the army, (Lee)—all in their interest, did they concentrate the army in the neighborhood of Richmond or Harper's Ferry, that they might at the opportune moment seize the capital and Government of the United States? Far from it. They placed it beyond the people's reach, virtually abolished it, and sent our ships of war into the furthest seas. They knew too well, when the hour of trial came, on which side the army and navy would be found; that "Yankee Doodle," and not "Dixie," would be the tune they would march and fight to.

At the close of the rebellion among no part of the people of the country was there a greater desire to be found than in the army for the immediate restoration of the people in the rebellious States to their rights of civil government, and the withdrawal, at the earliest practicable moment, of military authority from among them. And to-day, whatever may be said to the contrary, there are no men in all the United States more anxious to have the people of the South comply with the requirements of the Government, that they may be relieved of the exercise of the authority that has been imposed upon them, than are the five military commanders there. And whatever they may do, you may rest assured, is intended by them to facilitate the complete restoration of civil authority, and to end their military power.

No Danger from the Supreme Court.

Nor need the people have fears of danger to their liberties from the Supreme Court of the United States. Its recent decisions on the military commission and test-oath cases, that seemed to create such uneasy apprehensions in the public mind, were in the interest of individual liberty and the vindication of men's rights under the Constitution, and not the imposing of disabilities on them. They do not seek to deny the validity of military tribunals in States and districts where all civil tribunals were suspended or destroyed by actual war, or where, resultant from that war, the civil tribunals had ceased to protect society by the punishment of offenders against it. They are far different from the decision in the Dred Scott case, which, after denying a man's right to a hearing in court on the question of his freedom and remanding him to bondage, sought to doom the very earth to constitutional slavery.

Government, in the exercise of its war powers, may find it necessary sometimes to deal arbitrarily with individual rights, or in the tread of mighty armies they may be trampled under foot, but they are never lost sight of by an independent and honest judiciary. Much has been said of the power of one of the judges of the Supreme Court, in cases where the court is equally divided, to declare unconstitutional and void a statute or act of the United States which has met the approval of both the other departments of the Government, or been passed by the requisite majority in both houses of Congress, who, equally with the Supreme Court, are judges of the constitutionality of their own acts. By the Constitution the people vested the establishment of the Supreme Court in Congress, and extended its jurisdiction to all cases in law and equity arising under the Constitution, the laws of the United States, and treaties made, or which might be made, under the authority of the United States.

Suits are usually brought to obtain decisions, and the simpler and less difficult the mode of arriving at them is the better it is for the suitors. And Congress and the President in its establishment, perhaps, had more in view the interests of suitors than decreasing the chances of their own acts being declared null and void by requiring the concurrence of a greater number of the judges in any opinion having that effect. Otherwise they would have gone to the Constitution and ascertained what rule the people, whose agents they were, adopted relative to the other departments of Government, or affecting the Constitution, and applied the rule they there found to all decisions of the court invalidating any law or act of the United States.

If the executive department of Government disapproves of any law or resolution of Congress requiring its approval, two-thirds of both houses are required to concur in its passage or adoption. To convict the President in case of impeachment, two-thirds of all the Senators present must concur. To expel a member from either branch of Congress, two-thirds of the branch to which he belongs must concur. When the choice of President and Vice President devolves upon Congress, it requires a quorum of two-thirds of the several States to be represented in the House of Representatives to enable them to choose the President, and a quorum of two-thirds of the whole number of Senators to enable the Senate to choose the Vice President. To propose amendments to the Constitution, two-thirds of both branches of Congress must concur, or the Legislatures, or conventions of two-thirds of all the States must join in proposing them. To enter into any treaty with foreign nations, requires the concurrence with the President of two thirds of the Senate. To require the concurrence of all the judges would enable any one of them to prevent any decisions, and destroy the greatest constitutional purpose of the court altogether.

Freedom of Speech.

At the commencement of the rebellion, in fifteen States of this Union, except in one or two places, that provision of the Constitution that Congress shall never make any law abridging freedom of speech or of the press was, when they related to the subject of slavery, entirely nullified. No one could speak or print anything against the impolicy or evil of it, or in favor of its abolition, and in the other States and Territories it was seriously impaired by the same subject—the only one that ever did seriously affect it. Now that it is gone, and the people whose rights it involved are having those rights restored to them, may we not reasonably hope that freedom of speech and of the press may obtain to their pristine vigor in all the United States of America, never again to be impaired. When the measures of the Government for the restoration of the seceding States to their proper relations in the Union are consummated, the supremacy of the Constitution will be maintained, and the Union preserved with all the dignity, equality and rights of the several States unimpaired. There will be representatives in Congress from every one, and the State governments of each will alone afford protection to persons and property, and regulate in their own way their domestic affairs. . . .

51. SUPPLEMENT TO THE

RECONSTRUCTION ACT

July 19, 1867

Anticipating the sense of Rawlins' message, Republican Radicals and moderates had joined hands to produce another supplement to the basic March 2 statute on reconstruction. Passed over the President's unavailing veto on July 19, the new act countered his intrigues. It promised Grant and his area commanders in the South Congress' support if they complied with Congressional enactments, and it gave concrete expression to the theory that Thad Stevens, among other Radicals, had been trumpeting since early in the war, that the South was a political vacuum. It is a high point of Radical triumph; it is also a closing off of effective opportunity for the kind of reconstruction for which Sumner, Julian, and others had been pleading.

Here is the text of the act, July 19, 1867, supplementary to the statute on reconstruction of March 2, 1867.[1]

An Act supplementary to an Act entitled "An Act to provide for the more efficient Government of the Rebel States," passed on the second day of March, eighteen hundred and sixty-seven, and the Act supplementary thereto, passed on the twenty-third day of March, eighteen hundred and sixty-seven.

Be it enacted by the Senate and House of Representatives of the United States of America in Congress assembled, That it is hereby declared to have been the true intent and meaning of the act of the second day of March, one thousand eight hundred and sixty-seven, entitled "An act to provide for the more efficient government of the rebel States," and of the act supplementary thereto, passed on the twenty-third day of March, in the year one thousand eight hundred and sixty-seven, that the governments then existing in the rebel States of Virginia, North Carolina, South Carolina, Georgia, Mississippi, Alabama, Louisiana, Florida, Texas, and Arkansas were not legal State governments; and that thereafter said governments, if continued, were to be continued subject in all respects to the military commanders of the respective districts, and to the paramount authority of Congress.

SEC. 2. *And be it further enacted,* That the commander of any district named in said act shall have power, subject to the disapproval of the General of the army of the United States, and to have effect till disapproved, whenever in the opinion of such commander the proper administration of said act shall

---

[1] U.S. *Statutes at Large,* XV, 14–16.

require it, to suspend or remove from office, or from the performance of official duties and the exercise of official powers,
any officer or person holding or exercising, or professing to hold
or exercise, any civil or military office or duty in such district
under any power, election, appointment or authority derived
from, or granted by, or claimed under, any so-called State or
the government thereof, or any municipal or other division
thereof, and upon such suspension or removal such commander, subject to the disapproval of the General as aforesaid,
shall have power to provide from time to time for the performance of the said duties of such officer or person so suspended
or removed, by the detail of some competent officer or soldier
of the army, or by the appointment of some other person, to
perform the same, and to fill vacancies occasioned by death,
resignation, or otherwise.

SEC. 3. *And be it further enacted,* That the General of the
army of the United States shall be invested with all the powers
of suspension, removal, appointment, and detail granted in the
preceding section to district commanders.

SEC. 4. *And be it further enacted,* That the acts of the officers
of the army already done in removing in said districts persons
exercising the functions of civil officers, and appointing others
in their stead, are hereby confirmed: *Provided,* That any person heretofore or hereafter appointed by any district commander to exercise the functions of any civil office, may be
removed either by the military officer in command of the district, or by the General of the army. And it shall be the duty
of such commander to remove from office as aforesaid all persons who are disloyal to the government of the United States,
or who use their official influence in any manner to hinder,
delay, prevent, or obstruct the due and proper administration
of this act and the acts to which it is supplementary.

SEC. 5. *And be it further enacted,* That the boards of registration provided for in the act entitled "An act supplementary
to an act entitled 'An act to provide for the more efficient gov-

ernment of the rebel States,' passed March two, eighteen
hundred and sixty-seven, and to facilitate restoration," passed
March twenty-three, eighteen hundred and sixty-seven, shall
have power, and it shall be their duty before allowing the
registration of any person, to ascertain, upon such facts or
information as they can obtain, whether such person is entitled
to be registered under said act, and the oath required by said
act shall not be conclusive on such question, and no person
shall be registered unless such board shall decide that he is
entitled thereto; and such board shall also have power to
examine, under oath, (to be administered by any member
of such board,) any one touching the qualification of any person claiming registration; but in every case of refusal by the
board to register an applicant, and in every case of striking his
name from the list as hereinafter provided, the board shall
make a note or memorandum, which shall be returned with the
registration list to the commanding general of the district, setting forth the grounds of such refusal or such striking from the
list: *Provided,* That no person shall be disqualified as member
of any board of registration by reason of race or color.

Sec. 6. *And be it further enacted,* That the true intent and
meaning of the oath prescribed in said supplementary act is,
(among other things,) that no person who has been a member
of the legislature of any State, or who has held any executive
or judicial office in any State, whether he has taken an oath
to support the Constitution of the United States or not, and
whether he was holding such office at the commencement of
the rebellion, or had held it before, and who has afterwards
engaged in insurrection or rebellion against the United States,
or given aid or comfort to the enemies thereof, is entitled to
be registered or to vote; and the words "executive or judicial
office in any State" in said oath mentioned shall be construed
to include all civil offices created by law for the administration
of any general law of a State, for the administration of justice.

Sec. 7. *And be it further enacted,* That the time for completing the original registration provided for in said act may, in the discretion of the commander of any district be extended to the first day of October, eighteen hundred and sixty-seven; and the boards of registration shall have power, and it shall be their duty, commencing fourteen days prior to any election under said act, and upon reasonable public notice of the time and place thereof, to revise, for a period of five days, the registration lists, and upon being satisfied that any person not entitled thereto has been registered, to strike the name of such person from the list, and such person shall not be allowed to vote. And such board shall also, during the same period, add to such registry the names of all persons who at that time possess the qualifications required by said act who have not been already registered; and no person shall, at any time, be entitled to be registered or to vote by reason of any executive pardon or amnesty for any act or thing which, without such pardon or amnesty, would disqualify him from registration or voting.

SEC. 8. *And be it further enacted,* That section four of said last-named act shall be construed to authorize the commanding general named therein, whenever he shall deem it needful, to remove any member of a board of registration and to appoint another in his stead, and to fill any vacancy in such board.

SEC. 9. *And be it further enacted,* That all members of said boards of registration and all persons hereafter elected or appointed to office in said military districts, under any so-called State or municipal authority, or by detail or appointment of the district commanders, shall be required to take and to subscribe the oath of office prescribed by law for officers of the United States.

SEC. 10. *And be it further enacted,* That no district commander or member of the board of registration, or any of the officers or appointees acting under them, shall be bound in his action by any opinion of any civil officer of the United States.

SEC. 11. *And be it further enacted,* That all the provisions of this act and of the acts to which this is supplementary shall be construed liberally, to the end that all the intents thereof may be fully and perfectly carried out.

SCHUYLER COLFAX,
Speaker of the House of Representatives.
B. F. WADE,
President of the Senate pro tempore.

PART ELEVEN

Reconstruction and Impeachment

52. *THE NATION,* EDITORIAL

July 18, 1867

The Reconstruction Acts initiated the most concentrated, wide-sweeping alterations in American state and local governments, and in constitutional and political institutions, since the colonies wrested themselves free of the British Empire. Radical Reconstruction in the South was the most radical effort in the world's history to that time (and perhaps to the present) to accommodate in physical propinquity recent masters and slaves of different races, on terms of equality before the law, and to reach this improvement within a very brief time span.[1] At first under Army direction, then under civilian self-rule with Army support (forming what critical commentators decried as the "black-and-tan" state governments composed of carpetbaggers, scallawags, and Negroes), Southern states moved into the mainstream of nineteenth-century democratic practice. Tax-supported schools, hospitals, asylums, and roads came forth in unprecedentedly larger number—though in the schools, integration of races did not ensue. Judicial codes received review, and antiquated contents enjoyed fairer revision.

---

[1] And inexpensively as well. As example, the Congress provided by joint resolution on March 30, 1867, a maximum of only five hundred thousand dollars to cover Army expenses. U.S. *Statutes at Large,* XV, 29.

Tax loads fell into more equitable patterns. Electoral districts assumed shapes less likely to overweigh old centers of control. Not even the most ardent defenders of the Dunning tradition among historians have suggested that these advances would have been possible or even likely if Congress had not employed a prod.[2]

Most important to Northern Radicals was that Negroes participated in all this as voters and as officeholders in all branches of government and on all levels. What follows is an editorial from the influential journal of opinion, *The Nation*, in mid-July 1867, reflecting this primary reaction. Note how the success of biracial politics in the South inspired the editorialist to argue for Northern states to democratize themselves in like manner. The effect was further to concentrate the attention of Northern well-wishers of the Negro, and of supporters of Congressional reconstruction generally, on political aspects rather than on the economic questions that Sumner and Julian posed at different times. Further, the impact of the unexpectedly smooth course of reconstruction down South was to increase pressure in the North to count the job there finished.[3]

The Republican Party in the South.

Registration under military control has added one more to the hundred proofs of the utter failure of "Conservative" prophecies concerning the freedmen of the South. Notwithstanding all demonstrations to the contrary—in spite of the clearest evidence that science could draw from shins, hair, and cuticle, or wisdom draw from long experience, whip in hand, on cotton plantations—it is now admitted that the negro can fight, will work, and is both capable of receiving education and eager

---

[2] See John Hope Franklin, *Reconstruction, passim,* and Stampp, *Era of Reconstruction,* ch. 6, for the fullest analysis and soundest interpretations; and two articles by Jack B. Scroggs, "Southern Reconstruction: A Radical View," *Journal of Southern History,* XXIV (November 1958), 407–429; "Carpetbagger Constitutional Reform in the South Atlantic States, 1867–1868," *ibid,* XXVII (November 1961), 475–493.

[3] *The Nation,* V (July 18, 1867), 50.

for it. Almost the only predictions of "those who knew the
negro best" which have not long since been so thoroughly
overthrown by facts as to be ridiculous, are the assertions (1)
that the mass of the freedmen care nothing about the right of
suffrage, and (2) that in exercising that right they will be entirely controlled by their old masters. The war of races, which
Mr. Johnson dwelt upon with so much emphasis as certain to
result from the admission of negroes to vote, has long been
a public jest. Wade Hampton made it absurd in a single day.

There were certainly plausible grounds for believing that
the freedmen would be indifferent to the right of suffrage.
Never having had the privilege, and having been trained from
time immemorial to seek for happiness only in sensual indul-
gences to which such a franchise could not contribute, it did
not seem unlikely, from that point of view, that they would be
indifferent to it. But, on the other hand, those who believed in
the natural capacity of the colored race for improvement insisted that they had learned or would rapidly learn the value
of political rights, and would not fail to exercise them. The
result of the registration thus far in every Southern state has
justified the latter view. In every State and, as far as we know,
in every county, no matter how secluded from Northern influences, a far larger proportion of the resident colored voters
have registered than of whites. In Virginia the colored electors
are in a large majority on the roll, although the whites, if all
registered, would outnumber them by nearly 40,000. In Louisiana, where the numbers of the two races are nearly equal, the
colored voters on the register number twice as many as the
white. The case is much the same in Georgia, Alabama, and,
indeed, everywhere. The freedmen have, in every place where
they have been properly protected from intimidation, manifested an eagerness to be enrolled for which there is no precedent among white people North or South.

The only prediction that remains to be disproved is, that the
freedmen will vote under the dictation of their former masters.

It is abundantly proved that this will not be the case in large cities, and the registration of such vast numbers of the plantation negroes, contrary to the well-known wishes of their masters, affords strong evidence that they too will vote independently of local influences. Indeed, no reasonable man who has watched the course of affairs in the South can doubt that almost the entire body of the newly enfranchised race desire to cast their votes for men who are heartily in sympathy with the party and the policy which secured their freedom. The only real danger lies in the want of organization and information among the colored people, which leaves them open to imposition alike from secret enemies and from indiscreet and over-zealous friends.

A serious duty is thus devolved upon the Republicans of the North. They have the best organization ever known in the political history of this country, abundant wealth, and every facility for conducting political campaigns. They have now an opportunity to extend the same organization over the entire Union, and thus to secure the perpetuity of the nation even more effectually than has been done by war. They cannot with any wisdom or safety leave their Southern allies to carry on the work alone. Where all are inexperienced, the most presumptuous, and therefore the most unfit, are likely to rush to the helm, and guide a movement with which they ardently sympathize, but the perils of which they do not comprehend. There will be distracting quarrels for leadership, in which the power of the majority may be lost. Demagogues will raise false issues by the use of enticing programmes which can never be carried out. The large number of Southern white men who are now coming into the Republican party may be driven off by the jealousy of petty leaders anxious for office, and parties be thus divided strictly upon color—a result greatly to be deprecated, and which may, by a little prudence, be entirely avoided.

We do not wish that the course of Southern politics should

be absolutely dictated by Northern men; but it is well known that judicious Northerners have the confidence of all in the South who are disposed to act with the Republican party, and can reconcile conflicting interests more completely than any Southern man can do. A striking example of this has recently been given in Virginia, where the presence of a few gentlemen from the North resulted in healing a bitter feud in the party, and in starting a movement which is now spreading over the whole State, promising to bring within the Republican ranks almost every man who was sincerely for the Union before the late war.

The aid which the North can and ought to give will consist in giving money to defray necessary political expenses, in sending out public speakers, who should be men able to interest large audiences, and of moderate language, free from passion and revengeful feelings, in supplying sound advisers who can harmonize internal difficulties and suggest plans of organization, and in distributing political tracts or papers, which should be simple enough for children to read to their parents, short, plain, and to the point. Congressional speeches are not of much value for this purpose. They are calculated for Northern latitudes. Their tone is not often likely to attract Southern whites, and they are not simple enough for the colored people, who depend almost entirely upon their children for reading matter.

We are glad to see that Massachusetts has taken hold of this duty in earnest, and that an association has been organized under the presidency of Mr. George C. Richardson for this purpose. The names of the officers are all good, but we notice with special pleasure the names of Messrs. Andrew, Atkinson, Dana, and Loring whose abilities and discretion assure us that the work will be conducted under the best auspices. We need not urge such men to see to it that nothing is done to excite the freedmen to feelings of revenge or with delusive hopes of direct benefits from Government; while we are equally confident that they will seek to arouse the allies of the Republican party over all the South to a sense of the importance of the coming elections, and to give them an organization which will bring out their full strength and attract additions to their number. Similar associations might well be formed in every large State, or which would perhaps be better, the Massachusetts association might nationalize itself, and give to all who co-operate in the movement the benefit of the wisdom and efficiency which we are persuaded will characterize the parent society.

53. ARMY COMMANDS IN MISSISSIPPI,

AND DANIEL CHAMBERLAIN, SPEECH

October 4, 1870

During the last half of 1867, actions by the President and by many Southern whites made it clear that reconstruction was only as complete as the determination of Congressional Republicans would have it. Following up his efforts in June to cow the Army commanders in the South through the removal of Sickles and Sheridan, in August Johnson suspended War Secretary Stanton. In this instance the President acted conformably to the Tenure of Office law, enacted through Radical efforts on March 2, 1867. This law protected in their offices government personnel whose appointments had received Senate approval. Removals had to win senatorial assent as well. In a recess of Congress the President could suspend officials, then report on the matter within ten days of its reassembly. In turn, the Senate could confirm the President's action or reject it, and the latter decision required him to receive back the suspended officer.

As interim successor for Stanton, in August 1867 the President brought Grant in to the Cabinet. Wearing two hats as interim uniformed War Secretary, Grant secretly encouraged Army commanders in the South to hold fast until a political decision was clear.

Field officers needed stiffening. Suits swiftly maturing in state and federal courts were threatening them with heavy damages for enforcing the reconstruction statutes, and might result in decisions that these laws were invalid. Southern whites were resorting to violence against Negroes who ungratefully rejected leadership of old masters in favor of the proferred hands of new Republicans. And in elections in the North in the late autumn of 1867, several states returned Democratic candidates and/or rejected amendments to open polls there to Negroes.

Now unresting, the President employed his December 1867 message to Congress again to assault reconstruction legislation. In frankly racist terms he condemned all efforts to raise Negroes to political equality through government effort. He followed this with removals from Southern commands of Generals Ord and Pope. Then, to cap matters, Johnson refused to obey the Tenure of Office law, though in August 1867 he had suspended Stanton in conformity with its terms; and when soon after the turn of the new year 1868 the Senate ordered Stanton back into the Cabinet, Johnson refused to receive him.

Grant destroyed the President's weak lines. He turned over to Stanton the keys to the disputed war office. For weeks to follow, Stanton blockaded himself physically in the War Secretary's rooms. At last and too late, Johnson hesitated to push further; and the Supreme Court, his only ally in Washington, beat an undignified retreat when opportunity again came before it to void the reconstruction statutes.

Though comic elements existed in this complex interaction of personalities, ambitions, and institutions, the stakes were too high and the risks too great for much easy laughter. At least a stoppage of reconstruction was in the cards if the President's nominee to succeed Stanton and Grant as War Secretary managed to take over. At worst the Army could split into two antagonistic camps, in the pattern made fearfully familiar from events in Europe and Latin America. Either way, the aspirations for the betterment of millions of Negroes would have been swept into discard in 1868. Another civil war was not an inconceivable result.[1]

The following documents indicate what President Johnson was fruitlessly trying to block, first by obstructive interpretations of the reconstruction legislation, and then by his direct grabs at the reins of control of the highest echelons of the military institution. First in order are two regulations issued by an Army commander in the South, to provide conformity in matters of civil and political rights with the laws and intentions of Congress. Second is a campaign document of 1870, a speech by that "prince of carpetbaggers," Daniel Chamberlain, in support of Republican politicians and policies there.[2]

HEADQUARTERS 4TH MILITARY DISTRICT,
(DEPARTMENT OF MISSISSIPPI.)

Jackson, Miss., April 14, 1869.

GENERAL ORDERS, }
     No. 28.   }

The amount of poll tax levied under the existing laws of this State for state, county and municipal purposes being deemed exorbitant and oppressive on the poorer classes, it is hereby ordered:

That the following clause in an act approved February 21st, 1867, entitled "An act to amend an act entitled an act to raise a revenue to defray the expenses of the government of the State of Mississippi, approved December 5th, 1865," be annulled, viz:

"On each and every male inhabitant of this State between the ages of twenty-one years and fifty-five years the sum of

---

[1] William A. Russ, Jr., "Was there a Danger of a Second Civil War during Reconstruction?" *Mississippi Valley Historical Review*, XXV (June 1938), 39–58; Thomas and Hyman, *Stanton*, ch. 28.

[2] Originals of the Army orders are in possession of the author. Reprinted as a pamphlet, the Chamberlain speech is titled *The Facts and the Figures: The Practical and Truthful Record of the Republican Party of South Carolina, . . . Speech, October 4,* [1870] (n.p., n.d.).

two dollars, except disabled State and Confederate soldiers; to be assessed and collected in accordance with the provisions of the act to which this is an amendment."

And in lieu thereof tax collectors will be governed by the following:

"On each and every male inhabitant of this State, between the ages of twenty-one and fifty-five years, the sum of one dollar to be assessed and collected in accordance with the provisions of the Revised Code of 1857, for assessing and collecting a poll tax on free white persons:"

It is further ordered, That the special tax which the Boards of Police are authorized to levy by Article 22, page 417, of the Revised Code of 1857, shall not, so far as relates to poll tax, exceed fifty per centum of the State tax as established by this order. It is not the intention to deprive Boards of Police of the authority conferred upon them by Article 16, page 416, of the Revised Code of 1857, to levy a tax for county purposes not exceeding the State tax as fixed by this order.

It is further ordered, That no poll or capitation tax shall be levied by the corporate authorities of any city or town in this State.

It is further ordered, That the tax collectors of the several counties of this State and of the several cities and towns therein, shall be governed by the provisions of this order from and after its receipt by them. All proceedings which may have been instituted for the collection of taxes, shall, so far as they relate to poll tax in excess of what is required in this order, be discontinued. Tax collectors will continue the collection of so much of the taxes heretofore assessed and levied for state, county and municipal purposes as shall not be in conflict with the provisions of this order.

And it is further ordered, That upon the receipt of this order, the Tax Collector, Probate Clerk and President of the Board of Police of each county, or in case of vacancy in either of the last named offices, the Tax Collector and the remaining officer, shall forthwith prepare a schedule of the names of all persons within the county who have, prior to the receipt of this order, failed to pay the poll tax assessed upon them according to the last assessment roll, and the amount thereof; one copy of which will be forwarded to the Auditor of Public Accounts, one to be filed in the office of the Probate Clerk and one to be retained by the Tax Collector.

The receipt of this order will be acknowledged by letter to the Acting Assistant Adjutant General at these Headquarters.

By command of Brevet Major General Ames:

WILLIAM ATWOOD,
Aide-de-Camp,
Acting Assistant Adjutant General.

HEADQUARTERS 4TH MILITARY DISTRICT,
(DEPARTMENT OF MISSISSIPPI,)

Jackson, Miss., April 27, 1869.

GENERAL ORDERS,)
No. 32.   }

It is hereby ordered that all persons, without respect to race, color or previous condition of servitude, who possess the qualifications prescribed by Article 135, page 499, of the Revised Code of 1857, shall be competent jurors.

For the purpose of giving this order immediate effect, the Tax Assessors of the several counties in this State are hereby directed to proceed immediately in the manner prescribed in Article 135, page 499, of the Revised Code of 1857, to make out supplementary lists of the names of all persons found in their respective counties qualified to serve as jurors whose names are not now on the jury lists, and deliver the same to the Clerks of the Circuit Courts of their respective counties on or before the time prescribed by law for the meeting of the next Circuit Court of the county.

The Clerks of the Circuit Courts in the several judicial districts of the State are directed immediately upon the receipt of such supplementary lists, to record and give effect to the same in the manner prescribed by Article 136, page 499, of the Revised Code of 1857.

The provisions of this order are not intended to relieve the Tax Assessors of the several counties from the performance of the duties imposed on them to make out, annually, the lists of persons qualified to serve as jurors in accordance with the requirements of Article 135, page 499, of the Revised Code of 1857, provided, however, that in the preparation of such lists no distinction shall be made on account of race, color or previous condition of servitude.

By command of Brevet Major General AMES:

WILLIAM ATWOOD,
Aide-de-Camp,
Acting Assistant Adjutant General.

[Chamberlain's speech follows:]

. . . The close of the war found the State stripped of her wealth and prostrate at the feet of the Union. Those who had led the State in her mad career of attempted secession, expected that punishment of some sort would be visited upon them. Under the laws of the country, a crime had been committed which could justly consign the leaders to condign punishment. Yet I rejoice to think that our free Republic was strong enough and brave enough to say to every leader of a causeless and murderous war: "Your crimes have been great, but you are now conquered. Go in peace. The Republic you sought to destroy is strong enough to remit all penalties and invite you back, clothed with all your former rights, to a share in that government which you have vainly sought to destroy."

It was an act of unparalleled nobility; a scene of the highest moral sublimity; no confiscating property; no trials for treason; no imprisonments; no scaffolds; nothing but a full pardon for the past and a cordial welcome to forfeited rights and privileges.

Unfortunately for our State, the prejudices of education and habit were too deeply fixed, and spite of the hopes and advice of some of your ablest men, the North soon saw that color and caste, and not freedom and justice, were still the controlling sentiments of the State. Then followed the demand for guaranties that those whom the war had made free should be kept free; that the slavery which had been abolished in name should no longer exist in reality. Universal suffrage was decreed by the Congress of the United States, as the just and reasonable guaranty of national peace, and the common claim and right of all her citizens. This was the logical result of universal freedom, the legitimate fruit of those principles which inspired our fathers in their own struggle against oppression. Then for the first time our country redeemed the promise of her youth and made the words of her immortal declaration, the living and governing principle of the Republic. No result less ample and generous could have justified the sacrifices of the war. No basis less enduring and substantial could have upheld that Union which should be destined to lead the advance of civilization and progress for the centuries to come. . . .

The New Government and Its Attitude.

In obedience to a change so complete, but so unwelcome to a large portion of our fellow-citizens, as the result of a civic revolution so glorious and benignant, the present State government of South Carolina was called into existence.

In July, 1868, the present Administration, elected under the reconstruction acts of Congress, entered upon its work. I need hardly pause for a moment to remind you that it represented, politically, very few of the white voters of our State. So great was the opposition to impartial suffrage and to the general policy of Congressional reconstruction that the mass of the white people of our State either arrayed themselves against the present Administration, or stood aloof in silent dissatisfaction and chagrin. . . .

On the one side stood the newly enfranchised citizens of the State with comparatively few of the other race, destitute, in a great measure, of political experience, and strong only in numbers and in that cause which drew to them the hopes and prayers of the good and true everywhere. On the other side stood the old governing class of the State, chafing still under defeat, regarding universal suffrage as the last folly and indignity of their conquerors, and determined to lend no aid, no countenance, no support to the new Government.

I am sure I do not overstate the difficulties which stared us in the face in July, 1868. We were on the eve of a Presidential election, wherein was put to hazard the entire work of reconstruction. The Democratic party of the North boldly proclaimed its purpose to undo the work of a Republican Congress, and to reverse those great steps of justice and freedom which had brought the present Administration into power. The promises of the Northern Democracy were joyfully accepted by our political opponents here, and the expectation was fully indulged and expressed that by the success of the Democratic party in the Presidential election all the work accomplished under the reconstruction acts would become void and nugatory.

Such were the hopes of our enemies, and such were the fears of our friends. An angry and bitter spirit of opposition at home, encouraged and fostered by the sympathy and approbation of the Democracy of the North.

An Honorable Contrast.

Fellow-citizens, I have already reminded you that at every step since the close of the war the elevation and enfranchisement of the colored race has been opposed by the whites of our State. Look with me now, for one moment, at the contrast afforded by the conduct of our colored fellow-citizens from the hour they became possessed of political power to the present day.

The spirit and purpose of the white people found expression in that statute now familiarly known as the "Black Code," of which no less can be said than that while it recognized the fact of emancipation it sought to preserve the practical subordination and dependence of the emancipated race. I say to you to-day, what I do not believe you will dare to deny, that if ever retaliation would have been natural and excusable it was when at last the political power of the State was taken from the former ruling classes and placed in the hands of those who had hitherto known law and government only as the instruments of their slavery and degradation. But you will search in vain for an act in the three years which are now past which will betray a vindictive spirit, or which displays the old spirit of caste.

A Beneficent Constitution.

Look to the records of the Constitutional Convention of 1868. During the first days of its session a resolution was adopted in this Convention appealing to the Commanding General to stay the sales of property, real and personal, under the hammer of the Sheriff—an act which saved from immediate loss the homes of tens of thousands of those whose feelings toward the colored race had been expressed in the "Black Code."

Or look again at that provision of our Constitution which forbids the enforcement of debts due upon contracts for the purchase or sale of slaves; a measure whose only benefit was that it saved the former slaveholders and slave dealers of this State from the consequences of their own traffic in human flesh. No colored man in the State could have been personally interested in the enactment of such a law, but in the belief that when slavery perished, property in slaves, with all its incidents, perished, they desired that the burdens incurred by slavery, should be removed even from those who had no just claim to such exemption.

Fellow-citizens, I recall these events to show you again how groundless is the belief and the charge that the Republican party of this State was conceived and nurtured in hostility to the white men of the State. The facts to which I have just adverted are a record which I could well wish belonged to my own race. They are a tribute to the nobility of soul which characterizes the colored race of our State, a spirit which dwells not in the past, but rejoices in the present and looks hopefully to the future; which has no revenges to glut but is animated by a broad purpose to promote the welfare of all our people.

The Arduous Task.

Having framed a Constitution, just and liberal in all its provisions, abridging the rights of no man or class of men, but securing for all those inalienable rights to which our American Republic was from the first dedicated, the Republican party of South Carolina, in July 1868, assumed the practical control of the public affairs of the State. I need not further remind you, fellow-citizens, of the appalling task which confronted them on all sides. Behind them lay the dismal track of two centuries and a half of slavery, with all the inveterate prejudices and habits which that institution had nurtured. Around them were the fresh wastes and ruin of desolating war. The passions, the hatreds, the sufferings of the long struggle, were still fresh in the hearts and memories of our people. The new order of things was the final dashing of all their hopes, and the complete reversal of all the teachings of the statesmen and orators who had hitherto moulded and controlled the public opinion of our State. Surely, if ever a difficult task fell to human hands, it was the reconstruction of the civil and political fabric of our State, out of the materials which slavery and war had left us. Surely, if ever a party could invoke the charitable and sympathizing judgment of mankind, it was the party which in 1868 was charged with the work of laying the new foundations, of rebuilding the broken walls and the shattered columns of the political temple of South Carolina.

Now, fellow-citizens, it is not my purpose to claim for the Republican party of our State a record free from political errors or unmarked by political follies. I am speaking to men whose judgment I respect and whose intelligence I know; and I have recalled the circumstances which surrounded our advent to power, solely for the purpose of enabling them to form a more just and reasonable verdict upon our public policy and record. I am not anxious to claim that no acts have been done, during the past two years, of doubtful expediency and propriety. I am not anxious to claim that there have been no instances of incompetency, of dishonesty, of corruption among those who have been trusted with public office. Under circumstances so anomalous and conditions so untoward, I am sure that no thoughtful friend of freedom and progress will be astonished to find errors and shortcomings of a magnitude proportionate to the difficulties encountered.

I therefore, fellow-citizens, invite you, in a spirit of calm and dispassionate patriotism, as men who love our State and seek only the common welfare of all our citizens, to look at the general policy, the specific acts, and the practical results of the Republican administration of our State.

What has been done for the substantial growth and prosperity of our State, for her intellectual, moral and material advancement? I assume that a party which can point to a record which marks the progress of our State in all these aspects, can claim the commendations of the good people of our State.

Our Financial Record.

The Republican Administration of our State found itself face to face with the gravest financial questions at the threshold of its career. The treasury of the State was empty. The credit of the State was depressed to the lowest point. No assessment for taxation had been made for nearly two years. No taxes had been levied to meet the expenses of the new Government. I have already reminded you of the general tone of bitter hostility which characterized our political opponents. This hostility, overflowing in threats of repudiation, in open and repeated declarations of a purpose to starve out a party which they had failed to defeat at the ballot-box, enhanced greatly the natural difficulties of the situation.

The New Tax System.

First of all was the necessity of providing a system of assessment and taxation for our State, and it is to the features and principles which mark the new system that I now ask your attention.

The system of assessment and taxation of property which had prevailed for a long period in our State was a system which had its origin in the peculiar features of the social institutions of our people. It was an arbitrary and unequal system, having reference not to a just and equitable distribution of the burdens of taxation upon all the property of the State, but carefully adjusted to suit the interests of that portion of our community whose influence was predominant in the public affairs of the State—I mean the real estate and slave interests of the State.

Whoever will now examine a tax act under the ante-war system of assessment and taxation will discover that the burden of taxation was almost wholly removed from the primary property interests of the State and fastened upon those branches of industry and business which the peculiar institution of slavery had taught our people to regard as secondary to the great planting and slave interests. . . .

But, fellow-citizens, it is needless for present purposes to dwell upon the defects of the system which prevailed prior to the inauguration of the present administration. No one disputes its injustice and folly; and yet, fellow-citizens, the Republican party of our State is not more widely or bitterly assailed for any feature of its policy, than the ruthless sweeping away of the last vestige of such a system, and the substitution of a system which is based on the simple and just idea of placing upon all forms of property their just proportion of the public burden as *measured by their money value*. The new constitution of our State wisely declared that all taxes laid by the State should be strictly *ad valorem*. And following this enlightened principle, the act for the assessment and taxation of property has aimed to secure a just valuation of all the material interests and property of the State, and to lay upon each its just proportional burden of taxation.

Simple and just as such a system must be regarded, the difficulties of its application and the temporary dissatisfaction arising from its working have been great. No monopoly willingly yields its privileges. Immunities of long standing are surrendered reluctantly, and it is not wonderful perhaps that the land owners of the State saw with many regrets that henceforth the lands of South Carolina must contribute, like all other interests, according to their actual market value.

But is there any man here to-day who will undertake to defend the old system or to point out the injustice or unwisdom of the new? Ungracious as the task might be, what political party under our present Constitution, or according to the rule of justice, could have done otherwise? I am aware, fellow-citizens, that the planter who having lost his one hundred slaves, finds his lands on which he previously paid taxes at the valuation only of $4 an acre, now valued for taxation at $40 or $60 an acre, is apt to feel dissatisfied with the change and to denounce the Government or the party which has induced the change. But what privileged class, as I have already said, has ever willingly abandoned its privileges? The simple question is, which system is just? Which system is equal?

Which system distributes the burdens of supporting the government equally and fairly? And not, are those who have lost privileges and immunities heretofore granted, pleased with the change?

Fellow-citizens, I have heard expressions of dissatisfaction often enough, of denunciation of what men are pleased to call *the increased burdens* of taxation, but I have yet to see the first attempt made to prove or point out the inequality of the present system of assessment and taxation of property. . . .

Therefore, fellow-citizens, I place foremost among the acts of the Republican party of our State, which deserve the commendation of all fair men, the fact that it has given us a wise, just and equitable system of assessment and taxation of property.

I have called your especial attention to this subject, because I cannot be mistaken in regarding it as the basis, potential and actual, of all our financial health and credit. If the revenues of a State are based upon inequality and injustice, if privilege is substituted for equality and caprice for justice, it is easy to predict that the material stability of that government is but weakness and uncertainty. If the *bona fide* resources of a State, under a fair valuation of its property, are equal to a prompt and full discharge of her obligations, her financial standing is secured. The practical result of our present system has been to demonstrate the fact, that without increasing the per centum of taxation beyond the average of other States, and indeed by keeping considerably below it, the receipts from taxation are adequate to support a government which shall preserve the traditional good faith and honor of our State.

I pass now to consider the amount of taxes collected and expended under this system, as compared with the corresponding items of former years. . . .

For fairness of comparison, I select the years 1859 and 1860, the two years next preceding the outbreak of the war, and the years 1868 and 1869, the first two years succeeding the restoration of civil government to South Carolina. . . .

1858 and 1869—An Increase of 136,000.

If you will look into your Comptroller-General's report for the fiscal year 1859, you will find that the amount of taxes levied for general State purposes, was $635,000. The police assessments, so-called, for the same year, were $222,000—giving a total for the year 1859 of $857,000.

Now for the year 1868, the first year of Republican rule, the general tax of the State was $1,000,000. The estimated amount of the taxes levied by the several Counties of the State for County purposes during the same year, was $500,000, giving an aggregate for the year 1868 of $1,500,000.

Out of the general State tax for the latter year, $500,000 was appropriated to pay the interest on the public debt of the State, of which sum certainly not more than one-half, $250,000, is fairly chargeable to the year 1868. Deduct $250,000, and we have left of the entire amount levied in 1868, $1,250,000 for the ordinary current expenses of the year.

Now, fellow-citizens, you remember without my reminding you, that in 1859 your taxes were payable in coin, or its equivalent. A fair comparison will, therefore, require us to take note of the depreciated value of the currency in 1868. I deduct, therefore, from the amount of taxes in 1868, 30 per cent. of the taxes of 1859, namely, $257,000, which leaves a remainder of $993,000 as the true amount to be compared with $857,000 expended in 1859.

Instructive Comparisons.

The result of the comparison is an increase *in nine years*, of $136,000 in the annual expenditures of our State.

We are told by our political opponents, and the public are

asked to believe, that our annual expenses are *more than doubled*. We go to the authentic records, and the result is an increase of just $136,000 since 1859.

But let us go one step further and observe the other changes which have occurred since 1859.

In 1859, the *free* population of the State amounted in round numbers to 271,000. By the census of 1868, our *free* population amounted to 691,000.

From these figures you will therefore perceive that in 1859 the cost of governing our citizens was $3.15 per head!

In 1868, the cost was just $1.43 per head!

In other words, while the ratio of the cost of governing our State in the years now compared is that of 17 to 20, the ratio of population in the same years is that of about *three* to *eight*.

These facts are our answer to the wanton and wholesale charges of extravagance and profligacy which are now hurled at us by those who seek to gain control of the State.

1861 and 1869—An Increase of Only $68,000.

I proceed next to a similar comparison of the expenses of the year 1860, the last year before the war, with the year 1869, the second year of our Republican administration.

By the Comptroller-General's report for 1860, the current expenses of the State are found to have been for that year $549,251.09.

For 1869 the current expenses of the State are shown to be $1,103,372.20.

From this latter amount, I now deduct for extraordinary expenses the following items: for the new State House $20,000. For taking the census required by the Constitution of the State, $48,000. For completing the State Penitentiary, $75,000. For building new Quarantine buildings at the port of Charleston, $4,000. For the interest on the public debt for 1869,

$338,693.86. I make this last deduction for the reason that in 1860, the interest on our public debt was paid, not from the general taxes of the State, but by the Bank of the State. Whatever the merits or faults of that institution, it is certainly true that in 1860, the interest on our public debt was paid by this bank and formed no item in the regular current expenses of the State government.

The deductions now made amount to no less than $485,693.86.

Deducting this latter amount from the aggregate of expenses for 1869, we have left a remainder of $617,678.34, the true amount to be put against $549,251.09 in 1860. An increase of just $68,427.25, in *the nine years from* 1860 *to* 1869!

Applying to these amounts the test of population, and we again have as the cost of governing the State in 1860, $2.02 per head, and in 1869 the cost per head is *eighty-nine cents.*

The Expenditure for All the People.

Now, fellow-citizens, do I err in viewing the entire colored population of the State as so many added to the population of the State? In 1860 were not the slaves of this State your chattels, amenable not to the laws but to your will? Were they not maintained and governed at the expense of the master? For whom were your laws made? For whom were your public buildings erected? For whom were all your State expenses incurred? *For your free population solely.*

Mark the change! A whole race suddenly lifted from the legal level of brutes and placed upon an equality with you and me! An entire people, after two centuries and a half of slavery, emerge in the twinkling of an eye into the full liberty of citizens! From under the barbarous influence of a most brutal and degrading institution, 420,000 souls suddenly pass into the broad sunlight of Republican citizenship. Think of it for one moment! Think of the vices, the ignorance, which must result from such a condition continued from generation to generation! Remember that all this mass are now responsible no longer to the master but to the *law*, and then tell me where you will parallel this increase of population in its natural result upon the cost of the State Government!

No ordinary and gradual increase of population would ever add so greatly to our expenses, and yet the average cost of governing this whole population, so totally unprepared in many respects to weigh and appreciate the new conditions of life, has been but a little more than *one third of the cost of governing the free white population of the State before the war.*

The Debt of Our State.

Fellow-citizens, these facts are our second answer to the reckless slanders of those who seek to recommit this State to the control of those ideas which have brought nothing but disgrace and disaster upon our State. There is another topic connected with the material interests of the State to which I now invite your most careful attention—the management and condition of our public debt. I admit that no party could justly claim your suffrage which failed to administer this great trust with wisdom and fidelity. If the charges now made against the Republican administration of our State in this regard, can be substantiated, I will accept without further contest the just verdict of condemnation which our "Reform" opponents invoke upon us at your hands. Let an honest and faithful meeting of all the obligations of our State be, under all circumstances, the unqualified demand which you make of every party. . . .

At the date of the inauguration of our present State Government, July 1868, the valid public debt of our State existing in the form of bonds and stocks of the State—in other words, the *funded debt* of the State, is fixed by the Comptroller General's Report for the year ending October 31, 1869, page 87, at $4,925,314.47. This was the burden and the trust committed to us by those who had gone before.

Early Financial Difficulties of the Administration.

At the threshold of this part of my argument, I call your attention, fellow-citizens, to the condition of our Treasury at the date of which I have spoken, July 1868. I am stating a well-known and incontestible fact when I say to you that the Treasury was *empty*. For two years [under the Johnson state government] a large part of the expense of governing our State had been borne by the National Government. The taxes laid had been imperfectly collected and had been barely sufficient to meet the wants of the State Government up to the time of its expiration. The difficulty which met the new Government on the first day of its existence was the want of funds to pay the current expenses of the State Government. No taxes had been levied and none could be laid or collected until a new tax law should have been matured, and all the complex machinery of taxation put into practical operation.

It became necessary, therefore, to at once anticipate the taxes of the year on which we had entered—in other words, to borrow money. Here we encounter the most critical point of our experience.

The Democratic press of the State, in the overflow of its hate, boldly proclaimed its hope to starve out a party which they had failed to defeat at the ballot-box. Capitalists were warned that the property-holders of South Carolina would pay no debts contracted in support of a government forced on them by negro votes and Federal bayonets. If time would permit me, I could read you to-day column upon column in every Democratic paper of our State, in which the world was informed that no debts of the new administration, either in the shape of temporary loans or of State bonds, would be paid by the tax-payers of the State. At this distance of time, it is safe for me to say that this policy was nearly successful.

During the session of the Legislature from July to September 1868, there were times when the most hopeful of our friends saw nothing but starvation before us. . . .

We went to New York and asked the capitalists there to advance us money on the faith of the stability and honesty of our new government, and *they did it.* . . . They loaned us large sums of money—loaned it in the face of the open threat of repudiation, which came from the Democratic press and the Democratic leaders of the State. From July 1868 to August 1869, when our first taxes were collected under the present administration, our State Government was upheld by that faith which our administration, by its conduct and principles, had inspired in New York. You will see, therefore, that we had by necessity anticipated the taxes by one whole year, and the receipts from that source in the summer and fall of 1869, were nearly exhausted in the repayment of loans already made.

The Relief of Our Treasury.

In view of this fact, and of the hardships of putting two years' taxes into one, the Legislature of 1869 authorized the issue of $1,000,000 of State bonds, to be called "bonds for the relief of the treasury." These bonds were designed to be used as collateral securities to borrow money, so far as might be necessary, to meet the expenses of the State previous to the collection of our taxes for the year 1869 to 1870.

Fellow-citizens, is this issue of bonds unwarrantable and fraudulent, as now charged? Was it not demanded by a due regard to the welfare of the State? I admit that a larger rate of taxation might have given us funds sufficient to have paid the expenses of two years in one year. But I know that no party which had any regard for the popular will or the real welfare of our people would have counseled such a course. . . .

The Result Our Best Vindication.

Fellow-citizens, I should not do justice to this portion of my subject if I failed to call your attention to the splendid result which has followed the policy which I have now sketched, and which is after all the best answer to all the calumnies of our "Reform" opponents. In January, 1868, the average market value of the bonds and stocks of the State of South Carolina was *twenty-six cents on the dollar*. In January, 1870, after less than two years of Republican rule, the same bonds and stocks are worth in the markets of our State, and of New York, *from ninety to ninety-five cents on the dollar*.

In July, 1868, at the date of the inauguration of the present State Government, the bonds and stocks of the State were worth *from forty to forty-five cents on the dollar*. In July, 1870, after two years of Republican rule, the bonds and stocks of the State were worth *from ninety to ninety-five cents on the dollar*. Since that date the slanders of the "Reform" party, and the war now flagrant in Europe, have depressed the prices of our securities, in common with all other State securities, and yet to-day they rule at *more than treble their value two years ago*.

Fellow-citizens, such a record is proof against attack, and my only excuse for asking you to-day to consider these facts is to reassure our faith that wherever and whenever justice and freedom are the foundations of government, and honesty and good faith its rule of action, there and then financial prosperity is sure to prevail.

The Blue Ridge Railroad and Its Bonds.

There is another point in our financial record which I must not omit—the Blue Ridge Railroad bonds. Of all the charges

so recklessly made against the Republican party of our State,
I know of none more baseless than the pretence that our State
debt has been increased by the issue of $4,000,000 of bonds
in aid of the Blue Ridge Railroad. Let us look at this matter
fully and fairly.

The Blue Ridge Railroad is an enterprise which has long
enlisted the enthusiastic support of the best and wisest men
of our State. At its inception the State subscribed for no less
than $1,310,000 of the stock of the company, and in 1854 the
State issued $1,000,000 of State bonds to aid in its construc-
tion, and further authorized the endorsement of $1,000,000 of
the bonds of the company for the same purpose.

Thus it will be seen that prior to the war the State had invested no less a sum than $1,000,000 in this great work of
connecting the State of South Carolina, by an unbroken line
of railway, with the great West and Northwest. Bear in mind,
fellow-citizens, that the State had already expended $1,000,000
in this work.

At the session of the Legislature of 1868, among the questions presented and urged upon that body, was the proposition to aid further in the completion of this work. Among the
most effective arguments pressed upon that Legislature was
the fact that $1,000,000, already invested by the State, would
be lost without further aid. Under the influence of these
considerations, the Legislature authorized—*what?* The issue
of State bonds, as in 1854? The subscription of money in aid
of the work, as in 1854? No; the State did this, and no more:
she said to the road: "We have already given you $1,000,000
of the people's money. We cannot give you our money or our
bonds, but if you will mortgage us your entire road and
property we will endorse your bonds, payable in twenty years,
for $4,000,000." . . .

This is the miserable pretext upon which we are now ar-
raigned for squandering the public money in aid of railroads.
A simple endorsement of the company's bonds, secured by a
mortgage of the whole property of the company, is authorized,

and we are told that $4,000,000 is added to the debt of the State! . . .

But I need not argue to sensible men that this endorsement is not a *debt*. It has no place in our public debt, and the courts of our State have expressly held, as you all know, that the endorsement of these bonds does not constitute a *State* debt. . . .

The Land Commission.

Another topic connected with our general, and to some extent with our financial policy, is the Land Commission.

The Land Commission has its origin in the anomalous condition of the greater part of our agricultural laborers, and the fact that our available lands are held in tracts too large to be within the reach of our poorer fellow-citizens.

I am aware that I am now approaching a subject in which the colored people of this State are peculiarly interested. I regard it as among the most hopeful signs of the times that our colored fellow-citizens in all parts of our State are so keenly alive to the importance of owning a portion of the soil of our State. It is a tendency and desire which I am always ready to encourage. It is to-day an injustice and shame that two-thirds of our white laboring population, and four-fifths of those who perform the manual labor of our community, do not own a foot of the soil which they have tilled for centuries. In all ways and on all occasions, by all lawful means, I will aid in correcting this evil and in placing the lands of our State in easy reach of all who till our soil. I welcomed the establishment of this Land Bureau, therefore, as a means of ennobling our laboring classes and opening the door to higher aims, to more comfortable modes of living, to greater pecuniary and personal independence, to the inclination and leisure for self improvement and education—in a word, to a higher and truer discharge of the duties of citizenship.

The practical management of this Commission has been

attended with greater delays and more difficulties than were anticipated by its friends. But, in spite of all hindrances, this fact is clear, that over 110,000 acres of land have been purchased, and are now in preparation for sale to actual settlers and purchasers, according to the provisions of the law. It is charged by our "Reform" press and leaders that this Commission has been made the means of large profits to those who have made the sales of lands to the State. If this be true, and with the fullest opportunities on the part of our "Reform" friends no proof of individual delinquency or dishonesty has been discovered, our reply might still be that it was the only earnest effort to solve the problem which has yet been put forth in our State. When sufficient time shall have elapsed for a fair trial of the experiment, if the investment made shall not be a source of strength and prosperity to our State, it will be soon enough to ask your condemnation. With the follies and losses which have been brought upon our State by the systems of agriculture and labor which have hitherto prevailed in this State, it does not lie in the mouths of our former ruling classes to denounce this attempt to atone, in some measure, for the evils and inequalities of the past. With 110,000 acres of land within reach of our laboring people, capable of being divided into from 3,000 to 4,000 homesteads, I am content to wait for more than the vague charges of the "Reform" press before I admit that this great scheme has proved a failure or a fraud.

Public Schools.

Fellow-citizens, I next ask your attention to what has been accomplished for the educational interests of our State. I now approach a subject where my approval of the action of the Republican party cannot be unqualified.

I am compelled to admit that much less has been done in this greatest of all our duties, than was demanded at our hands. But it is my duty to present to you the *true* record of our administration in this respect. The slanders of our political opponents are nowhere more conspicuous than in their presentation of this subject.

Let me ask you, fellow-citizens, to remember that in 1868, the pressure of the financial and material questions, the taxation question, the public debt, the legal system of protection to our civil rights, were questions so urgent, so overshadowing, that naturally the consideration of a topic like popular education was jostled into the background. The Legislature of 1868 adjourned, without developing or setting in motion any general system of Public Common Schools. To illustrate, however, the comparative estimate placed upon this subject by the Legislatures of former years and that of 1868, look at the appropriations made in 1866 and 1868. In 1866, I find the following appropriations made for educational purposes: For the University of South Carolina, $13,600. For the education of the Deaf, Dumb and Blind, $4,000. For repairing Cedar Springs Asylum, $2,000. For the support of Free Schools, $25,000. Total, $44,600.

In 1868, I find the following appropriations made for Educational purposes: For the University of South Carolina, $26,800. For the support of Free Schools, $50,000, in addition to the entire capitation of the State, amounting to about $150,000. Total, $226,800.

During the first year of Republican rule a complete census of all the children of the State was taken as a basis for future plans and labors; and at the session of the Legislature for 1869 to '70, we find a careful, liberal and complete system of Free Common Schools, matured and adopted. This system is now in successful operation; amid a thousand obstacles, arising from the want of public interest in this subject on the part of those who had hitherto been the ruling class of our State, as well as from the absence of all the ordinary materials of conducting this work, we have made a most hopeful beginning for the education of all our children in the Common Schools of our State.

The appropriations made in 1869 for educational purposes were as follows: For Free Schools $50,000 in addition to the capitation tax, $150,000. For the University of South Carolina, $37,500. For the Deaf, Dumb and Blind, $8,000. Total $245,500.

When compared with the high test of our duty, as well as our truest interest, I lament that more has not been done, and I admit our failure to do our whole duty; but when called to account by the present "Reform" party or by any party or men who have heretofore had influence in South Carolina, I challenge comparison in all points, and I point with confidence and pride to the record which I have now placed before you. What man or what party in South Carolina has ever before done anything to bring education within the reach of every child of our State? The debt which this State, its property and its present intelligence, owes to the colored race, to all her uneducated children, can never be fully discharged. After centuries of enforced ignorance, with every book sealed and every avenue to knowledge closed, it is our high duty as well as our glorious privilege to lay the foundations of an educational system which shall cover our State from North to South and from East to West with the spirit, the power, the happiness which come from intellectual attainments and culture. To such a work, fellow-citizens, we are summoned by all our love of the free institutions of our country, by all our hopes of the future, safety and glory of our State, and by every dictate of humanity and patriotism.

As the tangible result of our common school system, I present these statistics: Number of schools in actual operation in July, 1870, 625; number of children in attendance, 23,299—exclusive of 5,000 children attending the free public schools in the city of Charleston.

Other Measures of Practical Value.

Fellow-citizens, there are many other topics in our political and legislative history during the past two years, upon which it would give me pleasure to speak, as evidences of the general wisdom which has marked our administration of the affairs of the State. Among such measures, let me specify the Act of 1870, providing for the payment of the interest on the public debt *in coin,* a measure of financial integrity and honor which needs no praise or defense; the act of the same session requiring insurance companies to secure their policy-holders by the deposit of a specified amount of our State securities with the Comptroller-General of the State; the act providing for a Commission of the Sinking Fund, whereby the unproductive property of the State is ordered to be sold, and the proceeds applied to the redemption of the public obligations of the State; the act by which the vast mineral wealth of our State, existing in the form of phosphatic deposits, is made a source of direct and immediate revenue to the State, as well as promoted to the rank of a leading article of export and commerce. I place each and all of these acts among the measures of practical material value to our State, calculated to enable her to enter upon a career of material and financial prosperity.

Looking at the more general interests of which our Legislature has taken note, I point you to the Homestead Act, which has already protected the homes of so many of our citizens; a measure which alone should entitle the Republican party in this State to the common gratitude of all our people.

Laws Which Benefit the Working People.

Again, I point you to the law which wiped out that disgraceful remnant of legal barbarism, imprisonment for debt; to the law hitherto unknown to this State, protecting married women

in the enjoyment of the rights of property independently of
their husbands; to the law which supplements and applies to
our domestic affairs the great principles embodied in the
"Civil Rights Act" of the Congress of the United States; to
the law which for the first time in this State makes the wages
of mechanics a lien on the property upon which their labor
is expended; to the law which exempts the wages or products
of agricultural laborers, mechanics, artisans and tradesmen
from attachment and sale, to the amount of $500; to the law
which protects our agricultural laborers from the cupidity
and fraud of the land-owners, and affords remedies for the
too frequent breaches of contracts made with those who have
little knowledge of the legal effect of such contracts; to all
these laws I point as evidences, clear and unquestionable, of
the general capacity, good sense, practical fidelity, and honesty of purpose which has marked the course of legislation
since freedom and justice, as represented by the Republican
party, have guided the policy of our State.

54. GENERAL E. R. S. CANBY,

GENERAL ORDER

July 1868

For Radicals more than for other Republicans, the impeachment
was wearying and disruptive. To be sure, it was impossible not to
applaud this supreme effort to hamstring the President. But recall
that Radicals believed that reconstruction must be a slow, patient,
educative process. A foreseeable result of the impeachment was a
pressure on Republicans for express speed in reconstruction, in

order to prevent similar crises from developing in the future. The impeachment further cracked the party's lines when a handful of Senate heavyweights decided not to vote in favor of convicting Johnson. Their "defection," though it did not result in the political suicides of the recusants as tradition has insisted, did permit Johnson to escape conviction by one vote.[1]

Closing ranks briefly at the height of the impeachment proceeding, the party nominating convention selected Grant as its Presidential candidate. Essentially, American voters were going to decide the validity of what had been done in reconstruction, however matters went in the Senate or before the Supreme Court. But Radicals, still forward-looking, were not encouraged.

They worried that the velocity of admission of "reconstructed" states was far too swift to permit true conversions of white men to biracial equality in politics and before the law. Only a month after the impeachment ended, in June, seven former Southern states gained readmission to Congress. They qualified under terms of Congress' statutes on reconstruction, including ratification of the Fourteenth Amendment and provision for Negro participation in voting and officeholding. The Freedmen's Bureau prepared to close up shop by early 1869. Army units on duty in the readmitted states withdrew from watchdog activity, as in the following order of General E. R. S. Canby.[2]

HEADQUARTERS SECOND MILITARY DISTRICT,
Charleston, S. C., July—, 1868.

GENERAL ORDERS, ⎱
    No. —.   ⎰

In view of the approaching termination of the military authority derived from and exercised by virtue of the Act of Congress passed March 2, 1887, and the Acts supplementary thereto, which laws are about to become inoperative by reason

---

[1] Ralph J. Roske, "The Seven Martyrs?" *American Historical Review,* LXIV (January 1959), 323–330.

[2] This order is in form of a galley proof, owned by the editor.

of the fulfilment of the conditions and limitations prescribed by the provisions thereof, the following instructions are promulgated for information and guidance of this command:

1. Upon the issue of the proclamation of the President of the United States required by Section 3 of the Act of June 25, 1868, announcing the ratification by the Legislature of the State of North Carolina of the constitutional amendment known as Article Fourteen, the commanding officers of posts in said State will cease to exercise any and all authority conferred under said reconstruction Acts of Congress, except so far as necessary for the inauguration of the new State government.

2. The term of office and all official functions of Registrars, Inspectors, Managers or Judges of Election, Military Commissioners, or other military agents in North Carolina, appointed under the authority of the reconstruction laws of the United States, will end at the date of the proclamation by the President, referred to in the preceding section, and all such officers or agents will, without delay, forward to these Headquarters, any books or records relating to their official duties that may be in their possession. They will also transmit a list of the property purchased with public funds, and exhibit the disposition made of it.

3. The Provost Courts now existing in North Carolina are abolished, and the records will be transmitted without delay to these Headquarters.

4. All appointments to civil office in the State of North Carolina under the authority of the reconstruction laws of the United States will terminate when the successors in such offices, elected or appointed under the Constitution and laws of the said State, are duly qualified.

5. All citizens who, at the date of the proclamation above referred to, may be in the custody of the military authorities, and held for trial for acts in violation of the reconstruction

laws of the United States, or in violation of military orders issued under the authority of the said laws, will be discharged from custody, and the prosecution dismissed.

6. At the same time all prisoners (citizens) held by military authority for trial, whether in confinement or on bail, for crimes or offences cognizable under the statutes of either State, will be turned over to the custody of the proper civil authorities; and all bonds, undertakings, deposits or other security for appearance of persons charged with crimes or offenses as above, taken by military authority in this District, in pursuance of the provisions of General Orders No. 105, series 1867, from these Headquarters, will be turned over to the Attorney-General of the State in which the parties bound, respectively, reside, with authority to enforce the same.

The Judge Advocate of the District will communicate to the Attorney-General of the State the history of each case so transferred, together with the depositions or other evidence or information upon which the parties accused have been arrested and held for trial. In like manner, the Provost Marshal-General will transfer to the Attorney-General all depositions, complaints or other information on file in his office in relation to persons accused who have avoided arrest or escaped from confinement.

7. All prisoners (citizens) who, when the Act of March 2, 1867, becomes inoperative under the conditions and limitations prescribed by the fifth Section thereof, may be in confinement or custody by virtue of the final judgment and sentence of a Military Commission or other military tribunal authorized by the said laws, will be continued in the said custody until entitled to discharge by expiration of sentence, or until their cases are otherwise disposed of by proper authority. Upon a writ of *habeas corpus* or other process issuing from a Court of the United States in the case of any prisoner so held, the writ will be promptly responded to, and the officer in making his return will set forth the material facts

of the case. If the writ be issued from a State Court, the officer having the custody of the prisoner will make a respectful return to the writ, setting forth the fact that the prisoner is held by virtue of the final judgment and sentence of a Court of competent jurisdiction, held under the authority of the laws of the United States, and that the jurisdiction is exclusively in the Courts of the United States.

The division between United States and State jurisdiction is not always distinctly marked; but officers will be guided in their actions by the principles laid down by the Supreme Court of the United States, in the case of Ableman *vs.* Booth, (21 Howard R., 506.)

8. At all forts, arsenals, light houses, custom houses and other public establishments, whether held by original cession or by capture and continued occupation, the jurisdiction will be held to be in the United States, regulated in the former case by the terms of the cession, and in the latter exclusive, until otherwise directed by law or other proper authority. Commanding officers are required to see that such places are not allowed to become asylums for criminals, and that no persons not in the service of the United States are allowed to establish themselves within the limits of any ceded or reserved jurisdiction.

9. The canvass returns, poll lists and ballots for the several elections held in said State, under the authority of the laws of the United States, will, as soon as practicable, be arranged and inventoried according to the several election districts, securely packed and transmitted to the Secretary of State at Raleigh for deposit and safe-keeping.

10. Authenticated copies of the registration in each County of the said State will be prepared as soon as possible, and deposited in the office of the Secretary of State.

11. Authenticated copies of all General and Special Orders, regulations and instructions issued by the District Commander, or by Post Commanders under authority duly delegated, will

be prepared; one set to be deposited in the office of the Governor of the State, and the other in the office of the Secretary of State.

12. Certified copies of all decisions affecting rights of property will be prepared and deposited in the office of the Secretary of State.

13. Commanders of Posts will immediately transmit to District Headquarters all records, correspondence, &c., that relate to the duties performed by them under the reconstruction laws—retaining only the military records.

By Command of Bvt. Major-General Ed. R. S. Canby:

PART TWELVE

The Issues of '68

55. E. L. GODKIN, EDITORIAL

July 18, 1867

With votes of the restored Southern states included, summer 1868 saw the Fourteenth Amendment added to the constitution. Despite his acquittal at the impeachment, President Johnson remained quiescent, save for vetoes, all through the year remaining of his White House term. Negro suffrage appeared to be working smoothly in the South and in the District of Columbia. Many Republicans expected that all reconstruction issues would disappear once Grant entered the White House.

Not so Radicals. Old antislavery front-runners such as Wendell Phillips were dubious at best on Grant's reliability. The new constitutional amendment obviously was not self-enforcing. Already the "reconstructed" state of Georgia, returned to Congress, had expelled Negro state legislators. In this instance Congress returned the state to military rule. But the future was cloudy. Would a new President of Grant's caliber and coattailing Republican congressmen ever again prove willing to expel a state for failing to meet minimal conditions?

To aid in providing a positive answer to this question, a fifteenth amendment to the Constitution appeared to be in order. Across the nation Radicals pushed one forward in 1869, but again they found to their dismay that what resulted did not positively forbid racial disfranchisement if a state concealed the color bar by obvious circumlocutions. Efforts to gain a better formulation proved unavailing. At the height of the victory in the impeachment and in Grant's election, and in the creation at last of Republican party organizations in the South, the earlier sharpness of Radical goals and weapons appeared blunted.

Workers in Republican vineyards did not find it difficult to assemble a catalog of reasons why their exertions were going adrift. Evidence accumulated that many Northerners were simply sick of what Orestes Brownson damned as the "eternal sambo," and as Walt Whitman wrote, "The Republicans have exploited the negro too intensely, and there comes a reaction."[1]

This reaction took on many, diverse, and sometimes paradoxical forms. Angry that Radicals sought equality for black men but not for white women, feminists split off. As noted in the introduction, enlarging acceptance for Darwinian notions made more effort on behalf of Negroes appear useless even to some old Negrophiles. Derivative notions grew of "natural law" limitations on the proper functions of government, and Radical ideas on augmenting what was already on the statute books ran into this heightening wall of opposition. Influential Republicans became devotees of clean—i.e., cheap, rational, efficient—government as a primary goal, transcending civil liberties.

The hurly-burly of the politics of reform, of war, and of reconstruction increasingly proved discordant to the altering tastes of a changing generation. Not only were some Radicals tarred with the darkening brush of concern for colored men; they also smacked of heretical advocacy of wildcat fiscal notions, of heretical ideas on the merits of organized labor, or of deviant panaceas about land confiscation. By 1870 Wade's and Julian's strong Congressional voices were stilled as result of losing election or renomination contests.

---

[1] Whitman to Moncure Conway, February 17, 1868, in Edwin Haviland Miller, ed., *Walt Whitman, The Correspondence, 1868–1875* (New York: New York University Press, 1961), II, 15. William Gillette, *The Right to Vote: Politics and the Passage of the Fifteenth Amendment* (Baltimore: The Johns Hopkins Press, 1965), is a valuable contribution to the literature.

Death snuffed out Radical sparks. Obituaries had appeared for Giddings, Rawlins, Stanton, Stearns, and Stevens, among others. Advancing age and physical infirmities hobbled survivors of the prewar and wartime crusade.

Remaining Radical makeweights in Congress, including Schurz and Sumner, increasingly found themselves out of sympathy with and cut off from the founts of power in Grant's administration. Newspaper publishers, always in the fore of Radical ranks, broke away from Radical causes, with Godkin and Greeley the two most prominent examples.

The upshot was that by 1870, for the first time since 1860, Radical Republicans were going adrift from the power structures that they had helped to build on all levels of the federal system. In largest part this weakening was a result of their successes. A Negro now sat in Jeff Davis' place in the United States Senate, swearing in there almost at the same time in 1870 that the arch-rebel was let out from under the weight of a pending treason indictment. Radicals had made it possible for abolition to triumph, and for three new amendments to grace the Constitution that in 1860 were impossible for most men even to hope for. Democratic platforms and candidates in 1864 and 1868, who had threatened to reverse the course of reform, were sunk in defeat. What was left to do, especially now that Andy Johnson was gone?

With Grant firm in the White House, anti-Johnson cement rapidly crumbled. "We can't run the machine [any longer] merely by making faces at Andy Johnson," worried Robert Ingersoll the night before Grant took office.

The people said why in hell . . . don't we have peace in the South —Andy Johnson—Why are not some of the traitors hung?— Andy Johnson— . . . What the devil makes the roads so muddy —measles so bad—whooping cough so prevalent—Why G-d d--n it, Andy Johnson. We can sing this song only until tomorrow.[2]

It is not that Radicals lacked goals. Sumner still pleaded against racial distinctions in education and sought federal laws against the practice. Philadelphia Radicals tried to push through a city ordinance prohibiting racial segregation in streetcars. The cause simply

---

[2] E. I. Wakefield, ed., *Letters of Robert G. Ingersoll* (New York: Philosophical Library, 1951), pp. 156–157.

failed to attract adherents. Even supporters realized that access to trolleys appeared puny compared to the majestic issues of secession, the Union, emancipation, and reconstruction. Only the anti-Johnson backlash finally resulted in a Pennsylvania state law in 1867, to forbid the racist practice in the Quaker city.[3]

Radicals lacked the capacity to recruit new rank and file. Young people no longer came to them. The congeries of reasons mitigating against the continuation of much concern for Negroes, especially by government, sent adventurous and energetic activists on to other pursuits.

With death, defections to other and sometimes contradictory causes, and failure to attract replenishing replacements weakening the humanitarian rhythm, the quality of reconstruction coarsened along with much else in the fabric of America. Of course men could not know this in 1868 as they celebrated the good news of the general's election to succeed Johnson. But straws were in the wind, and disquieting evidence was at hand that Radical Republican leaders, in redeeming campaign promises of 1864 and 1866, by 1868 had outstripped the desires of their constituents with respect to what rights Negroes should enjoy, North or South.

A scattering of sources to follow illustrates these manifold tendencies. The first is from that heavyweight Republican periodical, *The Nation*. It shared a page with a diatribe against Andrew Johnson. Here are Godkin's ideas on "True Radicalism."[4]

MANY well-meaning persons, impressed with a sense of the value of past reforms, and disgusted with the stupid conservatism which blindly adheres to every ancient abuse, are so anxious to be considered "radical" in their views that they fear to stop even when they have attained all that is really desirable or practicable. They distrust themselves if their common sense tells them to pause, and feel uneasy at the

---

[3] [Anonymous], *Why Colored People in Philadelphia are Excluded from the Street Cars* (Philadelphia, 1866); London *Freed-Man*, IV (June 1867), 24, surveys the issue.

[4] *The Nation*, V (July 18, 1867), 50–51.

thought that they have no more fields to conquer, and no progress, as it seems to them, to make. They dread the imputation of conservatism, and would almost prefer to have risked what they have gained rather than stand still. This class is never likely to form the majority of a community, but as its errors frequently afford an excuse for a reaction against wise reforms, it may be well to address a few words of advice to those who feel troubled by such fears.

The first thought that occurs to us is the folly of imagining that for hundreds of years to come, there will be any difficulty in finding subjects for radical reform. As fast as one topic of discussion is disposed of a dozen are ready to rise in its place—all important, involving much labor, needing long consideration, and sure to lead to animated controversy. It is a law of human nature that only one such controversy can be carried on at one time and place. Slavery, and the evils growing out of it, have absorbed the attention of this country for some years past, and so gigantic an abomination could never have been overthrown without an intense concentration of the public mind upon the work. It has been cut up by the roots, and the Congressional plan of reconstruction is rapidly extracting the last remnant from the ground. Universal suffrage is so nearly established, and appears so certain, that some who are more anxious to be radical than to be right are already casting about for some new demand for the benefit of those who were lately oppressed. But who cannot see that there are many other great questions which have been lying in abeyance during this great struggle, and which will give ample scope to the powers of the most radical reformer? Let no man be impatient for conflict. He will soon have quite enough in the legitimate path of duty. With a system of taxation which demoralizes a large part of the community, with rotten legislatures, municipalities, and judges, with systems of education grossly defective, with extravagance and inefficiency the rule in government rather than the exception, it is clear that no one need fear that the work of reform is at an end.

In the next place, genuine radicalism aims only to uproot evil, and to plant in its place that which promises good fruit. Having done this thoroughly, the wise radical is content to wait for final results, and slowly to build up when the work of pulling down is properly over. If we can never reach a state in which growth rather than destruction is desirable, then all destruction is useless, and the radical is the most unwise of men. But such is not the fact. We have already, in respect of many things, reached the stage in which development, and not simple uprooting, is the duty of the race. The Christian religion, the education of the young, the republican system of government, the family state, the liberty of commerce, and many other instances, might be given as illustrations of institutions or doctrines which need no change at the root, but have yet vast room for development and progress.

The practical application of these remarks at the present time relates chiefly to those persons who are uneasy lest by opposing confiscation and other punitory schemes they should cease to be radical. The party which claims to be conservative is so amazingly stupid that we cannot blame any one for doubting his own sagacity when he finds himself agreeing with it upon any point. But it should be borne in mind that, like a man who sings on one note the whole time, a party that persists in one line of conduct must be right occasionally and may happen to be right frequently. Let no one fear to act upon his own convictions of duty even if he does find himself sometimes in strange company.

All the propositions which are made by demagogues, looking toward special favors for special classes of people, are simply schemes of robbery which will, if carried out, despoil the majority of the very classes intended to be favored. Suppose the land of the South should be confiscated and divided among the negroes, as some advise. Not one-fourth of the negroes would get any land which they could live upon, while the other three-fourths would be deprived of a large part of their wages by the universal disorganization of the employing class. Suppose the eight-hour law should be made compulsory, as its friends insist. Who would suffer so much as the workmen, whose wages would be cut down and whose employers would largely abandon enterprises undertaken under different expectations?

It is not the mission of true radicalism to enter upon such schemes as these. In the sphere of politics it has long been the maxim of radicals that nothing can or should be done except to secure to every man the free use of his powers and a fair and equal opportunity for his development. In other spheres of action there is abundance of work for the most zealous reformer. Nay, in political affairs, as we have already intimated, there will always be enough to do. While the nation has been crushing one evil, others have sprung up which in their turn demand attention. Let us be content with securing equal justice at the South, and then combine to attack corruptions nearer home.

56. HOWARD M. JENKINS, PAMPHLET

1868

A somewhat similar fastidiousness, which subsequently would bring him to vote against conviction for President Johnson at the impeachment, is discernible in Senator Lyman Trumbull's concern of September 1867 that the national government *not* oversee state elections. An Illinoisan and old associate of Lincoln, Trumbull was traditionally accounted a Radical. He had taken a leading role in all reconstruction matters and strongly sustained Congressional jurisdiction over the defeated Southern states. But within those states

Congress had no jurisdiction once they reconstructed themselves, and it never had jurisdiction within Northern states, Trumbull asserted, in opposition to a growing sentiment among Radical spokesmen that all elections should become subject to national scrutiny.[1]

Radical spokesmen felt that his thrust was gratuitous and incorrect in its facts as well as judgments. A Delaware friend of War Secretary Stanton, Howard M. Jenkins, took issue with the learned Senator and voiced the conviction of advanced Radicals that the North as well as the South was due for a reconstruction.[2]

Senator Trumbull on Suffrage.

In a recently published letter, Senator Trumbull, of Illinois, presents, in advance of any exhaustive Congressional discussion of the question, what will seem, to many earnest friends of the principles to which he is presumably devoted, a hasty, *ex parte* decision, that Congress has no power to protect the voting right of citizens. Of course, it is no argument to say that Senator Trumbull's Conservative tendencies have induced this anticipation and pre-judgment of the hearing which the case will very probably have at the approaching session of Congress, and yet that conclusion will undoubtedly form in many minds. As an argumentative effort, however, the letter of the Senator is by no means creditable to him. It is deficient in logic, as it is inaccurate in statement.

Acknowledging, without hesitation, the necessity which he asserts, of adhering faithfully to the spirit and intention of

---

[1] See Trumbull's article, "Can Congress Regulate Suffrage in the States?" Chicago *Advance*, September 5, 1867. Ironically, Congress passed a law May 31, 1870 (16 *Statutes at Large*, 140), providing some overseership in local elections, but as a check on Northern urban political machines.

[2] Jenkins, *Our Democratic Republic: Its Form—Its Faults—Its Strength—Its Need* (Wilmington, 1868), pp. 16–21; and see David Plumb, "Citizenship and Suffrage: The Right and Duty of Congress to Enfranchise the Nation," *The Radical*, III (February 1868), 389–401.

our fundamental law, we propose to start also from that point, and discuss with him one single issue:—

DOES THE NATIONAL CONSTITUTION REQUIRE [or authorize] THE PROTECTION OF THE VOTING RIGHT OF CITIZENS, BY NATIONAL LAW?

This is the question, and just this, which in advance of any thorough examination, Senator Trumbull so promptly brushes aside. He asks in his letter "Can Congress *regulate* Suffrage in the States?" but his arguments are directed to the same point, and cover the same ground, as that which we have indicated in the query we propose, while the Senator confuses the issue, first by employing the term "regulate," and then by adding "in the States." To *regulate* the minor qualifications of tax-paying, registration, residence, &c., may be a privilege remaining with the States, but the protection of the citizen from disfranchisement is the duty of the national authority. The rights of person and property are protected by the Constitution, but the particular legislation by which their security is assured, and offences against them punished, is in the hands of the States. So perhaps with the voting right.

Mr. Trumbull says Congress cannot legislate relative to Suffrage:—

1. Because the Constitution provides that electors of Members of Congress, "shall have the qualifications requisite for electors of the most numerous branch of the Legislature."

2. Because he finds no other reference to "suffrage" in the Constitution.

In the first objection, he assumes what is certainly not justified by the language itself, that in providing for the qualifications of voters for Members of Congress, the qualifications of *all* voters are included. If that had been the intention of the Constitution certainly it would have been easy to say so. But with equal strain upon language it seems to be inferred that in providing that these qualifications must be the same as those of electors for the most numerous branch of the Legislature, the power to fix the latter was left in the hands of the States. Neither of these assumptions will stand by its own weight, and on the contrary, there is the strongest reason to believe, from their own declarations, that the framers of the Constitution intended this very clause, in conjunction with the authority given to Congress to "make or alter" the regulations of the States, concerning "the time, place and manner of electing Representatives," to form an ultimate power in the hands of Congress for the control of the suffrage. This is the plain import of Madison's language in the Virginia Convention called to consider the Constitution.

But even granting that this clause purposed to leave the regulation of suffrage to the States, what of it, while there exists in the Constitution a check which must always prevent them from restricting the suffrage to any privileged class, by the exclusion from the right of any other class of citizens? Although the States may act in the first instance, it is only within certain limits; the moment they take a step toward a non-Republican government, by raising one citizen or depressing another, the higher authority must interpose.

Necessarily our argument joins issue with that of Mr. Trumbull when he asserts that Congress receives no direction or authority to act in relation to Suffrage, from that clause which requires that "the United States shall guarantee to every State in this Union, a Republican Form of Government." For if the possession of the voting right, by the people, does not distinguish the Republic from other Governments, what does? If the United States is bound to preserve Republican institutions in its various parts, and yet cannot protect Suffrage, what is it to do? Strangely indeed for an American jurist and law maker, Senator Trumbull gives but one conclusive reason for his remarkable assertion, in these still more remarkable words:

"A Republican Government does not depend upon the number of the people who participate in the primary election of Representatives."

This is a strange doctrine for an American Senator! Upon

what, then, does a Republican Government depend? Have all American publicists erred in asserting the right of the people to rule, and that the Governments derive just power only from the consent of the governed? Madison must have been mistaken when he defined the only difference between a Democracy and a Republic, to be that in the former, "the people meet and exercise the Government in person; in a Republic they assemble and administer it by their Representatives and agents." For does not a Democracy require any specific number of voters? But, more than the force of any authority, is the convincement of logic. If a particular number of voters is not necessary in a Republic; if this form of Government does not depend upon that feature, then there is no such thing in reality. For we may not only confine suffrage to male citizens and yet have a Republic, to white citizens and do our Republic no damage; not only disfranchise one-half or two-thirds, but any number. If the number makes no odds, why stop, at all? Disfranchise all voters but one, and call him a King, an Emperor, a Sultan, what of it? You do not offend Mr. Trumbull. According to his definition, Turkey may be a Republic.

Such risks does the Senator run, such absurdities does he arrive at, when he attempts to show that the United States, in protecting a Republican Form of Government in the separate States, has nothing to do with Suffrage. Such absurdities must any one reach, who, for his argument's sake, needs to disregard the familiar noonday truth that there *is* a definite number of voters required in a Republic, viz: the whole of the mature citizens. Nothing less than this is a government of the people; nothing less is equality of rights; nothing less will give to the lawmaker and the executive, the consent of the governed.

It will be noticed that Senator Trumbull's argument that Congress derives no authority over suffrage from this clause, does not take any broad ground of reasoning, but is composed entirely of objections of detail, of such a character that they may all be generalized under a single head—a supposed difficulty in explaining what a "Republican Form of Government" really is. Some of these difficulties arise from his taking it for granted that all our existing institutions are essentially Republican. For, he says, some judicial and other officers are appointed, not elected; women do not vote; electors of the President are to be appointed in such manner as the Legislature shall direct; because these anomalous features exist in what we have been accustomed to regard as a Republic, our authority concludes there is no such a Government, or if there is that it has no distinct characteristic!

Finally, to refer to one or two allegations of fact. That at the time of framing the Constitution, "Suffrage was much more restricted in all the States than it is in any of them at present," is certainly not true. From 1787 to 1867, when for the first time, National authority interposed and gave their voting right back to the excluded class of nine States, there had been a steady restriction of suffrage, by the usurpation of local law. In the frame of their Constitutions, of the thirteen original States, South Carolina solitary and alone, excluded black voters, by placing the word "white" as a qualification. Yet of those thirteen, eight more have, since the adoption of the Constitution, excluded colored citizens from voting, and one has fixed so burdensome a property qualification as to amount to virtual exclusion.

Is this, as Senator Trumbull tells us, a widening of suffrage since 1787?

And more than this, it must be remembered that when the Constitution was framed slavery existed in most of the States. By the theory of that institution, the master, in his ballot, represented his chattels, as well as himself. In point of fact, he certainly was interested in their welfare as property, and voted to that extent in their behalf. But these human chattels have become citizens. Yet they have no vote in several States, and nobody pretends to represent them. Liberty is increased, but is the suffrage increased with it? Is it not more restricted now than in 1787?

If it be true, as we are told, that "the Republican form of Government required to be guarantied to each State is a government of such a character as existed in the States when the Constitution was framed," what follows? Certainly that we must put the States back into such Constitutions as they then had! If that was the particular form guarantied, any other was guarantied against, and the slightest departure from the original plan would require a check. If Mr. Trumbull is right on this point, the forms of State Constitution existing in 1787 were a cast-iron mould, and however inconvenient or impossible it may be, the Commonwealths of eighty years' existence must be taken back and forced into their unyielding baby clothes. And supposing that to be done, it would then re-establish negro suffrage in every State but South Carolina. In it, notwithstanding the rebellion, and the rights which, according to Mr. Trumbull's elaborate argument, Congress acquired by the conquest of the Southern territory, the negroes could *not* be allowed to vote, because it was forbidden in 1787! To such conclusion does this last logic of the Senator lead!

The guaranty of a Republican Government of the States is a simple and plain provision. To define the character of a Republic is easy, in the light of our history as a nation, and that done, there is no difficulty, beyond. The clause was necessary, for it is the only protection in the Constitution which of necessity, and in explicit language, prevents the States from being metamorphosed into aristocracies, oligarchies, and virtual despotisms. In this emergency, when many States have assumed the authority to tamper with the fundamental feature of the Government, and take from large classes of their people the right of suffrage, this guaranty is the sole safeguard of the nation. How fatal it must be for the Republic's homogeneity, and consequent unity, if Senators of the highest legislature shall presume to sweep it aside, as a mere abstraction, which can neither be explained nor applied! Calhoun or Davis struck never a more terrible blow at the Union.

That the guaranty power has never been exercised by Congress is no conclusive testimony that it does not exist. As an evidence from a parallel case, Congress has always had ultimate authority to take from the States the regulation of the time and manner of choosing U. S. Senators, yet down to 1866 that authority was not exercised. Till then the States had been allowed to regulate for themselves. What caused Congress to assume its reserved power? Abuse by the States of their suffered privilege.

That the guaranty by Congress of protection to the voting rights of the citizen, would interfere with present practice in several States is an argument for, and not against, the assumption of the duty. If the abuse is great, so much the greater necessity for action. If many States are trampling upon their citizens, it is surely time for the General Government to interpose its protection. If there is a growth of incongruous monsters in the family, it is time that the superintending power should promptly train them into homogeneity.

This is a Nation, not simply a Union—a Republic, not a mere Confederacy. If the great principle upon which its existence depends is not within its own protection, what a farce we are acting.

PART THIRTEEN

Thirty-Five Years of
Antislavery Agitation
Fittingly Rounded Out

---

57. THE AMERICAN FREEDMAN,

EDITORIAL

December 1868

Ever since Sumter, members of freedmen's aid societies had been a strong base for Radicalism. Scattered strategically across the North, centering in a dozen major cities, linking with Protestant church organizations, with business, fraternal, veterans' and other patriotic associations, and with local Republican party elements, zealous Negrophiles served state and national Radical legislators as sources of funds, news, and pressures on less ardent party colleagues.

But ever since Appomattox this essential contribution to Radical energy and insight had spasmodically ebbed away. News of Appomattox itself had caused some proportion of Negrophiles to give up efforts and to dry up funds. Similar reactions and secessions from active humanitarian politics were evident in December 1865 when the Thirteenth Amendment was ratified, in mid-1866 when the Civil Rights Act and the Freedmen's Bureau law pushed past the White House, a year later when the Reconstruction legislation succeeded in passage, and in 1868 with Johnson's impeachment and finally with Grant's election. Two years later the ratification of the Fifteenth Amendment symbolized the last curtain for a great many other tillers in the field of Negro-centered good works, and for many Radical Republicans of the rank and file.

They thought that they had won the fight, not that they were giving up too soon. We know their error. They knew their accomplishments and were proud of them.

Here is an editorial, "The Beginning of the End," from the periodical issued by the American Freedman's Union Commission, which speaks to many of these developments.[1]

"The Beginning of the End."

The objects for which the American Freedman's Union Commission was established are nearly accomplished. The end is not yet, but the end's beginning is visibly at hand.

The Central Commission was organized to do a specific and temporary work. This was: To gather up the tangled skeins of the Freedman's movement and weave them into a single strand; to incarnate in a national organization that spirit of humanity and enlarged patriotism which had before dwelt only in local Boards; to give it a habitation and a name which would better commend its claims to the people, to the government, and to other nationalities; and thus, in co-operation with other organizations, to prepare the way more efficiently for the hour when the Southern States, freed from the last shackle of slavery, could establish, by legislative action, those

---

[1] *American Freedman*, III (December 1868), 2–3; McPherson, *The Struggle for Equality*, ch. 18.

educational institutions for which public charities, however generously provided and wisely administered, are but an imperfect substitute.

This it has done.

The work of the American Freedman's Union Commission is a part of the history of the country. It has done much to prevent the scattering of the nation's gifts through irresponsible channels. It has checked, if it has not altogether overcome, that spirit of denominationalism which endangered the whole movement. It has given the cause standing abroad as well as at home. It has compelled recognition at the South as well as in the North. It has been a chosen channel of communication between private philanthropy and the Freedman's Bureau. Its school-houses have been planted in every Southern State. Its pupils are numbered by thousands, and its constituents by hundreds of thousands.

Its mission is not yet accomplished, but it will be in a definitely short period of time. At present, the unanimous conviction of its Secretaries and Board is, that it should terminate its existence at the end of this school-year.

To keep the black man before the public persistently as an object of commiseration would be to injure the black man's cause. To press even his educational wants upon the public a day longer than may be required by absolute necessity, would be to play into the hands of those who are seeking to promote a reaction against him.

The Freedmen will not have ceased to need aid at the end of the year, but by that time a national organization to raise this aid will have ceased to be a necessity.

The issues of the autumn's political canvass are now already settled. That now at last we shall "have peace" is rightly regarded by men of all parties as morally certain. And that among the first-fruits of this assured "peace" will be the provision of means for popular education at the South, can hardly be a matter of reasonable question. The rehabilitated States will find in our school-rooms models to their hand. In the graduates of our normal classes they will find teachers for their primary departments. The foundations will already have been laid. The skeleton of an educational system will already be there, waiting only to be filled up.

To this end the Commission has been steadily shaping its course. All that they need now is means to finish their work; that is, funds with which to send back for one more year the well-approved teachers who have been already in the field. For these funds reliance is placed not upon vague and general appeals to the public, but upon private applications to avowed and well-known friends of the cause.

That contributions to the Commission and its Branches are expended in the field, and not consumed in the support of agents and secretaries, will be evident when we state that the New York Branch has dismissed its salaried officers, and, with exception of the cost of one or two canvassers, temporarily engaged, will carry on its work another year without expense. The same, without the exception alluded to, is true of the New England Branch, and, with but little qualification, of the Philadelphia and Baltimore Branches. The Western Board has not a single salaried officer; and the Central Commission has been carried on by unpaid volunteers since the month of May last.

The Commission expends its resources mainly on schools for the training of native or colored teachers. Of the $275,000 raised last year, a large proportion was employed in this way. All the funds from abroad take this direction. These normal schools will become part of the permanent educational provision of the South.

Mr. McKim is at the West this season to lay for the last time the claims of the work before the friends of freedom. We bespeak for him the same cordial reception which was accorded to him last year. By his life-long service in this cause, he has earned the right to be heard when he appeals in its behalf. He testifies of what he has seen, and declares that which he personally knows. We trust the West will send back every last year's teacher to her post. We believe she will. And we moreover believe that East and West, finishing with patient perseverance a work which they began in faith, and have carried on undaunted in the face of obstacles, will yet see the fruit of their labors in a Southern system of education as beneficent as it will be catholic, and, in the best sense, American.

58. THE REVEREND ALEXANDER CLARK, SERMON

November 26, 1868

To be sure, contradictory voices argued that reconstruction remained uncompleted. During the war years Pittsburgh Methodist minister Alexander Clark had worked out a way to get his views into the White House and Capitol cloakrooms and committee rooms. He preached on a theme close to his concerns—the need for abolition, or employment of Negroes in the Union's armies—and through his friends found means to have his sermons read and discussed in Washington. These friends included Methodist Bishop Matthew Simpson and War Secretary Stanton, both intimates of Lincoln and of numerous congressmen. For his part, Clark served the political leaders as an invaluable source of transmontane opinion and as a powerful line directly into the widespread Methodist church network and into associated freedmen's aid organizations.

Exulting that the despised Johnson had found repudiation at the polls to cap his unparalleled humiliation in the impeachment, Clark expected to resume this role once Grant was seated in the White House. The sermon following, given at Pittsburgh's First Methodist Church on November 26, 1868, reflects this happy mood of the halcyon days immediately following Grant's election.[1] Radical goals

---

[1] Clark, *Radical Reconstruction: and Radicalism* (Pittsburgh: Bakewell & Marthens, 1869); and see Ralph E. Morrow, *Northern Methodism and Reconstruction* (East Lansing: Michigan State University Press, 1956).

still lay ahead. How could Clark know that his capacity to exert influence in the direction of these goals was in the past?[2]

A nation, to be righteous, must be so in three essential particulars: 1. *In its Constitution.* 2. *In its Administration.* 3. *In its People.*

1. Its framework must be put up of sound timber. . . . To change the figure: There must be no rottenness in the root of our liberty tree, if we expect strength in the trunk, symmetry in the branches, beauty in the foliage, and sweetness in the fruit. The seat of our national life must be, as the heart of man, the center and source of health. The plan and structure must be thorough, radical, Christian. The constitution of a nation must be righteous. It must recognize men, as such, from a deeper conception than that of their color, stature, or brogue. It must be harmonious with all the rights of a commingling people, whose capacities and tastes are varied, but whose privileges and opportunities are common. The Book of God furnishes the outline, and the Providence of God the particulars of a righteous constitution. The Constitution of the United States embraces the principles of the Declaration of Independence, and those principles are sprung from the Decalogue given directly to the Jewish nation of old. And the Gospel intensifies and magnifies the law,—"Thou shalt love the Lord thy God with all thy heart, and thy neighbor as thyself." Now, a man's neighbor is his equal, no matter whether he stand the same height in his boots, wear the same textured apparel, show the same tint to his skin, or manifest the same intellectual acumen. These differences do not touch the question of rights. Out in nature, the tall cedar of the mountain, the nodding violet of the plain, and the pale ground-ivy bloom of the valley, have each a right to the sunshine and the rain. Each has the privilege of perfecting itself according to its

---

[2] Edwin M. Stanton to Clark, December 26, 1868; letter owned by the estate of Benjamin P. Thomas.

capacity, and neither ever disturbs any other. The elm is not jealous of the daisy, but rather screens it beneath its spreading arms. The oak does not hurl acorns on the clasping fingers of the vine that seeks its strong protection. The eagle is not afraid that the lark may out-soar him toward the sun; each rises into the limitless heavens according to its strength of will and wing, for both are equally free. So every human being has the right to make the most of himself; and no man was ever appointed to lord it over his fellows by belittling them in church or state. "Love thy neighbor as thyself"—*square out*, and not obliquely, as if you stooped! There is no caste in genuine democracy. Nations are but neighborhoods, brotherhoods, indeed; and this makes the Gospel the interpreter of all international law. The nation that makes Christ divine, supreme, and every man the equal of every other, enjoys the true theocracy and the true democracy. The Jewish government, ordained of God and fashioned for humanity, was a Theo-democracy—a system which recognized, first, *the Lord* most high, and second *the people* all as lowly equals. . . .

This fundamental fact was understood by the framers of our national Constitution. It was conceived by the mind of the Infinite, languaged to the world in the Sinai law, and magnified by the Gospel of Jesus Christ. It has been the central glory of America's greatness from 1776 until now—obscured and misinterpreted until the day when Abraham Lincoln's hand, guided by the recording angel of the Lord, wrote four millions of bondmen free! That pen of the President, as it glided over the paper page, had mightier power than any warrior's sword that ever leaped from scabbard in the battle-field. For it moved in answer to the blessed will of God, and swept away from the old foundations the superstructures of the villainous builders; and it remains now for the people's Congress and the people's President in the incoming administration to go on until the broken ruins are completely removed from the base our fathers laid so wisely and so well. The reconstruction must be carried forward by honest men, who shall measure, weigh, square, fit, polish and cement every part by the standard of the Gospel.

The war has thrown down what was wrongly put up. The materials lie in wild confusion about us. They had been mischievously built in. Republicanism, Democracy, Abolitionism, Secession, Slavery, and all sorts of human fabrics piled in together, but without symmetry, beauty or strength—a worse than Babel tower of incohering parts. It was a monstrous deformity—an offence to the eye of all civilization. God wouldn't have such a pitiful structure rising up into His holy heavens. . . . and now He commands reconstruction on the basis of equal brotherhood. We are to rear again a national edifice that shall be fronted toward all races of men, and solid in every wall. Let us thank God to-day that we are permitted to do this—that we are not utterly destroyed, as a nation, for our sins. This is a grand work of ours. Let all the people take part in it by word, by prayer, and by solemn deed; and let us be glad that we may engage in such a blessed business. It is a rare privilege to live in these days, and through these duties of reconstruction—these times of special mercy and matchless opportunity. The Master says to the American people: You tried it once, but failed. You built in rubbish for rock, ice for granite, straw for cement; and your dangerous fabric was shaken down. Now, try it over again; and build, next time, after the model of the Gospel; build fair and square; build for souls, for eternity, for God. For only righteousness exalteth a nation.

Let us examine foundations. What our fathers merely implied, let us fully supply. . . . If States say we must swear by the God of the Bible, let States themselves stand by the Christ of the Bible. . . . To confess the authority of Jesus Christ is to acknowledge the equality of men. Now, let every word be taken from our Federal Constitution which slavery put in it—every letter, dash and dot which the Christ-rejecting and brother-hating iniquity caused to mar the Document our fathers traced out of God's law—let all be expunged and the blanks supplied by words from the Gospel of God's Son. . . . And let all State Constitutions accord with the central one; and let all ecclesiastical economies know no more forever such leveling words as "white" and "male" in the voices of fellowship and counsel.

The great danger now is in conciliation. Policy is always to be suspected. Compromise led to the great mistake at first, and apologized for its enormity till the last. This spirit led us as a people to build a false structure. It was conservatism before the war; let it be radicalism after the war. The one produced fraternal strife; the other leads to permanent peace. It was the rebel Beauregard who opened fire on Sumter; it was the loyal Grant who took Lee's sword at Appomattox. Let Congress insist upon it, in the face of Southern pride and party policy, *this stone of equal rights must go into the reconstruction*—IT MUST GO IN, without a scar or scratch, or stain of dishonor. To build without this, now, is doubly criminal; it would insult God and imperil man. Such reconstruction would be redestruction. There must be unswerving adherence to the masonry of the Architect who built the universe. . . .

We must not waste our time in answering questions of policy. We are simply to do our duty. "What shall be done with the negro?" Done *with* him? Thank God! he is not a chattel, nor a piece of commodity any more, that any such barbarous question as that need be asked. As well inquire, "What shall be done with the German, the Irishman, the Spaniard? These, in this land, are their own men, our neighbors, breathing freedom's air in common with us all; and the question now is, rather, "What shall we do *for* the negro?" If he be hungry, let us feed him; if he be naked, let us clothe him; if he be ignorant, let us teach him; if he be wicked, let us show him Christ by our own patience, our kindness, our forbearance, our love.

But we are told that there is no affinity between the African race and our own. We hear from the politicians of the South and their conservative sympathizers of the North, until it rings as the key-note of the party's plaint, "We hate the negro." "There is absolute antagonism," they say, "between the races." That would do to tell in a speech, or sing in a song, or write on history's page, if it were not for the one queer fact—*the mulattoes!* If these yellow faces argue natural antagonism, it is a pity for the logic as well as the instinct of the modern Democracy!

This so-called repugnance to color is mere pretence. . . . It is not repugnance to *color,* as they say: it is repugnance to *low condition.* And if they dared express it, the feeling is the same toward all who are poor and abject, and depressed. It is a political hypocrisy, itself darker than the badge it fain would throw over every child of poverty, of whatever name or nation.

There is a class of scant-idead men who say that this is the white man's country. So it is; but it is the black man's, the brown man's, and the red man's country, also. It is more the freedman's than the Irishman's, if birthright has any claim.

Thank God, this glad Thanksgiving day, I can stand in a free pulpit and say to you in those free seats, that *this is everybody's country.* It is broad enough for all kindreds, tribes and tongues; for rich and poor are here, weak and strong are here, learned and illiterate are here; while over all and first of all, God is here; for at last it is God's country! And if he permits black men in it, he'll see that they breathe its atmosphere, eat its bread, and enjoy it as creatures bearing his own image and destined to rise into his high heaven before their pale-faced fellows who hate them without a cause. Whoever hums this silly song, "The white man's country," deserves to be chased out of it by Indians;* for if it comes down to a simple question

---

* This passage has been especially frightful to the Democratic bodyhood. It has been itself *reconstructed,* set in quotation marks and made to mean any kind of perversion, according to the prejudice of the reviewer! It is alarming to think of the tomahawks and the scalps that have swung out of this little phrase. The bombs and bullets, the prisons and poisons of the broad Rebellion were nothing in comparison.

of prior occupancy, the copper-skin's claim is best of all. Shame on the tongue that has no better argument than "White man's country." For in wars with Britain and Rebeldom, soldiers in ebony contributed largely to save this republic from overthrow. If we relied upon the bullets of colored troops in time of war, surely we should be magnanimous enough to give ballots to colored freemen in time of peace. Suffrage does not necessarily lead to social equality. That is a matter of taste. Because a Dutchman votes in your ward is no reason why a Dutchman shall marry your daughter. Voting is a matter of right. Marrying is a matter of taste. Tastes and rights are not in danger of mixing any more than oil and water. Their equilibrium will not be disturbed by the innocent bits of paper that men deposit at the polls.

This whole nation needs to be recast on the model of the New Testament. Churches need reconstruction, until human creed and stately ritualism shall give place to simple Christianity. Schools need reconstruction, until physical and moral training shall stand equal in importance to mental culture. Labor needs reconstruction, until capitalists and employés see eye to eye as level men. Society needs reconstruction, until fashion's sickly sentimentalism shall hide before the light of common sense and warmth of neighborly affection. In all departments of life, the inalienable rights of all people should be recognized and honored, for nothing less or lower than thorough righteousness—unceasing righteousness—will exalt the nation.

2. A nation, to be exalted, must have a righteous Administration, as well as a righteous Constitution. . . . A nation, to be righteous, must be righteously governed. It will not do to commit a righteous instrument to unrighteous hands. But you may safely trust the sacred document with the man who exacted unconditional surrender from rebels in arms. You may be content while an unconquered soldier, an honest citizen, a lover of peace, an unpolicied President sits as central personage in the nation's cabinet—not as a king, not as a proclaimer

of vetoes, not as a presumptuous pronoun—but as an exponent of right as God reveals it anew and abroad from day to day. We may well thank God for a President who shall have no policy of his own. Surely we have had enough of "My Policy." We have had enough of party policy. We want honesty now. And there is no policy in honesty. It is always frank, and open, and free, and equal to the issues of the time. The word *policy* occurs but once in the Bible, and then in connection with a surly king who destroyed a whole people by his stubbornness, and who magnified himself in his own heart and stood up against the Prince of princes. "Through his policy," we are told, "he caused craft and conspiracy." Whenever you hear people talking of this or that "policy," refer them to the eighth chapter of the Book of Daniel, and let them see the real significance of the word.

The Chief Magistrate should recognize his relations to God and to the people—should comprehend the . . . democracy of the Constitution. And he should reflect these qualities in all his acts. . . .

We thank God for the result of the November ballot, for it has given us a leader to whom we can look with confidence and hope. We believe Grant will be as prudent, as patient, and as persistent in the chair, as he has been in the field. We will not be likely to hear that he has invited Toombs or Stephens to occupy the chair of Seward; and we may be confident that he will be colder towards Hampton and Forrest than Andrew Johnson ever was towards Charles Sumner. He has been tried and found equal to the veriest emergency when treason flourished in arms. He is not the man to be either flattered or fettered now. His silence has a magic power which the destructionists all dread, and which reformers note with thankful hearts. He shrinks from no labor; he indulges in no receptions; he makes no promises. He accepts his position as a man, and not as a monarch; as the people's fellow-friend, and not as the figure-head of a political party. He understands the situation now, as he did in the Wilderness; and again, as then, he will go through to the blooming apple-tree beyond.

3. A nation, to be righteous, must be composed of righteous People. A righteous Constitution and a righteous Administration are not enough. There must be a righteous citizenship. . . .

So the circle closes and links into itself. If the people are righteous, the economy of the nation will be safe and honorable. The more of Christ in the citizen, the more of religion in politics—until the religion is so much the stronger that the whole thing shall be called religious—until policy is lost in honesty—and then the Republic will rise and shine in all her agencies and departments.

And this thought brings us face to face with the wrongs and confusions in society. The Gospel of Jesus Christ, in its application to sinners, must be published to all as *glad tidings,* and not as *anathema.* There must be greater effort to reach the masses. Piety must come down from the pulpit where it whines and frowns, out from the pews where it sleeps and speculates, and be unsurpliced and unsabbathed as an everyday glory for the people. There should be more free churches, more sensational preaching, more advertising and less suppressing of Jesus, more missionary zeal, more venturing out into the darks and desolations after wandering outcasts, that they may be faced homeward and met with smiles and welcomes thither again. We must not be so fastidious. We must not permit ourselves to be porcupined by untouchable respectability. We must open our mouths and call things by their Bible names; we must open our pockets and help the poor according to Bible rules; we must open our hearts and love and get loved in New Testament style.

Our churches should be more aggressive—not as mere belligerent forces, battling and beating down for the sake of leaving society in ruins. As organizations, they must be perpetual reformers. These confused moral elements about us must be controlled and arranged, and all classes of people wrought up into Christly form and made symmetrical and sympathetic according to the standard of the Gospel. The Christian Church is not a mere little select company of the saved and sanctified who are expected to employ all their time and talent to keep themselves from backsliding into a lost condition. They are bound together for a more neighborly purpose—to do good to others—to represent Christ in the winning power of his life—to reconstruct society—to Christianize the world. The Church, to be really evangelical, must be the center of attraction and activity; it must have so largely the spirit of Christ as to draw men, to invigorate, to cheer, to comfort, to illuminate, to exalt, and to bless communities of common people.

The Church, to be true to its mission, must have not only words, but works for all. It must overwhelm the world's pleasures by floods of *greater* pleasure; it must outshine the world's allurements by heavenly transfigurations. . . .

Radicalism.

SUPPLEMENTARY.

Some persons fail to discriminate between *radicalism* and *fanaticism*. Newspapers, among some men, do the business of both Bible and dictionary, arranging beliefs and defining words. According to a popular political interpretation, the term radical means *evil* (with a *d* to begin with), and that in every question, evermore! So, by force of prejudice, this honorable word has been perverted to excite suspicion and awaken odium. Very often it is used in the puzzle of an indefinable idea, as an expression of something that writers and talkers know little or nothing about.

The word is derived from *radix—radicis*—a root. . . . It means, both in religion and politics, native, pure, thorough, clean, total, permanent. A radical is original, honest, and earnest. The Gospel of Jesus Christ, as heralded by John Baptist, brings out its significance in the announcement of a new order of thought and life—"Now the ax is laid unto the root of the trees." That means that the New Testament economy shall cut through forms and scums and shams, to the very core of real life—that the blade of truth shall penetrate heartward, probing down and striking in to the vital motives of thought and action. And any subject, however creeded or covered, that will not bear this deep searching, is unsound as a basis and dangerous as a structure. . . . Radicalism draws straight lines between right and wrong. It hews to the chalk-mark; it calls things by their right names. And this is sore business to double men, for it splits them asunder. It is the uncompromising antagonist of sin and wrong, however popular or powerful. Sometimes radicalism has been vehement, and ripped up the very foundations of society; but not sooner nor deeper than such bases needed just that ripping up! Radicalism cares not for numbers or position; it cares only for humanity and God. It is a heavenly principle let down from the blessed world of peace and purity, and aims to get all relations right in this. No wonder it makes a stir among the dry bones. It is about the livest thing that moves, and no marshaled conservatisms and rebellions have blades enough to kill it.

Radicalism means agitation. So do the sweet breezes of the ocean. If the vast deep were never stirred by storms, it would become a cesspool of death and abomination. The world of mental and moral being is kept alive and vigorous, and made beautiful by agitation. Radicalism is an early riser, a morning thinker, and an all-day worker. It is the impulse of all progress in Church and State. But conservatism is a lounger, a borrower, a cringing apologist, and the devil traps it drowsing, and makes it his uninquiring and servile agent. Radicalism deals with facts; conservatism plays with fancies. Radicalism attaches to duties, and faces right onward with a smile into oppositions; conservatism associates with caste and mammon, parleys with opinion, and skulks in times of peril. . . .

Almost any man could summon the courage to go into a battle when crowding comrades were around him, when the old flag floated broadly above him, when martial music pulsed the air all about him, and when the inspiration of a conquering host transfused his soul with the glory of apparent victory. . . . But not many men could do as old John Brown, the radical hero, did, when passing up the bleak hill-side along with his own coffin, toward the ignominious Virginia scaffold, where he must die alone and despised of the motley crowd; for as he ascended the hill he paused, took up in his arms a little wondering outcast colored child, and kissed it lovingly! It took a true man to do that! And he was a true man!

But the world does not produce many such brave men. John Brown, nearing the Charlestown gallows, is a grander sight than Jeff. Davis skulking away from his Confederate capital! O, by far—*how* grander the picture of an obscure man hanging by the neck that day for a principle, and dying for it, alone, than that of a traitorous Congressman—a rebel President—hanging for years, undead, in the infamy of a Benedict Arnold!

But a Christian radical has faith to pray for God's forgiveness to extend even to bitterest enemies. Down on the sand-grave of an Andersonville martyr, though the dust beneath were that of an only brother, he would kneel to ask mercy for the chief conspirator. For it is heart-work with the radical believer in Christ the Lord, and he has power with Heaven in quest of benedictions for humanity's meanest forms, because he pleads the merit of humanity's Sinless Image, and recognizes it in the face and life of the least of His little ones. . . .

59. CHARLES FRANCIS ADAMS, JR.,
AND HENRY ADAMS
1868–1869

Men of like concerns, especially the veterans of the antislavery and freedmen's aid crusades, in and out of Congress, pressed for a fifteenth amendment to the constitution forbidding states from restricting the enjoyment of citizenship because of race. Again Radicals proved themselves to be effective and practical politicians. Even Wendell Phillips supported the phrasing of the present Fifteenth Amendment when in February 1869 it emerged from Congress to go to the states for ratification.[1] It was to be one of the last times when Radicals and the main body of Congressional Republicans worked well together, when Radicals were in the van of public opinion, guiding it, reaching obtainable goals with it. But of course this was unknowable in early 1869.

Instead patriots congratulated themselves that in the year between Johnson's impeachment and the composition and passage of the Fifteenth Amendment, the nation had won another deadly battle and emerged high-stepping. The impeachment was the culmination of the War and Reconstruction, Charles Francis Adams, Jr., said in a July 4th tribute to his own generation:[2]

> We shall hereafter recognize only the great fact that the nation bowed to the law [i.e., the decision in the Senate not to convict Johnson], and, the object of an unprecedented popular odium, a chief magistrate who had shocked every sense of decency and humiliated every citizen—who was hated by the party in uncontrolled power and respected by no one—that this magistrate was retained in office with out a breath of resistance simply because one vote was lacking to convict him according to law. We may surely claim that this great episode will not discredit us in history.

His brother Henry Adams agreed and stressed particularly the view that 1869 properly closed off the period of emergency that since 1860 had justified Radical ways.

> Reconstruction naturally comes first on the list of subjects requiring public attention, although Reconstruction, thanks to the general acquiescence of the country in the result of the November [1868] elections, and thanks also to the increasing prosperity which has drawn the attention of the Rebel states to more profitable matters, has lost much of its old prominence in politics.

---

[1] McPherson, *The Struggle for Equality*, pp. 425–426.

[2] Adams, *The Double Anniversary, '76 and '63: Fourth of July Address, Quincy, Massachusetts* (Boston: Lunt, 1869), pp. 11–12.

Nevertheless, the point of Negro suffrage was thought to require attention, and even to need acknowledgment as part of the fundamental law of the land. Like most of the measures adopted by Congress, the [Fifteenth] Constitutional Amendment is more remarkable for what it does not than for what it does contain. . . . Congress . . . has had its failures, and the neck-tie with which it proposes at last to adorn the statue of American Liberty is the result of many efforts. Apart from the general doubt whether it is advisable to insert in the Constitution such special provisions, there is little in the 15th Amendment to which we can fairly object. The dogma that suffrage is a national right, and not a trust, is by implication denied. The "right" to hold office, as well as to vote, is not asserted. Education and even property qualifications [by state law] are not excluded. We know little of legal ingenuity, if it is not found that this Amendment is of small practical value. Its sting and its danger rest in the possible abuse of the power granted to Congress by the second section [of the proposed Fifteenth Amendment].[3]

60. WENDELL PHILLIPS, SPEECH

December 1869

The Fifteenth Amendment's "sting and danger" in Adams' depiction was the justification for Wendell Phillips and other Radicals to support the proposal, to the surprise of those who expected them to demand much more. Phillips expected that Congress and the federal courts would watchdog voting rights nationally under the new amendment, blocking the obvious loopholes it and its predecessor left in the improved American democracy. A Congress ever on the alert against wrongdoing by states in matters of race would fill in the gaps left by the evaporating Freedmen's Bureau and the contracting freedmen's aid organizations. These were the functions

[3] Adams, "The Session," *North American Review*, CVIII (April 1869), 610–640, with quoted material on 613.

"We Ask of Congress," Phillips told a Boston audience on December 4, 1869, the eve of the opening of the Congressional session, the members of which had been elected in November 1868, when Grant ran.[1] The Fifteenth Amendment was then close to ratification; military reconstruction was nearing a close in more than half the former Confederate states. Phillips' plea is in the Radical tradition of trusting that ever-enlarging democracy, literacy, and opportunity were the cures for the ills of democracy.

I am to speak to you to-night on "What we ask of Congress." . . . I have no criticism to make to-night on the [Grant] Administration; not that I do not blame it, as a unity, for very large and grave neglect; not that I do not see distinctly the cause of its weakness as an Administration. . . . The Administration represents a section, and a weak section—an unthinking, an unwilling, a reluctant section—of the Republican party. Congress is evidently the active element of our government for the next four years. What I demand of Congress is that it should assume the government, which the Executive has abdicated; that it take up the reins of civil government and put a hand on to the helm of the vessel of State; that it should not be allowed to drift without a policy, gravitate without any directing mind. What I ask of Congress, therefore, is the ingredients that shall harvest the results of the war. I want the elements which will enable the nation to get all the blood and treasure as fairly earned.

Now it seems to be that the one great idea symbolized in the war, against which the South protested, and on the wings of which the North was borne up, was "Nationality,"—not a partnership, but a nation; not a group of States, but a State. No element of race will ever make us a nation. No technicality and peculiarity of territory will make us a nation. We lie all around loose. Hitherto we have been only a herd of States

---

[1] In Boston *Commonwealth*, December 4, 1869.

hunting for our food in company. We never had an idea, nor an assertion, and our history was one like the dream of the morning. . . . We have learned only one thing by the war,— what the disease is. The matter with us is, that great, shrewd, persistent, bull-dog element at the South hates the Union. Now the question is, How is it to be appeased, to be conciliated, to be smothered if it cannot be conciliated? In my view, the war has just begun. We have fought the first skirmish. The state of society is never annihilated until it is replaced. You do not annihilate a social system when you decree its death. You only annihilate it when you fill its place with another. What is to be done with the reluctant section previously alluded to, is to replace it, not annihilate it; and what we are to, ask of Congress is the measure that shall replace, supersede, fill up, crowd out the elements which occasioned the war. If we expect any nationality, if we want anything that shall make a nation extending from ocean to ocean, I believe in a public opinion so vigilant and so exacting that from the gates of the Gulf to the Atlantic and the Pacific, we will have one flag and one law. I look to a popular education so advanced that under that one and that impartial law all creeds and all tongues and all races shall be gathered with an equal protection. But in order to do that we must use our time to-day; not that the experiment will fail in the end, for in that far future, if one may prophesy anything, I think I see it either through the forty years of the Wilderness, or I see it in a nearer view; I see it after the revolutions of 1715 and 1745 and 1688, as in England, after perpetual convulsions as in France; or I see it in a moment by the statesmanship and wisdom and determined purpose of the people. What I believe is that, if three years ago this people had had a leader, if we had had a President, not a representative, if we had Sully, or Cromwell, or Walpole even, or Chatham, we would have crystalized this reluctant section into a likeness of our own, and been to-day one people, with the same element of civilization, from Canada down to the Gulf. I look upon it in this light.

When our fathers started the constitution they only had one view. They thought that they took in a broad outlook. But very few take in a broad outlook; and it is very rarely that you find those men in the confidence of his race, or in the stations of power. Our fathers were hounded into the Union by pecuniary difficulties; the States could not pay up their debts; the nation could not raise its taxes; our money, paper, was worth nothing; our credit was gone. If you look in the constitution of the United States, you will be surprised to find an immense preponderance of provisions that relate to the financial provinces of government. It was a mercantile partnership, not a nation, that our fathers founded. You will be surprised to learn that this nation was a Yankee pedler for forty years. They forgot one great thing in framing the constitution. They forgot that social system at the South. Every drop of blood that they poured into the veins of the national government gave that strength. They nurtured their own enemy, and thence came the revolution of '61. All the subsidiary powers of government were left in the loosest possible condition. The only thing we guarded was the bank-vault of the country. Outside of our financial and mercantile arrangements the Union is all incomplete. Our fathers never finished their work. The Fourteenth Amendment is the first attempt, even, to define a citizen of the United States. In 1865 the United States government had never defined its own basis, its citizens. Nobody could tell, authoritatively, who was the substratum on which the government rested. We waited till 1867 before we made our own floor, and to-day, still more absurdly, there is not any recognized power of this government to protect its own citizens. What can we do to facilitate, to secure an impartial election of a President or a representative? is the question which arises, and the answer is—we can do nothing. We have no rights. We cannot touch the very elements out of which our own government is created. Our fathers trusted to the harmonious coöperation of the States. They left the United States to float like a balloon in the air. When the rebellion broke out, fortunately, our government had one power—war. Our fathers had secured to it the militia and the purse, and they are all it left. What we want to get now is a footing.

The first thing I ask of Congress is that it shall complete the construction of government. I do not ask this on the ground of a temporary measure on a report from Texas of so many murders, a report from Mississippi of so much turbulence. I ask it on this ground:—I undertake to say that now is the time to complete the machine which our fathers left incomplete. We have abolished slavery, one of their omissions; we have defined citizenship, another of their omissions. Now we want to protect citizenship. My claim of Congress is, now, before the helm passes out of the hands of the conquering idea, that we should, like statesmen, undertake to complete this portion of the machine committed to our care; that we should not allow a future difficulty to come across our path, and we not be able to reach into the States and remedy it. A government without a basis, that cannot reach down and protect its own citizens in doing a duty which it calls upon them to perform! If you need an amendment to the constitution, make it; but I do not believe it. The 14th Amendment covers it. If necessary, plant a squad of soldiers in every voting district in the thirty-eight States, but let the flag of the Union protect its own citizens wherever it floats. [Applause.] Announce the principle that whenever a State neglects its duty, whenever forty householders in any district calls upon the Union to protect its own ballot-box, that it shall be the duty of the President of the United States to send a company, or a regiment, into that section, and see that the polls are kept peacefully open. [Applause.] I know it may be a duty never called for in many States. I know that the very existence of the right may preclude the need of using it. I know that it looks towards despotism,—but better despotism than anarchy. What I want is a government so broad, so impartial, so founded on an average of national interests, that no local prejudice, no local malignity, no local wealth, can hold up its hand against the peaceful exercise of the citizenship under its flag.

Then there is another element. What made the rebellion? Eight millions of dunces [applause] led by a few hundred thousand knaves. And I say that the government which so far abdicates its rightful powers as to leave 8,000,000 of dunces under its flag deserves to be rebelled against. [Applause.] The foundation of a ballot-box is the common school. I want a common school system which shall not rest on the charity of the North. If Alabama doesn't set it up, we will, and send her the bill. [Applause.] I will complete their government. I will take hold with my feet off the ground on which it stands, and having done that, I will see what that soil is made of, and it shall be educated, men and women. Before I trust the great issues of the future, looming upon us from every side, I demand of Congress that they shall see to it that no State prejudice or obstinacy shall leave an ignorant mass to obstruct our progress. The great trouble of the South lies in its ignorance. Awake it to enterprise. Forgiveness is the watchword of the Democratic party. Non-resistance is the creed of a part of the Republican and the whole of the Democratic party. We have got an idea that forgiveness of everybody, in all circumstances,—shutting our eyes to the call to action,—is a virtue. We have got an idea that Christianity consists in putting our own eyes out, not knowing good from bad, black from white, and just from unjust. The stern, rigid, indomitable, unmixed idea of justice is intolerable to the American people. If the Republican party had a brave man at its head, it would marshal its forces, nail its colors. "No forgiveness to the mass," set every journal afloat, and absolutely impregnate the Northern mind with the state of the South so thoroughly that every man would be aghast at the very idea of forgiveness. It has the means in its hands, but it will never use them. It hasn't the pluck to use them. Therefore, what I demand of Congress is to fortify against the coming magnanimity.

God has given us one corner-stone upon which to fortify, and that is the negro. I demand of Congress that it should establish at the South lands, every acre of land that the North owns, as a gift to loyalty. There is a fearful problem looks to us from the Rocky Mountains. The immigration from Europe is probably drying up. . . . Europe is remodeling her governments, and she has need of all her people. . . . The epoch of European emigration is closing, and the vacant prairies of the West are to be filled up from the Pacific side. The great Oriental horde is opening. The four hundred millions of Chinese are to pour their surplus into our Western veins, a race as bold, as indomitable, as indestructible as the Yankee. The shock will strain to the utmost the capacity of Republican institutions. The very thought of it has scared from its seat the faith of many an American in self government. One half our statesmen are ready to sit down and surrender the principle that lies at the root of our government to this enormous danger. What I want is a government at Washington that can hold the States in their orbits while the great change needed goes on. . . .

61. CHARLES SUMNER, SPEECH

February 1869

Now it appears that Wendell Phillips and other Radicals were wise to accept the Fifteenth Amendment as the best obtainable. Probably a formulation more strongly restrictive of states' powers in matters of race would have failed to win passage through Congress. Alternatively, gaining exit, the conceivably more stringent versions that some Radical congressmen pleaded for would not have amassed enough support in states for ratification.

On February 5, 1869, Sumner had introduced a substitute for

the proposed Fifteenth Amendment, then under Senate consideration. He received almost no backing. Here is what was *not* possible,
even in the backwash of Grant's victory at the polls—or perhaps
because of the lack of a landslide on behalf of the general. The
Republican party had some sort of mandate, but clearly enough,
in the opinion of most congressmen, it was not for what Sumner
proposed.[1]

THE Senate having under consideration a joint resolution from
the House of Representatives proposing an Amendment to
the Constitution of the United States on the subject of Suffrage in the words following, viz.:—
"ARTICLE ——.
"SECTION 1. The right of any citizen of the United States to
vote shall not be denied or abridged by the United States or
any State by reason of the race, color, or previous condition
of slavery of any citizen or class of citizens of the United
States.

"SEC. 2. The Congress shall have power to enforce by proper
legislation the provisions of this Article."—

Mr. Sumner offered the following bill as a substitute:—

SECTION 1. That the right to vote, to be voted for, and to
hold office shall not be denied or abridged anywhere in the
United States, under any pretence of race or color; and all
provisions in any State Constitutions, or in any laws, State,
Territorial, or Municipal, inconsistent herewith, are hereby
declared null and void.

SEC. 2. That any person, who, under any pretence of race
or color, wilfully hinders or attempts to hinder any citizen of
the United States from being registered, or from voting, or
from being voted for, or from holding office, or who attempts
by menaces to deter any such citizen from the exercise or
enjoyment of the rights of citizenship above mentioned, shall
be punished by a fine not less than one hundred dollars nor

---

[1] Sumner, *Works*, XIII, 34–37, 46–49.

more than three thousand dollars, or by imprisonment in the common jail for not less than thirty days nor more than one year.

SEC. 3. That every person legally engaged in preparing a register of voters, or in holding or conducting an election, who wilfully refuses to register the name or to receive, count, return, or otherwise give the proper legal effect to the vote of any citizen, under any pretence of race or color, shall be punished by a fine not less than five hundred dollars nor more than four thousand dollars, or by imprisonment in the common jail for not less than three calendar months nor more than two years.

SEC. 4. That the District Courts of the United States shall have exclusive jurisdiction of all offences against this Act; and the district attorneys, marshals, and deputy marshals, the commissioners appointed by the Circuit and Territorial Courts of the United States, with powers of arresting, imprisoning, or bailing offenders, and every other officer specially empowered by the President of the United States, shall be, and they are hereby, required, at the expense of the United States, to institute proceedings against any person who violates this Act, and cause him to be arrested and imprisoned or bailed, as the case may be, for trial before such court as by this Act has cognizance of the offence.

SEC. 5. That every citizen unlawfully deprived of any of the rights of citizenship secured by this Act, under any pretence of race or color, may maintain a suit against any person so depriving him, and recover damages in the District Court of the United States for the district in which such person may be found.

On this he spoke as follows:—

Mr. President,—In the construction of a machine the good mechanic seeks the simplest process, producing the desired result with the greatest economy of time and force. I know no better rule for Congress on the present occasion. We are mechanics, and the machine we are constructing has for its object the conservation of Equal Rights. Surely, if we are wise, we shall seek the simplest process, producing the desired result with the greatest economy of time and force. How widely Senators are departing from this rule will appear before I have done.

Rarely have I entered upon any debate in this Chamber with a sense of sadness so heavy as oppresses me at this moment. It was sad enough to meet the champions of Slavery, as in other days they openly vindicated the monstrous pretension and claimed for it the safeguard of the Constitution, insisting that Slavery was national and Freedom sectional. But this was not so sad as now, after a bloody war with Slavery, and its defeat on the battle-field, to meet the champions of a kindred pretension, for which they claim the safeguard of the Constitution, insisting also, as in the case of Slavery, upon State Rights. The familiar vindication of Slavery in those early debates was less sickening than the vindication now of the intolerable pretension, that a State, constituting part of the Nation, and calling itself "Republican," is entitled to shut out any citizen from participation in government simply on account of race or color. To denominate such pretension as intolerable expresses very inadequately the extent of its absurdity, and the utterness of its repugnance to all good principles, whether of reason, morals, or government.

I make no question with individual Senators; I make no personal allusion; but I meet the odious imposture, as I met the earlier imposture, with indignation and contempt, naturally excited by anything unworthy of this Chamber and unworthy of the Republic. How it can enter here and find Senators willing to assume the stigma of its championship is more than I can comprehend. Nobody ever vindicated Slavery, who did not lay up a store of regret for himself and his children; and permit me to say now, nobody can vindicate Inequality and Caste, whether civil or political, the direct offspring of Slavery, as intrenched in the Constitution, beyond the reach of national prohibition, without laying up a similar store of regret. Death may happily come to remove the champion from the judgment of the world; but History will make its faithful record, to be read with sorrow hereafter. Do not complain, if I speak strongly. The occasion requires it. I seek to save the Senate from participation in an irrational and degrading pretension.

Others may be cool and indifferent; but I have warred with Slavery too long, in all its different forms, not to be aroused when this old enemy shows its head under an *alias*. Once it was Slavery; now it is Caste; and the same excuse is assigned now as then. In the name of State Rights, Slavery, with all its brood of wrong, was upheld; and now, in the name of State Rights, Caste, fruitful also in wrong, is upheld. The old champions reappear under other names and from other States, each crying out, that, under the National Constitution, notwithstanding even its supplementary Amendments, a State may, if it pleases, deny political rights on account of race or color, and thus establish that vilest institution, a Caste and an Oligarchy of the Skin.

This perversity, which to careless observation seems so incomprehensible, is easily understood, when it is considered that the present generation grew up under an interpretation of the National Constitution supplied by the upholders of Slavery. State Rights were exalted and the Nation was humbled, because in this way Slavery might be protected. Anything for Slavery was constitutional. Such was the lesson we were taught. How often I have heard it! How often it has sounded through this Chamber, and been proclaimed in speech and law! Under its influence the Right of Petition was denied, the atrocious Fugitive Slave Bill was enacted, and the claim was advanced that Slavery travelled with the flag of the Republic. Vain are all our victories, if this terrible rule is not reversed, so that State Rights shall yield to Human Rights, and the Nation be exalted as the bulwark of all. This will be the crowning victory of the war. . . .

If in the original text of the Constitution there could be any doubt, it was all relieved by the Amendment abolishing Slavery and empowering Congress to enforce this provision. Already Congress, in the exercise of this power, has passed a *Civil Rights Act*. It only remains that it should now pass a *Political Rights Act*, which, like the former, shall help consummate the abolition of Slavery. According to a familiar rule of interpretation, expounded by Chief Justice Marshall in his most masterly judgment, Congress, when intrusted with any power, is at liberty to select the "means" for its execution.* The Civil Rights Act came under the head of "means" selected by Congress, and a Political Rights Act will have the same authority. You may as well deny the constitutionality of the one as of the other.

The Amendment abolishing Slavery has been reinforced by another, known as Article XIV., which declares peremptorily that "no State shall make or enforce any law which shall abridge the privileges or immunities of citizens of the United States," and again Congress is empowered to enforce this provision. What can be broader? Colored persons are citizens of the United States, and no State can abridge their privileges or immunities. It is a mockery to say, that, under these explicit words, Congress is powerless to forbid any discrimination of color at the ballot-box. Why, then, were they inscribed in the Constitution? To what end? There they stand, supply-

---

* M'Culloch *v.* State of Maryland: 4 Wheaton, R., 408–21.

ing additional and supernumerary power, ample for safeguard-
ing against Caste or Oligarchy of the Skin, no matter how
strongly sanctioned by any State Government.

But the champions, anxious for State Rights against Human
Rights, strive to parry this positive text, by insisting, that, in
another provision of this same Amendment, the power over
the right to vote is conceded to the States. Mark, now, the
audacity and fragility of this pretext. It is true, that, "when
the right to vote . . . . is denied to any of the male inhabitants
of a State, ... or in any way abridged, except for participation
in rebellion or other crime," the basis of representation is reduced in corresponding proportion. Such is the penalty imposed by the Constitution on a State which denies the right
to vote, except in a specific case. But this penalty on the State
does not in any way, by the most distant implication, impair
the plenary powers of Congress to enforce the guaranty of
a republican government, the abolition of Slavery, and that
final clause guarding the rights of citizens,—three specific
powers which are left undisturbed, unless the old spirit of
Slavery is once more revived, and Congress is compelled again
to wear those degrading chains which for so long a time
rendered it powerless for Human Rights.

The pretension, that the powers of Congress, derived from
the Constitution and its supplementary texts, were all fore-
closed, and that the definition of a republican government
was dishonored, merely by the indirect operation of the clause
imposing a penalty upon a State, is the last effort of the champions. They are driven to the assumption, that all these beneficent powers have been taken away by indirection, and
that a provision evidently temporary and limited can have
this overwhelming consequence. . . . It is impossible to see
the application of this technicality. Because the basis of representation is reduced in proportion to any denial of the right
to vote, therefore, it is argued, the denial of the right to vote

is placed beyond the reach of Congress, notwithstanding all its plenary powers from so many sources. . . .

I make haste to the conclusion. Unwilling to protract this debate, I open the question in glimpses only. Even in this imperfect way, it is clearly seen, first, that there is nothing, absolutely nothing, in the National Constitution to sustain the pretension of Caste or Oligarchy of the Skin, as set up by certain States,—and, secondly, that there is in the National Constitution a succession and reduplication of powers investing Congress with ample authority to repress any such pretension. In this conclusion, I raise no question on the power of States to regulate the suffrage; I do not ask Congress to undertake any such regulation. I simply propose, that, under the pretence of regulating the suffrage, States shall not exercise a prerogative hostile to Human Rights, without any authority under the National Constitution, and in defiance of its positive texts.

I am now brought directly to the proposed [Fifteenth] Amendment of the Constitution. Of course, the question stares us in the face, Why amend what is already sufficient? Why erect a supernumerary column?

So far as I know, two reasons are assigned. The first is that the power of Congress is doubtful. It is natural that those who do not sympathize strongly with the Equal Rights of All should doubt. Men ordinarily find in the Constitution what is in themselves; so that the Constitution in its meaning is little more than a reflection of their own inner nature. As I am unable to find any ground of doubt, in substance or even in shadow, I shrink from a proposition which assumes that there is doubt. To my mind the power is too clear for question. As well question the obligation of Congress to guaranty a republican form of government, or the abolition of Slavery, or the prohibition upon States to interfere with the rights and privileges of citizenship, each of which is beyond question.

62. WILLIAM LLOYD GARRISON, SPEECH

April 9, 1870

Instead of embracing the content that Sumner advocated, the Fifteenth Amendment emerged from Congress in its present form, and almost precisely ten years after the attack on Fort Sumter, the Fifteenth Amendment received ratification and became part of the United States Constitution. Even case-hardened humanitarian campaigners such as Douglass, Phillips, and Theodore Tilton believed that at last the Negro was out of politics. Despite the pleas of some in attendance at the April 1870 session of the American Anti-Slavery Society, that the organization remain in being in order to combat race prejudice and especially to keep sentry watch over the condition of Southern Negroes, the membership chose overwhelmingly to dissolve.[1] Satisfied summings up were in order. William Lloyd Garrison set the tone in a reminiscence and an evaluation of "Thirty-five Years of Anti-Slavery Agitation Fittingly Rounded Out."[2]

. . . Forty years ago this time I was lying in the cell of a Baltimore prison for advocating the glorious cause whose triumph we are here to celebrate. Yet I believe I was then quite as happy in my mind and as confident in my spirit in that jail as today, because I saw the end which was the triumph we have met to celebrate. On coming to address the colored citizens of Boston for the first time, in commencing the conflict here, I said to them:—"I believe as firmly as I do in my own existence that the time is not far distant when you and the trampled slaves shall all be free and enjoy the same rights in this coun-

---

[1] Surveyed in McPherson, pp. 428–430.
[2] Boston *Commonwealth*, April 23, 1870, carried a reprint.

try as other citizens. If you will hold on with a firm grasp, I assert that liberty, equality, every republican privilege, is yours. I do not despair of the time when our State and national assemblies will contain a fair proportion of colored representatives." That was in my early days, when my fancy led me to dream of a comparatively easy conflict. Little did I then know of the strength of the slave-power, and how it had subjected to its sway all that was powerful, respectable, all that was deemed religious and good in the land. Little did I then imagine that the conflict would be rather with the North than with the South, and that here in the city of Boston the most determined opposition to the anti-slavery cause would be found. As the great struggle progressed I had given up the hope of living to see the abolition of slavery and citizenship conferred upon the people of the country. I thank God that I have lived to see every slave rejoicing in his freedom.

We have lived to see as great a miracle as ever we had read of. Who ever dreamed of seeing a nation, as it were, born in a day? Ten years ago the slave power seemed to be able to defy God. Ten years ago Jefferson Davis sat towering in his pride in his place in the Senate of the United States, plotting treason, and leading in open rebellion against the government of the country. . . . Look at the successor [in the U. S. Senate] of Jefferson Davis—a negro! Yes, [Hiram Revels] a negro! [Applause.] They might well rejoice and be filled with all jubilation, for they were having their *Revels* in the Senate of the United States. [Three cheers given.] There was nothing in all history to parallel this wonderful, quiet sudden transformation of four millions of human beings from chattelism to manhood, from the auction-block to the ballot-box, from a condition of slavery to the complete equipment of American citizenship. How have the emancipated slaves behaved themselves in the South since they came out of the house of bondage? Instead of inflicting violence upon those who had kept them so long in bondage, they, like the emancipated slaves in the British West India Islands, crowded to their churches, and on their bended knees offered up their thanksgiving to God, and had their hearts filled with the love of liberty, and had no desire of retaliating upon any man who had done them injury. I would like to know where are the eminent divines, where the sagacious statesmen, where the calculating merchants, who fondly prophesied all manner of evil consequences flowing out of the liberation of those people from bondage. Next came the experiment of arming the freedmen, in order to help us in our hour of peril and to save the Union, and make it possible for us to have a common country. O, what tribulation was felt far and near, even on the part of some friendly to the movement, lest, getting arms into their hands, they would make a bad use of them! But did ever a body of men behave more nobly than the enrolled colored soldiers of our country? Did ever any body of men show more heroic valor on the field of battle? He believed nobody now in this country undertook to question the valor of the colored population of America. They will undoubtedly be looked to in any emergency as those who will be foremost to uphold the flag and vindicate and save the free institutions of their country. Before emancipation it was said that they would be simply vagabonds; but no people in this world are laboring more industriously and effectively. So in regard to their education. It was said that they never could learn anything, that they were almost allied to the brute creation; yet they have among them more than five thousand schools in operation, and more than two hundred thousand have already been taught to read and write. They are really taking the lead in the South, and I believe it is the will of God, especially in regard to the cotton-growing States, that those States shall pass under the control of the colored people, and that they will lead off in a career of prosperity and honor and glory for our country. Since the suffrage was conferred upon them no voters in the land have shown more judgment and discrimination in voting than have the freedmen of the South. They have shown aptitude as legislators and done honor to the station to which they have been so suddenly called. The anti-slavery work was a great moral work, and was carried on up to the hour of the rebellion. I considered it concluded when the slave-power fired upon the flag at Sumter. Then it became a question of saving the country whatever might become of the slave, and so the conflict assumed a political form. I wish you to remember that the party which has given you the ballot, which in Congress has done everything that could be done to give liberty and justice and equality throughout the land, is the Republican party. [Applause.] And to that party belongs all the credit for those great acts of legislation over which you are rejoicing. And on the other hand it would stand forever in history that the Democratic party, so-called—a bastard democracy—opposed every measure for justice, for liberty and for equality; and it has rightly gone under. We are here to give thanks to President Grant. [Applause.] Yes, let the President know that here, in the old cradle of liberty, you mention his name with honor, and that you regard his course with admiration and gratitude in this matter of the ratification of the Fifteenth Amendment. [Three cheers for Grant.] If the President, since he has been elected to office, has seemed to be slow, he certainly has been sure.

63. WENDELL PHILLIPS, SPEECH

April 9, 1870

Even Wendell Phillips softened under the sweet sense of April. Agreeing with Garrison that finally the militants of the abolition and reconstruction crusade could relax, Phillips spoke on April 9 on "The Fulfillment of Our Pledge."[1] He was not wrong to be proud of the revolutionary alterations in American society that he and other activists had won. His error was in estimating that reconstruction was complete as to results as well as in form.

The purpose and pledge of the anti-slavery movement was to secure for the black race equality before the law with other races—to strike the word "white" from our laws and consti-tutions—to put the negro in possession of the same civil and political rights as are enjoyed by other citizens.

The New England Anti-Slavery Society—the parent of all the rest—formed in 1832—stated its object to be "to effect the Abolition of Slavery in the United States, to improve the character and condition of the free people of color, to inform and correct public opinion in relation to their situation and rights, and obtain for them equal civil and political rights and privileges with the whites."

The American Anti-Slavery Society, formed in 1833, aimed to secure the black an "equality with the whites of civil and religious privileges." Its declaration of sentiments pledged it "to secure to the colored population of the United States all the rights and privileges which belong to them as men and as Americans."

The ratification of the Fifteenth Amendment accomplishes this purpose and fulfills this pledge. In consequence of social prejudice and of other obstacles the exercise of these rights may be, for a longer or shorter time, neither easy nor wholly safe. But the law recognizes them, and the whole power of the nation is pledged to the negro's protection in the exercise of them. He holds at last his sufficient shield in his own hands; that which has always sufficed, in the long run, for the pro-tection of an oppressed class. Thwarted at one moment, bul-

---

[1] Reprinted in Boston *Commonwealth*, April 23, 1870.

lied or starved at another, the voter, if true to himself, always conquers and dictates his own fate and position in the end. Though this constitutional amendment does not cover all it ought, in present circumstances, still it contains within itself the cure for its own defects. A man with the ballot in his hand is the master of the situation. He defines all his other rights. What is not already given him he takes. As soon as the negro holds the ballot at the South, whatever he suffers will be largely now, and in future wholly, his own fault. At present, the anarchy in those States, the rule of assassins, social prejudice, his own poverty, ignorance and lack of combination, will postpone the full use of his power; but, in the end, the ballot makes every class sovereign over its own fate. Corruption may steal from a man his independence. Capital may starve and intrigue fetter him at times. But against all these his vote, intelligently and honestly cast, is, in the long run, his full protection. If in the struggle his fort surrenders, it is only because it is betrayed from within. No power ever permanently wronged a voting class without its own consent.

To-day, therefore, the anti-slavery movement may fairly leave its client to the broad influences of civilization and society. The American Anti-Slavery Society may dissolve, or adjourn indefinitely, only to be called together in case of some unexpected emergency. . . .

We have a right, then, as a society, to rejoice in the present condition of the negro's cause. We have seen one rebel State after another half reconstructed and then dashed to pieces by the indignation of the North. By dint of keeping the question open—a result to which our unintermitted demand of suffrage largely contributed—we have seen the misconduct of the South educate and rouse the North to its duty and the necessity of the hour; fortunately before it was too late to retrace its heedless steps. We have the satisfaction of having held up— a hundred-fold more than we could have done individually —the hands of the dozen men, in Senate and House, whose unflinching purpose and vigilant watch have saved the negro in spite of the weariness, the petty jealousies, the narrow technicalities, the ignorance, the prejudice, and the treason, of their party fellows. We have seen the Dred Scott decision set aside, and the negro's citizenship incorporated into the Constitution. We have seen his right to State office vindicated at the point of the bayonet. We have seen him preside over State Senates, and take his place on the Supreme Bench of one of the original thirteen States. We have seen a negro fill the Senatorial chair at Washington left vacant by the chief of the Rebel Confederacy. The hitherto partial law has resumed its sacred fillet, and, blindfold, can no longer distinguish black from white.

At length, panoplied in all the rights of citizenship, the negro stands under a Constitution which knows nothing of race, and for the first time in our history we can read without a blush our fathers' sublime declaration that all men are created equal. As we look back to the perils through which the path has led up to this august goal, we can have the satisfaction of knowing that no hesitation or mistake of ours increased those dangers or prolonged them one single instant. But that, on the contrary, straining every nerve, pressing into service every instrumentality, saving every tool that had in any hour availed our clients, we have contributed our utmost toward making the nation adopt the pledge of the American Anti-Slavery Society and bind itself to protect our clients in "all the rights and privileges which belong to them as men and as Americans."

Of course, in spite of this pledge, the negro, like every race just struggling into complete recognition, still needs the special sympathy and help of his friends. To be sure, the great elements of political security and of industrial protection are on his side. Already the Southerners tremble when they see anything tempt *labor* away from them. They see that a population tests the value of land and the possibility of growth. The ocean States are even now alarmed by the increasing emigration of black labor toward the valley of the Mississippi. On this alarm rests the negro's safety. States begin to compete with each other in tempting him by good treatment to remain within their limits.

Then the vote is a mighty bulwark. The Irish race among us still occupies, mostly, a humble place; is rarely defended by the possession of large wealth or by social position. But where does a politician dare to soil his lips with that name of contempt which used to be flung at the Irish? No, the class, a large one, has a vote; and ambitious men hunt up or invent any link which connects them with Erin. The day is close at hand when Americans will shrink just as carefully from spelling negro with two g's. How much was made out of Gen. Jackson's Irish descent? We may yet live to see the day when a Presidential candidate will boast his share of negro blood.

These two are chief among the strong forces which will cover the black with an ample shield and secure him the fairest opportunity. Ploughing its laborious, but no longer doubtful, course through heavy seas, the bark of that race nears a safe harbor.

Meanwhile, in his transition, he needs counsel, aid, education, land. Our long crusade for him is not therefore really and fully ended. We may break up our ranks, but we may not yet dismiss our care nor lessen our interest. . . .

64. DURBIN WARD, SPEECH

September 10, 1870

The Radical Republican success is represented in part by the nominal acceptance, however reluctant, by conservative Democrats of all these war- and Reconstruction-born novelties. By 1870 "the

new departure" among the Democracy was to act in surface obedience to the requirements of the nation's laws and constitutional
amendments dealing with race and Reconstruction. The speech of
Durbin Ward, an Ohio congressman and able political tactician,
reflects this improvement in his party's ways. It also gives voice to
the happy realization among Democrats that the Radical segment
of their Republican opposition was losing numbers, weight, and
inspiration.[1]

To all these things, as you well know, I was unalterably opposed. To the last moment, yea, on the very day of its final
adoption by this State, I raised my voice in indignant opposition to that final blow to State rights, the Fifteenth Amendment. But notwithstanding the open and active resistance of
the whole Democratic party, and the lukewarmness of many
Republicans, these Radical changes were clothed with the
forms of law and declared to be part of the Constitution. For
one, I have no doubt that, legally speaking, they are all revolutionary and void, and if it was in my power I would revoke
them and return to the Constitution of the fathers. But sad as
the admission may be, this is, in my judgment, plainly impossible. The peaceful revocation of these amendments would
require the ratification of three-fourths of the States, and this
no one can reasonably hope to obtain. Reluctant, then, as we
may be to admit it, the revolution is an accomplished fact.
Though it should lead to National ruin, still it is an accomplished fact. Nothing but a rebellion could revoke its work,
and that would not, for the great body of the people do not
feel with sufficient force the magnitude of the change. All
parties seek repose after a generation of strife. And though it
be the repose of political slavery, that is accepted rather than

---

[1] Durbin Ward, *Life, Speeches, and Orations of Durbin Ward of
Ohio; Compiled by Elisabeth Probasco Ward* (Columbus: Smythe,
1888), pp. 196–198. Ward spoke at Hamilton, Ohio, on September 10,
1870.

a resort to war for the revival of an institution. Control over suffrage is the corner-stone of the State government, and its removal leaves that government itself to rest only on the temporary prop of Federal consent, and to fall into ruin at the will of Federal power. But even to preserve their States from overthrow, the people have not stricken and will not strike one blow. The Constitutional guarantee by the imperial government of civil and political rights to the negro is as strong and will be as durable as any part of the Federal Constitution. There are many things which, though it were better they had never been done, when once accomplished can never be undone. And to this class belongs the late revolution. As well might Germany seek to undo the Reformation, England to recall the Great Rebellion, or Europe reverse Waterloo. Who would claim that the Stuarts could be re-seated on the throne of England? That the Arabs could regain power in Spain? or the feudal system be revised by a statute? Though this revolution is but a thing of yesterday, its results upon our political system are as irrevocable as if it had been over for a thousand years. It is not true that revolutions go backwards, but it is true that events never do. The enfranchisement of the negro is an event which, however brought about, can never be undone; and whether for better or for worse must be treated as accomplished. We may check the full fruition of the revolution, which seeks to absorb all State powers, and, for a time, preserve many of the benefits of States. But the negro is henceforth a political element in our system. He may have, and for a long time certainly will have, very little independence of action, but his vote will be counted, and he who ignores the fact counts without his host. In my own political action hereafter I shall recognize as a fact the new order of things and conform to it. What brought about this radical change in our institutions, how these changes might have been modified, and what is to be their ultimate result, are questions no longer profitable for discussion. They belong to the closet of the student rather than to the debates of the hustings. In my speeches to the people now and hereafter I shall no more discuss these old issues of the stormy past. Under whatever system of government we live, the present time will always be pregnant with questions deeply interesting to the people and eagerly pressing for practical solution.

But though no longer willing to discuss these "dead issues," let no one suppose that I can forget the mighty wrongs that these leaders have inflicted upon the country, or ever cease to struggle for their expulsion from the high places of power. All their ideas of government are at war with mine, and I can never either approve what they have done or intrust them with the ordinary interests of the present time.

But, my countrymen, we need concern ourselves but little about these old Radical leaders. From the very nature of things, the days of their political life are numbered. Parties cannot long survive the issues on which they are formed. The Republican party is in the last stages of dissolution. It was born amid agitation, and will die with repose. It drew its life from the slavery question, and they must be buried in a common grave. The old issues being dead, the party has to face new ones, and it is too old and effete to grapple with them. There is even now no harmony in its ranks, and its dissensions are daily growing greater. Nor ought the fall of the party to be regretted by the rank and file of its own members. Its mission is finished, and it must go with its work to the dread ordeal of history. . . .

PART FOURTEEN

1870 and Following

65. HENRY ADAMS, ARTICLE

July 1870

In one sense the American people by 1869–1870 had caught up with the survivors in politics of the old Radicals. Reviewing the work of Grant's first Congress, Henry Adams wrote:[1]

On the subject of Reconstruction little need be said. The merits or demerits of the system adopted are no longer a subject worthy of discussion. The resistance to [the adoption of] these measures rested primarily on their violation of the letter and spirit of the Constitution as regarded the rights of States, and the justification [for passage and enforcement] rested not on a denial of the violation, but in overwhelming necessity. The measures were adopted with reluctance by a majority of Congressmen, they were approved with equal reluctance by a majority of the people; but they have become law, and whatever harm may ultimately come from them is beyond recall and must be left to the coming generation, to which the subject henceforth belongs, to regulate according to circumstances and judgment. The present generation must rest content with knowing that so far as legal principles are involved, the process of reconstruction has reached

---

[1] Adams, "The Session, 1869–1870," *North American Review*, CXI (July 1870), 29–62.

its limits in the [Fifteenth Amendment] legislation of 1869. The powers originally reserved by the Constitution to the States are in future to be held by them only on good behavior and at the sufferance of Congress; they may be suspended or assumed by Congress; . . . . How far Congress will at any future day care to press its authority, or how far the States themselves may succeed in resisting the power of Congress, are questions which may be answered by a reference to the general course of events. Something may be judged of the [non-existent] rate of progress from the theories so energetically pressed during the past session by Senator Sumner, that the New England system of common schools is a part of the republican form of government as understood by the framers of the Constitution—an idea that would have seemed to the last generation as strange as though it would have been announced that the electric telegraph was an essential article of faith in the early Christian Church.[2] Something also may be judged from the condition of New York City and the evident failure of the system of self-government in great municipalities. Something more may be guessed by the rapid progress of corruption in shaking public confidence in state legislatures. Finally, something may be inferred from the enormous development of corporate power, requiring still greater political power to control it.

66. CARL SCHURZ, SPEECH

May 19, 1870

Henry Adams' contemporaries and more recent commentators have added substantially to the catalogue of reasons he offered to explain the waning of the Radical impulse. A consensus obtains that a

---

[2] See Kelly, "The Congressional Controversy over School Segregation," *American Historical Review*, LXIV (April 1959), 537–563.

change was in progress in the nation's mood. By 1870 this swift alteration in political currents was stranding the few holdfast Radicals on the wrong side of the nation's cape of good hopes.

Which is again to say that however various its numerous manifestations, Radical Republicanism was essentially an attitude toward man and toward the desirable functions of government. The most common Radical denominator was the conviction that government must do whatever appeared to be necessary to allow the machinery of political democracy to operate in an unimpeded manner, especially to equalize the position of men before the law and to enlarge the access of all men to the ballot, with the Negro deserving primary attention. The existence of the complex federal system—of the coexistence of national and state arenas of function—was no bar to Radical action. Neither was the booming capitalist base of the economy.[1]

This attitude combined with their impelling Negro-centered concerns and the opportunities the war opened in political activism for men of talent, energy, and determination, to carry Radicals to high peaks of power during the '60s. Its ebb turned these men of good will against one another. By the turn of the new decade, old comrades worked at cross-purposes, and many turned attention to what was wrong with political democracy rather than to means of improving it. Corruption in the electoral practices of Northern cities and growing racial violence in the South appeared to discouraged men to suggest that the Radical way of having the national government essay the creation of stable conditions was wrong or useless.

Resting on oars or trying to back water, Radical Republicans of prewar antislavery vintage observed the new breed of recent recruits into Radicalism, "regulars" within the Grant forces in Congress, pick up the ways and means and even some goals that Radicals had worked out since Sumter. Republican heavyweights took up consideration of a bill—opponents at once dubbed it a

---

[1] See the concluding chapters in earlier cited books by Brock, Cox and Cox, Franklin, Stampp, and Trefousse, and Richard Clark Sterne, *Political, Social, and Literary Criticism in the New York NATION, 1865–1881; A Study in a Change of Mood.* Unpublished doctoral dissertation, Harvard University, 1957.

"force bill"—to bring to action federal courts and *posses* if American citizens found political rights denied.

Long a Radical of large influence, Carl Schurz saw in the "force bill" as egregious an excess as the hated 1850 Fugitive Slave Law, to which he likened the novelty. Therefore he joined other anti-slavery greats to oppose it. Battling unsuccessfully against the regular party organization in Congress, Schurz and like-minded comrades further lessened their own effectiveness on Capitol Hill. Political effectiveness for a decade had been a brilliant characteristic of the Radicals. Schurz, speaking on May 19, 1870, in the Senate to oppose the "force bill," looked strange without it.[2]

In my opinion, and I say this to my party friends, it would be well for us to bridle that tendency which we have so frequently had occasion to observe, to thrust the hand of the National Government into local affairs on every possible occasion, and even to disregard and throw aside the most fundamental safeguards of popular rights for the correction of passing abuses.

I know it is fashionable to call that radicalism; but I apprehend it is false radicalism in the highest degree. We ought not to accustom ourselves, nor those who are to follow us in these seats, to the employment of arbitrary powers, and still less ought we to accustom the people to look always to the National Government for redress whenever anything goes wrong in their home concerns. Destroy their habit of holding themselves responsible for the management of their home affairs, deprive them of the great lesson of failure to be corrected by themselves, and they will soon cease to study and understand the nature of the evils under which they labor, as well as the remedies to be applied. Thus the educating power of our institutions will be fatally impaired.

There can be nothing more preposterous, in my opinion,

---

[2] Schurz, *Writings*, I, 500–503.

than the system prevailing in some foreign countries, where the people are permitted to vote upon the greatest and most complicated questions of general policy while they are not permitted to manage upon their own responsibility their home affairs at their own doors; the great popular school of political knowledge and experience, which consists in self-government, being thus closed to them. Certainly, it is not to be wondered at if in such countries universal suffrage becomes a mere instrument in the hands of despotism; an instrument which, indeed, may serve from time to time to subvert one form of despotism, but only to substitute for it another.

Therefore I am for State-rights as the embodiment of true and general self-government, and I am convinced that this is the prevailing sentiment among the American people. It would be a sad day for this Republic if it should cease to be so. It is true the exigencies of the civil war have quite naturally developed a tendency to accumulate and centralize power in the hands of the National Government, and while that accumulation was necessary to save the existence of the Republic, the people of the United States willingly and patriotically and cheerfully acquiesced in it; but as soon as the pressure of necessity ceases, as soon as it becomes apparent that the great problems for the solution of which we are struggling may be solved just as well by the simple operations of local self-government as by the interference of the National power, then the tide will just as certainly set in the opposite direction. I am sure the people of the United States will never countenance an accumulation of power merely for power's sake, and the Republican party will do well to consider whether it is not better for their usefulness and ascendency to direct than to resist that tide.

For this reason I earnestly deprecate those hazardous interpretations which have been applied to that clause of the Constitution which makes it the duty of the United States to guarantee to every State a republican form of government.

I certainly recognize that duty as a great, solemn and sacred one; but I deny that it confers upon the National Government the power to do all within the range of the human imagination. I deny that it authorizes or enables us to use the arm of the National authority for the purpose of realizing by force what conception each of us may entertain of the "ideal republic."

In whatever way political philosophers may define the term "a republican form of government," it seems to me that the Constitution of the United States in its amended, or, as our Democratic friends would have it, in its revolutionized state, has provisions which give a fair index of the powers conferred upon Congress by the guaranty clause. There we read that Congress shall see to it that no State establishes or maintains slavery or involuntary servitude; there we read that Congress shall see to it that every man born upon this soil or naturalized, and therefore a citizen of the United States, shall be protected in all the rights, privileges and immunities of citizens in every State of this Union; there we read that Congress shall see to it that every citizen of the United States shall be protected in his right to the ballot, irrespective of race or color.

But the Constitutional revolution has enlarged the powers of Congress for the purpose of establishing and securing true and general self-government in all of these States, not for the purpose of circumscribing its scope and functions within narrower limits. It has, indeed, overthrown what I call State wrongs; but it was not designed to abolish what I would call the legitimate sphere of State-rights. And I venture to say— and I cannot repeat this warning too often—the party which would attempt to carry that revolution much farther in the direction of an undue centralization of power would run against a popular instinct far stronger than party allegiance has ever proved to be.

But, sir, on the other hand, the party that would refuse to recognize and acquiesce in the great results of this beneficent revolution; the party that would attempt to subvert the institution of general self-government under National protection, as now established in the Constitution; the party that would strive to overthrow this new order of things, such a party certainly cannot fail to encounter the condemnation of the people and to meet disgrace and destruction, for such a party openly, by its own confession, constitutes itself the enemy of the peace and glory of this Republic. . . . I did not come to this country, where I hope to enjoy the blessings of liberty and self-government, to aid any party in designs like these. . . .

67. THE FORCE ACTS

1870, 1871, 1875

Despite the opposition of Schurz and other Republicans similarly troubled, as well as, of course, of Democrats, the "force act" became law on May 30, 1870. Defections in this instance preshadowed the Republican schism of two years later, when "Liberal Republicans" broke with the Grant regulars and compounded their grievous political sin with the worse offense of losing the 1872 election. Tainted from this uneasy and temporary alliance with the resurgent Democracy, the turncoat Radical-Liberal Republicans thereby lost influence within the regular party establishment, and Radicalism soon lost the meaning it had won in the sixties, of reformism combined with tough, effective politics.

The upshot was that in Congress, recent converts to Radicalism whose earlier careers exhibited little concern for the racial equalization of civil and political rights, reaped the benefits deriving from the rise after 1870 of Republican organizations in Southern states. Naturally these latecomers, who included in their number men of high talent and achievement such as James Blaine, Roscoe Conkling, James Garfield, and Oliver Morton, were interested in seeing to it that Negroes and other Republicans southward voted, and that Northern urban machines, traditionally Democratic, were cleansed as much as possible from this corruption. New "force acts" emerged out of these imperatives later in 1870 and again in 1871. These laws were designed to establish national supervision of elections at least as far as these statutes specified—and they went pretty far.

Too far? The tradition among historians is that these "force acts" represented the outworkings of partisan Republican selfishness, somehow clearly distinguishable from the enactments and motivations of the pre-1870 Radicals. Further, this tradition, echoing Schurz, has it that this legislation received frequent, excessive, and oppressive employment during Grant's White House years. In addition to these allegations, these statutes were supposed to have been injurious to relations between the races in the South by exacerbating whites without adequately protecting Negroes, thus providing fuel for the Klan movement to feed on and alienating "good-government" reformers from the central question of the Negro's condition.

Certainly the inadequacy of protection is accurate as an indictment. But as to other deficiencies and excesses, recent research suggests alternative judgments.

First, however, a capsule statement is in order on the contents of the "force acts"—the full texts are too long to include. The May 30, 1870, law forbade state officials from employing race or color as as discriminatory test of voters, and condemned the use of force, bribery, threats, or intimidation in elections. Masked or disguised organizations received specific prohibition. A second enforcement law, February 28, 1871, provided that federal supervisors oversee elections where irregularities might occur, and that they supervise returns.

On April 20, 1871, Grant signed into law a third "force act," also known as the Ku Klux Act.[1]

As to the recent scholarly re-evaluation of these much-maligned laws, Professor Everette Swinney has provided a careful and useful insight. Obviously the legislation of 1870–1871 moved the national government into unprecedented functional arenas, suggesting an ongoing reconstruction rather than the briefer process more com-

---

[1] U.S. *Statutes at Large,* XVI, 140–146, 433–440, XVII, 13.

monly sought. For one matter only, that of enforcement of these election-supervision laws, Swinney summarized their common provisions as follows:

The President was given authority to call out the army and navy and to suspend the [privilege of the] writ of habeas corpus; United States marshals were authorized to use the *posse comitatus;* and federal troops were empowered to implement [federal] court orders. In the hope of reducing the effect of local pressures against enforcement, exclusive jurisdiction in all suffrage cases was reserved to the federal courts.

Then, evaluating the claim of historians that these laws were dictatorial, Swinney came to this conclusion:

The Acts were comprehensive it is true; but the fact is that they did not go beyond the intent of the Fifteenth Amendment, which took a moderate and statesmanlike position on voting. The Fifteenth Amendment, unlike the Reconstruction Act of 1867, did not grant the Negro the right to vote; it merely outlawed the use of race as a test for voting. The Enforcement Acts of 1870–1871 accorded with the Fifteenth Amendment in leaving to the state full freedom to restrict suffrage on any basis except race or color.

Civil rights legislations of 1957 and 1960 according to Swinney . . . demonstrate that the United States Congress has returned to the principle of 1870 in its approach to [overseeing racial equality in] voting, and by its 1961 report the Civil Rights Commission shows that it has gone far beyond such principles in its demand for federal supervision of elections. Finally, the provisions for enforcement of the acts of 1870–1871—with the exception of the authorization to suspend the [privilege of the] writ of habeas corpus, which was done only once—were not innovations but were consistent with traditional usage. Whatever the motives of those who promoted the legislation, the laws as enacted were essentially in accord with the democratic credo.

Summing up, Swinney wrote that

. . . in 1870, measures to preserve the Negro's constitutional rights were desperately needed, and Congress responded with the passage of the Enforcement Acts of 1870 and 1871. These laws, essentially sound, worked fairly well for three or four years. Implementation, however, was difficult. The Grant administration, whose radicalism has perhaps been overemphasized, used federal power conspicuously on a few well-known occasions, but shortage of troops, money, and courts plagued law enforcement officers from the beginning. After 1874, the Acts were virtually dead letters. In the final analysis, Southern [white] intransigence and Northern apathy together brought about the collapse of the enforcement program; white supremacy proved [in the South] to be a more vital principle than Republican supremacy. The South, in its determination to win home rule, was willing to face the prospect of race war; the North was not. In the end, the policy of enforcement failed; but this does not mean that the policy was iniquitous nor that its failure was a blessing.[2]

On March 11, 1874, Charles Sumner died quite suddenly. Although his clashes with Grant five years earlier had cost him power save to obstruct, unlike many old abolitionists, Sumner had never lost faith in the capacity of the Negro to rise and in the need of American government to adapt itself to foster the black man's ascent. After 1870 Sumner's major contribution to the Radical Republican advance was to press (unavailingly) for national prohibitions against racial segregation in schools.

As a final statutory monument in this rich career so interwoven into the unfolding story of his nation, Sumner left a bill that since 1871 he had been advocating, and that a year after his death became the last civil rights law of the Reconstruction period. This law, of March 1, 1875, deserves exhibition.[3] It has required the passage of ninety years for Americans again to come close to its aspiration.

—An act to protect all citizens in their civil and legal rights.

Whereas, it is essential to just government we recognize the equality of all men before the law, and hold that it is the duty

[2] Everette Swinney, "Enforcing the Fifteenth Amendment, 1870–1877," *Journal of Southern History*, XXVIII (May 1962), 202–218 (quoted matter from pp. 203–204, 218); and see Robert A. Horn, *National Control of Congressional Elections.* Unpublished doctoral dissertation, Princeton University, 1942.

[3] U.S. *Statutes at Large*, XVIII, 335 ff.

of government in its dealings with the people to mete out equal and exact justice to all, of whatever nativity, race, color, or persuasion, religious or political; and it being the appropriate object of legislation to enact great fundamental principles into law: Therefore,

Be it enacted by the Senate and House of Representatives of the United States of America in Congress assembled, That all persons within the jurisdiction of the United States shall be entitled to the full and equal enjoyment of the accommodations, advantages, facilities, and privileges of inns, public conveyances on land or water, theaters, and other places of public amusement; subject only to the conditions and limitations established by law, and applicable alike to citizens of every race and color, regardless of any previous condition of servitude.

SEC. 2. That any person who shall violate the foregoing section by denying to any citizen, except for reasons by law applicable to citizens of every race and color, and regardless of any previous condition of servitude, the full enjoyment of any of the accommodations, advantages, facilities, or privileges in said section enumerated, or by aiding or inciting such denial, shall, for every such offense, forfeit and pay the sum of five hundred dollars to the person aggrieved thereby, to be recovered in an action of debt, with full costs; and shall also, for every such offense, be deemed guilty of a misdemeanor, and, upon conviction thereof, shall be fined not less than five hundred nor more than one thousand dollars, or shall be imprisoned not less than thirty days nor more than one year: *Provided,* That all persons may elect to sue for the penalty aforesaid or to proceed under their rights at common law and by State statutes; and having so elected to proceed in the one mode or the other, their right to proceed in the other jurisdiction shall be barred. But this proviso shall not apply to criminal proceedings, either under this act or the criminal law of any State: *And provided further,* That a judgment for the penalty in favor of the party aggrieved, or a judgment upon an indictment, shall be a bar to either prosecution respectively.[1]

SEC. 3. That the district and circuit courts of the United States shall have, exclusively of the courts of the several States, cognizance of all crimes and offenses against, and violations of, the provisions of this act; and actions for the penalty given by the preceding section may be prosecuted in the territorial, district, or circuit courts of the United States wherever the defendant may be found, without regard to the other party; and the district attorneys, marshals, and deputy marshals of the United States, and commissioners appointed by the circuit and territorial courts of the United States, with powers of arresting and imprisoning or bailing offenders against the laws of the United States, are hereby specially authorized and required to institute proceedings against every person who shall violate the provisions of this act, and cause him to be arrested and imprisoned or bailed, as the case may be, for trial before such court of the United States, or territorial court, as by law has cognizance of the offense, except in respect of the right of action accruing to the person aggrieved; and such district attorneys shall cause such proceedings to be prosecuted to their termination as in other cases: *Provided,* That nothing contained in this section shall be construed to deny or defeat any right of civil action accruing to any person, whether by reason of this act or otherwise; and any district attorney who shall willfully fail to institute and prosecute the proceedings herein required, shall, for every such offense, forfeit and pay the sum of five hundred dollars to the person aggrieved thereby, to be recovered by an action of debt, with full costs, and shall, on conviction thereof, be deemed guilty of a misdemeanor, and be fined not less than one thousand nor

---

[1] Sections 1 and 2 declared unconstitutional in *Civil Rights Cases,* 109 U.S. 3 (1883).

more than five thousand dollars: *And provided further,* That a judgment for the penalty in favor of the party aggrieved against any such district attorney, or a judgment upon an indictment against any such district attorney, shall be a bar to either prosecution respectively.

SEC. 4. That no citizen possessing all other qualifications which are or may be prescribed by law shall be disqualified for service as grand or petit juror in any court of the United States, or of any State, on account of race, color, or previous condition of servitude; and any officer or other person charged with any duty in the selection or summoning of jurors who shall exclude or fail to summon any citizen for the cause aforesaid shall, on conviction thereof, be deemed guilty of a misdemeanor, and be fined not more than five thousand dollars.

SEC. 5. That all cases arising under the provisions of this act in the courts of the United States shall be reviewable by the Supreme Court of the United States, without regard to the sum in controversy, under the same provisions and regulations as are now provided by law for the review of other causes in said court.

68. L. Q. C. LAMAR ON SUMNER

September 1874

One of the most impelling among Sumner's eulogists in Congress was the Mississippian L. Q. C. Lamar. Other former Confederates were surprised at the warmth of the encomiums Lamar offered on the life of the dead Senator and inquired as to his reasons for having spoken so fondly of a man commonly considered an enemy to the white South. Clement C. Clay, an Alabamian who almost ten years earlier had been suspected of complicity in Lincoln's murder, and who asked Lamar why he had enlarged the obsequies over Sumner further than he had warranty, received this reply on September 5, 1874.[1] It suggests how long a time had passed since Lee's surrender, as well as some of the characteristics of the "new departure" South, which nominally accepted the war's verdict and which kept Negroes off stage center.

I hope you believe me when I aver that my remarks on the death of Sumner were elicited by . . . no *pseudo* "magnanimity," but by a concern for the Southern people, a love for them with their helpless families which is a stronger feeling in my heart than the indignation I feel for their undeserved wrongs. At least I try to rein in the last feeling in order to obey the dictates of the former.

It will take more space & time, than I feel at liberty to occupy, to explain fully the processes of thought which led to the speech in question. I was most anxious to speak to the North on the condition & status of the Southern people. When I got to Washington & observed the indications of the temper of the Northern Representatives, I saw that what the Southern members said *never reached the masses of the North.* Indeed they were not *listened* to by the Republican side, unless some one should allow himself to be betrayed into intemperate & imprudent language. This would be caught up & circulated at the North to produce new irritations & inflame old passions. I prepared a speech on the Civil Rights Bill [referring here to Sumner's bill, enacted March 1, 1875]. I thought it a good one & it would have been very acceptable to my own people. But I very soon saw that every speech from our side strengthened the Bill. Our speeches were not listened to, & no representation that our men made of the condition of the Southern people, their convictions their necessities, their character—

---

[1] In Mattie Russell, ed., "Why Lamar Eulogized Sumner," *Journal of Southern History*, XXI (August 1955), 375–377.

received any attention. The splendid effort of Mr. [Alexander H.] Stephens made no impression at all. It was *answered* by a negro, [Robert B. Elliot, of Massachusetts, Congressman from South Carolina, 1871–November 1874] and the answer was applauded most vociferously. Had I followed the impulses of my nature I would either have sat silent or rose & hurled defiance at our oppressors. But the defiance would only have called down a greater wrath upon the defenceless head of the South. Silence would have been to acquiesce in the falsehood & misrepresentation that I heard every day uttered against our people. I mingled freely with the Northern Representatives & talked with them often to find out, if I could, whether there was any point upon which they could be approached successfully by the South—to ascertain if there was any ground upon which harmony, concord, peace & justice between the sections could be established. Bound together by force, the point with me was to search & see if there was any way in which they could be brought to *agree;* or whether the *instinct* of aversion of our people is based upon a melancholy remediless truth, that between them & the North there is no common union, no brotherly feeling—no bond of association. The result of that investigation was by no means a certain one. I found among the New Englanders & a few N. Westerners creatures egotistical, monstrously harsh & proud, with souls shut against every thing like commiseration, tenderness & charity, cynical, inexorable & contemptuous for the suffering people of the South. But such was not the spirit of even the *Republicans* in the North West, & there were some exceptions among the New Englanders. I thought I discerned a strong desire among them, & they declared it to be universal among the Northern people, to see the Southern States relieved from misgovernment & for the restoration of the whites to the control of their own affairs. But they are apprehensive & distrustful of reactionary measures if we get such control. They distrust the Northern democrats. They fear that the negroes will be put into a position of legal & civil subordination and an alliance formed with the Northern Democrats to reverse the results of the war.

They hear & believe stories of elections carried by fraud & intimidation. I tried to assure them that the results of the war were fixed beyond the power of reaction, at least until the North itself became satisfied with the experiment of negro freedom.

They said the real Representative men of the South had never so declared. I pointed to our support of [Horace] Greely [*sic*]. They said the people of the North believed Greely had sold out to us, But [*sic*] that the Greely Campaign had wrought a great change in the Northern mind towards the South. Stephens & other Southern men had declared the submission of the South to the results of the war, but the declaration was made in *arguments* upon subjects on which the northern mind was fixed & therefore, the declaration was unheeded. What was wanted was an *occasion* on which they would *listen*, & listen with something of a feeling of *sympathy*. I thought the death of Sumner was such an occasion. He was a man who had perhaps the largest personal following in the country. *Every word said about him, on the occasion of his funeral, would be read all over the North, especially among those classes who have never given us a hearing.* I know it is difficult . . . to think of him as a subject of eulogioum [*sic*] from such a man as I am. But his relation to parties & to us had been greatly changed if not entirely reversed. The most advanced & offensive assailant of our institutions, when you were his senatorial associate [in the early 1850's], he had become an advocate of amnesty & peace & fraternity with our people. He had been deposed by the Conklings, Chandlers, Mortons, Grants & Butlers from the leadership of his party & was very strongly in sympathy with our people. His own legislature had censured him. His death was a source of great regret to many of the best friends of the South. I ought to mention that among the caricatures of [Thomas] Nast, in Harper's pictorial, during the Greely canvass [in 1872], was Sumner strewing flowers over the grave of Preston Brooks [the South Carolina congressman who in 1856 ferociously attacked Sumner physically in the Senate]. [James G.] Blaine, the speaker of the House, in a letter jeered him for his 'association with the secessionist of the South & the ruffians who justified Preston Brooks in his brutal assault upon you in the Senate Chamber.' Sumner replied to him thus: 'I had not taken account of the Southern secessionists who, as you aver, are now co-operating with me, except to *rejoice that if among former associates some, like yourself, hesitate, their places are supplied from an unexpected quarter.* You entirely misunderstand me when you introduce an incident of the past & build on it an argument why I should not support Horace Greely. What has Preston Brooks to do with the Presidential election [?] *Never while a sufferer did any body hear me speak of him in unkindness & now, after a lapse of more than half a generation I will not unite with you in dragging him from the grave where he sleeps to aggravate the passions of a political conflict & arrest the longing for concord.* . . . Seven years have passed since we laid aside our arms, but unhappily during all this period there has been a hostile spirit towards each other.' &c. Seven years mark a natural period in human life. Should not the spirit be changed with the body? *Can we not after seven years commence a new life, especially when those once our foes repeat the saying* 'Thy people shall be my people, & thy God my God.'

The whole letter breathes a truly noble spirit. It is true he still advocated the civil Rights Bill which, in *my* opinion, is a measure of wrong & injustice & grievous injury to our people. I do not believe, however, that he meant it as a humiliation to us. It was, in his eye, a consummation of his life long struggle for equal rights. Intensely opposed as I am to that measure I must say that if Mr. S. had not supported it he would not have been in harmony with himself. . . .

PART FIFTEEN

Conclusion

Lamar had hit upon it. During the 1860 decade, Sumner and his coadjutors were "in harmony" with the nation's needs, interests, and energies.

Unquestionably Radicals made possible the fullest unleashing of those energies, at least during the crucial war years. Some Radicals tried to continue on this level of activity long after the war. Speaking in 1872 on his proposal for another civil rights law, Sumner repeated a theme he had marked out since the secession winter: the Constitution ". . . is overrunning with power. Not in one place or two places or three places, but almost everywhere."[1]

Radicals raised higher the nation's estimations of its own needs and the level of its interest in the often-seamy conditions of American life—at least for a score of years. Out of Radical prodding, Americans became aware of horrid depths and through brilliant political action brought light and reform to some of the worst of those conditions. Historians still have a large job to do in the matters of Radical Republican activity on local levels of government, and of achievements in expanding police and welfare functions of cities, towns, counties, and states.

But of course the Radical glory is Negro-centered; the American opportunity as well as dilemma. Radicals grew up to a vision of biracial coexistence and equality before law, a combination of conditions that existed nowhere in the world a century ago and that men of good will still seek today, and still with much pain.

---

[1] Sumner, *Works*, XIV, 424.

Never cynics or fanatics and rarely fools, the Radical Republicans tried very hard to bring their noble dream to action. There are worse judgments to make on men.

Still involved in 1870 with enterprises of great merit, the "old corps" of tough-minded (not hardhearted) reformer-politicians was fearfully weakening, reduced in numbers and vitality. The altering concerns of their countrymen left the Radical remnant seriously out of phase with newer political currents. Radicals did not lose principles; most white Americans lost interest in those principles. Negroes were no longer a "problem" that a militant minority among Republicans could put forward as an issue capable of evoking responses in the party, which would result in turn in the exertion of the power of government on behalf of what had been *the* good cause.

By mid-point of the '70's, only fitful resistance could be mustered against sweeping under the rug of conscience the question of the Negro's political condition. The Republican party had lost the Lincolnian heritage of sensitivity and honest self-appraisal, and sixty years were to pass before these necessitous qualities reappeared in politics and under a Democratic party banner.

Frederick Douglass tried to bring the Republican party back to its heritage. At the 1876 national convention he adverted to the great leaps forward that Negroes had made through emancipation and enfranchisement. He then demanded,

> What does it all amount to if the black man, after having been made free by the letter of your law, . . . is to be subject to the slaveholder's shot-gun? . . . I sometimes wonder that we still exist as a people in this country; that we have not all been swept out of existence, with nothing left to show we ever existed. . . . When you turned us loose, you turned us loose to the sky, to the storm, to the whirlwind, and, worst of all, . . . to the wrath of our infuriated masters. The question now is, do you mean to make good to us the promises in your constitution?[2]

But 1876 was the year of the disputed election returns with respect to the two Presidential candidates. It was also the centen-

---

[2] In *Proceedings of the Republican National Convention, Cincinnati, June 14–16, 1876* (Concord, N.H.: Republican Press Association, 1876), p. 27.

nial of American independence. In symbolic response to Douglass' question, the energies of the political institutions that year bent on avoiding hazards, not curing ills. The message of the time, and for a long time to follow, was expressed by a prominent Boston lawyer, William Giles Dix:

> We cannot better improve the centennial memories of this year and of the few coming years than by a thorough and, by the grace of God, a successful endeavor to eradicate the notion, so prevalent and so pernicious, that our form of government is a kind of political gospel, a civil revelation for the ultimate good of all mankind.[3]

The Radical Republican heritage is that "our form of government" is exactly what Dix denied. In 1966, is this Radical faith, optimism, and aspiration not the American creed?

---

[3] Dix, *The American State and American Statesmen* (Boston: Estes and Lauriat, 1876), p. viii.

Index

Abbott, Lyman, report on
Freedmen's Bureau (1867),
216–229
Abolitionists
Freedmen's Bureau and, 202–207
influence in Republican party of,
lxvii, 28–29
Lincoln and, 15–16, 29–31, 36,
46, 50
postwar change in attitude by,
xxvi, xlix–l, 199
prewar vs. postwar attitude of,
246–248
recommendations on reconstruc-
tion by, lxiii, 43, 69, 101–102
Sumner's speech on (July 7,
1862), 103–106
Whiting's memorandum on,
92–100
as villains, xxii, xliii
See also American Anti-Slavery
Society, Emancipation,
Radical Republicans,
Slavery
Adams, Charles Francis, Jr., 103,
477
Adams, Henry, 477–478
article by (July 1870), 503–504
Agassiz, Louis, xxvi
Alabama, 263, 411
Jim Crow laws in, 219n
American Anti-Slavery Society
dissolves, 492, 496–499
Douglass' speeches to, 85–89,
242–246
Garrison's last speech to, 492–495
American Freedman's Union
Commission, 224

American Freedman's Union
Commission (cont.)
editorial on (December 1868),
461–465
American Freedmen's-Aid Union,
224
American Freedmen's Inquiry
Commission reports,
113–123, 201–202
American Missionary Association,
224–225
American Union Commission, 224
Ames, General Adelbert, 418, 419
Andersonville prison, 274
Anti-Slavery Standard, 247, 328
Arkansas, 260
Lincoln-supported government
in, 136, 140–141
Army
civil suits against members of,
305–308, 415
in Civil War
elections, lvii–lviii, 64
influence of ministers, 62–63
Negro soldiers, 71, 82–83,
109–110, 167, 471
in plans for reconstruction,
90–91, 101
as political institution, 50–51
soldiers' resolutions, 107–109
Freedmen's Bureau and,
116–117, 195–196, 212–215
loyalty of, 398–399
occupation of South by
army policy toward slaves,
30–37, 47, 50–51, 69, 72,
116–117, 174